THE OXFORD HAN...

PUBLISHING

THE OXFORD HANDBOOK OF

PUBLISHING

Edited by

ANGUS PHILLIPS

and

MICHAEL BHASKAR

OXFORD

UNIVERSITY PRESS

OXFORD
UNIVERSITY PRESS

Great Clarendon Street, Oxford, OX2 6DP,
United Kingdom

Oxford University Press is a department of the University of Oxford.
It furthers the University's objective of excellence in research, scholarship,
and education by publishing worldwide. Oxford is a registered trade mark of
Oxford University Press in the UK and in certain other countries

Published in the United States of America by Oxford University Press
198 Madison Avenue, New York, NY 10016, United States of America

British Library Cataloguing in Publication Data
Data available

Library of Congress Cataloging in Publication Data
Data available

ISBN 978-0-19-879420-2 (Hbk.)
ISBN 978-0-19-284779-9 (Pbk.)

ACKNOWLEDGEMENTS

The idea for this volume dates back to a collaboration proposed by Michael in 2012, and the book's development has taken some time, a change of publisher, and the assistance of a variety of people. We express our appreciation to those who have contributed directly or through discussion of the themes in this Handbook.

First we owe a huge debt to the contributors to this volume, who responded cheerfully to our requests (and on occasion pleading), and came through brilliantly. They have been a pleasure to work with throughout.

Angus would like to acknowledge the unwavering support of colleagues at the Oxford International Centre for Publishing; as well as colleagues in the European E-READ working group, attendees at the By the Book conference, the editorial board of *Logos*, and the members of the Zadar Swimming Club. He would like to thank his family for their support: Ann, Matthew, Charlotte, and Jamie.

Michael would like to thank all his colleagues at Canelo, a company which came into being during the genesis of this book, and in particular his co-founders Iain Millar and Nick Barreto. All of us live the realities, the highs, and lows outlined in this book every day. The wider publishing and scholarly community is a constant source of inspiration, and we are lucky to work in such a voluble, sociable, and congenial area as this. Lastly, he would like to thank his wife Danielle for endless patience and support and his son Monty, another new arrival since the beginning of this project.

At OUP we would like to thank our editors, Adam Swallow and Jenny King, for their enthusiasm and expertise. To David Musson our special thanks for taking the book on shortly before his retirement. Cyril Cox may or may not know of his contribution to the birth of this volume—either way he is fondly remembered.

ACKNOWLEDGEMENTS

Contents

PART II THE DYNAMICS OF PUBLISHING

PART III PUBLISHING IN PRACTICE

CODA

LIST OF FIGURES

LIST OF TABLES

Editors and Contributors

Editors

Michael Bhaskar is a writer, digital publisher, researcher, and entrepreneur. He is Co-Founder of Canelo, a new kind of publishing company based in London, and Writer in Residence at DeepMind, the world's leading AI research lab. He has written and talked extensively about publishing, the future of media, the creative industries, and the economics of technology around the world. He has been featured in and written for *The Guardian, Financial Times,* and *Wired* and on BBC 2, the BBC World Service, BBC Radio 4, and NPR, amongst others. Michael has been a British Council Young Creative Entrepreneur and a Frankfurt Book Fair Fellow. He has written a prize-winning monograph *The Content Machine* (2013) as well as *Curation: The Power of Selection in a World of Excess* (2016). He is also the lead author of the *Literature in the 21st Century* report (2017) and can be found on Twitter as @michaelbhaskar.

Angus Phillips is Professor of Publishing and Director of the Oxford International Centre for Publishing at Oxford Brookes University. He formerly worked in the publishing industry as a trade editor at Oxford University Press. He has given talks and lectures about publishing all over the world and has carried out consultancy and training work with international publishers. He is on the European Advisory Board of Princeton University Press and was a judge for *The Bookseller* industry awards for four years in a row. He is the author and editor of a number of books including *Turning the Page* (2014) and *Inside Book Publishing* (sixth edition 2019, with Giles Clark). He is the editor of *Logos* and in 2015 published a book of selected articles from the journal's 25-year history: *The Cottage by the Highway and other essays on publishing.*

Contributors

Alison Baverstock PhD PFHEA is an Associate Professor at Kingston University, a publisher, and a pioneer of both Publishing Education and profession-oriented education within universities. She co-founded the Publishing MA at Kingston University in 2006 and has researched and written widely about publishing. *How to Market Books,* first published in 1990 and now in its sixth edition, has been widely licensed for translation and is an international bedrock of publisher education, both academically and professionally. She is a particular champion for the widening of literacy and the value of shared-reading. In 2007 she received the Pandora Award for a significant contribution to the industry.

Martin Paul Eve is Professor of Literature, Technology and Publishing at Birkbeck, University of London. He has written widely on open access to scholarly material and its economics and is a founder and CEO of the Open Library of Humanities.

Albert N. Greco is Professor of Marketing at Fordham University's Gabelli School of Business and the author/editor of 15 scholarly books and 10 professional books. He is the author of 33 journal articles, 112 book reviews, and 23 book chapters. He has presented research papers at The World Bank, Harvard, and the Library of Congress; and he did publishing consulting work for Goldman Sachs, Morgan Stanley, JP Morgan, among others. His research was cited by the Supreme Court of the USA, 3 Harvard Business School case studies and the *Journal of Marketing*. He is writing a book about World War 2's impact on scholarly publishing.

Frania Hall is Senior Lecturer at the London College of Communication, University of the Arts London, and Course Leader for the MA in Publishing. She also teaches on creative enterprise and publishing at undergraduate level and is teaching and learning Innovation lead for the Media School at LCC. She has worked across a variety of publishing sectors, including academic, education, and professional publishing. Her research focuses on creative collaboration, network behaviour, digital product innovation, as well as zine culture. She is author of *The Business of Digital Publishing* published by Routledge. She is a member of the Creative Industries Management Research Hub based at LCC.

Alex Holzman is CEO of Alex Publishing Solutions, a consulting firm, and co-editor of the *Journal of Scholarly Publishing*. During a forty-year publishing career he has served as director of Temple University Press, in various books, journals, and electronic publishing positions at Cambridge University Press, as assistant director at Ohio State University Press, and in sales and editorial positions at Charles Scribners Sons and Dodd, Mead. He served on the board of directors for the Association of American University Presses for six years, and as association president in 2008–09. Alex has contributed chapters and articles to publications ranging from *Publishing Political Science: APSA Guide to Writing and Publishing* and the *European Journal of Political Science* to *New York Yankees Magazine*. He also served on the Advisory Board for the sixteenth edition of the *Chicago Manual of Style* and has presented papers at a wide variety of academic and library conferences.

Miha Kovač is Professor at the Department of Library and Information Science and Book Studies at the University of Ljubljana. Before joining academia, he worked as a publisher for the two biggest Slovene publishing houses and was a consultant to textbook publishers in a variety of Central and East European countries. He is the author of more than fifty articles and four books on book publishing.

Sarah Kalikman Lippincott is the Assessment and Planning Librarian at the University of Massachusetts Amherst. She holds an MLIS from the University of North Carolina at Chapel Hill and a BA from Wesleyan University. She served as the inaugural programme director of the Library Publishing Coalition, an international non-profit membership association for academic libraries and has also contributed to communications and outreach work for the Association of Research Libraries (ARL), SPARC, and the open access journal eLife. She has conducted research on the information behaviour of scholars who use archival materials (particularly oral histories) and on the research and teaching practices of digital humanists and has consulted on a range of digital publishing and scholarly communications projects for cultural heritage organizations.

Paul Luna is an Emeritus Professor in the Department of Typography & Graphic Communication at the University of Reading, where he led the MA Book Design programme, and was formerly head of corporate design at Oxford University Press. He has designed editions of Shakespeare and T. S. Eliot, the Bible and Book of Common Prayer, and many dictionaries, including the *Oxford English Dictionary* and *Shorter Oxford English Dictionary*. His publications include *Typography: A Very Short Introduction* (OUP, 2018) and contributions to the *History of Oxford University Press* (Vol. I, 2014; Vol. IV, 2017). He co-edited *Information Design: Research and Practice* (Routledge, 2017) and *Typography Papers 9* (Hyphen Press, 2013).

John W. Maxwell is Associate Professor & Director of the Publishing Program at Simon Fraser University, where his teaching and research are on the impact of digital technologies in the book and magazine industries. John's research has focused on the cultural trajectories of personal and educational computing, the history of publication technologies, the emergence of digital genres, the evolution of digital media, and the future of the scholarly monograph. John regularly teaches a course on text processing histories at the Digital Humanities Summer Institute.

Alistair McCleery is Director of the Scottish Centre for the Book and Professor of Literature and Culture at Edinburgh Napier University. He is co-author of the two standard textbooks in his field, *An Introduction to Book History* (second edition, Routledge, 2012) and *The Book History Reader* (second edition, Routledge, 2006). He has recently contributed the chapter on 'Publishing' to *The Cambridge Companion to the History of the Book* (CUP, 2015) and co-authored 'Publishing 1914–2000' for *The Cambridge History of the Book in Great Britain* vol 7 (CUP, 2019, forthcoming).

Simone Murray is Associate Professor in Literary Studies at Monash University, Melbourne where her research centres upon sociologies of literature. Her book *Mixed Media: Feminist Presses and Publishing Politics* (Pluto Press UK, 2004) was awarded the 2005 SHARP DeLong Book Prize. Her second monograph, *The Adaptation Industry: The Cultural Economy of Contemporary Literary Adaptation* (Routledge, 2012) has been widely reviewed in English-, French-, German-, and Swedish-language publications. Her latest monograph, *The Digital Literary Sphere: Reading, Writing, and Selling Books in the Internet Era*, examines how the Internet is transforming literary culture (Johns Hopkins University Press, 2018).

John Oakes is an editor and publisher. Oakes is the co-founder of OR Books. He is also publisher of *The Evergreen Review*, and founding director of the New School Publishing Institute. Oakes has written for a variety of publications, among them *Publishers Weekly*, *The Review of Contemporary Fiction*, the *Associated Press*, and *The Journal of Electronic Publishing*. Oakes was named a *Chevalier de l'ordre des arts et des lettres* by the French government. He is the editor of *In the Realms of the Unreal: Writings of the Insane*.

Lynette Owen started her publishing career in rights at Cambridge University Press and then worked at Pitman Publishing and Marshall Cavendish before joining Longman (now Pearson Education) where she was Copyright Director. She now works as a freelance rights and contracts consultant and runs training courses in the UK and abroad. She is the author of *Selling Rights* (Routledge, eighth edition due Spring 2019) and is the General Editor of and a contributor to *Clark's Publishing Agreements* (Bloomsbury Professional, tenth edition 2017). She was awarded the second London Book Fair Lifetime Achievement Award in 2003 and received an OBE for services to publishing and international trade in 2009.

Mira T. Sundara Rajan is a law professor and expert consultant who specializes in copyright law. She holds a DPhil in copyright law from Oxford University, and has served as the Canada Research Chair in Intellectual Property Law at the University of British Columbia in Vancouver, Canada, as well as Professor of Intellectual Property Law and director of the LLM program in copyright law at the University of Glasgow and the CREATe copyright research centre in the UK. Mira has held visiting appointments at Oxford, Stanford, Monash, and other universities throughout Europe and India. She has published widely on copyright law, and has a special interest in the moral rights of authors and artists. Her book, *Moral Rights: Principles, Practice & New Technology*, was first published by Oxford University Press in 2011, and is now considered a leading text in the field. Mira is a great-granddaughter of Indian National Poet in the Tamil language, C. Subramania Bharati (1882–1921), and was the first person to undertake scholarly research into the unique copyright situation surrounding the poet's works.

Samantha J. Rayner is a Reader in Publishing at UCL. She is also Director of UCL's Centre for Publishing, co-Director of the Bloomsbury CHAPTER and series editor for Cambridge University Press's Elements series on Publishing and Book Culture. She is also the co-editor of the *Academic Book of the Future* BOOC (Book as Open Online Content) with UCL Press, and deputy editor of the *Journal of the International Arthurian Society* (JIAS). She was the lead investigator on the AHRC/British Library Academic Book of the Future Project.

Elizabeth le Roux is an Associate Professor and the coordinator of Publishing Studies in the Department of Information Science at the University of Pretoria. She is co-editor of the journal *Book History*, and her research focuses on the history of books and publishing in South Africa and in Africa more broadly. Her most recent publications include the books *A Social History of the University Presses in Apartheid South Africa* (Brill, 2016) and *A Survey of South African Crime Fiction* (with Sam Naidu, UKZN Press, 2017). Before becoming a full-time academic, she worked in the scholarly publishing industry in South Africa.

Carlos A. Scolari is Associate Professor and Coordinator of the PhD Program at the Department of Communication of the Universitat Pompeu Fabra—Barcelona. He has a PhD in Applied Linguistics and Communication Languages (Catholic University of Milan, Italy) and a degree in Social Communication (University of Rosario, Argentina).

He is the Principal Investigator of the H2020 Transmedia Literacy research project (2015–18) and is on Twitter @cscolari. His websites are Hipermediaciones.com and Modernclicks.net

Mojca K. Šebart is Professor of Sociology of Education at the University of Ljubljana. Her research topics include preschool and family education, authority, moral education, multicultural and Roma education, citizenship education, classroom and school culture, assessment in education, and textbooks. She is author and co-author of several books and numerous articles published in internationally recognized journals.

Niels Peter Thomas graduated from Technische Universität Darmstadt with a master's degree in industrial engineering and a PhD in political economy. In 2005 he started as an acquisitions editor for academic publisher Springer and moved to Beijing, China, in 2011, to set up editorial departments and business development. From 2014 he was Managing Director of several companies within the publishing group, and since 2017 he is Chief Book Strategist for Springer Nature, responsible for the long-term strategic development of books. Alongside his industry role, he is a lecturer for publishing business and the digitalization of media.

John B. Thompson is Professor of Sociology at the University of Cambridge and Fellow of Jesus College, Cambridge. His publications include *Ideology and Modern Culture* (1990), *The Media and Modernity* (1995), *Political Scandal* (2000), *Books in the Digital Age* (2005), and *Merchants of Culture* (2010). He is currently completing a new book on the digital revolution in the publishing industry. His books have been translated into more than a dozen languages and he was awarded the European Amalfi Prize for Sociology and the Social Sciences in 2001 for *Political Scandal*.

Adriaan van der Weel is Bohn Extraordinary Professor of Book Studies, teaching Book and Digital Media Studies at the University of Leiden. His research interests in book studies concentrate publishing studies and the digitization of textual transmission and reading. He is editor of a number of book series on these subjects, editor of *Digital Humanities Quarterly*, and the author of *Changing our Textual Minds: Towards a Digital Order of Knowledge* (Manchester UP, 2011). He is currently writing a book about reading together with Ruud Hisgen.

Rüdiger Wischenbart is the founder of 'Content and Consulting' and a writer specialized in culture, the cultural industries, global book markets, innovation in the book industry, literature, media, and communication. He researched and (co-)authored several reports on global publishing markets, notably the 'Global eBook' report (www. global-ebook.com), the 'Global Publishing Markets', and the 'Global Ranking of the Publishing Industry'. He coordinates its 'Global Market Forum, and is Director for Publishers' Forum in Berlin. In 2017, he co-founded BookMap, a non-profit initiative on international publishing statistics together with Miha Kovač of the University of Ljubljana.

CHAPTER 1

....

INTRODUCTION

....

MICHAEL BHASKAR AND ANGUS PHILLIPS

PUBLISHING is different. It is, for example, one of only a small but incredibly significant cluster of industries that can trace their origins back millennia, yet have, to an extraordinary degree, also modernized and embraced change. Banking or fashion might be others. But, at least in developed economies, most of us work in trades that would have been unimaginable five centuries ago. Not so the publisher.

In some ways publishing was, in the late fifteenth and early sixteenth centuries, a different universe. Culturally, technologically, economically: the contrast could hardly be starker. Yet threads of commonality are equally as arresting. Although publishers *avant la lettre*, the printing houses of Venice, Nuremberg, Paris, or Antwerp have startling similarities to today's publishing businesses. They too had to find and acquire content. They had to buy paper and manage plant. Production, distribution, text and book design, complex workflows and timescales, book fairs at Frankfurt, difficult authors, a constant pressure on working capital, the difficulty of assessing the right print run, relationships with bookshops and wholesalers, risk at times financial, cultural and legal, all define publishing then as now.

The fundamental economic model has not changed a great deal: you produce or facilitate the production of books, understood either as a physical codex or a specific information architecture, which are then sold above cost price. The more you can produce and sell, the more your unit cost comes down feeding a double success: books that sell a lot deliver not only the linear return of more sales but push down the unit cost of production. Likewise the central problem of publishing is consistent: that for any given book at any given time the likely pool of readers is small, smaller than either author or publisher would hope, and also difficult to reach. The average print run of an academic monograph is today measured in the hundreds, fewer than was managed by great publishers of the fifteenth and sixteenth centuries. A demographic and economic explosion and several technological revolutions have not, it seems, managed to solve this problem.

In many ways this historical aspect of publishing is still powerfully present. The book you are currently reading has been published by an organization dating back to 1586, although Oxford University was involved with printing for a century before that. The office of Oxford University Press on Great Clarendon Street in Oxford dates back to 1830. The Delegates that govern the Press meet in an even older home, the Clarendon Building on Broad Street, which dates back to 1715. The physical printing presses worked away in the basement of the adjacent Sheldonian Theatre, Christopher Wren's first large building. Even beyond still thriving and venerable institutions like OUP, publishing today is still an industry concerned with ink on paper, the thunder of presses, deals done with old friends over lunch. The great Venetian publisher Aldus Manutius had as his emblem a dolphin entwined around an anchor: today this same image is used as the colophon of Doubleday, an imprint of Penguin Random House, the world's largest trade publisher.

And yet this image of publishing, of gentlemanly, book-lined offices, stuffiness and tweediness, a leisurely pace, a backward looking and dilettante air is, while being grounded in truth, also hopelessly wrong. OUP is both an ancient institution and a modern one: it is a multinational corporation with a vast suite of print and digital products operating from Malaysia to Mexico with a turnover exceeding $1bn (Oxford University Press 2017). Many of its most famous books like the *Oxford English Dictionary* or *Dictionary of National Biography* are more digital than print products. You may be holding a physical book as you read this, but it is just as likely that you are looking at a screen. As Keith Robbins observes about the period from 1970 to 2004, 'the Press sustained and enhanced its position as the largest university press in the world', yet its history was not 'one of inexorable advance to comfort. The nature of its business and the ever-changing world in which it has operated make such a characterization implausible' (2017: 689–90).

Indeed publishing has never been a backwards looking industry. It has a long tradition to be sure, but one of radical innovation, powerfully continued today. Publishers have long been on the frontlines of change. They pioneered the first industrial technology, the printing press, the crucible of standardized mass production that defines the modern condition. With this they also pioneered industrial workflows, the complex division of labour in skilled and semi-skilled trades working in tandem around machines and intricate supply chains and dependencies. Concomitantly it was at printing houses that we see some of the earliest examples of organized labour and trades unions. Publishers drove forward the creation of intellectual property, the vital ingredient of the knowledge economy that predominates today. They adopted steam early and repeatedly revolutionized retail with everything from shops that were open to browse or Christmas presents that became essential ingredients of the festive season.

The invention of copyright and intellectual property owes much to the world of books. The first copyright law, the Statute of Anne, dates back to 1709 and gave the author ownership of the copyright: 'An Act for the Encouragement of Learning, by vesting the Copies of Printed Books in the Authors or purchasers of such Copies, during the Times therein mentioned'. The principle behind the concept of intellectual property is to foster creativity and innovation by allowing those with ownership rights to earn a return from their work.

More recently the ISBN was a harbinger of a new era of efficiencies. To watch a modern publishing warehouse, such as that of Hachette's new facility at Didcot in the UK, is to witness a dizzying dance of automated containers, robots, and gantries. While publishers' relationship with the Internet giant Amazon is complex, as we will see, it is undeniable and fitting that books had a pivotal role in the establishment of ecommerce. The world's richest person, Jeff Bezos, founded his business in an industry with a dizzying multitude of product lines that could never be encompassed by a physical store. And of course it was publishers that enabled so much intellectual and cultural transformation. Whether the Reformation or the Scientific Revolution; Romanticism, Modernism, or Communism; Newton's *Principia* or Mao's *Little Red Book*; the King James Bible or *Uncle Tom's Cabin*, the printed word has, at least as much as any other force, defined history. And behind those changes, were the people and organizations making these texts possible: publishers.

The interplay of history and modernity, tradition and innovation; the excitement of working at the frontiers of thought and culture; the ongoing ability to, just maybe, help change the world: this is why publishing is different.

DEFINING PUBLISHING

In this *Oxford Handbook of Publishing* one thing needs to be cleared up from the off: what is meant by publishing? As with many ideas, the closer one looks the more vexed the question becomes. Yet in essence our focus is simple. By 'publishing' this volume tends loosely to mean 'book publishing', echoing the colloquial use and understanding of the term.

Publishing describes not one but a host of industries. For example in the music industry, publishing denotes a specific activity aligned to the central work of record companies. Music publishers are essentially licensing and revenue collection agencies on behalf of artists and music rights holders. They typically collect income from subsidiary uses of music, and they are not concerned with the recording, production, and dissemination of music so much as various features of intellectual property around it. The structure of the industry assigns what in the book world would be publishing to record companies, while music publishing finds its bookish analogue across departments within book publishers and specialist agencies (such as literary agencies). Talk to a music executive about publishing, then, and you will have a different concept to both the authors of this volume and indeed its publishers.

Or take another industry, videogames, an industry with worldwide revenues of over $100bn (Batchelor 2018). In some respects this is closer to book publishing in that the publisher (usually) fulfils the functions of primary investor in a work and is then responsible for distribution and commercial exploitation. But videogame publishers have slightly different relationships with the creators of the work published: they work with development studios who might be in-house entities, often comprising hundreds or thousands of staff, or which could be separate companies altogether who license IP to the publisher or have been commissioned by the publisher. Neither model is foreign to book publishing. Educational publishers may produce significant quantities of material in-house and even a trade children's publisher such as Usborne does the same. Publishers of all stripes will commission work rather than passively wait for it to arrive. And yet when we think of companies like King, Ubisoft, or Electronic Arts they would not, for most people, be publishers in the way Gallimard, Bonnier, or Planeta are publishers.

Newspaper and magazine publishing echo the structure of videogame publishing inasmuch as, within a given publisher, the publishing team is generally responsible for business functions while the editorial team is responsible for content. While editorial is normally a separate department, this cleavage between 'editorial' and 'publishing' is not found in a book publisher. Instead the entire organization is devoted to publishing, rather than this being a function of specific areas of the company. Indeed, one understanding of publishing would be to simply view it as an emergent property of publishing organizations as a whole.

If books are one part of the equation, a further element, one encapsulating this emergent phenomenon, needs elaboration. Publishers are not just makers of books, and indeed the actual production, whether physical or digital, does not generally take place within the publishing firm. Publishers are about, at some level, and in various ways, making books public. Making books, yes; but making books *for* some purpose, for readers. As one of the editors has elsewhere discussed, the idea of 'making public', while common enough as an understanding of publishing, is still too fuzzy. Instead 'amplification' is the preferred term, bringing books to more readers than would otherwise have been the case. Whatever terminology we use then, we cannot say that publishers are just producing books. Publishers do not produce one copy of a book and lock it away. That is book making, not publishing. While publishers are usually concerned with maximizing audiences, there ultimately must be an audience in the first place for it to constitute publishing.

We have here then a working understanding of publishing: making books, and making them public, amplifying them, finding and building audiences for them, with everything that entails.

Publishing is a plural, variegated entity, not just an industry but a set of industries and industries within industries. Contrasting book publishing with other forms of publishing is helpful in focusing us but in turn raises another question: what is a book? In a time where the fundamental bases of books, in some senses stable for centuries, are now shifting fast, the nature of book publishing, is, unsurprisingly shifting with it.

THE PLACE OF THE BOOK

If publishing means book publishing, then publishing, and the editors of this book, have a problem. As we later discuss, reports of the death of the book are exaggerated. Books have proved a remarkably desirable, useful, and resilient media. This is not, however, to suggest that we are not living at a pivotal moment for the book, and that not only does this moment impact what publishing is and how it works, but the very emerging precarity of the book is, in some senses, driven by publishers.

This question of the place of the book in publishing and wider society works on many levels. For centuries the book dominated the intellectual and cultural landscape, certainly in what we would now call the West. If you wanted to store and disseminate knowledge or ideas; if you wanted to tell a story to the highest possible numbers; if you wanted to make a significant argument, be it religious, political, or personal; if you wanted to achieve fame or make an impact, then writing and publishing a book was probably your best bet. The edifice of learning and culture that accrued from the Middle Ages to the twentieth century was underpinned by print. This is a systemically important structural role in society that Adriaan van der Weel has called the Order of the Book (Van Der Weel 2011).

Although the place of the publisher was always ambiguous in highly stratified societies, somewhere between the merchant prince and grubby street trader, the equal of intellectual giants and also their fawning servant, both capitalist and aesthete, they eventually grew to have significant status in the metropolitan capitals of Europe and America. To read memoirs and biographies of great early twentieth-century publishers such as Allen Lane or Jonathan Cape is to read not only of the typical highs and lows of a life in publishing, but also to see powerhouse celebrities of their age dominating the gossip columns and societal scene of their time. Publishers were significant influencers, mavens, power-brokers, and party-goers at the very apex of their nations.

That Golden Age is gone. Publishers still carry significant clout as we will explore, but the gossip columns have, by and large, moved on. There are increasing question marks over the Order of the Book, that lettered system, driven and governed by publishers, and whether it can survive. The assault, if one wants to be brutal, has been sustained and unforgiving. From the late nineteenth century onwards, successive technological innovations gave rise to new media which have competed with books for functional elements in the overall communication and entertainment ecosystem, and have done so at arguably cheaper cost. Whether radio, television, or digital media, among others, books are no longer the only or even the most powerful mechanisms of communicating to wide audiences. Other media companies and entities, and other media forms, whether the BBC or Netflix, talk radio or the massively-multiplayer online game, have arisen to occupy spaces once inhabited by the book.

This is not necessarily a bad thing. After all, those new media in many if not most senses represent advances: of technology, living standards, choice. As per the eponymous law of Wolfgang Riepl, a newspaper editor, new media do not destroy wholesale older forms. Instead they accrete on top, creating a revised, expanded, more complex, and multilayered arrangement. Publishers produce more now, whether measured by turnover or number of products, than they ever have. In this expanded ecosystem they are still often the source of new ideas and the guarantor of quality even as other media, with more diffuse gatekeepers and less leeway for experimentation, lose touch with those roles.

What has changed is the relative place of the book. It has been nearly one hundred years since people started selling fake bookshelves, as recorded by the scholar Ted Striphas (2011). They wanted not real books but just the patina of learning, the cultural capital, associated with them. It indicated that the place of the book was, in this more competitive environment, shifting; that the role of books, maybe even of text, was, in some areas, becoming ornamental rather than structural. Today this continues. Whilst it could be argued that the superstore concept in the USA helped to pioneer the idea of retail as an experience—sofas, coffee, events—today the bookshop offers the prospect of symbolic capital. In China, for example, amongst the many new shopping malls built over the last few decades, bookshops are offered preferential rates by landlords. They are not really economically viable or intensively used by customers, but landlords like the idea of having them: they make shopping respectable. In many countries bookshops need a much wider range of stock in order to survive—toys, games, stationery, mugs…Some governments give financial support to independent bookshops. Newspapers have slowly but surely abandoned dedicated book sections; were it not for the continued status con-ferral of books, this process would have been completed. Books are no longer the central pillar of climbing the academic career path in many disciplines—the journal article is the unit of currency. Instead books are usually now something like a lap of honour for senior, tenured, end-of-career superstars to sum up their findings published elsewhere. With book chapters and journal articles merged in all-encompassing databases, will we even know that we are reading content from a book? We have seen a slow cultural shift in the meaning of books and, even, thanks to the ubiquitous force of the image, the priv-ilege of text. Publishers whose stock in trade are both of those things are bound to be impacted. Publishers have always dealt in signifiers; but their stock in trade has itself become a signifier as much as a trade.

Those watercooler or school gate conversations about popular culture are more likely to be discussions of the latest Netflix drama or continental crime series; although there was a brief appearance from *50 Shades of Grey*. Comparing the time use of different media is an inexact science, but estimates suggest that while reading time for pleasure is still significant, it has consistently lost ground to other media forms. Intensifying this trend is the fact that the most ardent readers are clustered in older age ranges. Whilst two-thirds of British adults read for pleasure, only 46.8 per cent had bought a novel in the last 12 months (DCMS 2015). Meanwhile the UK government media regulator Ofcom says people spend 8 hours and 41 minutes per day on media devices—more time than they spend asleep (Miller 2014). TV viewing per day is about four hours, while Americans watch over five hours of TV per day on average (Kafka 2016) (https://www.recode.net/2016/6/27/12041028/tv-hours-per-week-nielsen).

Most publishers have never simply been producers of books. Production has always been one department among many; marketing or even editorial is not involved in the 'production' of a book in the primary sense. What is more, to return to OUP, they not only produce books, such as this, but they also produce journals, class materials, research or learning resources, all in both physical and digital forms. Indeed, the world's biggest publishers are not conventional book publishers at all. Companies like Pearson and RELX, with multi-billion pound stock market valuations and revenues to match, increas-ingly produce fewer 'books': most of their output is non-book in form, and an increasingly large proportion is digital to boot.

Interestingly it is precisely these companies that are keenest to shed the label publisher. Instead they want to define themselves as information technology businesses. As valuable as they may be, their valuations pale compared to the swollen market capitalizations of the Silicon Valley giants. And, after all, like them, they are platforms, companies that trade off their IP, manipulators of data, symbols, systems, and information. The difference is that investors have far more patience with technology firms. Hence those major companies want to be Big Tech, not Big Text. Despite a public perception of resistance to change, and some internal turf wars, publishing has for the most part leapt into the digital milieu headfirst. Publishers, as much as anyone, drove the adoption of ebooks or online class materials. And yet they are still, despite diktats from the C-suite to avoid the word at all costs, publishers. Most young graduates going to work at an international publishing corporation still think of themselves as working in publishing not educational service provision, even if their corporate literature says otherwise. And despite moving away from books, the core elements of publishing, that key intermediating function, is still powerfully and clearly present.

We are, then, talking of book publishers. But books are in a complex place and publishing is largely composed of entities that can only be loosely understood as 'book publishers' if at all. As always publishing, part industry, part practice, part societal foundation, is protean, contradictory, and complex.

THE INFORMATION ENVIRONMENT

Another way of thinking about books, journals articles, or 'content' more widely is, to follow Cope and Phillips, to think of each not as a product or given piece of text, but as specific kinds of 'information architecture' (Cope and Phillips 2006). If we tend to think of publishers as either producers (of books or other textual media) or service providers (to authors or readers), here is something different: information architects at a high level whose buildings are 'constructed' by authors. If we couple this with the notion of making public then perhaps we can see a way forward: publishers design and sustain various information architectures, which they produce and 'make public' in various forms. They do this as both a service and and as creators and sellers of products.

This concept of information, in the form of all the stuff that goes into what publishers publish, raises a further critical point about publishing: that it is extremely important to any given society. Despite the changing, ambiguous place of the book then, publishing, as an idea, remains of paramount importance. Publishing is one of the crucial conduits via which information, knowledge, and culture are disseminated; and in so doing it has an integral role in regulating how we live, what we believe, what we can know, when and how, what stories define us. It is riven through our education systems, it sets boundaries at the forefront of research, it is the ultimate record of our civilizations. Publishing is both a mirror to society but also a shaper of it. If anyone ever questions why publishing is worth studying in detail here is the answer: because publishing, whether in its ancient forms in the scriptoria of medieval monasteries or today, in the server stacks and development hubs of web platforms, is the critical medium in creating and constantly reproducing our information environment. Without publishing, a society is, as a collective, essentially voiceless.

It is worth breaking this down. Education for example is generally seen as one of the key offerings of the state. In general governments set or at least monitor curricula. But, whether government-owned or private, it is educational publishers who are then responsible for translating this high-level work into the concrete outputs of textbooks and classroom materials. Publishers must interpret and deliver as best they see fit the educational matter handed to them, but this usually allows considerable leeway. A multitude of often small editorial, design, production, sales, and marketing decisions will inflect the content in various ways and so subtly (and not so subtly) inflect and shape the educations of entire generations; in today's world that means publishers have a powerful role in the upbringing of virtually everyone on the planet. When we think of powerful companies we would tend to see multinational banks, the energy majors, big pharma, technology, . . . We probably think less of educational publishers. And yet, in the day to day constitution of young people everywhere, educational publishers probably have as much influence as anyone; they have their hands on the tiller of the future.

Similarly, the novel is a form constantly called into question. But we should not forget that a novel is, at heart, a story, and is probably the most archetypal story architecture in common currency today. And stories are fundamental to humanity. At an evolutionary level, the ability to put events into meaningful explanatory sequences has been a key part of our development as a species. Basic building blocks of human social life, communication, cooperation, and shared norms arose through the power of stories (Kluger 2017). Those who told stories gained status, popularity, partners, and influence within nascent hierarchies and tight communities: all to the good in securing their and their children's futures (Gottschall 2013). Since then it has been stories from Gilgamesh to King Arthur that define countries. Oral stories like the *Iliad* and the *Odyssey* continue to resonate thousands of years after their first tellings. Today publishers are, as much as any industry and probably more so, on the frontlines of nurturing and sustaining the art of storytelling. Books are still the fountainhead of new stories and the place old ones go for renewal. While film, TV, and gaming are all arguably much bigger in the race for attentional market share, all are to a degree still reliant on book authorship and publishing. Once again, because of its role at the centre of the communications environment, publishing has a pivotal role in an essential human activity.

When we think of the cutting edge of research, we are thinking about an organized system of scrutiny and doubt. The Scientific Revolution of the sixteenth and seventeenth centuries was premised upon a new openness to empirical verification and falsification: knowledge was not to be taken on trust but was to be tested. Here is where the new industry of publishing was also to be vital, and continues in that role. Methods and results were to be made public and shared with peer scientists. They could then recreate the experiments and quiz all aspects of what happened. The key in this system of knowledge was precisely its public character. Openness to critical observation from all quarters was essential to the ongoing process of knowledge accumulation. Open publication and peer review is still to this day the gold standard of knowledge. Until something is officially published, it is not considered to have entered the lexicon of what is known. Until it is there, on the page or screen, for peers to critique and analyse, it has not yet proved itself. Publishing, then, has an extraordinary, unique, and under-appreciated epistemological role as an arbiter of truth; as a referee in the great and never-ending game of what can said to be known. Whether this role will continue in the form of the present day publishers, or will evolve into something new, or exist as it does now somewhere between the two, remains to be seen. But as long as there is a commitment to a set of scientific values prioritizing transparency and dissemination, publishing will have a role.

This is hardly an exhaustive survey of how publishing interacts with the wider information environment in crucial ways. But it is indicative. We can think of publishing as a set of companies and practices, which it is. Beneath that however lies something more significant and lasting, that survives the vicissitudes of an ever-changing marketplace where businesses come and go (even in a sector where companies last for hundreds of years). This is the deep structuring function publishing, as a concept, has in the world, a function which in various forms it has held for a long time. Even if the Order of the Book is challenged, the Order of Publishing remains. But while that function is not going away, it may be changing faster than ever.

THE STUDY OF PUBLISHING

Publishing has been studied within a host of disciplines, and this is reflected in its being taught in schools of media, communication, literature, sociology, business, and library and information science. Researchers from book history have examined all periods of the history of the book and publishing. One aim of the present volume is to present the study of publishing as an important new area of research and teaching, whilst continuing to draw on the allied areas mentioned above. We have sought to bring together leading international scholars of the subject to present a fully rounded picture of the ideas and approaches that make up the field of publishing studies.

The rapid growth in the number of programmes teaching publishing, from undergraduate level to PhD and postdoc research, shows the strong interest from the industry in greater professionalization, and new thinking is required all the time to keep abreast of the changes that have been taking place within publishing: from digitization to globalization. Theory has been adapted or applied from other subject disciplines, and fresh ideas have been put forward to explain what it is that publishers do, and how they can add value in a world of free content and self-publishing. What is exciting about this book is to see all this thinking put together in one place, alongside new approaches across a variety of dimensions.

The study of publishing comes of age with this volume. There are some who would argue that publishing studies simply applies to the study of the business aspects of the industry, and as such it should simply be subsumed elsewhere. This aspect is naturally important when focusing on one industry, but also of significance are the cultural, informational, and societal dimensions which make publishing so unique. If governments wish to control publishing and publishers, as they still do in many parts of the world, this can only highlight the valuable (and potentially challenging) contribution publishing makes to a flourishing society.

This Handbook provides a comprehensive and integrative exploration of current research and thinking, featuring contributions from both industry professionals and internationally renowned scholars from publishing and allied fields. It is divided into three distinct sections—context, dynamics, and practice—and covers subjects from copyright to corporate social responsibility. The contributors offer a range of viewpoints on how the industry is developing against a backdrop of globalizing markets, evolving strategies, and changing technology. They also reveal the continued importance of publishing and what publishers do—adding value whether through selection, design, or market awareness.

Publishing today is a major area of study with numerous undergraduate and graduate programmes on both sides of the Atlantic as well as significant presences in countries such as China, South Korea, the Netherlands, Germany, the Baltics, the Balkans, Argentina, Australia, South Africa, and Nigeria (Simon Fraser University Library 2018). From an ever-increasing number of influential and often cross-disciplinary monographs to scholarly articles in journals such as *Publishing Research Quarterly* and *Logos*, and the SHARP and *By the Book* conferences, there is a growing volume of high quality research, and this book is designed to put publishing in its full theoretical and business context whilst offering an invaluable multi-dimensional perspective. Publishing also attracts commentary in the industry and popular media, and the many conferences, blogs, and news articles show that there is an insatiable industry appetite for information about how digital in particular is changing the landscape. From the death of the book to the death of the ebook, the mainstream media remains fascinated by developments in book publishing.

Chapter topics and authors are carefully selected in order to give the Handbook the widest audience and most significant impact possible, of use to those studying publishing in the academy and also practitioners interested in the cutting edge understanding of their sector and discipline. Each chapter summarizes the present state of knowledge, with the inclusion of relevant authors, publications, and ideas. Where appropriate there is a view of the historical context as well as empirical data to help map the territory of the topic. The reader will find analysis, principles, key issues, and the essential context. When analysing market sectors or particular areas of practice, there is a view of the overall structures and dynamic. Illuminated are key questions and research areas for the future.

CHAPTERS

The Handbook is divided into three main sections: context, dynamics, and practice. In the first part we look at the fundamental influences on publishing, and how publishing interconnects with our society and culture.

Context: The chapter by Alistair McCleery discusses the nature of publishing history, and by implication how far back it stretches, and seeks to distinguish it from an amorphous, more elastic book history by exploring the nature and definition of publishing itself. In doing so, it will critically examine the 'great men' who constitute publishing's own historical vision of itself, as demonstrated in its many appeals to the past, before 'reverse engineering' aspects of the history of HarperCollins as representative of the contemporary industry.

Simone Murray argues that there is no inevitability about books being assigned to individual authors. Rather, it is because of a centuries-long process of copyright development and because of the dominance of a particular form of Western-European legal-aesthetic theory that the question of authorship appears so unproblematic. As digital communication facilitates self-publishing, enables texts to circulate anonymously, and provides global platforms for writers to read, critique, edit, and rewrite others' works, the intellectual struts that supported a print regime of textual fixity, standardized format, and individualized authorial control are being kicked out from under book culture.

Books need readers and over time reading became a necessary skill for gaining access to culture and knowledge. Yet it is not an easy activity for humans to engage in and screens offer many competing means of communication. Adriaan van der Weel suggests that the book industry has a great deal to learn from this newly arising awareness of the historically contingent role of reading in society. Because the status and position of reading depend on conscious decisions and continued efforts to make it relevant, in a world dominated by screens reading requires more conscious cultivation than one would like to think. The continued existence of the reader as a dependable customer of the book industry is rather more uncertain than it has ever been.

It would be no exaggeration to say that copyright is the foundation upon which the entire edifice of modern publishing has been built. Yet copyright, as we know it, is in transition. Given the closeness of the relationship between copyright and publishing, the implications of the modern copyright landscape for publishing could not be more fundamental or far-reaching. For better or for worse, the transformation of modern copyright law in the digital environment will shape the future of publishing. Mira T. Sundara Rajan asks whether the destruction of the copyright concept as we know it is inevitable, or is the prospect of a world without copyright absurd?

In her chapter on publishing and society, Elizabeth le Roux reflects on how publishing has taken different forms in different societies. The demographics of particular societies influence what is published and who controls the publishing process—thus, questions of gender, race, and class, and of diversity, are significant. The publishing of a controversial book can highlight fractures within the social identities of different societies, especially if it touches on issues such as religion, nationalism, politics, or sexuality. Debates around education, language, and culture all overlap with, or are centrally affected by, published products. Society can also directly impact on publishing, especially through government interventions, ranging from protectionism and promotion to regulation, and from textbook procurement to censorship.

John Oakes writes that the very concept of 'publishing and culture' may seem an oxymoronic combination: but if culture in its broadest sense is taken to mean the delimitations of a particular society, then book publishing plays an essential role in defining those delimitations. It is at the heart of cultural change, exchange, and interpretation. That is why publishing is not simply just another business; that is why it embodies the conflict between the commercially successful and the culturally substantive. Publishing traffics in the written transfer of ideas, of crafted messages that represent a direct appeal from the mind of the creator/author to that of the consumer/reader. It is a principle that applies as much to the works of Dale Carnegie as it does to those of Samuel Beckett.

Martin Eve addresses some of the conceptual challenges around speaking about publishing and 'information'. These range from the underlying philosophical distinctions between the various terms through to practical mutations in the non-fiction/ scholarly publishing spaces and the growing demands to publish new types of data objects and software. The focus here is specifically upon the turn to data and digital-artefactual publishing within the contexts of 'information'. He argues that the true challenges for publishing and information in the era of the Internet pertain to frames of cultural authority and truth but also to labour scarcity in publishing in a digital world that presents itself as infinitely abundant.

In his chapter on publishing and networks, Carlos A. Scolari gives a bird's eye view of the main transformations of media ecology since the emergence and spread of digital networks in the early 1970s. He analyses the most important 'commodity'—at least for publishers—that flows through the digital networks: the texts. His analysis focuses on the changes in the processes of production, distribution, and consumption of content, with phenomena such as collaborative production, user-generated content, filtering processes, and the emergence of a new figure: the hyperreader.

There are vital issues affecting our planet including climate change, inequality, and political freedom, and publishers have produced many books and articles on these topics. Companies are not obliged to consider the externalities, or side-effects, of their operations, but most now recognize these cannot be ignored, as Angus Phillips writes about corporate social responsibility. As the world has become increasingly globalized, the need for firms to adopt and enforce policies around social and environmental responsibility becomes ever more urgent. Further, if questions are asked about why we need publishers—what value do they bring?—addressing the area of corporate social responsibility throws up a key answer. A credible publisher assumes responsibility for, and believes in, its content and stands by its authors; this sets it apart from those who wish to be simply intermediaries in the distribution of content.

Dynamics: In the second part we analyse some of the fundamental drivers of the publishing industry. Ever since the times of Gutenberg, publishers have had to identify, understand, and create viable economic business strategies and models to cope with and minimize the pernicious impact of risk and complexity in a constantly changing business environment. In the first of his two chapters, Al Greco presents some of the major economists and their theories that provide an intellectual framework for publishers in a market that has been transformed from letterpress book formats to digital ebooks and streaming options. Very few industries release such a torrent of new products annually. This means that authors and editors experience considerable uncertainty since neither knows in advance with any certainty, except for a relatively small cluster of bestselling authors, if a book will be successful in the marketplace of ideas.

In a second chapter, on strategy, Greco shows that there has been a plethora of strategic theories that have influenced publishers. Publishers, editors, and authors face the fundamental question: what exactly do readers want? Companies have been able to craft strategies, and the structures needed to implement and execute strategies, to grow domestically and globally. While strategic theories have great value, there is always room for editors, publishers, and sales and marketing managers, in the diverse publishing industry, to use their judgement when confronted with randomness, chaos, or uncertainty in what is a constantly changing, shifting, and an exciting marketplace.

The international flow of bestsellers, global trade, universal production technologies and publishing skills, overseas printing, and international ownership of publishing houses have been around since the early days of the book business. Miha Kovač and Rüdiger Wischenbart examine how these common properties fuelled international book production throughout the twentieth and early twenty-first centuries, with a particular focus on which common features drove the overall expansion of the book industry, as well as what forces shaped differences along regional, cultural, or national lines.

Curation concerns what a publisher chooses to publish and why. Curation, which Michael Bhaskar defines as 'selecting and arranging to add value', is a proactive and wide-ranging process. To both outsiders and those working in other departments, there can be an air of mystery attached to the editorial process. Meetings are often closed to many employees. Editors traditionally wield power and status and are at the heart of critical business and creative decision making. Intersecting lines of financial and taste-making responsibility imbue the role with prestige. But it is vital, if we are to understand publishing, to demystify the editorial and understand the structural role of curation. Bhaskar here articulates an idea of the 'curatorial paradigm' which underpins and drives the editorial strategy of a given publishing house as a means of doing so.

While it is the most visible sector of publishing in the eyes of many, trade publishing is only one of the many worlds of publishing, and significantly smaller, in terms of overall revenue, than the combined sales of other publishing sectors that have a less prominent public profile, such as educational and professional publishing. It is also a riskier and less profitable sector, in part because customer prices are lower and the discounts offered to retailers are higher in trade publishing compared to educational and professional publishing. Trade publishing is, nonetheless, a central part of the industry, and it is the world in which many who want to work in publishing hope to build a career. John Thompson examines the field of Anglo-American trade publishing and four aspects of the field that are particularly important: the value of author brand; the relation between frontlist and backlist; the role of marketing and publicity; and the challenges and opportunities created by the digital revolution.

In turn Samantha Rayner explores the field of academic publishing. This includes monographs, journals, editions of texts, higher education textbooks, and collections of essays, all of which have undergone some sort of peer review process. Simply put, the field covers the production and dissemination of knowledge and research, but, intricately involved with political issues around education and the value of the knowledge economy, accessibility, and status, it is, and always has been, a complex, innovative, and reflexive industry. The drive to create content that is Open Access has been one of the transformative factors in academic publishing since the beginning of the twenty-first century, but the impetus to spread research and knowledge widely has arguably underpinned academic publishing since its beginnings in the late medieval period.

In many countries the publishing industry is, at its heart, educational publishing. Thanks to compulsory school attendance, educational publishers have the broadest audience of all book publishers, since they provide books for entire age cohorts and, for some people at least, textbooks are practically the only books they encounter in their entire life. Yet regardless of this wide audience, educational publishing remains an almost invisible field within the book industry. Indeed, there are no textbook bestseller charts, and textbook authors attract nowhere near the same level of media attention as bestselling fiction and non-fiction writers. Miha Kovač and Mojca K. Šebart analyse the impact of digital developments in this sector, and see educational publishing as a litmus paper of deep changes that are taking place in education. As such, it is becoming one of the main observation areas for those who wish to understand changes in the culture and anthropology of contemporary societies.

Practice: This book is in no way intended as a how-to guide for the profession, but there are areas of practice with distinctive ideas and approaches. Editorial was covered in the earlier chapter on curation, and we turn to other topics in the third part of the book, beginning with Frania Hall's examination of the structure of publishing companies. Publishing houses have recognizable organizational hierarchies that have evolved out of the management and production thinking which has been mimicked across many sorts of businesses through the twentieth century. Smaller publishing companies also generally adopt a functional approach to the business of publishing. But these structures can make it difficult to manoeuvre a company effectively in response to a rapidly changing environment and so there is an increasing awareness that new approaches to organizational design may be necessary in order for a company to position itself and adapt as needed for a constantly changing digital environment.

For more than five hundred years the aim of all publishing was to produce a physical product, and therefore design was concerned with the qualities of the book as an object, taking into account its haptic qualities and durability as well as the visual arrangement of text, illustrations, and binding. The development of electronic publishing channels alongside the printed book has radically changed this, as outlined by Paul Luna. Publishers may control every aspect of a physical book's design but, as content providers for electronic distribution, their influence over the appearance of an electronic book and how readers interact with it may be limited by the devices and platforms on which they publish. The design of both the material book and the virtual book therefore need to be considered, because design for publishing involves the creation of both engaging individual artefacts and complex design systems.

John Maxwell reminds us that should we think that digital media is somehow a break from the tradition of books and publishing, it it helpful to remember that publishing has always been a technological endeavour; its 'killer app' has always been the scaling up of audiences—publics—by technological means. What we see on the publishing landscape today is not so much a revolution but a flowering of possibilities: while the printed book trade continues to reach mass audiences as it has done for centuries, the Internet teems with myriad new channels, new forms, and new genres. Some closely resemble the print forms we have known, such as ebooks and online news sources; many do not, and challenge us to think about what we mean when we talk about 'publishing'. If we take a very broad definition of publishing—as nothing less than the infrastructure of modern liberal culture—then publishing and its long relationship to 'high tech' seems very robust indeed.

The chapter by Alison Baverstock shows how the marketing and public positioning of books has become critical to their success and marketers enjoy increasing clout in both organizational direction and publishing decisions. The mechanics through which they do this are, however, changing. Publishers have always had to balance the delivery of marketing and publicity, informally defined as promotion you do and do not pay for respectively, but new tools such as digital marketing and social media increasingly blur boundaries. The once classic intermediary mechanisms between author and reader— book reviews and serial extracts in the quality press—are changing as new methods of informing markets emerge; their significance is increasing as newspaper circulations fall and the impact of book bloggers and 'friends' on social media rises.

The author as the creator is normally the primary owner of copyright in a work together with all attendant rights; however, most authors will then delegate the handling of such rights to their literary agent or their publisher, depending on the terms of the publishing contract. Over the years the sale of rights has become increasingly important to the publishing industry; for some types of publishing, particularly in the area of illustrated books, rights sales may make projects financially viable and will make a crucial contribution to the profitability of the publishing company. As Lynette Owen writes, the function is crucial to the publishing industry and its importance is often underestimated by comparison with the primary editorial and sales functions—indeed, licence revenue is often wrongly compared with sales turnover, when the publisher share of licensing revenue should rightly be compared with the profit element of such sales.

When thinking of publishing, libraries may not spring to mind as customers with the same immediacy as bookshops, but Alex Holzman and Sarah Lippincott show why this is wrong in their chapter on libraries. They argue that libraries are the crucial outlets for large numbers of publishers, buying the majority of monographs and journals subscriptions, acting as repository, gatekeeper, and curator of publisher materials. But thanks to rising costs the relationship has become fraught, even as it has started to dematerialize in the digital context. At the same time they identify a comparatively new trend: that of libraries themselves becoming publishers in a number of different forms. As with bookshops, they describe a tense but ultimately symbiotic relationship, and it is to bookshops that Niels Peter Thomas turns his attention in the final chapter of the part. For centuries bookselling has been integral to the publishing process, but, as with so many areas of publishing, it has recently gone through immense change, from the rise of major book chains to the relentless growth of online bookselling. Competitive and innately open to the immediate whims of the book buying public, bookselling, whether on the retail or wholesale side, has never been easy. Nonetheless it is a vital and continuing part of the value and supply chain for books.

Coda: If we cannot predict the future of publishing, we can at least think about it. We can ask various questions of the form 'what if' and then pursue their consequences—an exercise carried out in the thought experiments of the coda, the final chapter of the Handbook. We can create miniature narratives based on extrapolated premises from the present and see what happens. We can do this firstly in a spirit of thinking with a rich intellectual lineage and secondly in terms of the new prevalence of thought experiments at extrapolating into uncertain futures. Thought experiments for publishing can throw the future—and the present—into relief; isolating salient features of publishing and extending them into extremes forces us to reconsider present trajectories. In turn this can help deepen an understanding of publishing and formulate strategies to navigate the future. We do not claim these thought experiments will in any way happen. They likely won't. But, in their various articulations and modalities, they should clarify what is important, what is at stake, what is within the boundaries of the possible for the future of publishing.

CONCLUSION

Publishing is different. That difference warrants interrogation, explanation, and articulation. Above all else, this is what the Handbook should do: understand what publishing is, does, and means, especially in the context of fast-changing markets, evolving technologies, and unstable structures of communication, to combine theory and practice at a deep level where each informs the other. Publishers are typically focused on the exigencies of their profession rather than its academic implications or understanding. Although it always has a bookish air, and although publishers are generally not the primary producers, publishers are still doers. The publishing schedule is an unforgiving and unending taskmaster that needs to keep rolling. Deadlines and bottom lines alike dictate most of the day to day of publishing activity, and each leaves little room for reflection. While most publishers have a stock they can rely on, their backlists, in truth most publishers are flow businesses: they rely on a constant stream of newness for their survival, and it is this stream above all that guides and governs their activities.

Yet precisely because of that new context, publishing is entering a new era of sophistication, where, as Al Greco makes clear in this volume, advanced business strategies are more commonplace. This in turn implies that deeper and more nuanced understandings of both the practice, the wider environment and techniques in general are both required and appropriate for publishers. In other words, theory and practice should not, and cannot, be as divorced as they once were. While scholars need, of course, to pay close attention to actions on the ground, publishers need to know what it is they do and how, where it is they add value in a world of extreme competition and information saturation. Whether it comes in the increasing use of data analytics or market research, a new attitude to testing making the most of tech-pioneered mechanics like A/B testing, in the understanding and appreciation of code, or the articulation of mission and purpose in an unstable world, never before has there been such a need to cross fertilize practice with theory.

Over the course of the twenty-first century, publishing, as it has traditionally been constituted, will face a series of existential challenges the likes of which it has only ever seen, in its modern incarnation, in the wake of catastrophic upheavals such as global conflict or events like China's Cultural Revolution. This time the pressures are economic and technological, although of course we can never discount other forms of disruption as well. All this means that publishing will not only need the best possible account of itself, a deep understanding of what it does and why it matters, but it will also need to understand how it can be improved, how it can constantly get better. On both fronts, a unity of theory and practice will be essential. As much as anything else, that is the goal of this volume.

References

Batchelor, James (2018). 'Games industry revenues in 2017'. *GamesIndustryBiz* [online]. Available at: https://www.gamesindustry.biz/articles/2018-01-31-games-industry-generated-usd108-4bn-in-revenues-in-2017 [Accessed 3 Apr 2018]

Cope, B. and A. Phillips, eds (2006). *The Future of the Book in the Digital Age*, Witney: Chandos.

DCMS, Department for Culture, Media and Sport (2015). *Taking Part 2013/14, Free time activities, Statistical Release*, March.

Gottschall, Jonathan (2013). *The Storytelling Animal: How Stories Make Us Human*, New York: Mariner Books.

Kafka, Peter (2016). 'You are still watching a staggering amount of TV every day'. *Recode* [online]. Available at: https://www.recode.net/2016/6/27/12041028/tv-hours-per-week-nielsen [Accessed 4 Apr 2018].

Kluger, Jeffrey (2017). 'How Telling Stories Makes Us Human'. *Time* [online]. Available at: http://time.com/5043166/storytelling-evolution/ [Accessed 8 Apr 2018].

Miller, Joe (2014). 'Britons spend more time on study than asleep'. BBC [online]. Available at: http://www.bbc.co.uk/news/technology-28677674 [Accessed 4 Apr 2018].

Oxford University Press (2017). *Annual Report of the Delegates of the University Press 2016/17* [online]. Available at: https://annualreport.oup.com/2017/report-of-the-secretary-to-the-delegates/ [Accessed 1 Apr 2018].

Robbins, Keith, ed. (2017). *The History of Oxford University Press*, Volume IV: 1970–2004, Oxford: Oxford Univesity Press.

Simon Fraser University Library (2018). 'Publishing programmes and conferences around the world'. Simon Fraser University [online]. Available at: https://www.lib.sfu.ca/help/research-assistance/subject/publishing/schools [Accessed 25 Apr 2018].

Striphas, Ted (2011). *The Late Age of Print: Everyday Book Culture from Consumerism to Control*, New York: Columbia University Press.

Van Der Weel, Adriaan (2011). *Changing Our Textual Minds: Towards a Digital Order of Knowledge*, Manchester: Manchester University Press.

PART I

PUBLISHING IN CONTEXT

CHAPTER 2

··

PUBLISHING HISTORY

··

ALISTAIR McCLEERY

INTRODUCTION

PUBLISHING houses are vain institutions: they trace, if at all plausible, their pedigrees as far back as possible; and they issue histories of themselves in a manner few other sectors dare. These house histories represent a constant and continuing form of institutionalized cultural capital (inherited also by the original company's heirs and successors) that, in turn, creates a social capital which disguises the commercial, or economic capital[ist], basis of those companies and their imprints. The house histories move, when issued, with the technologies available to their publishers: from the conventional print history of Longmans edited by Asa Briggs (1974), sponsored by the company, through the CD-based history of the German reference publisher Brockhaus, replete with documentation (Keiderling 2005), to the online history of HarperCollins (2017) that ascribes its origins to the earliest incarnations of its various components, no matter how recently acquired. Yet for all this autobiography, and self-aggrandisement, publishing itself, expressed as either the development of an industry, the preferred form of self-definition as witnessed by this flood of house histories, or as a function, the making available to the public of material, usually but not exclusively on a commercial basis, has become merely a sub-set of a more general book history. Academics categorize and compartmentalize and, in doing so, make publishing history subordinate to the history of the book, the function subordinate to the physical form. The pre-eminence, and uniqueness at one time, of the journal *Publishing History*, issued from 1977 onwards to complement its then owner Chadwyck-Healey's sale of publishers' archives on microfilm, gave way in academic precedence to the journal *Book History* from 1998 onwards, published on behalf of the all-encompassing Society for the History of Authorship, Reading and Publishing (SHARP). A critical, and growing, mass of researchers and scholars under this larger umbrella was enough to push publishing history to the margins of academe; it also created a student market for a wide range of introductions to Book History (now with acquired capitals) from Finkelstein and McCleery (2012) to Mole and Levy (2017).

This chapter will discuss the nature of publishing history, and by implication how far back it stretches, and seek to distinguish it from an amorphous, more elastic book history (minus the capitals) by exploring the nature and definition of publishing itself. In doing so, it will examine the 'great men' who constitute publishing's own historical vision of itself, as demonstrated in its many appeals to the past, before 'reverse engineering' aspects of the history of HarperCollins as representative of the contemporary industry. Such an exercise might, on the one hand, compensate for the complacent claims of the house histories, while, on the other, redressing the imbalance that has displaced publishing history from the centre of scholarly activity to its periphery. The wider academic field of book history had its roots in the distinct disciplines of textual criticism and social and economic history. Its presence in the academy was increasingly formalized from the 1980s onwards but its institutional base, in either Literature or History departments, and the wide range of outputs labelled as book history betrayed those discrete origins. Even the focus on the printed book was contested as scholars argued that the enabling technology of the book was script (and reading) and the scope of book history moved backwards from the near contemporary to the transition from orality to literacy, to the development from tablet and roll to codex, and to the movement from manuscript to print. However, four major approaches dominate the field as outlined by Howsam (2006): the book as a material object; the book as a vehicle for a (malleable) text; the book as the object of a series of (commercial) transactions; and the book as an agent in society—all of which tend to diminish the structures and function of publishing.

Book history not only traces the long development of the material forms of the book, with the concomitant risk of technological determinism, particularly in regard to ebooks and previous revolutions of the 'paperback' or of printing itself, but it also looks beyond that to identify and question the meanings of those material forms—something that can be illustrated from this very book: format, imprint, the absence or presence of an index—all reinforce its status as an academic text. This paratextual meaning, a term popularized by Genette (1997), complements the creation of meaning in the text itself (as well as influencing commercial decisions). While discussions of typography and layout treat words as images, examinations of the text, as it is given form in different books at different times, treat words as symbols to be interpreted through the act of reading. Book history traces the development of texts as they are given materiality in different shapes and kinds of container, including ebooks. The origins of this approach in textual criticism has privileged, with few exceptions, and sustained the centrality of, canonical texts within literature. In doing so, a clear focus on the publication of fiction has been created that obscures the actual dominance of other forms of publishing, particularly educational and scientific. Emphasis upon the creation of meaning has, in addition, focused attention on the nature of reading and, in distinction to the intentionalism that motivated much textual criticism, displaced the author, if not actually killed off that role, in favour of the reader—as much as it has erased the publisher altogether.

The transactional approach within book history does fully restore the role of the author in the latter's interaction with other agents involved in the creation, distribution, and reception of books, from publishers to readers, from libraries to institutions of the state—and all points in-between in the models developed by a number of prominent book historians such as Robert Darnton (1990). All tend to owe their origins to the communication circuit model developed by Shannon and Weaver in the 1940s for information theory: the point of origin (the author) is set, as is the point of reception (the reader) and in-between are the various agents (publisher, government, etc.) involved in either enhancing or inhibiting the transmission. The approach to book history based on variations of this model manages to squeeze in the publisher, and the publishing function, at some point between authors and readers. The study of the diversity of transactions involving books produces the richest range of materials in book history but also signals a move away from the book, as the vehicle for a particular text, to books, as a social and economic category of good. This approach relies on the methodologies, and forms of data, familiar within the social sciences, including economic history, as opposed to those of the humanities. Book historians have also plundered sociological theory, most recently the work of Pierre Bourdieu (1993), to enhance an understanding of the social roles and status of books (and reading). Bourdieu's notion of the social capital to be gained from books, both reading them and owning them, underpins much work on the aggregated, as opposed to the individual, nature of books, readers, and indeed publishers. With the development from the twentieth century onwards of other interactive pursuits, competing for our time, reading (and the purchase and borrowing of books) became more clearly only one of many lifestyle choices; the understanding derived in this area from book history informs how not only the imme-diate past but also the immediate future are viewed. Book history, in the interest of bal-ance here, does restore the external context (other than commercial rivalry) that most house histories lack and avoids the introspection that ignores, or loses sight of, wider movements within the publishing sector, of which any particular publishing house is only one component. A more specific publishing history is needed, however, to under-stand the contemporary industry and its practices.

THE ORTHODOX HISTORY OF PUBLISHING

Restoration of the emphasis upon the publishing function, rather than the material form or the social role of books, does, however, enable an even longer pedigree and trad-ition of service (to literature and the public) to be established, in much the same manner as Ulysses founded Lisbon or Aeneas settled Rome. These classical comparisons are not so far-fetched when Titus Pomponius Atticus (c110–32BC) is claimed as the first 'publisher'—and there have been at least eight publishers or imprints in the past century drawing on that name to indicate their lineage, including the contemporary Atticus Books in New York and the Atticus Bookstore in New Haven. 'Cicero could depend on [Atticus] to provide all the services of a high-class publisher [who] would carefully revise a work for him, criticize points of style or content, discuss the advisability of publication or the suitability of a title, hold private readings of the new book, send out complimentary copies, organize its distribution', claimed Reynolds and Wilson in their seminal and influential survey of the Roman book (1968: 22). That this has not continued to be the accepted scholarly wisdom may be due to the term 'publisher' initially being interpreted solely as the function of making public but then being associated by analogy with the range of roles played by the contemporary publishing industry. Debate (summarized by Phillips 1986) took place amongst distinguished classicists about whether Atticus merely sponsored private editions of Cicero's works and, as a knight, avoided the grubbiness of commercial transactions best left to freedmen or slaves; or whether he was the financial backer and organizational genius behind a system of production, distribution, and sales, perhaps through his own outlets or through independent booksellers (*librarii*—in a denial of the original meaning of that word as 'copyist', normally a slave copyist). However, both sides are guilty of viewing the Roman past through a contemporary lens. In discussing Atticus as the first 'publisher', and the Sosii brothers as the 'publishers' of Horace, and Tryphon as the 'publisher' of Quintilian, these classicists are also inviting the twenty-first-century reader to impose a contemporary understanding of publishing upon its history. 'The idea that these people [Atticus, etc.] can legitimately be called "publishers" with a ' "business", in anything like the way that these terms are used today, and with today's implications of commercial dealing between publisher and author, and between publisher, bookshops and reading public . . . is misconceived': Rex Winsbury (2009: 53) concluded, drawing on the authority of his own career in publishing. So, if publishing history rests on the general function of making available, then Atticus may well be the first 'publisher'. If, however, we are seeking a history of a publishing that evolves into the forms recognizable today, then a different starting point, and 'first publisher', will be needed.

Aldus Manutius (1449 or 1452–1515) represents another strong candidate for the title—and there have been many publishers or imprints drawing on his name as well, not necessarily all of a 'high-class' nature or acting as private presses. The Aldine Publishing Company of London produced, from the late 1880s onwards, reprints of American 'dime novels' such as the adventures of Buffalo Bill; while contemporaneously, the Aldine Company of New York issued *The Aldine, The Art Journal of America*; and Doubleday, founded in 1897 but whose name and history have now been acquired by Penguin Random House, appropriated his dolphin and anchor logo. Currently, Aldine Transaction is used as a social science imprint by Transaction Publishing, based in New Jersey, a relic of the Aldine Publishing Company bought from the Walter de Gruyter Publishing Group in 2004. Nor is the privileging of Manutius as primogenitor confined to publishers: Aldus PageMaker, the pioneering DTP software for Apple Macintosh, created by the Aldus Corporation, only became the more banal InDesign after acquisition by Adobe Systems in 1994; and, finally, the network of European Book Fairs is called ALDUS, a name that, despite appearances, is not an acronym but a tribute.

The case for Aldus Manutius, and for this nominative commemoration, lies in two aspects of his story: his position as the centre of a group of translators, writers, and printers that seems to underwrite the view of the publisher as manager of a process, or of a series of transactions; and his role in promoting and propagating the texts and values of the humanist movement that was the Renaissance. Ever since the pioneering biography by Martin Lowry (1979), we have been encouraged to picture the figure of Manutius at the eye of a whirlwind of intellectual activity: inspiring new editions and translations from classical Greek (and new editions of Latin texts, including Cicero's letters to Atticus in 1513), in conservation of a knowledge under threat since the fall of Constantinople in 1453; while overseeing the development of new fonts, such as Griffo's *italic*, in order to make his books more convenient and more accessible; and, last but not least, inventing the semi-colon. The resulting body of publications reminded Europe of its classical antecedents and permitted it to move beyond the strictures of medieval Christianity to a view of the universe with (Vitruvian) man at the centre of it. This combination of principled teacher and pragmatic creative contains a strong appeal in terms of the self-perception of contemporary publishers as guardians of culture as well as of shareholders' interests. He certainly appealed to Roberto Calasso: 'To understand what a great publishing house can be, all you have to do is look at the books printed by Aldus Manutius. He was the Nadar [an early photographer] of publishing. He was the first to imagine a publishing house in terms of *form*' (2015: 5). Indeed, Calasso views publishers as creative artists in their own right through the act of publishing beautiful books. The self-congratulatory stance that permeates his slim and shallow book, yet translated from Italian and published as a Penguin paperback, may well strike a chord with others. Aldus Manutius is picked out here, and by Calasso obviously, not because his career is paradigmatic but, like Atticus, it remains aspirational.

However, and the qualification was predictable, characterizing Aldus Manutius in this manner still imposes the template of the present, with its more assured and defined perspective, over the rougher and hazier picture of the past, with the attendant risks of simplification and distortion. In the twenty years of the Aldine Press, from 1495 until his death, Manutius printed just over 120 books in runs ranging from the standard 200 copies to the exceptional 1,000. His distinctive role in this was primarily that of techno-logical innovator. Although Martyn Lyons (2011: 78) may be rather grudging in his summing up—'One important pioneer of this revival of classical literature was the Venetian printer Aldus Manutius'—he is correct in his presentation of Manutius as offering skilled reproduction services (much as the Roman copyists, or *librarii*, had done). Manutius was principally a technologist seeking creative and commercial solutions to market challenges, particularly for more portable, and handleable, books containing texts that would fit the ongoing creation of a new educational canon as defined by Neil Harris (2017). These attributes may be necessary components of publishing but they are not sufficient in providing a historical starting point for the evolution of contemporary publishing.

There are perhaps two other distinct objections to the position of either Atticus or Aldus at the head of the development of publishing history: Eurocentrism and the cult of the individual creator. For the former, any emphasis upon the neat succession of Sumerian to Persian to Greek to Roman, in terms of the development of the Roman script and of the material book, reinforces and privileges a teleology that culminates in the triumph of a globalized English language and the domination of an Anglo-American publishing industry. It would seem to exclude from publishing history any other contribution such as that of the Chinese. Certainly, China provided three significant technical innovations, primary amongst which was the manufacture of paper. Paper was key to the rapid development of book production and distribution throughout the developed world as it provided a cheap medium for printing, drawing on relatively accessible materials. Rags, whether of cotton or linen, became the predominant raw material due to a perpetual and relatively abundant supply, particularly in towns and cities. By 150 AD, paper use and manufacture had spread to Turkestan, and subsequently made its way to Korea, Vietnam, and Japan. In the coming centuries, paper use and papermaking skills dispersed via key trade routes into Central Asia; by 1150 it was being manufactured in Spain by Moorish craftsmen, and ultimately from there diffused throughout Europe and into the Western world.

The second major innovation derived from China was ink. 'Indian Ink', as it was known in English-speaking countries but 'Chinese Ink' in the rest of Europe, thereby indicating its point of diffusion, was a type of solid ink originally perfected by the Chinese for undertaking rubbings of texts carved in stone. The portability of the hardened ink sticks enabled their spread beyond Chinese borders (including into India), and ultimately into Western Europe, where the manufacture of such ink would be refined and redeveloped for printing purposes.

The third element, more contentious in terms of tracing its influence and adoption (or adaptation), was the Chinese development of wooden block printing. This, in turn, originated in two other practices: stone rubbing, in which texts incised in stone, to create an unalterable permanency, were copied onto dampened paper laid on the stone by rubbing across it with ink sticks; and stamping, in which wooden blocks, engraved in relief and reversed as in a mirror, were inked and then stamped onto paper. The combination of both practices in the use of wooden blocks to reproduce the texts previously incised on stone represents for most Chinese scholars the invention of printing. Certainly, it enabled the mass production of literary works and textbooks, readily incorporating illustrations, albeit for a very small readership. There was 'no market for books outside the emperor's palace' (Lyons 2011: 58). Moreover, although smaller wooden blocks for individual characters had been developed and used in China, they were less economical, in the sense of both time and cost, than larger, whole-text blocks. And however essential the technologies of paper, ink, and moveable type were to the evolution of publishing, this history of printing technologies represents again only one aspect of it.

Whether in highlighting Cai Lun in terms of paper, Tien-Lcheu in terms of ink, or Gutenberg in terms of moveable type, humanity likes to create individual narratives for its achievements, rather than describe the slow accretion of knowledge through experimentation and dissemination. On the other hand, this privileging of particular 'names', including Atticus and Aldus, perhaps distracts from the ability to trace a clear evolutionary line for a contemporary publishing that is larger scale in its scope and more collectivist in its operation. The industrialization, and Taylorization, of the copying function may have begun earlier, in the monastic manuscript scriptoria or the secular manuscript workshop of Vespasiano da Bisticci (1421–1498), but the development in the sixteenth century of large printing factories, such as that of Plantin-Moretus in Antwerp founded in 1564, signalled a clear movement in the scale and collective nature of the reproduction enterprise. By 1575, Christophe Plantin had 16 presses, eventually rising to 22, and employed 56 men—32 printers, 20 compositors, 3 proofreaders, and an odd-job man (Clair 1960). Each press could produce 1,250 double-sided pages in a single day, an output well in excess of the artisanal Aldus Manutius. The Plantin Press was responsible for some 1,863 different editions over its lifetime, a 1,500 per cent increase over the total for the Aldine Press.

This model of more extensive (more titles) and intensive (more copies) operation spread across Europe, as war and the other horsemen of the Apocalypse allowed. Louis Elzevir, for example, who had been an apprentice of Plantin, founded his eponymous factory in Leiden in 1580; the company had its heyday under further seventeenth-century generations of the family involved, like Manutius, in producing reprints and portable editions, until it declined and disappeared in the eighteenth century. Similar businesses survived, based on a market for reprints rather than necessarily original work; like hot-metal Xeroxes, they printed what they knew would sell, hence the emphasis upon reprints, and what they were paid to produce, which, if popular, would then be reproduced by other printers, in a not-so-virtuous circle based on minimizing risk in an age without the concept of intellectual property. Once such a concept was introduced, and given statutory force, then the business model based on reprints was much less viable. The company name, now as Elsevier, was revived in 1880 for a new publishing enterprise that thrived to become one of the largest science publishers in the world, as Reed Elsevier from 1992 to 2015 after merger with the UK-based Reed International, then as the RELX Group from 2015, deriving in 2016 only 26 per cent of its revenue from Europe and only 20 per cent from printed as opposed to online publications (RELX 2016). So, the great reveal: what happened between the death of one company, Elzevir, and the birth of another, Elsevier, marks the beginning of publishing history per se; and what happened was the introduction of copyright as a legally enforceable principle, common to a particular jurisdiction but increasingly harmonized across many jurisdictions, and independent of any particular method of reproduction.

However, before this is taken up in more detail, it should be noted that the cult of the individual creator also affected authorship as much as it did technological innovation. Early anonymous works, once they had moved from an oral into a written form were accorded authors, much as inventions like paper were, out of this sense that one person must have created them. The well-known 'first Chinese novel', *Journey to the West*, grew out of the folk tales surrounding the monk Xuanzang's pilgrimage to India; the best-known version was published anonymously as a block print after AD 1590 but it has since been ascribed to the scholar Wu Cheng'en (Yu 1977). It seems as if the very fixing of a text in that written form demands a single creator; it also privileges the integrity of the form of the text that is first set down. The protection of that text and the ownership of that author becomes in consequence a statutory right enshrined in many copyright jurisdictions. Copyright, in other words, belonged, and belongs, to the 'first creator', the author or artist, who was then able to assign it, through absolute sale or a licensing agreement, to a publisher. It offers the possibility of remuneration for the author but, more importantly for the publisher, it also provides the opportunity for monopolistic exploitation of the work in question. Indeed, while supposedly enacted in the name of the author, 'protections for intangible property rights and their codification in copyright law... have been shaped more by the economics of "publishing" than by the economics of "authorship"' (David 2004: 5).

A Publishing History of Publishing

Publishers are neither essentially copiers of texts nor exclusively 'merchants of culture', to appropriate John Thompson's phrase (2010), but traders in intellectual property or 'masters of content' to echo Michael Bhaskar's (2013) emphasis. That function or role defines publishing, rather than printing or bookselling, and depends on this clear watershed at the beginning of the eighteenth century when the concept of intellectual property, developed by the philosopher John Locke, passed into UK law through the 1710 Statute of Anne, the first such legislation in the world. All the attributes of 'property' were considered to apply to intellectual creation apart from materiality: the property belonged to the first creator, as above, and much as a builder builds a house that can subsequently be sold or rented under a tenancy agreement, so too the right to reproduce the intellectual creation could be sold outright or leased through an author–publisher agreement; once the property was sold, the author lost all rights in it or, if leased, only retained those rights defined in the agreement; and, if the author was employed to create the work, much as the builder might be paid to put up a house for a client, then the publisher who gave the commission owned the copyright. Although the original term of copyright, this exclusive licence to reproduce, was severely limited (to 14 years from the date of publication), commercial pressure from publishers, in collusion with authors and literary estates, has resulted in a much longer period today of the author's lifetime plus 70 years within which the monopoly can be exploited. In continental Europe, the later development of protection for intellectual creation, coming after the idealism of the French Revolution, took an approach based not on the concept of property but on that of parentage, forming inalienable bonds between author and work and granting the former moral rights in the latter which could not be disowned in any commercial transaction. The *Urheberrechtsgesetz* in Germany and the *droits d'auteur* in France, for example, while recognizing the 'economics of publishing', gave more prominence to the persistence of author's rights (their literal translation).

The fledgling USA adopted the same principle as the UK of 'intangible property', which could be sold or leased much as physical property, in its first federal Copyright Act in 1790, itself copied from the 1710 precedent. However, it applied only to American authors: American publishers could continue (unabated until 1891) the profitable business of reprinting, without payment or penalty, the works of foreign, English-language writers. Indeed, the provision of the 1790 Act that there should be no prohibition to the 'reprinting, or republishing within the United States, of any map, chart, book or books, written, printed, or published by any person not a citizen of the United States, in foreign parts or places without the jurisdiction of the United States' (quoted in Spoo 2013: 21) survived in one protectionist form or another, through the Chace Act of 1891 with its clause demanding US manufacture to guarantee copyright recognition, to mandatory registration of works with the Copyright Office, until the USA acceded to the Berne Convention in 1988, over a century after the UK and many other European countries had ratified the Convention to regulate and police copyright on an international level. This insularity again benefited the economics of publishing rather than the interests of indigenous authors: US publishers such as Harper & Brothers issued libraries of non-copyrightable British reprints to the exclusion of US writers. Of the 54 titles in Harpers' Franklin Square Library, published in 1886 and selling for 10 cents a book, only one was by an American writer. Of the 62 titles in Harpers' Handy Series, also published in 1886 and selling for 20 or 25 cents a book, only four were by American writers.

Some US publishers, such as Harpers, did pay British publishers and authors for early access to proofs as even a matter of days might make a difference in issuing their edition first and cornering this very competitive market based on unlicensed reprints. Chambers, the Edinburgh-based publisher, tried, for example, to provide such a time advantage to its legitimate partners in the USA through the use of the new transatlantic steamships, such as those of Cunard. This form of payment to publishers such as Chambers, however calculated, did also give the US publisher the opportunity to promote that edition as the 'authorized' version to distinguish it, and the company's status, from other unscrupulous and 'cheaper' (in every sense) competitors. However, the lack of a publishing monopoly granted by copyright resulted in a US marketplace characterized by an accentuated sense of commercial rivalry and a reliance on predatory pricing. In 1881 Harper & Brothers had a very public dispute with Scribners over the publication of J. A. Froude's edition of Thomas Carlyle's *Reminiscences*: Harpers had an agreement with Carlyle, made before his death, for the publication of his works; but Scribner's had signed an agreement with Froude, Carlyle's literary executor, and argued that it superseded any earlier arrangement. As no resolution of this dispute was possible, both Harpers and Scribner's published editions of *Reminiscences* and each continued to argue, in a very public manner, that theirs was the 'authorized' one (Tebbel 1987). On other occasions, collusion rather than competition, with publishers acting as a cartel to exploit the non-copyrighted text, could characterize their actions: Harpers and Ticknor & Fields fought over Charles Dickens's *The Mystery of Edwin Drood* (left unfinished on his death in 1870) but resolved the matter amicably with Harpers issuing it as a serial in *Harper's Weekly*, while Ticknor & Fields published the novel in book form (McParland 2011).

In a sense, there is much to link a company such as Harper & Brothers with Aldus Manutius or even Atticus: James and John Harper, the founders of the firm in 1817, were printers by training (and outlook); in the American context of disregard for foreign copyrights, they were able to reproduce non-American texts freely; and, in doing so, they chased the market for books of proven popularity, such as Dickens, rather than primarily creating a new market for US writers. This demanded the adoption of the factory-system pioneered by Plantin for mass reproduction of texts: by 1853 Harpers had 41 presses, in total producing 25 books every minute of the 10 hours per day of a 6-day working week, an output exponentially well in excess of that of Plantin. After a disastrous fire in late 1853, that output was further improved upon through the introduction of additional steam-powered presses and new technologies such as electrotyping: 28 such powered presses were installed in the company's building in 1855; and such mechanization allowed the employment of relatively unskilled female labour (300 women in printing, gathering, and binding in 1855) rather than the time-served craftsmen of Antwerp. The building of this reproduction complex enabled a very fast turnaround after receipt of proofs. On occasion, only 24 hours elapsed between the docking of the transatlantic ships and the Harpers edition, authorized or not, being sold to American readers. Harpers had become the largest printer in the USA, so it was little wonder that in 1884 the company advocated the form of manufacturing clause that was eventually incorporated within the Chace Act of 1891. However, such efficiency also brought with it a need to feed those presses with sufficient material to keep them rolling at peak output. This could only be achieved by looking beyond reprints and packaged libraries of non-copyright material to move into textbook and religious publishing of original material, and more particularly in the case of Harpers, into magazines.

Their first magazine, *Harper's New Monthly Magazine*, was launched in 1850, rapidly attaining a circulation of some 110,000 copies. *Harper's Weekly* followed in 1857 (two years after the installation of the new presses), selling an average of 100,000 copies a week by 1865, with specific issues reaching some 300,000 in sales. Women readers were catered for through the introduction of *Harper's Bazar* [sic] in 1867. The company was now a publisher, rather than a technically very adept, mass reproduction factory. Henry James compared magazine publishing to running a railway: the trains and issues had both to leave on time but, unlike the carriages of the former, all the pages of the latter had to be full. Material had to be commissioned or bought; reliable, consistent authors were to be discovered and nurtured; and risks had to be taken on texts that had not already been successful in other markets. Success followed in book publishing as well as in magazines: *Ben Hur* was published in 1880, and in 1895 an exclusive contract was signed with Samuel Clemens for all the Mark Twain books. And after the entry into the marketplace for intellectual property of the literary agent, to mediate on behalf of the interests of the author, then the publisher had to accommodate these new negotiating partners, even coming to rely on them for initial selection of material for appropriateness and quality. Henry Mills Alden, who was Editor of *Harper's Weekly* from 1863 to 1869, and of *Harper's Monthly* from 1869 to 1919, and who acted generally as the company's editorial *eminence grise*, welcomed the opportunities that the new literary agents brought. He also ensured authors were properly named at the head of their contributions, rather than the traditional anonymity they had 'enjoyed'; he was open to new as well as established writers; he was a strong advocate of American writers such as Clemens, Longfellow, and Henry James and their contribution to a cosmopolitan culture; he encouraged female authors such as Mary E. Wilkins Freeman; and he employed on his staff other eminent literary figures such as William Dean Howells. He could rightly claim that 'periodical literature has done more for the American people than any other' (Alden 1908: 49): it had also placed Harper & Brothers on a sound footing as a preeminent *publisher*.

However, that degree of editorial success does not in itself account for the emphasis here upon Harpers, who, while distinguished publishers of relatively long standing, were not after all the largest US publisher of the early twentieth century, whether by number of titles, volume of sales, or size of revenue; the emphasis, in fact, derives from the company's forming a prominent part of the name of HarperCollins, currently the twelfth-largest publisher in the world (by revenue), and whose online lineage itself stresses that prominence (Publishers Weekly 2017—the RELX Group, including Elsevier, is second-largest). How Harpers arrived at that position provides, perhaps more so than Elsevier, a model for the history of publishing in the twentieth and early twenty-first centuries. McCleery (2014) places this model in a wider, not purely Anglophone, context. Indeed, European publishers, such as Bertelsmann, Hachette, and Planeta—respectively 4, 5, and 6 in the *Publishers Weekly* 2017 listing above—followed this model across not only national, political borders but also language-market, linguistic boundaries.

By the close of the nineteenth century, the editorial success of Harpers, and its cultural impact, was not reflected in commercial success, partly because of loans undertaken to invest in the manufacturing plant, and partly because, like many family enterprises, the third and subsequent generations of Harpers were more interested in drawing dividends from the company than in its effective operation. By 1900, the bankers (J. P. Morgan) had taken control and Harper was sold off to become part of Doubleday and McClure. Asset-stripping followed: *Harper's Bazar* was transferred to Hearst in 1913; *Harper's Weekly* was absorbed by the New York-based Congregationalist magazine, *The Independent*, in 1916; and the building that from the mid-nineteenth century had housed the editorial and printing operations was sold to Morgan in 1923. While cultural triumphs continued, particularly under the editorial aegis of Eugene F. Saxon from 1925 onwards, the challenge to find commercial stability and security also endured. This dichotomy could be considered the enduring tension in trade publishing: between culture and commerce. The persistence of this antisyzygy is reflected in a number of titles examining the development of contemporary publishing: from Lane and Booth (1980) through Coser (1982) to Greco et al. (2007) and beyond.

The response in the 1970s to the quest for commercial stability and security was growth and consolidation through merger and acquisition: if individual publishing houses were fragile, then the degree of that fragility could be mitigated through economies of scale. A movement took place away from family-owned companies and partnerships underpinning independent publishers towards an expanded shareholding dominated by financial institutions with little or no experience of the sector. The award-winning play, *The Substance of Fire* (1990), and the subsequent movie (1996), dramatized this transition through its consequences for one New York family.

Synergy ruled. Gillian Doyle (2013) provides an insightful, general discussion of this structural change in media organizations, while Stephanie Peltier (2004) supplies a more sceptical view of the expectations raised by these mergers and acquisitions in the late twentieth century. It should be noted also that by this period a threshold has been crossed from publishing to media, much as an earlier passage had been made from book production to publishing. 'Production to publishing to media' represents perhaps a more satisfactory schema than the standard 'script to print to digital' book history model in terms of understanding the evolution of contemporary publishing. In 1962 Harper & Brothers had merged with Row, Peterson & Company, a textbook publisher, to form Harper & Row, and in 1977 the firm acquired Crowell and in 1978 Lippincott. What was being added were intangible assets—rights, brands, and market penetration— and any fixed assets such as manufacturing plant (or staff) could be disposed of, in a situation that was the inevitable outcome of the development of publishing as a form of trading in intellectual property over 200 years previously. Staff could also be acquired: when HarperCollins took over the UK independent publisher, Fourth Estate, in 2000, one of the latter's chief assets was the dynamic and successful risk-taker, Victoria Barnsley, who had founded the innovative imprint in 1984; she immediately became the CEO of HarperCollins UK before taking on additional responsibility for HarperCollins International in 2008.

Size ruled. Harper & Row, itself by now the result of several mergers, was in turn acquired in 1987 by News Corporation, the media conglomerate, sparking further acquisitions such as Zondervan, a religious publisher, in 1988 and Scott Foresman, a textbook publisher, in 1989, until News Corporation merged it in 1990 with its other UK acquisition, William Collins & Sons, to form HarperCollins with the ambition of making the new company the largest Anglophone publisher in the world, an ambition reported in the *New York Times* (NYT) in 1990. Trading at this level took the form of buying and selling whole imprints rather than individual titles: Scott Foresman, for example, was sold off to Pearson in 1998 as HarperCollins moved out of educational publishing, while in 2012 HarperCollins consolidated its position in religious publishing by buying Thomas Nelson, then a leading US Christian publisher with no real link to its nominal Edinburgh ancestor (McCleery 2001).

The histories of both Thomas Nelson and William Collins, the other HarperCollins parent, would reveal, if developed in similar detail, an almost identical genetic pattern to that of Harpers. For Collins, founded across the Atlantic in Glasgow in 1819, the initial function was also printing, reproducing the sermons of Thomas Chalmers, a family friend, which in turn led to a specialism in religious works, including from 1862 the *King James* (Authorized Version of the) *Bible*. The production of stationery, especially diaries, provided stability in much the same manner as had the magazines of Harpers. Investment in the manufacturing operation in the 1850s resulted in the introduction of steam-powered presses; this had to be secured through an expansion in cheap reprint publishing, particularly of out-of-copyright texts such as the works of Shakespeare and Bunyan's *Pilgrim's Progress*, as individual titles or in libraries, including those destined for school use; and in the latter half of the nineteenth century, the expansion of compulsory schooling in the UK provided the opportunity for an increase in educational publishing. By 1895, Collins had over 1,900 employees and the 'total annual production of books printed and bound at Herriot Hill [its premises in Glasgow] was nearing two and a half million' (Keir 1952: 204). Collins Pocket Classics, launched in 1903 as a series of cheap, out-of-copyright literary titles, had sold over 25 million copies by 1953 (Stevenson 2007: 324). Collins also benefited, as did other UK publishers, from access to the large imperial market, both in the settled and administered territories of Empire, opening branches in Australia, India, New Zealand, and South Africa, while employing agents elsewhere. This represented a common pattern as confirmed by Kernan's (2013) work on Routledge and McCleery's (2013) on Penguin. That imperial outreach balanced the large internal (and protected) market of the USA. Collins, in fact, did not begin publishing original fiction, as opposed to reprints, or religious or educational books, until 1917.

By then, shortages of labour and rising production costs, the latter becoming a perennial problem, were undermining the business model behind cheap reprints. Instead, the company began to develop distinctive lists of original work, particularly of crime fiction, including the first (of very many) novels by Agatha Christie in 1926. Old habits died hard, however, or more accurately, the need to employ fully its manufacturing capacity persisted, and the Collins Crime Club was introduced in 1930. The company extended its paperback lists of reprints, following the precedent of Penguin from 1935 onwards, and this placed it in a good position for the consumer boom in paperbacks in the post-World War 2 'never had it so good' era. However, Collins misread trends in the late 1960s by investing further in manufacturing, including taking over the former Blackies factory, accentuating the existing weaknesses in the printing plus publishing structure, where the inflexibility of the former neutralized or, worse, damaged the nimbleness of the latter. By the end of the 1970s, the company was making severe losses; the London headquarters was sold off (and leased back); the workforce was reduced by 600: in sum, Collins had now become prey rather than predator. The Board had by 1989 to decide between being swallowed by a tiger or a hyena, choosing the former, the News Corporation of Rupert Murdoch, over the latter, the many enterprises, including Pergamon Press, Macmillan Inc. (the US publisher), and Prentice Hall Information Services, of Robert Maxwell. HarperCollins was formed, as noted above, in 1990.

THE END

And that might well have been the end of (publishing) history, with only the desultory trading in imprints indicating any activity in a relatively comatose sector. However, as with the Cold War itself, such complacency could not endure because of the entry of new, unexpected disruptive agents. It was not that these new companies competed with publishers in the trading of intellectual property; rather it was that they seemed to have no interest in trading (or respecting and protecting) intellectual property at all, other than their own proprietary platforms. Instead, they offered, as had the reprint printers of the nineteenth century and before, spaces for the reproduction of material without seeking to own or license the rights in it. More than that, unlike printers who have always been part of a chain of legal liability in terms of the distribution of defamatory or obscene material, companies like YouTube or Facebook denied any responsibility whatsoever for the 'user-generated content' they 'hosted' and, through its accessibility, distributed. Other companies, such as ResearchGate, seemed to host academic articles that were already copyright to scientific and academic publishers such as Elsevier; while Google embarked upon a large-scale programme of digitizing printed texts that appeared to confuse those in the public domain and those still in copyright. In both these cases, there are ongoing (late 2017) efforts to resolve conflicts with publishers and others who believe that their intellectual property rights have been infringed (Vaidhyanathan 2007; Van Noorden 2017). As far as the existing publishing industry was concerned, its first response to this new form of old competition was the familiar litany from the 1970s onwards: if you can't beat them, buy them. News Corporation bought the social networking site MySpace in 2005 to sit alongside the traditional HarperCollins as well as its other media components such as Sky and Fox. MySpace went into decline until by 2008 it had been overtaken by Facebook in terms of members and revenue. News Corporation sold it in 2011 for $35 million, compared to the $580 million it had paid for it (Saporito 2011). Nor was this exceptional: the Friends Reunited website was sold to the Scottish publisher D. C. Thomson in 2010 for £25 million; by 2011 its value had fallen to £5.2 million; in 2013 it was re-engineered as a family history site; and in 2016 Thomson closed it altogether (Fraser 2017).

The skills and knowledge built up in publishing over the past 300 years survive and thrive only in the context of intellectual 'property'. That concept creates a marketable commodity that underpins the contemporary publishing industry. As it operates in a global marketplace, the industry then seeks harmonization of international copyright to ensure equitable trading conditions. Once China, the last country to do so, had acceded to the World Intellectual Property Organization in 1980 and by 1990 had reformed its own copyright statutes to conform to the Berne Convention, such global trading conditions, with occasional hiccups over enforcement, had been created (Mertha 2005). What threw such equilibrium out of kilter was not just the commercial power of the new online platforms and social media at the beginning of the twenty-first century but the principled challenge to copyright itself that they represented and, consciously or not, encouraged by their very mode of operation. Whether these online companies will evolve, as Harpers and Collins did, from reproducers either disregarding (non-US) copyright or allowing only material that does not infringe existing rights, to publishers trading in intellectual property remains a matter of conjecture. The move of Apple and Amazon into original film and TV production, following the lead of streaming services such as Netflix and Hulu (30 per cent owned by Fox), might indicate that, at least for broadcast media, they will compete as 'masters of content'. The survival of the contemporary publishing industry, itself part now of general media structures, will, in turn, depend on the survival of the concept of intellectual property and its continued enforcement, since 1710, in law. If the 'new media' come to rely on copyright protection for content, then the argument that information is born free and put in chains by publishers (pushed by organizations such as the Electronic Frontier Foundation and the Public Library of Science) may be successfully countered in legislatures and courts (EFF 2017; PLOS 2017). History can only indicate echoes of the past in the present, not offer predictions of the future.

References

Adams, Thomas and Nicolas Barker (1993). 'A New Model for the Study of the Book', in *A Potencie of Life: Books in Society*. Edited by Nicolas Barker. London: British Library. pp. 5–43.

Alden, Henry Mills (1908). *Magazine Writing and the New Literature*, New York: Harper & Brothers.

Bhaskar, Michael. (2013). *The Content Machine*, London: Anthem Press.

Boehmer, Elleke, Rouven Kunstmann, Priyasha Mukhopadhyay, and Asha Rogers, eds (2017). *The Global Histories of Books: Methods and Practices*, London: Palgrave Macmillan.

Bourdieu, Pierre (1993). *The Field of Cultural Production*, New York: Columbia University Press.

Briggs, Asa, ed. (1974). *Essays in the History of Publishing: In Celebration of the 250th Anniversary of the House of Longman*, London: Longman.

Cadie, Nathaniel (2014). *The Mediating Nation: Late American Realism, Globalization and the Progressive State*, Chapel Hill, NC: University of North Carolina Press.

Calasso, Roberto (2015). *The Art of the Publisher*, London: Penguin Random House.

Clair, Colin (1960). *Christopher Plantin*, London: Cassell.

Coser, Lewis A., Charles Kadushin, and Walter W. Powell (1982). *The Culture and Commerce of Publishing*, New York: Basic Books.

Darnton, Robert (1990). 'What is the History of Books', in *The Kiss of Lamourette: Reflections in Cultural History*. New York: Norton, 107–36.

David, Paul A. (2004). 'The End of Copyright History', *Review of Economic Research on Copyright Issues*, 1(2), pp. 5–10.

Davies, David W. (1954). *The World of the Elseviers 1580–1712*, The Hague: Martinus Nijhoff.

Doyle, Gillian (2013). *Understanding Media Economics*, 2nd edition, London: Sage.

EFF (2017). https://www.eff.org/about/history [Accessed: 14 August 2017].

Eliot, Simon and Jonathan Rose, eds (2012). *A Companion to the History of the Book*, 2nd edition, London: Wiley Blackwell.

Exman, Eugene (1965). *The Brothers Harper: A Unique Publishing Partnership and Its Impact on the Cultural Life of America from 1817 to 1853*. New York: Harper and Row.[1]

Exman, Eugene (1967). *The House of Harper: 150 Years of Publishing*. New York: Harper and Row.

Finkelstein, David and Alistair McCleery, (2012). *An Introduction to Book History*, 2nd edition, London: Routledge.

---

[1] Exman was vice-president of Harper and Row until his retirement in 1965 when he became the archivist and historian of the company. This was a familiar pattern for the period, when house histories would be seen as best undertaken by insiders who had proven their loyalty, as well as themselves being complicit in that very history.

Fraser, Douglas (2017). 'D.C. Thomson's Friends Reunited continues fall in value', http://www.bbc.co.uk/news/uk-scotland-scotland-business-16210645 [Accessed: 14 August 2017].

Fyfe, Aileen (2012). *Steam-Powered Knowledge: William Chambers and the Business of Publishing, 1820–1860*, Chicago: University of Chicago Press.

Ganea, Peter, Thomas Pattloch, and Christopher Heath (2005). *Intellectual Property Law in China*, The Hague: Kluwer Law International.

Genette, Gerard (1997). *Paratexts: Thresholds of Interpretation (Literature, Culture, Theory)*, Cambridge: Cambridge University Press.

Greco, Albert A., Clara Rodriguez, and Robert Wharton (2007). *The Culture and Commerce of Publishing in the 21st Century*, Stanford: Stanford University Press.

Harper, Henry J. (1912). *The House of Harper: A Century of Publishing in Franklin Square*, New York: Harper & Brothers.

Harper, Collins (2017). http://200.hc.com/timeline [Accessed: 14 August 2017].

Harris, Neil (2017). 'Aldus and the Making of the Myth (Or What Did Aldus Really Do?)', in *Aldo Manuzio. La costruzione del mito*. Edited by Mario Infelise. Venice: Marsilio, pp. 346–85.

Hepburn, James (1968). *The Author's Empty Purse and the Rise of the Literary Agent*, Oxford: Oxford University Press.

Howsam, Leslie (2006). *Old Books and New Histories: An Orientation to Studies in Book and Print Culture*, Toronto: University of Toronto Press.

Keiderling, Thomas, ed. (2005). *F.A. Brockhaus, 1905–2005*. Mannheim: Verlag F.A. Brockhaus.

Keir, David (1952). *The House of Collins: The Story of a Scottish Family of Publishers from 1789 to the Present Day*, London and Glasgow: William Collins & Sons.

Kelly, W. A. and Giulia Trentacosti, eds. (2016). *The Book in the Low Countries*, Edinburgh: Merchiston.

Kernan, Mary Ann (2013). 'Routledge as a Global Publisher', *Publishing Research Quarterly*, 29(1), pp. 52–72.

Lane, Michael and Jeremy Booth (1980). *Books and Publishers: Commerce Against Culture in Postwar Britain*, Lexington: Lexington Books.

Lowry, Martin (1979). *The World of Aldus Manutius: Business and Scholarship in Renaissance Venice*, Oxford: Blackwell.

Lyons, Martyn (2011). *Books, A Living History*, London: Thames and Hudson.

Madison, Charles A. (1966). *Book Publishing in America*, New York: McGraw-Hill.

McCleery, Alistair (2001). 'Introduction', in *Thomas Nelson & Sons*, ed. David Finkelstein and Heather Holmes, Edinburgh: Tuckwell Press, pp. xv–xxii.

McCleery, Alistair (2013). 'Penguin and post-colonial publishing 1948–1972', *The Journal of Commonwealth Literature*, 48(1), pp. 131–44.

McCleery, Alistair (2014). 'Publishing in the Long Twentieth Century', in *The Cambridge Companion to the History of the Book* ed. Leslie Howsam, Cambridge: Cambridge University Press, pp. 162–80.

McParland, Robert (2011). *Charles Dickens's American Audience*, Lanham, MD: Lexington Books.

Mertha, Andrew C. (2005). *The Politics of Piracy: Intellectual Property in Contemporary China*, Ithaca, NY: Cornell University Press.

Mole, Tom and Michelle Levy (2017). *The Broadview Introduction to Book History*, Guelph: Broadview Press.

Needham, Joseph and Tsien Tsuen-Hsui (1985). *Science and Civilisation in China: Volume 5, Chemistry and Chemical Technology, Part 1, Paper and Printing*, Cambridge: Cambridge University Press.

NYT (1990). 'Birth of a Global Book Giant', *New York Times*, 11 June 1990, D1. Available at: https://www.nytimes.com/1990/06/11/business/the-media-business-birth-of-a-global-book-giant.html [Accessed: 14 August 2017].

Peltier, Stephanie (2004). 'Mergers and Acquisitions in the Media Industries: Were Failures Really Unforeseeable?', *Journal of Media Economics*, 17(4), pp. 261–78.

Phillips, John J. (1986). 'Atticus and the Publication of Cicero's Works', *The Classical World*, 79(4), pp. 227–37.

PLOS (2017). https://www.plos.org/open-access [Accessed: 14 August 2017].

Publishers Weekly (2017). https://www.publishersweekly.com/pw/by-topic/international/international-book-news/article/74505-the-world-s-50-largest-publishers-2017.html [Accessed: 14 August 2017].

RELX (2016). http://www.relx.com/investorcentre/reports2007/Documents/2016/relxgroup_ar_2016.pdf [Accessed 14 August 2017].

Reynolds, L. D. and N. G. Wilson (1968). *Scribes and Scholars*. Oxford: Oxford University Press.

Saporito, Bill (2011). 'Remember News Corp.'s Brilliant MySpace Buy?', *Business.time.com*, 12 January 2011, http://business.time.com/2011/01/12/remember-news-corp-s-brilliant-myspace-buy/ [Accessed: 14 August 2017].

Spoo, Robert (2013). *Without Copyrights: Piracy, Publishing and the Public Domain*, Oxford: Oxford University Press.

Stevenson, Iain (2007). 'William Collins & Sons', in *The Edinburgh History of the Book in Scotland Volume 4: Professionalism and Diversity 1880–2000*, ed. David Finkelstein and Alistair McCleery, Edinburgh: Edinburgh University Press, p. 323.

Stevenson, Iain (2010). *Book Makers: British Publishing in the Twentieth Century*, London: British Library.

Suarez, Michael F. and H. R. Woudhuysen, eds (2010). *The Oxford Companion to the Book*, 2 volumes, Oxford: Oxford University Press.

Tebbel, John (1987). *Between Covers: The Rise and Transformation of Book Publishing in America*, New York: Oxford University Press.

Thompson, John B. (2010). *Merchants of Culture: The Publishing Business in the Twenty-first Century*, Cambridge, UK: Polity.

Tucker, Amy (2010). *The Illustration of the Matter: Henry James and the Magazine Revolution*. Stanford, CA: Stanford University Press.

Van Noorden, Richard (2017). 'Publishers threaten to remove millions of papers from ResearchGate', *Nature*, 10 October, doi:10.1038/nature.2017.22793

Vaidhyanathan, Siva (2007). 'The Googlization of Everything and the Future of Copyright', *University of California Davis Law Review*, 40(3), pp. 1207–31.

Winsbury, Rex (2009). *The Roman Book*, London: Duckworth.

Yu, Anthony C. trans and ed. (1977). *The Journey to the West*. Volume I. Chicago: University of Chicago Press.

CHAPTER 3

....

AUTHORSHIP

....

SIMONE MURRAY

IN any conversation about a book, an utterly unremarkable question typically arises: who's its author? Whether the discussion occurs in a university tutorial, at the enquiries counter of a bookshop, or between friends at a suburban book club, the naturalness of inquiring about the author of a particular book masks the fact that 'authorship' is an historically and geographically-specific construct. In short, there is nothing inevitable about books being assigned to individual authors. Rather, it is because of a centuries-long process of copyright development and because of the dominance of a particular form of Western-European legal-aesthetic theory that the question of authorship appears so unproblematic. Conversely, the fact that digital technologies are eroding many of the previously taken-for-granted characteristics of Gutenbergian print culture means we can perhaps now see these characteristics more clearly. As digital communication facilitates low-cost and accessible self-publishing, enables texts to circulate anonymously, and provides global platforms for writers to read, critique, edit, and rewrite others' works, the intellectual struts that supported a print regime of textual fixity, standardized format, and individualized authorial control are being kicked out from under book culture. Consequently, the early decades of the twenty-first century offer an unparalleled vantage point from which to observe authorship's transmutation under the impact of digital culture.

The book industry's early responses to the advent of digital culture, in the years of the mass-access World Wide Web's nascence in the early-to-mid-1990s, tended towards doom-laden predictions of the death of the book and an either/or conception of print and digital mediums, all couched in rather alarmist rhetoric (Spender 1995; Nunberg 1996). Over the intervening period, print and digital culture have instead formed a relationship of complementarity whereby inherited print-based modes of thinking largely coexist with new, digitally-enabled processes. Change is undeniable, but it has been slower-paced, more nuanced, and more bidirectional than allowed for in 1990s forecasts.

A productive model for conceptualizing the relationship of print and digital formations is Tom Pettitt's (2007) 'Gutenberg parenthesis'. Rather than viewing Gutenbergian print culture as a natural state of being which finds itself suddenly under existential attack from digital culture, we can more accurately conceive of print's roughly 500-year-long dominance as an interregnum (hence 'parenthesis') between the period of pre-print manuscript transmission and contemporary digital culture. Viewed in this much longer historical timeframe, it is apparent that aspects of digital culture such as textual fluidity, collaborative creation, and freewheeling appropriation more closely resemble manuscript-era antecedents. Although the technology clearly differs enormously between the late Middle Ages and the early twenty-first century, there are historical precedents for written communication surviving epistemic technologically-induced changes. This counterintuitive logic of going back to the future may explain why academic medievalists have been largely sanguine about the rise of digital culture—at least more so than their print-centric literary studies counterparts (O'Donnell 2007). Steeped as they are in manuscript cultures, medievalists regard radically mutating, multiply-authored and extensively cross-referenced texts as their daily fare. Digital culture not only revivifies these pre-print modes of thinking, it also greatly aids their scholarly study.

While the digital revolution may be downgraded theoretically to a mere transition, this is not to deny the very real changes wrought to contemporary authors' professional status in practical terms. Authorial creativity has long been the bedrock of the publishing industry, and if practising authors find their prestige and income irrevocably eroded by digital changes they may cease to create. The following discussion thus sketches the historical preconditions for the rise of authorship and assesses the implications of the long reign of the author figure before surveying the current state of play in digital publishing, exploring contemporary realities of authorship, and forecasting potential future flashpoints. The chapter argues for a more complex, bifurcated model of digital culture's impact on authorship: simultaneously both democratizing and deifying the traditional author figure.

PRINT CULTURE CONSTRUCTIONS OF AUTHORSHIP

The legal origins of copyright in the English-speaking world lie in an Act of the British parliament known as the *Statute of Anne* (1710), which granted authors copyright in a literary work for 14 years from the date of publication. Importantly, this new form of property did not protect an idea (too vague a concept to be enshrined in law), nor did it protect the physical book itself (which was already protected under the law of chattels). Rather, the *Statute of Anne* demarcated an intermedial level of property ownership protecting the author's *expression* of an idea in a particular arrangement of words. In philosophical terms, this invention of the concept of 'intellectual' (because intangible) property effectively dematerialized the literary work from being solely a thing (book) to being *also* an abstract idea. The chief proponents of the new copyright law were the booksellers themselves (the publishers of the day) because of their desire to rein in piracy and its resultant erosion of their profits. However, one effect of copyright was to shift power gradually from material producers (printers, booksellers) to creators (authors) who could now profit from the sale of their works for a specified period before copyright expired and the works passed into the public domain (allowing anyone to copy them without payment).

While authors themselves may not have been at the forefront of lobbying parliament for copyright, they were—in the longer run—the chief economic beneficiaries of the changes. Copyright formed the essential foundation for the gradual professionalization of authorship during the eighteenth and, especially, nineteenth centuries. It removed authorship from the realm of patronage by a royal or noble sponsor to whom authors often dedicated their works, and instead created the possibility that authors (albeit, in reality, always a very limited number) could live on income generated by sale of their works to an expanding reading public. Because copyright, as it later mutated, secures income from creative works during the author's lifetime and to their estate for a delimited period after their death, authors were incentivized to devote time and effort to literary creation without the fear that others could simply reproduce a high-selling work without any payment to its creator. While the early eighteenth century represents the seedbed of copyright in English law, the reality of internationally-enforceable copyright did not coalesce until the late nineteenth century with the signing of the *Berne Convention for Protection of Literary and Artistic Works* (1886), enthusiastically lobbied for by famed men of letters with international readerships, such as Charles Dickens and Victor Hugo (Wirtén 2004). Even today, countries not signatories to the convention, or who do not rigorously enforce its regulations, render international copyright a decidedly leaky legal framework.

From the point of view of authors, copyright represented a double-edged sword: even as it promised to raise the economic status of authorship, it simultaneously tied authors to their texts in potentially disadvantageous ways. One of the chief legal motivations for copyright on the part of the state and crown was to aid the enforcement of blasphemy, sedition, and libel laws. Identifying a specific individual as the putative source for a particular text provided an individual human body that could be made to bear punishment for contraband ideas (Foucault 2006, [1969]). In this sense, the etymological source of the word 'author' in the Latin *auctor* (originator, founder, creator) is pertinent: the Author *authorizes* the text by standing behind or guaranteeing the ideas in it. While laws of sedition and blasphemy have all but disappeared from the law books of Western democracies, the power of authors to authorize their work in a more diffuse cultural sense remains potent (as the phenomenon of the writers' festival performance, explored in the section 'Contemporary authorial realities' below, attests). The ubiquity of the author figure can, inversely, be measured by its absence. Consider the extreme rarity of contemporary books being published anonymously and the unease generated when they do appear. In recent decades among the mere handful of high-profile examples are *Primary Colors* (1996), a satire on the Clinton administration, and *The Bride Stripped Bare* (2003), ostensibly the diary of a young wife's revolt against sexual boredom. In both cases, anonymous publication unleashed a media frenzy bent on identifying the book's author. As Michel Foucault wrote in his ground-breaking philosophical examination of authorship 'What Is an Author?' (2006 [1969]: 285), it appears that 'literary anonymity is not tolerable'. Even pseudonyms, providing some putative named 'source' for a text, trigger similar media campaigns to 'unmask' the 'real' author, as the cases of elusive Italian novelist Elena Ferrante and crime writer Robert Galbraith (later revealed to be J. K. Rowling) testify.

Precisely why the 'orphaned' text should provoke such disquiet takes us back to the eighteenth-century origins of copyright. For perhaps copyright's most influential legacy has been not legal nor economic but rather socio-aesthetic. The infancy of copyright coincided with and reinforced the rise of literary Romanticism in the later eighteenth century. Central amongst Romanticist precepts was an elevation of the writer from the status of a mere craftsman who reworks inherited ideas to the idea of the Author as creative genius—a unique individual whose originality instils their works with special significance (Woodmansee 1984: 427, 447). Romanticism's positing of the artist as a supremely inspired, even semi-divine, individual who channels his [sic] unprecedented ideas to the masses is encapsulated in a talismanic painting of the period, John Martin's 'The Bard' (1817).[1] It depicts a medieval bard (poet), accompanied by the traditional lyre, standing on the edge of a river gorge, defiantly shouting his artistic truth to the monarch and his soldiers below, their worldly power reduced by the spectacular scenery to a small patch of colour in the bottom foreground. The image is pure Percy Bysshe Shelley: celebrating poet-artists as 'the unacknowledged legislators of the World'.[2] The painting's latent proposition is that artists enjoy a special relationship with sources of creative inspiration and have a higher aesthetic sensibility which should be marvelled at by the common man, and even secular potentates such as monarchs. It distils a quasi-religion of Art in which the Poet-Author is prophet and the reader a mere worshipper (Sapiro 2016: 8).

Romanticism's long twilight explains why the cut-and-paste aesthetics of digital culture provoke such legal and cultural unease. In the print culture tradition, deeply imbued with the cult of authorial genius, a text is fixed in its final form by its author. Accordingly, the text predates and will outlast any given reader's interaction with it. To change a text (as was endemic and assumed in pre-Gutenberg medieval manuscript culture) was, to the print-based mindset, to debase or sully it. Of course, the notion of 'typographical fixity' (as print historian Elizabeth Eisenstein (1983, 78) termed it) was always something of a fiction. Book historians have amply documented how authorial corrections, new editions, later editorial interventions and the like render even printed texts in reality far more fluid than allowed for in Romanticist-inflected author theory. Traditional bibliography's exhaustive search to determine 'authorial intention' for a text was a concomitantly specious later scholarly invention, as interventions by other print culture agents during the publication and reception processes inevitably leave a range of individuals' fingerprints on any given work, including those of collaborators, publishers, editors, agents, illustrators, marketers, and the like. Despite the mainstreaming

---

[1]   See http://interactive.britishart.yale.edu/art-in-focus-wales/185/the-bard
[2]   The closing words of Shelley's 'A Defence of Poetry' (written in 1821).

of digital culture and its characteristic logics of borrowing, sampling, and remixing, Romanticism's individualist legacy retains power: purists offended by mash-ups such as *Pride and Prejudice and Zombies* (2009)—credited to 'Jane Austen and Seth Grahame-Smith'—take umbrage that Austen's classic, although long out of copyright, should be 'messed with' by others.

In terms of the academic institutionalization of literature, the author figure has long been theoretically disavowed yet has exerted what Roland Barthes (1986 [1968], 50) alleged was a 'tyrannical' power over interpretation of a given text. One potentially negative implication of the regime of copyright is that its conceptualization of the literary work as the individual property of an Author posits texts as discrete units, isolated from each other and each entirely unique (Landow 2006). The book format itself implicitly encouraged this sense of textual separation and self-sufficiency. For although printed books were produced in great volumes in standardized editions, their material form emphasized discreteness far more so than the manuscript written by multiple hands or the technologically interlinked hypertext. The New Critical and Leavisite schools of literary criticism which took root on both sides of the Atlantic during the first half of the twentieth century were quick to decry the reading of texts according to authorial biography as 'the intentional fallacy' (Wimsatt and Beardsley 1946). Nevertheless, both covertly reinstated authorial power through grouping together texts written by the same author and imposing upon them an interpretative unity (Foucault 2006 [1969]: 284). How then to account for connections between texts written by different individuals such as relationships of genre, intertextuality, allusion, influence, parody, and borrowing? More particularly, such an author-centric and implicitly Romanticist conception of literature is unable to account for more obvious authorial limit-cases such as oral narratives, translation, collaborative authorship, ghost-writing, and ever-evolving digital texts.

VARIETIES OF DIGITAL AUTHORSHIP

A characteristic feature of digital culture generally is disintermediation: the removal of intermediaries in the supply chain for products and services. In the book world this has manifested most dramatically in the rise of self-publishing, whereby would-be authors can bypass the industry's traditional gatekeepers such as publishers, editors, and literary agents to produce their own book through online publishing outfits such as Lulu, Lightning Source, Scribd, and Amazon's Kindle Direct Publishing. In return for facilitating and hosting publication, most self-publishing services receive a cut of all book sales. This greatly limits the risk traditionally assumed by print publishers in bringing out a new title as, in self-publishing, an individual book copy is only produced once an order is received, eliminating the physical costs of warehousing and supplying bookshops. Such online businesses increasingly also offer (for a fee) other services traditionally performed in-house by publishers: editorial advice; formatting, layout, and cover design; marketing and publicity assistance. Author advice columns abound with *caveat emptor* warnings about the uphill struggle self-published authors face to market, distribute, and gain reviews of their titles via mainstream book channels. Yet the rapid proliferation of self-publishing outfits demonstrates that the desire to see one's words in print, and thus to seize the prestigious mantle of Authorship, remains remarkably potent.

A second variety of digitally-enabled authorship, crowdfunded publishing, demonstrates clearly how contemporary digital practices frequently revive earlier book industry models in counterintuitive, back-to-the-future fashion. Crowdfunding allows a would-be author with a compelling book idea to pitch to a potential readership and to request individuals pledge money towards its publication (and often even writing) via crowdfunding websites such as Kickstarter and Indiegogo.[3] A crowd-funded publishing house, Unbound, has even emerged to precisely target the literary end of the more general crowdfunding market.[4] This model of individuals pledging capital up-front to facilitate a book's publication is strongly reminiscent of the practice of subscription publishing widespread during the eighteenth and nineteenth centuries, according to which donors were rewarded for their act of literary patronage by having their name listed in the end-pages of the resultant book.

Another salient characteristic of digital culture is interactivity. This finds expression in a further range of Internet-enabled authorship practices that are profoundly dialogic, in the sense that formerly passive readers now write back to texts and the authors who create them. Fan fiction (fanfic) denotes amateur rewrites/sequels/prequels/expansions and the like of published literary works both classic and pop-cultural. It tends to be medium-agnostic in that much fanfic is also based on movies, television, games, anime, manga, etc., and may freely cross-blend from multiple fictional universes (in the form of mash-ups or slash). The phenomenon long predates the advent of the Internet, having circulated in subterranean fashion among mid-twentieth-century fandoms in the form of niche science fiction periodicals and, later, photocopied zines. But it has exploded in membership and public prominence since the mid-1990s mainstreaming of the World Wide Web and more recently with the success of Canadian-based platform Wattpad.[5] Typically fanfic has a 'parasitic' relationship to already-published texts (note how the term itself betrays a very print culture/Romanticist worldview whereby 'originality' is the primary criterion for artistic success). Legally, fanfic occupies a grey area between copyright (and potentially also trademark) infringement and being a tolerated cultural practice engaged in principally by young people and especially women. The blurriness of fanfic's legal status is compounded by the fact that certain highly successful authors such as J. K. Rowling lend tacit approval for non-commercial fanfic reworkings of their stories, as well as by the fact that bestselling multi-book franchises such as E. L. James' *Fifty Shades of Grey* series (2011–15) had their origins in online fanfic. This fact suggests that publishers, for

---

[3] See https://www.kickstarter.com/; https://www.indiegogo.com
[4] https://unbound.com/. See also the firm's promotional video: https://www.youtube.com/watch?v=de9CQA7G6vk
[5] https://www.wattpad.com/

all their protestations at alleged copyright infringement, nevertheless have brokered a *modus vivendi* with fan fiction—conceiving it as traditional publishing's research and development arm. Legacy print publishers can cherry-pick demonstrably popular writing from the fanfic and self-publishing sectors and furnish it with the accoutrements of print publication at very low risk to themselves (Bradley et al. 2011). Problematically from the authorial point of view, such 'monetization of fan fiction' typically involves a writer who has benefited from the collective ethos of the fanfic community appropriating the financial benefits to herself (Guthrie 2013). For digital-realm aficionados this represents an incongruously old-fashioned conception of the singular author and a decidedly multinational publisher-friendly interpretation of copyright law.

Two final examples of digital literary practices reshaping the contours of contemporary authorship share affinities with fan fiction: mass-authored wikinovels and remix fiction. As with fan fiction, the conception of the text in both cases is formative, with the work of any individual author seen as at best provisional and open to reworking by subsequent hands. Mass-authored wikinovels are fictions written collaboratively online where anyone can contribute and edit anyone else's work (à la Wikipedia). However, unlike fanfic, these are usually written from scratch rather than reworking an existing text. *A Million Penguins* (2007), a five-week experiment devised by Penguin Books and the UK's De Montfort University, is one of the better-known examples of the phenomenon. The fact that *A Million Penguins* rapidly degenerated into narrative incoherence and was subject to trolling and outright vandalism demonstrates the difficulties of translating utopian ideas of digital community into actual practice (Mason and Thomas 2008). Additionally, the website supporting it ceased to be available within five years of the project's conclusion, raising unsettling questions about the longevity of digitally-published works.[6] It is likely for this reason that subsequent remix-fiction experiments have placed clear boundaries upon participation, often featuring an inner core of moderators with the power to vet or block others' contributions, and to select amongst them in creating a print-published version.[7] An example of such a modified literary remix project was the Australian-based Remix My Lit (2007), in which a number of established (i.e. print published) authors agreed to post short stories online under a Creative Commons licence permitting others to rewrite and reuse their work so long as derivatives were attributed and non-commercial. An editorially-selected 'best of' the remixed stories was published alongside the original stories in print-on-demand format as *Through the Clock's Workings* (Barker 2009). That remix practices long standard in the music and film sectors are only belatedly finding expression in such literary remix projects demonstrates how long a shadow the Romanticist conception of the singular Author has cast over the print medium.

---

[6] See http://www.katepullinger.com/website_archive/index.php/blog/comments/a-million-penguins-five-years-on

[7] See, for example, the Italian historical novel *In Territorio Nemico* (2013), credited to the authorial collective 'SIC', which involved contributions from over 100 writers.

DIGITAL CHALLENGES
TO THE AUTHOR CONCEPT

From the foregoing examples it is clear that the technological affordances of digital (and specifically Web 2.0) culture profoundly destabilize many aspects of the author function as traditionally conceived. By 'making strange' what—to print-habituated eyes—had appeared natural, the digital era has foregrounded the extent to which authorship was the product of a specific confluence of historical, technological, legal, and cultural forces. The most dramatic impact of digital culture on the publishing world has been to democratize authorship (Pugh 2005): the advent of technological access to publication by almost anyone, without any form of quality control, makes the high-Romantic cult of the singular Author as a semi-divine individual virtually impossible to maintain. As the aforementioned E. L. James phenomenon demonstrates, if 'amateur' fan fiction can be published in book form and become a global bestseller, how can authorship remain an elite category? It could be argued in response that authorship only ever really *was* an elite category at the high-cultural end of the book market represented by self-styled 'Literature' and that print culture has long supported a culture of semi-anonymous hack authors along Grub Street lines. While this is historically accurate, the truly democratizing aspect of digital culture is not its effect on the internal hierarchy of established writers so much as its ability to transform readers themselves into writers, and thus to radically disrupt the previously lopsided, read-only logic into which print culture's economy of scarcity cast the overwhelming majority of readers.

Varieties of digital publishing such as crowdfunding and self-publishing have empowered readers to become writers themselves, with reading and writing reconceptualized as inter-related activities with free traffic between the two modes. Not only has digital culture eroded previously accepted distinctions between the roles of 'author' and 'reader', but the role of 'critic' has been similarly reconceived. Fanfic has supported an emerging body of hybrid reader-critics in the form of beta-readers. These are readers, usually with established standing in the fanfic community, who review and edit other fanfic writers' works, making suggestions on plot, characterization, or expression as might an editor or literary agent (Jenkins 2006; Thomas 2011a, 2011b).[8] The practice, also known as 'feedbacking' stories, highlights by making-strange print-culture norms the extent to which literary reviewing and academia had enshrined the role of Critic as a type of super-reader (Busse 2013: 63). With digital culture undermining the barriers to access which had long characterized print culture, 'everyday' readers have eagerly seized the prestigious mantles of critic and reviewer for themselves—as Amazon's customer reviews, Goodreads ratings, the literary blogosphere, and booktuber videos amply demonstrate (Murray 2018).

---

[8] Beta-reader practices have also been adopted beyond the fanfic community. For example, the UK Arts Council-sponsored website You Write On (http://www.youwriteon.com).

At the more abstract level, the mainstreaming of digital literary activity has prompted a reconceptualization of the nature of text itself. Unlike in print culture, characterized since Gutenberg by the idea of the standardized, relatively fixed, and authorized text, readers of digital literature frequently have the technological capacity to amend, rewrite, or edit a text, or at a minimum to alter its display (e.g. the option to customize font size, colours, layout, formatting, and screen resolution, or the read-aloud functions offered with market-dominating ebook readers). This shift from a norm of 'typographical fixity' to one of assumed textual mutability is especially pronounced in the field of electronic literature: texts born digital rather than print books merely reformatted as ebooks. Electronic literature scholar Astrid Ensslin (2007: 34) notes born-digital literary works' common quality of 'processurality' (i.e. the text is always in progress, never finalized). This is most obviously true in relation to wildly unstable wikinovels, which often do not remain static even for the time it takes a reader to consume them prior to adding their own contribution. Temporality, in the form of literature's seriality, finds its modern reflection in fanfics posted in instalments and electronic literature formats such as Twitterature (narratives told via Twitter) (Andersen 2017). In both of these there is a sense of a writer–reader relationship sustained over time with a narrative being drip-fed in periodic instalments, much in the way that nineteenth-century novels were frequently serialized in weekly or monthly periodicals prior to being formatted in three-decker codex editions. What explanatory power can inherited bibliographical concepts of authorial intention and copy-text retain in a temporal sphere characterized by mass collaborative authorship and freewheeling textual mutability?

Considering the concept of time in relation to literature casts literary memory back well before the Gutenberg parenthesis to the period of oral culture's dominance. Prior to the invention of writing, and long after its appearance as well, narratives were experienced in face-to-face settings characterized by the embodied presence of a teller (note, not Author) whose tone of voice, facial expression, gestures, and body language all contributed powerfully to listeners' interpretation. Reconceptualizing text from being a primarily spatial entity (the volume, page, paragraph, or line of print culture) to an instance in time (digital culture's version, instantiation, or screengrab) has profound philosophical implications for literary culture. Is the resultant entity better considered a 'work' or a 'performance'? Such borrowing of vocabulary from the performing arts is revealing. The traditional conception of literary labour has the author producing a thing (the work) which hides to the greatest extent possible all signs of its construction (e.g. earlier drafts, edits, loose ends, proofreading errors). According to such a spatial, summative logic, the outcome is *all* that matters. This gives way in digital environments to the idea of writing as *performative*: something to watch, participate in, enjoy. The dominant metaphor becomes temporal, reflecting time spent formatively engaging in reading/writing as process, with eventual outcome a lesser concern. As electronic literature scholar and author Scott Rettberg (2011: 197) argues, 'Any type of collective narrative must be understood not only in terms of a resulting "work," but also as a performance'. For author and reader alike (if they have not already fused into a single entity), the literary journey here becomes more important than the destination.

CONTEMPORARY AUTHORIAL REALITIES

Such atomization and reconceptualization of the authorial role in the wake of digital culture's onslaught is all very well at the theoretical level, but the job description of contemporary authorship has changed in ways that are often detrimental to actual individual creators. In survey after survey across the Western world, authorial incomes are shown to be falling as the (in many ways laudable) democratization of authorship triggers a reluctance amongst large sections of the public to pay for content, especially if consumed in digital format. In the developing world, where Western concepts of copyright have often been dismissed as inhibiting national economic development, copyright has always exerted less force, with the effect that authors in nations with rampant piracy such as Russia or China have almost no possibility of living by their literary labours. Even in the Anglosphere, the fount of copyright, membership surveys conducted by professional associations such as the Authors Guild (US), the Society of Authors (UK), and the Australian Society of Authors reveal that median incomes derived by authors from their writing fall well below the poverty line, and are in long-term decline.[9] A significant majority of practising creative writers subsidize their writing time with income from another job/s, or are cross-subsidized by a domestic partner (Zwar et al. 2015: 4).[10] Granted, sales in digital formats such as ebooks are on the increase, but not sufficiently to offset the decline in print sales (and especially sales of hardbacks, on which authors have traditionally earnt a slightly higher royalty rate). A further complication is that dominant ebook retailers (principally Amazon and Apple) have, in the interests of building their own businesses, priced standard ebooks at such a low rate that authors' percentage cut results in a lower income, even on increased sales. Authors are moreover concerned that such practices normalize in the public mind the idea that creating a book-length work deserves only a low level of remuneration, and that the influx of self-publishing amateurs further reinforces this perception. Ebook piracy, a continuing threat in spite of e-reader developers' and publishers' investment in digital rights management (DRM) technologies, threatens to erode authorial incomes still further (Zwar et al. 2015: 6). Meanwhile, industry-wide belt-tightening in the face of digital uncertainties has seen advances to authors (upfront payments offset against future income) substantially reduced for all except star, front-list performers (who, in

---

[9] For example, the study *What Are Words Worth Now?* (2015) conducted on behalf of the UK's Authors' Licensing and Collecting Society (ALCS) found that authors' median pre-tax net earnings from their writing was GBP11,000 (against the national median earnings of GBP27,011). This represented a drop in real terms of 29% since 2005 (Johnson et al. 2015). Similarly, a 2015 study by Australian researchers Jan Zwar, David Throsby, and Thomas Longden found that the average income derived from practising as an author was A$12,900 (against an average national income of A$61,485) (Zwar et al. 2015: 3). Results from the Authors Guild's survey *The Wages of Writing* (2015) found a 30% decline in authorial incomes since 2009 among full-time writers and 38% among part-time writers. Declines were steepest among authors with 15+ years' experience.

[10] https://www.authorsguild.org/wp-content/uploads/2015/09/WagesofWriting_Final_10-22-15.pdf

the event, frequently fail to earn out their headline-making advances).[11] Such financial realities have contributed to a marked polarization of authorship into authorial celebrities at one end who may be marketed as virtual brand-names, and the mass of other authors, formerly denoted 'midlist', who struggle to maintain publisher support and must fight among themselves for editorial and marketing attention.

If the general public's fascination with authorship persists, despite the grim economic realities most authors face, it is largely attributable to the phenomenon of the celebrity author. While authors famous beyond merely literary readerships have existed for centuries (Byron is frequently identified as the first celebrity writer), the economic rationalization of the book industry during the 1980s and the concomitant emphasis on marketing drove the emergence of the author as brand-name. In this, publishers were on the back foot as readers' loyalty lies principally with authors, rarely to the publisher brand. Taking advantage of the situation, authors and their new career-managers—the literary agents who had stepped into the role of the in-house editor—began playing publishing houses off against one another in the search for the biggest advance and best promotional package. The growth of high-profile literary prizes such as the Booker spurred the growth of authorial visual branding, whereby a prizewinning author's back-list would be re-jacketed in a style reminiscent of their most recent, prize-winning title. (This visual shorthand for a star author or their characteristic genre then becomes ripe for imitation by other authors and publishers wishing to appropriate some of that writer's readership.) The authorial brand may even become inhibiting, as where a writer such as Iain Banks creates the sub-brand of Iain M. Banks to allow him to shift between mainstream fiction and SF genres without alienating his established readership for either. The apotheosis of celebrity authorship occurs with posthumous publication 'by' a deceased author-star such as Ian Fleming or Stieg Larsson (in truth by another writer commissioned by the author's estate). The persona of the celebrity author remains alluring to members of the general public and to aspirant writers for the creative kudos and cultural authority it seems to encapsulate. Yet the record-breaking advances and publicity oxygen enjoyed by star authors are made possible by whittling down advances and marketing budgets for midlist writers.

Coupled with the decline in incomes for the majority of writers is a gradual withdrawing of support functions previously undertaken by the publishing house. Marketing and publicity activities in particular are increasingly outsourced to authors themselves, with publishers advising authors (and their partial publisher-substitutes, literary agents) to ensure each author has a prominent social media presence (Thompson 2010; Adsett 2012; Killick 2013). Authors are expected to generate much of their own marketing and publicity 'buzz' for new titles through announcements via their homepage, email newsletters, blog, Facebook, Twitter and Instagram accounts, YouTube book trailers, and the

---

[11] http://www.alcs.co.uk/Documents/Authors-earning-2015-Download_version.aspx. See also Squires 2007 and Murray 2012.

like (Zwar et al. 2015: 6; Murray 2016, 2018).[12] Indeed, having a vibrant social media 'platform' has become in some quarters a prerequisite for gaining a book contract, as publishers try to minimize their risk by catering to already quantifiable communities of interest (Marshall 2006: 794; Clark and Phillips 2008: 88; Katz 2010: 47; Thompson 2010: 86). At the same time that all this additional labour of social-media maintenance is placed on the author's shoulders, for diminishing financial returns, authors are also being lectured on the right *kind* of social media persona to cultivate. Merely bombarding one's Twitter followers or Facebook friends with publicity for a new title or upcoming in-store appearance is insufficient, even poor form; making proper use of the collaborative, peer-to-peer nature of social media involves genuinely interacting with one's followers, tailoring individual replies, and being prominent on social media *between* publication dates and festival appearances (Baverstock 2008; Cannold 2011; Harrad 2012; Radford 2012). Potentially, the labour involved in maintaining an online authorial persona threatens to become an author's main work, with self-publicity and readership-cultivation crowding out time for actual writing (Zwar eta l. 2015: 5). The plaintive author who writes 'social media management has become a never-satisfied beast that I just can't keep feeding, if I want to write a novel a year' is far from alone.[13]

Even if this rather dire possibility remains more a worst-case scenario than an actual reality for many authors—admirably self-disciplined in their social media use and conscientiously quarantining their writing time—there is no doubt that twenty-first-century authorship has become an exercise in entrepreneurialism. In an echo of the neoliberal hyper-individualism which permeates creative industries rhetoric, would-be authors graduating from universities' burgeoning creative writing and MFA programmes are urged at all turns to take their authorial career into their own hands and to fashion a saleable persona (Horner 2015). As has been the case since the phenomenon of authorship emerged in the eighteenth century, this persona may in truth be wildly at odds with the actual flesh-and-blood creator (witness the long history of literary pseudonymity; Mullan 2008). What matters is that contemporary authors consciously construct a public presence which will enable their title to stand out from the hundreds of thousands published (let alone self-published) annually and will grab the attention of that sector of the general public which makes the book industry financially viable—readers.

One of the main fora for connecting with readers remains, in spite of the book industry's uptake of digital technology, writers' festivals. It is in the booming phenomenon of the writers' or literary festival that many authors see the upside of the industry-wide dictate to self-promote, in that such festivals are premised on bringing authors into face-to-face contact with actual readers. Typically at writers' festivals and their close cognates, book towns, writers address, are asked questions by, and interact socially with their readerships through formats such as author readings, panel sessions, and book signings. While potentially daunting, and not without risk of public humiliation, most

---

[12] 'Authors' time spent marketing and communicating with readers skyrocketed 59% since 2009' (https://www.authorsguild.org/wp-content/uploads/2015/09/WagesofWriting_Final_10-22-15.pdf).
[13] http://www.bookpromotion.com/authors-need-blog/

authors, even the most stereotypically introverted, acknowledge writers' festivals as stimulating and affirming interludes in a normally solitary creative life. Literary festivals have come to constitute their own annual circuit and are indisputably red-letter days on the literary calendar. In the festival context the writer acts as hybrid promoter, brand spokesperson, and potentially also political activist. This last role may be especially— even uncomfortably—pronounced for writers from minority backgrounds, whose embodied appearance is often used as a springboard for discussions of identity politics. Even when this is not the case, all writers' festival guests are in some sense publicly performing the role of authorship. It is a process strongly reminiscent of the writers' role in pre-Gutenbergian manuscript cultures where an author's reading in a courtly setting verified the circulating manuscript as his own creation (the intertwined etymology of the words 'author' and 'authority' is again pertinent here). The extent to which public performance of authorship is a key element of the contemporary authorial job description is readily apparent from the pages of author-society periodicals, which are replete with advice on how to give a polished book reading, conduct oneself on a school visit, produce a podcast series, start a blog, or observe appropriate Twitter netiquette.

Oral, print, and digital modes of communication are complexly braided in current authorial practice. While at the same time the writers' festival boom since the 1980s has revivified oral modes of authorial communication, the primacy of the printed book remains evident in festivals' on-site bookshop and signing-queues. In addition, book festivals have been keen adopters of digital media technologies to expand audiences for their events, both chronologically through audio-visual recordings, as well as geographically, with experiments in live link-ups and live tweeting expanding the audience catchment for an event beyond those resident in the host locale (Driscoll 2014; Murray and Weber 2017). As festivals are predominantly funded through public-sector cultural policy bodies, this gives festival managers quantifiable evidence of their events' public outreach and hence strengthens their claim on continued public funding. The digitally-saturated writers' festival is of course an ideal fit with the digitally-habituated performing author. Authors have used digital media, both during and outside festival dates, to engage in publicity and marketing, conduct informal market research and, less commercially, as a means of stoking their creative motivation. Especially techno-enthusiast authors such as Neil Gaiman, Jasper Fforde, Margaret Atwood, and John Green have even deployed digital media to engage in collaborative authorship or cover-design competitions with their fanbases (Skains 2010; Murray 2018).

It is a writers' festival cliché that no book is really finished until it has been responded to by an actual reader. But this has also been a dominant—albeit principally theoretical— concern in literary studies since the importation of French poststructuralist ideas of the 'writerly' text in the 1970s. The change is that digital media make these writer–reader interactions visible, archivable, and discoverable as never before. With this comes the risk that digital technologies—lauded for their interactivity—degenerate into usages more closely resembling broadcast architecture in which the celebrified few talk to the anonymized many. Even the aforementioned techno-enthusiast authors have social media followings hundreds or thousands of times larger than those whose accounts they are themselves following. Hence there is marked potential for authorial uses of social media counterintuitively to reinforce print culture's hierarchical author–reader relationship. A public spat between celebrity authors such as Jonathan Franzen and Salman Rushdie over Twitter (see Franzen 2013) reduces the vast majority of the reading public to the status of voyeurs, looking in at the spectacle of an authorial coterie in dispute rather than themselves participating in that dispute.

Conclusion

Authorship, as a conceptual category, was a legal-cultural-economic development specific to a certain time and place. It therefore stands to reason that some three centuries later, given vast changes in technology plus globalization, the author figure has itself undergone substantial change. By the early decades of the twenty-first century, the figure of the author looks both backwards and forwards. The Romanticist elevation of authors as culturally superior individuals possessing unique creative powers retains its allure, as demonstrated by the large number of self-published authors seeking to claim this status for themselves. Yet, paradoxically, the more writers who seek consecration as Authors, the less exclusive the category can remain. Authorship is thus experiencing a period of significant cultural devaluation. Sectors of the contemporary digital literary sphere have attempted to offset or counteract wholesale democratization of authorship via a variety of means: from the avant-gardist self-stylings of experimental electronic literature authors; through the editorial overseers of collaboratively-written wiki or remix projects; to the perversely hierarchical beta-reader protocols prevalent in fanfic communities. Meanwhile, at the top of the scale, celebrity literary authors circulate as virtual brand names, receiving adulation on the global writers' festival circuit, acting as figureheads for social and political causes, and sustaining ongoing, transmedial interaction with avid readerships. The landscape of twenty-first-century authorship is thus markedly polarized. It is those authors caught in the middle—publishing some books to modest critical and commercial success—who must battle hardest to maintain their precarious position.

References

Adsett, Alex (2012). 'Self-publishing in the Digital Age', *Island*, 128, pp. 132–9.

Andersen, Tore Rye (2017). 'Staggered Transmissions: Twitter and the Return of Serialized Literature', *Convergence*, 23(1), pp. 34–48.

Authors Guild (2015). *The Wages of Writing*, New York: Authors Guild. https://www.authorsguild.org/wp-content/uploads/2015/09/WagesofWriting_Final_10-22-15.pdf

Barker, Amy, ed. (2009). *Through the Clock's Workings*, Sydney: Sydney University Press.

Barthes, Roland (1986). 'The Death of the Author' [1968] *The Rustle of Language*. Trans. Richard Howard. Oxford: Blackwell. pp. 49–55.

Baverstock, Alison (2008). *How to Market Books*, 4th edition, London: Kogan Page.

Bradley, Jana, Bruce Fulton, Marlene Helm, and Katherine A. Pittner (2011). 'Non-traditional Book Publishing', *First Monday*, 16(8), http://firstmonday.org/ojs/index.php/fm/article/view/3353/3030 (1 August 2017).

Busse, Kristina (2013). 'The Return of the Author: Ethos and Identity Politics', in *A Companion to Media Authorship*. Edited by Jonathan Gray and Derek Johnson. Malden, MA: Wiley Blackwell, pp. 48–68.

Cannold, Leslie (2011). 'The Tweeting Truth', *Australian Author*, 43(3), pp. 13–15.

Clark, Giles, and Angus Phillips (2008). *Inside Book Publishing*, 4th edition, Abingdon, UK: Routledge.

Driscoll, Beth (2014). *The New Literary Middlebrow: Tastemakers and Reading in the Twenty-first Century*, Houndmills, UK: Palgrave Macmillan.

Eisenstein, Elizabeth L. (1983). *The Printing Revolution in Early Modern Europe*, Cambridge: Cambridge University Press.

Ensslin, Astrid (2007). *Canonizing Hypertext: Explorations and Constructions*, London: Continuum.

Foucault, Michel (2006). 'What Is an Author?' [1969] *The Book History Reader*. Edited by David Finkelstein and Alistair McCleery. 2nd edition, London: Routledge, pp. 281–91.

Franzen, Jonathan (2013). 'What's Wrong with the Modern World'. *Guardian* 13 September. http://www.theguardian.com/books/2013/sep/13/jonathan-franzen-wrong-modern-world (10 October 2013).

Guthrie, Meredith (2013). 'Whatever You Do, Don't Call It "Mommy Porn": *Fifty Shades of Grey*, Fan Culture, and the Limits of Intellectual Property Rights', *Infinite Earths* http://79.170.40.240/infiniteearths.co.uk/?p=993

Harrad, Kate (2012). 'Twitter—the Virtual Literary Salon', *Guardian* Books Blog 11 January. http://www.theguardian.com/books/booksblog/2012/jan/11/twitter-virtual-literary-salon (1 August 2017).

Horner, Damian (2015). 'The Author Brand', *The Author*, 126(4), pp. 120–1.

Jenkins, Henry (2006). *Convergence Culture: Where Old and New Media Collide*, New York and London: New York University Press.

Johnson, Phillip, Johanna Gibson, and Gaetano Dimita (2015). *What Are Words Worth Now?: A Survey of Authors' Earnings*, London: Authors' Licensing and Collecting Society. http://www.alcs.co.uk/Documents/Authors-earning-2015-Download_version.aspx (28 July 2017).

Katz, Christina (2010). 'Elements of a Successful Fiction Platform', *Writer's Digest*, November/December., pp. 46–51.

Killick, Ruth (2013). 'Meet the Publicist', *The Author*, 124(2), pp. 63–4.

Landow, George P. (2006). *Hypertext 3.0: Critical Theory and New Media in an Era of Globalization*. 3rd edition, Baltimore, MD: Johns Hopkins University Press.

Marshall, P. David, ed. (2006). *The Celebrity Culture Reader*, New York: Routledge.

Mason, Bruce and Sue Thomas (2008). *A Million Penguins Research Report*. Institute of Creative Technologies, De Montfort University, UK. http://www.ioct.dmu.ac.uk/documents/amillionpenguinsreport.pdf

Mullan, John (2008). *Anonymity: A Secret History of English Literature*. London: Faber and Faber.

Murray, Simone (2012). *The Adaptation Industry: The Cultural Economy of Contemporary Literary Adaptation*. Routledge Research in Cultural and Media Studies. New York: Routledge.

Murray, Simone (2016). ' "Selling" Literature: The Cultivation of Book Buzz in the Digital Literary Sphere', *Logos* 27(1), pp. 11–21.

Murray, Simone (2018). *The Digital Literary Sphere: Reading, Writing, and Selling Books in the Internet Era*, Baltimore, MD: Johns Hopkins University Press.

Murray, Simone and Millicent Weber (2017). ' "Live and Local"?: The Significance of Digital Media for Writers' Festivals'. *Convergence: The International Journal of Research into New Media Technologies*, 'Writing Digital' special issue 23(1), pp. 61–78.

Nunberg, Geoffrey, ed. (1996). *The Future of the Book*. Berkeley, CA: University of California Press.

O'Donnell, Daniel Paul (2007). 'Disciplinary Impact and Technological Obsolescence in Digital Medieval Studies', in *A Companion to Digital Literary Studies* edited by Susan Schreibman and Ray Siemens, Oxford: Blackwell, pp. 65–81.

Pettitt, Tom (2007). 'Before the Gutenberg Parenthesis: Elizabethan-American Compatibilities'. Plenary presentation to Media in Transition 5 conference, MIT http://web.mit.edu/comm-forum/mit5/papers/pettitt_plenary_gutenberg.pdf

Pugh, Sheenagh (2005). *The Democratic Genre: Fan Fiction in a Literary Context*, Bridgend, UK: Seren Books.

Radford, Ceri (2012). 'How Twitter is Changing the Literary World', *Telegraph* [UK] 12 March. http://www.telegraph.co.uk/culture/books/9137910/How-Twitter-is-changing-the-literary-world.html (1 August 2017).

Rettberg, Scott (2011). 'All Together Now: Hypertext, Collective Narratives, and Online Collective Knowledge Communities', in *New Narratives: Stories and Storytelling in the Digital Age*, edited by Ruth Page and Bronwen Thomas. Lincoln, NB: University of Nebraska Press, pp. 187–204.

Sapiro, Gisèle (2016). 'The Metamorphosis of Modes of Consecration in the Literary Field: Academies, Literary Prizes, Festivals', *Poetics*, 59, pp. 5–19.

Skains, R. Lyle (2010). 'The Shifting Author–Reader Dynamic: Online Novel Communities as a Bridge from Print to Digital Literature', *Convergence*, 16(1), pp. 95–111.

Spender, Dale (1995). *Nattering on the Net: Women, Power and Cyberspace*, Melbourne: Spinifex Press.

Squires, Claire (2007). *Marketing Literature: The Making of Contemporary Writing in Britain*, Houndmills, UK: Palgrave Macmillan.

Thomas, Bronwen (2011a). ' "Update Soon!": Harry Potter Fanfiction and Narrative as a Participatory Process', in *New Narratives: Stories and Storytelling in the Digital Age*, edited by Ruth Page and Bronwen Thomas. Lincoln, NB: University of Nebraska Press, pp. 205–19.

Thomas, Bronwen. (2011b). 'What Is Fanfiction and Why Are People Saying Such Nice Things about It?' *StoryWorlds: A Journal of Narrative Studies*, 3, pp. 1–24.

Thompson, John B. (2010). *Merchants of Culture: The Publishing Business in the Twenty-first Century*, Cambridge, UK: Polity.

Wimsatt, William K., and Monroe C. Beardsley (1946). 'The Intentional Fallacy', *Sewanee Review*, 54(3), pp. 468–88.

Wirtén, Eva Hemmungs (2004). *No Trespassing: Authorship, Intellectual Property Rights, and the Boundaries of Globalization*, Studies in Book and Print Culture. Toronto: University of Toronto Press.

Woodmansee, Martha (1984). 'The Genius and the Copyright: Economic and Legal Conditions of the Emergence of the "Author" ', *Eighteenth-Century Studies*, 17(4), pp. 425–48.

Zwar, Jan, David Throsby, and Thomas Longden (2015). *Australian Authors—Industry Brief No. 1: Key Findings*. Sydney: Department of Economics, Macquarie University. http://www.businessandeconomics.mq.edu.au/our_departments/Economics/econ_research/reach_network/book_project/authors/1_Key_Findings.pdf (28 July 2017).

CHAPTER 4

....

READING

....

ADRIAAN VAN DER WEEL

THE discovery of writing some six millennia ago was the overture to a world in which texts—and in particular books—became the chief vehicle for recording and disseminating knowledge and culture. One would be forgiven for thinking of the discovery and development of writing as an historical accident. In fact it was not. Writing evolved as a 'convergent' phenomenon in three different parts of the world independently, suggesting that its discovery was probably inevitable. That we can read and write is one of the most extraordinary cultural achievement of our species. Although it takes years to learn, in all Western countries literacy has become part of a compulsory educational curriculum. We don't have to go to school to learn to speak. Without apparent effort—except on the part of our parents—we all manage to become amazingly sophisticated mother tongue users. But all the parental time, energy, and patience—freely and lovingly donated to the cause of getting our offspring to communicate through speech—pale to insignificance compared to the machinery set in motion to teach each and every young child to read and write. Long years of formal instruction demand arduous and ceaseless exertion: a severe toll exacted by society on all new entrants. The development of fine motor skills accounts for a large part of this tremendous effort. More fundamentally, unlike for spoken language, our brain is not wired for its written counterpart.

To achieve the formidable feat of reading we repurpose a collection of brain areas that evolved for other, older tasks, such as 'reading' tracks in nature. One well-known neuroscientist has therefore gone so far as to call reading 'unnatural'. A deliberate provocation perhaps, but it does help to drive home the point about the artificiality of the practice. Compared to other media, from music to the spoken word, from games to film, writing demands an extra decoding effort over and above what the brain has to do when it sees and hears people speak. Neuroscientifically there is no difference between listening to someone speaking in person or through a medium such as radio, television, or an audio recording. But when we *read* the same words, whether from paper or from a screen, we first have to link the visual *image* of the characters that make up the words to the linguistic utterance they represent. Only then can we access their meaning in our mental dictionary. Unlike spoken language (and yes, that includes audiobooks), written language is always mediated and reading always involves this extra decoding step. Whether or not audiobooks should be included in reading statistics therefore depends on what they are intended to measure: the number of 'stories' consumed or the amount of text decoding performed.

We have the tremendous recent growth in reading research to thank for many new insights into the extraordinary phenomenon of reading and writing. What has triggered this sudden advance in reading research is the evident need for a better understanding of the impact of digitisation. In assessing this impact, one of the first, and rather sobering, realizations has been that the role of reading in society is by no means as securely established as is normally assumed. Over time reading became a necessary skill for gaining access to culture and knowledge. Yet it is not an easy activity for humans to engage in and screens offer many competing means of communication. The book industry has a great deal to learn from this newly arising awareness of the historically contingent role of reading. The status and position of reading depend on conscious decisions and continued efforts to make it relevant and, in a world dominated by screens, reading requires more conscious cultivation than one would like to think. This is emphatically not to say that reading is in any way endangered as such. Rather, how and what readers read today is rapidly changing, notably in the direction of fewer books. This is making the continued existence of that reader as a dependable customer of the book industry rather more uncertain than it has ever been.

The position of readers at the end of the value chain could easily suggest that they are a mere appendage to what the industry is really about. In a curious way for a long time that was probably indeed the case. To the industry, the reader was chiefly relevant as 'the end user', or even more abstractly, 'the market'. In that capacity readers were chiefly the concern of the bookseller. The reader was perhaps always an elusive entity, but readers were known to be out there. They just needed to be hunted down so they could be turned into buyers. Nor was the issue that there were not enough of them; merely that they might be hiding in fragmented and diffuse markets. Even if readers could occasionally only be reached indirectly, through the library, their existence, and even their ongoing willingness to read books and thus to become potential customers were not fundamentally in doubt. The prevalence of reader–buyers followed naturally from the Order of the Book (Chartier 1994; Van der Weel 2011) that slowly established itself over the last few centuries. By the second half of the nineteenth century the socialization of book reading through formal education had become institutionalized in most Western countries. In reality never more than a relatively small proportion of the population—an elite few—may have turned into active readers, and again not all of them turned into buyers. Nevertheless, that proportion used to be fairly stable. The expectation was that there would always be a significant reading class for whom the continued existence of a book industry, supplying a constant stream of fresh books, from the most popular and ephemeral to the most erudite and classic, was essential.

With the Internet as one of the main drivers, this is now changing. Reading has of late become a subject of (renewed) concern and an object of study. The question is not so much *whether* people read: it is glaringly obvious that they do. The Internet is to a large measure a textual medium. Accessible through an endless variety of screen devices, it adds significantly to the amount of reading time its users chalk up. A substantial proportion of the massive amount of time that the average person spends online is spent reading—even if it is only navigation instructions, comments, or text messages. As shopping and banking and myriad other ways of servicing our lives increasingly move online, they too now involve reading. The issue is that such brief and fragmented texts as web pages, emails, status updates, blogs, and so on are not of book length, and are not products of the publishing industry. The same goes of course for the massive amount of analogue 'other' reading that we are not aware we are doing. Think of advertising leaflets and government brochures; subtitles and credits; guidelines and instructions, to mention just a few genres.

READING STATISTICS

Much of this diverse reading remains undocumented and is therefore barely visible. There are no reliable statistics on the total amount of text an ordinary person might read in a day, let alone in a lifetime. It is safe to assume that in twenty-first-century Western society more reading is done than ever before in history. However, despite—or precisely because of—the deluge of text in people's daily lives, that mainstay of the publishing industry, book reading, is in decline. Changing reading habits are focusing attention on the extent to which the reader is the one truly indispensable actor in the chain—for all of his being the last. Unfortunately in this transformation, with so much reading taking place outside of the industry, the reader as consumer is probably becoming even more elusive than ever.

Time surveys and library loan statistics show that the amount of time spent reading books, magazines, and newspapers is going down. In the USA, from 2005 to 2015, the average amount of time Americans spent reading for personal interest on weekend days and holidays fell by 22 per cent to 21 minutes per day and 17 minutes on normal work days. Younger Americans (age 15 to 44), read less than older Americans, spending an average of 7 to 12 minutes reading. Predictably, over the same decade this decrease in reading was matched by increases in leisure-related screen use such as gaming and watching television (Humanities Indicators 2016). In Germany the number of regular readers who read a book at least once a week fell from 49 per cent in 2002 to 42 per cent in 2017. Again the decline is disproportionately high for the young (14–29 years) and middle (30–59 years) age groups, regardless of educational level (Boersenblatt 2018). In the decade 2005–14 the proportion of adults in the UK who had visited a library over the last year dropped by 28 per cent from 48.2 to 34.9 (Department for Culture, Media and Sport 2014). In the Netherlands, between 1994 and 2015, the number of library loans plummeted from over 180 million to less than 80 million (Centraal Bureau voor de Statistiek, Statline 2017). Meanwhile the percentage of 'intensive readers' (here defined as people reading more than twenty books a year) decreased from 19 per cent to 12 per cent between 2012 and 2016, while the number of 'non-readers' (people reading zero books per year) increased from 11 per cent to 21 per cent (Stichting Lezen 2016). The gloomy trend suggested by these figures was confirmed when GfK reported in 2017 that the proportion of non-readers of books around the globe was highest in the Netherlands and South Korea, while China at 36 per cent (against a global average of 30 per cent) has the highest percentage of every-day book readers (GfK 2017).

The Dutch national time use survey published in 2018 once again corroborated the finding that the decrease was especially strong in the younger cohorts. Almost half of 13–19-year-olds, and almost three-quarters of 20–34-year-olds, are now non-readers (Wennekers et al. 2018: 60, 62). This is a greater cause for concern because one revealing outcome of reading research has been that this decline is not made up for in later years, but is maintained throughout people's life spans (Huysmans 2007: 179–92). There is no reason to assume that this is not indicative of a more general trend.

Surprisingly perhaps in this light, children's books tend to perform strongly in most markets, and this may be taken as a proxy for a strong and continuing reading activity in the relevant age group. Nevertheless, as research shows, in spite of all attempts at socialization at schools, in their mid-teens adolescents are inclined to abandon long-form reading in favour of social media and other screen reading (Eyre 2015). It is easy to blame the smartphone and the computer, but the decline in reading probably set in much earlier. Leisure time has been spent on media other than books, notably television, for much longer.[1] Now the computer and the smartphone add significantly to the numerous popular alternatives for leisure time spending. Screens are agents of distraction especially because those alternatives compete for attention on the same few square inches of screen real estate—and they are, as we have seen, less demanding in terms of brain processing. This goes for gaming, scouring image-based social networks such as Instagram (but also increasingly Facebook, whose algorithms seem to favour video and images), watching TED talks, series, or Youtube films, which are all in direct competition with reading, both for information-seeking and leisure purposes. An additional factor that may drive people to seek out media other than text when it comes to their leisure time is that many people spend much of their working day reading on screens for work.

Public libraries were instituted everywhere from the second half of the nineteenth century with the explicit brief to make books broadly available, particularly to those who could not afford to purchase them. In this perspective the downward trend in library loans, which is much sharper than the decline in book sales, means that we can be fairly sure that the economic cost of reading is not a crucial factor in its decline. Indeed, perhaps somewhat surprisingly, the statistical data show book sales to have been more stable in recent years than the decrease in reading time would lead one to expect.[2] Even after correction for inflation, we thus find a discrepancy between buying

---

[1] While no firm data are available, the effect would appear to correlate with lower education levels.
[2] The combined turnover of European publishers (29 countries) in 2016 amounted to 22.3 billion euro, leaving the value of the book market unchanged from 2015 (Federation of European Publishers 2016).

and reading behaviour, offering a twenty-first-century confirmation of the old book historical truism that buying and reading are not necessarily closely related.

How can this discrepancy be accounted for? This has not been researched, but a number of interrelated factors may be assumed. First of all books are relatively cheap, so people can afford not to consume the books they purchase. Compare, for example the expendable music file with how the expensive LP record used to be treated. There is much less incentive to learn to appreciate media in which we have not invested economically. At current price levels, a disappointed reader who gives up reading one book does not have to think very long about buying another. More importantly books continue to be favoured as gifts. The symbolic capital books represent accrues both to the recipient and to the giver. Giving a book as a present assumes that value is attached to reading both by the giver and by the receiver. The book gift thus acts like a sign of mutual intellectual or cultural appreciation. Related to this, a third factor is likely to be that among certain social groups reading itself accrues symbolic capital. If book ownership is a cue suggestive of a reading mind, it is one of the features of print that it makes that ownership, and by extension the presence of a reading mind, visible. Today the symbolic capital effect of print probably still accounts for a significant portion of sales, dampening the statistical evidence of a decline in book consumption. In the short term each such sale may represent one bird in the hand, but it does not of course provide a stable basis for the continued health of the industry.

While the statistics are revealing in themselves, it is necessary to look beyond them at readers and readership more fundamentally and in an historical perspective. The digital developments are too diverse and still too new to be easily explained through figures alone. Seen in a longer historical context, the digital revolution is one more punctuation in that 'punctuated equilibrium' that characterizes the evolution of text and reading technology from its origins in handwriting. As a result of this revolution once again the amount of information, the number of readers and the speed of dissemination increase with a jolt—just as happened after the invention of printing with moveable type. It is of course to be welcomed that reading is yet again finding a broader base, but just as in the case of earlier revolutions it comes at a price. In the transformation of the book culture shaped by print into a reading culture shaped by digital text, the stark reality seems to be that though reading may be increasing overall, book reading is decreasing and the book as such is starting to carry less prestige. Reading as a pursuit in its own right (in contrast to more functional reading) does not seem to rank as highly as it used to. Consequently, it is no longer the conventional book and print industry that is supplying the changing demand. Rather it is the digital behemoths, the handful of popular platforms where people tend to spend most of their online time: Google and the social media, particularly Facebook.

Both these trends seem undeniable. And even if the prevalence of screens in the modern world may not explain the whole story, it is equally undeniable that digitization is one major contributing cause. As our lifestyle is rapidly becoming more digital, it looks like the decline in long-form reading may not be a temporary phenomenon either. That the future of reading and a (paying) readership can no longer be simply taken for granted has obvious long-term implications. More than being a merely economic problem affecting the industry, changing consumption habits are part of—and reflect—a fundamental change in the place of books and reading in society. At the same time, in capitalist societies governments are progressively abandoning such tasks and responsibilities as supporting and promoting the writing, production, and distribution of books to the market, diminishing their potentially corrective influence. This presents a vastly different challenge than the book industry is accustomed to handling. That is not to say that it has no role to play; in fact it is indispensable. But before examining what that role might be it will be instructive to take a moment to survey what the spate of recent reading research has to teach the industry about this extraordinary cultural phenomenon.

LEARNING FROM READING RESEARCH

Fortunately the benefits of reading are no longer in doubt as they once were. Especially in the last few decades of the nineteenth century and the first quarter of the twentieth century, the reading habits of the fast growing mass of newly educated readers were often met with suspicion and even contempt. Since then learning to read has effectively become a precondition for being able to function in society. With the social emancipation of the 'lower classes' their reading habits were less patronized by people who conceived of themselves as their betters. The latest research concentrates on showing the benefits of reading with much less prejudice to content.

So why then is reading good for people? Before attempting to answer that question it must be recognized that readers may engage with texts on many levels. PISA[3] tests the ability to read only at a very technical level. Even a literary text may be read variously for the narrative as a story, for the enjoyment of the author's stylistic skills and vocabulary, for the psychological insights proffered, and so on. But perhaps the very first point to note, and this is no less important for being a millennia-old cultural phenomenon, literacy changes the way humans think. Whether one considers these changes as advantageous— or even literate ways of thinking as superior to non-literate ones—is not relevant. The point is simply that literate thinking is different from non-literate thinking. Notably, literacy fosters abstract thinking and reasoning skills that have defined the cultural history of the literate part of the human species.

More recently, a variety of fascinating correlational statistical patterns have been remarked. Perhaps not surprisingly, the prevalence of books in households turns out to correlate with the educational achievements of the children who grow up with them. That correlation holds for all cultures around the world, and is not affected by socioeconomic status (Evans et al. 2010). In a similar vein, reading books (but not newspapers and other types of texts) turns out, for example, to correlate with longevity (Bavishi et al. 2016). As the authors of that particular study conclude, their findings suggest that

---

[3] Programme for International Student Assessment, pisa.oecd.org.

'the benefits of reading books include a longer life in which to read them' (Bavishi et al. 2016: 44). Of late, reading research has been particularly interested in empirically demonstrating the direct benefits to people's personal lives. Three main, but somewhat overlapping categories of effects can be distinguished.

First, reading broadens our thinking. Fiction and non-fiction alike tend to present perspectives different from our own, stimulating reflection on our beliefs and opinions and training the imagination and creativity. In fact, reading is frequently documented as having been life changing.

Secondly, reading helps us to understand others and train our social abilities. Readers are prompted to contemplate the writer's (or persona's) thoughts, feelings, and wishes. This effect is, as we shall see, especially strong in fiction.

Thirdly, reading improves our well-being. It does so in a direct way through the pleasure furnished by the reading act itself. More indirectly it helps to create meaning and order in the happenstance of life. Meaning and order offer a greater sense of being in control and, by extension, a means of coping with difficult or even adverse circumstances.

Besides these—and other—reasons why reading is a good use of one's time, there are less visible—but not therefore less important 'side' effects of reading. It is likely—though hard to prove in the absence of a representative non-reading control group—that reading is a crucial source of such of essential life skills as, notably, concentration and mental discipline. It teaches us sustained attention for something that does not compel it, but that we expect to repay the investment. More generally reading promotes well-being because solitude can lead to relaxation and stress reduction. When carried out in 'fertile solitude' reading fosters readers' resilience, offering greater impermeability to social pressures and expectations, such as those encountered on social media (Salgaro and Adriaan van der Weel 2017).

In response to the decline in book reading some commentators like to say that if it is *reading* that matters, that is being done more than ever. It is true that reading of any sort will help keep up or develop fluency in reading. However, short texts not written by skilled authors are unlikely to do much for concentration and mental discipline or vocabulary. Length may not be crucial per se, but for obvious reasons, long-form sustained arguments or serious fiction require greater concentration and are more likely to correlate with a broader range of vocabulary.

Fiction reading is often singled out from reading at large as having beneficial effects all of its own. Fiction is thought to stimulate reflection on one's own feelings and concerns; contemplation of alternative life scenarios; and the development of intercultural sensitivity and empathy. By offering possible acting scenarios, it is thought to help the reader in resolving moral issues, negotiate difficulties in interpersonal relationships and so on. The jury is still out about the extent to which literary fiction affects readers differently than popular fiction, but it makes sense to assume that literature makes greater cognitive demands. Genre fiction tends to effect immersion in the same way as do, say, computer games, while literary fiction, serious non-fiction (such as academic writing), or poetry demand deep reading.

Insofar as the benefits of fiction reading are singled out, some critics object that any form of storytelling—in games, series, films—would have the same effects. So, their thinking goes, book promotion activities need to be aimed at emphasizing the importance of stories rather than reading habits. It may of course be countered that given the popularity of films, series, and games such marketing is not likely to benefit *reading* very much, and that anyway films, series, and games do not stand in need of as much promotion as reading does. The salient point, however, is that the imagination is stimulated more by reading fiction than by watching a film. This goes for reading in general. Requiring a more active mental contribution than any other medial form, it stimulates a particular brain development, enhancing particular thinking skills. Certainly the passive consumption stigma that was once attached to reading fiction has been largely removed or, insofar as it still exists, has moved from reading in general to reading genre fiction, and from books to series and films. This is one fascinating illustration of the contingent status of reading in society.

Besides requiring greater concentration and subjecting the reader to a broader range of vocabulary, long-form reading offers other strengths. Because they are associated with greater complexity, longer texts promote memorization and mental organization abilities. Understanding and analysing textual arguments is an important prerequisite for responsible citizenship in democratic societies. It has often been noted that reading from screens tends to involve shorter text units while long-form reading tends to be more associated with paper. That is not to say that people will not read full-length books from screens. The most suitable type of screen for that purpose is the e-ink or e-paper screen of some dedicated e-reading devices. Its reflective surface provides a paper-like reading experience. However, most digital texts are read from backlit screens: smartphones, tablets, and laptop and desktop computers, and most are short: social media, emails, blogs, texts, news, web pages. When they do read long-form texts from screens, many readers report difficulties in sustaining their attention. So another intriguing research question is whether or not it matters if we read from screens or from paper, and if we read in long form or not.

The short answer is that the substrate does indeed matter. Just like a story—as we just saw—is not a story, a text is not a text. The question is just *how* screens affect the reading experience and whether the effect is significant. The history of concern about the effects of screens on reading is a long one. It started by pointing at the inferiority of screens compared to paper in terms of flicker; reflection and glare; resolution and legibility. Especially some of the earlier concerns regarding screens now appear a little naïve. A new generation of screen hardware has seen improvements in portability, resolution and legibility, lighting, and so on beyond anything imaginable even twenty years ago. More recently the different haptic experience has been under scrutiny. It seems possible that the absence of a haptic experience similar to that of paper hampers immersion, but this has not been conclusively shown. So far, the evidence that the difference in physical substrate really affects the reading experience is mixed. In the absence of decisive outcomes, there has been a tendency to regard all concern about the move from paper to screen as alarmist. There is a distinct risk here of throwing out the baby with the bathwater.

Screens present issues on a more fundamental level: a different picture emerges when we look at the 'infrastructure' underlying online screen use. It is below the 24/7 connected onscreen textual surface that the elephant in the room is hiding.

As unconnected devices, books are remarkably straightforward and predictable in terms of interface and navigational possibilities. By contrast hardware and software navigational possibilities differ per device, per operating system, and per software iteration. Research has found that even something as relatively simple as the presence of hyperlinks places attention demands on the user by presenting the need for a decision whether or not to follow them. This so-called cognitive overhead disadvantages weaker readers. Something similar may be said about the enhancement of children's books with multimedia. Unless the enhancement clearly supports the narrative, clicking for an instant reward may easily become just a distraction from the effort of comprehending the story. Cognitive overhead adds to the already often noted existence of an economic digital divide. Enriching e-books with digital enhancements, often presented as the future of books, is therefore to be approached with caution.

Also, the screen is a natural temptation space anyway, with promises of newness and excitement ever a mere button click away. Something better—a text, a solution, a new source of entertainment—might always be on the next page. The screen holds out a constant promise of novelty that print lacks, but thereby also that particularly modern anxiety, FoMO. Attention and concentration are thus easily dissipated. Even the very presence on the table of a turned-off smartphone has been shown to be a source of distraction.

Most alarming—but in the light of the preceding not surprising—is a substantial body of evidence showing that digital forms of text tend to be taken less seriously by readers than printed text (Singer and Alexander 2017; Delgado et al. under review [2018]). This shows itself in, for example, a reduced willingness to engage in metacognitive learning regulation when reading texts on screens. In an educational setting especially, this is of course problematic. While the precise cause remains unclear, the fluidity and ephemerality of screen text must be one prime factor. The association with distraction—and perhaps in particular distraction by less serious and more entertaining screen uses—is probably another likely factor. So is the greater onus on the reader to evaluate every snippet of information found in the confused jumble of the Web: who is its author; who published it; is it an opinion or a fact; how reliable is it? The largest digital platform, Facebook, for example, is not in the business of providing 'content' (including reading matter). It is in the business of selling consumer attention. Facebook can do this by creating user profiles on the basis of the time spent on the platform. Therefore it is imperative for the company to make users stay as long as possible. Crudely speaking, to Facebook veracity and quality of information are irrelevant; popularity (a prevalence of click bait) and addiction (to dopamine-generating behaviour such as collecting likes) are. That the need to evaluate and discriminate represents an increasing challenge to readers was well illustrated by a noticeable revival of the appreciation of conventional, print-based journalism after the outcome of the 2016 US presidential elections.

Moreover, the perception that less has been invested in screen texts gives rise to the 'cheap speech' phenomenon. When Eugene Volokh first described this phenomenon as early as 1995, he cast it as an exciting and democratizing effect of the digital medium. It would give everyone a voice, not silenced or even muted by intermediaries like editors, publishers, and booksellers. More recently, it has become increasingly evident that this 'cheapness' comes with unintended darker side effects. These range from what Andrew Keen has called 'the cult of the amateur' (Keen 2008) to the debilitating political effects of fake news (Hasen 2017).

Lastly, digital text is characterized by fluidity and impermanence. Cutting-and-pasting and remixing make it hard to think of it in terms of ownership, either by a named and attributed author or on the part of the consumer. (The terms of service tend to emphasize that what the 'purchase' grants the consumer is only ever a temporary licence to access.) Although this has not yet been investigated, such a tentative hold on the text may not be conducive of learning. In fact, the trend—which *has* been found—from just-in-case (learning to memorize) to just-in-time (looking up, searching for) knowledge seems unstoppable (Sparrow et al. 2011).

Another outcome of the digital turn has been that, paradoxically in view of the unprecedented and much vaunted wealth of readily accessible 'content' on the Web, digital reading actually reduces diversity. This is chiefly the result of the algorithmic means by which this wealth of content is usually accessed. Most of these means are designed, for commercial or other reasons, to please. One of the main criteria by which Google ranks its search results, for example, is by 'popularity', whether measured by your own previously divulged interests or by other people's. Similarly, Amazon's recommendations are meant to cause sales, and will favour the most popular titles based on their capacity to generate them. Already back in 2008 UK economists Will Page and Andrew Bud found that in the case of music, of 13 million 'songs' available for sale, a staggering 10 million had *never* been downloaded, and a paltry 52,000 songs (4 tenths of one per cent) created 80 per cent of income (Page and Garland 2009). If the long tail exists, it is found only by those who actively set out to find it. Even reading for academic research has shown itself not to be immune to such narrowing effects. Counterintuitively, 'as more journal issues came online, the articles referenced tended to be more recent, fewer journals and articles were cited, and more of those citations were to fewer journals and articles' (Evans 2008).

Being so diffuse, and affecting society in such diverse ways, the effects of these and other infrastructural differences between paper and screens on reading are not always easy to measure. It also requires defining what we expect from reading, both as individuals consciously and deliberately engaging with text to a particular end (say, a temporary escape from reality, reflection on life, learning something new) and as a complex society in need of means of efficient communication. The number of variables in reading research is large. Prominent among them is the ever-changing combination of age and digital experience, which makes extrapolation towards the future particularly hazardous. Yet there can be little doubt that in their long-term consequences the introduction of digital text will surpass even the invention of printing almost 600 years ago. It is more likely to resemble the transmogrifying effects on human culture of the introduction of writing some six millennia ago.

Cultivating Readership

Screen reading clearly comes with a number of distinct challenges to the publishing industry. The publishing industry is and always has been a Janus-headed one, with (often longer-term) cultural considerations and (usually shorter-term) economic imperatives often fighting for the upper hand. Given the structural nature of the digital transformations, the challenge will be to bring both imperatives into harmony in the industry's response to sweeping changes in reading patterns. As is only natural—and healthy in a largely profit-driven industry—economic considerations are usually taken care of first as a matter of course. What needs more conscious cultivation is the social responsibility that comes with the territory of it also being a creative cultural industry. If each new cohort of younger readers reads less than the preceding one, how can new readers be cultivated? What can the book industry do in particular to stem the decline of long-form reading, whether E or P?

In view of the fast changes and the contingent status of reading in society, it makes sense to treat reading and readers as a much more dynamic phenomenon than they have historically been recognized as being. In addition to thinking of readers as demographically discrete markets (including micro-target groups) it is vital also to study closely readers' development over their lifetime, with particular attention to adolescence when so many readers are currently abandoning reading and the crucial role of education in the socialization of reading.

The unwonted responsibility for fostering a future readership can only really be borne collectively. In many countries there are already forms of collective reading promotion, whether instigated by governments or by the industry. But the current massive changes in reading patterns demand an even broader strategy of developing not just a market for (long-form) reading as such, but a culture in which such a market can thrive. In particular, trade publishing is increasingly supply driven as title production keeps accelerating. Customary commercial book marketing, focused on titles, authors, characters, series, imprints, is necessarily in direct competition with other publishers. The ever increasing competition among publishers resulting from this is inevitably more wasteful than is spending resources on the marketing of reading as a collective interest.

Books being relatively cheap, the marketing of reading is a matter less of competing for consumer spending than for that rarest of commodities: attention and time. What is needed to do such marketing effectively is demographic research on time spending habits and purchase behaviour, especially on media; (non-)reading motives; and the perceived status of books and reading for various purposes, such as leisure and entertainment or as an information source. The book trade may not be a match for Silicon Valley's ability to transform itself into an addiction industry—not all that different from the tobacco industry. Nevertheless, data should clearly play a more important role in strategic thinking than they have hitherto, and again, except in the case of a moloch like Amazon, this can only be achieved in a more collective scenario.

A greater emphasis on the cultural importance of reading—as against book buying—also legitimizes an appeal to other than industry resources. Obvious existing partnerships are with reading promotion agencies (insofar as they operate independently from the book industry) and libraries. Partnerships with libraries have traditionally suffered from a vague notion that libraries service consumers who are not, or at least not necessarily, buyers. Because lending tends often to be regarded as a natural competition to sales, collaboration has on the whole remained low key. Concentrating on reading promotion as a common goal would offer a subtle but productive change of perspective.

Less obvious partnerships that are tentatively beginning to be explored are with a diffuse range of organizations promoting health, democracy, responsible citizenship, etcetera. A traditionally strangely neglected but essential partner is the educational field. Given the contingent nature of reading, education clearly plays a formative role in fostering a book (as against a mere reading) culture. School is one of the most pivotal because authoritative means for the socialization of young people as readers—although the way it currently goes about it may be counterproductive to judge by the massive desertion of adolescent readers. The parental example may be equally conducive, but this is much harder to influence. Students are a captive audience. It should be a matter of some concern—not just to the book industry—that the chief impetus for the current mushrooming of digital learning environments seems to be coming from the tech industry. By skilfully exploiting the widespread fear of educational policy makers that their field may be 'left behind', it manages to gloss over the fact that there is scant evidence if, and if so how precisely, technology aids learning (Selwyn 2016). If anything the evidence, as we have seen, goes the other way. As book use in schools diminishes, one of the two chief sources for the socialization of book reading threatens to fall away. This is a cause for alarm.

One hopeful recent trend that the industry has been quick to play into is that of younger readers fleeing the online herd. Although it is early to say, this may well augur a broader movement in which reading could even become imbued with a new social chique. Many young and dynamic startups in publishing have already begun to cater to this. At first blush somewhat surprisingly, they emphasize the very materiality that digerati would have been inclined to spurn as Old Skool. In an age of mindfulness and individual development, reading is being (re-)discovered as a 'technology of the self'. There seems to be a growing sense that much online time is being frittered away on idle pursuits whose only fleeting reward is a hit of dopamine in the short run, leaving one feeling empty and drained of energy when its effect subsides. Offline reading may thus be pitched successfully as an antidote to an unhealthy addiction to the screen world and its cheap online thrills. Contemplative and 'slow reading', including of books that challenge the reader and need savouring, may be an unsuspected hole in the market.

The unique selling points (USPs) of paper books that may thus be profiled more are the fact that they are offline (the absence of distraction aiding concentration); that they may be owned (e.g. they can be annotated, so as to appropriate the intellectual content; that they can be archived as a physical record of cognitively and emotionally meaningful memories; that they can be shared (lent out) in a way that digital rights management

(DRM) does not permit; and that they have an aesthetic, a weightiness, a visibility, capable of representing symbolic capital as much as satisfying our haptic needs as embodied people. A likely but so far unresearched USP of paper books is the value perception resulting from the very need for a serious economic investment to be made, in the purchase of course, but even more so in the very production of the book, making it worth purchasing (Van der Weel 2018). For convenience, utility, and disposability there is digital text; for symbolic value, ownership, and emotion there is the material book. There is a great deal of scope here for the industry in that only for the latter are people prepared to pay premium prices. By contrast, consumer demands for convenience and utility—epitomized by the e-book—command little opportunity to add value that can easily be turned into profit.

Collective efforts aimed at the marketing of reading rather than books also demand a recalibration of marketing efforts by individual publishers. In this connection facilitating reading and book communities, highlighting the social role of reading, are perceived as a particularly valuable contribution by publishers and booksellers as cultural middlemen. A continuing emphasis on curation as a service is likely to be particularly welcome and valuable to new readers.

CULTURAL CONSIDERATIONS VERSUS ECONOMIC IMPERATIVES

The future of the book industry ultimately demands a healthy economic basis no less than a strong cultural one. That brings us to the subject of the economic issues of e-reading—and e-commerce at large. One major factor here is the value of E. E-books have been most popular as replacements for the mass market paperback, characterized by disposability. Given that e-book pricing tends to be distinctly lower than that of paper books, the promotion of e-reading in the short term reduces turnover and perhaps profitability. Someone reading a 5 euro chicklit or 1 euro self-published e-novel (never mind a fragment of free fiction) is spending attention and valuable reading time that could also have been spent on a more expensive title, whether E or P.

Much more significantly, in the longer term, the undeniably lower value perception consumers have of E services compared to that of P products could compromise the value perception of books and writing as a whole. Another factor is the reduced visibility of digital books and reading to a potential readership in society at large. For reading to be marketed and 'branded', it must be visible. To be seen to be reading is (still) a proxy for being regarded as a cultured person. However, the act of reading on screens is not easily identifiable as such. Also, as more bookselling moves online, not only will booksellers experience greater difficulty surviving in the main street, but it reduces the presence of books and reading in society overall, making them less a natural part of our habitat.

Some say that for e-reading to come into its own it needs to develop the 'true' strengths inherent in the digital form, and that these have yet to be discovered. A few years ago gamification and other forms of bells-and-whistles thinking dominated talk about the future direction for publishing. However, the tremendous investment that such treatment of an authorial text requires means that only an exceptional popular success could possibly repay it. Moreover, readers do not seem to be clamouring for bells and whistles, which are perceived as a hindrance rather than an attraction in the reading process. The prediction that hypertext novels were to be the natural evolution for literature was never fulfilled (Mangen and Van der Weel 2017). What reasons are there to assume that enhanced books are the answer to real reader needs? That is not to say that there will not be a place for enhancement; just that enhanced books may be more in the nature of a remediation, like games or films, resulting in what would be perceived as a type of medium distinct from text for reading.

For the continued health of the book industry as part of the 'content industry' there is no need to eschew multimediality. There is a healthy performance in audiobooks—although we have seen that their consumption cannot technically be called reading. Bookshops usually carry a variety of entertainment media, including DVDs (as long as that format lasts). Especially the larger, internationally operating publishing conglomerates have long been part of a tendency toward the horizontal convergence of media and modalities. Yet this only serves to accentuate the industry's central quandary: which distinct identity—both of itself and of its market—should it be (does it want to be) promoting. Is that the textual reading experience, or that of a media industry? As the theory of disruptive innovation suggests, the industry might find it challenging to compete on such alien territory and might risk alienating the faithful core readership that sustains it. Also, the more the book industry evolves into a content industry, the less it will be a force for a book reading culture in the long term.

Mere figures and statistics do not do justice to the disruption and complications the digital revolution is bringing. Identifying the reader with the (potential) buyer no longer suffices. In the face of such transformations, it is not enough to care about a *reading culture*: both the book industry and society at large need to aim at fostering book reading in a *book culture*. Reading is as unstable as human culture, and there is no doubt that we will adapt to any new reality. However, we may consider (aspects of) a book culture to be worth preserving, such as, in particular, the benefits of long-form reading on paper. That paper books persist when other media have long turned almost completely digital; that books are beginning to be considered as a welcome counterbalance to the fragmentation and more superficial consumption of digital text, and that students and even children brought up in a digital world continue to have a clear preference for paper, are all signs that there *are* such aspects (Baron 2015: ch. 4).[4]

Beyond its purely economic perspective, the industry has to consider seriously how it can continue to make itself relevant as an intermediary, taking seriously the cultural side

---

[4] Cf. Scholastic's finding that 'nearly two-thirds of children (65%)—up from 2012 (60%)—agree that they'll always want to read print books even though there are ebooks available' (Scholastic 2015).

of its two-faced nature. To take co-responsibility for maintaining and creating an audience is a new and unaccustomed role for the industry. Beyond the traditional foci of reading promotion this requires collaboration. If not active lobbying, it requires at least strong support for fostering a reading culture that supports the presence of books and reading in the streetscape, in particular shops and libraries, but also in schools. The good news is that the industry's interests turn out to align very nicely with those of society at large. As reading research shows, letting the digitization of reading simply run its course would not be in society's best interests, but in the longer term it may also not be the most helpful policy for industry.

REFERENCES

Baron, N. (2015). *Words Onscreen: The Fate of Reading in a Digital World*, New York: Oxford University Press.

Bavishi, A., Martin D. Slade, and Becca R. Levy. (2016). 'A chapter a day: Association of book reading with longevity', *Social Science & Medicine*, 164, p. 44.

Boersenblatt. (2018). 'Der Buchmarkt verliert vor allem jüngere Käufer'. https://www. boersenblatt.net/artikel-studie_des_boersenvereins.1422566.html

Centraal Bureau voor de Statistiek, Statline. (2017). 'Openbare bibliotheken'. http://statline. cbs.nl/Statweb/publication/?DM=SLNL&PA=70763NED&D1=20&D2=13-19&VW=T.

Chartier, R. (1994). *The Order of Books: Readers, Authors, and Libraries in Europe between the Fourteenth and Eighteenth Centuries*, Stanford, CA: Stanford University Press.

Delgado, P., C. Vargas, R. Ackerman, and L. Salmeron. (2018). 'Don't throw away your printed books: A meta-analysis on the effects of reading media on reading comprehension', *Educational Research Review*, 25, pp. 23–38, https://doi.org/10.1016/j.edurev.2018.09.003.

Department for Culture, Media and Sport. (2014). 'Taking Part 2014/15: Quarter 1'. https:// www.gov.uk/government/uploads/system/uploads/attachment_data/file/360011/Taking_ Part_2014_15_Quarter_1_Report.doc.

Evans, J. A. (2008). 'Electronic Publication and the Narrowing of Science and Scholarship', *Science*, 321(5887), p. 395. DOI: 10.1126/science.1150473.

Evans, M. D. R., Jonathan Kelley, Joanna Sikora, and Donald J. Treiman. (2010). 'Family Scholarly Culture and Educational Success: Books and Schooling in 27 Nations', *Research in Social Stratification and Mobility*, 28, p. 171. doi:10.1016/j.rssm.2010.01.002

Eyre, C. (2015). 'Nielsen highlights mid-teens reading dip'. https://www.thebookseller.com/ news/nielsen-says-18-25s-more-likely-read-young-teens-314777.

Federation of European Publishers. (2016). 'European Book Publishing Statistics'. https:// www.fep-fee.eu/European-Book-Publishing-922.

GfK. (2017). 'Frequency of reading books'. http://www.gfk.com/global-studies/global-studies-frequency-of-reading-books/.

Hasen, R. L. (2017). 'Cheap Speech and What It Has Done (to American Democracy)'. https:// papers.ssrn.com/sol3/papers.cfm?abstract_id=3017598.

Humanities Indicators (American Academy of Arts & Sciences). (2016). 'Time Spent Reading'. https://www.humanitiesindicators.org/content/indicatorDoc.aspx?i=11094.

Huysmans, F. (2007). 'De openbare bibliotheek in Nederland en de veranderende leescultuur sinds 1975', *Jaarboek voor Nederlandse Boekgeschiedenis*, 14, p. 179.

Keen, A. (2008). *The Cult of the Amateur: How Blogs, MySpace, YouTube and the Rest of Today's User Generated Media Are Killing Our Culture and Economy*, London: Nicholas Brealey Publishing.

Mangen, A. and Adriaan van der Weel. (2017). 'Why don't we read hypertext novels?' *Convergence: The International Journal of Research into New Media Technologies*, 23(2), pp. 166–81. DOI: 10.1177/1354856515586042.

Page, W. and E. Garland. (2009). 'The long tail of P2P', *Economic Insight*, 14. https://www.prsformusic.com/-/media/files/prs-for-music/research/economic-insight-14-the-long-tail-of-p2p.ashx?la=en&hash=E60A0106A1890DF49C6D103766BF354C37069133

Salgaro, M. and Adriaan van der Weel. (2017). 'How Reading Fiction Can Help You Improve Yourself and Your Relationship to Others', *The Conversation*, 19 December. https://theconversation.com/how-reading-fiction-can-help-you-improve-yourself-and-your-relationship-to-others-88830

Scholastic. (2015). *Kids & Family Reading Report*, 5th edition. http://www.scholastic.com/readingreport/Scholastic-KidsAndFamilyReadingReport-5thEdition.pdf?v=100

Selwyn, N. (2016). *Is Technology Good for Education?* Cambridge: Polity.

Singer, L. M. and P. A. Alexander. (2017). 'Reading on Paper and Digitally: What the Past Decades of Empirical Research Reveal', *Review of Educational Research*, 87(6), p. 1007. DOI: 10.3102/0034654317722961.

Sparrow, B., J. Liu, and D. M. Wegner. (2011). 'Google Effects on Memory: Cognitive Consequences of Having Information at Our Fingertips', *Science*, 333, p. 776. DOI: 10.1126/science.1207745

Stichting Lezen. (2016). *Leesmonitor*. https://www.leesmonitor.nu/nl/leestijd.

Van der Weel, Adriaan. (2011). Changing Our Textual Minds: Towards a Digital Order of Knowledge. Manchester: Manchester University Press.

Van der Weel, Adriaan. (2018). 'The Persistent Predilection for Paper', *TXT* 2018.

Wennekers, A., Frank Huysmans, and Jos de Haan. (2018). *Lees:Tijd: Lezen in Nederland*, The Hague: Sociaal en Cultureel Planbureau. https://www.scp.nl/Publicaties/Alle_publicaties/Publicaties_2018/Lees_Tijd.

....

CHAPTER 5

COPYRIGHT
AND PUBLISHING

Symbiosis in the Digital Environment

....

MIRA T. SUNDARA RAJAN

INTRODUCTION

....

COPYRIGHT and publishing are as intimately related as parent and child. Publishing cannot exist without copyright; it is fundamentally dependent on copyright for its operation. Indeed, it would be no exaggeration to say that copyright is the foundation upon which the entire edifice of modern publishing has been built.

This is a grand claim, but it is both a necessary and an important one. Copyright, as we know it, is in transition. Given the closeness of the relationship between copyright and publishing, the implications of the modern copyright landscape for publishing could not be more fundamental or far-reaching. For better or for worse, the transformation of modern copyright law in the digital environment will shape the future of publishing.

Copyright can be defined, quite simply, yet with surprising accuracy, as the 'right to copy' an original work. It governs the relationship between the author of a work and its publisher. The publisher must acquire copyright from the author—in principle, and in the first instance, the holder of the initial copyright in the work—in order to proceed with any publication related activity. Copyright can either be transferred outright by the author to the publisher, or, alternatively, licensed, in whole or in part. I in the latter case, these detailed arrangements for the publication of the work are generally accomplished by contract.[1] It must be emphasized that agreement on the treatment of copyright

---

[1] But the work-for-hire, or employment, rule, should be duly noted. In modern copyright practice, if the author works as an employee, his or her prerogatives under copyright law can be superseded by those of his or her employer, who then becomes the owner of the work. In the important but, from a theoretical

precedes absolutely everything that the publisher is entitled to do with the work. Copyright, and copyright alone, confers on the publisher the right to act.

Modern copyright law operates in an increasingly complex environment—one that differs, in fundamental ways, from the copyright context of the past three centuries. Digital technology, in particular, challenges many of the foundational concepts underlying copyright law. What does a 'right to copy' mean, when, practically speaking, the moment a work is digitized, it becomes susceptible to infinite replication, flawless and integral modification, and potentially limitless public availability? Like the notion of 'copying', itself, the sophisticated conceptions of authorship, originality, publication, and use that have served as the underpinnings of copyright law throughout the modern age no longer mean what they used to. The very existence of copyright is under threat.

Given the symbiosis of copyright and publishing, there can be little doubt that the developments transforming modern copyright law will have a tremendous impact on publishing. In this dynamic and rapidly evolving context, what are the key challenges facing copyright law and practice, and what do they imply for the present and future of publishing as we know it? This chapter will consider some of the most exciting and unnerving developments in modern copyright law, and it will draw a number of conclusions on how publishing might ultimately be affected.

COPYRIGHT: AN EXTREMELY BRIEF HISTORY

Copyright fundamentally seeks to protect the rights of both authors and publishers. The author has right to decide on the publication of his or her own work, and on the terms surrounding publication. From the author, the publisher acquires the right to control the communication of the work to the public. Copyright law then prevents anyone from infringing upon the publisher's exclusive right to control the dissemination of the work.

Neither of these rights is absolute. Instead, the law aims to achieve balance in order to promote important objectives of public policy. The purpose of copyright is to support, and potentially encourage,[2] the creation of culture, by providing a practical means for its sustenance. Simultaneously, copyright is said to facilitate the dissemination of works to the public by encouraging their commercialization. When an appropriate balance is achieved between these two, public policy objectives, copyright law is said to support the worthy goals of education, cultural progress, and the betterment

---

perspective, exceptional case of employment relationships, the transfer of ownership is accomplished by the direct operation of copyright law, itself, which, rightly or wrongly, shifts ownership directly to the employer. A publisher must then negotiate with the *owner* of the work for its use—the creator's employer—and these transactions, once again, are governed by the broader context of copyright law.

[2] In copyright parlance, one of the purposes of the law is to 'incentivize' creativity—although it is a much less controversial proposition to focus on the role that copyright plays in support of culture by generating economic support for its creators: authors.

of society. For example, in its famous 'Copyright Clause', the United States Constitution explicitly affirms that the purpose of copyright is the 'Progress of Science and useful Arts'.[3]

Accordingly, copyright law accomplishes three important functions. First, it establishes a right in intellectual creation, and, as part of that process, generally vests that right in the creator of the work, its author. Secondly, as noted above, it defines the fundamental terms of the relationship between the author and the person, organization, or entity responsible for the dissemination of the work—its publisher. Thirdly, it establishes an equilibrium between the interests of right-holders and those of the public. Of these three roles, the final one has become a source of extraordinary conflict in the digital age—but, to varying degrees, the other relationships protected by copyright, including that between author and publisher, are also under strain.

It is therefore worth considering the roles of all three parties involved in publishing matters—author, publisher, and public—since the adoption of modern copyright law. Curiously, the author was a relatively late addition to the landscape of publishing, but ultimately became the anchor to which the entire system was moored. Copyright has focused on the role of the author since the adoption of the first modern copyright statute, the celebrated Statute of Anne of 1710, which broke apart the existing structures of publishing in the United Kingdom to create a revolutionary new context for publishing. The innovation introduced by the Statute was tremendous, yet astonishing in its simplicity: for the first time in Western history, authors owned their own, unpublished works. They did so by virtue of having created them. Thereafter, it was up to authors to negotiate with publishers for their publication.

The radical nature of this remarkable change may not be immediately apparent to modern eyes. It is worth remembering that the landscape of publishing prior to the Statute of Anne was an extremely restrictive one, more or less entirely dominated by the prerogatives of state censorship. In particular, the Sovereign exercised tight control over publishing through the grant of royal charters that conferred exclusive powers to publish upon the holder of this printing 'privilege'.[4] The publishers, themselves, were a tight-knit and powerful group known as the Stationers' Company, and, in particular, the Conger.[5] They fought against the sacrifice of their privileges, with cunning and ruthlessness, in court proceedings over the following half-century and beyond. Their struggles ultimately influenced the interpretation of the Statute in profound ways.[6]

But the Stationers were fighting the tide of history. The adoption of the Statute of Anne, with its focus on authorship, was the result of immense social pressures, and

---

[3] Available at https://fairuse.stanford.edu/law/us-constitution/.

[4] This history has been insightfully explored by scholars interested in copyright, including Lyman Ray Patterson's pioneering work, *Copyright in Historical Perspective*. Patterson notes: 'In 1710, copyright was the right of a publisher to the exclusive publication of a work, and functioned to prevent literary piracy; by 1774, copyright had come to be the right of an author, and still functioned to protect the exclusive right of publication' (1968, p. 151).

[5] Patterson (1968, pp. 151–52).

[6] Among the notable cases were *Millar v Taylor* (1769) 4 Burr. 2303, 98 Eng. Rep. 201, five years later by *Donaldson v Beckett* (1774) 2 Brown's Parl. Cases 129, 1 Eng. Rep. 837.

reflected historical forces that had been building throughout the previous century. Riding the crest of this wave, the Statute was championed by writers and thinkers from Milton to Locke, who argued eloquently in favour of freedom of speech and individual rights of authorship based on the act of creation.[7] The conferring of individual rights on authors was a defining element of the statutory scheme, and it continues to inform copyright law today. However, the formal recognition of authors under copyright law is arguably eclipsed, in modern times, by the power acquired by publishers through the operation of copyright—and by the controversy generated by growing public perceptions that the influence exercised by the owners of copyright works is excessive, and goes against the public interest.

Copyright in the Digital Era: A Paradigm Transformed

The technological possibilities of the digital environment have brought new challenges to copyright, primarily as a result of the newfound accessibility and, correspondingly, vastly altered public perception of the value of works of authorship. In terms of copyright, these changes will undoubtedly prove to be paradigm-shifting forces in the relatively long term. The following sections examine some of the most interesting of these developments, and consider their implications from a publishing perspective.

Authorship and Originality

Publishers must negotiate with the author of a work in order to be able to publish it. However, the nature of authorship has been transformed by technology in a number of respects, leading to ambiguity about ownership and control. This issue can be broken down into three phenomena of interest: the use of new technological methods in the creation of works, automatic means of disseminating works through technology, and the democratization of authorship.

New Works

To varying degrees, creative works have always drawn upon earlier works for their creation. This applies, not only in the sense of inspiration, but also, in the explicit use—notably, in literature, but also, in music—of actual quotations and extracts from earlier works.[8] This process of assimilating existing literature, and the mysterious alchemy by which it

---

[7] See, for example, Milton's famed polemic on free speech, the Areopagitica, available at https://www. dartmouth.edu/~milton/reading_room/areopagitica/text.html.

[8] The musical examples from classical music are numerous; for example, Robert Schumann 'quotes' from a Beethoven song in his famous Fantasy, Opus 17, for piano.

supports new and original creation, is brilliantly explored by T. S. Eliot in a 1919 essay entitled, 'Tradition and the Individual Talent.'[9]

In the environment of digital technology, however, our relationship with culture has changed. It is now possible to draw upon the established world of culture and tradition in a way that is entirely new— quite literally, by exploring data, rather than (or in addition to) the facilities of memory, vision, and dream that Keats must have meant when he spoke of the 'viewless wings of poesy'. It is worth noting that, in the long run, an environment so richly super-endowed with information is likely to bring a new emphasis to creativity in its most traditional sense. Where information is abundant, creativity, representing an infinitely greater level of engagement with knowledge, may ultimately prove to be valued more highly than ever before. At the moment, however, pragmatic concerns and practical temptations abound.

Books written today can easily integrate text from the past; and works of art such as collages can draw upon a virtually limitless library of digitized images to create new and unique juxtapositions of existing art. Indeed, the seamlessness of digital technology enables perfect integration to be accomplished, so that there may even be no 'physical' way to distinguish between new and re-used text. The sheer proliferation of material that is available—images of artworks alongside personal photographs, classic literature as well as student exam papers—suggests that the curation of information will increasingly be recognized as a subtle, complex, and valuable activity in its own right.

These technological changes have been accompanied by aesthetic and moral shifts. The early part of the digital era has, perhaps quite naturally, favoured experimentation over restraint, freedom over control, and innovation over originality in the usual sense of the term. Instead, enthusiasm for technology predominates. In this environment, a novel made entirely out of passages from pre-existing works by a teenage author created an online sensation; as Randy Kennedy of the *New York Times*, writing in 2010, commented:

> A child of a media-saturated generation, [Helene Hegemann] ... presented herself as a writer whose birthright is the remix, the use of anything at hand she feels suits her purposes, an idea of communal creativity that certainly wasn't shared by those from whom she borrowed. In a line that might have been stolen from Sartre (it wasn't) she added: 'There's no such thing as originality anyway, just authenticity.'[10]

In a more sombre tone, the husband of an elderly and ailing concert pianist, a sound producer himself, created a world of new recordings, ostensibly of her playing, by combining a variety of samples from existing recordings. His questionable yet quite understandable purpose was to establish his wife's reputation as a leading concert artist who had struggled against, and overcome, extraordinary odds. Joyce Hatto was warmly welcomed by a largely unsuspecting classical music community as a great pianist in the late bloom of a frustrated career; but, by a fitting irony, the fraud that was made possible

---

[9] Eliot (1964, p. 3).   [10] Kennedy (2010).

through technology was also unveiled by it. When a music-lover inserted a Hatto CD into his iTunes program, the Gracenote service, which matches tracks from CDs to works already within its database, found matches between 'Hatto's' recordings and those of other, both well-known and lesser-known, pianists.[11]

In the world of publishing, the abundance of material available in the digital environment, and the corresponding difficulty of knowing its source, can lead to difficulties. As suggested by the examples noted above, these difficulties range from relatively easy to more complex to resolve. The use of software can help to detect copying. However, it can be a far more subtle issue to determine whether copying is plagiaristic or permissible. If the publisher has an agreement with an author, and the author has made use of source material in the creation of his or her work, is there a bright line telling us how much existing material can be incorporated before it ceases to be considered that author's original work? Alas, no: copyright no longer clarifies this issue at all, with courts agreeing that a single word can be a significant part of a work,[12] and that an extract of eleven words made by a machine can still amount to a work protected by copyright because those eleven words *may* represent the original creation of an author whose work is included in the database.[13] When does the point at which the author may be deemed a plagiarist arrive, leading to legal liability or, what may be an equally or more serious problem in the digital environment, loss of reputation for the publisher?

Indeed, it is worth noting that this determination may vary depending on whether the question of plagiarism is examined from a social or a legal point of view. Once again, the publisher may face liability or reputational damage, or both, with the protection of reputation being a sensitive and increasingly important issue in the digital context.

Technological Means of Dissemination

Just as information can be manipulated by human beings, it can also be manipulated by machines. When this happens, the results range from the banal to the spectacular—basic text and data mining, at the base of the pyramid of knowledge, to independently operating artificial intelligence at its apex, like the Deep Blue and Deep Mind computers, trained to play chess and the Asian game of Go at the highest levels. Machines like these can match and possibly exceed the skills known to humanity—and can even, in the astonishing words of Go master Fan Hui, attain 'beauty'.[14]

As noted above, it seems reasonable to expect that, as the technological era progresses, the mere provision of information will be of decreasing value and interest. However, the proliferation of immense volumes of information suggests a corresponding need for guidance. Here is surely an important opportunity for publishers—to play a role in publishing guides, indices, abstracts, and summaries, and to develop the various tools needed to help the public to find information that it needs and wants, and to understand

---

[11] Singer (2007).   [12] *Frisby v BBC* [1967] Ch 932.

[13] The European Court of Justice decision of 16 July 2009, which offered an interpretive ruling on the issues later followed by the Danish Supreme Court, is available at https://www.ippt.eu/files/2009/IPPT20090716_ECJ_Infopaq_v_DDF.pdf.

[14] See Metz (2016).

the information that it discovers. However, as in the *Infopaq* case described earlier (see note 13), the use of technological tools in this endeavour, necessary as it is, can lead to situations where even machine-led 'creation' arguably implicates the original creations of human beings—leading to the subsistence of copyright and infringement problems of a new and rather startling kind. At the other end of the spectrum, 'purely' machine-made creation is currently outside the scope of copyright protection in most jurisdictions, including the United States,[15] making this an area that is open to development, though without the usual incentives offered by the copyright system, and, in the absence of copyright ownership, potentially difficult to protect.

The Democratization of Authorship

Adding to these complexities is the changing nature of authorship itself. The digital environment offers an unprecedented opportunity to develop new material using existing matter. In this sense, the ability to create works lies within the grasp of more people than ever before. Some of these people will already think of themselves as authors—like the essayist quoting from pre-existing articles, or the artist making a collage out of pre-existing photographs. However, some creators of works in the digital context will be generating material such as photographs and writing with no real, pre-conceived notion of being an 'author' at all. What happens to these works when, for example, they appear online? Is this a form of publication? In what circumstances can existing works, or new compositions based on those works, be used or reused in other, newly published works?

The Creative Commons licensing system attempts to address at least some of these questions. The only true 'alternative to copyright' to emerge in the digital era so far—apart from the option of making works freely available online, with the expectation of no further association or control—Creative Commons allows the creator of a work to release his or her work online under the terms of a general licence to the public. The licence is freely available on the Creative Commons website.[16] The system is American in origin, developed by law professor Lawrence Lessig and inspired by Richard Stallman's model of Open Source protection for computer software,[17] but it has since spread to many countries. The licences are available in adapted versions on international websites.

Despite the aim of clarifying the status of works appearing online, the Creative Commons licensing system remains quite complex in its own right. Virtually all of the licences require some measure of recognition by the user of a work—attribution of its creator, for example—and some of them go much further, imposing conditions on the

---

[15] Compendium of U.S. Copyright Office Practices (29 September 2017 version), s. 313.2, 'Works That Lack Human Authorship,' available at https://www.google.co.in/search?q=U.S.+COPYRIGHT+OFFICE%2C+COMPENDIUM+OF+U.S.+COPYRIGHT+OFFICE+PRACTICES&oq=U.S.+COPYRIGHT+OFFICE%2C+COMPENDIUM+OF+U.S.+COPYRIGHT+OFFICE+PRACTICES&aqs=chrome.69i57.1031j0j9&sourceid=chrome&ie=UTF-8.

[16] See https://creativecommons.org/choose/.

[17] See e.g. https://creativecommons.org/2005/10/12/ccinreviewlawrencelessigonhowitallbegan/.

further use of works, such as requiring subsequently published works that use Creative Commons material to be released to the public under similar Creative Commons licences. The implications are clearly significant for publishing: failure to respect the conditions of a given licence can lead to liability and, indeed, reputational damage—if the creator of the work is ultimately tracking its use and discovers the re-publication. Creative Commons adds to the diversity of options available in the publishing environment, and, given the shortcomings of copyright in the technological context, this is undoubtedly a good thing. However, in order to benefit from the options that the system offers, publishers not only need to be aware of its existence; they also need to find new ways of integrating its terms into their own business and creative practices.

An unanswered question remains how the greater potential for involvement in the creative process will affect many of these trends. Attitudes towards copyright are likely to fluctuate depending on where in the cycle of cultural production an individual finds himself or herself—perhaps tending towards a greater appreciation of access when in the audience for creative works, but recognizing the imperatives of control as a creator. However, this comment should not be taken for anything more than a general observation about an increasingly diverse and unpredictable environment. Authors often want and need a degree of control over the works, at least to the extent that they seek attribution of their authorship, but, as recognized by the Creative Commons system, some authors are not in search of any further need to control their work at all. However, practically no author seeks control at the expense of the dissemination of the work to the public. Every writer wants to be read—every author's goal, fundamentally, is communication with the public. Extreme restrictions on the communication of works, including extreme reactions to copying and piracy, make little sense for authors, who typically have every interest in maintaining a constructive relationship with their public, rather than allowing their audiences to be antagonized.

Publication and Communication to the Public

As suggested by these remarks, new technologies have theoretically made it easier than ever before to 'publish' works—or, in the up to date terminology of modern copyright law, to 'communicate them to the public'. This terminology specifically seeks to reflect the reality of online publishing, which may differ from publication in the traditional sense, but still serves the purpose of releasing the work to the public—with all of the practical implications following from that act.

In particular, the attempt to stretch traditional notions of publication under copyright law to embrace technological means of disseminating works leads to two interesting situations. First, technology is constantly evolving, leading to the likelihood that there will be new methods of disseminating works, and new formats for doing so, in the future—including curated formats that reflect the 'added value' of publishers in the digital environment. It is likely that these new approaches to publication will fall within the ambit of copyright law, leading, for example, to requirements for permission from copyright owners, and royalty payments, in new contexts. This may be the case whether or not the new publishing arrangements are, or can be, explicitly referenced in contracts.

An issue that has already proven to be difficult is the question of how much should be paid for the use of a work in a new and specific technological context. New online publishing platforms, for example, such as the video platform YouTube or the music streaming service Spotify, may secure licences on behalf of authors or performers from the collective societies that represent them; but these arrangements can prove unsatisfactory in terms of the royalties that they generate, leading to conflict. This situation is exemplified by controversy and lawsuits surrounding Spotify. Once again, reputational damage also has a cost: objections to Spotify by major pop music figures have been at least as influential as lawsuits in encouraging Spotify to try to improve its compensation to artists.[18]

A second, and truly fascinating, consideration is the increasing accessibility of publication itself. Just as authorship is experiencing a process of democratization, publishing, too, is being 'democratized' through the rise of opportunities for self-publication of works. The technology to 'publish' without the intervention of a publisher is now well-established. Possibilities range from the extremely simple technique of posting one's work online to the more sophisticated options made available by online publishing platforms for authors. For example, tech giant Amazon's CreateSpace platform not only allows authors to design and publish their own books; it also offers services, including editorial assistance and cover design, on a pay-per-use basis, to allow authors to professionalize their own publications. In these situations, Amazon receives payment for its work based on cost of production, and calculated according to the number of books sold in a given region of the world; the author receives the remaining revenues from sales. In some cases, authors who are self-publishing their work on platforms such as these become inordinately successful, even reaching heights of financial achievement and reputation where they are able to create publishing houses of their own, offering editorial advice and support to other authors in their genres. The publishing industry as a whole, for the written word, is experiencing a kind of democratization.

Crucially, in these scenarios, copyright is no longer a focus. An author who self-publishes is under no constraint to negotiate his or her ownership of copyright. On the contrary, the point of departure for that author is that he or she will retain copyright. Copyright is not implicated in self-publishing arrangements; rather, they are carried out on the basis of contractual arrangements whereby the publishing platform provides a service. That service may be quite a simple one, as where an author makes a PDF file of his or her book and uploads it to the publishing platform of his or her choice. The PDF is then printed as a book and made available for sale online via that

---

[18] See, for example, https://djbooth.net/features/2017-07-19-spotify-unreliable-royalty-payment-system-artists-scrambling, https://www.rollingstone.com/music/lists/wixens-16-billion-spotify-lawsuit-what-you-need-to-know-w514878, https://www.theverge.com/2017/6/9/15767986/taylor-swift-apple-music-spotify-statements-timeline.

platform, with the hosting company, Amazon for example, agreeing to print and deliver books on demand. Alternately, if editorial input and book design are involved, the service may be more complex and sophisticated in nature.

It is worth noting that, in both cases, there is significant scope for competitive new industries to arise. Which organizations can provide the best and most rapid facilities for printing and production, and for distribution? Will the same actors be the most sophisticated in terms of editorial and design work, or will others respond most competitively to those needs? And, of course, a crucial question: how do these new, 'democratized' forms of publication interact with the traditional publishing landscape? Do they compete, complement, supersede, or subsume those industries—or does the future hold some combination of all of these eventualities, depending on genre, geography, and other factors, including the flexibility, responsiveness, and vision of industry players?

In these scenarios, the practical redundancy of copyright is obvious, and is similarly mirrored by—to put it brazenly—the increasingly superfluous character of the traditional publishing industries overall. Copyright is relevant only in the sense that it rests with the author; it exists, at least for the moment, because it is conferred upon him or her by law; it confirms his or her right to publish a work, without which, no further action is possible. It is redundant, yet fundamental. Nevertheless, there is no doubt that the weakness of copyright in the new publication landscape described here follows an overall pattern, whereby copyright, in the traditional sense, may increasingly find itself superseded by new technological means of dealing with works.

This leads to one last, but incredibly significant point to consider: the role of large organizations dealing with online matter, including search engines—Google, in particular.

The case of Google Books, a project of unparalleled ambition aimed at digitizing the world's books and making them available in an online library, illustrates a fascinating trend: the suppression of copyright by technology, on the one hand, and the attempts of the publishing industry to adapt to technology, on the other, by seeking new allegiances that transcend the traditional relationship of author and publisher in the copyright paradigm.

In the case of Google Books, Google's revolutionary proposal was to scan books and make them available online. In the case of books that were still protected by copyright, Google planned to make excerpts available online—*unless* the owner of the work chose to 'opt out' of the service by communicating directly with Google. As Judge Denny Chin observed in his initial ruling of 2011 against Google's plan, the proposal turned copyright 'on its head', in the words of both participants and commentators, by dispensing with the need to obtain the author's consent before publication—the essence and foundation of copyright law. At the time of the initial lawsuit, the Association of American Publishers brought suit against Google alongside authors and their representatives. As Google appealed the ruling, however, a quiet discussion developed between the publishers and Google, with the publishers increasingly practical in their attitude towards Google Books in the light of the ongoing progress of the technology during the near-decade of controversy surrounding the project. By the time the case returned to Judge Chin, in

2013, he pronounced a new ruling that essentially reversed his earlier finding—Google Books should be allowed to carry on because of the immense public interest that it fulfilled.[19] By this time, publishers had largely re-aligned themselves with Google and settled.[20] The Authors Guild, however, continued to pursue its suit even after the publishers had settled with Google—pointing to a jarring disjuncture between the perceptions of at least some authors and publishers in the online context.[21] Interestingly, this conflict was arguably due, not to the traditional imbalance of power issues that have dogged author–publisher relations from their earliest days, but, instead, to the unprecedented power of leading tech companies to manage and manipulate knowledge, information, and culture online, leaving authors with questions about their own status in this environment. In its summary of the case, the Authors Guild comments:

> The Authors Guild remains committed to the notion that the digital revolution cannot come at the cost of authors' rights to preserve writing as a livelihood. Copyright protection is one of the main reasons this country has built such thriving cultural industries over the course of its existence; we need to ensure that the next generation of writers and other creators have the same opportunities as those who came before them.[22]

Technology is as exciting in the cultural domain as in any other. Will the opportunities outweigh the costs—and will the author be primarily beneficiary or victim of technological change? I and, in this environment, will he or she continue to need or want copyright? If not, what will the alternatives be?

Reputation and Moral Rights

While the transformations of the digital age have offered a bold challenge to many aspects of copyright—even threatening its very existence—there is one notable exception to this pattern: the 'moral rights' of the author. Moral rights are an aspect of copyright law that protects the personal interests of authors. The principal moral rights are the author's right to attribution as the creator of the work, and his or her right to protest damage to, or mutilation of, the work. These rights are part of the standard 'bundle of rights' protected by copyright laws in all countries, although they are greatly

---

[19] The ruling is available at https://www.scribd.com/document/184176014/Judge-Denny-Chin-Google-Books-opinion-2013-11-14-pdf.

[20] See the analysis in http://www.nytimes.com/2012/10/05/technology/google-and-publishers-settle-over-digital-books.html.

[21] The case failed, and leave to appeal to the US Supreme Court was denied. See https://law.justia.com/cases/federal/appellate-courts/ca2/13-4829/13-4829-2015-10-16.html and http://www.scotusblog.com/case-files/cases/authors-guild-v-google-inc/.

[22] See https://www.authorsguild.org/where-we-stand/authors-guild-v-google/.

limited in the United States,[23] and in international copyright agreements. In contrast to other aspects of copyright, they cannot generally be assigned, although, controversially, it is possible to waive them, in part or in whole, in some jurisdictions—notably, countries of common law heritage such as Canada and the UK.

The curious combination of these diverse legal features amounts to a powerful set of rights whose purpose is, fundamentally, non-commercial in nature: the protection of the relationship between the author and the work that he or she has created, and of the integrity of the work, itself. Accordingly, these moral rights are known as the author's rights of attribution and integrity.

Historically, moral rights have been considered an area of secondary importance within copyright law—due, no doubt, to their personal and non-commercial character. The economic aspects of copyright have taken precedence. In the digital environment, however, it has gradually become apparent that the interests protected by moral rights have gained a new importance. While it is increasingly difficult for authors and owners of copyright works to prevent the unauthorized, commercial exploitation of their works, technology, as in the Joyce Hatto case discussed earlier, tends to reinforce attribution and integrity interests—a point that has been analysed in appropriate depth by this author, in another work.[24] In this sense, moral rights reinforce the fight against copyright piracy by encouraging attribution and integrity to be maintained. But the issues at stake are much broader than the problem of copyright piracy. As noted above, the viability of copyright as a means of support for authors in the digital environment is questionable.

In contrast, what is beyond doubt in the digital context is the dependence of authorship on reputation. While reputation has always been at the core of authorship, its significance appears to be changing in the digital environment. The ability of an author to reach the public now depends, more than ever, on his or her reputation—on the ability to build and maintain a viable reputation, rather than the ability to restrict 'copying', that is to say, the use, of his or her work. Accordingly, it could be said that reputation, rather than copyright, is increasingly at the heart of an author's ability to make a living. Reputation, already recognized as a moral right, has, in a sense, become the currency of the digital environment. And so, by an interesting paradox, these ordinarily disparate strands of copyright theory, the economic and the personal, are tightly interwoven, and united in a new and unfamiliar pattern.

Moral rights have traditionally been an area of both potential cooperation and potential conflict between authors and publishers. Publishers, because of their special relationship with authors, are in a unique position to inflict harm on the author's moral rights, by neglecting the author's attribution and integrity interests. At the same time, if a third party were to malign the author's personal interests in the work, or the integrity of the work itself, authors and publishers have an extremely strong, shared interest in

---

[23] The moral rights provisions in the United States apply exclusively to visual artists, and were enacted in the Visual Artists Rights Act of 1990, 17 U.S.C. s. 106A, available at https://www.law.cornell.edu/uscode/text/17/106A.

[24] Sundara Rajan (2011, ch. 5; new edition pending).

combating that harm. In the digital environment, the interests of author and publisher are further united by their shared and interdependent reliance on reputation—the reputations of both author and publisher. The evolution of technology suggests that publishing, as a whole, should pay greater attention to the cultural imperatives of moral rights—for practical and social reasons, rather than primarily legal ones. The recognition of moral rights should be real and reasoned, reflecting the shifting landscape of copyright and publishing in the digital environment. Lip service, alone, to moral rights would represent the loss of a peerless opportunity to adapt. Both copyright and the culture of publishing would benefit from an exploration of moral rights in the light of the realities of the digital era.

Conclusion

The perspectives offered in this article should help to show why copyright is among the most dynamic areas of law in the digital context—at once embattled and potentially revivified, though much of the expert discussion surrounding copyright focuses naturally on the threat of piracy that technology presents. Is the destruction of the copyright concept as we know it inevitable, or is the prospect of a world without copyright absurd? Whatever may be the ultimate outcome of the 'Copyright Wars', and despite all the efforts to forestall it, change is inevitable. Given the central importance of copyright for publishing, there can be little doubt that the evolution of copyright will have a profound impact on publishing in all its forms. Rationalization, modernization, and vision are needed. An understanding of copyright, in all the complexity of the digital environment, can help publishing to evolve with it—and offers a shared hope, common to authors, publishers, and the public at large, of discovering new and creative ways to support the continuing vitality of the world's cultures.

References

Eliot, T. S. (1919 [1964]). 'Tradition and the Individual Talent', in *Selected Essays*, new edition, New York: Harcourt, Brace & World.

Kennedy, Randy. (2010). The Free-Appropriation Writer, *New York Times* (26 February 2010). http://www.nytimes.com/2010/02/28/weekinreview/28kennedy.html.

Metz, Cade. (2016). 'The Sadness & Beauty of Watching Google's AI Play Go', *Wired* (3 November 2016). https://www.wired.com/2016/03/sadness-beauty-watching-googles-ai-play-go/

Patterson, Lyman Ray. (1968). *Copyright in Historical Perspective*, Nashville, TN: Vanderbilt University Press.

Singer, Mark. (2007). 'Fantasia for Piano', *The New Yorker* (17 September 2007). https://www.newyorker.com/magazine/2007/09/17/fantasia-for-piano

Sundara Rajan, Mira T. (2011). *Moral Rights: Principles, Practice & New Technology*, Oxford: Oxford University Press.

CHAPTER 6

....

PUBLISHING
AND SOCIETY

....

ELIZABETH LE ROUX

How do we conceptualize the role of publishing in society? In China and Japan, the history of the Sino-Japanese War is presented differently in school textbooks, to the extent of having different starting and ending dates. In South Africa, a book on the last years of Nelson Mandela was withdrawn from circulation after pressure from the family, while in India a controversial book on Mahatma Gandhi was banned in the state of Gujarat. Religious tensions flared in France and Denmark, after apparently Islamophobic books and comics were published. Authors of colour and female authors in the USA and UK regularly claim that they are being unfairly treated by publishers, book reviewers, and award committees. A trend towards anti-intellectualism sees the public's faith in and the credibility of publishers and the media generally declining.

All of these examples show that books and publishing are an integral part of society. Our interactions with the publishing industry and its products raise questions of socio-political debates, diverse audiences, and social change. As Jonathan Rose (2003) has put it, 'all written and printed documents can be used to transmit culture, broadcast information, preserve human memory, distribute wealth, and exert power.' Many scholars since Elizabeth Eisenstein (1979) have acknowledged that the printing press and its products have been an agent of change in society, even if opinions may differ as to the extent and direction of that change. Desmond Hesmondhalgh (2012) has updated Eisenstein's formulation in his work on *The Cultural Industries*, referring to these as 'agents of economic, social and cultural change', and arguing that publishing and the other media industries influence our understanding and knowledge of the world, through the texts they produce and circulate. Publishing is thus intimately connected with the articulation and transmission of a society's underlying ideologies and values.

To explain the relationship between publishing and society, a number of different theoretical models have been proposed, mainly emanating from cultural studies or sociology. In each of these, publishing is seen as being inevitably influenced by the particular social context in which it is taking place. In Robert Darnton's Communications Circuit, for instance, the 'economic and social conjuncture' is placed at the centre of the model, and he emphasizes that the model can be applied in different societies and historical periods. Itamar Even-Zohar's polysystem theory and Pierre Bourdieu's sociology of culture theories have both been used to situate publishing within a broader, and historically and culturally specific, social context. Bourdieu's field theory, which distinguishes the symbolic capital (the prestige or reputation) of publishing from its economic capital, has been particularly influential. Benedict Anderson's (1983) concept of imagined communities has also been used to examine publishing in relation to social issues such as representation and identity. More recently, theorists like Ted Striphas in *The Late Age of Print* (2009) have examined books as social artifacts, 'through which social actors articulate and struggle over specific interests, values, practices, and worldviews'. This view, of books as a social artefact and as a cultural mediator, is increasingly widespread.

As a creative industry, publishing is a central facet of the identity and culture of a community, as well as reflecting cultural shifts over time. Culture in this sense is closely tied to what societies value, as well as to identity, and the next chapter will highlight this connection in more detail. In many societies, books are invested with a distinctive social and cultural value (or what Bourdieu calls symbolic capital); in other words, books are seen as having a special status that distinguishes them from other kinds of products. At the same time, books are seen as having a special value because they can help different communities to better understand each other. Books are also often read as being representative of their authors' national or cultural identities; as Ponzanesi puts it, 'texts can become ambassadors of identity, nationhood and cosmopolitanism' (2014: 3).

As scholars applying these models seek to show, publishing has taken very different forms in different societies. The demographics of particular societies influence what is published and who controls the publishing process—thus, questions of gender, race and class, and of diversity, are significant. The publishing of a controversial book can highlight fractures within the social identities of different societies, especially if it touches on issues such as religion, nationalism, politics, or sexuality. Debates around education, language, and culture all overlap with, or are centrally affected by, published products. Society can also directly impact on publishing, especially through government interventions, ranging from protectionism and promotion to regulation, and from textbook procurement to censorship. However, the element of politics or power is not always foregrounded in such analyses; the links between publishing and ideology have not been as explicitly theorized as they are in studies of the press, for instance. Theoretical models from fields like cultural studies describe how cultural products reflect social inequalities and may be used to entrench the interests of powerful groups, including governments. Such dominance may also be resisted through strategies of resistance and subversion (see Lassen et al. 2006, for a discussion of the links between media and ideology). This aspect of the interaction between publishing and society deserves further attention.

This chapter will deal with a few key areas relating to socio-political debates: publishing and its interactions with diversity, with nationalism, and with censorship. These issues of culture, diversity, and power occur differently in various social contexts.

DIVERSITY

If publishing reflects society, then it reflects both its demographic makeup and its inequalities and injustices. Products like books thus mirror inequalities among diverse groups in a society (some would go further, to argue that they entrench these inequalities). Diversity is a significant social issue worldwide, partly due to migration and its effects. The issue of 'diversity' has become a buzzword around the world, referring to factors of social identity such as gender, race, class, and language. Problems of diversity are much more severe in countries that are ethnically and linguistically diverse, like India. In relation to publishing, Claire Squires (2017) notes that diversity can be considered in terms of the publishing workforce (including its staff and authors), in terms of content (i.e. its output), and in terms of readership (i.e. its potential consumers). These questions are linked to issues of control and power: Whose voices are heard? What products are available to the public? And which audiences are seen as core? Publishing employs a significant number of workers worldwide, and as such the publishing industry has been criticized for its lack of diversity—the workforce is overwhelmingly white and female in countries like the USA and across Europe. It should be noted that actual evidence or statistics are lacking in many cases, and the research in this field is often carried out by interest groups or NGOs rather than academics. To really understand diversity in publishing, we need further research on the ownership of publishing houses, and their employers and employees; analyses or profiles of authors; and studies of readers and their access to information. In terms of the latter point, it has been assumed that access has been democratized and made available to a much broader group of readers through digital innovations, but the limited research on the topic shows that, contrary to expectations, digitization has not necessarily improved unequal access.

Diversity is often examined quite simplistically, in terms of quotas or numbers—how many children's books feature black characters, for instance, or how many women are published each year. The issue of how to measure diversity more holistically has been examined by Benhamou and Peltier (2007) using the French publishing industry as a case study. They emphasize that sheer numbers are insufficient for understanding the scope and complexity of an issue like diversity, and thus suggest looking at three different dimensions when considering diversity in publishing: variety, balance, and disparity. Their study also acknowledges that the parameters of diversity will vary from one society to the next, according to the fault lines and social markers that create different tensions in different parts of the world.

Much of the research on diversity in the publishing industry has focused on authors, and on the dimensions of gender and race—there has been markedly less attention paid to the dimensions of religion, class, language, and sexual orientation. A few studies that can be highlighted that raise these issues include Yao's (2014) study of the workforce in China, which examines class as an important factor, Adams' (1998) research into lesbian publishing, and studies of Islamic cultural production (e.g. Watson 2005). The gender-focused research is necessary as a baseline for creating awareness and drawing attention to diversity problems, because there is still bias and discrimination in the publishing, packaging, and reception of works by women and by writers of colour. Evidence shows that women writers still get published less than men, are reviewed less than men, and win fewer prizes than men. For example, in research conducted in France, Germany and the USA, Marc Verboord (2012) found that women are underrepresented in a wide variety of genres and across the bestseller lists. While his research did show an improvement over time, a gender gap still persists. Yoshio (2012) found a similar gender gap in Japan, which seems to indicate that this issue cuts across different social contexts.

It is interesting that this gap persists despite the growing numbers of women in the publishing industry, and indeed they are the majority in many cases. However, workforce analysis in some contexts has shown that the most influential decision-making positions are often still held by men. At the same time, the presence of women in publishing houses does not automatically change inherent attitudes towards and bias against women as authors and as readers. Prevailing social attitudes will shape what books are selected for publication. Publishing houses have been deliberately established and special prizes started in an attempt to counter this ongoing discrepancy, such as Virago in the UK and Modjaji Books in South Africa. Women-run or feminist publishing houses such as Virago started as a reaction to the perceived bias against women in publishing, as part of the women's liberation movement during the 1970s (see Murray 1999; Travis 2008)—although they may now be perceived to have declined in importance. Menon (2001) notes that, in recent years, 'several feminist presses in different parts of the world have either closed down or been bought by mainstream publishers' and their publishing output has declined significantly. However, she argues that 'the very power structures of wealth and knowledge that we continue to resist' have not declined, but in fact strengthened.

A similar bias against people of colour has led to accusations of racism against the publishing industry. It is argued that there are insufficient representations of black people in children's books, for instance, and that authors of colour face even greater structural inequalities than women or other minorities when seeking to be published. The intersection of race with factors like gender or class complicates the situation still further. Ownership and decision making are also still predominantly white. In the USA, a quite vibrant area of research is the 'rediscovery' or foregrounding of African-American and Hispanic writers and publishing. A number of studies have examined the 'textual construction of race' in US history, to use the phrase George Hutchinson and John K. Young employ in their edited collection, *Publishing Blackness* (2013); these include studies by Eric Gardner (2015), Lara Langer Cohen and Jordan Alexander Stein (2012), and Christopher Hager (2013), while Shirley Moody-Turner (2015) has analysed the intersection of gender and race. In the United Kingdom, there has been growing interest in the plight of so-called BAME (black, Asian, and minority ethnic) authors and publishers (see e.g. Chambers 2010; Fowler 2013). In South Africa and Australia, publishing is still overwhelmingly white-owned, and this is seen as a key issue of transformation in these countries.

One of the key concepts that emerges from studies of diversity is that of authenticity, referring to the tendency for either women or authors of colour to be seen as representative of their entire ethnic or racial group. As a result of 'the reader's expectation of cultural difference and ethnic authenticity' (Slaughter 2014: 59), publishers package authors in certain ways, to the extent that 'writers of colour...feel that their work is often marginalized unless it fulfils a romantic fetishisation of their cultural heritage' (Squires 2017). An example is Heinemann's African Writers Series, which was criticized for only publishing works that fit the editors' ideas of what was 'African'. More recently, the Nigerian author Chimamanda Ngozi Adichie has described this stereotyping as the 'danger of a single story' (2009), arguing that she sees her own work categorized as both 'African' and as 'not African enough', depending on readers' reductive expectations and on the publishers' packaging of her books for particular audiences. Eileen Julien uses the theoretical concept of 'an extro-verted novel' to explain the phenomenon of books that are expected to 'explain Africa to the world' (Julien 2006: 695). This can be clearly seen in the designs of books by African authors for Western markets—many of which feature acacia trees against a sunset, regardless of setting and theme—and which has been satirized by Binyavanga Wainaina in his article, 'How to Write about Africa' (2006).

But this is not only the case for African authors, as other non-Western authors are also subject to stereoptyping—a similar, single book cover design has been identified for books by Muslim women, which almost all depict veiled women. The marketing and reception of minority and postcolonial writers have been the subject of incisive analysis, examining the exoticism, tokenism, and fetishization of minority cultures within the broader global publishing and cultural industry (see Ponzanesi 2014). It has also been placed within a broader trend of the commodification of culture more generally, with key works being Graham Huggan's *The Postcolonial Exotic: Marketing the Margins* (2001), and Sarah Brouillette's *Postcolonial Writers in the Global Literary Marketplace* (2007). These studies examine the intersection between race and nationalism, or the politics of location.

NATIONALISM AND INTERNATIONAL NETWORKS

These stereotypes arise because of unequal geopolitical relations, a macro social issue. Which countries dominate cultural production? The rise of English as a global language, and the associated strength of the English-speaking publishing industries, influences what is published and what is circulated. This effect has continued because of the dominance of multinational publishing companies in smaller countries, and the greater credibility or authority still accorded to publishing in the global North: 'the book industry underpins and perpetuates certain geographies of knowledge whereby periphery creators and scholars gravitate towards countries of the centre, while their places of origin remain economically and culturally reliant on imports from dominant book producers' (Murray 2007: 6). The political and social issues relating to location and the nation thus remain of importance even in an apparently global era. Many studies of publishing are still national in focus—examining 'the book in China', or 'the Mexican book', for instance—but they are often situated within a broader global context, sometimes as a reaction to the perceived homogenizing effects of globalization. This raises issues of the politics of nationalism and of internationalism, as well as the cultural and economic forces influencing national and regional publishing industries.

Nationalism and nation-building are often closely linked to the publishing industry, with some countries actively seeking to develop their national identity through the construction of 'national literatures' or a 'national heritage' of written works. This has been the key driver behind Unesco's support for books and publishing, since just after World War 2. Unesco was established to promote 'the free flow of ideas by word and image', with the specific aim of creating greater dialogue and mutual understanding among different societies. Books were seen as one of the tools in the United Nations' post-war peacebuilding efforts. According to the charter of Unesco, and a number of its publications since then, books are an essential aid to social progress, enabling societies to develop faster, especially economically, and thus to elevate people's education and well-being. Unesco argued strongly that, 'A sound publishing industry is essential to national development' on the basis that cultural development would lead to other forms of development (Barker and Escarpit 1973: 138). The sharing of scientific and technical information was also promoted, as it was expected that this would also lead to both development and the alleviation of social problems.

Some of the programmes Unesco supports reveal a direct concern with the social impact of publishing and reading: for instance, the promotion of literacy among schoolgirls, so that they could have access to opportunities for improved livelihoods; or the training of a new generation of publishers in the newly decolonized nations in what was then called the 'developing world'. Book development programmes were touted as a solution. As a result, books were seen as 'key tools in decolonizing nations' struggles to achieve literary, educational and professional standards requisite for competitive, post-industrial economies' (Murray 2007: 14). Such attempts at book development were often a deliberate attempt to increase the visibility or presence of national products in the global cultural marketplace. While the link between publishing and social development has not been quite as direct as Unesco's rather optimistic predictions had hoped, it is still a major concern that books and ideas should be freely circulated.

Translation is the major medium for books to circulate to different societies, in spite of the dominance of English as a world language. Even-Zohar (2005) theorized that languages have different places in a cultural hierarchy, which affects the international circulation of texts in any given language (see Pickford, 2011, for a discussion of translation and literary awards using this model). It was not surprising, then, that Unesco also supported a flagship project to develop a shared 'world literature' collection through translation. Known as the *Collection of Representative Works*, this project aimed to 'encourage the translation, publication, and distribution in the major languages—English,

French, Spanish and Arabic—of works of literary and cultural importance that are nevertheless not well known outside their original national boundaries or linguistic communities' (Giton 2015). Through its support, 866 books were published, in 91 different languages, between 1948 and 1994. However, as Céline Giton (2015) points out, the success of such translation projects in really bridging social divides is ambiguous; she notes that the project only reached 'a select Western or Westernized elite and encountered many difficulties in its efforts to reach the general public'. Unesco's aim of building 'inclusive knowledge societies' may remain elusive but is an ongoing project.

Such translation projects may also not be successful because they perceive certain social values to be universal. But different social groups still maintain different collective beliefs and values, especially at the national and local level. This can be seen in the different values assigned to books and publishing in different countries, and indeed to their national traditions of reading and writing. To use Bourdieu's (1986 [2011]) terms, there remains an opposition between symbolic capital and economic capital, with a society such as France promoting and protecting its national publishing industry through the use of subsidies and fixed book pricing. The survival of independent booksellers has been linked to supportive government policies on pricing and culture—to the extent that the Minister for Culture in the Macron government, Françoise Nyssen, is a publisher. In Germany, too, publishing is seen as a significant factor in the national identity, and this country was the first to study and thus valorize its national book trade history. In contrast, the Anglophone societies of the UK and USA are seen as much more commercial in their focus.

Of course, the UK and USA may not see the need to protect their publishing industries because they are already so dominant worldwide. Smaller nations have to respond to this perceived threat. The Canadian government, for instance, offers grants to promote local publishing and writing, in part because of fears that Canadian publishing is often over-shadowed by their large and economically more powerful neighbour. The Scottish publishing industry also keenly promotes a separate, regional identity that is not simply subsumed within the larger UK. Similar impulses may be seen among other smaller minority cultures or what Ramdarshan-Bold and McCleery (2012) call 'small nation publishing' (see also Henningsgaard (2008) on Australia; Boswell (2014) on Scotland and Catalonia; or Kovač and Squires (2014) on Scotland and Slovenia). Noorda (2016, 2017) has examined how a small nation markets its works within the broader international literary marketplace, while also considering how the identities of members of the Scottish diaspora are expressed. Certain studies also examine national interests within a regional identity, such as the interaction between different countries belonging to La Francophonie or the common Iberian market and identity shared by Spain and Portugal, referred to as *Iberismo* (Faustino 2009) All of these initiatives represent attempts to propagate specific national ideals via literary culture and national book policies.

Some literary prizes, too, aim to promote certain nationalities. Literary prizes help to shape the literary publishing industry in particular, affecting who is published, who is translated and distributed, and how many copies of a book are sold. Gillian Roberts (2011), examining literary awards in Canada, sees such awards in terms of a discourse of 'national celebration' (as can be seen in the sub-title of her study: 'The celebration and circulation of national culture'). However, she complicates the notion of the 'national' by relating it to corresponding issues of citizenship and hospitality to immigrants, as well as concepts of national identity and belonging—which is at least unifying in impulse, if not unified in practice. Using Bourdieu in her theoretical framework, she develops the notion of a 'national habitus' rather than class habitus to describe the context. Similarly, Edward Mack has examined publishing and prize culture in the context of Japan, in his study, *Manufacturing Modern Japanese Literature* (2010).

This impetus to promote the national remains so relevant because of the unequal distribution of power in the world. This power imbalance may be seen in the (often unconscious) bias against non-Western countries in studies of print culture and publishing. Studies undertaken within the centres of publishing production often seem to be placed within a cultural vacuum, without understanding the cultural specificity of their contexts. Other research is seen as 'peripheral'. In such studies, books are clearly associated with the idea of civilization, especially Western civilization, while downplaying the role of indigenous authors, printers, and publishers. For instance, while India is the second largest English-language book market, analyses of Anglophone publishing often concentrate on the USA and UK. Even more extreme, overviews of African publishing often portray it as impoverished, emergent, or even entirely lacking. A lack of basic evidence such as publishing statistics has enabled certain myths to propagate, such as the 'book famine' in developing countries (which is in fact a problem of access rather than an actual gap, as Zell and Thierry (2015) show). Moreover, while critiques raise very real problems associated with publishing in developing countries—including low literacy rates, low disposable incomes and thus small reading publics, poor infrastructure, and so on—very little attention is paid to the historical and ongoing impact of the former colonial powers and the multinational companies that still control much of the lucrative schoolbook market. One example of such research has been conducted by Caroline Davis (2011; 2013), who has examined some of the contradictions inherent in Oxford University Press's publishing programme in Southern Africa in the twentieth century; there has not been similar attention given to the recent corruption scandals involving Macmillan and Oxford University Press in East Africa. It is difficult to maintain a national publishing industry in the face of such competition.

GOVERNMENT CONTROL
AND CENSORSHIP

In some cases, the nationalist impulse behind the development of national literatures is taken to extremes. This may be seen in countries that have aimed to limit the amount of information available on specific topics or to examine them only from a specific perspective, especially if these relate to potentially embarrassing or damaging historical events. The presentation of historical events in school textbooks has often been seen as an opportunity for governments to inculcate certain values among the youth, especially patriotism. In Japan, for instance, the textbook authorization process in the 1980s was tightened up to 'cultivate the Japanese spirit and foster national pride' (He 2009: 211). Tanaka Tatsuo, the Education Minister, instructed publishers to 'soften their approach to Japan's excess during World War II', in other words, to downplay Japanese war crimes. This has led to some diplomatic protests, in 1982 and again in 2000, with criticism from both China and South Korea over the use of terms like the Japanese army 'advancing into' China, rather than 'invading' it. The Japanese Society for History Textbook Reform has been particularly criticized for its right-wing publications (Kasahara 2010). More recently, though, a similar case arose in China in 2017, when the Ministry of Education mandated a revision of the presentation of the Sino-Japanese War in all school textbooks, to refer to the '14-year Chinese People's War of Resistance Against Japanese Aggression'—a war that had previously been acknowledged to have lasted eight years (1937–1945). Interestingly, though, a comparative study of textbooks by Stanford University (see Shin and Sneider 2011) found recent Japanese textbooks to be largely 'muted, neutral, and almost bland', with a majority promoting pacifism, while Chinese and South Korean textbooks were more nationalistic. Textbooks from the USA were similarly found to be 'overly patriotic' in their approach. As this example shows, governments still readily intervene in publishing to promote their national interests, and publishing—even in the form of school textbooks—can readily be used for propaganda.

The role of governments in regulating the publishing industry has usually been examined in the context of extreme cases of censorship: studies may be found of the censoring of books in repressive environments such as the Soviet Union (e.g. Sherry 2015), East Germany or GDR (e.g. Beate Müller; Spittel 2015), Spain under the dictatorial regime of Francisco Franco (Herrero-Olaizola 2007), Myanmar (Wiles 2015), and apartheid South Africa (McDonald 2009). There is also a wealth of studies on censorship of the media more generally. Such studies reveal certain similarities in the manner in which repressive governments deal with the circulation of information, although there are of course historical and regional peculiarities associated with each of these cases.

However, what these studies also show is that censorship and government control are in fact still prevalent all over the world, but to different degrees, and for different reasons—ranging from the protection of minors from obscenity (often a factor behind book banning in libraries in the USA), to religious control, to issues of confidentiality and state security. This is clearly depicted in Nicole Moore's edited collection, *Censorship and the Limits of the Literary: A Global View* (2015), which offers case studies from across the world. What is significant is that a degree of information control exists in almost all societies, but often for unwritten reasons: the extra-textual factors that underpin censorship, book banning, or regulation are largely based on accepted social beliefs, norms, or behaviours, rather than overt policies. This insight is given a theoretical basis in the work of Bourdieu (1986 [2011]) on structural censorship. He posits that there is implicit social control in any given field of cultural production: 'It follows that structural censorship occurs in the field within which a text circulates, and is determined by the habitus of the agents belonging to that field. In this respect, censorship has to be seen not as an institutional set of rules, or even as an overtly repressive means of controlling public opinion and discourses: rather as a set of unwritten rules, shaped both by the current habitus and by the symbolic capital a text enjoys in a certain field' (Bourdieu, quoted in Billiani 2014: 8). This set of unwritten rules is taken to the extreme in a country like Iran, where, as Arash Hejazi shows, the government is at pains to deny its involvement in censorship; he refers to the effects of the ensuing system, which 'despite being untraceable, leaves them with absolute free reign to control the content of every publication' (2011: 56).

Historical studies of publishing in former colonies show that the circulation of information and publications in such societies was always closely tied to government control and censorship. This has sometimes continued to the present day, in the form of state-sponsored publishing houses. Research in this area often traces the role of print culture in resistance and decolonization. A good example may be found in Kenya for instance, in Shiraz Durrani's *Never Be Silent* (2016), which depicts the history of publishing in that country as a 'history of struggles'. While it is a compelling image to portray publishers, writers, and readers as agents of resistance, this may be an over-simplification. The present author's research on university press publishing under apartheid (Le Roux 2016) has shown that responses to censorship can be highly compli-cated, on a spectrum from complicity to resistance, depending on shifting circumstances and often on individuals.

Has government regulation changed in recent years? The general belief appears to be that the publishing industry and communications more broadly have become looser and more deregulated. This is generally associated with the impact of information tech-nology and the Internet, as well as a greater commercial focus. But this view may reflect our preoccupation with certain kinds of dominant societies (especially Anglophone societies) when studying publishing: in countries like Iran, as mentioned above, as well as China, strong centralized control remains. In other contexts, a generally repressive atmosphere leads to fear and thus self-censorship—in Turkey, for instance, Bilge Yesil (2014) has identified 'networks of state power, commercial pressures, and self-censorship' as the dominant modes restricting the free flow of information, rather than overt gov-ernment control. Moreover, while some scholars warn that the kind of state censorship previously experienced may have waned, it is generally acknowledged that it has been replaced by a market-led censorship. What this means is that the economic interests of the media and publishing company owners determine what is published, and inevitably exclude certain viewpoints and voices. Since the 1990s, in particular, amid increasing centralization of ownership of publishing companies, there have been warnings about the dangers of market censorship and its possible implications for diversity (see e.g. Moran 1997). Generally, cultural theorists consider commercial imperatives as leading to greater conservatism in decision making.

Commercial and Digital Determinism

In spite of concerns about the dominance of market forces, more recent scholarship on publishing increasingly focuses on commercial aspects, and especially the economics of the book market. This is seen as natural and even inevitable in some cases, as commercialism is seen as being central to every publishing decision. However, it has meant that books, in particular, are being portrayed as commodities rather than cultural products. Similarly, the pervasive influence of digital technology is seen as a central axis for publishing studies. While the hype around the assumed rise of ebooks and the predicted decline of print has died down somewhat, there is a preoccupation with the impact of 'the digital' in most areas of publishing, sometimes to the exclusion of other social issues and of the wider context. For example, research on educational textbook publishing now tends to focus on the uptake and use of ebooks in schools and universities. Research on what used to be called reading habits and patterns is now often framed as 'consumer behaviour patterns' or 'user experience'—a common blend of a commercial and digital focus. Business-oriented studies examine publishers' and booksellers' 'changing' business models and 'innovation' in the face of what are framed as digital threats and challenges. Indeed, in such studies, 'social change' is reframed as the effects of technology on publishing (see e.g. Feather 1997). More recent theoretical models for the publishing industry also use this lens as the primary construct: Michael Bhaskar in *The Content Machine* (2013) portrays books as 'content' that is 'framed' according to a model and then 'filtered' and 'amplified'. This may be a useful perspective for understanding publishing generically, but it tends to downplay the political and social specificity of publishing in different contexts.

This is not just an issue for publishing studies, as there has been criticism in fields such as cultural studies that there is too little sustained, historically informed analysis of the 'knowledge society' or the 'creative economy'. Rather, the focus on increasing commercialization and commodification, and on the impact of technology, demonstrates a step back from engaging with issues of the social and, especially, of the political. Do we still see a social and political role for the publishing industry in the twenty-first century? Are we still interrogating the links between publishing and ideology? There is a great deal of scope for further research that engages directly with the social role of publishing, and that recognizes its political dimensions. Scholars who think their work is 'apolitical' may simply not be considering the underlying ideological issues of culture, diversity, and power that shape the context they are examining.

References

Adams, Kate. (1998). 'Built out of books: Lesbian energy and feminist ideology in alternative publishing', *Journal of Homosexuality*, 34(3–4), pp. 113–41.

Adichie, Chimamanda Ngozi. (2009). 'The danger of a single story' TED Talks. https://www.ted.com/talks/chimamanda_adichie_the_danger_of_a_single_story

Anderson, Benedict. (1983). *Imagined Communities: Reflections on the Origin and Spread of Nationalism*, London: Verso.

Barker, Ronald and Robert Escarpit. (1973). *The Book Hunger*, Paris: UNESCO.

Benhamou, Françoise and Stéphanie Peltier, (2007). 'How should cultural diversity be measured? An application using the French publishing industry', *Journal of Cultural Economics*, 31(2), pp. 85–107.

Bhaskar, Michael. (2013). *The Content Machine*, London: Anthem Press.

Billiani, Francesca. (2014). 'Assessing Boundaries: Censorship and Translation', in *Modes of Censorship: National Contexts and Diverse Media*. Edited by Francesca Billiani, Abingdon: Routledge, pp. 1–25.

Boswell, Daniel. (2014). 'Publishing and the Industrial Dynamics of Biblio-cultural Identity in Catalan and Scottish Literary Fields'. PhD Diss. Edinburgh Napier University.

Bourdieu, Pierre. (1986 [2011]). 'The forms of capital', in *Cultural Theory: An Anthology 1*. Edited by Imre Szeman and Timothy Kaposi, Malden, MA; Oxford: Wiley-Blackwell, pp. 81–93.

Brouillette, Sarah. (2007). *Postcolonial Writers in the Global Literary Marketplace*, Basingstoke: Palgrave Macmillan.

Chambers, Claire. (2010). 'Multi-Culti Nancy Mitfords and Halal Novelists: The Politics of Marketing', *Textus*, 23(2), pp. 389–403.

Cohen, Lara Langer and Jordan Alexander Stein, eds (2012). *Early African American Print Culture*, Philadelphia: University of Pennsylvania Press.

Davis, Caroline. (2011). 'Histories of Publishing under Apartheid: Oxford University Press in South Africa', *Journal of Southern African Studies*, 37(1), pp. 79–98.

Davis, Caroline. (2013). *Creating Postcolonial Literature: African Writers and British Publishers*, London: Palgrave Macmillan.

Durrani, Shiraz. (2016). *Never Be Silent: Publishing and Imperialism 1884–1963*, Nairobi: Vita Books.

Eisenstein, Elizabeth L. (1979). *The Printing Press as an Agent of Social Change: Communications and Cultural Transformations in Early-modern Europe*. Volume 2, Cambridge: Cambridge University Press.

Even-Zohar, Itamar. (2005). 'Polysystem theory (revised)', *Papers in Culture Research*, 38–49.

Faustino, Paulo. (2009). 'The Potential of Book Publishing in Iberian American and African Countries', in *The Handbook of Spanish Language Media*. Edited by Alan Albarran, London: Routledge.

Feather, John. (1997). 'Book publishing and social change', *Logos*, 8(1), pp. 55–61.

Fowler, Corinne. (2013). 'Publishing Manchester's black and Asian writers', in *Postcolonial Manchester: Diaspora Space and the Devolution of Literary Culture*. Edited by Robert H. Crawshaw, Corinne Fowler, and Lynne Pearce. Manchester: Manchester University Press.

Gardner, Eric. (2015). *Black Print Unbound: The 'Christian Recorder,' African American Literature, and Periodical Culture*, New York: Oxford University Press.

Giton, C. (2015). Unesco's World Book Policy and its Impacts. UNESCO. Available online: http://en.unesco.org/news/unesco-s-world-book-policy-and-its-impacts-according-celine-giton.

Hager, Christopher. (2013). *Word by Word: Emancipation and the Act of Writing*, Cambridge, MA: Harvard University Press.

He, Yinan. (2009). *The Search for Reconciliation: Sino-Japanese and German-Polish Relations since World War II*, Cambridge: Cambridge University Press.

Hejazi, Arash. (2011). '"You don't deserve to be published": Book censorship in Iran', *Logos*, 22(1), pp. 53–62.

Henningsgaard, Per. (2008). 'Outside Traditional Book Publishing Centres: The Production of a Regional Literature in Western Australia', PhD Thesis, University of Western Australia.

Herrero-Olaizola, Alejandro. (2007). *The Censorship Files: Latin American Writers and Franco's Spain*, Albany: State University of New York Press.

Hesmondhalgh, David. (2012). *The Cultural Industries*, 3rd edition, London: Sage.

Huggan, Graham. (2001). *The Postcolonial Exotic: Marketing the Margins,* Abingdon: Routledge.

Hutchinson, George and John K. Young, eds (2013). *Publishing Blackness: Textual Constructions of Race Since 1850*, Ann Arbor: University of Michigan Press.

Julien, Eileen. (2006). 'The extro-verted African novel', in *The Novel: History, Geography and Culture*. Edited by Franco Moretti. Princeton, NJ: Princeton University Press.

Kasahara, Tokushi. (2010). 'Reconciling Narratives of the Nanjing Massacre in Japanese and Chinese Textbooks'. Presented at Center for Philippine Studies & Japan Society for the Promotion of Science.

Kovač, Miha and Claire Squires, (2014). 'Scotland and Slovenia', *Logos*, 25(4), pp. 7–19.

Lassen, Inger, Jeanne Strunck, and Torben Vestergaard, eds (2006). *Mediating Ideology in Text and Image: Ten Critical Studies*, Amsterdam: John Benjamins Publishing.

Le Roux, Elizabeth. (2016). *A Social History of the University Presses in Apartheid Souh Africa*, Leiden: Brill.

McDonald, Peter. (2009). *The Literature Police*, Oxford: Oxford University Press.

Mack, Edward. (2010). *Manufacturing Modern Japanese Literature: Publishing, Prizes and the Ascription of Literary Value*, New York: Duke University Press.

Menon, Ritu. (2001). 'Kali for Women in India in 1984', *Logos*, 12(1), pp. 33–8.

Moody-Turner, Shirley. (2015). '"Dear Doctor Du Bois": Anna Julia Cooper, WEB Du Bois, and the Gender Politics of Black Publishing', *MELUS: Multi-Ethnic Literature of the United States* 40(3), pp. 47–68.

Moore, Nicole, ed. (2015). *Censorship and the Limits of the Literary: A Global View*, London: Bloomsbury.

Moran, Joe. (1997). 'The role of multimedia conglomerates in American trade book publishing', *Media, Culture & Society*, 19(3), pp. 441–55.

Murray, S. (1999). *Mixed Media: Feminist Presses & Publishing Politics in Twentieth-Century Britain*, London: University College London.

Murray, S. (2007). 'Publishing Studies: Critically Mapping Research in Search of a Discipline', *Publishing Research Quarterly*, 22(4), pp. 3–25.

Noorda, Rachel. (2016). 'Transnational Scottish Book Marketing to a Diasporic Audience, 1995–2015', PhD Diss. Stirling University.

Noorda, Rachel. (2017). 'From Waverley to Outlander: Reinforcing Scottish diasporic identity through book consumption', *National Identities* (2017), pp. 1–17.

Pickford, Susan. (2011). 'The Booker Prize and the Prix Goncourt: a case study of award-winning novels in translation', *Book History*, 14(1), pp. 221–40.

Ponzanesi, Sandra. (2014). *The Postcolonial Cultural Industry: Icons, Markets, Mythologies*, London: Palgrave Macmillan.

Ramdarshan Bold, M. and A. McCleery. (2012). '"What is my country?": Supporting Small Nation Publishing', *Journal of Irish and Scottish Studies*, 6(1), pp. 115–131.

Roberts, Gillian. (2011). *Prizing Literature: The Celebration and Circulation of National Culture*, Toronto: University of Toronto Press.

Rose, Jonathan. (2003). 'The horizon of a new discipline: inventing book studies', *Publishing Research Quarterly*, 19(1), pp. 11–19.

Sherry, Samantha. (2015). *Discourses of Regulation and Resistance*, Edinburgh: Edinburgh University Press.

Shin, Gi-Wook and Daniel Sneider, eds (2011). *History Textbooks and the Wars in Asia*, New York: Routledge.

Slaughter, Joseph R. (2014). 'World literature as property', *Alif: Journal of Comparative Poetics*, 34, pp. 39–73.

Spittel, Christina. (2015). 'Reading the Enemy: East German Censorship across the Wall', in *Censorship and the Limits of the Literary: A Global View*. Edited by Nicole Moore, London: Bloomsbury.

Squires, Claire. (2017). 'Publishing's Diversity Deficit', *CAMEo Cuts No.2*. Leicester: CAMEo Research Institute for Cultural and Media Economies, University of Leicester.

Striphas, Ted. (2009). *The Late Age of Print*, New York: Columbia University Press.

Travis, Trysh. (2008). 'The women in print movement: History and implications', *Book History*, 11(1), pp. 275–300.

Verboord, M. (2012). 'Female Bestsellers: A cross-national study of gender inequality and the popular-highbrow culture divide in fiction book production, 1960–2009', *European Journal of Communication*, pp. 396–409.

Wainaina, Binyavanga. (2006). 'How to write about Africa', *Granta*, 92.

Watson, C. W. (2005). 'Islamic books and t,heir publishers: notes on the contemporary Indonesian scene', *Journal of Islamic Studies* 16(2), pp. 177–210.

Wiles, Ellen. (2015). *Saffron Shadows and Salvaged Scripts: Literary Life in Myanmar Under Censorship and in Transition*. New York: Columbia University Press.

Yao, Jianhua. (2014). *Knowledge Workers in Contemporary China: Reform and Resistance in the Publishing Industry*, Lanham, MD: Lexington Books.

Yesil, Bilge. (2014). 'Press Censorship in Turkey: Networks of State Power, Commercial Pressures, and Self-Censorship', *Communication, Culture & Critique*, 7(2), pp. 154–73.

Yoshio, H. (2012). *Envisioning Women Writers: Female Authorship and the Cultures of Publishing and Translation in Early 20th Century Japan*, New York: Columbia University Press.

Zell, Hans M. and Raphaël Thierry, (2015). 'Book Donation Programmes for Africa: Time for a Reappraisal? Two Perspectives', *African Research & Documentation*, 127.

CHAPTER 7

PUBLISHING AND CULTURE

The Alchemy of Ideas

JOHN OAKES

SINCE the days of Gutenberg and probably long before, publishers have depended on what was most popular, and therefore profitable, for their existence. From breathless, half-imagined travelogues to more salacious material, from puzzle books to sycophantic portraits of wealthy patrons, publishing has always displayed its commitment to commerce. The very concept of 'publishing and culture' may therefore seem an oxymoronic combination: but if culture in its broadest sense is taken to mean the delimitations of a particular society, then book publishing plays an essential role in defining those boundaries. It is at the heart of cultural change, exchange, and interpretation. That is why publishing is not simply just another business; that is why it embodies the conflict between the commercially successful and the culturally substantive. Publishing traffics in the written transfer of ideas, of crafted messages that represent a direct appeal from the mind of the creator/author to that of the consumer/reader. It is a principle that applies as much to the works of Dale Carnegie as it does to those of Samuel Beckett. That transfer of ideas, pushed a bit further, becomes the essential leap from 'writing' to 'publishing': the first requires a single physical act, the second demands a complex relationship involving a readership beyond a circle of one. Publishing yearns for an audience, a community of readers—to have a cultural impact.

The transition from idea to page represents a commitment on the part of the creator to the recipient that is missing in any other medium: a reader sees precisely the marks made for her, in precisely the sequence intended. Dance, theatre, music, art: all lose in the translation; the physical transference from concept to stage, canvas, or concert. Writing comes closest to being a focused, accurate conveyance of thought.[1] While it may

---

[1] But not so fast: in Plato's *Phaedrus*, Socrates quotes a legend concerning an Egyptian pharaoh who is approached by the god Thoth, the scribe of the gods and the god of scribes, with various gifts that

be too much to claim that there is no culture without books—oral traditions abound in human history, past and present—it is safe to assert that books are a powerful tool in creating, preserving, and furthering a cultural message in an effective, easily transmissable way. (Here, by a 'book', I mean an object that conveys an extended, pre-fixed message based on the written word: that definition applies to print books, electronic books, and audio books.)

If we imagine how culture—the expression of a people's identity—occurred in a pre-book era, we can see that its evolution and practice was dependent on personal relationships developed over a period of time. Dialogue and debate are integral to a living culture, and in the pre-book era, information travelled slowly, transmitted person to person, orally or by manuscript across vast distances, via small groups of people. Even relatively major debates took place gradually, over decades, sometimes involving a new generation. The result of these exchanges was to create commonality, and gradually re-shape society: as David Foster Wallace observed in *Consider the Lobster and Other Essays*, 'The whole point of establishing norms is to help us evaluate our actions (including utterances) according to what we as a community have decided our real interests and purposes are.' That is, to establish its culture.

What follows is of necessity an incomplete and personal overview of the relationship made manifest by the tenacity of publishers and their advocates over the centuries, and matched by the ferocity of their opponents: the Inquisition, the Crown, the Texas School Board, the Reichskulturkammer, the New York Society for the Suppression of Vice, and so on.

With the arrival of the printing press and in particular moveable type in mid-fifteenth-century Europe, the slow-motion pace of cultural development became headlong, and the 'solitary scribe' an anachronism. The press immensely multiplied the impact of manuscripts, making possible timely cultural debate across a continent. As the Babel of learned voices increased, so did the authorities' concern: because of their role as fixed propaganda, books engendered intellectual unrest on a level not previously encountered.

It is this period that marks the beginning of modern publishing, because, apart from technological innovations that do not challenge the basic principles of the book business, the profession has remained essentially the same for 500 years. Reviewing the personalities and events surrounding the advent of the press and movable type, a twenty-first-century publisher cannot help but be struck by the distant parallels of her predecessors: the Mainzian Johannes Gutenberg, the man credited with giving us moveable type, himself lost his presses and his business to a creditor; the Venetian Aldus Manutius battled counterfeit copies of the books published by his Aldine Press; the

---

Thoth explains should be shared with the people. After going through a lengthy catalogue of wonders, finally he presents the king with his greatest gift: something that will be an 'elixir of memory and wisdom'. The gift, of course, is writing. The king demurs: whether out of error or malice, Thoth has ascribed to letters 'a power the opposite of what they really possess' (274c, H. N. Fowler translator; Harvard University Press). Words can never precisely describe a thought or an occurrence: they convey only an approximation thereof. Until Zeno of Elea (*fl.* fifth century BCE), Greek philosophers conveyed their arguments via poetry; all things considered, this may be a more effective means of transmitting complex ideas.

life of the peripatetic Dutch humanist Desiderius Erasmus—priest and publisher—is bracketed by scholarship and a constant search for patrons who will enable him to continue his work. These are all issues—irregular cash flow, violation of copyright, and the constant need for underwriting pioneering but financially risky books—familiar to any publisher today.

The quick turnaround, the vastly lowered cost-per-unit of these technological innovations had results beyond the enrichment of the merchant printer/publishers: it solved the 'shortage of reading matter,' exulted Jacobo Cromberger, one of Seville's most highly regarded printers of the sixteenth century.[2] Cromberger is a prime example of the cultural mix that resulted from the flurry of activity necessitated by the newfound demand for books, readily transportable and affordable sources of entertainment, knowledge, and propaganda. A Nuremberger working in Spain, Cromberger was most likely a *converso*, a converted Jew. At the request or perhaps direction of Juan de Zumârraga, the first bishop of Mexico, in 1539 Cromberger sent one of his surrogates, the Italian Giovanni Paoli (also known as Juan Pablos), to establish the first printing press in the New World in Mexico City (the original house where it was installed still stands at the corner of Moneda and Licenciado Primo Verdad streets).[3] Six years later, the Casa de Cromberger produced the first printed book in the Americas, in both Spanish and Nahuatl (*Breve y más compendiosa doctrina Christiana en lengua Mexicana y Castellana*, by none other than Zumârraga). Zumârraga, head of the Inquisition in Mexico and reputedly the creator of the first public library, knew the value of publishing.[4] He was renowned for his steady assault on native culture, and he did this most effectively through his relentless hunt for Aztec codices: in 1530, he made a bonfire of them in Texcoco. Thus was the book an essential complement to the sword in incinerating the old culture and imposing the new.

From the earliest days of the printing press, perhaps no group was more involved in the culture of books than the self-styled 'People of the Book', the Jews, members of a religion that has at its core the delivery of a two-page 'book' to Moses—the stone tablets of the Ten Commandments. In every Jewish temple, the focal point of the house of worship contains a written document, usually a scroll of the Torah, or Old Testament, safeguarded within a cabinet known as the Ark. Apart from the Torah itself, several books were considered essential to ongoing Jewish cultural vitality and stability, and therefore Jews provided a ready market for the nascent publishing industry. The deeply engrained rabbinical traditions of debate and analysis are exemplified by the Talmud—a collection of discussions about Jewish law and tradition, the earliest of which date back more than 2000 years. But it was particularly due to the standardization of prayer books that the printing press changed how Jews acted as a culture, and unified them across vast

[2] As paraphrased by Lisa Jardine 1998: 141.

[3] In *The Library at Night* (2008), Alberto Manguel writes that Zumârraga, a zealous book burner of heretical texts, may not have 'understood the paradox of on the one hand creating books, and on the other destroying them'; I would argue that it was precisely because the bishop recognized books' numinous power that he focused on them. To create a new world it was necessary to destroy the old.

[4] Fernando Báez 2008: 131.

distances: for the first time, Jewish gatherings from Kochin to Warsaw to Amsterdam could read from books that shared the same texts and songs. In short order, all established congregations had printed books. Although in Venice, home to the world's most vibrant Jewish community of the Renaissance, Jews were forbidden to publish books, the steady demand for prayer books became a profit base for the early printer/publishers, and allowed the print market to thrive there for 150 years.

Thanks to the collaboration demanded by publishing, different cultures came together as they never had before: for the first time, Christians, Jews, and *conversos* worked together in business. The act of publishing itself, not only the dissemination of its products, led (and leads) to cultural exchange. In short order, via the books that Martin Luther so detested, Humanism (of which Erasmus was the great proponent), Judaism, but also Arab thought (and hence the catalytic advances brought by Arab science and philosophy) made its way to the enlightened princes of the Renaissance, who were prodigious collectors of Jewish and Arab manuscripts.

As those in authority have argued since the concept of book-focused censorship first arose, if books could spread culture and 'wrongful' ideas, their absence would logically prevent ideological contamination. Even the books that were permitted to be published could be corrupting in the wrong hands. In 1546, responding both to the threat of Protestantism and the increasing number of independent observers who were making use of the new technologies, the Second Degree of Session IV of the Council of Trent condemned 'printers, who now without restraint,—thinking, that is, that whatsoever they please is allowed them,—print, without the license of ecclesiastical superiors, the said books of sacred Scripture, and the notes and comments upon them of all persons indifferently'. It therefore decreed:

> ...It shall not be lawful for any one to print, or cause to be printed, any books whatever, on sacred matters, without the name of the author; nor to sell them in future, or even to keep them, unless they shall have been first examined, and approved of, by the Ordinary; under pain of the anathema and fine imposed in a canon of the last Council of Lateran....As to those who lend, or circulate them in manuscript, without their having been first examined, and approved of, they shall be subjected to the same penalties as printers: and they who shall have them in their possession or shall read them, shall, unless they discover the authors, be themselves regarded as the authors.

This gave impetus to the authoritarian cry, in the words of the Council, that 'what ought to be condemned, may be condemned'—and in practice led to a frenzied destruction of books as agents of subversion. In 1559, following on a smattering of other such decrees, Pope Pius IV published the first edition of the *Index Librorum Prohibiturum* (*Index of Prohibited Books*). The Index had many local variants in France, Spain, the Holy Roman Empire, the New World, and this sometimes resulted in now-astonishing decrees: in 1565, the Mexican Second Provincial Council restricted the circulation of Bibles, including in the Vulgate (the Church-approved, fourth-century Latin translation) and expressly forbade non-Europeans from possessing them. The Index continued through various editions and was held as Church doctrine until 1966, by which time some 4,000 titles—by authors such as Martin Luther and John Calvin, but also ranging from Voltaire to René Descartes to Simone de Beauvoir—had been included.

Across the English Channel, 1534 marked the passage both of the Acts of Supremacy, which asserted the role of Henry VIII as head of the Church of England, and the related founding of Cambridge University Press, a convenient way to control dissenting voices. Under Henry, but continuing under the reign of Edward VI, the government waged relentless war on books by 'papists' including Thomas Aquinas and Duns Scotus, destroying their work wherever found. In 1548, for example, Henry destroyed a 300-year-old centre of Celtic scholarship, Glasney College, together with its unique collection of books in the Cornish language. With the restoration of Catholicism under Mary I, oppression continued, but in a different ideological direction. In 1557 the Stationers' Company, founded 150 years previously, was chartered by the Crown, and the right to publish was restricted to two universities and twenty-one existing printers. As officially sanctioned censors, the Stationers had the right and obligation to pursue measures against offending books, their authors and printers, and so served as proxies of authority.

Publishing and books were integral to the extended confrontations between Puritans and Royalists in the mid-seventeenth century, and the disputes there were only slightly less bloody than the fights that occurred on the battlefields. One among many examples is that of the unyielding William Prynne, a Puritan critic and publisher notable for his own attacks on 'bawdy' actors as laid out in *Histriomastix: The Player's Scourge, or Actor's Tragedy*. All copies were publicly burned and Prynne's ears were cut off, and when this did not dissuade him from his publishing, subsequently the stumps of the ears were cut off as well, and he was branded and sentenced to life in prison. (Remarkably, Prynne later became an advocate for the return of the monarchy.)

The ruling class was not wrong in its fascination with, and fear of, the cultural powers of a well-argued book. More than three centuries after their expulsion from England, the 'humanization' of Jews brought about by Rabbi Leone da Modena's 1637 *Historia de' riti hebraici* ('History of Jewish Rites'), a book addressed to gentiles, opened up the way for their return under Cromwell.[5] On the Continent, radical change was presaged by a literacy rate that surged to 50 per cent of the French population, simultaneous with a concerted and failed attempt by the monarchy to control the publishing business: the publisher Guillaume Desprez went to prison for printing Pascal's *Provinciales*, but he also became wealthy from its sales.[6]

As the Enlightenment took hold across Europe and the Americas, the focus of publishers' transformative cultural output became less religious and more political and social in nature. And controversy went hand-in-hand with good publishing: if Thomas Paine's books were bestsellers (the perpetually impoverished revolutionary contributed his considerable royalties from *Common Sense* to the Continental Army for the purchase

[5] Alessandro Marzo Magno, 'Bound in Venice: The First Talmud'. http://primolevicenter.org/printed-matter/bound-in-venice-the-first-talmud/#_edn11

[6] Vincent Giroud 2013: 336.

of mittens), his works were the ones printers, publishers, and booksellers (usually one and the same) were 'most often prosecuted for disseminating, on the grounds of seditious libel and blasphemous libel respectively'.[7] Unless it was the Bible, reading of any sort was suspect: eighteenth-century moral guardians were on the alert for 'the moral laxity that could stem from ungoverned fiction reading'.[8]

'Blasphemous' publishing was more often than not synonymous with political radicalism; the books by revolutionaries such as Giacomo Casanova, Henry Fielding, and the Marquis de Sade were no less assaults on established society than books by similarly forbidden and equally scandalous writers such as Jean-Jacques Rousseau, Baruch Spinoza, and John Stuart Mill. The danger of books lay not only in their transmission of ideas, but in their ability to allow a recognition of the commonality of interests. 'Once Weymouth, on the Dorset coast, became fashionable in the 1780s, a bookseller named James Love... marketed his bookshop as a house of public entertainment, named "The Pantheon of Taste." The venue, open from six o'clock in the morning to ten in the evening, housed, in addition to its books, a billiard room, musical circulating library, and public exhibition room...'[9] Books, then and now 'extended bodies', in the words of the philosopher Alva Noë, were both focal points for communities formed by their readers and a means to personal and cultural transformation. From Cervantes on, the most substantive excesses in literature are book-centred; it was books that drove Don Quixote mad, and it is the book itself that is celebrated as the most intoxicating of worldly possessions by experts on the matter as disparate as François Rabelais, William S. Burroughs, and H. P. Lovecraft.

With the advent of more complex economies, the days of writer/printer/publishers such as Benjamin Franklin were on the wane: the roles of printer (the tradesman), publisher (the amalgamator), and writer (the creative force) became increasingly specialized throughout the nineteenth century. At least in theory, professionalism on all sides of the equation increased in tandem with the distinctions.

The dangers of increasing mass literacy demanded a matching response from regimes and ideologies struggling to maintain their grip on society. Industrialization was accompanied by an unending stream of official efforts around the globe to shape newly developing publishing programmes—or eliminate them entirely. Emblematic of this oppression was the notorious Anthony Comstock, the founder in 1873 of the New York Society for the Suppression of Vice (aptly called 'a modern inquisitor' by Fernando Báez), the man who still holds the record for destroying the most books in the USA.[10] The Anglo-American establishment of the period was desperate to fend off incursions first from the likes of Oscar Wilde, and later from writers such as George Bernard Shaw and James Joyce: and one of the enduring tragedies of this reaction is that the reverberations of such savage counter-attacks were felt well into the twentieth century, when American publishers and booksellers still faced the prospect of being sent to jail for simply publishing and/or selling a book. Brave and obstinate publishers such as Maurice

---

[7] Elisabeth Ladenson 2013: 174.   [8] Abigail Williams 2017: 3.
[9] Williams 2017: 111.   [10] Báez 2008: 224.

Girodias, John Calder, and Barney Rosset, invoking the spirits of their antecedents Prynne and Desprez, defied the authorities and faced fines and prison time in pursuit of their commitment to the work of their writerly counterparts, including Vladimir Nabokov, Henry Miller, and D. H. Lawrence. New York bookseller Sam Roth, a translator of French avant-gardist Alfred Jarry, was only one of many in the profession who were convicted and sent to prison multiple times. But despite the seeming vulnerability of its protagonists, as the publishing industry continued to chip away at the rules laid down by Church and State, there was no question that cultural mores were changing, and the 'eroticization of leisure was a force no warning voice could stop'.[11] The twentieth century adage not to pick a fight with a man who buys ink by the barrel seems to have truth at its core: although practically from the moment the profession was founded publishers have been sued, thrown in jail, and driven to bankruptcy—their products condemned, banned, and burned—they persevere, and so does the material they propagate. Once conceived of and transmuted to paper (or the electronic screen), ideas still have remarkable, authority-defying tenacity.

As far back as Benvenuto Cellini's memoir (1563)—a wonderful, extended classic of shameless self-promotion—artists have recognized the aesthetic fiefdom conferred by literary creation. Whether for commercial gain, to influence society at large, or 'simply' as an extended artistic exercise in a different medium, artists' and writers' movements have often undertaken the establishment of publishing houses. William Morris' Kelmscott Press (1891) was essential to the development of the Arts and Crafts Movement and to promoting socialist values in England. On the Continent, the symbolists had their Mercure de France, which published works by Guillaume Apollinaire, André Gide, and others. A few decades later, in 1917, Virginia and Leonard Woolf founded the Hogarth Press to further the interests of the Bloomsbury Group. Around the same time, the 'Literary Company of Futurists' was thriving in Russia, as was the Edizioni Futuriste di Poesia, founded in Milan by the artist Filippo Tommaso Marinetti, author of both the Futurist and Fascist Manifestoes (1909 and 1919, respectively). The tradition continues: in 2010, artist Paul Chan founded his Badlands Unlimited, a raucous New York-based enterprise that has published erotica, an interview with Marcel Duchamp, and ex-Iraqi dictator Saddam Hussein's speeches on democracy, among other titles. To effect aesthetic change it helps to be the ruler of a literary demesne.

The threat posed by freethinking publishers to a particular definition of 'civilization' came on two fronts, social and political. Thus it was that Emma Goldman, the great anarchist of the early twentieth century, was an early advocate of 'free love'. And publishers who fought censorship were well aware that writing that celebrated pleasures of the flesh, even as it occasionally sold well, was writing that challenged social stability. Barney Rosset, for example, was taken to court repeatedly by the US government for publishing Henry Miller's *Tropic of Cancer*; he was also the American publisher of Che Guevara's diaries, Frantz Fanon's *The Wretched of the Earth*, and so many other radical works. The legal battles raged for decades, culminating in the Anglophone world with

[11] Jay Gertzman 2002: 106.

the million-copy selling satirical novel *Candy*, written on a lark by Terry Southern and Mason Hoffenburg for Girodias' Olympia Press.[12] Its odyssey from underground success (1958) to number one commercial blockbuster (1965) 'can be attributed to America suddenly growing up after the relaxation of the "decency laws" that had kept such works as *Lady Chatterley's Lover*, *Howl*, and *Last Exit to Brooklyn* from sullying America's Doris Day-hallucination of cheerful, neutered perfection.'[13] After *Candy*, American and English governments skirmished with publishers, but they knew they had lost the war.

No discussion of authority's hatred and fear of the power of publishing would be complete without mention of Germany in the 1930s. As Gary Stark has documented in *Entrepreneurs of Ideology* (1981), a string of German publishers had over a period of decades set the ideological stage for the rise of the radical right in that country, and may even have been instrumental—by providing a 'solid' base philosophy—in the rise of National Socialism. Publishers such as Eugen Diederichs, Julius Lehmann, and others in the late nineteenth and early twentieth centuries took advantage of what was then perhaps the largest literate market in the world, playing to fears of immigrants and Marxists, and stoking nationalism. The books sold well, by all accounts. After Hitler was named chancellor of the Weimar Republic in 1933, laws were passed to restrict 'dangerous' material, and the infamous, brilliant Joseph Goebbels, a novelist and propagandist possessed of a doctorate in philology, began his book burnings. Texts were destroyed, libraries ransacked, and publishers' warehouses 'sanitized'. 'In Frankfurt, books were brought in on trucks, and the students made human chains to get them to the bonfire.'[14] Germany's allies in the war, the Japanese Empire, undertook a similarly systematic destruction of libraries throughout China, part of the strategy of conquest. As the persecution of books and their producers and defenders intensified, it became clear the process was only a prelude to more intensive and human-focused oppression: the care of books, and a vibrant publishing environment, closely parallels a society's assessment of the worth of its human components. 'Where they burn books, they will also ultimately burn people.'[15] Burning a book or repository of books sacred to a particular people is the penultimate insult, or so biblioclasts like to think. In the years following the destruction

---

[12] Girodias' career ended in bankruptcy after repeated legal clashes. Although Girodias, the first publisher of Vladimir Nabokov's *Lolita* and J. P. Donleavy's *The Ginger Man*, was as notorious for his commitment to 'erotica' as he was for fleecing his authors, it was his political engagement that most enraged the authorities: in 1947 he was sued by the French minister of culture (the writer André Malraux) for publishing *Le pain de la corruption* (*The Bread of Corruption*), a book attacking the state of the economy, and in 1959 he was condemned again by Malraux for publishing books legal in France but banned in their home countries. In 1963, he wrote his fellow publishing maverick, Barney Rosset: 'The situation here is really most awful and disgusting. I am being sentenced once a week, or nearly, and for the most ludicrous reasons. It seems difficult to continue publishing books in France, and I am now trying to start a branch abroad—perhaps several branches' (Barney Rosset 2016: 249.) He moved to New York when the Olympia Press went bankrupt in 1970, and a mere four years later his pornographic fantasy *President Kissinger* caused US State Department officials to tell him to leave the country, a situation perhaps facilitated by his expired visa. (Nile Southern 2004: 284).
[13] Southern 2004: 13.   [14] Báez 2008: 210.
[15] 'Das war ein Vorspiel nur, Dort wo man Bücher verbrennt, verbrennt man auch am Ende Menschen.'—Heinrich Heine, 'Almansor'.

of the World Trade Center, American Pastor Terry Jones made a name for himself burning copies of the Koran, and following the Chinese invasion of Tibet in 1950, ethnocide (and the death of approximately 200,000 people) was complemented by a highly focused campaign to destroy the extensive network of monasteries, which doubled as publishers for Tibetan Buddhism: 'the Great Monastery of Derge had a collection of more than half a million woodblocks that was systematically deposited in more than ten halls... the use of such blocks made possible printing on demand'.[16] Not content with destroying thousands of monasteries, their libraries, manuscripts, and woodblocks, the Chinese 'forced Tibetans to burn or shred sacred scriptures, mix them with manure, or lay them on the ground and walk on them'.[17] Destruction was so thorough that by the 1990s, most Tibetans had no concept of what a library was.[18]

Russians famously venerate the status of publishers, writers, and their output, so much so that their governments have a long tradition of attempting to control the process: both by tightly regulating the business and by incarcerating writers and publishers on the pretext of their threat to the state. In 1553, it was the first tsar, Ivan the Terrible, notable for his wars against the Mongols and his enthusiasm for torture on a mass scale (and the Massacre of Novgorod), who founded Russia's first publishing company, the Moscow Print Yard. Throughout the centuries, Russian rulers recognized the connection between publishing and mass influence: one of the world's all-time bestsellers, and a book with particularly pernicious consequences, *The Protocols of the Elders of Zion*, is widely believed to have been fabricated in 1903 under the direction of Pyotr Rachkovsky, chief of the foreign branch of the Romanov secret police. Thirty years later, the Soviets imposed rigid layers of control over the publishing process: 'first by the Writers' Union, then by the appropriate state-appointed commissar, finally by the Central Committee of the Communist Party'.[19] Stalin himself was a famously insatiable reader who held authors and their books in high regard—and consequently had no hesitation about imprisoning and executing them and their publishers. For Stalin, the ultimate editor/publisher, 'the power to edit was power itself'.[20] In the post-war period, the State Committee for Publishing in the Soviet Union, or Goskomizdat, held sway; private (non-governmental) publishers were enjoined from doing business until the 1980s. Even when the restrictions eased, the lack of infrastructure and the tightly-controlled paper supply meant that almost no books could be printed privately, giving rise to samizdat publishing, underground publishing where a 'print run' often consisted of a few copies of a manuscript passed illicitly from hand to hand. After 1989, there was a surge in literary and radical publishing in the former Soviet states, but to no one's surprise (except, perhaps, ever-optimistic publishers'), the publishing scene quickly came to be dominated by the same commercial works (romance, how-to, potboilers) long seen in the West. And publishers were once again in the sights of those who resented

[16] Rebecca Knuth 2003: 205.   [17] Knuth 2003: 213.   [18] Knuth 2003: 225.
[19] Isaiah Berlin, *The New York Review of Books*, 19 October 2000: accessed at http://www.nybooks.com/articles/2000/10/19/the-arts-in-russia-under-stalin/
[20] Holly Case, *The Chronicle of Higher Education*, 7 October 2013: accessed at https://www.chronicle.com/article/Stalins-Blue-Pencil/142109

their products: in 2006, for example, the Moscow offices of Alex Kervey, publisher of T-ough Press, were firebombed (as Barney Rosset's Grove Press offices had been in 1968, as was the London home of Gibson Square publisher Martin Rynja in 2008).

'People die, but books never die', said FDR in 1942.[21] Recognizing that the Nazi campaigns against books and 'decadent' art could be used as counterpropaganda, Roosevelt authorized the establishment of the Council on Books in Wartime (CBW), a publisher's committee headed by the publisher W. W. Norton. 'Books are weapons in the war of ideas', became the CBW's slogan. The culmination of the Roosevelt Administration's remarkable series of book-centred cultural programmes in the USA both during the Depression and World War 2, the CBW instituted its own publishing programme during the war, eventually engineering the manufacture and distribution of close to 123 million paperbacks to soldiers overseas. Authors included in the programme ranged from Zane Grey to F. Scott Fitzgerald. Books were also printed and distributed to newly 'liberated' populations, sometimes in wanton violation of copyright (including unauthorized editions of *The Abruzzo Trilogy* by the socialist writer Ignazio Silone).[22] More than any speech or overt indoctrination, the publishing programme became a palpable expression of what the Allies saw themselves as fighting for.

At the end of World War 2, as part of its effort to stymie the forces that were 'destined to shake civilization to its roots', in the words of FBI chief J. Edgar Hoover, the USA doubled down on its efforts to influence the world of publishing. Publishers were manipulators who themselves could be manipulated, potential if not actual 'masters of deceit', to borrow Hoover's (1958) marvellously crystallizing phrase, the title of his bestselling tome assessing the communist threat. As they had with the Axis powers, the American propagandists found they could use their opponents' intransigence to their own advantage: in 1957, after being denied publication by Goslitizdat, the Soviet state publishing house, Boris Pasternak handed the manuscript of *Doctor Zhivago* to an agent for the left-wing Italian publisher Giangiacomo Feltrinelli. Despite explicit pressure from Soviet emissaries (which included a personal visit to his offices), Feltrinelli proceeded to publication. The entire Italian print run sold out in one day, and the novel, disseminated throughout Europe with the help of the CIA, became a runaway success. Wrote one American agent regarding *Doctor Zhivago*: 'It is requested that Headquarters keep us informed of its plans concerning the book so that we may continue to discuss its exploitation with the [British] as closely as possible.'[23] In the UK, Secker & Warburg was used to channel CIA money to friendly publications, and the Free Europe Press was an out-and-out CIA-run publisher, managed by the CIA's 'Office of Policy Coordination'.[24] Years after the fact, publishers themselves saw no need to disavow their CIA connections, which stretched from Beacon Press (through the editor and publisher Sol Stein, a prominent member of the CIA-funded American Committee for Cultural Freedom) to

[21] [Author uncredited], 'Book Trade hears appeal by M'Leish: He Urges a Return to Old-Time Standards of Responsibility for Works Dealers Sell Message from President "Books Never Die," He Writes in Referring to Anniversary of the Nazi Bonfire', *The New York Times*, 7 May 1942, p. 17.
[22] Alexander Stille, foreword to Ignazio Silone 2000: vii–viii.
[23] Joel Whitney 2016: 62–5.   [24] Whitney 2016: 38.

Farrar, Straus & Giroux (whose publisher Roger Straus acknowledged his CIA-funded and -hired literary scouts to a writer for *The New Yorker*).[25]

In the modern era, no political movement has taken shape without a published presence, and no would-be leader seems to achieve legitimacy without a book to his or her credit (even if it is ghost-written). There is no enduring ideology without at least one book providing its cultural foundation. From the fascists to the Zapatistas, from Lenin to Trump, the popular conception of a leader is underpinned by two things: a prevailing visual image (Hillary Clinton in her pantsuit; Donald Trump in his red tie and com-bover) and a book (*It Takes a Village* and *The Art of the Deal*, respectively). Titles in this category include Lenin's *What Is to Be Done?*, Hitler's *Mein Kampf*, Mao's *Little Red Book*, Merkel's *So wahr mir Gott helfe*, Gaddafi's *Little Green Book*, Kennedy's *Profiles in Courage*, Obama's *Dreams of My Father*, Thatcher's *Statecraft*, and many more. Each was written to further its purported author's ambitions; each succeeded to various degrees.

As countries moved out from under the weight of overbearing outside forces, publishing industries—in Egypt, in China, in India—sprang up as part of an effort 'to understand ourselves, our past, our future', says V. Geetha, publisher and co-director of Tara Books in Chennai, India. In French North Africa, Algerian-born writers knew that for a book to be considered professional, it had first to be published in the language of the colonizers. A sense of self-worth, anti-colonialism, and a thriving literary culture are part of the same package, and occupying forces have always been alert to the challenge. In Algeria during the war for independence, the library and campus of the University of Algiers were targeted and set on fire in 1962 by the Organisation de l'armée secrète (OAS), a catastrophe commemorated throughout the Arabic-speaking world.[26] In India, various iterations of the hated Sedition Laws were imposed beginning in the nineteenth century, with punishment for infractions ranging from banishment to life imprisonment. As always in trials of sedition, books provided clinching evidence for the prosecution (bringing to mind contemporary American cases, where mere possession of a book such as William Powell's *Anarchist Cookbook* or Abbie Hoffman's *Steal This Book* has been cited as evidence of a commitment to violent revolution). Towards the end of the 1800s, the Hindu Free Thought Union founded a publishing house which brought out books with a distinctly atheistic, rationalistic bent. In the 1920s, populist reading rooms sprang up, along with books for people 'who didn't read, but liked to listen', says Geetha. 'The connections between popular oral and written worlds were close: and what would often happen is that older women and younger women developed a bond there. For the first time, people were exposed to Indian content in a formalized setting, giving them a chance to fraternize with strangers and bring in 'new worlds'. Publishing democratized knowledge in a big way', as it sidestepped the traditions of the caste system,

---

[25] 'Appealing to Straus's patriotism, the man asked if Farrar, Straus could provide cover for two men in Europe. They would do real work for Straus as literary scouts, but they would also be reporting to this government agency, which would pay their salaries.... Straus (who has always been a fan of spy fiction) agreed to the plan. A dedicated telephone line was put into his office for calls to and from his contact.' Ian Parker, 'Showboat: Roger Straus and his flair for selling literature', *The New Yorker*, 8 April 2002.

[26] http://www.libraryhistorybuff.com/bibliophilately-algiers-library.htm

which imposed cultural taboos against sharing knowledge. Suddenly, culture and history were acknowledged as a part of public memory, rather than the 'property' of privileged familial or communal circles. Publishers began asserting the vitality of their regional culture by the not-so-simple act of rejecting English and publishing in one of the many languages spoken and written by the pre-colonial population—Hindi, Tamil, Mayalam, Urdu, Bengali, Kannada, and many more.

In modern Turkey, despite the ascension to power of an intensely nationalist regime at the turn of the twenty-first century, literary publishers by and large have been spared harassment, with one notable exception: Ragıp Zaraklou, publisher of Belge Publishing House, brought to trial at least seven times. What makes Zaraklou distinct? His determined commitment to publish the work of Greek, Kurdish, and Armenian authors, thus perpetuating minority cultures in a nation ruled by a government that has no patience for non-Turkish voices. In China, while the enforcement of laws is widely acknowledged by editors to be inconsistent, the threat of jailtime is a very real one for publishers: the State Administration of Press, Publications, Radio, Film, and Television has complete power over the industry, both print and electronic. Typically, books dealing with the Cultural Revolution, Tibet, and border provinces from anything other than a tourist's point of view, or containing even a mention of the Tienanmen Square protests, will be refused publication. In the 1990s, among the books banned outright by what was then known as the General Administration of Press and Publication was Dr Seuss' *Green Eggs and Ham*: more recently, under President Xi Jinping, censorship has become more focused and the consequences of running afoul of the government more dramatic. In 2015, five Hong Kong publisher/booksellers, all connected to Mighty Current Media, known for books exposing government officials, disappeared. One of them, Gui Minhai, a Swedish citizen who reportedly had been working on a book about President Xi Jinping's love life, remains in government detention as of this writing.

Publishing provides a means to document a culture. A foundationless, undocumented culture is vulnerable, a fact recognized, for example, by Palestinians living in the West Bank and the Gaza Strip, a displaced, impoverished population of five million that enthusiastically supports close to thirty publishing houses. The industry thrives, in spite of restrictions on paper deliveries and arrests of writers and editors on charges of sedition. While the assault on culture via the emphatic repression of books and publishing is not limited to wartime or occupied territories, war of course provides conditions that accelerate the process. Remarking on the looting of the National Library of Baghdad in 2003, 'in the land where the book was born, where libraries were born, where the first legal codes were created',[27] the journalist Robert Fisk famously wrote, 'All over the filthy yard they blew, letters of recommendation to the courts of Arabia, demands for ammunition for troops, reports on the theft of camels and attacks on pilgrims, all in delicate hand-written Arabic script. I was holding in my hands the last Baghdad vestiges of Iraq's written history. But for Iraq, this is Year Zero; with the destruction of the antiquities in the Museum of Archaeology on Saturday and the burning of the National Archives and

[27] Báez 2008: 278.

then the Koranic library, the cultural identity of Iraq is being erased. ....For almost a thousand years, Baghdad was the cultural capital of the Arab world, the most literate population in the Middle East. Genghis Khan's grandson burnt the city in the 13th century and, so it was said, the Tigris river ran black with the ink of books. Yesterday, the black ashes of thousands of ancient documents filled the skies of Iraq.'[28]

Despite the obstacles, across eras and languages, publishers often see themselves as, at least in part, cultural knights errant. In fact some, such as Barbara Epler, editorial director of the venerable publisher New Directions, see such pioneering work as crucial to their job: 'I want to live up to the legacy of [James Laughlin, founder of the house in 1936], to be the kind of publisher he wanted to be, to allow writers to make their experiments in public, doing things that somehow move the walls around inside your brain. You're not going to do that if your first objective is to make money.' Beacon Press, once a conduit for CIA-funded propaganda, is now one of the leading outlets for defenders of civil liberties. In a company blog, Tom Hallock, its associate publisher, proudly observed: 'To meet the needs of our times, we don't have to publish bestsellers. On the day that SCOTUS [the Supreme Court of the United States] handed down their decision on marriage equality, Hillary Goodridge (a lead plaintiff in the Massachusetts case that rocked the nation) publicly thanked Beacon Press for publishing *What Is Marriage For?* by E. J. Graff. She said that it had provided her with the intellectual framework to take a stand. The book sold modestly, but has so far helped make it possible for almost a million gay and lesbian people in the US to marry.'[29]

For many publishers, the spectre of profitless seasons without end, and accelerating cash-drain—the pressures of the market—were and are a danger more immediate than the threat of lawsuits, jail, or officially-sanctioned violence. Publishers have always attempted to defy the laws of supply and demand—that there are many more books than readers does not keep them from attempting to maintain the steady value of their product. But as commercial forces put more pressure on publishing firms, more writers are taking matters into their own hands founding companies such as Fiction Collective and AK Press, echoing the anti-commercial, cooperative tradition of the Woolfs and their Hogarth Press. The latest incarnation of individual writers-as-publishers, online and off-, the techno inheritors of the samizdat tradition (albeit in a corporatized version), is represented via the offerings of companies such as Wattpad, Smashwords, and Lightning Source, all of which can lay legitimate claim in different ways to helping blast open the doors to the Palace of Culture. Wattpad, for example, allows writers to publish directly on the site, without editorial 'interference'—and a number of commercial books and at least one movie have been the result.

If war, the heavy hand of authority, and the equally oppressive demands of profit are united in their assault on culture, the undying obstreperousness of publishers makes for a formidable foe.

---

[28] Robert Fisk, 'Library books, letters and priceless documents are set ablaze in final chapter of the sacking of Baghdad', *The Independent*, 15 April 2003.

[29] Tom Hallock, 'The work of publishers in an authoritarian age', Beacon Broadside, 19 January 2017. http://www.beaconbroadside.com/broadside/2017/01/the-work-of-publishers-in-an-authoritarian-age.html

As the act of publishing has become more accessible to each generation through successive technological advances, we see the profession in a kind of historical loop, where authors can once again act as their own publishers, as they did in the pre-modern era. The result has been a tsunami of published books, an overwhelming if joyful chaos. The distinction between publisher and author, between author and reader continues to diminish, and the tools of culture are no longer in the hands of a few.

ACKNOWLEDGEMENTS

I am indebted to Alessandro Cassin, director of the Centro Primo Levi; the writer and critic Dale Peck; to V. Geetha, publisher and co-director of Tara Books; Barbara Epler, editorial director of New Directions; Matthew J. Boylan, senior reference librarian, the New York York Public Library; and to Carin Kuoni, director of the Vera List Center for Art and Politics at The New School University, all of whom expanded on and refined a number of the ideas contained herein.

REFERENCES

Báez, F. (2008). *A Universal History of the Destruction of Books: From Ancient Sumer to Modern Iraq*. Translated by A. MacAdam. New York: Atlas and Co.

Gertzman, J. (2002). *Bookleggers and Smuthounds: The Trade in Erotica, 1920–1940*, Philadelphia: University of Pennsylvania Press.

Giroud, Vincent. (2013). 'The History of the Book in France', in *The Book: A Global History*. Edited by Michael F. Suarez and H. R. Woodhuysen, Oxford: Oxford University Press, pp. 328–48.

Hoover, J. (1958). *Masters of Deceit: The Story of Communism in America and How to Fight It*, New York: Henry Holt and Company.

Jardine, L. (1998). *Worldly Goods: A New History of the Renaissance*, New York: W.W. Norton.

Knuth, R. (2003). *Libricide: The Regime-Sponsored Destruction of Books and Libraries in the Twentieth Century*, Westport, CT: Praeger.

Ladenson, Elisabeth. (2013). 'Censorship', in *The Book: A Global History*. Edited by Michael F. Suarez and H. R. Woodhuysen, Oxford: Oxford University Press, pp. 1639–82.

Manguel, A. (2008). *The Library at Night*, New Haven, CT: Yale University Press.

Rosset, B. (2016). *Rosset: My Life in Publishing*, New York: OR Books.

Silone, Ignazio. (2000). *The Abruzzo Trilogy*, Hanover, NH: Steerforth Italia.

Southern, N. (2004). *The Candy Men: The Rollicking Life and Times of the Notorious Novel Candy*, New York: Arcade Publishing.

Stark, Gary D. (1981). *Entrepreneurs of Ideology: Neoconservative Publishers in Germany, 1890–1933*, Chapel Hill: University of North Carolina Press.

Suarez, M. and H. Woudhuysen, eds (2014). *The Book: A Global History*, Oxford: Oxford University Press.

Whitney, Joel. (2016). *Finks: How the C.I.A. Tricked the World's Best Writers*, New York: OR Books.

Williams, A. (2017). *The Social Life of Books: Reading Together in the Eighteenth-Century Home*, New Haven, CT: Yale University Press.

CHAPTER 8

··

PUBLISHING AND
INFORMATION

··

MARTIN PAUL EVE

IN the era of the so-called knowledge economy, the vocabulary of computational information is abundant. Data, metadata, information, blogs, bits and bytes, posts, software, code, bandwidth, 4g, routers, wifi, smartphones, and smart-homes all surround us. Indeed, the early twenty-first century is replete with neologisms to describe the technological phenomena of our binary times.

Two aspects of these vocabularies stand out, though. First, the precise relationships and definitional distinctions between knowledge, information, and data are unclear. Second, were one to ask an audience for associative terms with the above list of words, 'publishing' would fall fairly low down the guesses that might be ventured. For there is something about publishing that continues to be associated with print in the popular imagination, even when XML-first print publishing processes are born digital.[1]

In this chapter, I address some of the conceptual challenges with speaking about publishing and 'information' that will range from the underlying philosophical distinctions between the various terms through to practical mutations in the non-fiction/ scholarly publishing spaces and the growing demands to publish new types of data objects and software. While there is, inevitably, some confluence with Chapter 16 (on 'Academic Publishing'), the focus here is more specifically upon the turn to data and digital-artefactual publishing within the contexts of 'information'. In particular, I argue that the true challenges for publishing and information in the era of the Internet and World Wide Web pertain to frames of cultural authority and truth but also to labour scarcity in publishing in a digital world that presents itself as infinitely abundant. This argument is structured across a first section on what we mean by 'information', a second on the history of digital reproduction as it emerged in the twentieth century, a third on the challenges for labour and authority in information publishing, and finally a set of case studies and practical observations on preprints, replication studies, and data.

---

[1] N. Katherine Hayles (2012: 6).

DATA, INFORMATION, KNOWLEDGE, AND TRUTH

Academic/professional sources and dictionary definitions hold no consensus on the precise definitions of information, knowledge, and data.[2] Indeed, the rise of knowledge fetishism within corporate cultures has taken place without a shared understanding of what the term 'knowledge' actually means. This is unsurprising, since the quest to understand different epistemological modes and concepts has been core to Western philosophy from Ancient Greece until the present day.[3] That said, and while hardly the final word on the subject, Anthony Liew helpfully distinguishes between these terms by positing data as 'recorded (captured and stored) symbols and signal readings'; information as 'a message that contains relevant meaning, implication, or input for decision and/or action'; and knowledge as 'the (1) cognition or recognition (know-what), (2) capacity to act (know-how), and (3) understanding (know-why) that resides or is contained within the mind or in the brain'.[4]

Care must be taken even with these definitions. For instance, note that in Liew's phrasings, the term 'relevant' is present for 'information' but not for 'data'. This leads to the idea that data is somehow a 'raw' form, as though it were an unmediated capture of some phenomenon that can later be whittled into sub-groups of relevance. As Lisa Gitelman et al. have forcefully pointed out, however, 'raw data is an oxymoron'.[5] The act of collecting and storing is determined in the last instance by human judgement and selection. Even supposed 'comprehensive' data-collection processes will involve decisions about the bounds of relevance that are implicit within the systems that are designed to support them. These data are then recorded to degradable media in encodings and file formats that require active preservation and interpretative action to be usable. The relevance of data is already pre-determined by the time it comes to recording.

Likewise, Liew gives a utilitarian definition of information that is clearly born within enterprise cultures: 'a message that contains relevant meaning, implication, or input for decision and/or action'. It is unclear from Liew's syntax here whether 'relevant meaning' or 'implication' are also meant to be for the purposes of 'decision and/or action' or whether this solely pertains to 'input'. However, we may wish to consider whether information has always to be for a purpose in the way that this suggests. Various forms of information may hold esoteric or intrinsic values that pertain neither to decision nor action and exist merely for interest; to inform.

---

[2] See, for example, Anthony Liew (2007) and the comparison between Merriam Webster's Collegiate Dictionary 10th ed. and Juris Kelley (2002); Pentti Sydänmaanlakka (2002); Amrit Tiwana (2001); George Von Krogh, Kazuo Ichijō, and Ikujirō Nonaka, (2000); Nancy M. Dixon (2000); Frances Horibe (1999); Debra M. Amidon (1997); Andrew P Garvin and Robert I. Berkman (1996); Ikujirō Nonaka and Hirotaka Takeuchi (1995); Thomas H. Davenport and Laurence Prusak (2010).
[3] Dick Stenmark (2001: 1).   [4] Liew (2007).   [5] Lisa Gitelman (2013).

Finally, each of Liew's three sub-definitions of 'knowledge' rest upon contingent value judgements about the *truth* of the information received. For 'know-what', 'know-how', and 'know-why' must all be subjected to truth tests that are verified within a specific epistemic context. As just one example, it was 'known' that the sun revolved around the Earth for many centuries. When we speak, therefore, of 'knowledge production', 'knowledge transfer', and other terms around knowledge, we rely upon an implicit social contract that suppresses the fact that knowledge is at its core *belief*. We suppress this in favour of pragmatics—and the basis of the belief may be empirical evidence—but the challenge here is that knowledge claims are always socially rooted. This has implications for the world of publishing.

Publishing, Information, and the Digital Age

Ever since Gutenberg and probably since time immemorial, a branch of publishing has been about the dissemination of information, however one so chooses to define that term. Various legislative apparatuses have also emerged as a result of information publication. As Adrian Johns controversially traces it, for example, current copyright legislation (such as the US Constitution's provision 'To promote the Progress of Science and useful Arts, by securing for limited Times to Authors and Inventors the exclusive Right to their respective Writings and Discoveries') came about as a direct result of the increase in reproductive capacity of printing technologies.[6] Diderot's *Encyclopédie* was also an important milestone in this respect. As many historians have traced, the increase in technological publishing potential here caused an epistemic revolution. For, while earlier efforts at the encyclopaedic form, from Varro and Pliny the Elder through to Vincent of Beauvais, were thought to reflect a divinely-imparted wisdom, Diderot's model was more rhizomatic and open, albeit also more prone to a totalizing positivism; a quest for interlinked, total knowledge.[7] At the same time, though, as Robert Darnton has famously noted, the *Encyclopédie* cost 980 livres. At two and a half times the income of a common labourer, the 'openness' of the new printed knowledge was severely restricted and certainly not democratic.[8]

Despite their practical limitations, the models of knowledge dissemination and information publishing implied by Diderot's work have been extended and facilitated by more recent changes to the available ecosystems of publishing in the twentieth century. This began, in fact, around the 1930s when Paul Valéry wrote that

> [o]ur fine arts were developed, their types and uses were established, in times very different from the present, by men whose power of action upon things was

---

[6] Adrian Johns (2011: 291–326).   [7] Robert Lewis Collison (1964: 42).
[8] Robert Darnton (1987: 11).

insignificant in comparison with ours. But the amazing growth of our techniques, the adaptability and precision they have attained, the ideas and habits they are creating, make it a certainty that profound changes are impending in the ancient craft of the Beautiful. In all the arts there is a physical component which can no longer be considered or treated as it used to be, which cannot remain unaffected by our modern knowledge and power. For the last twenty years neither matter nor space nor time has been what it was from time immemorial. We must expect great innovations to transform the entire technique of the arts, thereby affecting artistic invention itself and perhaps even bringing about an amazing change in our very notion of art.[9]

Likewise, Walter Benjamin, who cited Valéry as the epigraph to his *The Work of Art in the Age of Mechanical Reproduction*, wrote that

> [i]n principle a work of art has always been reproducible. Man-made artifacts could always be imitated by men.... Around 1900 technical reproduction had reached a standard that not only permitted it to reproduce all transmitted works of art and thus to cause the most profound change in their impact upon the public; it also had captured a place of its own among the artistic processes.[10]

While it took another thirty years for the development of the computing systems that would carry Valéry's and Benjamin's respective ideas to their logical conclusions, the essential stakes here centre around the idea of non-rivalrous objects and the nature of knowledge and/or information.

The notion that knowledge and information might be forms that are 'non-rivalrous' has a long history. A non-rivalrous object is one that can be copied perfectly without the original owner losing it. For instance, Thomas Jefferson wrote that '[i]f nature has made any one thing less susceptible than all others of exclusive property, it is the action of the thinking power called an idea, which an individual may exclusively possess as long as he keeps it to himself; but the moment it is divulged, it forces itself into the possession of every one, and the receiver cannot dispossess himself of it.'[11] This is a sentiment that was echoed in recent years by the Internet hacktivist, Aaron Swartz, who wrote that 'by their very nature, ideas *cannot* be property.'[12]

Until very recently, however, all of the containers with which publishing dealt were essentially rivalrous. These containers, such as printed books, were essentially *not like knowledge*. As Peter Suber puts it:

> for all of human history before the digital age, writing has been rivalrous. Written or recorded knowledge became a material object like stone, clay, skin, or paper, which was necessarily rivalrous. Even when we had the printing press and photocopying machine, allowing us to make many copies at comparatively low cost, each copy was

---

[9] Cited in Walter Benjamin (1999: 211).   [10] Benjamin (1999: 212).

[11] Thomas Jefferson (1853:, VI, 180).

[12] I am grateful to Mark Carrigan for pointing out to me this correlation between Swartz and Jefferson. Mark Carrigan (2016); Aaron Swartz (2015:. 24).

a rivalrous material object. Despite its revolutionary impact, writing was hobbled from birth by this tragic limitation. We could only record nonrivalrous knowledge in a rivalrous form. Digital writing is the first kind of writing that does not reduce recorded knowledge to a rivalrous object.[13]

In the digital age, this changes. The new technological capacities of the Internet that are available to publishing appear, for the first time, to have matched the underlying philosophies of knowledge/information in a process that has been building since the 1930s. There is a move towards supposed unlimited abundance of replication, mirrored in Google's assertion that it wishes to 'organize the world's information' and is perhaps best captured in its massive-scale book-scanning enterprise; a move itself that causes challenges for information discoverability in such a space of potential information overload.[14] However, it is also clear that the rapid changes in the technological affordances of the digital space are not yet being replicated across the labour and economic structures of information publishing as it currently exists.

DIGITAL LABOUR, DIGITAL AUTHORITY, AND INFORMATION PUBLISHING

The convergence of digital forms as the first mass non-rivalrous systems with the underlying structures of knowledge and information has significant consequences for publishing. The two aspects that are a challenge for publishing in such a space are: labour and authority. I will turn, first, to labour.

The digital space has the capacity to make labour invisible or to seem unnecessary. For, consider that, in the digital world, most of the costs of publishing inhere within the less visible realm of cost-to-first-copy.[15] Marginal dissemination costs are lowered to a near-infinitesimal level by the capacity of the digital. Yet there are a variety of forms of labour that require remuneration for both fixed and variable costs. At the infrastructure level, ongoing maintenance, feature development, programming, graphical design, format creation, digital preservation, forward-migration of content, security design, marketing, social media promotion, implementation of semantic machine-readability, licensing, and legal costs are all important. For every unit, there may also be additional typesetting, copy-editing, proofreading, design, marketing, and legal costs.[16]

Yet, these forms of labour must be remunerated within a system of marketing and sales that has grown around print media and there is evidently confusion among consumers about what is being purchased. A good example of this can be seen in the

---

[13] Peter Suber (2012: 46–7.   [14] James Somers (2017).
[15] Martin Paul Eve (2014: 16); John B. Thompson(2005: 16–20).
[16] I first made these arguments in Martin Paul Eve (2017).

case of electronic books and VAT in the United Kingdom.[17] Consumers often express shock that an eBook could cost more than its print analogue since the tangible materiality of the item purchased is so much less. Yet we also know that the final print and distribution costs do not form a major component here.

This prioritization of the physical object is a problem that we can trace back to Marx's thinking on commodity fetishism. In Volume I of *Capital*, Marx wrote that

> the commodity reflects the social characteristics of men's own labour as objective characteristics of the products of labour themselves.... It is [actually] nothing but the definite social relation between men themselves which assumes here, for them, the fantastic form of a relation between things ... I call this the fetishism which attaches itself to the products of labour as soon as they are produced as commodities.[18]

In other words, what is happening here is that, in our rush to perceive publishing processes as being akin to information—that is, non-rivalrous and free (and, particularly, free of *labour*)—we can easily mistake the relationships we have to the objects of publishing as relations to artefacts, rather than relations to labour. In a world where the publication of data, information, and knowledge becomes ever more important—even as the non-rivalrous nature of the digital threatens to mask labour through its promise of unlimited dissemination—information publishing must transform to a service industry that foregrounds the *work* of publication.

The second challenge in the realm of information publishing posed by the digital age pertains to authority. As I explored in the first section of this chapter, there are definitional challenges in speaking about knowledge and truth. The traditional approach to truth evaluation in publishing consisted of high-quality framing outlets, as Michael Bhaskar has partially suggested.[19] Such venues were designed to serve as proxies for the evaluation of quality, with a presumed commensurate scarcity of publication correlating to pre-selection of material. In other words, the authority of long-standing publishing entities (for instance, long-established university presses) was predicated on a print scarcity and a supposed quality scarcity. Authority was bestowed upon work through the recognition of two interlinked facts that it was (1) difficult to get a university press (for example) to publish one's work because there was a cost involved in the printing and dissemination of work; but (2) the procedures for the selection of material to be published were rigorous and difficult to pass. Indeed, authority works a little like a symbolic economy: the scarcer it is, the more worth it has. If everything can make the equal claim to be true, then there are problems for judgement.

This is not to say that the system was perfect. Indeed, I have argued strongly elsewhere that peer review is an extremely flawed system that is poor at predicting future quality.[20] I have also argued that the use of a brand name of a press or journal as a proxy for quality is far too broad a measure to helpfully appraise work at the article or book level and that it comes with serious consequences for university library budgets.[21] When the spread of

---

[17] Marion Dakers (2015).   [18] Karl Marx(1992: 165).
[19] Michael Bhaskar (2013: 103–6).   [20] Samuel Moore et al. (2017).
[21] Eve (2014: 44–55).

this expertise is legitimized by the traditional print media (who also have an authority based on material scarcity) the results can, in fact, be devastating. A good example of this is the case of Andrew Wakefield's now-retracted article in *The Lancet* claiming a link between the MMR (mumps, measles, and rubella) vaccine and the development of child-hood autism.[22] Despite appearing in one of the most prestigious medical journals in the world with the most challenging selection criteria, Wakefield's study was unethical in subjecting children to unnecessary medical procedures for research without ethical approval, for not disclosing financial conflicts of interest, and for the falsification of its results.[23] The tabloid press seized upon this, using the cultural authority of *The Lancet* as a basis for truth in information publication, and it has proved incredibly hard to undo the popular false perception that Wakefield's paper was true. Certainly, one may argue that this situation could have been *worse* without peer review and that many more untruths would have made it through. However, I disagree: it is the legitimating power of peer review and its failure in this case that leads some, even now, to believe erroneously that the retraction is a cover-up and that scientific consensus is still, in reality, being suppressed. Put otherwise: even in a time before the full ascent of the digital, the markers of scarcity that were supposed to equate information or knowledge with truth were highly problematic.[24]

In the digital realm this problem is no worse than before but it is more acutely exposed. For it is not difficult to establish a website that can present a veneer of professionalism or sleek visuals atop shady social practices for the evaluation of truth. This 'abundance' of the digital space leads to a difficulty in comparing relative truth claims between outlets, even if the pre-digital markers of truth were problematic. In fact, the single largest challenge for the future of information publishing will be to find markers or frames that can accurately denote quality or truth at the level of the article or book (or other form) while still bene-fiting from the abundance of dissemination that the digital space can offer. This poses difficulties at the organizational level for publishers and paying institutions who remain orientated towards both a sales, rather than service, model (and therefore struggle with the infinite reproduction within digital modes) and a set of marketing and revenue strategies that rely upon aggregating brand, correlated to truth, upwards to the publisher level (that create overly broad frames of reference for truth evaluation).

INFORMATION AND DATA PUBLISHING

In the closing words of this chapter, I want to turn to the new formal demands that are being placed on information publishing in a time of digital abundance (even if that remains a time of labour scarcity). As digital media more closely mirror the underlying

---

[22] A. J. Wakefield et al. (1998).   [23] Fiona Godlee, Jane Smith, and Harvey Marcovitch (2011).
[24] In fact, Wakefield used the prestige of the journal to defend his fraud, specifically denigrating claims by a critic on the basis that they were 'from the Internet' A. J. Wakefield (1998).

structure of information and/or knowledge, the theorized structures of science and verification are superimposed upon publishing. The clearest examples of this yet are the phenomena of preprints, of replication studies, and of data publishing. Let us examine each of these in turn.

In scientific and information publishing, a 'preprint' is a version of an article made available before the formal publishing processes of peer-review, typesetting, copy-editing, and proofreading have been completed. There are a number of reasons why preprints have become popular in some disciplines, such as high-energy physics.

The first pertains to *priority*. Academic accreditation systems are typically structured around novelty. That is, the first person to claim an idea takes credit for a discovery. Subsequent work that repeats an already-staked claim is plagiarism. For many years, academic publishing in the natural, social, and human sciences has adhered to a so-called 'Ingelfinger Rule' that stipulates that a journal would not publish work that had previously appeared elsewhere.[25] However, with the advent of the Internet and enough commonly shared, even if proprietary, file formats, some disciplines saw the emergence of preprint servers, such as arXiv.[26] These sites are repositories where communities of scholars or researchers can share working papers and/or preprint versions of articles openly. When a preprint server has enough attention from a community of scholars, this establishes priority at the earliest possible moment, since papers in the arXiv can be cited. However, it raises thorny questions for the Ingelfinger Rule and what counts as being 'published'. As of 2016, many publishers have had to admit that preprints may be desirable to academics and to accept work that has previously appeared. Consider, for just one example, the statement of the journal *Palgrave Communications*: 'Palgrave Communications allows and encourages prior publication on recognized community preprint servers for review by other academics in the field before formal submission to a journal. The details of the preprint server concerned and any accession numbers should be included in the cover letter accompanying submission of the manuscript to Palgrave Communications.'[27]

The second reason for the uptake of preprints pertains to speed and accelerationism. In many scientific disciplines, such as biomedicine, speed may be of the essence. Indeed, people's lives may depend upon the rapid uptake and practical implementation of published information. Clearly, the processes of publishing take time and labour that decelerate this process of information circulation. For some disciplines, this loss of speed is unacceptable and preprints are billed as the answer.

Both of these changes, in priority and speed, put pressure on information publishing as it has existed until recently. For example, if a journal is the last place to formally publish work that has already seen mass circulation in the media and on preprint servers, what is its actual function? Does the journal become a repository for preservation? Or is it merely an accreditation mechanism? Could it be that the journal is actually a site of discovery; a social curation site for discoverability and filtering in a world of information

---

[25] Arnold S. Relman (1981).   [26] arXiv (2013).
[27] Palgrave Communications (2016).

overload? The answer to these questions is presently unclear but it is apparent that changing workflows of information publishing are altering the demands for speed and acceleration.

In many ways, preprints are also a challenge to the unspoken notion that a *work* and a *text* are synonymous in information-publishing circles. In an influential book from the 1980s, Jerome McGann worked against this idea in the field of textual editing, claiming that the *work* was a *social event* but that a text was but a single, fixed, media-encoded moment of the work.[28] For many years, the idea of a 'version of record' for scholarly information publishing being the only version in circulation attempted to conflate the work and the text; as though the fixity of a version could present a truth in coherence through the convergence of scientific truth, the textual representation of that truth, and the work that was identical to that text. The challenge is that, in the digital age, texts are ever-more mutable than they even were in the print era. Ideas of versioning bring a decoupling of text and work, in which a single work of information publication may have several different textual versions (a preprint, version 1, an updated version 2). The question for the evaluation of truth then, likewise, becomes much harder to ascertain. Which version should one consult? Is it always the case that the *later* textual version of an article is the more truthful? Is this some kind of temporal positivism of text for information publishing? The epistemology of print fixity and its relation to truth comes under fire in the digital age. This is not necessarily a bad thing but it does appear as a change.

The second core area of change in contemporary discourses around information publishing is concerned with replication studies and negative results. In disciplines that work on a hypothesis and experiment model, a replication study is an attempt to re-perform an experiment in order to verify that the results are consistent when following the methods described in an article. By contrast, a negative result occurs when a hypothesis is proved incorrect (for instance when someone hypothesizes that 'substance Y cures malaria' but the experiments conducted unfortunately do not show this). Both replication studies and negative results contribute to science as a process of knowledge accumulation. For instance, if a replication study can correctly show that the results of the experiment are repeatable, then trust should grow in a research article (or *vice versa*). Yet, one recent paper estimated a cumulative total prevalence of irreproducible preclinical research exceeding 50 per cent at an annual cost of $28bn.[29] On the other hand, negative results are important in many disciplines since they prevent much wasted time and effort. If, say, a second group of scientists decided that it would be a good idea to test 'substance Y' against malaria, it would be useful for them to know that a previous group had already tried this, without success.

In the era of digital information publishing, which appears abundant, there are increasing calls for the publication of these replication studies and negative results. After all, it is asked, since we can replicate material ad infinitum in the digital realm, why can we not just publish more and more, especially when such information might be helpful for

---

[28] Jerome McGann (1983).
[29] Leonard P. Freedman, Iain M. Cockburn, and Timothy S. Simcoe (2015).

science? Such an approach has both benefits, but also challenges. Clearly, the publication of replication studies and negative results would contribute positively to the cumulative process of knowledge acquisition in science. However, it would also complicate the discoverability ecosystem. As more and more replication studies are published, the reader-side act of sorting the wheat from the chaff becomes a harder task. In a limited time-economy for the reader it is not clear what systems, amid the currently disaggregated and dispersed corporate publishing model, would be required to see through the 'article' to the underlying set of replication studies and the cumulative literature review. There is also the question of where/when the value of replication studies might end. Is it helpful to publish a replication study of the boiling point of water? It could be methodologically sound and the result could be correct, but this is a fact that is known so well that a further replication study here would be of little use. Likewise, publishing a negative result of an experiment based on a hypothesis that appears ludicrous (e.g. 'water will boil at 30 degrees centigrade on the third day of each month') may add very little to our collective understanding. Perhaps the biggest challenge posed by this discourse for information publishing, though, is the spiralling labour costs of publishing ever more information, at a time when library budgets are scarcely able to afford it.[30]

The third and final area in which the digital era has expanded for information publication is linked to the second: data publishing. Before discussing this, it is worth noting that data sharing is controversial. An editorial in *The New England Journal of Medicine*, for example, recently wrote in an editorial of a concern 'that someone not involved in the generation and collection of the data may not understand the choices made in defining the parameters' or that someone might 'use another group's data for their own ends, possibly stealing from the research productivity planned by the data gatherers, or even use the data to try to disprove what the original investigators had posited', describing such work as conducted by 'research parasites'.[31] Yet, this is troubling. For, surely, to disprove claims or to find new work within an existing data set is one of the *very core* functions of science: falsifiability. Indeed, this is extremely common practice in the humanities, where the 'data' or evidence are openly available cultural artefacts, such as a work of fiction in literary studies where multiple interpretations of the 'data set' are worked upon. Indeed, in contrast to this more conservative view, posts on the *British Medical Journal* blog have gone so far as to repeat claims of proponents that 'publishing articles without making the data available is scientific malpractice' or that 'publishing research without data is simply advertising, not science'.[32] Such a call has been ongoing for over a decade now and the earliest reference that I can find is from a 1995 book in which it is stated that '[a]n article about computational science in a scientific publication is *not* the scholarship itself, it is merely *advertising* of the scholarship. The actual scholarship is the complete software development environment and the

[30] See Association of Research Libraries (2014) for the way in which library serial expenditure has spiralled out of control since the 1980s, partly as a result of the mass expansion of higher education and partly due to the domination of the information-publication space by a small number of very large corporations making profits in excess of 20%.
[31] Dan L. Longo and Jeffrey M. Drazen (2016).   [32] Claire Bower (2013); Graham Steel (2013).

complete set of instructions which generated the figures'.[33] This debate has led to many large research funders developing policies for open data and software sharing.[34]

On whichever side of this data debate one falls, it is clear that calls for data publishing have serious implications for information publishers. This is because 'data' is so vague a term as to be almost universally replaceable with the word 'stuff'. Indeed, for publishers, the call to publish data is a call to make available and to indefinitely preserve arbitrary digital objects that range in size from a few kilobytes up to tera- or exo-bytes. To 'publish' software might necessitate the creation of new software preservation systems and runtime environments that can be permanently accessed by virtual machines if we are not to encounter a digital dark age.[35] All of this requires labour, time, and expense, as well as the training of those who are 'publishing' in new technologies and methods. However, it is just another facet of the changes to information publication that we are currently seeing in the digital age.

To conclude: publishing and information have a long history together, even though the terms surrounding its practices ('data', 'information', and 'knowledge') are not well understood or defined. Even the types of publication to which we refer when we talk about 'information' are not wholly clear. Yet, the changes to information publishing in recent years as a result of the Internet and World Wide Web—which extend well beyond the trite example of Wikipedia mirroring Diderot's *Encyclopédie*—pose new challenges for verification/truth, and for the labour of publishing. For, while the digital world appears to offer a chance to synthesize the non-rivalrous nature of knowledge with its to-date rivalrous manifestations, there are still serious hurdles to be overcome in the information space for publishing businesses. It is also the case that the infinite replication of the digital space poses difficulties for an underlying epistemology of publishing that once relied on a supposed print fixity to guarantee a correlation with truth. New technologies of distributed write-once databases such as the blockchain might offer ways in which we could re-inscribe such artificial scarcity and fixity in the digital space. However, the more important question that we need to address is whether or not this is what we want in the age of the digital. It might, instead, make more sense for us to embrace the pluralism of the web and to acknowledge that the multiplicity that we now see in the digital space is, in fact, a better representation of the underlying messiness of the scientific process itself.

REFERENCES

Amidon, Debra M. (1997). *Innovation Strategy for the Knowledge Economy: The Ken Awakening*, Boston: Butterworth-Heinemann.
arXiv (2013). 'FAQ'. Available at: http://arxiv.org/help/support/faq [accessed 22 December 2013].
Association of Research Libraries (2014). 'ARL Statistics 2009–2011'. Available at: http://www.arl.org/storage/documents/expenditure-trends.pdf [accessed 1 July 2014].

---

[33] Jonathan B. Buckheit and David L. Donoho (1995: 55–81). With thanks to Cameron Neylon and Todd Vision for helping me to find this reference.

[34] For instance, Research Councils UK (2016).   [35] Terry Kuny (1998).

Benjamin, Walter (1999). 'The Work of Art in the Age of Mechanical Reproduction', in *Illuminations*, Pimlico, 332, Pimlico ed London: Pimlico, pp. 211–44.

Bhaskar, Michael (2013). *The Content Machine: Towards a Theory of Publishing From the Printing Press to the Digital Network*, New York: Anthem Press.

Bower, Claire (2013). 'Publishing Articles without Making the Data Available Is Scientific Malpractice', *BMJ Blogs*. Available at: http://blogs.bmj.com/bmj-journals-development-blog/2013/05/24/publishing-articles-without-making-the-data-available-is-scientific-malpractice/ [accessed 13 November 2016].

Buckheit, Jonathan B. and David L. Donoho (1995). 'Wavelab and Reproducible Research', in *Wavelets and Statistics*. Edited by Anestis Antoniadis and George Oppenheim Dordrecht: Springer, pp. 55–81. Available at: http://link.springer.com/10.1007/978-1-4612-2544-7_5 [Accessed 14 November 2016].

Carrigan, Mark (2016). 'Like Air, Ideas Are Incapable of Being Locked up and Hoarded', *Mark Carrigan*. Available at: http://markcarrigan.net/2016/04/06/like-air-ideas-are-incapable-of-being-locked-up-and-hoarded/ [Accessed 6 April 2016].

Collison, Robert Lewis (1964). *Encyclopaedias: Their History throughout the Ages; a Bibliographical Guide with Extensive Historical Notes to the General Encyclopaedias Issued throughout the World from 350 B.C. to the Present Day*, Royal Oak, MI: Hafner.

Dakers, Marion (2015). 'Controversial VAT Change Means E-Books Are about to Get More Expensive', *The Telegraph*. Available at: http://www.telegraph.co.uk/finance/businessclub/11320318/Controversial-VAT-change-means-e-books-are-about-to-get-more-expensive.html [Accessed 10 November 2016].

Darnton, Robert (1987). *The Business of Enlightenment: A Publishing History of the Encyclopédie, 1775–1800*, Cambridge, MA: Harvard University Press.

Davenport, Thomas H. and Laurence Prusak (2010). *Working Knowledge: How Organizations Manage What They Know*,(Boston, MA: Harvard Business School Press.

Dixon, Nancy M. (2000). *Common Knowledge: How Companies Thrive by Sharing What They Know*, Boston, MA: Harvard Business School Press.

Eve, Martin Paul (2014). *Open Access and the Humanities: Contexts, Controversies and the Future*, Cambridge: Cambridge University Press. Available at: http://dx.doi.org/10.1017/CBO9781316161012

Eve, Martin Paul (2017). 'Scarcity and Abundance', in *The Bloomsbury Handbook of Electronic Literature*. Edited by Joseph Tabbi, London: Bloomsbury.

Freedman, Leonard P., Iain M. Cockburn, and Timothy S. Simcoe (2015). 'The Economics of Reproducibility in Preclinical Research', *PLOS Biology*, 13, p. e1002165. Available at: https://doi.org/10.1371/journal.pbio.1002165

Garvin, Andrew P. and Robert I. Berkman (1996). *The Art of Being Well Informed*, Garden City Park, NY: Avery Pub. Group.

Gitelman, Lisa, ed. (2013). *'Raw Data' Is an Oxymoron*, Infrastructures Series, Cambridge, MA: The MIT Press.

Godlee, Fiona, Jane Smith, and Harvey Marcovitch (2011). 'Wakefield's Article Linking MMR Vaccine and Autism Was Fraudulent', *British Medical Journal*, 342, p. c7452. Available at: https://doi.org/10.1136/bmj.c7452

Hayles, N. Katherine (2012). *How We Think: Digital Media and Contemporary Technogenesis*, Chicago: University of Chicago Press.

Horibe, Frances (1999). *Managing Knowledge Workers: New Skills and Attitudes to Unlock the Intellectual Capital in Your Organization*, Toronto: J. Wiley.

Jefferson, Thomas (1853). *The Writings of Thomas Jefferson*, ed. by H. A. Washington, Washington, DC: The United States Congress, VI.

Johns, Adrian (2011). *Piracy: The Intellectual Property Wars from Gutenberg to Gates*, Chicago: University Of Chicago Press.

Kelley, Juris (2002). *Knowledge Nirvana*, Fairfax, VA: Xulon Press.

Kuny, Terry (1998). 'The Digital Dark Ages? Challenges in the Preservation of Electronic Information', *International Preservation News*, 17, pp. 8–13.

Liew, Anthony (2007). 'Understanding Data, Information, Knowledge And Their Inter-Relationships', *Journal of Knowledge Management Practice*, 8. Available at: http://www.tlainc.com/articl134.htm [Accessed 5 November 2016].

Longo, Dan L. and Jeffrey M. Drazen (2016). 'Data Sharing', *New England Journal of Medicine*, 374, pp. 276–77. Available at: https://doi.org/10.1056/NEJMe1516564

McGann, Jerome (1983). *A Critique of Modern Textual Criticism*, Charlottesville, VA: University of Virginia Press.

Marx, Karl (1992). *Capital*, London: Penguin, I.

Moore, Samuel, Cameron Neylon, Martin Paul Eve, Daniel O'Donnell, and Damian Pattinson (2017). 'Excellence R Us: University Research and the Fetishisation of Excellence', *Palgrave Communications*, 3. Available at: https://doi.org/10.1057/palcomms.2016.105

Nonaka, Ikujirō and Hirotaka Takeuchi (1995). *The Knowledge-Creating Company: How Japanese Companies Create the Dynamics of Innovation*, New York: Oxford University Press.

Palgrave Communications (2016). 'Editorial and Publishing Policies'. Available at: http://www.palgrave-journals.com/palcomms/about/editorial-policies [Accessed 12 November 2016].

Relman, Arnold S. (1981). 'The Ingelfinger Rule', *New England Journal of Medicine*, 305, pp. 824–26. Available at: https://doi.org/10.1056/NEJM198110013051408

Research Councils UK (2016). 'Concordat on Open Research Data Launched', *RCUK*. Available at: http://www.rcuk.ac.uk/media/news/160728/ [Accessed 13 November 2016].

Somers, James (2017). 'Torching the Modern-Day Library of Alexandria', *The Atlantic*, 20 April. Available at: https://www.theatlantic.com/technology/archive/2017/04/the-tragedy-of-google-books/523320/ [Accessed 9 July 2017].

Steel, Graham (2013). 'Publishing Research without Data Is Simply Advertising, Not Science', *Open Knowledge International Blog*. Available at: http://blog.okfn.org/2013/09/03/publishing-research-without-data-is-simply-advertising-not-science/ [Accessed 13 November 2016].

Stenmark, Dick (2001). 'The Relationship between Information and Knowledge', *Proceedings of IRIS 24*, pp. 11–14. Available at: http://citeseerx.ist.psu.edu/viewdoc/summary?doi=10.1.1.21.965

Suber, Peter (2012). *Open Access*, Essential Knowledge Series, Cambridge, MA: MIT Press. Available at: http://bit.ly/oa-book

Swartz, Aaron (2015). 'Jefferson: Nature Wants Information to Be Free', in *The Boy Who Could Change the World*, London: Verso, pp. 23–25.

Sydänmaanlakka, Pentti (2002). *An Intelligent Organization: Integrating Performance, Competence and Knowledge Management*, Oxford: Capstone.

Thompson, John B. (2005). *Books in the Digital Age: The Transformation of Academic and Higher Education Publishing in Britain and the United States*, Cambridge: Polity Press.

Tiwana, Amrit (2001). *The Essential Guide to Knowledge Management: E-Business and CRM Applications*, Essential Guide Series, Upper Saddle River, NJ: Prentice Hall PTR.

Von Krogh, George, Kazuo Ichijō, and Ikujirō Nonaka (2000). *Enabling Knowledge Creation: How to Unlock the Mystery of Tacit Knowledge and Release the Power of Innovation*, Oxford: Oxford University Press.

Wakefield, A. J. (1998). 'Autism, Inflammatory Bowel Disease, and MMR Vaccine', *The Lancet*, 351, p. 1356. Available at: https://doi.org/10.1016/S0140-6736(05)79083-8

Wakefield, A. J., S. H. Murch, A. Anthony, J. Linnell, D. M. Casson, M. Malik, and others (1998). 'RETRACTED: Ileal-Lymphoid-Nodular Hyperplasia, Non-Specific Colitis, and Pervasive Developmental Disorder in Children', *The Lancet*, 351, pp. 637–41. Available at: https://doi.org/10.1016/S0140-6736(97)11096-0

....

CHAPTER 9

NETWORKS

*From Text to Hypertext, from Publishing
to Sharing, from Single Author
to Collaborative Production*

....

CARLOS A. SCOLARI

WRITING about media and technology is not easy. Any discourse on 'new' media or technological issues that does not go beyond the analysis of the latest available product to grasp the more *strategic* or *organic* meanings (as proposed by Antonio Gramsci) of the problem, runs the risk of becoming outdated in a few weeks.

How can we deal with such a fast, deep transformation of the media ecosystem? This text starts with a bird's eye view of the main transformations of the media ecology since the emergence and spread of digital networks in the early 1970s. The second section analyses the most important 'commodity'—at least for publishers—that flows through the digital networks: the texts. In the last section the analysis focuses on the changes in the processes of production, distribution, and consumption of contents. The section deals with phenomena such as collaborative production, user-generated contents, filtering processes, and the emergence of a new figure: the *hyperreader*.

THE RISE OF THE NETWORKS

From Arpanet to the World Wide Web (and beyond)

After a trial period, Arpanet, the first computer network funded by the state agency ARPA (Advanced Research Projects Agency) based on the transmission of data packets, was officially launched in 1972 during the sessions of the International Conference on Computer Communication (ICCC). It was originally designed for remote computing and, from a military perspective, as an intercommunication tool in case of nuclear war.

However, in these first years of digital life, rather than using the network to solve complicated mathematical problems taking advantage of the computing power of a computer located on the other side of the country, many researchers used Arpanet to exchange personal messages and simple videogames. Arpanet was used for sharing propaganda against the Vietnam War, information about the Watergate affair and the first copies of Adventure, a digital version of *Dungeons and Dragons* created by Bill Crowther and perfected by computer science students (Hafner and Lyon 1998; Berners-Lee 2000).

In the early 1970s similar networks spread in Europe, especially in Italy, the UK, Norway, and Germany. Researchers began to think about interconnecting these networks, that is, creating a 'network of networks' or 'inter-network' ('inter-net'). There were, of course, many problems to solve, from defining the protocols so that all these systems could talk to each other (thus TCP-IP/Transmission Control Protocol—Internet Protocol was born) to creating gateways capable of directing and distributing the data packets. Between 1973 and 1975 the network grew at a rate of knots; in 1978 the TCP/IP was finally defined and adopted and is still used today as the standard for Internet connections.

As almost everyone knows, the World Wide Web was created by a group of researchers in the late 1980s. In 1990, Berners-Lee and other members of CERN (Geneva), excited about the possibilities offered by graphical interfaces, and developed the first version of a software to browse digital networks. The program, which used the object-oriented technology and the Hypertext Transfer Protocol (HTTP) for client–server communication, allowed editing and WYSIWYG (what you see is what you get) viewing of information. One year later the technology was transferred to other platforms and disseminated to various research centres, where programmers worked on these protocols to improve their performance.

In 1993 a group from the University of Illinois introduced the alpha version of Mosaic, a browser with a graphical interface that spread rapidly among Internet users. Shortly after, the group left the university to set up the company Netscape, which, against all business logic, distributed a free program to navigate in the new digital network. From this moment on the conflictive emergence of new browsers (Internet Explorer, Firefox, Safari, Opera, Chrome, etc.), the accelerated evolution of web page contents (animated GIF images, high compression formats and quality like JPG or PNG, videos, animations, etc.) and the incorporation of multimedia and interactive features (Shockwave, Java, Flash, new versions of HTML, etc.) have never stopped. The first pages were simple containers of static information, but with the advent of new browsers the situation decisively changed: the World Wide Web transformed itself into a *metamedium*, a mega-niche inside the media ecology that generates a never-ending series of new media and communication platforms.

From the World Wide Web to Social Networks

In the early 2000s many researchers and professionals detected a series of transformations in the World Wide Web. The spread of new collaborative platforms like

Wikipedia, new sharing tools like BitTorrent or Napster, and a new communication logic based on participation rather than just the publication of information, was forming a new paradigm. The 'new' web was called *Web 2.0* (O'Reilly 2005).

The rise of the new collaborative web evidenced the limits of the initial web of the 1990s: even if it was based on a network infrastructure, the conceptions and uses were still those of traditional broadcasting (one-to-many communication). In the specific field of media and communication, the Web 2.0 expressed a new many-to-many communication paradigm. New phenomena like the advent of narrow niches of all kinds of products along the 'long tail' (Anderson 2006), the explosion of big data research and services (Mayer-Schonberger and Cukier 2013), the emergence of a collective intelligence (Lévy 1997) based on participatory cultures (Jenkins et al. 2016) and the crisis of traditional legal systems like copyright (Lessig 1999) are some of the emerging traits of this paradigmatic passing from broadcasting to networking.

The logic of the Web 2.0 reached its highest expression with the emergence of social networking platforms: Linkedin, MySpace (2003), Facebook, Flickr (2004), Twitter, GoodReads, Wattpad (2006), Tumblr (2007), Academia.edu (2008), Foursquare (2009), Instagram (2010), and Pinterest (2011). There are several types of social networking platforms: social network sites that promote interpersonal contact; user-generated content media that support creativity and promote the exchange of contents; trading and marketing sites like Amazon or eBay; and finally, play and game sites, ludic environments designed for gaming, like FarmVille, Angry Birds, or PokemonGo.

How has the evolution of social networking platforms affected textual content? According to Jose van Dijck

> It is instructive to recall the early promise that Web 2.0 platforms would liberate content. The production of music, films, videos, art, and texts would no longer be limited to professionals, as the tools for creative production would be yielded to amateurs and citizens. . . . However, over the past decade, users and platform owners have appreciated the value of online content differently. Whereas the first regarded it as something to be created and shared, the latter increasingly defined it as something to be managed and exploited. Whereas users cared mostly about the *quality* and form of content, platform owners were preoccupied by data *quantities* and traffic volume.   (van Dijck 2013: 161–2)

The evolution of the media ecology is always under construction. As van Dijck put it, social media platforms, rather than being finished products, are 'dynamic objects that are tweaked in response to their users' needs and their owners' objectives, but also in reaction to competing platforms and the larger technological and economic infrastructure through which they develop' (van Dijck 2013: 7).

Power and Conflict in the New Media Ecology

Throughout this section there has been constant mention of the (new) 'media ecology'. The research into the emergence of the World Wide Web included an element that was not present when former 'new media' like cinema or radio were born: an ecological vision of the media system. Traditionally, cinema, radio, and even television were studied as a single medium and not as a part of a complex ecology of communication. Marshall McLuhan's often polemical but always pertinent contributions have led to media research taking on a more integrated and ecological view of the communication system:

> A new medium is never an addition to an old one, nor does it leave the old one in peace. It never ceases to oppress the older media until it finds new shapes and positions for them.   (McLuhan 1964: 278)

In a few words: it is almost impossible to continue analysing a single medium (cinema, radio, television, press, the Internet, etc.) isolated from the rest of the media ecosystem; media research needs to abandon single-media approaches and adopt an ecological vision of the media system, paying particular attention to inter-media relationships. In the same context, it is almost impossible to continue talking about 'new media'. Is television a 'new media'? It used to be a new media in the 1950s. The same may be said for radio in the 1920s or cinema at the beginning of the twentieth century. In other words: all media were once new media (Gitelman and Pingree 2003; Gitelman 2006; Zielinski 2006). Typewriters, optical telegraphs, vinyl record albums, eight-track tapes, and walkmans are (today) old media, but 'they were not always old, and studying them in terms that allow us to understand what it meant for them to be new is a timely and culturally important task' (Gitelman and Pingree 2003: xi). Therefore, 'new media' is a relative concept: in twenty or thirty years time blogs, eBooks, and online journals will be considered 'old media'.

If we want to understand the transformations that publishing has undergone since the emergence of digital networks, we must start from the changes of the whole media ecology. Since the diffusion of personal computing in the 1980s and the expansion of the web in the 1990s, digital technology has been a catalyst for social change in contemporary societies. From economy to politics, from education to culture, practically all aspects of human life have been transformed due to the different ways of developing and using ICT. As we have seen, the media ecology is undergoing a metamorphosis from the traditional broadcasting system to the networking paradigm, where the old 'media species' (radio, cinema, television, books, etc.) must compete with the new ones (YouTube, Twitter, Facebook, PokemonGo, etc.) and adapt in order to survive (Scolari 2012, 2013).

A couple of final reflections on networks, power, and hegemony. The networks are not a paradise of democracy and transparency as some utopians thought they would be in the early 1990s: corporate media, grassroots activists, social movements, and hundreds of social actors have found in the networks a new battleground for confrontation. In the networks we live, learn, share, discuss, and dispute power at different levels. According to Manuel Castells, one of the most lucid analysts of these metamorphoses,

> the structures of power are rooted in the structure of society. However, these power structures are reproduced and challenged by cultural battles that are fought to a

large extent in the communication realm. And it is plausible to think that the capacity of social actors to set up autonomously their political agenda is greater in the networks of mass self-communication than in the corporate world of the mass media.   (Castells 2007: 257)

Three of the most critical issues regarding networks are the increasing loss of privacy, the extensive exploitation of personal data by a small group of companies and the creation of algorithm-based filter bubbles around subjects. In 2011 Eli Pariser warned: 'the digital world is fundamentally changing. What was once an anonymous medium where anyone could be anyone … is now a tool for soliciting and analysing our personal data' (2011: 6). Pariser introduced the concept of *filter bubble* to describe the new situation:

> The new generation of Internet filters look at the things you seem to like—the actual things you've done, or the people you like—and tries to extrapolate. They are prediction engines, constantly creating and refining a theory of who you are and what you'll do and want next. Together, these engines create a unique universe of information for each one of us … which fundamentally alters the way we encounter ideas and information.   (Pariser 2011: 9)

The bubble reduces serendipity; it creates a comfortable niche where we grow up and interact with people, watch videos, and read books already selected (or at least recommended) by a digital engine. According to Pariser the bubble is invisible and we are alone in it; and neither do we choose to get in it. Is the filter bubble an upgraded and sophisticated version of Foucault's panopticon?

The transformation process we have been describing in this section is less than 10,000 days old. In the context of the long-term evolution of Homo sapiens, that is almost the last nanosecond of a human life. The big transformation and its conflicts have just begun.

The New Textualities

In this section we will analyse the emergence of new textual structures and narratives as a consequence of the spread of digital networks in the media ecology. Digital textualities made of millions of binary units of minimal information are especially suited to network circulation: they flow like liquid, they are easy to modify and share, and they adapt to different interactive devices, from smartphones to tablets, personal computers, and digital television screens. Digitalization processes have also introduced other changes into traditional media contents: hypertextuality, multimediality, and interactivity seem to be the basic features of this transformation. Their origins can be condensed into a single concept: hypertext.

Every field of knowledge has its founding fathers, the apostles, and their mythical characters. In the 1930s a new utopia took shape in the imagination of some scientists operating in the field of information retrieval: How can we manage huge amounts of scientific data? What began in the immediate post-war period as a utopia, led to the project of building a vast digital network to interconnect all documents produced by our culture.

The Founding Father: Vannevar Bush

The problem of managing a large mass of data is not recent:

> Complaints about information overload, usually couched in terms of the overabundance of books, have a long history—reaching back to Ecclesiastes 12:12 ('of making books there is no end', probably from the 4th or 3rd century BC). The ancient moralist Seneca complained that 'the abundance of books is a distraction' in the 1st century AD, and there have been other info-booms from time to time—the building of the Library of Alexandria in the 3rd century BC, or the development of newspapers starting in the 18th century.   (Blair 2010)

Despite these warnings the number of texts has continued to increase at a relentless pace. The introduction of the mechanical reproduction of images and sound in the nineteenth century, and the arrival of electronic supports in the twentieth century, contributed to the growth of textual production.

But this textual abundance did not only come from the cultural industry: the mass of scientific texts also grew incessantly, creating imbalances in the production, distribution, and consumption of specialized knowledge. The management of these text masses of scientific information particularly concerned Vannevar Bush, an American engineer who in the 1930s had worked in the design of a Rapid Selector of information for the US Navy. For Bush it was perfectly clear that textual production expanded at a greater rate than people's ability to understand and control it. How can information be selected? Is it possible to mechanize this process?

In *As We May Think* (1945) Bush analysed the main forms of organization and selection of information: linear and hierarchical. However, for Bush

> The human mind does not work that way. It operates by association. With one item in its grasp, it snaps instantly to the next that is suggested by the association of thoughts, in accordance with some intricate web of trails carried by the cells of the brain. It has other characteristics, of course; trails that are not frequently followed are prone to fade, items are not fully permanent, memory is transitory. Yet the speed of action, the intricacy of trails, the detail of mental pictures, is awe-inspiring beyond all else in nature. Even if we cannot hope fully to duplicate this mental process artificially.... Selection by association, rather than indexing, may yet be mechanised.   (Bush 1945)

To mechanize this associative mental process was Bush's objective. In that classic article published by *The Atlantic Monthly* in 1945 he described an imaginary machine—the

Memex (Memory + Extension)—a sort of mechanized private file and library that stored books, records, and communications, which could be consulted with exceeding speed and flexibility. The main feature of the Memex was the creation of personal links and trails between documents that any other user could navigate later: 'Wholly new forms of encyclopedias will appear, ready made with a mesh of associative trails running through them, ready to be dropped into the Memex and there amplified' (Bush 1945). The idea of a flexible and open textual network, crossed by links and navigation trails, was born.

The Myth: Douglas Engelbart

On 24 May 1962, the engineer Douglas Engelbart wrote to Vannevar Bush and asked him for permission to quote a few paragraphs from his article on the Memex. Working in the Stanford Research Institute, Engelbart was developing one of the first digital systems of collective production (groupware). The Augment project, which allowed a group of workers to share information within a network of computers, constituted a fundamental stage in the evolution of digital networks.

The aim of Engelbart's research programme was to significantly increase the effectiveness of human problem solvers and develop new techniques, procedures, and systems to support this change. According to Engelbart, Bush's trails 'provide a beautiful example of a new capability in symbol structuring that derives from new artefact-process capability, and that provides new ways to develop and portray concept structures' (Engelbart 1962). The philosophy that animated this research was summarized three decades later by the cyberphilosopher Pierre Lévy with these words: 'different concatenations of media, intellectual technologies, languages and working methods available at a particular time, mainly determine the mode of thinking and working in groups of a society' (1992: 61). According to Lévy, people like Engelbart are 'politicians of a special type' distinguished by working on the 'molecular scale interfaces', an area where the passages between different systems are organized, representations are retranslated, and the sense of human–device relationships is constructed. Douglas Engelbart foreshadowed in the 1960s a world of direct access to information and a new way of working in groups. Today, we live in that world.

The Apostle: Ted Nelson

In 1965 Nelson published 'A File Structure for the Complex, the Changing, and the Indeterminant', an article where he introduced for the first time the concept of *hypertext*:

> Let me introduce the word 'hypertext' to mean a body of written or pictorial material interconnected in such a complex way that it could not conveniently be presented or represented on paper.   (Nelson 1965)

In 1974 he expanded the concept to *hypermedia*:

> Hypermedia are branching or performing presentations which respond to user actions, systems of prearranged words and pictures, for example, which may be explored freely or queried in stylised ways.... Like ordinary prose and pictures, they will be media; and because they are in some sense 'multidimensional', we may call them hypermedia, following the mathematical use of the term 'hyper'.   (Nelson 1974)

Nelson's main initiative, the Xanadu system—a digital platform to store, link, and navigate through an open network of interconnected documents—integrated in a single environment the utopian vision of Vannevar Bush and the cognitive dimension of Douglas Engelbart's Augment Project. In a poster presented in 1987 Nelson described the Xanadu storage system as

> A new form of software with potentially revolutionary implications... for personal computing, word processing, file management, the office of the future and its software, teleconferencing, electronic mail, electronic publishing, libraries of the future, and tomorrow's education. He saw it as offering 'a plan for a world wide network, intended to generate hundreds of millions of users simultaneously for the corpus of the world's stored writings, graphics and data.... It is a design for a new literature, a system of order to make such a network understandable, usable, and readily expansible to any degree.... The Xanadu system provides a universal data structure to which all other data structures will be mapped'.   (cited by Boyd Rayward 1994)

Nelson's conception was a source of inspiration for a couple of generations of programmers, visionaries, writers, and literature scholars. Thanks to his ideas and the diffusion of software such as HyperCard, hypertext fiction became popular in the late 1980s. According to Daniel M. Russell, a veteran researcher at Google,

> Hypertext is a large and hugely successful idea. Such ground cracking ideas always have many fathers. But everyone recognises that Nelson's book provided a huge amount of the vision and evangelism to motivate the masses. At the time, nobody was writing about hypertext with the depth and clarity of *Computer Lib/Dream Machines*.   (Russell 2008: 16)

Also around that time, in March 1989, Tim Berners-Lee submitted a proposal for an information management system to his boss, Mike Sendall. 'Vague, but exciting', were the words that Sendall wrote on the proposal, allowing Berners-Lee to continue. In *Information Management: A proposal* Berners-Lee (1989) explained the following:

> Most systems available today use a single database. This is accessed by many users by using a distributed file system. There are few products which take Ted Nelson's idea of a wide 'docuverse' literally by allowing links between nodes in different databases. In order to do this, some standardisation would be necessary. However, at the standardisation workshop, the emphasis was on standardisation of the format

for exchangeable media, nor for networking. This is prompted by the strong push toward publishing of hypermedia information, for example on optical disk. There seems to be a general consensus about the abstract data model which a hypertext system should use.   (Berners-Lee 1989)

The standardization proposed by Tim Berners-Lee included an application protocol for distributed, collaborative, hypermedia information systems (Hypertext Transfer Protocol/HTTP), a language to create 'web pages' (HyperText Markup Language/HTML), and a Uniform Resource Locator (URL) for identifying each 'web address'. A particular experience—to create links and to navigate in a textual network following trails—imagined in the 1940s and first developed in the 1960s in the labs of California, was finally available for millions of users with no specific knowledge of programming or computer science.

New Textual Species

The World Wide Web did not only generate new 'media species': new 'textual species' were also created inside this environment. If we focus on the new interactive and collaborative textualities, the development of new formats has run parallel to the expansion of digital networks since the 1970s. In 1975 *Colossal Cave Adventure* was created, the first widely used adventure game for computers. Three years later a student from Essex University developed a multi-user adventure game called MUD (Multi-User Dungeon). MUDs were one of the favourite hobbies on US and UK campuses in the 1980s and early 1990s. These online text-based role-playing games attracted the interest of researchers like Sherry Turkle (2004), who detected the complexity behind these interactive environments:

> For many, computer programming is experienced as creating a world apart. Some create worlds that are highly predictable and use their experiences in them to develop a sense of themselves as capable of exerting firm control. Others have different needs, different desires, and create worlds whose complexity is always on the verge of getting out of hand, worlds where they can feel themselves to be wizards of brinkmanship.   (Turkle 2004: 21)

In the late 1970s, with the production of games like *Adventureland* or the *Zork* saga, interactive fiction entered a commercial era that would last until the 1990s. All of these text-based role-playing games were progressively substituted by immersive videogames that exploit the possibilities of 3D high-resolution environments and real-time interaction with other players.

Any map of the new textual species born in the digital environment should include a reference to hypertextual fiction. Works like *Afternoon, A story* by Michael Joyce (1990) have been objects of theoretical reflection for over twenty years and have entered the canon of digital literature. Although hyperfiction is not as popular as videogames or mobile apps, it is a very active field and generates a seamless flow of new creations every year. At the same time, many novels, like Mark Z. Danielewski's *House of Leaves* (2000), have been greatly influenced by hypertextual fiction. What was born in literature (Cortazar's *Hopscotch*) stays in literature (Danielewski's *House of Leaves*).

Many of the new textual species that emerge from the new media ecology share a common trait: they have very short, ephemeral contents perfectly adapted to the digital networks where they are born, reproduce, and circulate. Tweets, trailers, recaps, sneak peeks, micro fiction, information capsules, breaking news, webisodes, mobisodes, and other expressions are born of the *snack culture* (Miller 2007). As representative data to exemplify the idea: the duration of the average online content video in 2014 was 4.7 minutes, while the average online video ad was 0.4 minutes (comScore 2014).

Nancy Miller, in her *Minifesto for a New Age* published by *Wired* magazine, focused on these short media formats:

> Music, television, games, movies, fashion: We now devour our pop culture the same way we enjoy candy and chips—in conveniently packaged bite-size nuggets made to be munched easily with increased frequency and maximum speed. This is snack culture—and boy, is it tasty (not to mention addictive).   (Miller 2007)

In recent years *microfiction* (also known as *flash fiction*) has flourished, and not only in English (beyond societies with a centennial tradition in very short stories like China and Japan, the activity in this field in Spanish-speaking countries is remarkable). The spread of the World Wide Web in the 1990s and social networking platforms in the next decade enhanced an awareness of flash fiction, inspired the creation of new stories and online publications (like *SmokeLong Quarterly*, *wigleaf*, *NANO Fiction*, *Flash Fiction Online*, and *Flash Fiction Magazine*) and promoted research (the scientific journal *Short Fiction in Theory and Practice* was launched in 2011).

As can be seen, the new textual formats and narrative structures that emerged from the digital networks have a strong relationship with literary expressions in traditional supports. All texts, digital or analogue, and all narrative structures, linear or hypertextual, coexist in the same environment and are subject to the laws of remediation, translation, and hybridization.

New Actors and Processes

In this section we will see the transformation of old media actors, the emergence of new ones, and the changes of relationships and processes in the specific area of publishing as a consequence of the transformations in the media ecology. Just to order the description, we will start with the changes in the production process, continue with the transformations of distribution and then conclude with the new reading practices.

Content Production in the New Media Ecology

Digital networks have transformed the way textual contents are created. This change includes the spreading of innovative production logics and the appearance of new professional routines and profiles. We will focus in particular on the main transform-ations in these two fields.

The World Wide Web spread new forms of collaborative writing, a practice that expanded with the arrival of the Web 2.0 in the early 2000s. Obviously, Wikipedia is the most visible and important initiative of collective writing of the new century. The statis-tics are impressive (January, 2019): the English Wikipedia includes more than 5.7 million articles and has involved more than 35 million users since it was launched on 15 January 2001; more than 122,000 users can be considered active users (that is, registered users who have performed an action in the last 30 days). The whole Wikipedia is available in 301 languages, mobilizes more than 79 million users (290,000 active) and includes more than 49 million articles (Wikipedia:Statistics). Nevertheless, in the last two decades there have been many experiences of collective writing in different countries at the crossroads of literature and digital networks; these kinds of projects increased with the spread of social media such as Twitter (for example the experimental interactive novel *Twovel* started by Neil Gaiman in 2009 and continued by users).

Any map of the transformations of textual production should include an area dedicated to fanfiction and user-generated content. Even if fanfiction is as old as mass culture, the arrival of the World Wide Web and the spread of social networking platforms took user-generated content to a new dimension. Now any fan can be a content creator and share any kind of production at a global level. In Fanfiction.net alone there are more than 800,000 stories about Harry Potter written by fans around the world (January, 2019). For Shirky, user-generated content is not just the output of ordinary people with access to creative tools such as word processors and drawing programs: it 'requires access to-*re*-creative tools as well, tools like Flickr and Wikipedia and weblogs that provide those same people with the ability to distribute their creations to others' (Shirky 2008: 83).

According to Henry Jenkins (2003, 2006a, 2006b), transmedia storytelling is a practice that emerges from the convergence of the media industry and collaborative cultures. Transmedia stories 'are stories told across multiple media. At the present time, the most significant stories tend to flow across multiple media platforms' (Jenkins et al. 2009: 86). User-generated contents are a basic component of any transmedia narrative world. Blogs, social media, wikis, and fanfiction platforms should be considered open-source story-creation machines that allow users to enrich a narrative world.

Beyond the emergence of collaborative forms of creative production, digital networks also promote new forms of editing. Phenomena like collaborative translations or comic scanlations are part of the same open and participatory process. In many non-English speaking countries the fans of Harry Potter did not have to wait for the publication of the official translations into their mother tongue: the network of fans in Germany, France, Venezuela, Sri Lanka, and China translated the text in a few hours through online translation processes. All of these translations were considered a violation of copyright and the translators were persecuted and in many cases arrested.

Comic scanlation is a more complex process that involves many steps and a highly organized collaborative structure. Scanlation (scan + translation) is the scanning, translation, and editing of comics by fans from one language into another language. The process goes far beyond the simple translation, for example, the lettering of the new text reproduces the style of the original text. In the USA the term *scanlation* refers to the translation of Japanese manga into English, but in other countries such as Brazil it is used for the translation of American superhero comics into Portuguese (Lee 2009, 2011; Silva 2014). It is not easy to delimit the scanlation practices. As Manovich, Douglass, and Huber put it

> The creative activity of scanlation groups is neither 'authorship' nor 'remix.' It also cannot be adequately described using a well-known distinction by Michel de Certeau between 'strategies' and 'tactics' (because in contrast to the unconscious tactics described by de Certeau, scanlation groups add new pages to manga series they publish quite consciously.) Similarly, scanlations are neither 'remediations' (Jay David Bolter and Richard Grusin) nor 'transmedia' (Henry Jenkins). In short, we currently lack proper terms to describe them—and this is already an important reason why we should study them.   (Manovich et al. 2011: 193)

All of these collective writing practices should be placed under the wide umbrella of the open-source movement and participatory cultures. For Steven Weber, the open source is an 'experiment in building a political economy—that is, a system of sustainable value creation and a set of governance mechanisms' (2004: 1) based on the right to distribute a product freely. These experiences challenge 'some conventional theories about the organisation of production, and how it affects and is affected by society' (2004: 8). Many digital journalists, bloggers, and free information partisans have adopted this philosophy and adapted it to digital content (Gillmor 2004). As the old world dies (or, at least, as it changes deeply), and the new world struggles to be born, tensions and conflicts emerge and challenge its main actors. For example, many of these new 'experiments' are situated on the borderline or directly outside the legal system; new forms of protection of rights beyond traditional copyright (like the Creative Commons licences) try to set new rules for these innovative and valuable creation practices.

Regarding participatory cultures, according to Jenkins and collaborators

> A participatory culture is a culture with relatively low barriers to artistic expression and civic engagement, strong support for creating and sharing creations, and some type of informal mentorship whereby experienced participants pass along knowledge to novices. In a participatory culture, members also believe their contributions matter and feel some degree of social connection with one another (at the least, members care about others' opinions of what they have created).
>
> (Jenkins et al. 2009: xi)

Weblogs, social networking platforms like Wattpad, or web portals like Fanfiction.net are based on the free distribution of textual contents. Wiki technology, in this context, empowers user modification and the sharing of digital texts. This combination of open-source philosophy and many-to-many distribution is one of the most important challenges for the established publishing production logic.

A new production logic needs a new workforce and productive routines. Publishing was one of the first professional fields hit by the digital wave in the early 1980s. Desktop Publishing (DTP) radically changed the production process of printed publications, a revolution that later expanded to photography, music, and video production in the 1990s. New professional profiles and actors emerged in a couple of decades, from inter-action designers to web content managers, online marketing experts, and vbloggers. In the specific field of textual content production, traditional profiles like the archivist have become almost extinct as they are replaced by digital content management systems. Figures like the bookseller or the production manager have been forced to redefine their skills and adapt to the new conditions of the media ecology.

Now that we have described the new production logic, it is time to talk about the distribution of these textual contents.

Content Distribution in the New Media Ecology

The transformations of text distribution as a consequence of the changes in the media ecology include practices like digital print on demand, online publication, open reposi-tories, Creative Commons licences, etc. In this section we will focus on just one of these: the inversion of the traditional professional publication logic in the context of the increasing spread of disintermediation and re-intermediation processes. In the new media ecology, content is published and distributed based on a single law: *first publish, then filter*. According to Clay Shirky

> The media landscape is transformed because personal communication and publish-ing, previously separate functions, now shade into one another. One result is to break the older pattern of professional filtering of the good from the mediocre before publication; now such filtering is increasingly social, and happens after the fact.
>
> (Shirky 2008: 81)

This inversion of the publishing–filtering sequence is a consequence of the emergence of digital networks and the explosion of digital contents. The old system—first filter, then publish—rested on the scarcity of media content. In the old media ecology, the textual production was in the hands of professionals (authors, editors, artists, illustrators, musicians) and filtering was supported by social institutions (newspapers, publishers, radio and television stations, etc.). The multiplication of digital content thanks to user-generated production and the emergence of the long tail of little niches has made that scarcity part of the past. The expansion of social networking platforms 'means that the only working system is publish-then-filter' and, in the same movement, we have 'lost the clean distinctions between communications media and broadcast media' (Shirky 2008: 98).

These changes in textual distribution may be framed into the transformations of traditional intermediation processes. What is disintermediation? In short, it can be defined as 'cutting out the middleman' in the production/distribution/consumption chain. Traditional professions like real estate agents, publishers, and journalists, as well as service providers in areas like travel agencies and video rental, have already faced this dilemma (Scolari et al. 2013). In the 1990s the potential of the World Wide Web as a revolutionary distribution channel was evident for most professionals. The Web potentially offered providers the opportunity to participate in a market in which distribution costs or cost-of-sales shrank to zero, especially in certain sectors like publishing, information services, and digital product categories. Introducing the appropriate information technology allowed the manufacturer to leap over all intermediaries and reduce the cost of the entire process (Hoffman et al. 1995). According to Sarkar et al. (1995), reducing costs and internalizing activities are the main arguments for cutting out intermediaries. On the web, buyers and sellers can find and contact each other directly, thus eliminating some of the marketing costs and constraints imposed by these interactions in the real world. In this context, it is not surprising that new distribution processes and actors like Amazon Kindle, Fanfiction, Scribd, Wattpad, and Academia, which challenge traditional publishing intermediaries, have emerged.

But the reader may ask: are publishing platforms like Amazon or Scribd—so different from each other—a good example of disintermediation? Or are they proposing a new type of intermediation? It is in this context we can talk about *cyberintermediation* or *distributed intermediation*. In these platforms the traditional middlemen (the publisher or the book seller) has been substituted by an interface based on algorithms, databases, and fulfilment of data centres around the world and, last but not least, the information provided by millions of user interactions. In this context the original disintermediation proposal—based on the so called 'killer-car salesman' idea—derived into a mixed clicks-and-bricks economy. The emergence of cyberintermediaries or distributed intermediaries can be expected in a context where the organizational forms perfected for industrial production have been replaced with structures optimized for textual content abundance, big data, and digital networks.

Content Consumption in the New Media Ecology

Digital networks are making researchers reflect on their traditional conception of mass media interaction. It seems clear that the user experience in digital interactive media is not the same as flicking through TV channels or turning a page: the sense of immersion and the consequences of interaction are radically different in digital environments. Traditional concepts like 'audience' should be revisited from an 'interactive' point of view (Burnett and Marshall 2003; Marshall 2004).

Another important issue of textual consumption in digital networks is political: many hypertext theoreticians agree that the division between author and reader (producer–consumer) should be erased. George Landow suguested that 'hypertext blurs the boundaries between reader and writer' (1991: 5). If first generation hypertexts transferred power from the author to the reader, current forms of digital communication in social networks and media collaborative platforms are definitely socializing the production and distribution of contents.

In 2009 Néstor García Canclini published a small volume entitled *Lectores, Espectadores e Internautas* (*Readers, Spectators and Internauts*) that included a draft map of these transformations of the cultural consumer sphere:

> The concept of *reader* worked within the framework of a theory of fields, either in a restricted way as a literature reader (Iser, Jauss) or, in a more sociological sense, as a receiver of the editorial system (Chartier, Eco).... The notion of *spectator*, although it is more popular, was defined in relation to specific fields like the cinema, television or music spectator.... If we talk about *internauts*, however, we refer to a multimodal actor who reads, sees, listens and combines various materials from reading and entertainment.   (García Canclini 2009: 31–2)

García Canclini concluded that 'to be an internaut increased, for millions of people, the possibilities of being readers and spectators' (2009: 78). This expansion of reading practices is one of the key traits of the new media ecology. However, the changes in reading practices are not precisely a new thing: over the past 6,000 years (at least since something called 'writing' was invented) reading practices have been changing. After many centuries, reading evolved from an oral and group practice to a silent and individual exercise. For Marshall McLuhan (1962) that change was the consequence of the introduction of printing; other researchers, such as Ivan Illich (1996), have argued that silent, individual reading was born at least a couple of centuries before Gutenberg. In any case, it is clear that a specific kind of practice that until recently was regarded as 'normal' (the silent reading of a book) is now expanding to include a broad spectrum of textual consumption experiences. Once again, what is surprising and what makes contemporary transformations so disruptive, is the speed of the change. The move from group and oral to individual and silent reading took several centuries; the transformation of traditional readers into spectators and internauts took a few decades.

How does reading mutate in the new media ecology? The space that used to be occupied by extensive and intensive reading practices is now the territory of *weak* or *precarious readers* (García Canclini 2009). As early as 1997 Nicholas C. Burbules had already introduced the term *hyperreader* and *hyperreading* to describe how reading in a digital textual network 'involves the reader making connections within and across texts, sometimes in ways that are structured by the designer/author (for example, following footnotes or quotations), but often in ways determined by the reader'. Now readers have gone beyond that practice: they write and edit, either by cutting, moving, changing the order or just introducing their own text. Vicente Luis Mora, in *El Lectoespectador* (*The Lecto-Spectator*), delves into this line of thought and wonders: How does the *lecto-spectator* read? They read the page 'like an electronic surface emission, a landscape or a painting.... Turning the pages, looking at them without reading them, the *lecto-spectator* can identify textual and page treatments aimed to a literature closer to his imagination than the nineteenth century's one' (2012: 109–18).

All of these new forms of reading are situated far beyond the figure of the 'critical reader' that hermeneutics and Cultural Studies have vindicated since the 1980s or even earlier: in the contemporary media ecology, there emerges a *hyperreader* identified by the high-level interpretative skills necessary for navigating in a textual network. At the same time, this skilled *hyperreader* is also a *prosumer* (textual producer + consumer), a concept introduced by the futurist Alvin Toffler (1980) and popularized in recent years. New generation interactive media researchers like Bruns (2008) have proposed an even more radical concept: *produser* (producer + user). In short: readers are no longer where they used to be: alone, locked in the reading bubble, immersed in a printed volume.

THE BARBARIANS ARE COMING

In *The Barbarians. An Essay on the Mutation of Culture* (2013) Alessandro Baricco wrote the following:

> If I had to summarise, I would say this: there's a sense of incomprehensible apocalypse in the air—we all feel it—and there's a rumour going around: the barbarians are coming. I see subtle minds with eyes glued to the television, scanning its horizon for the imminent invasion. From their university chairs, clever professors survey, in their student's silences, the ruins left behind by a horde that nobody actually manages to see. And over what is written or imagined hovers the bewildered gaze of exegetes who tell in dismay of an earth sacked by predators with no culture or history.   (Baricco 2013: 2)

It is not only readers who are no longer where they used to be. All traditional actors in the media ecology have been displaced: authors, publishers, translators, distributors, agents, librarians, booksellers, and, obviously, readers. At the same time the emergence of novel actors—like booktubers, maybe the most powerful book prescribers in the second decade of the twenty-first century together with Amazon top reviewers—has introduced new conflicts and tensions into the publishing niche. The Barbarians are here. Will the armoured fortresses resist?

In the last two decades we have also seen how consolidated oppositions that used to organize our interpretation of society (i.e. professional–amateur, private–public, paid–free, closed–open, etc.) have been radically transformed. The dislocation of these oppositions adds another level of complexity, in this case at an interpretative level: how can we make sense of publishing when pirated versions of books are awaiting their readers on a server in the deep dark Web and any teenager can transform themselves into a book prescriber after uploading a couple of videos to YouTube? At the same time the

Publisher's Dictionary has also been enriched with new concepts: Creative Commons, DRM, fandom, filter bubbles, long tail, open-access, produser, prosumer, scanlation, transmedia…New words for a new media environment.

At first Baricco thought of titling his book *Mutation*. This is another key concept: the media ecology is going through a deep mutation whose outputs are impossible to predict. As it is a complex system, it is very difficult to forecast the future evolution of the media ecology. However, we can learn a lot from its previous transformations. In this chapter we have mapped some of these mutations. In many cases it was the creative combination of technologies, actors, and processes that generated deep transformations in the media system. In other words, the future of the media ecology and the publishing subsystem lies in the new combinations generated by the different human and technological actors in the media ecology. As Alan Kay put it, 'the best way to predict the future is to invent it'.

REFERENCES

Anderson, C. (2006). *The Long Tail: Why the Future of Business is Selling Less of More*, New York: Hyperion.

Baricco, A. (2013). *The Barbarians. An Essay on the Mutation of Culture*, NewYork: Rizzoli Ex Libris.

Berners-Lee, T. (1989). *Information Management: A proposal*, CERN, Geneve, Switzerland. Available from: https://www.w3.org/History/1989/proposal.html [Accessed 1 March 2018].

Berners-Lee, T. (2000). *Weaving the Web: The Original Design and Ultimate Destiny of the World Wide Web by its Inventor*, New York: Harper Collins.

Blair, A. (2010). 'Information overload, the early years', *Boston.com*, 28 November. Available from: http://archive.boston.com/bostonglobe/ideas/articles/2010/11/28/information_overload_the_early_years [Accessed 1 March 2018].

Boyd Rayward, W. (1994). 'Visions of Xanadu: Paul Otlet (1868–1944) and Hypertext', *Journal of the American Society for Information Science*, 45(4), pp. 235–50. Available from: http://polaris.gseis.ucla.edu/gleazer/260_readings/Rayward.pdf [Accessed 1 March 2018].

Bruns, A. (2008). *Blogs, Wikipedia, Second Life, and Beyond: From Production to Produsage*, New York: Peter Lang.

Burbules, N. C. (1997). 'Rhetorics of the Web: Hyperreading and Critical Literacy' in *Page to Screen: Taking Literacy Into the Electronic Era*. Edited by I. Snyder. New South Wales: Allen and Unwin, pp. 102–22. Available from: http://faculty.education.illinois.edu/burbules/papers/rhetorics.html [Accessed 1 March 2018].

Burnett, R. and D. Marshall (2003). *Web Theory. An Introduction*, London: Routledge.

Bush, V. (1945). 'As we may think', *The Atlantic Monthly*, August 1945. Available from: http://www.theatlantic.com/magazine/archive/1945/07/as-we-may-think/303881/ [Accessed 1 March 2018].

Castells, M. (2007). 'Communication, Power and Counter-power in the Network Society', *International Journal of Communication*, 1, pp. 238–66. doi: 1932-8036/20070238. Available from: http://ijoc.org/index.php/ijoc/article/viewFile/46/35 [Accessed 1 March 2018].

comScore (2014). *comScore Releases January 2014 U.S. Online Video Rankings*, 21 February. Available from: http://www.comscore.com/Insights/Press-Releases/2014/2/comScore-Releases-January-2014-US-Online-Video-Rankings [Accessed 1 March 2018].

Danielewski, M. Z. (2000). *House of Leaves*, New York: Pantheon Books.

Engelbart, D. (1962). *Augmenting Human Intellect: A Conceptual Framework*, Menlo Park, CA: Stanford Research Institute. Available from: https://web.stanford.edu/dept/SUL/library/extra4/sloan/MouseSite/EngelbartPapers/B5_F18_ConceptFrameworkPt3.html [Accessed 1 March 2018].

García Canclini, N. (2009). *Lectores, espectadores e internautas*, Barcelona: Gedisa.

Gillmor, D. (2004). *We the Media. Grassroots Journalism by the People, for the People*, Sebastopol, CA: O'Reilly. Available from: http://www.oreilly.com/openbook/wemedia/book/ [Accessed 1 March 2018].

Gitelman, L. (2006). *Always Already New Media, History, and the Data of Culture*, Cambridge, MA: MIT Press.

Gitelman, L. and G. Pingree, eds (2003). *New Media, 1740–1915*, Cambridge, MA: MIT Press.

Hafner, K. and M. Lyon, (1998). *Where Wizards Stay Up Late: The Origins of the Internet*, New York: Touchstone.

Hoffman, D., T. Novak, and P. Chatterjee (1995). 'Commercial Scenarios for the Web: Opportunities and Challenges', *Journal of Computer-Mediated Communication*, I(3). Available from: http://onlinelibrary.wiley.com/doi/10.1111/j.1083–6101.1995.tb00165.x/full [Accessed 1 March 2018].

Illich, I. (1996). In the Vineyard of the Text: A Commentary to Hugh's Didascalicon, Chicago: University of Chicago Press.

Jenkins, H. (2003). 'Transmedia storytelling. Moving characters from books to films to video games can make them stronger and more compelling', *Technology Review*, 15 January. Available from: http://www.technologyreview.com/biotech/13052/ [Accessed 1 March 2018].

Jenkins, H. (2006a). *Fans, Bloggers, and Gamers: Exploring Participatory Culture*, New York: New York University Press.

Jenkins, H. (2006b). *Convergence Culture: Where Old and New Media Collide*, New York: New York University Press.

Jenkins, II., R. Purushotma, M. Weigel, K. Clinton, and A. J. Robison (2009). *Confronting the Challenges of Participatory Culture: Media Education for the 21st Century*, Cambridge, MA: The MIT Press.

Jenkins, H., M. Ito, and d. boyd (2016). *Participatory Culture in a Networked Era: A Conversation on Youth, Learning, Commerce, and Politics*, Cambridge: Polity Press.

Joyce, M. (1990). *Afternoon, A story*, Watertown, MA: Eastgate Systems(floppy disc).

Landow, G. (1991). *Hypertext: The Convergence of Contemporary Critical Theory and Technology*, Baltimore, MD: Johns Hopkins University Press.

Lee, H.-K. (2009). 'Between fan culture and copyright infringement: manga scanlation', *Media Culture and Society*, 31(6), pp. 1011–22. doi: 10.1177/0163443709344251.

Lee, H.-K. (2011). 'Participatory media fandom: a case study of anime fansubbing', *Media Culture and Society*, 33(8), pp. 1131–47. doi: 10.1177/0163443711418271.

Lessig, L. (1999). *Code and Other Laws of Cyberspace*, New York: Basic Books.

Lévy, P. (1992). *Le Tecnologie dell'Intelligenza*, Bologna (Italy): ES/Synergon (orig. edition: *Les Technologies de l'intelligence. L'avenir de la pensée à l'ère informatique*, Paris: La Découverte, 1990).

Lévy, P. (1997). *Collective Intelligence: Mankind's Emerging World in Cyberspace*, New York: Basic Books.

McLuhan, M. (1962). *The Gutenberg Galaxy: The Making of Typographic Man*, Toronto: University of Toronto Press.

McLuhan, M. (1964). *Understanding Media: The Extensions of Man*, New York: McGraw Hill.

Manovich, L., J. Douglass, and J. Huber (2011). 'Understanding scanlation: how to read one million fan-translated manga pages', *Image and Narrative*, 12(1), pp. 190–227. Available from: http://www.imageandnarrative.be/index.php/imagenarrative/article/view/133 [Accessed 1 March 2018].

Marshall, D. (2004). *New Media Cultures*, London: Arnold.

Mayer-Schonberger, V. and K. Cukier (2013). *Big Data: A Revolution That Will Transform How We Live, Work and Think*. London: John Murray.

Miller, N. (2007). 'Minifesto for a New Age', *Wired*, March 2007. Available from: http://www.wired.com/2007/03/snackminifesto/ [Accessed 1 March 2018].

Mora, V. L. (2012). *El Lectoespectador*. Barcelona: Seix Barral.

Nelson, T. H. (1965). 'A File Structure for The Complex, The Changing and the Indeterminate', *Proceedings of ACM 20th National Conference*, pp. 84–100. Available from: http://csis.pace.edu/~marchese/CS835/Lec3/nelson.pdf [Accessed 1 March 2018].

Nelson, T. H. (1974 [1987]). *Computer Lib/Dream Machines*. Self-published. 2nd edition, Redmond, WA: Tempus Books/Microsoft Press.

O'Reilly, T. (2005). *What Is Web 2.0. Design Patterns and Business Models for the Next Generation of Software*, 9 September. Available from: http://www.oreilly.com/pub/a/web2/archive/what-is-web-20.html [Accessed 1 March 2018].

Pariser, E. (2011). *The Filter Bubble. What the Internet is Hiding from You*, New York: The Penguin Press.

Russell, D. M. (2008). 'Deeply Intertwingled: The Unexpected Legacy of Ted Nelson's Computer Lib/Dream Machines' in *HCI Remixed. Essays on Works That Have Influenced the HCI Community*. Edited by T. Erickson and D. W. McDonald, Cambridge, MA: MIT Press, pp. 13–18.

Sarkar, M. B., B. Butler, and C. Steinfield (1995). 'Intermediaries and Cybermediaries: A Continuing Role for Mediating Players in the Electronic Marketplace', *Journal of Computer-Mediated Communication*, I(3). Available from: http://onlinelibrary.wiley.com/doi/10.1111/j.1083–6101.1995.tb00167.x/full [Accessed 1 March 2018].

Scolari, C. A. (2012). 'Media Ecology: Exploring the Metaphor to Expand the Theory', *Communication Theory*, 22(2), pp. 204–25. doi: 10.1111/j.1468–2885.2012.01404.x

Scolari, C. A. (2013). 'Media Evolution: Emergence, Dominance, Survival, and Extinction in the Media Ecology', *International Journal of Communication*, 7, pp. 1418–41. doi: 1932–8036/20130005.

Scolari, C. A., C. Cobo Romaní, and H. Pardo (2013). 'Should We Take Disintermediation In Higher Education Seriously? Expertise, Knowledge Brokering, and Knowledge Translation in the Age of Disintermediation', in *Social Software and the Evolution of User Expertise: Future Trends in Knowledge Creation and Dissemination* Edited by T. Takševa, Hershey, PA: IGI Global, pp. 73–92.

Shirky, C. (2008). *Here Comes Everybody: How Change Happens when People Come Together*, New York: Penguin.

Silva, A. H. da (2014). 'Shared Values in Social Media and Comics Scan Communities as New Belonging-Marks', in *Handbook of Research on the Impact of Culture and Society on the Entertainment Industry*. Edited by R. Gulay Ozturk, Hershey, PA: Information Science Reference/IGI Global, pp. 558–77.

Toffler, A. (1980). *The Third Wave*, New York: Morrow.

Turkle, S. (2004). *The Second Self: Computers and the Human Spirit*, Cambridge, MA: MIT Press.

van Dijck, J. (2013). *Culture of Connectivity. A Critical Story of Social Media*. New York: Oxford University Press.

Weber, S. (2004). *The Success of Open Source*, Cambridge, MA: Harvard University Press.

Wikipedia:Statistics. Available from: https://en.wikipedia.org/wiki/Wikipedia:Statistics [Accessed 1 March].

Zielinski, S. (2006). *Deep Time of the Media: Toward an Archaeology of Hearing and Seeing by Technical Means*, Cambridge, MA: MIT Press.

CHAPTER 10

PUBLISHING AND CORPORATE SOCIAL RESPONSIBILITY

ANGUS PHILLIPS

PUBLISHING is a special kind of business, given the important place the book and knowledge still hold in our history, society, and culture. How should we view the publisher as a corporate citizen? What responsibility do publishers have towards society? How sustainable for the planet is the business model of publishing? Since publishing is a global business, how broadly should we think about the impact of the operations of companies? How can publishers follow ethical principles whilst pursuing the profit motive? Examination of corporate social responsibility (CSR) also clarifies the role of the publisher in an age of open content and self-publishing.

Archie Carroll set out that 'The social responsibility of business encompasses the economic, legal, ethical, and discretionary expectations that society has of organizations at a given point in time' (Carroll 1979: 500). Society expects businesses to contribute to the economy and obey the law, and also to be mindful of ethical norms around such issues as the environment, the fair treatment of their employees, and inclusion. To meet discretionary expectations, companies could make philanthropic contributions or encourage their employees to volunteer during their paid employment.

This chapter will make the assumption that publishing firms make a positive contribution to the economy and abide by the laws of their country (for example around employment law and health and safety), and concentrate on the two areas of ethical and discretionary expectations. The expectations of the general population and the relevant stakeholders of a publishing firm should inform how that company operates so that it acts as a good corporate citizen.

An immediate counter-argument to this process comes from the economist Milton Friedman, who said that 'The social responsibility of business is to increase its profits' (Friedman 1970). If the actions of a firm around social responsibility were to reduce the returns to shareholders, or the wages to employees, then these would be detrimental.

It is up to the shareholders or the employees to spend their own money on such causes. However, it would be difficult to find many people in the publishing business who do not believe that their companies have a wider social responsibility, and many firms are keen to display their credentials in this area, from sponsoring reading programmes through to ensuring that they minimize the impact of their activities on the environment. At the heart of publishing is a belief in the importance of books and other content to education, entertainment, personal development, and society. In 2017, Hilary Murray Hill, the CEO of Hachette Children's Group in the UK, said: 'Publishing is a business, but our product has a wider social meaning. And this is the key to thinking about our future success' (*The Bookseller*, 20 September).

There are vital issues affecting our planet including climate change, inequality, and political freedom, and publishers have produced many books and articles on these topics. Companies are not obliged to consider the externalities, or side-effects, of their operations, but most now recognize they cannot be ignored (Meyer and Kirby 2010). As the world has become increasingly globalized, the need for firms to adopt and enforce policies around social and environmental responsibility becomes ever more urgent. The aim will also be to protect the company's reputation and manage any potential risks, for example around labour practices in the supply chain. According to the mission of the UN Global Compact:

> Corporate sustainability starts with a company's value system and a principled approach to doing business. This means operating in ways that, at a minimum, meet fundamental responsibilities in the areas of human rights, labour, environment and anti-corruption. Responsible businesses enact the same values and principles wherever they have a presence, and know that good practices in one area do not offset harm in another. By incorporating the Global Compact principles into strategies, policies and procedures, and establishing a culture of integrity, companies are not only upholding their basic responsibilities to people and planet, but also setting the stage for long-term success.   (www.unglobalcompact.org)

Smaller firms will be keen to act along these principles but it is the larger firms that have the resources (and influence) to act in a more concerted manner and to report regularly on their aims and the results. 'The CSR report . . . provides a company with an opportunity to communicate its CSR efforts to the company's stakeholders and to discuss (within the confines of a single document) certain company successes and challenges on a wide array of CSR issues, including corporate governance, climate change, employee and supplier diversity initiatives, and community investments and partnerships' (Noked 2013).

For the learning company Pearson, their approach to corporate social responsibility connects together their sustainability vision and their commercial vision: 'We identified three key pillars which were "be a trusted partner", "reach more learners" and "shape the future of learning". If you look at our business strategy, be a trusted partner and reach more learners are also part of that commercial strategy piece. The thinking around sustainability and the commercial strategy are very much integrated' (Hughes 2017).

There are indices of CSR and sustainability but these were thrown into question by the scandal over emissions from Volkswagen cars. When the story broke in September 2015 that the car company was manipulating emissions tests, it was shortly after the Dow Jones Sustainability Index had crowned the company as the world's most sustainable car company (VW was soon to be suspended from the index). There are newer certification routes available to companies: one example is B Corp, which offers the business equivalent of the Fairtrade label in food production. Organizations have to operate to strict standards of social and environmental performance, accountability, and transparency. (www.bcorporation.net) Value-led firms will also find that being ethical is good for business in the long term, as those values feed into their products and brands in the eyes of their employees, customers, and other stakeholders.

Working with Stakeholders

The list of the stakeholders of a publishing company can be lengthy, including their employees, authors and readers, shareholders, customers, suppliers, governments, non-governmental organizations, society more widely, and the environment (Figure 10.1). Consultation with stakeholders by Axel Springer in 2015 revealed questions about the participation of women in leadership (from employees), the credibility of content (from readers), and the company's environmental footprint (from an environmental NGO) (Axel Springer 2015).

Interaction with stakeholders can be two way and complex. Employees would certainly expect their companies to act in an ethical manner, not just towards them but also across

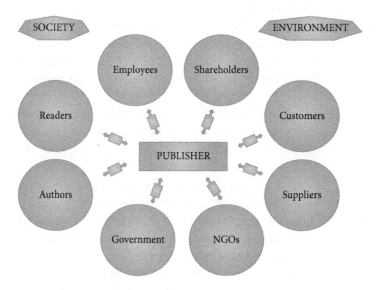

FIGURE 10.1 Map of the stakeholders of a publisher

the business; and trade unions are recognized by many employers. However, there are parts of the world where union activity is disrupted or illegal, and the actions of government can severely impact on the operations of the publishers themselves. There is censorship in countries such as China and Iran; and in Turkey in 2016 a number of publishers were closed following the failed summer coup. In 2017 Cambridge University Press faced criticism over its decision (subsequently reversed) to take down content at the request of Chinese authorities. '*China Quarterly* is the highly respected journal whose website had been pruned, to comply with Chinese demands, of articles on subjects including the Tiananmen Square massacre, the Cultural Revolution and President Xi Jinping' (Kennedy and Phillips, 2017).

There are also countries where a vibrant publishing community is believed to be important for culture and society, and publishers and booksellers receive aid from the state. For example, the Canada Book Fund (CBF) supports financially the production, marketing, and distribution of Canadian-authored books; whilst in France alongside fixed book prices, designed to support the independent bookshop sector, there is financial support for small publishers and bookshops in order to maintain the country's cultural identity. Contrast this approach with the UK and the USA, where independent bookshops have become endangered as a result of competition from chain bookstores, supermarkets, and online retailers such as Amazon. The response of bestselling author James Patterson in 2014 was to start 'a program to give away $1 million of his personal fortune to dozens of bookstores, allowing them to invest in improvements, dole out bonuses to employees and expand literacy outreach programs.... "I'm rich; I don't need to sell more books," Mr Patterson said. "But I do think it's essential for kids to read more broadly. And people just need to go into bookstores more. It's not top of mind as much as it used to be." ' (*New York Times*, 19 February 2014).

There are issues around taxation and the large technology companies—are they pursuing an ethical stance in relation to their contribution to the societies in which they operate? In the financial year to June 2016, it was reported that in the UK Google paid £36.4 million in tax on revenues of around £1 billion. In their defence Google said that 'its UK offices, employing just under 3,000 people, are not big enough to count as a "permanent establishment" and that it therefore should pay the majority of its taxes elsewhere' (*Independent*, 31 March 2017). It was also reported, from the retail sector, that 'UK bookshops pay ... 91p per £100 of turnover, which is 11 times the amount of tax paid by online retailer Amazon, which contributes 8p per £100 of turnover' (*The Bookseller*, 11 September 2017).

Publishing companies seek best value when sourcing suppliers, whether freelance editorial work, typesetting, printing, or more general business services. The growth of outsourcing exposes domestic suppliers to international competition, and raises questions about working conditions in the supply chain. Freelance staff will not have access to the same set of rights and benefits as those given to employees of publishers: 'Atypical workers in the media and culture industries often do not benefit from the same protection as employees, such as unemployment benefit, pensions, maternity leave and sick pay; they may be excluded because of their independent or self-employed status.

In some cases, taking on self-employed status may be a positive choice for media and culture workers wishing to develop their own enterprise, while in others it could be a negative necessity to avoid unemployment' (ILO 2014: 10).

Publishers need to be aware of working conditions at key suppliers overseas, whose workers are also stakeholders in their operations. There is a reputational risk if those conditions are not monitored on a regular basis and examples of abuse or malpractice come to light. The printing of colour books, for example, is typically located in those countries offering the optimum combination of quality and price. It is common to send work to Hong Kong or Mainland China, and a 2014 report examined working conditions at the Hung Hing Heshan printing house in China's Guangdong Province, which produces books for Finnish publishing houses. The report did not recommend that the printer should not be used, but did raise concerns over health and safety, as according to the workers interviewed, the factory does not enforce rules on wearing protective clothing. Also the levels of pay were low and employees worked on average 80 hours of overtime a month to make ends meet: 'Overtime pay at Hung Hing accounts for a very important part of the total monthly salary. If workers only work during standard working hours, their salary is around CNY 1,479 (194 euros), which is slightly above the minimum wage . . . yet it is barely enough to cover basic costs of life in Heshan' (Finnwatch 2014: 7). In the UK, as part of the Book Chain Project, the PRELIMS tool offers an industry code of conduct, to ensure that suppliers meet standards around labour and environmental practices. In turn the tool helps suppliers since they can share their audit results with a number of publishers (bookchainproject.com).

Publishers need to remain aware of the activities of their subsidiary organizations overseas. Oxford University Press and Macmillan had to pay substantial penalties as a result of bribes paid by their operations in Africa. Both organizations admitted the making of improper payments with the aim of securing World Bank funded contracts in Kenya and Tanzania (OUP), and Southern Sudan (Macmillan). The publishers were pursued through civil rather than criminal proceedings by the Serious Fraud Office in the UK: in 2012 OUP paid a fine of £1.89m plus a contribution of around £2m to not-for-profit organizations in sub-Saharan Africa; and in 2011 Macmillan was ordered to pay £11.3m.

Should stakeholders also not include the fledgling operations of publishers in less developed countries? They can suffer severe effects from the activities of multinational companies. In Africa the international publishers vanished and reappeared as the conditions changed, withdrawing and then reintroducing competition for local companies. 'In some cases, for example in Tanzania, multinational companies pulled out when the economic crisis struck in the 1980s, only to return promptly when the World Bank allocated $60 million for educational supplies. Survival was made difficult for both parastatals and the fledgling independents in the private sector. The combination of the decline of GDP in Africa, generally, and aid policies favouring the donation of foreign books resulted in a number of closures' (Bgoya and Jay 2015: 12).

Most contracts with authors are subject to negotiation, with or without the involvement of agents, and should it be recognized that no advantage is taken of writers? Is there a fundamental tension between the interests of authors and publishers: does success for one side come at the expense of the other? Would a more transparent offer to authors enable a greater level of fairness? Publishers would argue that they must be able to agree the best contract with an author on an individual basis, one that leads to a profitable outcome for the company, which is bearing the risk of publication. Yet in the UK, in the light of falling author incomes, the Society of Authors is pushing for legislation to ensure that authors are treated fairly. Nicola Solomon, their Chief Executive, pointed out that for 2016, 'Even if we take out journal revenue—where authors are, shockingly, paid next to nothing—authors were receiving less than 5 per cent of turnover in the same year that (major) publishers' profits were around 13 per cent (Solomon 2018).

Users of digital content may be concerned about privacy and the responsible use of any data about them and their interests and behaviour; whilst readers of books and articles will not expect excessive profits to be made from publications through unfair pricing. For example, high profit margins and price increases in the area of journals publishing have helped to stimulate the cause of open access to research articles. This issue has attracted the support of governments and research funders, keen to see greater access to publicly funded research. There are those who see this as a clearly ethical issue: research is a public good, similar to clean air, which should be freely available rather than exist within a toll system of subscription.

Books and the Environment

Is the supply chain efficient in its use of resources and how does book production impact on the environment? In 2007 the then Penguin Managing Director Helen Fraser said that 'If we wanted to scare ourselves we could be described as an industry that chops down forests, takes them in lorries to printers and warehouses, then to bookshops, and then all too often back to be pulped and thrown into landfills' (*The Bookseller*, 5 April 2007). Indeed it was reported that the new M6 toll road in the UK was built on two and a half million copies of returned and unsold Mills & Boon romances. 'Unsold copies of the books were shredded into a paste and added to a mixture of asphalt and Tarmac...preventing the surface from splitting apart after heavy use' (*Telegraph*, 18 December 2003).

Developments in the industry have led to a reduction in waste: the arrival of ebooks for genres such as romance leads to a decline in print production; the use of point of sale data to inform printing and buying decisions, and the growth of digital printing, have reduced overstocks. Distributed printing in local markets should reduce the need to ship books long distances and lower the book miles travelled by titles. However, paper production has shifted its location in the search for lower costs, as highlighted in a 2007 report: 'To meet growing demand for paper products, the pulp and paper industry is expanding its production capacity, primarily in developing countries with lower raw material and labor costs and looser environmental regulations.

Increasingly, the largest consumers of paper products are exporting the environmental consequences of production, such as damage to forests and discharges of pollutants from paper mills' (EPN 2007: vi).

In terms of natural resources, books consume water, ink, and paper. Water is one of the key ingredients in papermaking and steps have been taken to reduce the quantity used and to minimize effluent through its recirculation. 'The effect of the closed-water systems has been to reduce the amount of fresh water needed in paper-making from 132,000 gallons per ton to below 2,640 gallons per ton, with a corresponding reduction in the amount of waste water effluent to virtually zero' (Bullock and Walsh, 2013: 99). The growing use of vegetable inks is also a positive step. Conventional inks are petroleum-based and release volatile organic compounds (VOCs) into the atmosphere, a source of pollution and lower air quality.

One estimate is that around 30 million trees are used to make books sold in the USA each year (BISG 2008)—1,500 times the number of trees in Central Park in New York. Consumers would expect books to be printed on environmentally friendly paper, and the two alternatives are to use recycled paper or that derived from sustainable sources. In 2015 the use of recycled paper by the Hachette Book Group (HBG) in the UK was around 9 per cent of overall usage, whilst 90 per cent was Forest Stewardship Council (FSC) certified. Under the FSC label those trees that are harvested are replaced or allowed to regenerate naturally. HBG was looking to increase the share of recycled paper but identified problems of scarcity, low quality, and high cost. There is a much higher use of recycled paper in other goods such as tissue products and newsprint. Virgin fibres cannot be recycled more than six or seven times as 'each time you recycle, the fibres get shorter and shorter because of the mechanical process...that says, you are going to need a virgin supply coming into the supply chain somewhere' (Sammons 2018). Many companies state that they will not knowingly use paper from ancient woodland or endangered areas, such as tropical rainforests.

The PREPS grading system (Book Chain Project) gives companies a tool to assess the papers they are purchasing. The tool was developed in response to uncertainty about the origins of the paper used by publishers—one paper may have five different forest sources, all from different countries. 'The task was to make sense of that big pile of uncertified paper: understand where it is from, what tree species were used in making it, what risk was associated with those tree species and the countries they came from, and identify the less risky papers out of that bunch' (Sammons 2018). PREPS now works with mills across over 100 countries and has data on forests and species for more than 800 papers.

The World Wildlife Fund suggests that a 10 per cent reduction in paper and paperboard consumption in North America and Europe matches one year's consumption in Africa and South America combined. 'Reducing wasteful consumption, like over-printing or over-packaging, would also ease the pressure on forests and land use, as paper use grows in developing countries' (WWF 2012: ch. 4). Over time the usage of paper in the book industry should decline in some markets with the arrival of ebooks, yet figures from the UK showed the use of paper rising between 2011 and 2015 by 17 per cent

(PA 2015: 104). It is believed the increase was due to the growing production of colouring books and children's books (Hughes 2017). Other studies suggest that print production in the UK was in decline from the turn of the millennium, with UK consumption of paper and board reaching a peak in 2001, falling back since with a further decline in book and newspaper reading. 'As the circulation of newspapers falls, and the sale of books decreases, these trends are highly likely to continue. Digital reading is widely thought to have a much smaller greenhouse gas impact than reading from paper' (Goodall 2011: 11).

We can test this argument by comparing the carbon footprint of a tablet computer and the printed book. Apple's environmental report on the iPad suggests that over the product's total lifecycle it is responsible for 135 kg, or 297 pounds, of CO_2: 86 per cent through its production, 10 per cent in its use, 3 per cent through transport, and 1 per cent through the transport and energy involved in its recycling (Apple 2017). By contrast a study of the book industry discovered that the carbon footprint of a printed book, through all the steps of production through to its sale, emits 8.85 pounds CO_2 per book (BISG 2007). If, say, a user spends 10 per cent of their time on the iPad reading books, during its whole life, this is equivalent to the purchase of three or four printed books. The picture is more complex with any reuse of the printed book—or of course the book may not even be opened and read. For the learning company Pearson, which is investing heavily in digital resources, 'where the impact lies is different: for print, it is in the paper, print piece; on digital it is around usage, how the content is accessed. It is not necessarily better or worse, it is just different' (Hughes 2017).

There are other trends that could impact on book production. As further biological products are developed from tree fibre, there are implications for book paper and its availability and pricing. These products could include waterproof and fire retardant paper, or clothing made from viscose. 'The price of those bio products could rise above the price manufacturers are getting from book paper' (Sammons 2018).

As a growing share of print sales has gone online, how might this impact on environmental considerations? The available research suggests that an environmental comparison of shop visits and home delivery is dominated by the local level—the last mile. There appears to be no increase in our carbon footprint from the growth in Internet shopping: 'Some forms of conventional shopping behaviour [e.g. the use of public transport] emit less CO_2 than some home delivery operations. On average, however, in the case of non-food purchases, the home delivery operation is likely to generate less CO_2' (Edwards et al. 2009: 36–7).

The environmental journalist, Justin Gillis writes about climate change: 'The changes we need to make are hard, and they demand large-scale, collective action: to rebuild our energy system, to save our forests, to change our cars, to create radically better buildings' (New York Times, 18 August 2017). Publishers can play their part in efforts to reduce greenhouse emissions, from the use of renewables to the creation of energy efficient workplaces, alongside carbon offsetting, through to reductions in book miles through localized printing and distribution.

DIVERSITY AND THE BOOK TRADE

Publishers have to answer questions from stakeholders about the diversity of their books and content. At the same time there are sound business reasons for the companies to widen their recruitment pool to ensure that their workforce properly represents the population as a whole. How else can they produce publications that will reach all parts of the reading public, and that will attract new readers? Society more widely should expect publishers to produce books that match the interests of a population that is diversified by, for example, gender and ethnicity. The challenge is to build inclusivity from the inside, rather than simply pay lip service to the ideal of diversity. As Rebecca Nicholson observes: 'Whenever I see a big brand adopting the rainbow as a sign of its social conscience, I instinctively think, that was never the point of the flag' (*Guardian*, 3 July 2017).

The book critic Ron Charles writes, 'More than a half-century ago, Ezra Jack Keats published *The Snowy Day*, his groundbreaking picture book that featured an African American child. The intervening years have seen many sincere efforts to provide children and young readers with more books that reflect the rich diversity of the United States, but by and large, the shelves have remained as white as freshly fallen snow' (*Washington Post*, 3 January 2017). In *The Good Immigrant*, edited by Niksh Shukla, writers explore what it means to be black, Asian, and minority ethnic in today's Britain. Publication was crowdfunded through the Unbound platform and the project received a pledge of £5,000 from J. K. Rowling. One contributor, Darren Chetty, observed great uncertainty amongst publishers about how to create stories featuring people of colour: 'A South Asian author told me that she was advised to change her name for a book cover to broaden its appeal, and another writer was advised that unless they were writing an "issue" book, their book-cover protagonist should not be black, as this would result in fewer copies being purchased' (Shukla 2016: 98).

Organizations such as We Need Diverse Books, in the USA, have set out to put 'more books featuring diverse characters into the hands of all children'. By diversity they recognize all diverse experiences, including 'LGBTQIA, Native, people of color, gender diversity, people with disabilities, and ethnic, cultural, and religious minorities'. They offer grants to fund internships from diverse backgrounds, alongside reading lists for booksellers, and give awards for books that address diversity in a meaningful way. In the UK Tanya Byrne argues that authors must be more disruptive: 'We must tell our own stories and if there is no space for us to do so, then we will make space for ourselves. Like Rupi Kaur did when she self-published *Milk and Honey* and Issa Rae did with her web series, *The Misadventures of Awkward Black Girl*, which now has over 25 million views on YouTube' (*Guardian* 19 August 2017).

A US industry survey from 2015 highlighted the lack of diversity in publishing: in the industry overall, 79 per cent of employees were white, 78 per cent female, 88 per cent heterosexual, and 92 per cent non-disabled; at executive level, the figures were 86 per cent, 59 per cent, 89 per cent, and 96 per cent (Lee and Low Books 2015). As *Publishers Weekly* pointed out, there are difficulties in turning the position round: 'Most jobs in publishing houses require college degrees and recent census data shows 73 per cent of Americans with college degrees are white. Looking at the situation through this lens, the roots of the problem can be seen to extend well beyond the publishing industry itself' (11 March 2016). In response to this dilemma Penguin Random House in the UK removed the requirement to have a degree for applicants for new jobs.

The practice of internships in publishing on little or no income must surely impact on the diversity of the workforce. This discriminates against those without a friend or family member near the workplace, and the many who cannot afford to work unpaid for a long period. Naomi Klein, who has written about low paid work in the service sector, comments: 'Perhaps predictably, the culture industry has led the way in the blossoming of unpaid work, blithely turning a blind eye to the unglamorous fact that many people under thirty are saddled with the mundane responsibility of actually having to support themselves.... Of course, the media conglomerates—the broadcasters, magazines and book publishers—insist that they are generously offering young people precious experience in a hard employment market.' (Klein 2010: 245).

The statistics show an industry with a predominantly female workforce, yet the British writer Naomi Alderman believes that there is a subtle sexism at work in the publishing industry:

> Publishing is still a man's world in some respects.... I work in video games and I work in publishing and the sexism in video games is very overt. The sexism in publishing is subtle—and that does not mean the sexism in publishing is better. Subtle is sometimes much harder to deal with. Overt sexism you can point out, you can say 'please do not use mostly naked ladies in bikinis to advertise your video games, that's horrible'. The women's publishing thing is more subtle—if you are a woman writing fiction you are construed as writing 'women's fiction' and you get a flower on your book jacket and you get put in the women's section.
>
> (*The Bookseller*, 8 June 2017)

Published data on pay in publishing in the UK shows quite marked differences between companies, with the median pay gap at Elsevier of 40 per cent in favour of men (the highest reported by a publisher) but at Penguin Random House there was a small median gap of nearly 2 per cent in favour of women (Page 2018). Gaps may be a product of the gender balance amongst senior roles in the company but they have rightly prompted serious reflection at many publishers and new programmes to encourage and mentor women into top roles.

There are other dimensions to diversity from class to sexual orientation. Attitudes towards the gay community have changed markedly in both employment and society generally, although this must be set against a global context in which being homosexual is still illegal in seventy-one countries, and punishable by death in eight nations (http://www.equaldex.com). Publishers increasingly recognize that being gay friendly is important for recruiting and retaining talent in the job market. In 2013 Elsevier launched the Elsevier Pride network, which runs a series of educational events within the company to create and sustain a positive environment for LGBT employees; it also fundraises for local initiatives such as HIV/AIDS outreach, and takes part in the annual Amsterdam Pride event. *The Economist* suggests: 'It is hard to give your best if you have to conceal an important part of who you are. Straight workers routinely plaster their offices with pictures of their families, which not only creates a pleasant working environment but also broadcasts the message: "I have kids. Please don't sack me." Closeted gays find it harder to socialize with colleagues and build informal networks' (*The Economist* 2012).

HELPING COMMUNITIES

It is hard-nosed business sense that without new generations of readers and continued visibility for books, the publishing business will cease to exist. Is it philanthropy or self-interest that encourages publishers to launch or participate in reading promotions, library campaigns, and support for independent bookshops? With increased competition for books from other media such as games and music, social media such as Facebook and YouTube, added urgency is in the air. In any case publishers are active in reading promotions in developed countries and literacy campaigns in less developed countries. Education is a key driver of economic success and governments are keen to expand provision and make best use of both digital and print resources.

In July 2015 France launched its first national promotional reading campaign, titled Lire en Short, aimed at children on holiday. The first campaign involved many hundreds of events and attracted over 300,000 youngsters and their parents, and has been repeated in subsequent years under the name Partir en Livre. Publishers donate books and organize events alongside libraries and bookshops.

Broader campaigns to encourage book buying and reading include World Book Day, supported by publishers since its inauguration by UNESCO in 1995. The idea originates from Catalonia in Spain where on Jordi Day, St George's Day (23 April), there has been a long-standing tradition for men to give women roses and for the women to give men a book. Today women also receive a book and there is a substantial uplift in sales, particularly of fiction. In 2017 retail book sales in Spain were €73m euros in the week of the celebration, compared to €52m in the previous week (Nielsen Bookscan). 'With book signings and rose-selling events scheduled to take place in 30 countries, the celebration is global. Albert Royo, head of Catalonia's Diplomatic Council said: "We are trying to spread this festivity beyond our borders. Books and roses promote positive universal values: literacy, culture, peace, civility—and that is something we all share" ' (*Guardian*, 23 April 2017).

There are notable examples of publishers wishing to give back to the wider community. In the UK the Paul Hamlyn Foundation was established in 1987 by one of the pioneers of colour publishing. Upon his death in 2001, Hamlyn left most of his estate to the Foundation, creating one of the largest independent grant-making foundations in the UK. There is a particular focus on disadvantaged young people and the arts. The multinational learning company Pearson donates at least 1 per cent of its operating profits to charitable purposes in the communities in which it works.

But should companies go further in this area? Some under challenging financial circumstances would find it difficult, but there are examples of companies wishing to throw aside conventional routes and turn upside down the notion of CSR. From the area of craft brewing, BrewDog announced in 2017 that it would give away 20 per cent of its profits each year, half to employees and half to charities. Cofounder James Watt said: 'Outdated CSR policies have zero consideration for their real-world impact, existing merely for the purpose of an oversized cheque and an awkward photo shoot. This is a call to arms for businesses to democratise the impact their charitable contributions can have on their community, their people, and the world' (www.brewdog.com).

The Corporate Citizen

Being an effective and moral corporate citizen is not necessarily easy. Operating as an ethical business, a publisher should take into account the expectations of a range of stakeholders to ensure that social and environmental concerns inform its activities. This can extend from the use of energy from renewable sources and a responsible attitude to authors and key suppliers, through to hiring and employment policies and salary structures. But how should a publisher navigate the broader waters of moral and political concerns? If they are receiving a subsidy from government, can they be free to publish views contrary to those of the party in power? Should a company publish views with which the staff themselves are uncomfortable?

In 2017 the autobiography of the British right-wing provocateur Milo Yiannopoulos was due to be published by Simon & Schuster in New York. His editor, Mitchell Ivers, had worked with other conservative figures, including Donald Trump, but the book was dropped by the publisher after a recording became public of Yiannopolous appearing to endorse sex between 'younger boys' and older men. The book *Dangerous* was self-published by Yiannopolous and he attempted to sue the publisher (the case was later dropped). Documents submitted to the court included an edited draft of the text. In a section in which 'Yiannopoulos claimed that feminist ideology was a "made up fairy tale", the editor . . . displayed little patience. "I will not accept a manuscript that labels an entire class of people 'mentally ill'," he wrote' (Buncombe 2017). The book deal had been condemned by many who did not want the author's controversial views to be given a serious platform, yet how should we have reacted if publication had gone ahead? Is it the job of the publisher to censor unpalatable opinions? In a world of content bubbles on social media, how do we encounter views contrary to our own? It can be the job of the publisher to swim against the tide, or to stand up for what is right. But if the work is of insufficient quality, it should not be published.

There are special features of a publishing company and its responsibilities around the defence of free speech and the integrity of what is published. For example, Penguin took notable stands on the publication of *Lady Chatterley's Lover* in the early 1960s and then in its defence of the author Deborah Lipstadt. The academic from Emory University wrote *Denying the Holocaust: The Growing Assault on Truth and Memory* (1993), in which she called David Irving a 'Holocaust denier'. Previously a respected historian, Irving had come to the conclusion that the genocide of the Jews was a myth. He decided to sue and launched a case in the High Court in London, in which Lipstadt and Penguin were forced to defend the book: 'Lots of people told me not to fight, including leaders of the Jewish community, who were fearful that I was giving him a platform. Many of them told me to settle. Don't fight, ignore it. But if I lost, it would become illegal to call the world's leading Holocaust denier a denier. And what he would then say is, "Ok, I'm not a denier, but the court ruled in my favour, ipso facto, the David Irving version of the Holocaust is the genuine version"' (*Guardian*, 14 January 2017). The civil case in 2000 (and subsequent appeal in 2001) were won by Lipstadt and Penguin, and Irving was both bankrupted and thoroughly discredited.

In a world of alternative facts, claims, and counter claims, many believe we are losing our grasp on what is the truth. At the same time publishers feel they have to justify their existence alongside the growth of self-publishing and user-generated content. The stakeholder engagement carried out by Axel-Springer in 2015 brought out the expectation from readers that content should be credible and this surely highlights a key value that publishers can bring, and ought to bring, to their content. Investment in selection, quality control, and editing is not wasted and must be highlighted to readers and consumers. Taking responsibility for content is a key element of what a publisher does—why they are necessary.

The content should also meet standards around decency, and for example, many publishers would feel unhappy about making profits out of murder. When the publication of a book by O. J. Simpson, *If I Did It*, was announced in 2006 this led to universal condemnation and the book's cancellation. The author was planning to give a hypothetical account of how Nicole Brown Simpson and Ronald Goldman were murdered. The book's editor and publisher (Judith Regan and HarperCollins) were 'pressured to drop the project because they were, in effect, paying Simpson at least $880,000 to tell how he might have committed the murders, money that should have gone to satisfy the $33.5 million judgment a 1997 civil jury ordered him to pay to the victims' families' (*Newsweek*, 21 January 2017). The book was later published, after a court order, with the rights owned by the Goldman family: the new title was *If I Did It: Confessions of the Killer*.

In April 2017 a Facebook user in Cleveland posted a live video of himself killing a 74-year-old man in a random attack. The content was taken down but Facebook was not able to stop the live coverage and it took some hours for the video to be removed. This raised questions about what the social media company would allow to be posted, and had they become a publisher? This meant that they had responsibilities about what content should be approved on the platform. Sara Fischer asked: 'There have long been questions as to whether Facebook is a media company or a technology company. It may be easier to think of it this way: Is Facebook a publisher that monetizes quality, or a distributor that monetizes quantity?' (Fischer 2017). The UK newsreader Jon Snow said, regarding a bogus news story circulating on the social network that claimed the Pope had endorsed Donald Trump for the US presidency, that 'Facebook has a moral duty to prioritise veracity over virality. It is fundamental to our democracy. Facebook's lack of activity in this regard could prove a vast threat to democracy' (*Telegraph*, 23 August 2017).

A transparent adherence to values and principles is a vital part of the case for the continued existence of publishing. As technology gives us access to a vast range of content of variable quality, and also limits our encounters with opposing views, we need to value the work of publishers around selection and quality. If questions are asked about why we do need publishers—what value do they bring?—addressing the area of corporate social responsibility throws up a key answer. A credible publisher assumes responsibility for, and believes in, its content and stands by its authors; this sets it apart from those who wish to be simply intermediaries in the distribution of content.

References

Apple (2017). *iPad Environmental Report*, 21 March.

Axel Springer (2015). *Sustainability Report*, Berlin: Axel Springer.

Bgoya, Walter and Mary Jay (2015). 'Publishing in Africa from Independence to the Present Day', *Logos*, 26, p. 3.

BISG, Book Industry Study Group (2007). *Environmental Trends and Climate Impacts*, New York: Book Industry Study Group.

Book Chain Project (2017). *The Future of the Printed Book*, London: Carnstone.

Bullock, Adrian and Meredith Walsh (2013). *The Green Design and Print Production Handbook*, How Books.

Buncombe, Andrew (2017). 'Milo Yiannopoulos's book torn apart by Simon & Schuster editor, court documents reveal', *Independent*, 28 December.

Carroll, A. B. (1979). 'A three-dimensional conceptual model of corporate social performance.' *Academy of Management Review*, 4, pp. 497–505.

Edwards, J. B., A. C. McKinnon, and S. L. Cullinane (2009). *Carbon Auditing the 'Last Mile': Modelling the Environmental Impacts of Conventional and Online Non-food Shopping*, Edinburgh: Heriot-Watt University, March.

The Economist (2012). 'Of Companies and Closets', 11 February.

EPN, Environmental Paper Network (2007). *The State of the Paper Industry: Monitoring the indicators of environmental performance*, Lochinver, Scotland: Environmental Paper Network.

Finnwatch (2014). Books from China: Working conditions at the Hung Hing Heshan Printing Factory, July.

Fischer, Sara (2017). 'Murder in Cleveland: Facebook's latest fiasco', *Axios*, 17 April.

Friedman, Milton (1970). 'The Social Responsibility of Business is to Increase its Profits', *The New York Times Magazine*, 13 September 1970.

Goodall, Chris (2011). ' "Peak Stuff" Did the UK reach a maximum use of material resources in the early part of the last decade?', 13 October. Available from www.carboncommentary.com

Hughes, Peter (2017). Director, Sustainability, Pearson, interviewed by the author, 4 August.

ILO, International Labour Organization (2014). *Employment relationships in the media and culture industries*, Geneva: International Labour Organization.

Kennedy, Maev, and Phillips, Tom (2017). 'Cambridge University Press backs down over China censorship', *Guardian*, 21 August.

Klein, Naomi (2010). *No Logo*, 10th anniversary edition, London: Fourth Estate.

Lee and Low Books (2015). *Diversity in Publishing*, available from www.blog.leeandlow.com

Meyer, Christopher, and Kirby, Julia (2010). 'The Big Idea: Leadership in the Age of Transparency', *Harvard Business Review*, April.

Noked, N. (2013). 'The Corporate Social Responsibility Report and Effective Stakeholder Engagement', https://corpgov.law.harvard.edu/2013/12/28/the-corporate-social-responsibility-report-and-effective-stakeholder-engagement/ [Accessed 30 September 2017].

PA, Publishers Association (2015). *Statistics Yearbook*, London: Publishers Association.

Page, Benedicte (2018). 'Elsevier reports 40% gender pay gap', *The Bookseller*, 29 March.

Sammons, Nick (2018). Book Chain Project, Carnstone Partners, interviewed by the author, 1 March.

Shukla, Nikesh (2016). *The Good Immigrant*, Unbound.

Solomon, Nicola (2018). 'The Profits from Publishing: Authors' perspective', *The Bookseller*, 2 March.

World Wildlife Fund (2012). *Living Forests Report*, World Wildlife Fund.

PART II

THE DYNAMICS
OF PUBLISHING

CHAPTER 11

....

ECONOMICS
OF PUBLISHING

....

ALBERT N. GRECO

Ever since the day in 1450 that Gutenberg first used moveable type and a make-shift printing press to print the first book,[1] publishers and editors have had to identify, understand, and create viable business economic strategies and models to cope with and, hopefully, minimize and reduce the pernicious impact of risk and complexity in a constantly changing business environment. Clearly, some strategies adopted by publishers since the fifteenth century were based on well-tested business strategies, policies, and economic theories and procedures developed in other industries, from agriculture to textiles to international trade. However, as economic theories became more available, because of the growth of universities and the printing of books and scholarly journal articles,[2] a more coherent understanding and utilization of various economic theories were understood and adopted, changing how many publishing houses operated.

In the following sections, a review is presented of some, but clearly not all, of the major economists and their theories that provided an intellectual framework for publishers in

---

[1] Eisenstein (1980: 22–182). Also see Eisenstein (2012: 78–115); and Dittmar (2011: 1133–172).

[2] As for universities, book printing production started in 1478 at Oxford and in 1584 at Cambridge. The first scholarly journal was the *Journal des Savants*, launched in January 1665. In March 1665, the first English language scholarly journal was *Philosophical Transactions*, published by the Royal Society. Copies of the *Journal des Savants* are available for the years 1665–1944, see http://gallica.bnf.fr/ark:12148/cb343488023/date; for the years 1909–2010, see http://www.persee.fr/collection/jds. For access to the modern version of the *Journal des Savants*, see http://www.persee.fr/web/revues/home/presscript/revue/jds. See also McCutcheon (1924: 626); Vittu (2005: 527–45); and Banks (2015: 1–17). See the Royal Society's web site for historical information: https://royalsociety.org/about-us/history. Its list of authors includes: Isaac Newton (in 1672); Charles Darwin (1837); Michael Faraday (1857); James Clerk Maxwell (1865); Alan Turing (1952); and Stephen Hawking (1983). It is still published today; and the Royal Society's website has every issue back to March 1665. For information about *Philosophical Transactions A* and *Philosophical Transactions B*, see http://rsta.royalsocietypublishing.org/about. See the Royal Society's web site for information: https://collections.royalsociety.org/?dsqIni=Dserve.ini&dsqApp=Library&dsqDb=Catalog&dsqCmd=Overview.tcl&dsqSearch=((text) per cent3d per cent27first+issue per cent27); and the Royal Society: http://rstb.royalsocietypublishing.org/citation-metrics.

a market that has been transformed from letterpress print-oriented book formats to digital ebooks and streaming options. That theory is then applied more directly to the book business.

MAJOR ECONOMIC THEORIES

Smith and Marshall

Adam Smith (1723–90) in *The Wealth of Nations* analysed the benefits of economies of scale and mass production to increase pin manufacturing output in Scotland. 'This industry is now carried on, not only the whole work is a peculiar trade, but it is divided into a number of branches....One man draws out the wire; another straights it; a third cuts it; a fourth points it; a fifth grinds it at the top for a head; to make the head requires two or three distinct operations...'[3] Smith also commented on prices, free trade, the role of the government in the economic affairs of a nation. He also did important work on the basic concept behind the gross domestic product and the powerful 'invisible hand' of the market.[4]

Alfred Marshall (1842–1924) in *Principles of Economics* pioneered the use of mathematics to make economics more rigorous. Marshall wrote about value, the cost of production, wealth, and consumer surplus and demands.[5] But he made major contributions regarding the price elasticity of demand, which shows the percentage relationship between a change in price and the quantity of demand. He also wrote in detail about the changing consumer demand for a product;[6] and his detailed comments about the pivotal importance of supply and demand influenced countless other economists in the UK and abroad.[7]

Three Major Twentieth-century Economists:
Keynes, Friedman, and Samuelson

John Maynard Keynes (1883–1946) shaped economic thought and influenced economists for decades. In his monumental work *The General Theory of Employment, Interest, and Money*, Keynes addressed a series of substantive issues. His views about classical economic theories, risk, output, and employment are still hotly debated today. Keynes commented that, if certain economic theories were faulty, it was because of a 'lack of clearness and of generality in the premises'.[8] Keynes began 'pushing monetary theory back to becoming

---

[3] Smith (2003: Book 1, ch. 1, 8–9).
[4] Smith (2003: Book 1, ch. VII, 69; Book 1, ch. X, 136; Book IV, Introduction, 459; Book IV, ch. II, 488–9; Book IV, ch. VII, Part Third, 667; Book IV, ch. 1, Part II, 775). See also Chandler (1962: 78, 81–112).
[5] Marshall (2013: 54–60, 63–6).   [6] Marshall (2013: 86–91, 92–100).
[7] Marshall (2013: 124–30, 153–69).   [8] Keynes (2008: 4).

a theory of output as a whole'.[9] His 'fundamental equations were an instantaneous picture taken on the assumption of a given output'.[10] Yet his 'method of analysing the economic behaviour of the present under the influence of changing ideas about the future is one which depends on the interaction of supply and demand, and is in this way linked up with our fundamental theory of value'.[11] Lastly, Keynes developed a general theory 'which includes the classical theory…'[12] Keynes' legacy was monumental in economics and public policy (especially his work at the Bretton Wood Conference during World War 2.[13]

Milton Friedman (1912–2006) was a proponent of the 'Chicago School of Economics' that rejected Keynes. Friedman strongly supported the idea that free markets and minimal governmental restrictions were the best way to allocate scarce resources and grow an economy. Friedman maintained that markets were efficient. This meant that stock prices contained all of the available information; and economic 'actors' were making rational business decisions, had access to 'full information', and used 'full information' to maximize 'utility function' (i.e. self-interest).[14]

Friedman was also concerned with all types of risk, including the supply of money and interest rates. In *Capitalism and Freedom*, Friedman addressed the pivotal importance of international trade, monetary policies, and inflation.[15] He was the equal to Keynes in terms of impact within the economic community, although they rarely agreed on economic issues.

Paul Samuelson (1915–2009) also stressed the importance of monetary theory and its intrinsic relationship with the dynamics of supply and demand and insidious inflation. Yet he was deeply concerned about what he maintained was the limited rationality of consumers when making decisions to buy products.[16] Samuelson also did groundbreaking research on the importance of mathematical optimization economic topics, including his early work on what became known as the efficient market hypothesis (EMH)[17] and the pricing of options. He was influenced by a long-forgotten doctoral dissertation by Louis Bachelor (1870–1946)—*The Theory of Speculation*.[18] Once again, Samuelson was ahead of his economics colleagues in realizing that option pricing was a topic that needed more research by economists.[19]

Another important twentieth-century economist was Harry Markowitz (1927–) who developed the modern portfolio theory (MPT) of diversification, which had a dramatic impact on finance, publishing, and other industries.[20]

---

[9] Keynes (2008: 4).   [10] Keynes (2008: 4).   [11] Keynes (2008: 5).

[12] Keynes (2008: 5).   [13] Steil (2014: 61–98, 125–64).

[14] Friedman (1993: 1–18). See also Friedman and Schwartz (1993: 15,47–9, 52–61, 301–11, 475).

[15] Friedman (2002: 1–6, 37–50, 108–18, 177–96). See also Hicks (1982: 6, 28, 340).

[16] Samuelson and Crowley (1986: 5). Also see Samuelson, 'Maximum Principles in Analytical Economics', 62–9; available at: http://www.nobelprize.org/nobel_prizes/ecpnomic-sciences/laureates/1970/samuelson-lecture.pdf. Also see Samuelson (1983: 22, 26–33, 39–44, 55–64, 92–9, 148–52).

[17] Samuelson (1965, 1973a: 1–42, 1973b). See also Cassidy, 'Postscript: Paul Samuelson', *The New Yorker*, 14 December 2009; available at: http://www.newyorker.com/news/john/cassidy/postscript-paul-samuelson. Samuelson (1966a: Vol. 1, chs 13 and 14, 1966b: Vol. 2, ch. 7); Fama (1963, 1965, 1970, 1991, 1998).

[18] Bachelier et al. (2006: 1–14 on mathematics and finance, and 15–79 on the theory of speculation).

[19] Merton (2006). Also see Scholes (1972); Black and Scholes (1973); Black (1986).

[20] Markowitz (1952: 77, 79).

The Rise of Behavioural Economics

Subsequently 'behavioural economic' theories emerged, influenced by psychological research,[21] questioning the idea that economic 'actors' were always rational, and markets were always efficient. The 'behavioural economists' argued that an economist should consider economic, psychological, social, and emotional issues when analysing the decisions of individuals who were, at times, completely rational, and, at times, emotional in deciding to buy or not to buy a product or a service. They called into question many well-established economics and finance theories.

Two prominent 'behavioural economists' included Richard H. Thaler (1945–) and Robert J. Shiller (1946–). Thaler addressed the issue of economic 'actors' who had limited or incomplete information in *Nudge: Improving Decisions About Health, Wealth, and Happiness*, where he outlined his ideas about biases, blunders, and following the herd.[22] In *Misbehaving: The Making of Behavioral Economics* he wrote that 'the core premise of economic theory is that people choose by optimizing'.[23] While traditional economic theory had merit, he insisted that 'adding humans to economic theories is to improve the accuracy of the predictions made with those theories...'.[24] Thaler also wrote about 'mental accounting', bargains, finance, and the efficient market hypothesis.[25]

Shiller in *Irrational Exuberance* warned that 'economists usually like to model people as calculating optimally their investment decisions based on expectations of future price changes....In fact, the typical investor's actual decision about how much to allocate to the stock market overall, and into other asset classes...tends not to be based on careful calculations.'[26] Shiller posited that 'many popular accounts of the psychology of investing are simply not credible....Psychologists have shown that people's decisions in ambiguous situations are influenced by whatever anchor is at hand.'[27] Shiller joined Thaler in also writing about herd behaviours and epidemics.[28]

APPLIED ECONOMIC THEORY

The Years after the End of World War 2

Before 1939, most US book publishing operations were small companies privately owned by a few partners. An interesting example is Random House which was started in 1925 by Bennett Cerf and Donald Klopfer when they acquired the Modern Library,

---

[21] Kahneman (1991). Also see Kahneman (2003: 1449–75); Kahneman and Tversky (1979, 1984).
[22] Thaler (2009: 17–36 and 53–73).   [23] Thaler (2015: 5).   [24] Thaler (2015: 9).
[25] Thaler (2015: 55, 58–63, 202–15). See also Thaler (1990, 1999); Thaler and Johnson (1990); Sendhil Mullainathan and Thaler (2000).
[26] Shiller (2000: 55).   [27] Shiller (2000: 135, 137).   [28] Shiller (2000: 148–68).

which published reprints. In 1934, they took a gamble and the financial and legal risks associated with publishing James Joyce's *Ulysses*.[29]

World War 2 impacted most nations. While the USA was able to demobilize after 2 September 1945 and resume book publishing, albeit slowly,[30] most of the European nations sustained devastating damage to its populations, cities, infrastructure, and publishing operations.[31] However, both the Americans and Europeans had to develop effective economic strategies and structures to resume publishing programmes and generate enough profit to hire personnel, find and develop authors, and enter into contracts with printing plants that could handle complex printing, paper, binding, and distribution operations; they assumed that new bookstores would open when prosperity returned and damaged bookstores would be restocked.

So, the state of book publishing in late 1945 was dominated by small companies staffed primarily with college graduates who majored in the humanities and the social sciences; very few had degrees in economics or business administration. But they were well educated, and they either read or learned about certain theoretical economic concepts, which dominated economic thought before 1939, practices that were successful in the past, or became aware of recent theories in other industries that were applicable to the inherent risks associated with building, or rebuilding, publishing into a successful national or international endeavour.

The Importance of Scale and Supply and Demand after 1945

While most economic ideas and beliefs before 1945 were theoretical, applied economic theories came to the forefront after the end of World War 2 in order to revive or create viable new publishing operations. What were the applied pivotal economic theories that were utilized by many publishers in the decades after the end of the war?

First, they paid more attention to the following: scale and the mass production of books, hardcover and paperbacks (Smith); supply and demand (Keynes; Marshall; Samuelson); sensitivity about book prices (Smith); discount rates for books (Marshall); value (Keynes); 'utility function' of consumer book buyers (Friedman); and substitution of books (hardcover to paperback to ebooks).

An unusual example of supply and demand, and elasticity of demand, is a new hardcover book. Assume it is a 'Harry Potter' book, with total US sales in excess of 160 million copies for all of the books in this series. For the first four books in the series, the publisher had a suggested retail price (SRP) of $25.00 for the books; and each of the first four 'Potter' book sold between 9.3 million and 9.75 million copies in the USA. However, because of the tremendous publicity for the title, and intense demand from consumers

---

[29] Cerf (1977: 53–89).   [30] Tebbel (1980: 98–104).   [31] Judt (2006: 13–40).

to buy the book, the publisher decided to order an initial hardcover print run of the fifth 'Potter' book of ten million copies and increase the SRP the publisher charged for the book. The publisher posted a suggested retail price (SRP) of $30.00 for this title; and this higher SRP had little impact on the projected sale of this new hardcover book since all ten million hardcover copies were sold; and the publisher had to order an additional 200,000 copies to satisfy consumer demand.

This is an example of the basic concept of elasticity, which is a measure of the percentage change in the demand of consumers (i.e. readers) to an increase in the SRP of a product (i.e. the new book). Elasticity is calculated by dividing the percentage change in the quantity demanded by consumers by the percentage change in price. Theoretically, an increase in price should generate a decrease in the quantity demanded. Yet this did not happen with the fifth 'Potter' book, perhaps an unusual example of a theory that works only in seminar rooms on white boards and not always in the rough and tumble world of publishing a 'Harry Potter' book.

In addition, the publisher can also offer 2,500 copies of the 'Potter' book signed by the author for an SRP of $200.00 each, a premium price for this book. This is an example of first degree price discrimination, sometimes called perfect price discrimination, and the publisher is able to capture all of the consumer surplus. The publisher can also have different discount rates (in the USA books are sold generally into the channels of distribution at reduced rates) for wholesalers (perhaps 30 per cent off the SRP) and distributors (perhaps 50 per cent), examples of second degree price discrimination. The publisher could also offer discounts to consumers buying the book based on age (perhaps a 10 per cent senior discount), employment (15 per cent discount to individuals in the military), etc.; this is known as third degree price discrimination.[32]

However, the fifth 'Potter' book is an exceptionally unusual title. Since 1985, the present author conducted hundreds of interviews with authors, editors, publishers, business managers, book researchers, book industry reporters at major newspapers and magazines and news organizations, executives in charge of book retailing (in the big chains and in independent book stores), and book distribution. Book publishing is unquestionably a risky endeavour. The generally accepted belief, based on these interviews, is that for every ten new hardcover adult trade books published in the USA, seven lose money, two break-even financially, and one is a financial hit. So why would anyone ever invest in or work in a book publishing firm since the economics of book publishing are unquestionably harsh and unforgiving? Quite simply, book publishing is arguably the best business in the world. It is involved in the transmission of ideas and theories, from the ethics of Aristotle to the dreams of people living in a ghetto in a developing country. Books spark individuals to think, to challenge the status quo, to run for public office, or to try and make the world a better place for everyone.

---

[32] Greco (2015: 168–72, 211–21).

A Sample Profit and Loss Statement

The profit and loss (P&L) statement for a hardcover book (Table 11.1) illustrates some of these substantive financial issues. This is a P&L for a highly successful book; and it is not typical of all adult trade fiction books.

Assume a book publisher has great confidence that this new adult trade fiction title will generate significant interest, sales, and become a number one bestseller; and an initial print of 300,000 copies is ordered, which sells out. Second, third, and fourth print runs are ordered, totaling 500,000 copies in print. Of that total, it is common for a publisher to allocate approximately 1 per cent of the initial print run (in this instance 3,000 copies) that are not sold; that is, copies given to the author, employees, copies placed in the publisher's display cases, provided to various book award committees, etc. The publisher also assumes a modest 5 per cent return rate (25,000 copies), well below the industry's 20 per cent in 2018; and net sales totalled 472,000 units. With a suggested retail price (SRP) of $28.95, this book was sold into the various channels of distribution (e.g. online book retail sites; bookstore chains; independent bookstores; mass merchants; price clubs; etc.) at an average discount rate of 47 per cent (the industry's average in 2018); and the publisher nets $15.34 per copy. However, the discount rate does not include any additional promotional expenses paid by the publisher (often called 'points') to a retailer. These include 'placement fees' to have the book displayed prominently in a window, on a table, a rack, or an end-cap. 'Points' also covers placing a book face out on a shelf and not spine out, in an ad, on the retailer's website, etc.

The author's contract was negotiated by the author's agent who received 15 per cent of all of the author's revenues (this is the most common percentage for an agent in 2018 in the USA). The contract stipulated that the author received a $500,000.00 advance against earned royalties; and the publisher and agent agreed on a 'step' royalty structure ranging between 10 per cent and 15 per cent depending on the total number of sold copies. Since this was a bestseller, certain rights were listed in the author's contract, including filmed entertainment and subsidiary rights (i.e. reprints, book clubs, and serial rights if the book were sold to periodicals). The author is a 'star;' and the agent insisted that the author, and not the publisher, received all of the rights income (i.e. $2,500,000).

Table 11.1 outlines the various revenues (net sales of $7,240,480; gross sales minus returns equals net sales; all numbers were rounded off and may not always equal 100 per cent); and the various expenses associated with this book (e.g. cost of goods sold, COGS, $3,276,549). When marketing expenses ($750,000; for an author tour, sales and marketing personnel working on this book, advertisements, etc.) and corporate overheads ($2,172,144; costs include the office of the publisher, editor, sales and marketing, legal, warehouse and distribution, information technology, etc.) are calculated, the book had a net profit of $1,041,787; and a contribution of $3,963,931 to the publishing house. The author earned $1,527,973 in royalties and another $2,500,000 in various rights fees, for a total of $4,027,973. The agent's 15 per cent generated $604,196 for the agent's work on this one book.

Table 11.1 Sample P&L adult trade fiction hardbound book published by a major US trade book publisher

Business model assumptions: 320 printed pages; colour cover, spine, and back cover; no photographs or illustrations.

Print run:				
1st print run	300,000 copies			
Gross sales:	297,000 copies	[−3,000 copies; −1 per cent of 1st print run]		
2nd print run	100,000			
3rd print run	50,000			
4th print run	50,000			
Total print run	500,000			
Gross sales	497,000	[minus initial 3,000 copies]		
Returns:	25,000 copies	[5 per cent return rate; and copies never sold and in warehouse; 20.34 per cent was the 2016 average return rate; and copies never sold and in warehouse]		
Net sales:	472,000 copies			
Suggested Retail Price:	$28.95	[2017 industry average for this type of book was $27.95; publisher charged a premium price because of the author's popularity]		
Average discount:	47 per cent	[publisher nets $15.34 per copy; industry average]		
Royalty advance:	$500,000	[this is an advance against royalty income;]		
Royalty rate:		[per cent of suggested retail price of $28.95, 10 per cent: first 300,000 copies 12 per cent 301,000 − 400,000 copies; 15 per cent + 400,001 copies]		
Subrights:				
Other income:	Gross	Author's percent*		Publisher's percent
Filmed entertainment subsidiary rights	$1,000,000	100 per cent		0 per cent
Reprints	$1,000,000	100 per cent		0 per cent
Book clubs	$500,000	100 per cent		0 per cent
1st Serial:	0	100 per cent		0 per cent
2nd Serial:	0	100 per cent		0 per cent
Total:	$2,500,000	100 per cent		0 per cent

*This is typical for a major author. His or her agent sells North American rights (or US rights) to a publisher, retaining all foreign and subsidiary rights (which are sold directly by the agent). The 'typical' agent collects 15 per cent of all revenues, domestic, foreign, and subsidiary rights.

Revenues and expenses		
1. Gross sales	$7,623,980	[497,000 copies × $15.34 each]
2. Returns:	$383,500	[25,000 copies × $15.34 each]
3. Net sales:	$7,240,480	[#1 − #2 = net sales]
4. Plant:	$289,619	[4 per cent of net sales; includes editorial, art, design, layout, and page make-up costs]
5. PPB:	$1,375,691	[19 per cent of net sales; industry average; printing, Paper, and binding costs]]
6. Earned Royalty:	$1,527,973	[royalty rate: per cent of suggested retail price] 10 per cent [$2.895] first 300,000 copies = $868,500; 12 per cent [$3.470] 300,001 − 400,000 copies = $346,997; 15 per cent [$4.340] + 400,001 = $312,476;
7. Inventory write-off:	$83,266	[#4 plant + #5 PPB = $1,665,310 divided by 500,000 printed copies = $3.33 × 25,000 returns]
8. Royalty write-off:	$0	
9. Total cost of goods sold:	$3,276,549	[COGS: #4 + #5 + #6 + #7 +#8 = #9]
10. Initial gross Margin:	$3,963,931	[#3 − #9 = #10]
11. Other publishing income:	$0	
12. Final gross margin:	$3,963,931	[#10 + #11 = #12]
13. Marketing:	$750,000	[$1.50 × 500,000 copies; $1.50 industry average]
14. Corporate overhead:	$2,172,144	[standard 30 per cent of net sales revenues]
15. Net profit:	$1,041,787	[#12 − #13 − #14 = #15]
16. Contribution:	$3,963,931	[#13 + #14 + #15 = #16; book's contribution to the publisher]

N.B. All numbers rounded off. Author's expenses for the agent's fees and taxes were excluded from the publisher's P&L. Shipping and handling costs were excluded; some publishers provide free shipping; actual shipping and handling costs vary due to numerous variables (e.g. geographical location; rush versus normal delivery schedules, etc.).

Source: Albert N. Greco based on numerous discussions with industry's executives.

The Growth of Technology
and the Rise of the Machines

A major development since 1945 and especially after 1990 was the growing importance of technology and technological change. Since Gutenberg, books were printed (originally letterpress and now lithography). Yet a series of events transformed reading and access to the book. The emergence and wide acceptance of the Internet significantly changed how readers could access book content.

One substantive event was the development of lightweight laptops with colour screens, 'adequate' storage capacity, and attractive prices. The second event was the creation of effective smartphones capable of a variety of functions including downloading book content. A third development was the creation of reliable e-readers. In 2007 Amazon released the Kindle, the first effective and popular e-reader; and in 2009 Barnes & Noble released its e-reader the Nook. The fourth significant event took place in 2010 when Apple released the iPad, a tablet capable of sending and receiving emails, using Google for search, offering music, and the ability to access and read ebooks. The wide acceptance of laptops, smartphones, and tablets also increased the ability of readers to have immediate access to books. E-readers, laptops, and tablets were to Clayton Christensen, in *The Innovator's Dilemma*, examples of what he called 'disruptive and sustaining technologies'.[33]

The purchase of millions of smartphones, e-readers, tablets, and laptops, and the availability of ebooks from publishers, found many eager consumers eschewing printed books in favour of instant downloads of ebooks on to their machines. Many publishers responded by creating a hybrid publishing strategy, simultaneously releasing a new book in a printed and ebook format.

The Self-publishing Movement

Alongside these developments, the movement toward an author self-publishing a book has gained traction in the last few years. According to a report released by Bowker,[34] which issues all ISBNs in the USA, 786,935 self-published books were released in 2016 in the USA, an increase of 8.2 per cent over 2015's totals, and a staggering 218 per cent increase from 2011 (247,210).[35] Not every self-published book has an ISBN; so it is likely that the total number of self-published books is higher than Bowker's tallies.

Table 11.2 (which concerns the same adult trade fiction book in Table 11.1) illustrates the economics of self-publishing a book as an ebook. Assume that the author of the hardcover book outlined in Table 11.1 decided to self-publish the book and assumed all of the expenses related to the ebook's publication. So, there was no print run; the market demand was 472,000 copies (as in Table 11.1). Since ebooks have a lower SRP than printed books, the ebook's SRP was $14.99 (a typical ebook SRP for a major 'star' author in 2018). The average discount rate (70 per cent) for ebooks is higher than for printed books. And the author did not use an agent, keeping what would be the agent's 15 per cent of royalties and rights revenues.

The ebook had gross and net sales of $7,075,280 (there were no returns or write-offs). The author paid $70,752 for plant (i.e. editorial, art, design, and page make-up, etc.) and $200,000 for marketing (the author's tour and other expenses related to direct mail,

[33] Christensen (2011: xi–xxxi, 33–55).
[34] Bowker, 'Self-Publishing ISBNs Climbed 8 per cent Between 1015–2016' at: http://www.bowker.com/news/2017/Self-Publishing-ISBNs-Climbed-8-Between-2015-2016.html.
[35] Bowker, 'Self-Publishing ISBNs'. Also see Milliot (2017c) at: https://www.publishersweekly.com/pw/by-topic/industry-news/manufacturing/article/75139-self-published-isbns-hit-786-935-in-2016.html.

Table 11.2 Sample self-published P&L adult trade digital fiction book (same book as in Table 11.1)

Business model assumptions: 320 pages; colour cover, spine, and back cover; no photographs or illustrations.

Print run:	0 copies		
Ebook gross sales:	472,000 copies		
Returns:	0 copies		
Net sales:	472,000 copies		
Suggested Retail Price:	$14.99	[2017 industry average for this type of ebook was $9.64, although the range was between 99 cents and $14.99; author charged a premium price because of the author's popularity]	
Average discount:	70 per cent	[Author nets 30 per cent $4.50 per copy; industry average; on-line book retailer keeps 70 per cent]	
Royalty advance:	$0		
Subrights:			

Other income:	Gross	Author's percent*	Publisher's percent
Filmedentertainment subsidiary rights	$1,000,000	100 per cent	0 per cent
Reprints	$1,000,000	100 per cent	0 per cent
Book clubs	$500,000	100 per cent	0 per cent
1st Serial:	0	100 per cent	0 per cent
2nd Serial:	0	100 per cent	0 per cent
Total:	$2,500,000	100 per cent	0 per cent

*This is typical for a major author who retains all foreign and subsidiary rights (which are sold directly by the agent). The 'typical' agent collects 15 per cent of all revenues, domestic, foreign, and subsidiary rights.

Revenues and expenses		
1. Gross sales	$7,075,280	[472,000 copies × $14.99 each]
2. Returns:	$0	
3. Net sales:	$7,075,280	[#1 − #2 = #3]
4. Plant:	$70,752	[1 per cent of net sales; includes digital page make-up; author's expenses; hired freelancers]
5. PPB:	$0	
6. Earned royalty:	$2,124,000	[royalty rate: 30 per cent of suggested retail price; $14.99 × 30 per cent = $4.50 × 472,000]

(continued)

Table 11.2 Continued

Revenues and expenses

7. Inventory write-off:	$0	
8. Royalty write-off:	$0	
9. Total cost of goods sold:	$70,752	[1 per cent of net sales; includes digital page make-up; author's expenses; hired freelancers; COGS to author: #4]
10. Initial gross margin:	$2,053,248	[to the author #6 – #7 – #8 – #9 = #10]
11. Other publishing income:	$2,500,000	
12. Gross margin:	$4,553,248	[to author #10 + #11 = #12]
13. Marketing:	$200,000	[author's expenses for author's 20 city tour, travel and per diem costs; direct mail, social media, and Internet/web expenses; etc.
14. Corporate overhead:	$0	
15. Net profit:	$4,353,248	[#12 – #13 – #14 = #15]

N.B. All numbers were rounded off.

Source: Albert N. Greco based on numerous discussions with industry's executives.

social media, Internet/web expenses, etc.). The author's earned royalty from the sales of the ebook was $2,124,000, versus $1,527,973 with the printed book, and the $2,500,000 in rights revenues for both versions. Total income was $4,027,973 for the printed books; and $4,353,248 for the self-published ebook.

Clearly, the author became an entrepreneur assuming all of the costs, risks, and worries associated with handling the ebook's production, distribution, and marketing; but the author earned an additional $325,275 with this ebook. However, the agent's 15 per cent commission for the printed book cost the author $604,196, reducing the author's total profit from $4,027,973 to $3,423,77 (the author did not use an agent for the ebook). This meant that this author kept significantly more money by self-publishing this book and eschewing a traditional book publisher and an agent, which helps explain the staggering growth in the number of self-published books and the companies created to assist the authors.

The Crisis of the Old Order: Bookstores and International Trade of Books

Another technological development was the growth in the market share of online bookstores and the decline in bricks and mortar bookstores. Amazon.com was launched on 5 July 1994; and its market share of all books sold in the USA in 1995 (its first complete year of business) was about 0.003 per cent; by 2010 its market share of book sales stood at approximately 26 per cent; and in 2018 Amazon.com accounts for +50 per cent to +70 per cent in some categories.[36]

Publishing firms also focused on the dramatic growth of the book chains in the 1960s and in the following decades (e.g. Barnes & Noble) and book sales in non-bookstore retail establishments (e.g. mass merchants; price clubs; supermarkets; convenience stores; etc.). These general retailers caused a steep decline in the number of bookstores. In 1990, there were 22,926 bookstores; and a little more than 14,000 in 2018, a decline of 39 per cent.[37] This meant there was a large reduction in the amount of shelf space for trade books, which impacted the ability of consumers to discover books. All bookstores are critically important to authors and publishers who need readers to discover their books; and this is why publishers support booksellers. And they also closely monitored disintermediation (consumers buying books online); and reintermediation (bookstores offering online book purchases, home delivery, store pick-ups, and returns). Ultimately 'better' data provided publishers with a more realistic understanding of the mercurial habits of book buyers in the USA, although book focus group data collection is rarely conducted.

There was also an increase in the importance of free trade markets for books (e.g. the European Union) and minimal governmental restrictions and controls over book publishers (Friedman). A prime example is the creation of the economic (with a monetary union; a single market; and a customs union) and political organization (laws covering all of the members) known as the European Union (EU). The EU allowed for the trade of books between nations, which supported the growth in the book industries in the twenty-eight members.[38] However, while the USA allows the discounting of books to consumers, discounting is not always allowed in every EU nation.

An Acceptance of Behavioural Theory

There has been the growth and recognition of the importance of 'behavioural economics' and how consumers make decisions to buy or not to buy books (e.g. authors; genres; bookstores; book clubs; online) (Thaler; Shiller). The availability of somewhat 'limited' book sales collection systems (e.g. NPD BookScan Data) provided book publishers with information; NPD BookScan collects sales data for about 85 per cent of all book sales in the USA) regarding who buys, but not why they buy, books.[39] An intriguing example is the marketing research conducted by the Romance Writers of America (RWA; a trade association of romance authors and publishers). Using NPD BookScan statistics, as well as data from other sources, RWA created superb data about who buys romance fiction, what genres they by, when they buy, where they buy, how they buy (credit

---

[36] Greco et al. (2015: 46, 221, 259).   [37] Bogart (2003a: 535, 2003b: 476–77).
[38] Pinder and Underwood (2013: 56–69).
[39] NPD BOOKSCAN Data; at: http://www.ecpa.org/?page=npd.

cards; debit cards; bookstore discount coupons; bookstores; online), and why they buy romance books.[40]

The Need for Reliable Data

The US book industry has been able to capture some timely economic statistical information about total sales (Marshall; Samuelson). *Publishers Weekly* reported that, in 2016, the US trade book industry (print and ebooks) had sales of $15.9 billion. The largest of the major trade book categories is the eclectic adult hardcover and paperback fiction ($4.43 billion) and non-fiction book ($5.87 billion) categories. The second largest one is the popular juvenile/Young Adult hardcover and paperback fiction ($3.82 billion) and non-fiction ($650 million) book sector. While small, religious hardcover and paperback fiction, non-fiction, Bibles, testaments, hymnals, and prayer books ($1.13 billion) has been an important book category since the first book was printed in what is now the USA (Cambridge, Massachusetts) in 1640 (*The Bay Psalm Book*).

Publishers also have access to book buyer demographic data, including the fact that adult females, in the 45–54 age cohort, comprise the largest, most important book buying and book reading category; and trade books represent 60.59 per cent of US book sales.[41]

Another factor was the creation of effective metrics (Marshall; Friedman) to gauge book returns, book costs, and the appeal of self-publishing.[42] The Association of American Publishers reported that the value of all book returns in 2016 was $3.076 billion (e.g. adult books $1.2135 billion; children's/Young Adult $368.1 million).[43]

The Acceptance of Portfolio Theory, Diversification, and Conglomerates

The industry has also seen the increased importance of portfolio theory and diversification of books (Markowitz) and financial management (Samuelson). Penguin Random House is an example of a successful diversified book publishing house with many imprints or strategic business units (SBUs). Over the decades, it published titles in a series of distinct book categories, including: arts and entertainment; biography and memoir; classics; cooking; fantasy; fiction; history; humour; mystery and suspense; non-fiction; poetry; politics; reference; romance; science fiction; travel; and young adult. The company clustered these book categories under various imprints, including: Vintage; Bantam Books;

---

[40] Romance Writers of America; at: https://www.rwa.org/p/cm/ld/fid=580.
[41] Milliot (2017a).   [42] Bogart (2003a: 535, 2003b: 476–7).
[43] Association of American Publishers. 'Monthly Stat Shot December 2016', 24 May 2017, p. 3; sales from 1,207 publishers; available at http://newsroom.publishers.org/aap-statshot-book-publisher-trade-sales-flat-for-2016.

the Crown Publishing Group; Modern Library; Knopf Doubleday; Bantam Spectra; Random House Audio; Random House Children's; and DK.[44] If sales of YA fiction are up but politics are down, the company's diversification portfolio offers some protection against such vagaries of the marketplace.

The Scholastic Corporation and Wall Street

Diversification strategies within many publishing houses worked successfully for decades; and this caught the attention of a number of financial service companies that viewed book publishing as an interesting investment (at least when compared to other sections; e.g. retail). The Scholastic Corporation is an example of a book publishing operation that caught the interest of certain financial service companies, and many invested in this well-known, well-established, and overall successful publisher. Scholastic is the world's largest publisher and distributor of children's and YA books, a leading provider of core literacy curriculum and professional services, and a producer of educational and entertaining children's media. Scholastic had $1.673 billion in revenues in 2016 (up from $1.635 billion in 2015).[45] While revenues can vary annually, and Scholastic certainly has had some difficult years, the company publishes a series of very successful book series (e.g. Harry Potter; Clifford the Big Red Dog; etc.) with strong frontlist and backlist sales; and some books were also made into popular motion pictures). Scholastic has book clubs; and its book fairs take place annually in about 90 per cent of the 98,271 public K-12 schools in the USA (and a large percentage in the private and religious schools).

Table 11.3 lists some of the major institutional and mutual fund companies that have taken a position in Scholastic. The institutional investors include some of Wall Street's elite firms, including: Blackrock, Inc.; The Vanguard Group; Alliance, Bernstein LP; and T. Rowe Price. Collectively, these nine firms held 17.767 million shares worth in excess of $666.762 million. The nine mutual funds, including Vanguard and T. Rowe Price, held 8.048 million shares worth $336.585 million. Overall, these investors held a total of 25.816 million shares worth slightly more than $1 billion. Why?

A review of Scholastic's financial performance explains why these financial service companies have such a large position in this company. Table 11.4 has data for 2016 for: various financial valuation metrics, including: Scholastic's low Beta (β; Beta is a measure of the volatility, or systematic risk, of a security or a portfolio in comparison to the market as a whole). To financial analysts, a Beta of 1.0 indicates that the stock's price moves with the market; and a Beta less than 1.0 means that the security is less volatile than the market. This means that, for example, a Beta of 1.2 is theoretically 20 per cent more volatile than the market. So, Scholastic's 0.8 Beta is theoretically 20 per cent less volatile the market; and its EBITDA (i.e. earnings before interest, taxes, depreciation, and

---

[44] Penguin Random House; at http://www.penguinrandomhouse.com. Also see Milliot (2017b: 57).
[45] Scholastic; at https://finance.yahoo.com/quote/SCHL/holders?p=SCHL.

Table 11.3 Major institutional and mutual fund investors in the
Scholastic Corporation

Institutional holder	Number of shares	Value of shares
Blackrock, Inc.	3,504,513	$130,052,479.00
Dimensional Fund Advisors LP	2,606,160	$104,136,599.00
The Vanguard Group, Inc.	2,354,763	$87,385,256.00
Royce & Associates LP	2,218,324	$82,322,004.00
Alliance Bernstein LP	1,946,771	$72,244,672.00
T. Rowe Price Associates Inc.	1,586,637	$58,880,160.00
Fairpoint Capital LLC	1,478,614	$54,871,366.00
Northern Trust Corporation	1,199,847	$44,526,322.00
Bank of New York Mellon Corporation	871,565	$32,343,777.00
Mutual funds	Number of shares	Value of shares
Royce Special Equity Fund	1,620,000	$67,878,002
AMG Managers Fairpoint Mid-Cap Fund	1,281,026	$53,674,991
DFA U.S. Small Cap Value Series	1,237,437	$54,905,078
iShares Core S&P Smallcap ETF	1,192,772	$49,416,544
T. Rowe Price Mid-Cap Value Fund	633,420	$23,506,216
Vanguard Total Stock Market Index Fund	548,733	$24,160,713
Ab Discovery Value Fund	526,020	$22,182,262
iShares Russell 2000 ETF	520,685	$21,571,979
T. Rowe Price Small-Cap Value Fund Vanguard Small-Cap Index Fund	488641	$19,289,778

Source: https://finance.Yahoo.com/quote/SCHL/holders?p=schl; accurate as of 18 November 2017.

amortization was $106.7 million, its total cash was $311.9 million, and it had a very low debt of $12 million.

Table 11.5 has Scholastic's economic data for the fiscal years 2013 through 2017; and this data points out that stockholders made a profit investing in Scholastic. Total revenues increased 12.39 per cent between 2013 and 2017. Net income grew 62.5 per cent during those same years. However, the company's net income, net profit margins, and return on equity surged in 2015. Scholastic's 2015 annual report revealed why 2015 was an anomaly. 'In May, we closed on the sale of Scholastic's Educational Technology and Services (EdTech) business to Houghton Mifflin Harcourt (HMH) for $575 million pretax. This significant event was recorded as a discontinued operation in our FY2015 results.'[46]

---

[46] The Scholastic Corporation. Annual Report 2014–2015; at http://files.shareholder.com/downloads/ABEA-28S6DN/5588957146x0x847824/8B6E17B7-BF08-4472-A71C-75DDF43AD84D/web_enabled_final_2015_annual_report.pdf;

Table 11.4 The Scholastic Corporation: financial analysis for the fiscal year ending 30 April 2017 (US dollars)

Valuation measures

Market cap:	$1.31 billion
Enterprise value:	$1 billion
Beta (β):	0.80
Stock price range:	$33.51 – $49.38 [52-week range]

Profitability

Profit margin:	1.71 per cent
Operating margin:	4.86 per cent

Management effectiveness

Return on assets:	2.83 per cent
Return on equity:	2.30 per cent

Income statement

Revenue:	$1.65 billion
Revenue per share:	$47.22
Gross profit:	$927.1 million
EBITDA:	$106.7 million

Balance sheet

Total cash:	$311.9 million
Total cash per share:	$8.91
Total debt:	$12 million

Source: The Scholastic Corporation. Annual Report 2016–2017; available at http://files.shareholder.com/downloads/ABEA-28S6DN/5588957146x0x904587/0420F02A-5288-400E-8169-0D57F0233A85/2016_Annual_Report.pdfhttp://files.shareholder.com/downloads/ABEA-28S6DN/5588957146x0x953550/5E26BBB0-391B-4380-B619-52C3D4640D95/final_2017_annual_report.pdf.

Table 11.5 The Scholastic Corporation: historical data for fiscal years 2013–2017

		Revenues	Net income
Performance:	2013	$1.550 billion	$32 million
	2014	$1.562 billion	$44 million
	2015	$1.636 billion	$295 million
	2016	$1.673 billion	$41 million
	2017	$1.742 billion	$52 million
		Gross margins:	Operating margin:
Profitability ratios:	2013	53.84 per cent	1.36 per cent
	2014	53.57 per cent	0.67 per cent
	2015	53.63 per cent	2.01 per cent
	2016	54.43 per cent	4.04 per cent
	2017	53.23 per cent	5.10 per cent

(continued)

Table 11.5 Continued

		Revenues	Net income
		Net profit margin:	Return on equity:
Profitability ratios:	2013	2.01 per cent	3.60 per cent
	2014	2.84 per cent	4.85 per cent
	2015	18.01 per cent	24.45 per cent
	2016	2.42 per cent	3.22 per cent
	2017	3.0 per cent	4.0 per cent
Equity ratios: Year		Return on capital earnings per share:	Return on dividend per share:
	2013:	$0.15 cents	$0.50
	2014:	$0.41	$0.55
	2015:	$0.46	$0.60
	2016:	$1.26	$0.60
	2017:	$1.15	$0.60
		Book value per share:	Cash value per share:
Equity ratios:	2013	$27.22	$2.75
	2014	$28.34	$0.65
	2015	$36.29	$15.27
	2016	$36.56	$11.62
	2017	$37.26	$12.65
		Return on capital employed:	Return on assets:
Profitability ratios:	2013	2.07 per cent	2.16 per cent
	2014	0.95 per cent	2.90 per cent
	2015	2.58 per cent	16.17 per cent
	2016	5.06 per cent	2.36 per cent
	2017	6.47 per cent	2.97 per cent

Source: The Scholastic Corporation. Annual Report 2012–2013; at: http://files.shareholder.com/downloads/ABEA-28S6DN/5588957146x0x709522/0E586EC3-7852-43FA-8EFA-ABD50FCE84E9/73994_Annual_Report_Web_0731123616.pdf; The Scholastic Corporation. Annual Report 2013-2014; at: http://files.shareholder.com/downloads/ABEA-28S6DN/5588957146x0x775130/F1778701-3A0C-4E64-A4E8-7AD0BC90140D/SCHL_ANNUAL_REPORT_-_2014.pdf; The Scholastic Corporation. Annual Report 2014–2015; at: http://files.shareholder.com/downloads/ABEA-28S6DN/5588957146x0x847824/8B6E17B7-BF08-4472-A71C-75DDF43AD84D/web_enabled_final_2015_annual_report.pdf; The Scholastic Corporation. Annual Report 2015–2016; at: http://files.shareholder.com/downloads/ABEA-28S6DN/5588957146x0x904587/0420F02A-5288-400E-8169-0D57F0233A85/2016_Annual_Report.pdf; The Scholastic Corporation. Annual Report 2016–2017; at: http://files.shareholder.com/downloads/ABEA-28S6DN/5588957146x0x904587/0420F02A-5288-400E-8169-0D57F0233A85/2016_Annual_Report.pdfhttp://files.shareholder.com/downloads/ABEA-28S6DN/5588957146x0x953550/5E26BBB0-391B-4380-B619-52C3D4640D95/final_2017_annual_report.pdf.

Scholastic's gross margins declined slightly between 2013 and 2017; yet its operating margins, which vacillated during those years, ended significantly up by 2017. Gains were also posted in many other metrics, including return on capital earnings per share (up a staggering 666.7 per cent), return on dividend per share (+20 per cent), book value per share (+33.88 per cent), cash value per share (a dramatic 360 per cent increase), return on capital employed, and return on assets. While financial service companies pay a great deal of attention to understanding a company's valuation,[47] many traditional valuations are unable to capture the value of intellectual properties or the fact that books are capital assets.[48]

Conclusion

Anyone who is familiar with publishing's history[49] knows that it is a dynamic industry, constantly re-inventing itself with new authors and genres (and sub-genres) as cultural, business, and economic conditions change. While it tends to be product oriented, an issue addressed by Theodore Levitt in his insightful article 'Marketing Myopia',[50] industry leaders have tried to change the industry into a more market-oriented business, seeking to understand the 'behavioural economics' of who, what, when, where, how, and why readers find and buy a specific title. In addition, publishers and editors (and some authors) have adopted more economic metrics to gauge the financial success of a book.

Yet book publishing since 1450 has been, and will remain, one of the major creative copyright industries. This means that certain economic concepts work, and some do not work, because book publishing is not like most businesses that sell products or services to consumers (e.g. athletic apparel; automobiles; computers; etc.).

For example, the USA experienced an annual surge of new books, averaging well beyond 1 million new titles annually, since 2009 (topping 4.1 million in 2010) according to data released by Bowker.[51] The Association of American Publishers' data on the US market is relevant: in 2016 publishers had revenues of $26.24 billion (+1.5 per cent over 2015) in net revenues on the sale of 2.7 billion books (+2.8 per cent over 2015; also net data); and trade books posted net revenues of $15.9 billion (versus $15.67 billion in 2016) with units topping 2.48 billion units (in 2015 it was 2.415 billion).[52]

Very few industries release such a torrent of new products annually. This means that authors and editors experience dual-sided uncertainty[53] since neither know in advance with any certainty, except for a relatively small cluster of about a dozen bestselling authors (e.g. Mary Higgins Clark; Dan Brown), if a book will be successful

---

[47] Barclay Hedge; at https://www.barclayhedge.com/products/best-hedge-funds-database.html. Also see Hill and Zeller (2008); Goebel (2015).

[48] Soloveichik (2014).

[49] Excellent examples include: Coser et al. (1983); Davis (1984); Tebbel (1987); Silverman (2008); Hall (2012); Kachka (2013); Bernstein (2016); Claridge (2016).

[50] Levitt (1975).

[51] Bowker, 'ISBN Output Report, 2002–2013' at http://media.bowker.com/documents/isbn_output_2002_2013.pdf. Also see Bowker, 'Self-Publishing in the United States, 2011–2016' at http://media.bowker.com/documents/bowker-selfpublishing-report2016.pdf

[52] Association of American Publishers. 'Book Publishing Annual StatShot Survey Reveals Religious Crossover and Inspirational Books Supported Trade Book Growth in 2016' at http://newsroom.publishers.org/book-publishing-annual-statshot-survey-reveals-religious-crossover-and-inspirational-books-supported-tradebook-growth-in-2016.

[53] Cramton (1984).

in the marketplace of ideas. The proliferation of new titles also poses a sizeable economic challenge because of the complex nature of the book publishing, book buying, and book reading ecosystem. Complexity in the marketplace has been analysed by Gokce Sargut and Rita Gunther McGrath, who wrote that 'complex organizations are far more difficulty to manage than merely complicated ones. It's harder to predict what will happen, because complex systems interact in unexpected ways.... It's harder to place bets, because the past behavior of a complex system may not predict its future behavior.'[54]

So, not every publisher has been able to take advantage of the various applied economic theories. But most publishers have realized that the economics of the book publishing industry are harsh and unforgiving unless publishers come to grips with the fact that book publishing is a business, and a demanding domestic and global business today, in a complex, adaptive, partially chaotic, constantly changing, and shifting marketplace. Publishers who understood, and applied well-established economic theories, or modified some of the theories listed above, profited. The ones that did not ended up going out of business or were acquired by a larger firm. This has been true for decades; and it will be true in the foreseeable future.

REFERENCES

Association of American Publishers (2017). 'Monthly Stat Shot December 2016', 24 May, p. 3; sales from 1,207 publishers; available at http://newsroom.publishers.org/aap-statshot-book-publisher-trade-sales-flat-for-2016.

Axelrod, Robert and Michael D. Cohen (2000). *Harnessing Complexity: Organizational Implications of a Scientific Frontier*, New York: Basic Books.

Bachelier, Louis (2006). *Louis Bachelier's Theory of Speculation: The Origins of Modern Finance*, trans Mark Davis and Alison Etheridge, Princeton, NJ: Princeton University Press.

Banks, David (2015). 'Approaching the Journal des Savants, 1665–1695: A Manual Analysis of Thematic Structure', *Journal of World Languages*, 2(1), pp. 1–17.

Bernstein, Robert L. (2016). *Speaking Freely: My Life in Publishing and Human Rights*, New York: New Press.

Black, Fischer (1986). 'Noise', *The Journal of Finance*, 41(3), pp. 529–543.

Black, Fischer and Myron Scholes (1973). 'The Pricing of Options and Corporate Liabilities', *Journal of Political Economy*, 81(3), pp. 637–59.

Bogart, Dave, ed. (2003a). *The Bowker Annual: Library and Book Trade Almanac 2003*, 48th ed. Medford, NJ: Information Today.

Bogart, Dave, ed. (2003b). *The Library and Book Trade Almanac 2015*, 60th edition, Medford, NJ: Information Today.

Bowker, R. R. 'Self-Publishing ISBNs Climbed 8 per cent Between 2015–2016', available at http://www.bowker.com/news/2017/Self-Publishing-ISBNs-Climbed-8-Between-2015-2016.html.

Cassidy, John (2009). 'Postscript: Paul Samuelson', *The New Yorker*, 14 December, available at http://www.newyorker.com/news/john/cassidy/postscript-paul-samuelson.

---

[54] Sargut and McGrath (2011). Also see Axelrod and Cohen (2000: 11–20).

Cerf, Bennett (1977). *At Random*, New York: Random House.

Chandler, Alfred D. (1962). *Strategy and Structure: Chapters in the History of the American Industrial Enterprise*, Cambridge, MA: MIT Press.

Christensen, Clayton M. (2011). *The Innovator's Dilemma*, New York: HarperCollins.

Claridge, Laura (2016). *The Lady With the Borzoi: Blanche Knopf, Literary Tastemaker Extraordinaire*, New York: Farrar, Straus and Giroux.

Coser, Lewis A., Charles Kadushin, and Walter W. Powell (1983). *Books: The Culture and Commerce of Publishing*, Chicago: University of Chicago Press.

Cramton, Peter C. (1984). 'Bargaining with Incomplete Information: An Infinite-Horizon Model With Two-Sided Uncertainty', *The Review of Economic Studies*, 51(4), pp. 579–93.

Davis, Kenneth C. (1984). *Two-Bit Culture: The Paperbacking of America*, Boston, MA: Houghton Mifflin.

Dittmar, Jeremiah E. (2011). 'Information Technology and Economic Change: The Impact of the Printing Press', *Quarterly Journal of Economics*, 126, pp. 1133–72.

Eisenstein, Elizabeth L. (1980). *The Printing Press as an Agent of Change* (Volumes 1 and 2 in one volume), Cambridge: Cambridge University Press.

Eisenstein, Elizabeth L. (2012). *The Printing Revolution in Early Modern Europe*, Cambridge: Cambridge University Press.

Fama, Eugene F. (1963). 'Mandelbrot and the Stable Paretian Hypothesis', *The Journal of Business*, 36(4), pp. 420–9.

Fama, Eugene F. (1965). 'Random Walks in Stock Market Prices', *Financial Analysts Journal* 21(5), pp. 55–9.

Fama, Eugene F. (1970). 'Efficient Capital Markets: A Review of Theory and Empirical Work', *The Journal of Finance*, 25(2), pp. 383–417.

Fama, Eugene F. (1991). 'Efficient Capital Markets: II', *The Journal of Finance*, 46(5), pp. 1575–617.

Fama, Eugene F. (1998). 'Market Efficiency, Long-Term Returns, and Behavioral Finance', *Journal of Financial Economics*, 49(3), pp. 283–306.

Friedman, Milton (1993). *Why Government Is the Problem*, Stanford, CA: Hoover Institution Press.

Friedman, Milton (2002). *Capitalism and Freedom: 40th Anniversary Issue*, Chicago: University of Chicago Press.

Friedman, Milton and Anna Schwartz (1993). *A Monetary History of the United States, 1867–1960*, Princeton, NJ: Princeton University Press.

Goebel, Viktoria (2015). 'Estimating a Measure of Intellectual Capital Value to Test its Determinants', *Journal of Intellectual Capital*, 16(1), pp. 101–20.

Greco, Albert N. (2015). *The Economics of the Publishing and Information Industries: The Search for Yield in a Disintermediated World*, New York and London: Routledge.

Greco, Albert N., Jim Milliot, and Robert M. Wharton (2015). *The Book Publishing Industry*, 3rd edition, New York and London: Routledge.

Hall, James W. (2012). *Hit Lit: Cracking the Code of the Twentieth Century's Biggest Bestsellers*, New York: Random House.

Hicks, John R. (1982). *Money, Interest, and Wages* (Collected Essays on Economic Theory Vol. 2), Cambridge, MA: Harvard University Press.

Hill, John W. and Thomas L. Zeller (2008). 'The New Value Imperative for Privately Held Companies: The Why, What, and How of Value Management Strategy', *Business Horizons*, 51(6), pp. 541–53.

Judt, Tony (2006). *Postwar: A History of Europe Since 1945*, New York: Penguin Books.

Kachka, Boris (2013). *Hot House: The Art of Survival and the Survival of Art at America's Most Celebrated Publishing House, Farrar, Straus & Giroux*, New York: Simon & Schuster.

Kahneman, Daniel (1991). 'Judgment and Decision Making: A Personal View', *Psychological Science*, 2(3), pp. 142–5.

Kahneman, Daniel (2003). 'Maps of Bounded Rationality: Psychology for Behavioral Economics', *The American Economic Review*, 93(5), pp. 1449–75.

Kahneman, Daniel and Amos Tversky (1979). 'Prospect Theory: An Analysis of Decision Under Risk', *Econometrica*, 47(2), pp. 267–91.

Kahneman, Daniel and Amos Tversky (1984). 'Choices, Values, and Frames', *American Psychologist*, 39(4), pp. 341–50.

Keynes, John Maynard (2008). *The General Theory of Employment, Interest, and Money*, New York: BN Publishing.

Levitt, Theodore (1975). 'Marketing Myopia', *Harvard Business Review*, 53(5), pp. 26–9.

McCutcheon, Roger Philip (1924). 'The Journal des Savants and the Philosophical Transactions of the Royal Society', *Studies in Philology*, 21(4), p. 626.

Markowitz, Harry (1952). 'Portfolio Selection', *The Journal of Finance*, 7(1), pp. 77, 79.

Marshall, Alfred (2013). *Principles of Economics*, New York: Palgrave Macmillan.

Merton, Robert C. (2006). 'Paul Samuelson and Financial Economics', *American Economist*, 50(2), pp. 18–21.

Milliot, Jim (2017a). 'AAP's First Report on 2016 Shows Sales Down', *Publishers Weekly*, 15 June; available at https://www.publishersweekly.com/pw/by-topic/industry-news/financial-reporting/article/73991-industry-sales-dropped-6-6-in-2016.html.

Milliot, Jim (2017b). 'Pearson Rises Above', *Publishers Weekly*, 28 August, p. 57.

Milliot, Jim (2017c). 'Self-Published ISBNs Hit 786,935 in 2016', *Publishers Weekly*, d; available at https://www.publishersweekly.com/pw/by-topic/industry-news/manufacturing/article/75139-self-published-isbns-hit-786-935-in-2016.html.

Mullainathan, Sendhil and Richard H. Thaler (2000). 'Behavioral Economics', NBER Working Paper No. 7948; October; available at http://www.nber.org/papers/w7948.

Pinder, John and Simon Underwood (2013). *The European Union: A Short History*, 3rd edition, Oxford: Oxford University Press.

Samuelson, Paul (1965). 'Proof That Properly Anticipated Prices Fluctuate Randomly', *Industrial Management Review*, 6(2), pp. 41–9.

Samuelson, Paul (1966a). *The Collected Scientific Papers of Paul Samuelson*, Vol. 1, ed. Joseph E. Stiglitz, Cambridge, MA: MIT Press.

Samuelson, Paul (1966b). *The Collected Scientific Papers of Paul Samuelson*, Vol. 2, ed. Joseph E. Stiglitz, Cambridge, MA: MIT Press.

Samuelson, Paul (1973a). 'Mathematics of Speculative Price', *SIAM Review*, 15(1), pp. 1–42.

Samuelson, Paul (1973b). 'Proof that Properly Discounted Present Values of Assets Vibrate Randomly', *The Bell Journal of Economics and Management Science*, 4(2), pp. 369–74.

Samuelson, Paul (1983). *Foundations of Economic Analysis*, Cambridge, MA: Harvard University Press.

Samuelson, Paul and Kate Crowley (1986). *The Collected Scientific Papers of Paul Samuelson*, Vol. 5, Cambridge, MA: MIT Press.

Sargut, Gokce and Rita Gunther McGrath (2011). 'Learning to Live with Complexity: How to Make Sense of the Unpredictable in Today's Hyperconnected Business World', *Harvard Business Review*, 89(9), pp. 69–76.

Scholes, Myron (1972). 'The Market for Securities: Substitution Versus Price Pressure and the Effects of Information on Share Prices', *The Journal of Business*, 45(2), pp. 179–211.

Shiller, Robert J. (2000). *Irrational Exuberance*, Princeton, NJ: Princeton University Press.

Silverman, Al (2008). *The Time of Their Lives: The Golden Age of Great American Publishers, Their Editors, and Authors*, New York: St. Martin's Press.

Smith, Adam (2003). *The Wealth of Nations*, New York: Bantam Books.

Soloveichik, Rachel (2014). 'Books As Capital Assets', *Journal of Scholarly Publishing*, 45(2), pp. 101–27.

Steil, Benn (2014). *The Battle of Bretton Woods: John Maynard Keynes, Harry Dexter White, and the Making of a New World Order*, Princeton, NJ: Council on Foreign Relations—Princeton University Press.

Tebbel, John (1980). *A History of Book Publishing in the United States Vol. IV The Great Change*, New York: R.R. Bowker.

Tebbel, John (1987). *Between Covers: The Rise and Transformation of American Book Publishing*, New York: Oxford University Press.

Thaler, Richard H. (1990). 'Anomalies: Saving, Fungibility, and Mental Accounts', *Journal of Economic Perspectives*, 4(1), pp. 193–205.

Thaler, Richard H. (1999). 'Mental Accounting Matters', *Journal of Behavioral Decision Making*, 12(3), pp. 183–206.

Thaler, Richard H. (2009). *Nudge: Improving Decisions About Health, Wealth, and Happiness*, New York: Penguin Books.

Thaler, Richard H. (2015). *Misbehaving: The Making of Behavioral Economics*, New York: W.W. Norton & Company.

Thaler, Richard H. and Eric J. Johnson (1990). 'Gambling with the House Money and Trying to Break Even: The Effects of Prior Outcomes on Risky Choice', *Management Science*, 36(6), pp. 643–60.

Vittu, Jean-Pierre (2005). 'Du *Journal des Savants* aux *Memoires Pour L'Historie des Sciences et des Beaux-Arts*: L'Esquisse d'un Systeme European des Periodiques Savants', *Dix-Septieme Siecle*, 3, pp. 527–45.

CHAPTER 12

....

THE STRATEGY
OF PUBLISHING

....

ALBERT N. GRECO

There is a tide in the affairs of men
Which, taken at the flood, leads on to fortune;
Omitted, all the voyage of their life
Is bound in shallows and in miseries...

William Shakespeare, *Julius Caesar*
[Act IV. Scene iii]

MOST marketing and strategy researchers, including Theodore Levitt, Peter Drucker, and Michael E. Porter, believe that the purpose of a business is to satisfy the wants and needs of customers, including current, potential, and former customers. If this is achieved, then a company has an opportunity, but not the guarantee, to earn a profit. And this means that a book publisher needs to find and keep customers willing to buy and read the publisher's books.

An entrepreneur running a small publishing house in Paris (with annual revenues of €200,000) or the president of Penguin Random House (2016 annual revenues of $3.697 billion)[1] need a coherent strategy and a realistic structure to achieve the strategy. The basic building blocks of strategy are well known (e.g. analysis; formulation; and execution and implementation). However, this is not an easy task since it involves complex research activities, including: scanning the overall business environment (e.g. interest rates; unemployment rates; Gross Domestic Product; domestic consumer expenditures; etc.); researching the industry's environment (e.g. direct competitors; channels of distribution; the firm's skills; human and capital resources; gross and net margins; cost of goods sold; debt levels; etc.); and then creating and analysing its current and future strategy. There has been a plethora of strategic theories, a few of which have stood the test of time and influenced book publishing editors, marketing and sales personnel, and publishers.

[1] Milliot (2017b). All of the revenue data used in this chapter came from various Milliot articles that appeared in *Publishers Weekly*.

THE DEVELOPMENT
OF STRATEGIC THEORIES

In this section, an overview of various strategies is presented. The goal is to provide the reader with a sense of the development of some of the important substantive strategic theories that influenced managers over the centuries in different industries including the book publishing sector. Marketers and strategy researchers always write about the '4Ps' (i.e. product; price; placement; and promotion) and markets (i.e. consumer; business; and governmental). Some of the following authors were not marketers. And they did not specifically address products or markets. However, their comments do relate, directly or indirectly, to strategies and structures utilized in the book publishing industry since the day Gutenberg used moveable type and a make-shift printing press (based on the wine press) in 1450 to print his Bible; and this new printing press was used by Martin Luther to trigger the Reformation, perhaps the first use of a 'book publishing strategy' in the nascent world of publishing.

The Ancient World

Heraclitus (535–475 BCE) was known for his thoughts on constant change. 'No man ever steps in the same river twice.'[2] Heraclitus was not interested in business endeavours, but his comment on change relates specifically to the fact that business environments change constantly, from the impact of the introduction of electricity in the printing and production of books, the creation of national bookstore chains, or the launch of the Internet and its impact on the development of ebooks.

Gaius Julius Caesar (100–44 BCE) wrote about military strategy. One of his most famous quotes was 'veni, vidi, vici' (i.e. 'I came. I saw. I conquered')[3]; and many business executives embraced the notion that business was war. Kevin O'Leary, an entrepreneur on the US television show *Shark Tank*, who was involved at one time in the digital publishing sector, said, 'My attitude is business is war.... You want to steal their market share. You want to destroy them and get their customers.'[4]

Ricardo and Comparative Advantage

David Ricardo (1772–1823) was influenced by Adam Smith's *The Wealth of Nations*. Ricardo's *The Principles of Political Economy and Taxation* addressed many important

---

[2] Heraclitus. His quote appears in Plato's *Cratylus: The Comedy of Language*, ed. Shane Montgomery Ewegen (Bloomington, IN: Indiana University Press, 2013), paragraph 402A.

[3] Gaius Julius Caesar. This quote appears in Suetonius, *Vol. 1 The Lives of the Caesars—Julius, Augustus, Tiberius, Gaius, and Caligula.* Trans J. C. Rolfe (Cambridge, MA: Harvard University Press, 1914), 177.

[4] Kevin O'Leary. Available at http://www.businessinsider.com/shark-tank-investor-kevin-oleary-2015-2.

economic ideas, including the value of money, rent theory, prices, and commerce.[5] However, his ideas on comparative advantage were exceptionally important and influential, especially to Michael E. Porter as well as many book publishers. 'Under a system of perfectly free commerce, each country naturally devotes its capital and labor to such employments as are most beneficial to each.'[6] Ricardo posited that Portugal should make wine, and England should concentrate on activities where it possessed a natural competitive advantage, for example wheat production. A book publishing firm that specializes in, perhaps, ebook romance novels reduces risks by avoiding large advances typically found in the adult trade hardcover fiction sector, creates economies of scale and mass production by eschewing printing and paper production expenditures, printed book inventories, and costly book returns (e.g. in 2015 in the United States, book returns for hard cover books was 26 per cent, mass market paperbacks was 46 per cent, and trade paperbacks was 20 per cent).[7] Some of these savings can be passed along to consumers with lower prices for their digital products.

Twentieth-century Strategists: Taylor and Barnard

Frederick W. Taylor (1856–1915) was a management consultant who attempted to melt the scientific methods of industrial engineering and manufacturing process into what he called *The Principles of Scientific Management*. Taylor insisted that managers develop effective work strategies and then train workers; and these trained workers would implement these strategies by avoiding traditional methods based on 'learning on the job'. 'It is only through enforced standardization of methods, enforced adoption of the best implements and working conditions and enforced cooperation that . . . faster work can be assured. And the duty of enforcing the adoption of standards and enforcing this cooperation rests with management alone.'[8] A relevant example includes the practices at most of the large 'Big 5' US trade publishing houses (Penguin Random House; HarperCollins; Simon & Schuster; Hachette/Little Brown; Holtzbrinck/Macmillan) where, before a book contract is issued, highly trained and experienced editorial, sales, marketing, and publicity personnel review and analyse the book's proposal and the book's projected profit and loss (P&L) statement; and then vote on issuing a book contract to an author. If the sales people insist they cannot sell the book, or if publicity has doubts on its ability to publicize the book, the book proposal might be revised or rejected.

Chester Barnard (1886–1961) was a business leader who crafted strategies about how organizations functioned, ideas similar to those developed by Taylor. 'An organization comes into being when: (1) there are persons able to communicate with each other; (2) who are willing to contribute action; and (3) to accomplish a common purpose.'[9]

---

[5] Ricardo (2004: Preface 1; ch, I, 11, 32; ch. II, 41; ch. XXIV, 220; ch. XXXII, 276).
[6] Ricardo (2004: ch. VII, 81). Also see Costinot and Donaldson (2012).
[7] Rosen and Milliot (2016).   [8] Taylor (1911: 83).   [9] Barnard (1938: 82).

Drucker: 'The man who invented management'

Peter Drucker (1909–2005) influenced countless numbers of managers and scholars with his extensive publication record, consultations, and university instruction. He was so important that Alan Kantrow published 'Why Read Peter Drucker?' in the *Harvard Business Review*.[10] Drucker's *The Practice of Management* set forth his overarching theories about management, marketing, and the business firm. Some of his major opinions include: 'there is only one valid definition of a business purpose: to create a customer',[11] and not just to make a profit; and 'a manager sets objectives; a manager organizes; a manager motivates and communicates; a manager, by establishing yardsticks, measures; a manager develops people',[12]—ideas influenced by the writings of Taylor and Barnard.

Drucker's *Management: Tasks, Responsibilities, Practices* is, arguably, his most important book. 'A management decision is irresponsible if it risks disaster this year for the sake of a grandiose future.'[13] 'The fault is in the system and not in the men.'[14] 'The purpose of an organization is to enable common men to do uncommon things.'[15] And 'there is a point of complexity beyond which a business is no longer manageable.'[16]

In 'What Makes an Effective Executive', Drucker analysed the strategy of Jack Welch. 'Jack Welch realized that what was needed to be done at General Electric when he took over as chief executive was not the overseas expansion he wanted to launch. It was getting rid of GE businesses that, no matter how profitable, could not be number one or number two in their industries.'[17] Drucker insisted that an effective executive needed to ask two substantive strategy questions. 'What needs to be done?' 'Is this the right thing [strategy] for the enterprise?'[18]

Important Strategists who Refined Strategic Thinking: Andrews and Chandler

Kenneth R. Andrews (1916–2005) played a major role in the development of business strategy. In *The Concept of Corporate Strategy*, Andrews posited that 'corporate strategy is the pattern of major objectives, purposes, or goals; and essential policies and plans for achieving those goals stated in such a way as to define what business the company is in or is to be in.... In a changing world, it is a way of expressing a persistent concept of the business so as to exclude some possible new activities and suggest entry into others.'[19]

---

[10] Kantrow (1980: 74, 76).   [11] Drucker (1954: 37, 344).   [12] Drucker (1954: 344).
[13] Drucker (1974: 43).   [14] Drucker (1974: 140).   [15] Drucker (1974: 455).
[16] Drucker (1974: 681).   [17] Drucker (2004: 59).
[18] Drucker (2004: 59, 60).   [19] Andrews 1987: 28).

Again, this strategy explains why most of the 'Big 5' trade book publishers avoided entering the complicated K-12 educational textbook publishing sector of English, mathematics, language, arts, etc.

Alfred D. Chandler (1918–2007) believed that a firm must first craft a realistic strategy based on economic, organizational, and industrial considerations, and then craft the structure to achieve the strategy. He observed that 'planning and carrying out the new strategy of diversification required more complex and more numerous strategic decisions than did the older one of consolidation, integration, and expansion within a single industry'.[20] Chandler's book, based on an extensive analysis of US business history (e.g. du Pont, Standard Oil of New Jersey, General Motors, etc.), formed the intellectual foundation of business strategy, a firm bedrock that other management and marketing authors built on in the future. An example is a new publishing operation's strategy to publish a series of juvenile fiction books. The firm must create the organizational structure (e.g. finding authors and illustrators who understand what interests an eight-year old child; book distribution to the bookstore chains, mass merchants, convenience stores, supermarkets) to reinforce and achieve the desired strategy.

Levitt and 'Marketing Myopia'

Theodore Levitt (1925–2006) believed that every firm must be customer and not product oriented, ideas that formed the foundation for his classic article 'Marketing Myopia'.[21] He approached strategy with a series of questions and observations. 'What business are you in?' 'Is your firm global'? He is credited with creating the term 'globalization'.

Writing about du Pont, Levitt insisted that 'without a very sophisticated eye on the customer, most of their new products might have been wrong; their sales methods useless'.[22] His observations about business failures, which he felt were indicative of myopic thinking, included Detroit's auto makers who failed because they never really researched consumer preferences.[23] Levitt also believed that far too many industries were totally focused on a specific product(s): they believed their product was indispensable (e.g. the printed encyclopedia); and they did not see how the product was being made obsolete (by online streaming of content),[24] Based on his research, Levitt came to believe that sales personnel knew the product, but not what the customer wanted. In some instances, they knew how the channels of distribution operated but not much about the ultimate consumer (e.g. few trade publishers conducted marketing studies of consumer preferences). For example, in 2015 some trade book publishers were surprised to find out that: romance book buyers spent $1.08 billion purchasing these books, representing 3 per cent of the entire US fiction book market; the average buyer and

---

[20] Chandler (1962: 78).   [21] Levitt (1975: 26).
[22] Levitt (1975: 27).   [23] Levitt (1975: 38).
[24] Levitt (1975: 28, 33, 44). Also see The Encyclopedia Britannica at https://www.britannica.com.

reader of romance novels was a female 30–44; and 61 per cent of them preferred ebooks versus only 26 per cent who preferred mass market paperbacks.[25]

Buffett: 'The Sage of Omaha'

Warren Buffett (1930–) is one of the most influential investors in the past fifty years because of his successes at Berkshire Hathaway, with 2016 annual revenues of $232.8 billion and a gross profit of $179.85 billion.[26] However, Buffett's musings on strategy caught the attention of investors and academics. 'If you understand a business perfectly and the future of the business, you would need very little in the way of a margin of safety. So, the more vulnerable the business is...the larger margin of safety you would need.'[27]

To achieve a level of safety, Buffett was a strong proponent of what he called the 'castle and moat' theory. If the 'castle' is the brand—perhaps the Penguin Classics with over 1,300 titles[28]—then the 'castle' must be protected with as wide a 'moat' as possible. A 'moat' is a competitive advantage that one company has against it competitors (copyrights; trademarks; patents); and to Buffett companies with defensive moats tend to outperform competitors financially. The concept of the 'wide moat' has been adopted by many financial service companies, academic researchers, and most of the large trade book publishers.[29]

Michael E. Porter and Strategy

All the authors listed so far in this section made substantive contributions to strategic theories and practices. However, the scholarly articles and books of Michael E. Porter (1947–) have had an inordinate influence on countless researchers and managers.

Porter, borrowing the idea of competitive advantage from Ricardo, believed that a firm needed to differentiate itself in the marketplace by creating products or services different or more attractive from the competition. 'Strategy is about making choices, trade-offs; it's about deliberately choosing to be different.'[30] The structural elements of strategy, to Porter, can include one or more of the following. First, a company should locate a potentially profitable niche (perhaps young adult books; YA). Second, once this is done, then it is necessary to develop products designed to satisfy the needs of the customers in this market segment. Third, since firms are all active in the same sector, it is imperative to create a defensive plan designed to withstand the intense competitive thrusts of other companies eager to gain market share and profits in this niche (ideas

---

[25] See the statistics issued by the Romance Writers of America at: www.rwa.org/p/cm/id/fid=580; also see Hayes and Abernathy (1980: 68).

[26] Berkshire Hathaway, Inc., the 2016 annual report at: http://www.berkshirehathaway.com/2016ar/2016ar.pdf.

[27] Kirkpatrick (2000: 1615).   [28] Penguin Classics; at: www.penguinclassics.com.

[29] Boyd (2005).   [30] Porter (1996: 70).

borrowed from Buffett). Fourth, accounting and financial issues must be analysed; and this means evaluating existing economies of scale, capital requirements, and cost disadvantages independent of size. Fifth, a review of substantive marketing issues is needed to determine product differentiation (perhaps YA mystery books); make sure that all of the diverse sales and marketing strategic business units (SBUs) constantly convey the benefits offered by the differentiated offerings; and also consider existing and/or new distribution channels. Sixth, current regulatory agency rules, and any relevant laws, must be scrutinized. Seventh, for some, but not all companies, the creation and support for outstanding research and development (R&D) operations allows the firm to stay ahead of its competitors while delivering consistently high-quality products or services that can change as the market changes. Eight, a successful firm stays agile in the marketplace (perhaps drop YA mystery and add YA romance if the market changes, as it inevitably does).[31]

Porter's overarching theory to achieve strategic advantages was his innovative 'Five Forces' model; and it includes understanding and coping with: (1) supplier power; (2) barriers to entry; (3) the threat of substitutes; (4) buyer power; and (5) the degree of rivalry.[32] Almost every firm requires some type of 'raw material' (i.e. manuscripts to be evaluated and possibly published; ink, paper, and binding for the printed book; etc.). So, every book house, small or large, has a 'buyer–supplier' relationship with potential authors, printers, warehouse-distribution operations, bookstores, mass merchants, price clubs, etc. And in book publishing, 'suppliers' can and do exert a powerful influence on publishing enterprises. They are 'powerful', according to Porter, if they exhibit any of the following: the ability to develop forward integration operations (e.g. a book author using a self-publishing option); and powerful customers, which can include boycotts of a book publisher because of authors on its list.

Other important ideas for Porter included that a firm must concentrate on core competencies and competitive positioning. A successful firm must understand the basic difference between operational effectiveness and strategy. Operational effectiveness is critical if a firm is to compete effectively in the marketplace; but operational effectiveness alone is not sufficient to win in the complex, always changing marketplace. In essence, operational effectiveness means doing things better than the company's competitors; and strategic positioning means doing different things than competitors.[33]

Lastly, Porter developed additional suggestions for firms (often based on ideas put forward by Drucker and Levitt). 'The essence of strategy is choosing what not to do.'[34] Business is not war; all firms in an industry can profit if the economic 'pie' gets bigger. Strategy means using the right metrics, including the 'value chain'. 'The essence of formulating strategy is relating a company to its environment.'[35] The idea of 'low cost relative to competitors becomes the theme running through the entire strategy, though quality, service, and other areas cannot be ignored.'[36]

[31] Porter (1998b: 5–32, 34–44, 47–71). Also see Porter (1998a: 4–10, 14–25).
[32] Porter (2008b: 80).
[33] Porter (1998a: 14–25, 120–49; 2008a: 117–54).   [34] Porter (1996: 70).
[35] Porter (1998a: 3).   [36] Porter (1998a: 35).

Clearly, Porter has had a tremendous influence on strategic research, managers, and publishers. However, some researchers have questioned some of the basic tenets of strategic theories.

Mintzberg and Portfolio Theory

Henry Mintzberg (1939–) insisted that, all too frequently, there are limits to the implementation of strategies. 'When strategic planning arrived on the scene in the mid-1960s, corporate leaders embraced it as "the one best way" to devise and implement strategies.... Planning systems were expected to produce the best strategies as well as step-by-step instructions for carrying out those strategies so that the doers, the managers of businesses, could not get them wrong. As we now know, planning has not exactly worked out that way.'[37]

Based on his research, Mintzberg described how managers really deal with business problems as 'planners as strategy finders'. He stated that 'some of the most important strategies emerge without the intention or sometimes even the awareness of top managers. Fully exploiting these strategies, though, often requires that they be recognized and then broadened in their impact, like taking a new use for a product [or event] accidentally discovered by a salesperson and turning it into a major new business.'[38] Firms and their employees are communities, where people work together, where theory is just an idea in a textbook, where managing is both an art and a science (and more art than science to Mintzberg); facts that Mintzberg believed escaped the attention of many researchers.

An example of what Mintzberg described was the creation and development of Post-Its, those ubiquitous small yellow rectangles of paper with an adhesive on the back that consumers use to mark pages in a book. It was discovered in 1968 by Spencer Silver a chemist at the 3-M company. Silver was at his church choir practice, and he dropped his book with all of the important hymns marked with small pieces of paper. To address this annoying problem, he developed an adhesive for a piece of paper that would stick but not damage the page. By 1974, he had a practical application for an early version of the Post-It. His employer, 3-M, field tested the product, and in 1980 the company released the first Post-Its for consumer and business use. And the result was a product that created a new strategic business unit, Post-Its. A product that was created without the use of any major strategic plans; it was the 'solution to a problem nobody realized existed'.[39] For decades, many book editors marked up a book manuscript with yellow Post-Its before the development of more efficient on-line editorial systems.

---

[37] Mintzberg (1994: 107).   [38] Mintzberg (1994: 113).
[39] CNN. 'The 'Hallelujah Moment' Behind the Invention of the Post-It Note' at http://www.cnn.com/2013/04/04/tech/post-it-note-history/index.html.

Mintzberg raised substantive issues. Sometimes the unexpected occurs that shakes the very foundation of a successful publishing company. Some family-managed firms struggled and had to sell to a larger publishing house (e.g. Scribner's to Simon & Schuster); and some ceased operations because of steep financial losses (e.g. Duquesne University Press). Other authors also addressed the impact of the unknown and unknowable.

Other Important Authors on Strategy

Nassim Nicholas Taleb (1960–) in *The Black Swan: The Impact of the Highly Improbable* wrote that Europeans believed all swans were white, until black swans were discovered in the New World. 'The central idea of this book concerns our blindness with respect to randomness, particularly the large deviations.... Black Swan logic makes what you do not know far more relevant than what you do know.'[40]

David Levy (1957–) wrote that 'it is almost impossible to predict the impact of the advent of a new competitor or technology in an industry. The fundamental problem is that industries evolve in a dynamic way over time because of complex inter-actions.... Indeed, many strategic theories attempt to classify firms and industries and to describe appropriate strategies for each: examples include the Boston Consulting Group matrix for resource allocation.... Although these models are based on recurring patterns that we recognize in the real world, there are usually far too many exceptions for the models to have much predictive value.'[41]

Arthur De Vany (1937–) and W. David Walls (1957–) insisted that many of the creative industries, including the book publishing industry, have certain common characteristics. Book publishing is 'semi-chaotic' to DeVany and Walls in that the business is trying to make sense of changing consumer interests and needs for printed and ebooks and genres with remarkably little precise information about why consumers buy, or do not buy, books. Book publishing is, in reality, a business where no one knows very much for sure.[42]

Roger L. Martin (1956–) and Tony Golsby-Smith (1956–) in 'Management Is Much More Than A Science: The Limits Of Data-Driven Decision Making', wrote that 'trans-forming customer habits and experiences is what great business innovations do.... To be sure, innovators often incorporate scientific discoveries in their creations, but their real genius lies in their ability to imagine products or processes that simply never existed before. The real world is not merely an outcome determined by ineluctable laws of science.... A scientific approach to business decision making has limitations, and managers need to figure out where those limitations lie.'[43]

---

[40] Taleb (2007: xix).   [41] Levy (1994: 167).   [42] De Vany and Walls (1996: 1513).
[43] Martin and Golsby-Smith (2017: 30). Library of Congress, United States Copyright Office. 'Circular 15T; at: https://www.copyright.gov/circs/circ15t.pdf. Also see 17 U.S.C. (the Copyright Law of the United States) regarding copyrights; at: https://www.copyright.gov/title17/92chap1.html.

IMPACT OF STRATEGIC THEORIES

This section examines the impact that some of these strategic theories had in the book publishing sector. Strategic management and marketing theories and practices impacted managers in the USA and elsewhere because of a number of important trends and developments. First, in the years after 1945, and especially by the 1950s and 1960s, many different economic and social forces were at play, including: the need to consider market and not just product marketing considerations; globalization and the emergence of the global marketplace; and the creation of regional economic and political organizations, including the European Union. These developments impacted business schools and their curricula. By the 1970s, business schools began to stress strategic management and marketing theories in their undergraduate and graduate curricula. The transformation of business education, and the concomitant outpouring of scholarly articles and books about strategy, reinforced existing strategic publishing practices utilized since the nineteenth century and/or influenced generations of corporate leaders who read those books and journal articles, were trained in business schools, or who came to industry from another field (perhaps law).

Penguin Random House

It was only a matter of time before many publishing firms began to implement, sometimes successfully and sometimes unsuccessfully, many of the managerial and marketing strategies that augmented or reinforced many of their existing strategies. Consolidation and corporate ownership were two of the dominant strategic trends in US book publishing industry; and the creation of Penguin Random House is an interesting case study of consolidation.

In 1945 Bantam Books was a very small paperback reprint house issuing out-of-print (OP) titles. It grew slowly and then rapidly because of the proliferation of and interest in the paperback books provided to American service personnel during World War 2, followed by the post-war interest in hard-to-find titles.[44] Due to the over-supply of paperback books at prices as low as 25 cents, Bantam sustained severe losses. New management was hired, but ultimately Bantam was sold to a series of companies unable to turn it around, including: (a) National General Cinema in 1968—motion picture and entertainment companies became very interested in book publishers because of their copyrighted content; (b) American Financial Corporation in 1973—financial service companies have long been interested in publishers again because of their content, copyrights, and revenue streams; and (c) *Instituto Finanzario Industriale* (IFI), an Italian company, in 1974.[45]

---

[44] Hench (2010: 19–131). See also Davis (1984: 1–55); Manning (2014: 41–92).

[45] Greco et al. (2014: 109–15).

Stability was attained when Germany's Bertelsmann AG decided to enter the large, lucrative US book publishing market by purchasing Bantam Books in 1981; Bantam Books had a large backlist of titles which produced impressive annual revenues. Bertelsmann AG was founded by Carl Bertelsmann in 1835 in Germany, and the company originally specialized in publishing religious books. Bertelsmann eventually published fiction, non-fiction, and other media products. The company decided to embark on an international expansion, first buying a Spanish publisher. Bertelsmann's successful purchase of Bantam Books triggered additional major acquisitions. In 1986, Bertelsmann acquired Doubleday Dell, creating a consolidated Bantam Doubleday Dell, allowing Bertelsmann to have a major presence in hardcover and paperback books as well some other domestic activities. Bertelsmann increased its international reach with operations in North and South America, Europe, and Asia.[46] In 1998, they purchased Random House, long considered by some industry observers as the most prestigious publishing house in the USA. In 2013, Penguin Books (owned by the UK's Pearson) and Bertelsmann created a partnership with a new publishing venture Penguin Random House (2016 revenues of $3.697 billion: 53 per cent owned by Bertelsmann; Pearson has the remaining 47 per cent). In October 2017, the parties agreed to a new corporate structure, with Bertelsmann buying 22 per cent of Pearson's share, increasing its ownership to 75 per cent, for approximately $1 billion.[47] Penguin Random House's imprints include: Penguin; Random House; Knopf; DK; Dutton; Viking; Ballantine Books; The Dial Press; etc. The company publishes 15,000 new printed books and 70,000 digital books annually.[48]

Bertelsmann has a number of strategic business units, including: RTL Group; Gruner + Jahr; BMG; Arvato; Bertelsmann Printing Group; and Bertelsmann Investments.[49] Bertelsmann's corporate strategy is as follows. 'Bertelsmann is going to make the Group a faster-growing, more digital, more international, and more diversified company in the years ahead, and gradually reshape the group over a period of five to ten years.... Strengthening the core, digital transformation, building growth platforms, and expanding the Group's presence in growth areas.'[50]

The other major 'Big 5' trade houses also had corporate ownership, launched global operations, and utilized the same strategic plans to sign the best 'big' trade authors able to generate consistently in excess of 1 million in unit sales domestically and globally.[51]

[46] Bertelsmann SE & Co. KGaA; at: https://www.bertelsmann.com/company/company-profile.
[47] Milliot (2017a).
[48] Penguin Random House; at http://www.penguinrandomhouse.com/imprints; see also: http://www.penguinrandomhouse.com/about-us.
[49] Bertelsmann SE & Co. KGaA; at https://www.bertelsmann.com/company/company-propfile.
[50] Bertelsmann SE & Co. KGaA; at https://bertelsmann.com/strategy.
[51] HarperCollins Publishers; at https://www:harpercollins.com. See also Simon & Schuster; at https://www.simonandschuster.com; Hachette Book Group; at https://www.hachettebookgroup.com; and Macmillan Science and Education and Macmillan Publishers; at https://www.macmillan.com.

Educational Publishers

The five largest educational book publishers in the K-12 and higher education sectors (Prentice Hall/Pearson; McGraw-Hill; John Wiley; Cengage; and Houghton Mifflin) originally published printed textbooks (e.g. reading, languages, arts, mathematics, science, social studies), supplementals, and teacher's editions primarily for a domestic market. And they modified their basic strategies and structures and moved eventually, in the late 1990s and early 2000s, into digital products; and many of these products worked in global markets, especially certain higher education textbooks (e.g. marketing; statistics; strategy), supplementals, online tests, chapter outlines, and learning management systems (LMS) that allowed a student to take online tests and quizzes that were graded by the computer systems, providing the teacher or college instructor with instant grades for each student on each question. These publishers also developed language programmes (e.g. English language LMS) for the global markets, perhaps students in China, Argentina, or Germany who wanted to study English.[52]

Oxford University Press and Cambridge University Press

The two largest university presses in the world are Oxford University Press (2016 revenues: $939 million) and Cambridge University Press ($332 million).[53] Both utilized successfully strategic theories of diversification, an emphasis on core competencies, and tremendous brand recognition (both are top ranked universities in the world; in 2017, Oxford was ranked first, and Cambridge was fourth) to reach global audiences.[54]

Oxford University Press, a department of the University of Oxford, publishes books (and scholarly journals) in an 'extremely broad academic and educational spectrum, and we aim to make our content available to our users in whichever format suits them best. We publish for all audiences—from pre-school to secondary level schoolchildren; students and academics; general readers to researchers; individuals to institutions.'[55] With roots in the fifteenth century (1478),[56] the press publishes 'more than 6,000 titles a year worldwide, in a variety of formats. Our range included dictionaries, English language teaching materials, children's books, journals, scholarly monographs, printed music, higher education textbooks, and schoolbooks.... We sell more than 110 million units each year, and most of those sales are outside the U.K.'[57]

---

[52] Pearson PLC. 'About Pearson;' at https://www.pearson.com/corporate/about-pearson.html; John Wiley & Sons; at www.wiley.com; Cengage Learning Holdings; at www.cengage.com; McGraw-Hill Education (not a public company); at www.mheducation.com; and Houghton Mifflin Harcourt; at hmhco.com. See also Milliot (2017c).

[53] Milliot (2017b).

[54] *The Times Higher Education.* 'World University Rankings 2016–2017'; at https://www.timeshigh-reducation.com/world-university-rankings/2017/world-rankings#1/page/O/length/25/sort_by/rank/order_order/asc/cols/stats.

[55] Oxford University Press, 'About Us'; at https://global.oup.com/about/introduction?cc=us.

[56] Oxford University Press, 'History'; at https://global.oup.com/about/oup_history/?cc=us.

[57] Oxford University Press, 'Publishing'; at https://global.oup.com/about/publishing?cc=us.

Cambridge University Press has as its mission 'to unlock people's potential with the best learning and research solutions. Our vision is a world of learning and research inspired by Cambridge, where we enable people to achieve success by providing the best learning and research solutions.... We use our profit for purpose, contributing to society by furthering the mission of our university.'[58]

Cambridge University Press has its origins in the sixteenth century (1584), 'making it the oldest publishing house in the world. Over the next four centuries, the press's reputation spread throughout Europe, based on excellence in scholarly publishing of academic texts, poetry, school books, prayer books, and Bibles. Along the way Cambridge published ground-breaking works such as Newton's *Principia Mathematica*.'[59] Cambridge expanded over the centuries, and it 'has over 50 offices across the globe... publishes over 50,000 titles by authors from over 100 countries.'[60]

Because of Cambridge's traditions, it has been able to adapt to a changing and expensive academic publishing ecosystem. The press made substantial investments in Cambridge Core (its digital platform), solutions, and services while expanding its already significant partnerships with educational institutions in Latin America, China, and other parts of the Pacific Rim.

In order to fulfil their publishing mission, Cambridge, along with Oxford, stressed the importance of Open Access scholarly book and journal publishing. Collectively, these two presses are among the leaders in offering both gold and green options to authors.[61] In addition, both capitalized on the growing interest in 'shorter' scholarly books (Oxford's 'Very short Introductions' and Cambridge's 'Cambridge Elements'), with lengths of around 20,000 to 30,000 words.[62]

The Size of the Major Book Publishing Firms

Any review of either financial metrics (e.g. revenues) or the global reach of these firms (Bertelsmann; HarperCollins; Simon & Schuster; Hachette; Macmillan; Pearson; McGraw-Hill; Wiley; Cengage; Houghton Mifflin; Oxford; and Cambridge) reveals that the publishing operations followed the generally accepted managerial and marketing strategies; and they achieved measures of success, and, in several instances, impressive levels of success, generating $21.83 billion in 2016. Table 12.1 lists the publishers, annual revenues, corporate owners, and some of their imprints.

---

[58] Cambridge University Press; at http://www.cambridge.org.
[59] Cambridge University Press, 'About Us'; at http://www.cambridge.org/about-us/what-we-do.
[60] Cambridge University Press, 'History'; at http://www.cambridge.org/about-us/who-we-are/history.
[61] Cambridge University Press, 'Annual Report for the Year Ended April 30, 2017'; at http://www.cambridge.org/about-us/annual-report-2017. See also Oxford University Press, 'Open Access Journals'; at https://academic.oup.com/journals/pages/open_access?
[62] Oxford University Press, 'Very Short Introduction Book Series'; at https://global.oup.com/academic/content/series/v/very-short-introductions-vsi/?cc=us&lang=en&; and Cambridge University Press, 'Individual Elements'; at https://www.repository.cam.ac.uk/bitstream/handle/1810/268209/PRE_ChrisHarrisonCUPSTM_V1_20171101.pdf?sequence=1.

Table 12.1 Major US trade and educational publishers: 2016 revenues

Publisher	Annual revenues 2016	Corporate owner	Major imprints
Prentice-Hall/ Pearson	$5.617 Billion*	Pearson PLC	Prentice-Hall; Pearson
Penguin Random House	$3.697 Billion	Bertelsmann AG and Pearson PLC	Penguin; Dial Press; Random House; Knopf; DK; Dutton; Viking
Hachette Book Group	$2.39 Billion	Hachette Livre	Little, Brown; Grand Central
McGraw-Hill	$1.757 Billion	Apollo Global Management	McGraw-Hill
John Wiley	$1.727 Billion**	John Wiley & Sons	Wiley
HarperCollins	$1.646 Billion	News Corp.	Harper Collins; William Morrow; Avon Books; Harper Academic
Cengage	$1.631 Billion	Cengage	Cengage Learning Holdings
Houghton Mifflin	$1.373 Billion***	Houghton Mifflin Harcourt	Houghton Mifflin
Macmillan Publishers	$1.226 Billion	Verlagsgrouppe Georg von Holtzbrinck	Henry Holt; St. Martin's Press; Tor/Forge; Farrar, Straus & Giroux
Simon & Schuster	$767 Million	CBS Television Network	The Free Press; Pocket Books; Simon & Schuster
Total	$21.83 Billion	–	–

*Pearson PLC's total includes trade books and educational books.
**Wiley's total includes trade, educational books, and scholarly journals.
***Houghton Mifflin Harcourt's total include trade and educational publishing.
Source: Corporate Annual Reports; and *Publishers Weekly.*

CONCLUSION

The world learned a bitter lesson between the 1920s and 2 September 1945 (the day the peace treaty ending World War 2 was signed on the deck of the *USS Missouri*). Books are, have always been, and will remain important; they are a primary format in the transmission of ideas, culture, and history. Dictators burn books because books inform, educate, and, in some instances, entertain the reader. The Gordian knot that publishers, editors, and authors faced since 1450, and still face today, was what exactly do readers want? Trying to get answers to this fundamental question makes the book publishing industry an exceptionally interesting and exciting industry.

After the end of World War 2, book publishers and editors returned home to build, or in some cases rebuild, viable publishing operations. A review of historical and statistical data indicates clearly that many strategic models influenced and aided countless publishing houses trying to cope with the uncertainty of volatile business changes. For example, in 1947, new book title output in the USA stood at 9,182; and the average hardcover fiction book had a suggested retail price of $2.66.[63] By 2015, depending on which statistical database you use: more than 1.4 million new titles were published; the average hardcover fiction book had a suggested retail price of $24.84; and 662.7 million printed books were sold.[64] These statistics reveal the renaissance of the book publishing industry from the ashes of World War 2.

Yet an objective analysis compels you to realize that the reliance, or the total reliance, on strategic models or formulas, whether it be value-chains, SWOT analyses (strengths; weaknesses; opportunities; and threats), the Boston Consulting Group grid (stars; cash cows; question marks; and dogs), websites, social media, trade meetings, trade shows, Book Expo America, the Frankfurt Book Fair, etc., must be tempered with the fact that people, markets, and governments are not always predictable. Sometimes unexpected legal barriers can emerge. Under the terms of the 'Copyright Term Extension Act' (1996),[65] on 1 January 2021, *The Great Gatsby* will fall out of copyright protection and into the public domain unless Simon & Schuster (or its parent owner the CBS Corporation) can convince the US Congress to extend copyright protection for this important novel; and on 1 January 2023, the Walt Disney Company will lose copyright protection for Mickey Mouse, its most important symbol.

Paul Samuelson (1915–2009), a great economist and a staunch supporter of using mathematical formulas and models, once said, 'there is a tempting and fatal fascination in mathematics. Albert Einstein warned against it. He said elegance was for tailors; do not believe in something because it's a beautiful formula. There will always be room for judgment.'[66] Samuelson was correct. While strategic theories have great value, and the ten largest US trade and educational publishers generated $21.83 billion in revenues in 2016, there is always room for editors, publishers, and sales and marketing managers in the diverse publishing industry to use their judgement when confronted with randomness, chaos, or uncertainty in what is a constantly changing, shifting, and exciting marketplace.

---

[63] Greco (2015: 183, 185).

[64] Nielsen. '2015 U.S. Book Industry Year-End Review'; at http://www.nielsen.com/us/en/insights/reports/2016/2015-us-book-industry-year-end-review.html. Also see Jonathan Segura. 'Print Book Sales Rose Again in 2016'; at https://www.publishersweekly.com/pw/by-topic/industry-news/bookselling/article/72450-print-book-sales-rose-again-in-2016.html; and GBO New York: German Book office. 'The U.S. Book Market'; at https://www.publishersweekly.com/pw/by-topic/industry-news/bookselling/article/72450-print-book-sales-rose-again-in-2016.html http://www.buchmesse.de/images/fbm/dokumente-ua-pdfs/2013/buchmarkt_usa_market_updated_november_15_2013.pdf_40487.pdf.

[65] Library of Congress, United States Copyright Office. 'Circular 15T'; at https://www.copyright.gov/circs/circ15t.pdf. See also 17 U.S.C. (the Copyright Law of the United States) regarding copyrights; at https://www.copyright.gov/title17/92chap1.html.

[66] Greco (2015: 33). Also see Paul Samuelson, 'The Trillion Dollar Bet' PBS transcript; at http://www.pbs.org/wgbh/transcripts/2704stockmarket.html.

References

Andrews, Kenneth R. (1987). *The Concept of Corporate Strategy*, Homewood, IL: Richard D. Irwin.

Barnard, Chester (1938). *The Functions of the Executive*, Cambridge. MA: Harvard University Press.

Boyd, David P. (2005). 'Financial Performance of Wide-Moat Companies', *Journal of Business & Finance Research*, 3(3), pp. 49–56.

Chandler, Alfred D. (1962). *Strategy and Structure: Chapters in the History of the American Industrial Enterprise*, Cambridge, MA: MIT Press.

Costinot, Arnaud and Dave Donaldson (2012). 'Ricardo's Theory of Comparative Advantage: Old Idea, New Evidence', *American Economic Review Papers and Proceedings*, 102(3), pp. 453–8.

Davis, Kenneth C. (1984). *Two-Bit Culture: The Paperbacking of America*, Boston. MA: Houghton Mifflin Company.

De Vany, Arthur and W. David Walls (1996). 'Bose–Einstein Dynamics and Adaptive Contracting in the Motion Picture Industry', *The Economic Journal*, 106(439), p. 1513.

Drucker, Peter (1954). *The Practice of Management*, New York: Harper & Row.

Drucker, Peter (1974). *Management: Tasks, Responsibilities, Practices*, New York: Harper & Row.

Drucker, Peter (2004). 'What Makes an Effective Executive', *Harvard Business Review*, 82(6), p. 59.

Greco, Albert N. (2015). *The Economics of the Publishing and Information Industries: The Quest for Yield in a Disintermediated World*, New York and London: Routledge.

Greco, Albert N., Jim Milliot, and Robert M. Wharton (2014). *The Book Publishing Industry*, 3rd edition, New York and London: Routledge.

Hayes, Robert H. and William J. Abernathy (1980). 'Managing Our Way to Economic Decline', *Harvard Business Review*, 58(4), p. 68.

Hench, John B. (2010). *Books As Weapons: Propaganda, Publishing, and the Battle for Global Markets in the Era of World War II*, Ithaca, NY: Cornell University Press.

Kantrow, Alan (1980). 'Why Read Peter Drucker?' *Harvard Business Review*, 58(1), pp. 74, 76.

Kirkpatrick, Andrew (2000). *Of Permanent Value: The Story of Warren Buffett*, Vol. 2, New York: McGraw-Hill.

Levitt, Theodore (1975). 'Marketing Myopia', *Harvard Business Review*, 53(5), p. 26.

Levy, David (1994). 'Chaos Theory and Strategy: Theory, Application, and Managerial Implications', *Strategic Management Journal*, 15, p. S2167.

Manning, Molly Guptill (2014). *When Books Went to War: The Stories That Helped Us Win World War II*, Boston. MA: Houghton Mifflin Harcourt.

Martin, Roger L. and Tony Golsby-Smith (2017). 'Management Is Much More Than A Science: The Limits of Data-Driven Decision Making', *Harvard Business Review*, 95(5), p. 30.

Milliot, Jim (2017a). 'Pearson to Sell Stake in Penguin Random House', Publishers Weekly, 18 January, at https://www.publishersweekly.com/pw/by-topic/industry-news/industry-deals/article/72524-pearson-to-sell-stake-in-penguin-ramdom-house.html

Milliot, Jim (2017b). 'The World's 50 Largest Publishers, 2017', Publishers Weekly, 25 August, at https://www.publishersweekly.com/paper-copy/by-topic/internat5ional/international-book-news/article/74505=the-world-s-50-largest-publishers-2017.html

Milliot, Jim (2017c). 'Tough Year for Educational Publishers', Publishers Weekly, 25 August, at https://www.publishersweekly.com/paper-copy/by-topic/international/international-book-news/article/74505-the-world-s-largest-publishers-2017.html

Mintzberg, Henry (1994). 'The Fall and Rise of Strategic Planning', *Harvard Business Review*, 72(1), p. 107.

Porter, Michael E. (1996). 'What is Strategy?' *Harvard Business Review*, 74(6), p. 70.

Porter, Michael E. (1998a). *Competitive Advantage: Creating and Sustaining Superior Performance*, New York: The Free Press.

Porter, Michael E. (1998b). *Competitive Strategy: Techniques for Analyzing Industries and Competitors*, New York: The Free Press.

Porter, Michael E. (2008a). *On Competition, Updated and Expanded*, Cambridge, MA: Harvard Business School Press.

Porter, Michael E. (2008b). 'The Five Competitive Forces That Shape Strategy', *Harvard Business Review*, 86(1), p. 80.

Ricardo, David. (2004). *The Principles of Political Economy and Taxation*, Mineola, NY: Dover Publications.

Rosen, Judith and Jim Milliot (2016). 'With Print Book Sales Stabilized, Return Rate Lowers', Publishers Weekly, 6 May, at https://www.publishersweekly.com/pw/by-topic/industry-news/bookselling/article/70298-with-print-book-sales-stabilized-return-rate-lowers.html

Taleb, Nassim Nicholas (2007). *The Black Swan: The Impact of the Highly Improbable*, New York: Random House.

Taylor, Frederick W. (1911). *The Principles of Scientific Management*. New York: Harper & Brothers.

CHAPTER 13

GLOBALIZATION AND PUBLISHING

MIHA KOVAČ
AND RÜDIGER WISCHENBART

GLOBAL AND LOCAL VALUES

As a starting point, we will use Manfred Steger's definition of globalization as a 'social condition, characterized by tight global economic, political, cultural, and environmental connections and flows that make most of the current borders and boundaries irrelevant' (Steger 2013: 9). In such an interconnected world, people buy the same products, watch similar television shows and movies, dress similarly, eat the same fast food, and engage in similar recreational activities. However, it would be a mistake to assume that this level of similarity is all that there is. As stressed by Hofstede et al. (2010: 347), this globalized surface hides an underlying level of different values, 'which moreover determine the meaning for people of their practices'. These meanings differ from country to country, even when people engage in similar activities and use similar goods and services.

Research into this 'underlying level of values' has been ongoing since the late 1960s, when Dutch psychologist Geert Hofstede conducted a value survey among employees of more than seventy IBM subsidiaries worldwide. He published his initial findings in the 1980s and then developed a set of six indicators describing the value differences that exist among countries (power distance, individualism, uncertainty avoidance, masculinity, long-term orientation, and indulgence vs. restraint). His work was widely debated, and it received a significant upgrade as a result of the Global Value Surveys that have been run since 1981 (after 2000, the surveys have been conducted in waves, every five years, in approximately 100 countries).

Despite their impressive size and statistical excellence, these research projects did not result in any new basic findings regarding human behaviour. They merely formalized, systematized, and statistically confirmed what any educated and culturally aware global traveller would know on an anecdotal level, namely that even similarly developed countries differ significantly in terms of the attitudes that their inhabitants exhibit towards authorities, economy, immigrants, sex, thrift, and other similar issues. For instance, being an immigrant in Germany in the mid-2010s was not the same as being an immigrant in Belgium or Hungary, while being gay was easier in Sweden than in Poland—all this in addition to the fact that people in those countries bought the same Korean cars, wore underwear made in India or Bangladesh, ate pizzas, read E. L. James' novels, drank Coke, and enjoyed 'Game of Thrones' on the HBO TV network.

Even more so, at the turn of the century, any literary agent or publisher with global experience knew that save for a few blockbuster titles, people in similarly developed countries read different books and accessed those book in different ways. Notably,

- in some countries, people preferred translations to local originals, while in other countries the situation was reversed;
- in some countries, people borrowed more books from public libraries than they purchased, whilst in others, public libraries were much less relevant and bookstores shaped reading trends;
- in some countries, self-publishing took over in genres such as romance and science fiction, while in other countries this trend was barely significant;
- in smaller markets in particular, bookshops were owned by publishers, while in bigger markets, such vertical ownership integration was unimaginable until the advent of Amazon; and
- online book sales became crucial for many publishers in both the USA and the UK, although such sales were less important in continental Europe.

Therefore, a Murakamian question must be asked: what are we talking about when we talk about the globalization of book markets? As with any good story, the answers lie in the detail.

PUBLISHERS, READERS, AND GLOBAL BOOK MARKETS

From its very beginnings in early modern Europe, the book publishing industry positioned itself at a strange intersection between local and global trends. As shown by Benedict Anderson some forty years ago, the combination of printing technology and market forces caused early printers and publishers to look for alternatives to the saturated Latin book market, which eventually led to book production in vernaculars. These vernaculars subsequently evolved into standardized national languages, which became one of the pillars of modern national and ethnic identity. A universal technology—the printing press—thus produced 'localized' cultural outcomes. This universality of printing technology is most visible in the fact that early books in many languages were printed in territories where the utilized language was not spoken, or else the printer did not speak it. Indeed, the first book in Serbian, for example, was printed in Venice, the first book in English in Bruges, the first book in Slovene in Tubingen, and the first book in Lithuanian in Konigsberg. Furthermore, experienced bookmen with sufficient knowledge and social networks travelled with their printing presses across Europe, selling books in a wide variety of languages in various territories. For instance, the first printer in Poland was a German named Caspar Straube; further, in both Denmark and Slovenia during the seventeenth and eighteenth centuries, the prominent local booksellers were of Dutch origin, while much of the Norwegian publishing trade during the nineteenth century was conducted by Gyldendal Norsk, a company of Danish origin (for more on this, see Appel and Skovkgaard-Petersen 2013: 398; Dular 2002). In terms of German-speaking countries, German publishing companies traditionally dominated the Austrian book market (see Flood 2013), while the British and French book industries controlled the book trade in their respective colonial empires even after their dissolution (see Squires 2013; Stevenson 2010).

This marriage between the universality of the book business and localized products can still be seen in the early twenty-first century, since it is predominantly newly expanded publishing conglomerates such as Penguin Random House, Hachette, or Macmillan, with a centralized infrastructure, but diversified title catalogues in their local daughter companies, which dominate the publishing industry. In this regard, a new chapter in the history of consumer publishing was opened in 1998, when the German media group Bertelsmann acquired the largest North American trade publisher, Random House, and decided to coordinate all their international publishing activities from New York. Yet, as part of the same move, it was made clear both in-house and to the general public that all the individual publishing ventures housed under the same vast corporate roof would maintain a high degree of editorial autonomy in order to cater to their differing audiences (for more on this, see Dohle 2013). This basic formula was not only applied to Random House's subsequent acquisition of Penguin and various Spanish-language operations; the model notably also applies to the French Hachette, which has strong holdings in the US and British markets; the German Holtzbrinck's ventures in both their original domestic market and in the English language market under the Macmillan brand; and the American HarperCollins, which is the publishing arm of the media giant NewsCorp. Remarkably, the latter did not use its parent company's global holdings to broaden the international scope of its book publishing. Instead, the New York-based company acquired a Canadian publisher specializing in romance, Harlequin, for their specific penetration of popular reading audiences in countries as diverse as Germany, Russia, and Japan.

In addition to the global flow of printing technologies and publishing skills, there also exists a long tradition of the global flow of content in the form of translations. Goethe's *The Sorrows of Young Werther* was not only one of the first trans-continental bestsellers, but also the first book to cause an international moral panic concerning the dangers of mass reading after being translated into French (1775), English (1779), Italian (1781), and Russian (1788), thereby preceding debates about the perils of television and mass digital media by roughly one and a half centuries (see Furedi 2016). This international flow of book content during the eighteenth and nineteenth centuries mainly took place in the form of 'pirated' editions that did not result in any financial rewards for either their authors or the original publishers, which subsequently triggered calls for international copyright protection. Following long discussions, the first rules governing the international rights trade were embodied in the Berne Convention in 1886, which remains the guiding principle behind the globalization of publishing (for more on the Berne Convention, see Chapter 5 in this book).

To sum up, within the field of publishing at least, there is nothing new under the sun. The international flow of bestsellers, global trade, universal production technologies and publishing skills, overseas printing, and the international ownership of publishing houses have been around since the early days of the book business. In the next section, we will examine how these common properties fuelled international book production throughout the twentieth and early twenty-first centuries, with a particular focus on which common features drove the overall expansion of the book industry, as well as what forces shaped differences along regional, cultural, or national lines.

TITLE EXPLOSION

Around the globe, the backbone of the statistics concerning the number of published titles is the International Standard Book Number (ISBN). Since its creation in the late 1960s, a unique ISBN has been assigned by publishers to every edition or adaptation of a book. This means that a book published in paperback and hardcover formats will have two ISBNs, while a book published in hardcover and paperback formats, as a club edition, and as an ebook in Epub, mobi/Kindle, and PDF formats will have six ISBNs. Therefore, the number of ISBNs issued should not be confused with the actual number of unique books written; the increase in the number of the latter is smaller than the increase in the number of the former. Yet, as people likely do not read the same book six times in six different formats, it is reasonable to assume that each copy of the same book in different formats is bought or borrowed by a different user. Consequently, the growing number of issued ISBNs results from the growing diversification of book production, and it is thus one of the indicators of growing book consumption.

The available statistics show that the number of published titles has been on the rise ever since the early days of printing, with a dramatic increase being seen during the second half of the twentieth century. In 1911, B. Iwinski calculated that between 1450 and 1910, more than 10 million books were published in the West. To this number, an additional 3.5 million titles were added by 1940. In 1986, P. J. Curwen calculated that between 1955 and 1981, global book production increased 2.71 times, with the largest growth being seen in North America (8.3 times; Krummel 2013: 200). On 28 August 2009, Google declared that there were 168 million titles in the world (Krummel 2013: 195), while in 2013 alone, more than 1.8 million books were published in thirty-three countries in which publishers' trade organizations had become members of the International Publishers Association (IPA 2014: 16). In short, between 1911 and 2009, the total number of published titles grew from 10 million for the period 1450 to 1911, to 168 million by 2009—an increase of 1,580 per cent. On average, between 1451 and 1911, 21,000 titles were published annually, while between 1912 and 2009, an average of 1.6 million titles were published annually, which represents a 7,600 per cent increase in annual production. Furthermore, the annual title production grew by 1,026 per cent between 1940 and 2009. As we shall see later, this growth was made possible by advances in printing technology, with new marketing and sales techniques as well as a growing number of sales channels for books being additional pull factors.

As it is reasonable to assume that more people will produce and consume more books, these numbers must be considered in relation to the growth of the world's population. It is estimated that the world's population reached one billion in 1804, doubled to two billion in 1923, grew from three to five billion between 1959 and 1987, and reached seven billion in 2011.[1] Hence, between 1804 and 2011, the world's population grew by 500 per cent. Between 1923 and 2011 alone, it grew by 250 per cent, while between 1959 and 2011, the population increased by 133 per cent. This shows that global title production grew faster than the global population. In the seven decades between World War 2 (1940) and 2010, the world's population grew by 180 per cent, while global title production grew by around six times more, that is, by 1,144 per cent.

Following the introduction of the Kindle in 2007, title production received yet another boost from the rapid growth of ebook sales, especially in Anglo-Saxon book markets, as authors started to self-publish their works on a massive scale. In 2013, for example, some 304,912 new titles and re-editions were published by American publishers. This already impressive number was dwarfed by self-published literature, for which the ISBN registrar for the USA, Bowker, registered 725,125 new titles by 2015, up a remarkable 375 per cent from 2010, when 152,978 standard numbers had been purchased for self-publishing (Bowker.com 2016).

Yet, domestic market power is not the only generator of growth in newly published titles. The British book industry, with 173,000 new releases in 2015, or 2,621 releases per one million inhabitants, in relative numbers, easily dwarfs the USA, which saw the release of a modest 935 titles per million consumers. The UK is by far the global leader in book exports (similar to its export muscle in other creative industries), with its tradition of a colonial empire being a helpful historical factor. Even Spain, which was severely hit by the financial crisis of 2008, produced a relatively high 1,686 new titles per million inhabitants in 2015, mostly thanks to its primordial role in Latin America.

However, growing title production may tell us a lot about the increasing diversity in book production (in terms of both content and format), but less so about the overall number of books consumed, that is, the number of books printed, sold in bookshops, and borrowed from public libraries in any given society and worldwide. For this, we

---

[1] http://www.census.gov/popclock/; http://en.wikipedia.org/wiki/World_population#cite_note-USCBcite-68

need data regarding the number of copies printed and sold in all formats, in addition to statistics concerning library loans.

Unfortunately, local and global statistics concerning library loans, book sales, and print runs for longer periods of time are mostly non-existent.

LIBRARIES: A GROWING
OR DISAPPEARING SECTOR?

The total number of books borrowed from US public libraries was 2.2 billion in 2012 (including print books, audiobooks, DVDs, and ebooks). This represents a 16.8 per cent increase from 2002 (Swan et al. 2014: 6) and a 57 per cent increase from 1990, when the circulation of library materials in US public libraries was around 1.4 billion (ibid). Data regarding the circulation of library materials in US public libraries are not available for earlier periods; nevertheless, as circulation growth was known to be 57 per cent in 1990–2012, it is reasonable to speculate that the growth of library circulation was above 60 per cent between 1975 and 2013.

Unfortunately, we have only a few samples of data that show longitudinal trends in the number of library loans in European public libraries. In Slovenia, similarly to the situation in the USA, the data indicate an almost 100 per cent growth in library loans between 1990 and 2013 (from eight million to 16 million, or 24 million including renewals).[2] Iceland witnessed 50 per cent growth in library loans between 1998 and 2012 and Spain saw 10 per cent growth between 2000 and 2012, whilst Norway, which has some of the best library statistics in Europe, witnessed 100 per cent growth in library loans between 1970 and 2012.[3] In some countries such as the Netherlands and Finland library loans started to decrease after 2010 yet it remains to be seen whether such trends will emerge elsewhere and be long-lasting enough to reverse the growth that occurred globally between the 1970s and 2010s. Quite the opposite to continental Europe, the number of books borrowed in England halved between 1997 and 2013, standing at 209 million in 2013/2014 and 411 million in 1997 (Farrington 2014). However, during the same period in the UK, book buying by the general public increased by around 25 per cent, coinciding with improvements in bookshop environments and increased competition between online retailers and the high street (Macdonald 2012).

In the absence of better data, let us conservatively assume that, save for the stagnation found for lending in English libraries, trends in aggregate library loans were also growing, and they had a positive impact on increasing book consumption. In some countries at least, the growth seen in the number of loaned copies was higher than the growth in

---

[2] http://bibsist.nuk.uni-lj.si/statistika/index.php and Slovene Book Reading Research
[3] https://plinius.wordpress.com/data-bank/nordic-countries/norway/

the number of copies sold, which indicated that in such countries, the role of the public sector in the business of books was increasing.

Nevertheless, as data concerning public libraries in developing countries are practically non-existent (see, for example, https://librarymap.ifla.org/map), we will assume that their impact on both the information gap and the publishing model in developing countries was not relevant.

Decreasing Print Runs
and Turnover per title

With a few exceptions such as UK (Phillips 2017) the data concerning the number of copies printed and sold in the second half of twentieth century and first years of twenty-first century are similarly incomplete. Most of the available data are anecdotal or, at best, based on statistical projections, circumstantial evidence, and educated guesses. The numbers that follow should therefore be treated with caution and considered only as an approximation of trends.

In 1954, R. E. Barker estimated that the annual number of copies of books printed globally stood at 5 billion. Eight years later, based on paper sales to printing houses as well as UNESCO data on the number of titles published, the French sociologist Robert Escarpit estimated that it was only in 1962 that global book production reached 4,500 million copies (Escarpit 1966: 64–5). In their introduction to the fourth edition of *Inside Book Publishing*, Clark and Phillips (2008) noted that in 2006, including exports, UK publishers sold 787 million books, of which 472 million were sold in the domestic market (a number which had decreased a decade later to around 360 million units, according to the UK Publishers' Association 2016 Report). For the year 2006, *Publishers Weekly* estimated that 659.3 million books were sold in the US market. For 2015, the market research firm Nielsen BookScan (2016) reported 653 million sold units. In both the UK and US markets, print book sales had at first declined, likely in reaction to the advent of ebooks, before expanding again slightly from around 2013.

Publishing statistics are *terra incognita* in Africa and for the majority of countries in the Middle East and Asia. African book production is usually estimated to account for 2–3 per cent of global book production; however, we have no evidence to substantiate this estimate (Zell 2014). The same is true for many Asian countries. As an absence of book statistics is usually the result of an underdeveloped book industry—and a lack of exact data—let us make an educated guess that the aggregate book sales of Australia, Africa, and the rest of Asia do not exceed 1 billion copies.

In a very rough ballpark estimate, we can therefore assume that, at the beginning of the new millennium, annual global book consumption stood at around 7 billion copies. If this is correct, then the number of copies sold increased by only 35 per cent between the 1960s and the first decade of the twenty-first century.

Therefore, relative to global population growth, global book consumption has actually decreased. In the 1960s, on planet Earth, 1.6 books per head were sold annually, compared to 0.9 after the year 2000. Throughout the twentieth century, most books were produced, sold, and consumed in the book markets of developed countries, while population growth was fastest in underdeveloped countries. Hence, we can assume that the main reason for the global drop in book consumption per head was the discrepancy between population growth and the near non-existent book production and professional distribution networks in less developed Latin American, Asian, and African countries.[4] In other words, global book statistics confirm the growing information gap between developed and non-developed countries, which indicates that reading habits correlate with the population's inclusion in education (see Kovač 2015).

However, it would be wrong to assume that the information gap is the only reason for globally decreasing book production. At least in last decade, the available data reveal declines in the majority of developed book markets.

BOOK SALES IN THE SIX BIGGEST MARKETS

No standardized approach is available for measuring and comparing book sales internationally, and even within markets, measuring methodologies have changed regularly, so that historical comparisons are always accompanied by a degree of uncertainty. Nevertheless, even a few random snapshots help to illustrate the wide disparity between the scope and penetration of books around the world. A good example of this can be found in the case of the six largest book markets.

According to recorded consumer spending on books and related publications, six markets account for two-thirds of the world market, namely the USA with 30 per cent and China with 17 per cent, which together amount to almost half of global share, as well as Germany (8 per cent), Japan (5 per cent), the UK (4 per cent), and France (3 per cent). Even large countries with an outstanding reading tradition such as Russia, newly emerging economies with substantial populations such as Brazil and Mexico, not to mention nations like Indonesia or Pakistan, with only limited domestic publishing traditions, follow far below those levels. Among the market leaders, only China demonstrates continuous growth in the total spending on books and other publishing products, while over the past decade, the big Anglo-Saxon markets have only recently been able to recuperate the losses seen in earlier years. The largest non-English markets, from an aggregated perspective, by and large saw a decline in sales (Figure 13.1).

In terms of published titles, with 475,800 new releases in 2015, of which 866 million copies have been sold, China arguably sits at the global pinnacle. Yet, when considering its

[4] http://en.wikipedia.org/wiki/World_population

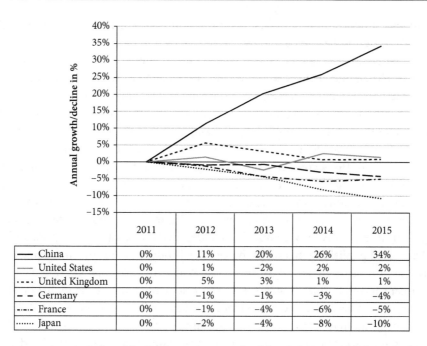

	2011	2012	2013	2014	2015
—— China	0%	11%	20%	26%	34%
—— United States	0%	1%	−2%	2%	2%
···· United Kingdom	0%	5%	3%	1%	1%
− − Germany	0%	−1%	−1%	−3%	−4%
−·−·− France	0%	−1%	−4%	−6%	−5%
······· Japan	0%	−2%	−4%	−8%	−10%

FIGURE 13.1 Aggregated positive and negative growth of the six largest publishing markets

population of almost 1.4 billion, this amounts to 344 new titles per 1 million inhabitants, which results in 0.6 copies per head. Neighbouring Japan reported 76,465 new releases, selling 644 million copies to a population of 127 million, or 613 new releases per million (although this also includes the very popular and quickly consumable Manga genre, of which each consumer bought an average of five units). Germany, the largest European book market, reported slightly less than 90,000 new titles, amounting to 1,078 copies per 1 million inhabitants, which was similar to France at 1,001 copies, with 6.5 units per head, or almost tenfold the level in China.

To sum up, with the exception of China, top global book markets are suffering declines in print-runs and in consumer spending for books. Globally, these trends might be reversed (and the global 'book gap' shortened) if the growth in book production seen in the other BRIC countries (Brazil, Russia, and India) follows trends in China.

BOOK SALES IN THE EUROPEAN UNION

A similar trend of a growing number of published titles and a decline in publishers' turnovers occurred in the European Union. According to data collected by Groenlund et al. (2000: 26) in 1997, 23 billion euro were spent on books in the (by then) fifteen member states, and 400,000 titles were published. Two decades later, in 2015, in an EU of twenty-eight member states, the Federation of European Publishers (FEP)[5] estimated

[5] https://fep-fee.eu/-Annual-Publishers-Statistics-

the combined net revenues of all publishing companies in Europe to total 22.5 billion nominal euro, down from 23.25 billion in 2006.

The difference between total consumer spending on books, which was the parameter chosen by Groenlund et al. (2000), and publishers' net revenue, as reported by FEP, can be estimated to be around 60 per cent of the value of the books at end consumer prices, which includes the mark-up for retail. Adjusting for the difference in used parameters, and for inflation, European publishing showed solid and continuous growth over the first decade, from 1997 to 2006, while it ran out of steam after 2007 and the economic crisis in 2008. In the second surveyed decade, from 2006 to 2015, according to FEP's statistics, the publishing sector lost around 15 per cent of its real value, which equals accumulated inflation of around 15 per cent for the Eurozone over the same period. (Our comparison does not factor in the expansion in European member states in 2004 and 2013, from fifteen to twenty-eight, which added several small and (with Poland) one medium sized publishing market to the Union). Production, meanwhile, had continuously risen in the same period to 475,000 new titles in 2006, and 575,000 by 2015, or 44 per cent in total. This confirms both our calculations about the global decline of per head book sales and anecdotal evidence shared among book professionals that the average print runs have come down dramatically.

Such trends received a significant impetus after Amazon's launch of the Kindle reading device in 2007. The combination of books and reading has found many more ways to reach consumers than simply replicating a long form text in the closed container format of an ebook. As a consequence, new publishing models occurred. These diverse patterns in market developments are well in accordance with the initially chosen theory of globalization as a paramount process, albeit with ample variations on many levels, both geographically and over time. In order to better understand this process, we need to investigate the traditional publishing model.

Changes in the Traditional Publishing Model

A number of research papers and books agree in their basic description of both the publishing value chain and the implied business model (see, for example, Darnton 1982; Greco et a l. 2007; Phillips 2010, 2014; Thompson 2010). Simply put, by using financial and intellectual capital in combination with organizational, marketing, and editing skills, publishers turn manuscripts into books that are then taken over by a set of intermediaries, including distributors, booksellers, and other traders, who sell them to their final customers (either to readers, private and public institutions, or libraries). The income from the book trade is generated from the number of copies sold, multiplied by the retail price of each copy, covering the costs and profits of all the players in the value chain (i.e. booksellers' discounts, printing and software costs, the author's earnings, and the publisher's profits and overheads, etc.). At least in theory, the mathematics of this model are straightforward: the more copies sold, the lower the cost—and the higher the number and retail price of the sold copies, the higher the income of authors, publishers, and booksellers.

For the majority of the era of print, due to relatively high fixed costs, it has been economically unwise to print less than a few hundred or even a few thousand copies of a given title, since the cost per copy would be too high to permit the publisher to sell the book at a competitive and acceptable price. As a result, a kind of censorship by market forces had been imposed. Publishers became the gatekeepers of the book world, predominantly publishing titles for which they assumed a sufficient demand to recover production and overhead costs when sold at a price that consumers would still accept.

Since mid-twentieth century, one of the crucial triggers that put such a business model under pressure were the changes that occurred in production technology, followed by developments in bricks and mortar and online retail, with the underlying innovation in logistics further re-enforced by the introduction of ebooks in the first decade of new millennium. With Amazon, a new competitor entered the marketplace, one that was betting on radical expansion, backed by stock market capital, and committed to taking advantage of the muscle provided by digital technology. The main change that resulted from the introduction of digital technologies was the dilution of fixed production costs to the extent that online and on-demand services could introduce a new level of flexibility and cost efficiency for the production and delivery of both printed as well as digital copies of books to any customer, anywhere, in minuscule quantities and at a low retail price.

As we have seen, as a first step, this resulted in a massive increase in the number of new title releases in both continental Europe and Anglo-Saxon countries. In the UK, these processes were enhanced by the abolition of fixed book prices, which resulted in harsh competition between the online retailer Amazon and traditional retail chains that led to a battle over discounts to both print and, even more aggressively, ebook editions, with publishers caught in the middle.

As a second step in the developed book markets, these processes led to the disintermediation of the publishing chain. The traditional value added by a publisher to a book, which was the result of editing the text and organizing its distribution, suddenly became substitutable by new specialized entrants, who catered to authors on a massive scale by digitally integrating and optimizing the entire publishing process online. Consequently, many authors started to perform the traditional publisher's role by controlling the editing, publishing, and marketing processes at their own cost and risk (for more on these processes, see Gaughran 2014). As a result, a new book ecosystem was born.

New Book Ecosystem(s)

By 2015, based on Amazon's online sales data, independently (or self-) published books had for the first time overtaken those published by the 'Big Five' largest publishers in the USA. In the UK, self-published titles have been estimated to account for 22 per cent of the domestic book market. In Germany, in 2016, around 40 per cent of ebooks sold through Amazon were self-published. In addition to crime, romance, and fantasy being the genres that most massively migrated to this new book ecosystem, self-publishing started to offer opportunities to bring books to large audiences that were otherwise difficult to reach through more traditional means. In 2016, in the USA, for example, 71 per cent of African-American fiction was self-published. In the Philippines, a country that lacks a well-established bookselling infrastructure, the self-publishing service Wattpad has been instrumental in the rapid success of romance fiction. In much of sub-Saharan Africa, local author services have in many cases substituted conventional publishing and distribution enterprises.[6]

In China, yet another approach to reading on a screen has been successfully pioneered, with pay-per-view platforms bringing together authors and readers by the millions as early as the mid-2000s. These ground-breaking schemes were elevated to an industrial scale a decade later by leading Chinese Internet giants, especially by the messaging and digital services conglomerate Tencent and the telecommunications giant China Mobile. They were facilitated by the massive penetration of smartphones and affordable mobile data connections. These operators rapidly extended the new digitally integrated value chain beyond reading, since successful authors have been systematically offered contracts for the secondary exploitation of their intellectual property in other formats, especially games and movies.

On the other side of the globe in Scandinavia, ebooks were initially a format almost exclusively relevant for library loans, before the emergence of a combination of subscription—or flat rate—models and streaming offers, with a remarkably prevalent role played by streamed digital audiobooks. In Russia, ebooks became hugely popular, albeit primarily in illegally disseminated, pirated editions that allowed cheap access to reading through affordable domestically produced reading devices.

All these changes rendered small Eastern European book markets such as Slovenia, Croatia, Lithuania, Latvia, Estonia, and Serbia the last bastions of the traditional publishing model. In such countries, the role of self-publishing and ebooks was almost non-existent. Even more so, in some of these countries the prevalent format was still hardcover. Nevertheless, they all faced the growth of titles, shrinking average print runs, and diluted incomes, which made the role of public money spent by governments to encourage domestic book production as a means of fostering national cultural identity more important than ever.

However, that is not the entire story. Similar to the situation of Latin in medieval Europe, English became the *lingua franca* of the early twenty-first century as the number of English speakers in non-English countries rapidly increased (for more on this, see McCrum 2010; Montgomery 2013; Kovač 2014). Although there is no globally reliable data, anecdotal evidence suggests that imports of books in English represent a

---

[6] For more on developments in the USA, see the AuthorEarnings report, February 2016 edition— www.authorearnings.com; for the UK, see data published by Nielsen, quoted in *The Bookseller*, 23 March 2016; for Germany, see Matthias Matting's Self-Publisher Bibel—www.selfpublisherbibel.de; for a summary and overview of international developments, see the Global Ebook Report 2017, www.global-ebook.com; and for a fundamental analysis, see Shatzkin 2017; AuthorEarnings.com 2017.

visible part of the overall book sales in some parts of continental Europe, Asia, and Africa. In Slovenia, for example, together with textbooks, English book sales represented up to 20 per cent of the book market in 2012 (Gregorin et al. 2013), while even in some bigger markets such as Germany, blockbusters in English would make it onto the best-seller lists if editorial rules permitted (for more on this, see Bowen, 2010; Global Ebook Reports 2013–2017 and Diversity Report 2016). In Norway, three out of every fourteen books sold per year per head were in English (for more on this, see Norwegian Book Reading Survey 2014[7]).

In short, the native and secondary English-reading population has become the biggest language group in the world. Consequently, even the small book markets of continental Europe, which seem not to have been affected by the birth of the ebook ecosystem, might be suffering due to growing imports of English (e)books via sales channels invisible to official statistics, for example, Amazon.

These processes have been enhanced by global trends in the sales of bestselling books.

Impact of Bestsellers on Changes in Publishing Models

In last two decades, three important characteristics of bestselling authors have arisen. First, globally successful authors started to emerge in regions that were considered publishing peripheries during the mid-twentieth century; second, for an author to reach the very top of the charts, writing a series of at last three books is a must; and third, the top of the charts is dominated by only a few titles and authors represented by influential agents.

For example, in 1997, a debut novel by an unknown author living far away from the action nodes of international publishing—London, New York, and the Frankfurt Book Fair—was able to build a bestselling career that would span continents within less than a year, by travelling along lines of professional connections that were already well established. The writer Arundhati Roy, who was born in the South Indian backwater of Kerala, had finished her autobiographical tale *The God of Small Things* in New Delhi in 1996. However, she had the intuition to hand over the manuscript to carefully chosen middlemen such as HarperCollins editor Pankaj Mishra and London-based agent David Gowin, who in 1997 had the book published in English. Translation rights for the book were sold in twenty-one languages, and earned advances worth half a million pounds sterling as well as winning the prestigious Man Booker Prize.[8] In the same year, and again in London, another debut novel launched the global career of an unknown writer, albeit more modestly, with an initial print run of just 500 copies, of which 300 were

[7] http://www.bokhandlerforeningen.no/leserundersokelsen-2014
[8] https://de.wikipedia.org/wiki/Arundhati_Roy

distributed to libraries. By 2017, all seven volumes of J. K. Rowling's *Harry Potter* series had sold 450 million copies in seventy-nine languages.[9]

The new and globally pervasive pattern established by the *Harry Potter* books was not individual. Individual titles topped the charts, but more often, they were part of a series of three to seven books, recognizably linked by a compelling story, and targeted at a core audience that would follow the epic or in some cases also the author, over a longer period. These characteristics apply to authors as varied as J. K. Rowling and her *Harry Potter* series, Stieg Larsson and his *Millennium* thriller trilogy (which was similar to the case of Roy in terms of coming from a publishing periphery), E. L. James and her *Shades of Grey* erotic fantasies, and Ken Follett and his historically inspired *Fall of Giants* series. For the decade beginning in the mid-2000s, by which time the model had been firmly established, we could document the process across seven Western European markets (France, Germany, Italy, the Netherlands, Spain, Sweden, and the UK), plus the USA, by analysing the fiction bestseller charts since 2006 (for more on this, see Kovač and Wischenbart 2018).

For the ten years between 2006 and 2015, all fiction titles with a presence in the top ten of any of the surveyed charts in eight selected major book markets have been attributed 'impact points' as a measure of the duration of their stay among the top ten, in months, weighted by the occupied rank. Overall, for each single year, only a handful of these annual bestsellers had far outperformed all the rest. On average, a year's top five titles accounted for 22 per cent of all the attributed impact points for that year. Even among these blockbusters, a few again stand out. Swedish crime author Stieg Larsson and British eroticist E. L. James, with a total of 7,937 and 6,830 impact points, respectively, outperformed more conventional non-series authors such as Khaled Hosseini (*Kite Runner, And The Mountain Echoed*), Paolo Giordano (*The Solitude of Prime Numbers*), and Muriel Barbery (*The Elegance of the Hedgehog*) by a factor five to ten (Figure 13.2).

OLD AND NEW BOOKISH ELITES

On the basis of these findings, we can assume that during the first twenty years of this millennium, four global trends have stood out in the international book industry. First, the number of published titles has rapidly increased. Second, the overall number of major bestsellers has decreased, while the average print run across the board has also declined. Third, self-publishing and the inclusion of new actors in the market have both started to rise and new book ecosystems have emerged. Fourth, due to the first three trends, publishers' income per title has decreased, while the whole industry has become more dependent on bestsellers. In developed markets, all these forces have worked to the advantage of the largest economic actors, who were in a better position to leverage scale. This pattern operates in favour of the strongest author brands, the predominant

---

[9] https://harrypotter.bloomsbury.com/uk/harrypotter20/.

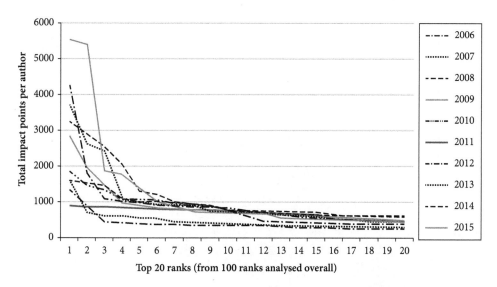

FIGURE 13.2 Number of bestsellers and months they were on selected bestseller lists in Europe

corporate publishing groups, and the expansion of Amazon, as the industry's most successful new entrant on a global level over the observed period. In combination, these factors have deeply shaken an industry that had long been defined by medium-sized, local or, at best, regional companies.

By considering book production, consumption, and overall wealth on a per capita basis in order to balance the sheer size of countries, an overview is able to take shape that clearly highlights how the business of books, at least in terms of its more conventional practices, is still rooted in the world order of the late nineteenth and much of the twentieth centuries. A few nations from Western Europe and North America, plus a few exceptional cases such as Japan and Korea, largely predominate in the global commerce of knowledge, education, and entertainment in which books are a central element and format.

Figure 13.3 further emphasizes how a few countries, both small and medium sized, have successfully developed their book industries and book culture to position themselves particularly high up among the 'Bookish Elite' by supporting the sector with regulations and subsidies. This makes Norway stand out, since the small, but oil-rich nation has traditionally spent some of its wealth on fostering domestic culture. However, even in Germany, Switzerland, and Austria, books and reading are considered to represent a special domain, which is not meant to be subjected to the brutal forces of unhinged market developments. The figure also emphasizes the above-mentioned role of the UK and of Spain as important exporters.

In the lower left corner of Figure 13.3, a new and so far more loosely knit group has taken shape, which is composed of Brazil, Russia, India, and China, together with countries like Poland, Turkey, and Mexico. In these countries, new middle classes have formed over the past two decades, which has resulted in the expanding consumption

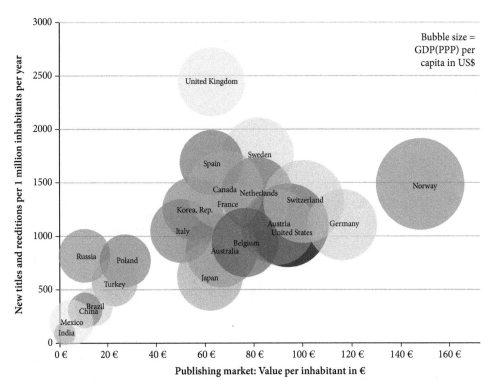

FIGURE 13.3 Title production per million, value of the book market per head, and GDP. Compilation and analysis courtesy Rüdiger Wischenbart Bookmap.org 2017

and domestic production of books. In Mexico and Brazil, the governments have started to dedicate public money to educational publishing in order to lower the dependence on overseas imports. China has defined a long-term strategy for its media sector, which includes publishing, selecting a few of the most promising ventures, turning them into larger holding structures, and encouraging the resulting corporations to 'go out' and compete in the world markets. Similarly, in Brazil, two of the leading educational publishers have engaged in a merger in order to strengthen their position against turbulent economic conditions as well as to occupy a better position for cooperation with global market leaders. In Russia, the consumer book sector and educational publishing have each been consolidated into two predominant publishing conglomerates, if not with the active support, at least with the consent of the federal government. Mexico, similar to other developing countries with a tradition of the state as a public entrepreneur, has been pursuing a centrally controlled and fostered national book strategy for a long time.

In many of the above-mentioned strategies, digital transformation has become a central focus. Building a conventional infrastructure, with decentralized publishers and retail infrastructures that expect learners as well as passionate individual readers to pick up books one copy at a time, seems too costly from a public planning perspective. As we have seen in the cases of China and the Philippines, digital books and, even more so, digital learning tools appear to offer an appropriate alternative approach.

NEW MODELS, NEW CLASHES

The conventional book business and the digital outlook therefore appear to clash in several regards. Independent small-scale publishing, often founder and owner driven, requires a high degree of autonomy, having made books a genuine vehicle for the freedom of expression as well as opposition to the state and government in many countries and during different periods. Across different times, territories, and cultures, even seemingly trivial works of literature have occasionally assumed a political role in challenging authorities with novel ideas and conceptions, while new, groundbreaking bestsellers such as the Harry Potter series began their march to the top in small- or mid-sized companies. Additionally, as evidenced by the success of Stieg Larsson and the Nordic Noir trend, fresh impulses can travel from books to other storytelling media and then back into books.

On the other hand, the digital format has the inherent potential to centralize services and play to the strengths of new, large entrants whose leverage does not stem from the originality, diversity, and richness of the proposed content. Together with these centralizing trends, the increasing economic dependency of the entire book industry on a very limited number of bestsellers limits the viability of exploring experimental and innovative narratives.

Hence, deep shifts and rifts have been seen, and it seems to be too early in the game to arrive at a definitive conclusion. Those corporations that shape the Internet, though, excel at fostering and subsequently gating and owning the communities of their users, while content is commoditized. It is therefore expected that the clash between local, segmented, and hence fundamentally decentralized publishing actors and the identified new super-players is likely to represent the next frontline in global publishing during the coming decade.

As of autumn 2017, when the present chapter was being written, this transformation is still ongoing, while the associated winners and losers remain unknown.

REFERENCES

Appel, C. and K. Skovgaard-Petersen (2013). 'The History of the Book in Nordic Countries'. In *The Book: A Global History*. Edited by M. F. Suarez and H. R. Woudhuysen. Oxford: Oxford University Press.

AuthorEarnings.com. (2017). Print vs. Digital, Traditional vs. Non-Traditional, Bookstores vs. Online: 2016 Trade Publishing by Numbers. Available at http://authorearnings.com/report/dbw2017/ [Accessed 5 February 2017].

Bowen, K. (2010). International bestsellers get Germans reading in English. Available at http://www.dw-world.de/dw/article/0,,4199574,00.html [Accessed on 11 September 2017].

Bowker.com. (2016). Report from Bowker Shows Continuing Growth in Self-Publishing. Available at http://www.bowker.com/news/2016/Report-from-Bowker-Shows-Continuing-Growth-in-Self-Publishing.html [Accessed 11 September 2017].

Clark, G. and A. Phillips (2008). *Inside Book Publishing*, 3rd edition, London: Routledge.

Curwen, P. J. (1986). *The World Book Industry*, New York: Facts on File.

Darnton, R. (1982). What is the History of the Book? Available at https://dash.harvard.edu/bitstream/handle/1/3403038/darnton_historybooks.pdf?sequence=2 [Accessed 1 February 2017].

Diversity Report (2016). Ruediger Wischenbart Content & Consulting. Available at https://www.mecd.gob.es/dam/jcr:4313636f-998d-4c71-99cb-ea877ebb2c89/diversity-report-2016.pdf [Accessed 16 January 2017].

Dohle, M. (2013). Talk at Frankfurt Book Fair CEO panel. Available at https://www.youtube.com/watch?v=RyYp082Laqo&t=89s [Accessed 13 July 2017].

Dular, A. (2002). *Živeti od knjig*. Ljubljana: Zveza zgodovinskih društev Slovenije.

Escarpit, R. (1966). *The Book Revolution*. Paris and London: Harrap and UNESCO.

Farrington, J. (2014). 'CIPFA Stats Show Drops in Library Numbers and Usage', *The Bookseller*, 8 December.

Flood, J. (2013). 'Austria'. In *The Book: A Global History*. Edited by M. F. Suarez and H. R. Woudhuysen, Oxford: Oxford University Press.

Furedi, F. (2016). *The Power of Reading. From Socrates to Twitter*, London: Bloomsbury Continuum.

Gaughran, D. (2014). *Let's Get Digital: How to Self-Publish and Why You Should*, 2nd edition, Kindle Books.

Global Ebook Report (2013–2017). Ruediger Wischenbart Content & Consulting. Available at Wischenbart.com [Accessed 13 July 2017].

Greco, A., C. E. Rodriguez, and R. M. Wharton (2007). *The Culture and Commerce of Publishing in 21st Century*, Stanford, CA: Stanford University Press.

Gregorin, R., M. Kovač, and A. Blatnik (2013). 'The Curious Case of Bestsellers in Slovenia', *Logos*, 24(4), pp. 12–23.

Groenlundd, M., R. Piccard, and V. Ponni (2000). *Competitiveness of the European Union Publishing Industries*, Bruxelles: European Commission, Enterprise Directorate-General.

Hofstede, G., G. J. Hofstede, and M. Minkov (2010). *Cultures and Organizations: Software of the Mind*, Columbus, OH: McGraw Hill.

International Publishers Association (IPA) (2014). Annual Report. Available at https://www.internationalpublishers.org/images/reports/2014/IPA-annual-report-2014.pdf [Accessed 15 August 2017].

Kovač, M. (2014). 'Global English and Publishing Trends at the Turn of the 20th Century', *Knygotyra*, 62, pp. 7–17.

Kovač, M. (2015). ' "Bokes be not set by, there times is past, I gesse": reflections on the end of the book', Logos, 26(4), pp. 7–21.

Kovač, M. and R. Wischenbart, (2018). 'Bestsellers 2008 to 2014: the last king of analogue and the first dame of the digital pleasure house', Logos, 29(1), pp. 18–27.

Krummel, D. W. (2013). 'The Heritage of Boleslas Iwinski', *Library Trends*, 62(2), pp. 456–64.

Macdonald, L. (2012). *A New Chapter: Public Libraries in 21st Century*, Dunfermline: Carnegie Trust.

McCrum, R. (2010). *Globish: How the English Language Became the World's Language*, London: Viking.

Matting, M. Self-Publisher Bibel—www.selfpublisherbibel.de. Available at [Accessed 16 September 2017].

Montgomery, S. L. (2013). *Does Science Need a Global Language?* Chicago: University of Chicago Press.

Nielsen BookScan. (2016). Year in Books. Review 2015. PowerPoint Presentation.

Phillips, A. (2010). 'Where is the Value in Publishing? The Internet and the Publishing Value Chain'. In *The Future of the Book in The Digital Age*. Edited by B. Cope and A. Phillips, Oxford: Chandos.

Phillips, A. (2014). *Turning the Page: The Evolution of the Book*, Abingdon on Thames: Routledge.

Phillips, A. (2017). 'Have we Passed Peak Book? The Uncoupling of book Sales from Economic Growth', *Publishing Research Quarterly*, 32(3), pp. 310–27.

Shatzkin, M. (2017). 'Agency pricing didn't restrain Amazon; it strengthened it'. Shatzkin Files, 1 February. Available at http://www.idealog.com/blog/agency-pricing-didnt-restrain-amazon-strengthened/ [Accessed 4 February 2017].

Squires, C. (2013). 'Britain from 2014'. In *The Book: A Global History*. Edited by M. F. Suarez and H. R. Woudhuysen, Oxford: Oxford University Press.

Steger, M. (2013). *Globalization. A Very Short Introduction*, 3rd edition, Oxford: Oxford University Press.

Stevenson, I. (2010). *Book Makers. British Publishing in 20th Century*, London: British Library Publishing Division.

Swan, D. W., J. Grimes, T. Owens, K. Miller, J. Arroyo, T. Craig, S. Dorinski, M. Freeman, N. Isaac, P. O'Shea, R. Padgett, and P. Schilling (2014). *Public Libraries in the United States Survey. Fiscal Year 2012*, IMLS-2015_PLS-01, Washington: Institute of Museum and Library Services.

Thompson, J. (2010). *Merchants of Culture*, Cambridge: Polity Press.

UK Publishers Association. (2016). The UK Book Industry in Statistics 2016. Available at https://www.publishers.org.uk/resources/uk-market/ [Accessed 11 September 2017].

Zell, H. (2014). 'How Many Books are Published in Africa? The need for more reliable statistics', *African Book Publishing Record*, 40(1), pp. 1–14.

CHAPTER 14

CURATION IN PUBLISHING

Curatorial Paradigms, Filtering, and the Structure of Editorial Choice

MICHAEL BHASKAR

BEYOND FILTERING

WHAT does publishing do? The question is more difficult than it first appears. Publishers differ greatly over time, geography, and sector; the boundaries between published and unpublished texts are not clearly drawn. Exactly what constitutes publishing shifts according to underlying technological and market conditions, and to prevailing attitudes about what ensures 'public' display of a work.

Elsewhere I have explored the twin concepts of filtering and amplification: between them they broadly underwrite ideas of publishing across a broad spectrum of contexts (Bhaskar 2013). While amplification can be succinctly defined, the term filtering requires further elaboration. Filtering registers that a publisher cannot publish everything, because if they did, they would simply be a medium. Any publisher, however large, must choose. They must say no to some items and they must do so according to some criteria: in other words, they must filter. Filtering is, however, the maximal limit of publishing, the extreme case. Filtering implies a near-passive sifting. In fact, this is rarely how publishing occurs. The processes of selection enacting filtration mechanisms are usually active, engaged, working according to complex and often unspoken models. They are contested and shifting; they are critical points of differentiation and competitive advantage.

A better phrase for the filtering function is curation. Publisher curation broadly relates to commissioning and editorial departments but is implicated in everything a publisher does. Publisher curation concerns what a publisher chooses to publish and why. Curation, which I define as 'selecting and arranging to add value' (Bhaskar 2016) is a proactive and wide ranging process. To both outsiders and those working in other departments, there can be an air of mystery attached to the editorial process. Meetings are often closed to many employees. Editors traditionally wield power and status and are at the heart of critical business and creative decision making. Intersecting lines of financial and taste-making responsibility imbue the role with prestige. But it is vital, if we are to understand publishing, to demystify editorial and understand the structural role of curation.

At the heart of publisher curation is this question: why do some works gets published and not others? What impact does this have? What role does curation play in constituting the publishing industry? To answer them I will introduce the concept of the curatorial paradigm.

These questions take on a heightened importance as we move, over centuries, from a position of textual scarcity to super-abundance. Even in the distant past it was felt there was too much to read: in Antiquity Plato, Seneca, and Hippocrates all bemoaned a surfeit of written material, not to mention more recent complainants like Leibniz and Boswell. Even before the printing press, industrial production techniques and digital replication, humanity had (or at least perceived itself to have) an abundance problem.

Today we have vastly more texts than ever before. In 1800 the UK published around twelve books a week (St Clair 2004). By 2011 it was more like 2,800 a week, with many more published unofficially. In the year 1800, one book was published for every 17,500 people, whereas in 2011, the country was publishing one book for every 348 people (Flood 2014). While the population increased sixfold, the number of books published went up 250 fold. Even accounting for the rise in literacy and disposable income, the growth is enormous. A report from the bibliographic information company Bowker suggests the total number of ISBNs in the United States, a useful proxy for published books, increased 375 per cent between 2010 and 2015 (Bowker 2016). The trend had been rising for years but was supercharged by the boom in self-publishing: in 2010 152,978 ISBNs were issued to self-published titles, but this rose to 727,125 by 2015. Even accounting for multiple ISBNs ascribed to one title, Bowker estimates 625,327 individually self-published titles appeared in 2015 (Anderson 2016a). All of this increase takes place amidst an unprecedented explosion of available media and data powered by the Internet and digital technology. Few if any industries face this daunting level of new product. The dream of writing a book is alive and well (see Chapter 3 on Authorship). Supply-side super-abundance is a fact of life for publishing.

Every publisher thus works in a saturated market. Copyrights can carve little islands of monopoly in this sea of material. But the question of what a publisher chooses to do, how it constitutes its curatorial paradigm, in this context of radical excess, is not only a question of identity or strategy: it is quite simply a question of survival.

MODELS AND THE CURATORIAL PARADIGM

Publishers publish for a variety of reasons: to make money, spark the revolution, glorify a deity, further a scientific discipline. Whenever they publish, they do so according to what I term a model: a model for what they want the book or project to achieve which then guides the publishing. One common mistake is to view publisher models in simplistic terms—to see each book as trying to do only one thing. This is rarely the case; publishers have multiple, contrasting expectations and divergent models for books which blend together to form an overarching model. For example a radical press may publish a book simultaneously to advance an anti-capitalist political agenda *and* to recoup the costs of production and even deliver a surplus to help ensure the publisher's ongoing survival (ongoing survival also being part of that political project). Every item published, then, is done so according to an intricate set of blended models.

At the level of the firm we can aggregate the total set of blended models. This set of models is what I call the curatorial paradigm: the guiding and limiting architecture behind what a publisher may publish. Each publishing house, or imprint, division, or list, has a unique editorial signature, their curatorial paradigm, which delimits their space of possible publishing. When publishers say 'This is our kind of book' or 'Oh, that's definitely not one for us' they are obliquely referring to the curatorial paradigm. The concept can be depth adjusted for different scales of analysis: each imprint within a large firm for example has its own curatorial paradigm, the sum of which goes to produce the overall curatorial paradigm of the wider group. And we can escalate the concept to sectoral and societal levels. Just as a curatorial paradigm is the sum of blended models deployed by a publisher, so societies' have a kind of Ur-curatorial paradigm: the total set of curatorial paradigms at work in that society. Collectively these configure and delimit the public sphere. In future this will be a valuable area of research but is out of the scope of this chapter.

The curatorial paradigm should not be thought of as simply an emergent abstract that lies mute. To some degree all staff members of a publisher, and especially those with acquiring capacity, are aware of the curatorial paradigm, or parts of it; and this awareness then powerfully conditions the publishing decision making. So the curatorial paradigm is both active and dynamic, constantly changing and exerting pressure; it is part roadmap, part set of strategies and tactics, part list of dos and don'ts, part tribal identity, part business plan and financial forecast.

One idea in some respects analogous to the curatorial paradigm is what the scholar Walter W. Powell calls the 'premises of the firm' (Powell 1985). Given its centrality to publishing, editorial has received remarkably scant scholarly attention within publishing studies, but Powell was amongst the first and most comprehensive researchers (Coser and Powell 1982).

To understand how these 'premises of the firm' introduce a unique curatorial DNA, we need to understand how they work and what influences go into their creation. These influences happen on two main levels: within the company (endogenous factors) and outside the firm (exogenous factors). In other words we are dealing with a range of factors from an individual's micro-strategies to the most expansive society-level boundary conditions. We will explore the former first, looking at the curatorial paradigm at the firm level and drawing on work in publishing studies, organization theory, and sociology. Then, at the exogenous level, we will zoom out to unpick the complex and mutually reinforcing connections between societal contexts and curatorial paradigms.

Exogenous and endogenous influences should be understood as operating at once. Publishing decisions, at the level of an individual editor, editorial team, imprint, and group, are massively overdetermined. Following media sociologists Reese and Shoemaker we can unravel that overdetermined knot by seeing such decisions occurring on many levels: the individual level, the level of media routines and team cultures, the organizational level, the extramedia level, and the ideological level (Shoemaker and Reese 1996). The former three broadly equate to the endogenous context of the curatorial paradigm, the latter the exogenous; but in practice, as should become clear, all factors are always present. Distinguishing between endogenous and exogenous is a useful heuristic for understanding curatorial paradigms rather than a claim on the nature of publishing curation.

Endogenous Factors

Commissioning starts with individuals. While teams tend to be responsible for publishing decisions (the Editorial Department), typically one person is the champion and originator of a project. Often these decisions are private: editors only generally discuss successful projects and conversations within Acquisitions Meetings, and this key assembly for publishing curation is (usually) confidential, both for business reasons and to enable frank, even combative discussions.

Claire Squires has conducted an in-depth study of an editor's gatekeeping role and the force of editorial 'taste' (Squires 2017). She wants to know why, in an age when so many corporate decisions are becoming data-driven, editorial selection is still to some extent based on 'gut' or subjective choice? Publisher curation is, in other words, a redoubt of an older form of business less prevalent in publishing than is sometimes imagined; curation it is still, in part, the province of an individual's subjective tastes or opinions. Interviewing editors at a range of trade publishers, Squires finds many of them use embodied language to describe their publishing decisions. Their publishing reflected, in their view, their taste. Arguments for publishing that might appear rational and cost-driven could, in fact, be guided more by symbolic or emotional logic than economic considerations. Where taste ends and business begins is not clear-cut, to editors as much as anyone else.

Individual editors operate within a wide range of conditioning factors, as Powell highlights. People's sense of their careers, for example, and how their publishing advances or stymies that career, has a substantial impact on their choices. Powell also underscores how an editor's network powerfully shapes their field of decision making:

> Personal friendships and extended networks among authors and publishers generate strongly defined standards of behaviour. Bonds of allegiance shape the processes of access and discovery. Networks of personal relations are also vital to economic success.   (Powell 1985: 193)

Every editor approaches publishing decisions from a tightly situated place. Their experience and position in the hierarchy may dictate how they approach the curatorial paradigm: more senior or experienced editors might feel empowered to push that paradigm, but equally someone young and keen to prove themselves may pursue risky acquisition strategies with big potential pay offs. Factors like gender, race, and class all condition an individual's taste and positionality within the editorial structure. Educational levels, personal beliefs (religion, politics, aesthetic preferences), and temperament play a role. Squires, for example, comments that in the course of her research most editors she encountered in trade publishing where white, middle class, university educated women. While there can be no simplistic causation between such factors and publishing decisions, it is unlikely they played no role.

There is also a personal element built on mutual admiration, trust and long-term relationships that Powell likens to a 'mating process' with authors (Powell 1985: xii). He acknowledges serendipity plays an outsized role in publishing—random encounters, friendships, or decisions can have large knock-on effects. Chance works in other ways. For example, if an editor already has a significant number of difficult or 'big' books they may turn down something simply for the reason that that 'slot' is already taken on the list.

Both Powell and Squires highlight how powerfully the 'premises of the firm', in my language the curatorial paradigm, weighs upon editors. Take Squires: 'What was evident in the interviews was that editors needed to fit their editorial taste-making and selection to their company environment. Gut reactions were, in actuality, learned business decisions, in constant negotiation with the environment' (Squires 2017).

The context of a publishing house, its ambience, make up of people, hierarchies, and distinct culture, has a powerful and often hidden impact on editorial selection. Interdepartmental conflicts create their own editorial dynamics. There is a tension between the 'occupational autonomy' ascribed to editors and the force of the curatorial paradigm. For the most part this is not an overt form of control. It isn't necessarily spelled out, there is no manual, but rather, in Powell's words 'editorial decision-making is guided by a number of informal control processes' (Powell 1985: 145), it is 'a process that relies on the internalization of organizational values and preferences' (1985: 146).

How then does the curatorial paradigm exert control? Partly this is down to an overt editorial strategy adopted by the house. A publisher may focus on publishing numerous romance titles, or concentrate on excelling in economics, or only in illustrated fiction for the under fives. This conscious editorial strategy sets clear boundaries and guidelines for all editors and acts as a key differentiator for publishers: focused editorial strategies enable publishers to improve through specialization and also become well known in a given area. The more focused and distinctive the editorial strategy, the more it may be a competitive advantage in a crowded field. This is a matter of positioning, if not in the eyes of the public then in business-to-business terms: editorial identity is a useful marker for literary agents, booksellers, for suppliers and customers of all kinds. It allows those in the supply chain to auto-identify with given publishers to the mutual benefit of both. And just as an automotive manufacturer will have a portfolio of brands (say Volkswagen going from Porsche to Skoda) so large groups spread their editorial activity. Groups like Penguin Random House have august imprints catering to an editorial strategy of literary prestige, as well as self-consciously 'commercial' imprints with an ethos of popular entertainment and large sales. Even within much smaller houses there may be distinct imprints or lists that service a similar purpose: to diversify the curatorial paradigm overall and enable a spread of editorial strategies, even where these are not obviously complementary. Those working within one paradigm will be conscious of the strategy and how it plays out in this differentiated wider plan.

But in terms of control, the strategy, and the curatorial paradigm underlying it are usually operationalized through the process of internalization or buy-in rather than a 'command and control' structure. Most editors are not directly told to acquire specifically this or that. Instead individual editors tie organically into the curatorial paradigm, becoming conditioned by anything from the nature of the backlist, to the philosophical opinions of a founder or an explicit company mission. There is a then a significant grey area encompassing what is overt about the paradigm and what is implicitly known and understood by members of the team. The key interface, that is, the concrete manifestation of the curatorial paradigm in day to day acquisition decisions, is the notion of social scripts or routines.

These are both formal and tacit, encompassing both sides. At the level of formal routines we see things (beyond editorial strategy) including a structure of meetings such as editorial or acquisitions meetings (the former typically attended by editors only, the latter by senior members from across departments and management); the process of forecasting revenues and costs for a title (the appraisal) and filling in various forms of documentation to describe a book; the process of getting people onside around the company and in the meeting by pitching and finding internal and external comparisons that look on the book favourably.

But the idea of social scripts (or script theory) has a powerful tacit dimension (St Clair 2008 and Meng 2008). When, say, we meet an acquaintance in the street this interaction is governed by certain social scripts, whereby each person knows the form of the conversation and their role within it—so they may talk about the weather and other phatic elements in a mutual acknowledgement. Sometimes scripts are much more elaborate, such as when hosting a wedding or a business conference. To some extent all interactions are governed by such scripts and this is powerfully the case for editorial decisions.

For our purposes scripts are in essence how all the information—from the nature of the backlist to the operating assumptions of senior management to the state of the market—are encoded into concrete discussions and decisions within the firm. It represents the mutual inter-internalization of the curatorial paradigm and its manifestation across the editorial programme, the way complexity and uncertainty are managed into a set of unspoken protocols which govern them. Editors must learn and perform social scripts for editorial choice in their company. These are not, however, fixed. First, unlike in a profession such as medicine or engineering, publishing is based to a degree on subjective factors (which is not to say it does not utilize a body of technical knowledge and hard skills). It is not only understanding a body of technical knowledge that matters for an editor, but things like their network of contacts, appreciation of writing or judgement of the market. Secondly actors within social scripts can transform them. Editors all have varying degrees of authority to challenge and morph the paradigm. More senior editors may be explicitly and implicitly granted leeway to bypass or alter social scripts and push the paradigm's boundaries; a junior editor may have a smash hit which then enables them to do likewise. Social scripts are neither stable nor monolithic; they are idiosyncratic and dynamic. That, however, does not mean they are not always powerfully present.

Publishing is messy. Chance plays an outsized role. Every aspect of list-building represents an over-determination of factors. Company hierarchy, personal taste, the backlist and trajectory of the firm, individual aspiration, tradition, finances...all tie together in an intricate knot that is is ultimately impossible to unpick: while there may be simplistic stories we can say about a decision, the full range of factors behind it are likely inordinate.

Nonetheless, as John Thompson (2010) has argued, there is still a large mythos and misunderstanding around publisher curation, especially in the trade arena. Thompson identifies a set of widely held views on publisher decision making which are not supported by the complexity of actual processes. Simplistic models for endogenous factors lead to erroneous ideas about publisher curation. For example, it is often assumed that publishers do not curate as such, that they simply go for whatever makes them money; that corporate owners exert undue editorial pressure to further their own agenda (the paradigmatic case being Rupert Murdoch nixing a book critical of China); that publishers only want established authors rather than debuts and, lastly, that editorial departments have lost all power anyway: decision making has been ceded to an ascendant trinity of sales, marketing, and management (Thompson 2010).

Thompson proceeds to show how each is mistaken. Take a look at publisher lists and you will find plenty of 'difficult' and varied books. It needs only a cursory glance at what gets published, and indeed the bestseller lists, to see a huge range of work available and selling well. A thousand curatorial paradigms do indeed bloom as any good bookshop can attest. Instead of total control Thompson finds only 'mild nepotism' and 'subtle self-censorship' (Thompson 2010: 141); there is an element of control then, but it fits into the tacit, 'premises' mould rather than anything more overt. A good deal of Thompson's argument is built around the idea that, contrary to being undesirable, debuts present the hottest properties of all. Unsullied by a commercial track record, debut books are creatures of pure potential. They could be the next bestseller. Moreover, editors may be motivated by finding such a breakthrough. Bidding wars for new writers are often the most intensely fought and the sums can escalate to eye watering levels (Bosman 2013).

Lastly, as for the perception that editors ceded all ground, the reality is again more complex. The idea that editors reign supreme has been replaced with what he calls a 'dialogical' model, whereby editors extensively consult with sales, marketing, and publicity departments to reach collective decisions. Having both their perspective and support became important. However this does not mean editors are powerless. In fact, they are still the crucial people proposing and championing titles and building lists.

Indeed, Thompson situates the shift as part of a change in publishing's dominant social scripts underwritten by a change in curatorial paradigms: 'The importance of sales and the market is not something that is simply imposed on recalcitrant editors by an increasingly powerful triumvirate of sales, marketing, and finance directors; it is something that editors themselves have internalized and incorporated into their own practices' (Thompson 2010: 143).

One question is why this should happen. Why would a common shift in the curatorial paradigm occur across a range of publishers that represents an incorporation of a sales mentality? For that we must look beyond the publisher to exogenous factors.

Exogenous Factors

There can, of course, be no clean boundary between what is internal and external to a publisher: the two are necessarily, as with any institution, in constant and ill-defined dialogue. Nevertheless, things like the economy or societal trends exist mostly outside a publisher but still forcefully inform the curatorial paradigm. In an extreme theocracy, for instance, it is unlikely that most publishers would have models deemed blasphemous. Most paradigms are much more subtle. I will sketch a framework for a publishing social theory which draws on work in sociology, media studies, and cultural theory to situate publishers and their curatorial paradigms in the widest social context.

This takes us back to the idea of concentric rings of influence. Having explored the 'inner rings' of individuals and firm-level cultures, we now look to the outer rings: things like the book retail market right up to macro ideological and economic factors further out. It should be stressed, though, that these concentric rings of influence exert bidirectional force. Organizations are not simply passive respondents in the face of the market or ideology, but are also part of the forces that, in turn, condition and shape markets and ideologies. The market often obviously conditions paradigms. If vampire novels start doing well, you tend to see many more; if popular science has a smash hit more publishers produce popular science. Curatorial paradigms can be relatively unchanging and impervious to influence. But more commonly they are dynamic and reactive, in constant states of re-adjustment to reflect market conditions as understood by the participants. These reactions in turn become part of the market and then themselves become factors in readjusting other publishers curatorial paradigms. These concentric circles then really model a system of feedback loops, flows and counterflows, recursive lines of influence.

Marxist cultural theory promotes the idea, popularized by thinkers like Georg Lukács, that the cultural field is part of a superstructure firmly underwritten and shaped by an economic base. Much work subsequently added nuance to this picture, which provided an important counterweight to ideas that cultural production is somehow separate from material concerns. Useful work came from the cultural materialists, including thinkers like Raymond Williams. Cultural materialism was alive to the undercurrents of power, politics, and economics that undergird products and practices in the cultural field, publishing included (Milner 2002). It meant connecting specific forms of culture, in various senses, to the material practices, the means of production, which created them. Cultural and technico-economic formations were imbricated. This was not a straightforward causal or simplistically hegemonic system, but something like a series of mediations and transitions and found a counterpart in the work of poststructuralist thinkers such as Michel Foucault or the sociology of Pierre Bourdieu.

The key argument here is that informational and cultural production, the work of publishers, non-simplistically mediates wider contexts. And one primary fulcrum for this is the decision-making process. Which prompts a further question: to what extent do publishers have autonomy from these contexts? How much does that mediation impact on publishing in day-to-day terms? The communications theorist Denis McQuail talks about the 'continuum of media autonomy': 'at one extreme the media are totally penetrated by, or assimilated to, outside interests, whether state or not; at the other end the media are totally free to exclude or admit as they will' (McQuail 2010: 319). But we need to extend this analysis and see where publishing as a whole sits before coming back to the specifics of a given publisher.

Publishing is marked by the curious nature of blended models. There has to be an economic component of some kind in any publishing model, as publishing requires the mobilization of resources. The old equation is starting to change in a digital world which holds out potential for a radically reworked cost structure, but for most publishers the inputs, whether that is the labour of copy-editors or the paper on which to print, are not free.

Artists, even perhaps scientists, can give themselves the illusion of autonomy; and to some extent, perhaps they are, in certain circumstances, granted the maximal possible extent of autonomy. The publisher, because of the innately resource intensive nature of their activities, never has this capacity. The publisher as an entity is always forced to confront markets directly, even when it pretends such influences have no bearing. A writer may ultimately be subject to the dictates of the market but only at a remove. The publisher, always sitting at the heart of a chain of markets, is directly implicated in them. For non-market systems, the same holds for the governing ideology/means of organization—resources are still required and they must come from somewhere.

So what is true of the ideological prism out of which content emerges, is doubly true of the publishing that filters or curates that content. We should envisage autonomy on a sliding scale (the continuum); and as a rough rule publishing is usually (but not always) further away from the autonomous pole than the material upon which it works. We feel this above all in the field of curation, in the choices a house makes. It should be noted there is within publishing, and even within publishers and individual imprints, departments and amongst editors, a further sliding scale in this social autonomy. There is no default mode of contextual engagement or governance for publishing; only specific constellations of influencing factors for each business, imprint, department, and decision maker. What we have then are layers of autonomy and conditionality that are unevenly applied across the curatorial paradigm.

These outer concentric layers demarcate the sum total of possible curatorial paradigms (and within that individual publishing models) available to a given publisher. The precise constitution of the paradigm is then down to a series of innumerable specific and contingent factors, but they are all contained within the umbrella of that wider context. What kind of factors are we talking about? Some are fairly local in nature. For example the level of freedom of speech and regulation of cultural and informational spheres has an impact, as does the nature of that regulation. Then there is the constitution of society: liberal or conservative, authoritarian or open, capitalist or non-capitalist? Government policies or institutional structures in, say, education, funding of science or dissemination of cultural products will all condition paradigms. The constitution of the economy matters greatly. Not just whether or not an economy is doing well, but also how it is made up: do public or private ownership structures dominate and how do they interact? What levels of competition are there? How does retail work? What is the state of technology?

Returning to the shift within British and American publishing houses whereby editorial accommodates sales and marketing as part of the decision-making process, we can understand this as part of a wider shift to a more aggressive form of shareholder capitalism sometimes called neoliberalism.

A set of exogenous factors bears on the Anglo-American curatorial paradigm, including but not limited to the ownership of publishers by publicly listed multi-nationals and the concomitant demand for growth and profits to underpin share prices. A deflationary pressure on the price of content stems from increasingly competitive and, in some cases, deregulated markets (the UK abandonment of the Net Book Agreement being a prime example). One hypothesis views this as adding to the return on investment (ROI) component of curatorial paradigms. That is to say, a high ROI on a given project becomes a more important part of the decision to publish in the context of such markets. Certainly, and in line with Thompson's (2010) findings, there will be no straightforward manner in which this has changed publisher curation, but it will have had an impact. More research is needed, but it will be a fruitful area of investigation.

In Practice

Faber & Faber became an iconic British publisher in the twentieth century, noted for its poetry list and stylish typographic jackets using the Albertus font. The publishing was a distinctive mix but tended to focus on modernist works. More than any other publisher the movement of literary modernism was embedded and embodied in Faber's publishing. In asking how this came about, we can see all levels of the curatorial paradigm operating. In doing so I am indebted to the critic John Mullan's history of Faber & Faber (Mullan 2004, 2016). More than anything else this is not just the story of a particular publisher, but a particular editor: T. S. Eliot.

Eliot wasn't just the great poet of Anglophone modernism, he was also an editor and publisher at Faber for over forty years. His influence on the world of letters is therefore threefold: as a poet, a critic, and an editor actively selecting many of the most important works of his time for publication. Moreover Eliot was extremely engaged in the business as a Director. In the words of Mullan, 'It was largely thanks to Eliot that this small, independent company shaped literary modernism' (Mullan 2004).

Faber itself started life as Faber and Gwyer, founded by Geoffrey Faber, a Fellow of All Souls College, Oxford, and former editor at Oxford University Press. Largely publishing medical textbooks, Eliot was nonetheless involved from an early stage thanks to Faber's interest in avant-garde poetry. After several years in the City, he joined as a Director. Eliot had edited the quarterly magazine *The Criterion* since 1922, which he soon brought into the orbit of Faber until it closed in 1939. From his poetry and *Criterion* connections Eliot would soon introduce a host of writers to the press. One notable figure was Ezra Pound. His *Selected Poems* was published by Faber & Gwyer in 1928. On the back of Siegfried Sassoon's *Memoirs of a Fox-Hunting Man*, Geoffrey Faber became the sole owner and renamed the company Faber & Faber.

In 1930 Faber's first catalogue pinned the firm as a modernist enterprise, something confirmed by a commentary on *Ulysses* published that year. Some years later Eliot was to correspond with Joyce offering him publication 'when feasible'. While the Bodley Head eventually published *Ulysses*, it was thanks to their old connection and Eliot's patience that *Finnegan's Wake* was later published by Faber alongside a panoply of great writers. There was W. H. Auden, initially rejected but encouraged by Eliot; Louis MacNeice; Stephen Spender; Marianne Moore; William Empson; Wallace Stevens; Thom Gunn; the seminal *Faber Book of Modern Verse*; more, of course, from Pound and Eliot himself, including the *Cantos* of the former and *Ash-Wednesday* from the latter. *The Faber Book of Modern Verse* set the whole tone and agenda for Modernist poetry. Its choices were bold and controversial, carefully curated to reflect the best of what was still the cultural frontline.

Later, in the 1950s, Samuel Beckett became another major Modernist to publish with Faber. In addition to the poets other modernists were represented including the artist Eric Gill, architect Walter Gropius, and the critic Herbert Read, alongside figures like André Breton. These lived side by side with writing from the likes of G. K. Chesterton and John Betjeman. Later additions to the list read like a who's who of late twentieth-century poetry: Sylvia Plath, Ted Hughes, Seamus Heaney, and Derek Walcott, amongst others.

Eliot worked alongside editors such as Walter de la Mare in an atmosphere redolent of the time: donnish, erudite, somewhat eccentric, with a commitment to new and often difficult writing. It was male, wealthy, educated, and elite. Editors were given latitude to follow their instincts and tastes (which lead to an idiosyncratic catalogue that ran from abstract poetry to popular fiction like crime and science fiction). Eliot was always deeply involved. He was in the office most days, and made sure to attend the weekly editorial meetings (known then as the 'book committee'—lunch and drinks were served). The system employed for the meeting was that everyone would read and respond to comments made about books being proposed for publication. There was a standard form, in yellow, which recorded these and was then circulated for every book. Members of the committee would sit around a large octagonal table in the boardroom and systematically go through these over the course of an afternoon. All of them maintained a commitment to reading and commenting upon unsolicited manuscripts.

From here we can unpick how the differing factors that made up the curatorial paradigm intersect—and also find a twist in the tale. First, from the writers, from the collected volumes, the consistency of aesthetic, we can see the paradigm at work; this is not necessarily the case for many publishers, where the paradigm results in a far more diffuse and, on the surface, contradictory output. In Faber's case the curatorial paradigm is visible, this is a constant and heightened curation. We can also see the importance of individuals, notably Eliot. Bringing a sensibility that married Boston Brahminism with cutting edge aesthetics, scholarship and tweedy banking with literary radicalism, Faber's publishing is shot through with his (and other editors like de la Mare's) distinctive habitus. Moreover it was Eliot's influential position in the writing community, as author of the seminal *The Wasteland* and editor of *The Criterion*, that not only attracted poets through existing personal connections but made the house a magnet for talent, drawing in names like Auden from the slushpile. Privileges of class, race, and gender are never far from the surface here; this is very much a white, male, 'gentlemanly' model of publishing that dominated the early twentieth century.

We can also see how it connects with wider currents outside the house itself. Modernism was a distinctive form that both sprung from and took inspiration from the dislocations of modernity, from new technological forms like faster transport and cinema, to a sense of ennui or anger with capitalism and the contemporary; it was a creature, a complex and often contradictory one, of the metropolitan West in those years. Likewise Faber & Faber operated in a world of independent bookshops to a small, educated, and discerning audience. It could both connect to an old world of book publishing, a newer world of the emergent literary Modernism and, underlying it all, a cut-throat world of book industry capitalism.

Behind the elegant books of poetry there was another strand to Faber's publishing, one there from the beginning but largely forgotten today: medical publishing. It was this that enabled the company to start, and through all the years of literary stardom to continue. Including perennials like one of the biggest textbooks on nursing, even as late as 1947 Faber's medical catalogue filled some sixty pages. One nursing author, Evelyn Pearce, earned far more than Eliot from her books. This veiled element of the paradigm undergirded the aestheticism; publishing medical texts buttressed the financially unrewarding work of poetry. Faber & Faber's model hence has a huge further dimension that situates it within two additional strands of its twentieth century context: the growth and professionalization of the medical profession and the financial exigencies of running a business in competitive capitalist markets while maintaining an air of self-consciously running counter to those very markets. Geoffrey Faber is central here: it was his set of connections and interests, in both academic textbook publishing and new poetry that enabled this curious balancing act, a very particular curatorial paradigm that encompassed a diverse range of inputs to produce something distinctive. In its seeming contradiction however, in uniting apparently oppositional elements (a focus on art with an emphasis on making money from medical students) we should not see Faber & Faber as a curious outlier. In fact it is just an extreme case of the norm. Curatorial paradigms are complex for a complex world, obeying many different masters and limiting factors at once, aiming to bring them into some kind of functioning and meaningful but still dissonant whole.

OUT OF HOUSE

Although the focus here is on the publisher's curatorial paradigm, we shouldn't forget it is part of a wider chain. Given the sheer mass of reading matter, there is a vast system of sequential mechanisms through which a work must pass before it finds a reader: not so much a single gatekeeper, as a long series of gates only one of which is the publisher. Publisher's curatorial paradigms are thus part of a wider process, what I call an 'ecosystem of curation' (Bhaskar 2016), which filters and curates the mass of text.

In the case of written matter this ecosystem encompasses anything from freelance reader reports and literary agents to librarians and book buyers and merchandisers. It includes literary editors and peer reviewers. This is the formal ecosystem: comprised of professional actors whose living, like that of the publisher, is at least in part derived from their ability to effectively curate. Literary agents, newspaper review pages, and booksellers all, in different ways, are about filtering. Their value to readers, on whom they ultimately depend, is directly correlated to the success or failure of that curation. Literary agents in particular have careers defined by what may be understood as micro or individual curatorial paradigms; in essence the agent is a maximally concentrated version of a publisher's curatorial paradigm. Agents thus function as a vital part of solving publishing's abundance problem. Selection is hence of paramount importance to agents, not least as they themselves operate in a crowded and competitive market. Historically speaking the formal ecosystem of curation of books is simply another description of the publishing industry and its value chain.

But there has always been a shadow side to this: the informal ecosystem, otherwise known as word of mouth. Whether in the margins of an academic conference or the intimacy of a book group, what people read is influenced by such informal filters. In the present age this is super-charged by the ubiquity and potential power of digital social networks (Thompson 2017). The informal ecosystem is thus made visible and foregrounded to an extent never previously possible. At the same time the formal ecosystem has experienced a range of challenges, like literary pages closing (Wasserman 2007) and the ongoing troubles of bookshops (although there is evidence that, in fact, a renewed focus on curation is paying dividends; Kean 2017).

Publishers are part of the formal ecosystem, yet they must engage with the informal side, which in turn becomes part of the curatorial paradigm. Eliot's contacts and friendships were a vital part of what made Faber's publishing so distinctive. An editor of commercial fiction today would be remiss if they weren't closely aware of the blogger community. A publisher's curatorial paradigm may sit at the heart of the wider ecosystem; but it should always be remembered that, beyond it, lies a sequence of curatorial paradigms, and that in turn these impinge upon and become part of the publishers own paradigm.

CONCLUSIONS

As the number of books, and beyond books the number of media and informational choices more widely, continues to grow so the importance of the curatorial paradigm grows. Publishers have always thrived or declined partly on the basis of their curatorial paradigm; but as the field becomes more crowded, and as certain logistical and production matters are streamlined, this element becomes ever more central. We can feel it in the growing role and changing nature of imprints, the signature form of modern trade publishing. As publishers grow in size and scale, so they become more internally diversified as a multiplicity of imprints. In the past few years, for example, the publisher Hachette UK has either acquired or launched imprints including Two Roads, Trapeze, Wildfire, riverrun, Spring, Fleet, Dialogue, Bookouture, and Nicholas Brealey. Penguin Random House alone has nearly 250 distinct imprints (Penguin Random House 2017).

Why this expansion of imprints? Because each imprint has an element of editorial independence, each imprint is thus able to occupy different parts of the all-encompassing curatorial paradigm, expanding and shaping it. The growth of imprints is then an essential strategy, first in growing the business and expanding the output, and secondly as a hedge; if the curatorial paradigm (e.g. the editorial selection) of one imprint starts to systematically fail, others are there to take its place. The wider the curatorial paradigm, the more open to serendipity the publisher is. Publishers operate with something akin to the portfolio theory of investing, whereby investors maximize returns and minimize risk using a careful construction of a diverse basket of investments. What is more, large groups by definition cannot concentrate on a small number of small niches as eventually they will cannibalize themselves.

As imprints proliferate, so the politics of their curation grows. One example was Penguin Classics' controversial decision to include the singer Morrissey's autobiography in its prestigious black classics range, apparently at the author's insistence. The decision was unusual not only because calling an original publication a classic is somewhat presumptuous, even when the writer is an undoubtedly gifted lyricist. It was also that black classics are reserved for dead authors—Plato, Milton, Austen...and Morrissey. Because the curatorial paradigm of a given imprint is more obvious than the publisher it sits within, so both readers, writers, and those in the trade are more likely to feel they have a stake in that paradigm, that they, to some extent, act as guardians should the editorial filters 'fail'.

One way of understanding this is to borrow the idea of the 'form' of a publisher from the Italian writer and publisher Roberto Calasso, seeing the curatorial paradigm as a key factor that goes into producing that form (Calasso 2015). While there have been a number of metaphors for the act of cultural intermediation—as a window, a mirror, a filter, a gatekeeper or portal, a signpost, guide or interpreter, as a forum or platform, a disseminator, an interlocutor (McQuail 2010: 84–5)—Calasso's concept is grounded in the day-to-day of being a publisher as well as the world of media theory. The form of a publisher maybe considered that which is unique, that which defines and distinguishes a publisher, the medley of methods and strategies and judgements that make up their publishing.

As Calasso puts it 'Form is crucial, first of all, in the choice and sequence of titles to be published.' (Calasso 2015: 5). He goes on to acknowledge that 'all books published by a certain publisher could be seen as links in a single chain, or segments in a serpentine progression of books, or fragments in a single book formed by all the books published by that publisher' (Calasso 2015: 6). This is a particularly poetic evocation of the curatorial paradigm; it elevates the paradigm to the status of something apparent, the 'single book', a lovely image although something actually better understood as a kind of underlying and unspoken meta-book behind all the actual outputs of a publisher. 'By looking at publishing houses in this way,' he writes, 'one of the more mysterious aspects of our profession might perhaps become clearer: why does a publisher reject a particular book? Because he realizes that publishing it would be like putting the wrong character into a novel, a figure who might throw the whole thing off balance' (Calasso 2015: 6). For Calasso, then, this positions publishing as a kind of literary genre or form akin to say lyric poetry, what is more one replete with its own canon of 'classics': Aldus Manutius, Gaston Gallimard, Samuel Fischer, Ernst Rowohlt, Leonard and Virginia Woolf, Alfred Knopf, and Giulio Einaudi, for instance.

We needn't go as far as Calasso, however, in acknowledging that publishers have a specific profile in their publishing, and this arises from the curatorial paradigm. Curation is so significant as this is the foundational moment for all publishers. All other aspects that produce the form of a publisher are dependent on curation. Filtering, curation, must be at the centre of our discussion of publishing because, quite simply, they are at the centre of publishing. Above everything the choice of what to publish is the starting point.

The implications of this are enormous and warrant much further research. If the central question of book publishing—who will read what and why—is and always has been one of curation this means the public sphere, our base of knowledge, swathes of our common culture, are all dependent on the panoply of curations attending the world of words. The health of all those structurally integral factors must, to a large degree, depend on the makeup and weighting of the curatorial paradigms that support them.

And a further questions looms: if self-publishing continues to rise, and indeed one day becomes a dominant mode of publishing, what then for the curatorial paradigm? Like other publishing functions this would become outsourced, but in doing so it would become so splintered it could hardly be said to exist. Marketing and production would survive the death of publishers as distinct organizations; it is less clear whether curation, editorial selection, would do so. There would still be filters; writers and others would still be choosing work to publish or display; but the curatorial paradigm as the central nexus of this would appear to become redundant. But there is an alternative scenario: that in an age of content oversupply it will precisely be this curatorial function that serves as a bulwark for professional publishers, that gives them their *raison d'etre* in an age when other functions can in theory be unbundled. More research is urgently needed on this question.

Readers curating their bookshelves and reading decisions; bookstores curating their offering, choosing which books to highlight; the media and others curating their pages and discussion; and of course publishers, carefully curating their lists... Curation is the necessary thread, the deep centre of choice, selection, filtering which defines the world of books and text, a store of value in a competitive and confusing marketplace, the heart-beat of publishing.

References

Anderson, Porter (2016a). 'Bowker Now Cites at Least 625,327 US Indie Books Published in 2015'. *Publishing Perspectives*. Available at http://publishingperspectives.com/2016/10/bowker-indie-titles-2015-isbn/#.WGaOf_krKUk [Accessed 3 June 2017].

Anderson, Porter (2016b). 'Bowker: 727,000 US Self-Published ISBNs Registered in 2015', *Publishing Perspectives*. Available at http://publishingperspectives.com/2016/09/bowker-isbn-self-published-us/ [Accessed 3 June 2017].

Bhaskar, Michael (2013). *The Content Machine: Towards a Theory of Publishing from the Printing Press to the Digital Network*, London: Anthem Press.

Bhaskar, Michael (2016). *Curation: The Power of Selection in a World of Excess*, London: Piatkus.

Bosman, Julie (2013). ' "City on Fire", a Debut Novel, Fetches Nearly $2 million', *New York Times*. Available at http://www.nytimes.com/2013/11/11/business/media/city-on-fire-a-debut-novel-fetches-nearly-2-million.html [Accessed 8 July 2017].

Bourdieu, Pierre (1993). *The Field of Cultural Production: Essays on Art and Literature*. Cambridge: Polity Press.

Bourdieu, Pierre (1996). *The Rules of Art: Genesis and Structure of the Literary Field*, Cambridge: Polity Press.

Bowker (2016). 'Self Publishing in the United States 2010–2015'. *Bowker*. Available at http://media.bowker.com/documents/bowker-selfpublishing-report2015.pdf [Accessed 3 June 2017].

Calasso, Roberto (2015). *The Art of the Publisher*, New York: Farrar, Straus and Giroux.

Coser, Lewis A. and Walter W. Powell (1982). *Books: The Culture and Commerce of Publishing*, New York: Basic Books.

Flood, Alison (2014). 'UK publishes more books per capita than any other country, report shows', *The Guardian*. Available at https://www.theguardian.com/books/2014/oct/22/uk-publishes-more-books-per-capita-million-report [Accessed 3 June 2017].

Kean, Danuta (2017). 'Waterstones boss attacks "godawful uniformity" of chains such as WH Smith', *The Guardian*. Available at https://www.theguardian.com/books/2017/mar/06/waterstones-boss-attacks-godawful-uniformity-of-chains-such-as-wh-smith [Accessed 12 August 2017].

McQuail, Denis (2010). *McQuail's Mass Communication Theory*, 6th Edition, London: SAGE.

Meng, Hangdong (2008). 'Social Script Theory and Cross-Cultural Communication', *Intercultural Communication Studies* (online) XVII(4), pp. 132–8. Available at http://web.uri.edu/iaics/files/14-Hongdang-Meng.pdf [Accessed 7 May 2017].

Milner, Andrew (2002). *Re-Imagining Cultural Studies: The Promise of Cultural Materialism*, London: SAGE Publications.

Mullan, John (2004). 'Style Council', *The Guardian*. Available at https://www.theguardian.com/books/2004/sep/25/classics.thomasstearnseliot [Accessed 8 June 2017].

Mullan, John (2016). 'The History of Faber', *Faber Blog*. Available at https://www.faber.co.uk/blog/about/faber-1940s/ [Accessed 8 June 2017].

Penguin Random House (2017). 'Imprints', Penguinrandomhouse.com. Available at https://www.penguinrandomhouse.com/imprints [Accessed 6 August 2017].

Powell, Walter W. (1985). *Getting Into Print: The Decision-Making Process in Scholarly Publishing*, Chicago IL: University of Chicago Press.

Schiffrin, André (2001). *The Business of Books*, London: Verso.

Schiffrin, André (2010). *Words and Money*, London: Verso.

Shoemaker, Pamela J. and Stephen D. Reese (1996). *Mediating the Message: Theories of Influences on Mass Media Content*, New York: Longman.

Squires, Claire. (2017). 'Taste and/or big data?: Post-digital editorial selection', *Critical Quarterly*, 59(3), pp. 1–15.

St Clair, Robert N. (2008). 'Social Scripts and Three Theoretical Approaches to Culture', *Intercultural Communication Studies* (online) XVII(4), pp 173–83. Available at http://web.uri.edu/iaics/files/13-Robert-StClair.pdf [Accessed 7 May 2017].

St Clair, William (2004). *The Reading Nation in the Romantic Period*, Cambridge: Cambridge University Press.

Thompson, Derek (2017). *Hit Makers: How Things Become Popular*, London: Allen Lane.

Thompson, John B. (2010). *Merchants of Culture: The Publishing Business in the Twenty-First Century*, Cambridge: Polity.

Wasserman, Steve (2007). 'Goodbye to All That', *Columbia Journalism Review*. Available at http://archives.cjr.org/cover_story/goodbye_to_all_that_1.php [Accessed 12 August 2017].

CHAPTER 15

....

TRADE PUBLISHING

....

JOHN B. THOMPSON

PUBLISHING is not one world but many worlds, and the ways that publishers operate vary greatly from one publishing world to another. Trade publishing is one of these worlds: it is the world of general-interest books, both fiction and non-fiction, that are written for a non-specialist readership and sold through the general retail trade, including retail chains such as Barnes & Noble in the USA and Waterstones in the UK, independent booksellers, and online retailers such as Amazon. For many people, this is the world they think of first when they think of books and publishing: it is the public face of publishing, the world of bestsellers and celebrity authors, of literary prizes and accolades, of books turned into movies and adapted for TV, of novels, memoirs, biographies, and histories—the books that form an indispensable part of the public conversation and of our public culture. While it is the most visible sector of publishing in the eyes of many, it is only one of the many worlds of publishing, and is significantly smaller, in terms of overall revenue, than the combined sales of other publishing sectors that have a less prominent public profile, such as educational and professional publishing. It is also a riskier and less profitable sector, in part because the prices are lower and the discounts offered to retailers are higher in trade publishing compared to educational and professional publishing (discounts in trade publishing are typically around 50 per cent, although they can be 60 per cent or more, compared to discounts of 20–30 per cent that are common in educational and professional publishing). Trade publishing is, nonetheless, a central part of the industry, and it is the world in which many who want to work in publishing are hoping to build a career.

Like other sectors of publishing, trade publishing can be conceptualized as a particular field, where by 'field' I mean, following the French sociologist Pierre Bourdieu, a structured space of social positions that can be occupied by agents and organizations, and where the position of any agent or organization depends on the type and quantity of resources or 'capital' they possess.[1] Publishing fields are spaces of power and competition, where publishers compete with one another to acquire rights from authors and

---

[1] See Bourdieu (1993a, 1993b: 72–7).

agents and to maximize the sales of their books through the retail channels available to them. Each field of publishing has its own distinctive properties and characteristics. There are some publishing practices that are common to different fields, and the boundaries between fields are, in any case, often blurred; but many publishing practices are specific to the particular field in which they occur. Most people who work in the industry tend to work within a particular field. They become experts in that field and may rise to senior positions of power and authority within it, but they may know very little or nothing at all about what goes on in other fields.

Publishing fields also have linguistic and spatial boundaries, and there are important differences in the ways that publishing fields work in the English-speaking world compared to those in other languages and other regions of the world. In part this is linked to the global dominance of the English language, which has given English-language publishers—especially those who are able to operate in an international market—an enormous advantage vis-à-vis their counterparts in other languages. The USA and the UK are among the top book producers in the world, and books and authors originally published in English tend to dominate the translation market. Translations from English often feature prominently on the bestseller lists in Europe, Latin America, and elsewhere, whereas translations from other languages seldom appear on the bestseller lists in Britain and the USA. In the international marketplace of books, the flow of translations and bestsellers is skewed heavily in favour of books and authors originating in the English-speaking world.[2]

The account of trade publishing in this chapter will be focused on the USA and the UK—the field of Anglo-American trade publishing. It begins by looking back at how this field has changed over the last 50 years or so, in the period since 1960. Four aspects of this field are particularly important: the value of author brand; the relation between frontlist and backlist; the role of marketing and publicity; and the challenges and opportunities created by the digital revolution.

TRANSFORMATION OF THE FIELD OF TRADE PUBLISHING

The world of trade publishing in the first half of the twentieth century and before was very different from the world we know today. There were dozens of independent publishing houses in New York, London, and elsewhere, many run by charismatic founders-owners who had strong views and forceful personalities. They knew what they wanted to publish and they built their lists on the basis of their own judgement and taste. Editors tended to work at the same publishing house for many years, often for their entire career, and authors tended to remain loyal to the house that published

---

[2] See Wischenbart (2008).

them. These publishing houses were run with varying degrees of efficiency and financial discipline. Some, like Penguin in the UK and Random House in the USA, flourished and grew into large and successful publishing companies while others struggled; in some cases the struggling firms were acquired by other companies and folded into their operations, in other cases they went out of business and disappeared from the publishing scene.

In the early 1960s the landscape of trade publishing in the USA and the UK began to change in significant ways. Three developments were particularly important.[3] The first key development was a transformation in the nature of the marketplace and the way books were sold—in essence, the rise of the retail chains. During the first half of the twentieth century, books were commonly sold in the USA and the UK by a plethora of small independent booksellers, on the one hand, and by various non-book retailers such as newsagents, drug stores, and department stores, on the other.[4] This began to change in the 1960s with the rise of mall stores in the USA, like B. Dalton and Waldenbooks. The 1970s were the heyday of the mall bookstores, but these were soon eclipsed by the rise of the 'book superstores' in the 1980s, especially Barnes & Noble and Borders in the USA and Waterstones in the UK. The rise of the retail chains had several consequences in the field of trade publishing. First, it led to the dramatic decline of the independent booksellers. They simply could not compete with the book superstores and hundreds were forced into bankruptcy. Second, the rise of the retail chains led to a shift in the ways that books were stocked and sold. The methods of selling and stock management that were developed in other retail sectors were now applied to books. This meant using display tables and dumpbins to stimulate impulse buying and multiple purchases. It also meant using computerized methods of stock management to monitor stock levels and stock turnover, so that fast-selling titles could be reordered and slow-selling titles could be returned. (Bookselling is one of the only retail sectors where unsold stock can be returned for full credit, a practice that took hold during the Great Depression of the 1930s as a way of encouraging booksellers to increase stockholdings and subsequently became a key feature of the way the industry is organized).

A third consequence of the rise of the retail chains was what we could call 'the hard-cover revolution'. Much has been written about the paperback revolution started by Allen Lane in the UK, with his launch of the Penguin imprint in the 1930s, and exemplified by the rise of Pocket Books, Bantam, Dell, Fawcett, the New American Library, and other paperback houses in the USA in the period after World War 2. Mass-market paperback sales became the financial driving force of the industry, and the sale of paperback rights became a principal source of revenue for the hardcover houses. By the 1960s the industry itself had bifurcated into two separate businesses—hardcover publishing, on the one hand, and paperback publishing, on the other. In the 1970s this began to change. Paperback houses began to originate their own hardcovers in order to gain more control over their supply chain. They also began to apply some of the techniques

---

[3] For a more detailed analysis of these changes and their consequences, see Thompson (2012).
[4] For an excellent account of bookselling in the USA, see Miller (2006).

they had developed in the world of mass-market paperback publishing, such as the use of bold and attractive covers, to their hardcover publishing. With the roll-out of the book superstore chains, publishers were able to achieve hardcover sales that were far in excess of anything they had known previously. In the 1970s and before, a hardcover that sold 500,000 copies would have been a huge success; by the early 2000s, sales of hardcovers commonly numbered in the millions. Dan Brown's *The Da Vinci Code*, published in 2003, sold more than 18 million copies in hardcover in the USA alone—this was the hardcover revolution. As the sales of hardcovers increased, the old relationship between hardcover and paperback publishing was gradually inverted: whereas in the 1950s and 1960s, paperback publishing was the financial driving force of trade publishing, in the 1980s and 1990s hardcover publishing became the financial foundation of the industry.

In the last decade, the retail landscape has changed still further with the rise of online retailers such as Amazon and with the growing role of the mass merchandisers and supermarkets, like Tesco in the UK. We shall return to this later.

The second key development in Anglo-American trade publishing was the rise of the literary agent. This is something specific to the Anglo-American field of trade publishing: there are literary agents in France, Germany, Italy, and elsewhere, but they are nothing like as numerous or as powerful as they are in the UK and the USA. The history of the literary agent goes back to the late nineteenth century: a Scotsman, A. P. Watt, is usually regarded as the first professional literary agent, and he began representing authors in London in the late 1870s.[5] For two decades, Watt had the field pretty much to himself, but by the end of the nineteenth century others had seen the potential and entered the field as competitors. The role of the agent remained pretty much unchanged for a century or so: they were cultural intermediaries who saw their role as one of mediating between authors and publishers, serving their authors by negotiating deals that both parties—authors and publishers—would regard as fair and reasonable. But in the late 1970s and early 1980s, things began to change. A new breed of literary agent began to appear—what I call the 'super-agents'. These were outsiders—that is, people who came into the publishing field from outside and were not attached to the traditional practices of publishers and agents. In their eyes, the traditional agent was too imbued with the ethos of the publishing world. They were too close to the publishers and they maintained a kind of gentlemanly relationship with them; they never pushed hard because they didn't want to rock the boat. But this traditional conception of the agent was anathema to the new super-agents, who thought of themselves not as intermediaries but as advocates of their clients'—that is, the authors'—interests. They took a more combative attitude: they were prepared to fight hard and make enemies. The perfect examples of this new breed of super-agent were Morton Janklow and Andrew Wylie, two well-known New York agents. Neither had come out of publishing: Janklow was a lawyer and Wylie went straight into agenting from college. Andrew Wylie is somewhat notorious in the business—he is often referred to as 'the jackal' for his willingness to poach authors

---

[5] On the early history of literary agents, see Hepburn (1968); Gillies (2007).

(generally regarded as a despicable practice by other agents) and for his tough-minded pursuit of high advances. In the world of Anglo-American trade publishing, Andrew Wylie is feared, loathed, and admired in roughly equal measures, but no one doubts that he has had a huge impact on the way agents work.

The third key development was the consolidation in the industry and the emergence of large publishing corporations. Since the 1960s, many of the formerly independent publishing houses have been bought up and merged with other publishers to form large publishing corporations, which are themselves part of, and owned by, large multimedia conglomerates.[6] Today there are only five large publishing corporations in the USA and the UK, and for the most part they are the same corporations operating on both sides of the Atlantic. The largest trade publisher in the world is now Penguin Random House, formed through the merger in 2013 of Random House, owned by the German conglomerate Bertelsmann, and the Penguin Group, owned by British media conglomerate Pearson. Hachette, a major trade publisher in the UK and, following the acquisition of the Time Warner Book Group in 2006, a major trade publisher in the USA too, is owned by the French conglomerate Lagardère. HarperCollins is owned by Rupert Murdoch's News Corporation. Simon & Schuster is owned by CBS. The German-based Holtzbrinck Group owns Macmillan and a variety of other imprints including Pan, Picador, and Farrar, Straus & Giroux. Many publishing imprints that were once independent publishing houses—Knopf, Doubleday, Viking, Scribner, Hutchinson, Heinemann, Hamish Hamilton, Jonathan Cape, etc.—are now imprints operating under the umbrella of one of the large publishing corporations. 'The Big Five' are the dominant publishers in the field of Anglo-American trade publishing and together they account for around half of total trade sales in the USA and the UK.

These three developments had a profound impact on Anglo-American trade publishing. Among other things they produced a polarization of the field: there are now a small number of very large publishing corporations, on the one hand, and a large number of very small publishing operations, on the other, but very little in between. It is very difficult to be medium-sized in the field of trade publishing. Medium-sized publishing houses are not big enough to compete with the large corporations when it comes to acquiring the most desirable authors and books: with agents controlling access to new content, publishers have to be able to offer large advances—often in the high six figures, sometimes seven figures—in order to acquire the rights for the most sought-after authors and books. Hence medium-sized publishers tend to lose their most successful authors to the imprints owned by the large corporations. On the other hand, medium-sized publishers have much higher overheads than the very small publishing operations that exist on the margins of the field. Unlike these small operations, which often get by on low and erratic revenue streams, the medium-sized publishers need a steady flow of bestselling titles to cover their costs and generate a profit. They find themselves in a very vulnerable position, always at risk of losing their bestselling authors to the large

---

[6] This development and its consequences for trade publishing have been discussed in various works including Schiffrin (2000); Epstein (2001); de Bellaigue (2004).

corporations and of failing to publish enough bestselling titles to remain profitable. Most eventually get bought up by the large corporations.

The developments that shaped the field of Anglo-American trade publishing also helped to produce a preoccupation with 'big books'. This preoccupation stemmed from a simple business problem faced by all of the large publishing corporations: these corporations were expected by the conglomerates that owned them to grow year on year and to generate a good level of profit, ideally in excess of 10 per cent, but they had to do this in a market that was largely static. The book market in the USA and the UK was a mature market that was not expanding in real terms, and if it grew at all, it did so only at the rate of inflation. Hence all of the publishing corporations were faced with the same fundamental problem: how could they achieve growth in a static market? They could not solve this problem by just increasing the number of books they published: their sales forces were already overstretched and had far too many books to sell, and adding more would only exacerbate the problem of title overload. So there was tremendous pressure within these organizations to try to cut out the bottom range of what are known in the business as 'mid-list' titles—that is, books selling in modest quantities—and focus more of their publishing effort on a small number of big books. The aim, in short, was to maximize your sales on a smaller number of books—that's the golden rule.

Big books are not necessarily bestsellers: they are more accurately described as 'hoped-for bestsellers'. Big books exist well before they are published, and therefore well before anyone knows whether they will actually become bestsellers. For most of the new books that are being offered by agents and bought by editors and publishers, no one really knows just how well they will do. They are placing bets on books in the hope that some of them will turn out to be bestsellers. This creates a large space at the heart of trade publishing for what we could call 'the web of collective belief'. A great deal of time and effort is invested in agents trying to persuade publishers that the book being offered to them is, indeed, a big book. And a great deal of weight is placed on what other people—especially trusted people, like trusted agents with a good track record—think and say about the book and how big it is. The buzz and excitement that is generated around a new book project becomes contagious, and this in turn tends to drive up the stakes in the auctions that agents orchestrate for the sale of the rights for books that are deemed to be big.

The more a publisher ends up paying for a book, the bigger the book tends to be. Much more is riding on a book for which a publisher has paid a million dollars than one for which it has paid $50,000, and the expectations, prioritizations and investments within the publishing house are adjusted accordingly. Ironically, this creates a perverse incentive within the large publishing houses to pay more for books rather than less, because the more you pay, the bigger the book is, and the more likely it is that the book will be treated as a big book all the way down the line, from the allocation of marketing spend to the prioritization of titles by sales teams. There is just one hitch: a big book is not a bestseller, it is merely a hoped-for bestseller. It is the publisher's best guess supported by various more-or-less reliable considerations, ranging from the author's track record and the sales of comparable books to the views and opinion of others, that is, the web of collective belief. But the guess could be wrong, and more often than not it is. The challenge for the publisher is to try to ensure that you win enough times to compensate for the books that fail, and that, on those occasions when you do win, you are able to turn it into a success on a scale that will make up for all the failures. Trade publishing is a business of risk and hope: you have to be willing to take risks, and you have to hope that the occasional investment that succeeds will have a disproportionate payoff. By its very nature this gambling game favours the big corporate houses with deep pockets, as they can afford to place more bets and bigger bets than the smaller houses, and they have the financial wherewithal to survive when the majority of these bets fail.

While frontlist trade publishing is inherently risky, there are two areas where trade publishers can count on more reliable revenue streams: brand-name authors and the backlist. Both forms of publishing are very important for trade publishers because they provide counterweights that offset the inherent riskiness of frontlist publishing.

The Value of Brand-Name Authors

Brand-name authors are important for trade publishers because their sales are predictable. They have readerships that are loyal to them: readers become 'fans' of a particular writer, or of a series of books by a particular writer, and they want to read more. The publisher can therefore count on a market that is to some extent captive, and the sales of the author's previous books become a good guide to the sales of the author's next book. In a world where so much frontlist publishing is a crapshoot, predictability of this kind is a gift. Reader loyalty is more common in fiction than in non-fiction, and more common in commercial fiction than in literary fiction. It is in the genre categories of commercial fiction, such as thriller, horror, mystery, romance, science fiction, and fantasy, where the loyalty to brand-name authors—Stephen King, James Patterson, John Grisham, Nora Roberts, Dean Koontz, Patricia Cornwell, Lee Child, Tom Clancy, etc.—is particularly strong.

There is another reason why brand-name authors are important for trade publishers: they are repeaters. They write a book a year, or maybe a book every two years. This means that the publisher with a number of brand-name repeaters can plan their future programme with much more accuracy and reliability than a publisher who is relying on the normal hit-and-miss business of frontlist trade publishing. They know when each of their repeaters will deliver and they can plan their publishing strategies for each author and each book in order to maximize their sales potential—each year a new hardcover, which is subsequently re-launched as a trade or mass market paperback, etc. The regular, predictable output of repeaters also enables the publisher to build the author's brand over time, feeding new books into the marketplace at regular intervals to maintain the interest and loyalty of existing fans and to recruit new readers.

One of the first trade houses to appreciate the value of brand-name authors was Putnam. An old American publisher dating back to the middle of the nineteenth century,

Putnam was taken over in 1975 by MCA, the multimedia entertainment conglomerate. MCA wanted steady growth and steady cash, and Putnam delivered this by importing into the world of trade publishing a model that was used by MCA in other sectors of their entertainment empire. They found commercial fiction writers who were publishing with other houses, brought them over to Putnam by paying good advances and lavishing personal attention on them, and then worked closely with them to build their brand and their sales. Authors wrote a book a year and publication was spaced out so that new books by big-name authors were not competing in the same slot. The sales force developed strong relationships with the accounts and worked hard to push each new book up the bestseller lists, so that the author, not just the title, became more and more visible. At the same time they kept the author's backlist constantly in front of the public. The model was hugely successful and was soon imitated by other publishers. Putnam itself was acquired by the Penguin Group in 1996 and its brand-name author model became a cornerstone of Penguin's growth and success in the USA.

While publishing brand-name authors is a very effective way to build a trade publishing programme, it has a significant downside for the publisher: the importance of the author brand puts the author and the agent in a very strong position when it comes to negotiating terms and advances. The agent knows how valuable the brand-name author is to the publisher and is able to use this to secure higher advances. What this means, in effect, is that the advance ceases to be a guarantee on future royalty earnings and becomes a premium paid to the brand-name author for the benefits that accrue to the publisher from having him or her on the list. This reduces the profitability of the author's books and puts pressure on the publisher's margins, since it means that the brand-name author is taking a larger share of the publisher's revenue. It also means that there is always a risk that a bestselling brand-name author will leave a publishing house, where they may have been for many years, and move to another house that is prepared to pay a higher premium. High-profile moves of this kind are not uncommon in trade publishing and are a testimony to the poaching game that is played out in that sector of the field where brand-name authors are leveraged by large corporations seeking to grow their revenues and increase their market shares in a market that is largely static.

FRONTLIST VS BACKLIST

The second area where trade publishers can count on reliable revenue streams is the backlist. The virtues of the backlist are numerous: the revenue is relatively predictable and stable from one year to the next; the major investment costs have already been incurred and any unearned advances have usually been written off by the time a book becomes a backlist title; marketing expenditure and promotion costs are minimal; and returns are generally low. With backlist titles the publisher is simply reprinting books to meet ongoing demand and the only costs they incur are the costs of printing, the costs of warehousing and distribution and the royalty payments to the author (and, in the case of books no longer in copyright, not even the latter). Backlist publishing is therefore much more profitable than frontlist publishing. Not only does it make a relatively stable contribution to the publisher's top line, it also makes a disproportionately large contribution to the bottom line.

So why don't trade publishers do more of it? The simple explanation is that building the backlist is a slow and laborious process, especially in trade publishing. It takes a long time to build up a list of books that backlist well. Good backlists were built by publishing houses that were founded in previous centuries, or in the first half of the twentieth century, when the conditions in the field of trade publishing were very different. Most of those backlists have now been acquired by the large publishing corporations, which bought up houses and imprints partly in order to acquire the kind of backlist that would be very difficult to create ex nihilo today. So there are very few opportunities left for the large publishing houses to grow their backlist by acquisition.

Moreover, with the growing importance of the retail chains and of other mass-market retail outlets like the discount stores and supermarkets, the major trade houses were able to ship large quantities of new hardcovers to the major retail accounts, thus shifting their publishing programmes towards a model that was increasingly reliant on a regular flow of frontlist bestsellers. Many trade houses found themselves increasingly drawn into the bestseller syndrome where their ability to meet the financial expectations of their corporate owners was increasingly dependent on their ability to acquire and successfully publish a regular stream of frontlist bestsellers. This in turn ratcheted up the stakes for big books—that is, for those books that were seen as potential bestsellers— and increased the value of the brand-name authors. The publishers with the smallest backlists were most exposed to this dynamic. A publisher with a backlist that accounts for only 25 or 30 per cent of its sales, like Simon & Schuster, would have to generate 70 or 75 per cent of its revenue each year from new books. Publishers with more substantial backlists, like Penguin Random House, are able to rely on their backlists to generate a higher proportion of their revenue, and this eases somewhat the pressure on frontlist publishing—although even in this case, around 60 per cent of the revenue each year will need to come from new books. The heavy reliance of the major trade publishers on frontlist publishing creates a powerful incentive to pay large advances for big books and do everything they can to turn them into bestsellers.

THE ROLE OF MARKETING
AND PUBLICITY

Creating a regular stream of frontlist bestsellers requires not just a willingness and ability to pay large advances to acquire big books and brand-name authors, it also requires a substantial investment in marketing and publicity. Marketing and publicity play a particularly important role in trade publishing because they are the activities through which publishers seek to make readers and consumers aware of the books they are publishing and create a desire to buy them and read them. This is where the real challenge for trade publishers lies—in part because there are many other demands on the time, attention and resources of individuals, and in part because of the sheer number of new books that are being published every year. The book market is a very crowded marketplace—and today, with the lowering of entry costs associated with the digital revolution, this is truer than ever. How can publishers make their books stand out and get noticed despite all the competition and noise in the marketplace?

There are two main arenas where the struggle for attention has traditionally been played out in the field of trade publishing. One arena is the battle for eyeballs in the bookstores and other retail outlets. The physical spaces at the front of bookstores, and especially the big retail chains, become key battlegrounds for the attention of consumers. Many consumers walk into bookstores and browse the tables and shelves at the front, picking up books that catch their attention; many books are bought as impulse purchases, so getting your books stacked on the front tables, or displayed face-out on the shelves at the front of the store, can be crucial. How do publishers get their books into the high-visibility spaces at the front of bookstores? Essentially, they pay for it, through a system known euphemistically as 'co-op' (or cooperative advertising). Co-op is a cost-sharing arrangement between the publisher and the retailer in which the publisher pays for part of the retailer's promotion costs. Most trade publishers calculate what they are prepared to make available to a particular account as a percentage of that account's net sales in the previous year; the amount can vary from 2 to 4 per cent, depending on the publisher. This money goes into a pool which can be used by that account to promote the publisher's books in their bookstore or on their website. To get a book in a front-of-store display in a major retail chain like Barnes & Noble is not entirely within the control of the publisher. What typically happens is that the publisher's sales managers for the national accounts present the new titles to the central buyers at the retail chains and let them know what their expectations are for the book—how big a book it is for them, how many copies they'd like the retailer to buy, etc. The buyers decide which titles they want to buy in what quantities based on their own assessment of the book and other factors, such as the sales histories of the author's previous books, and they can tie co-op money into the order by negotiating an in-store promotion funded through co-op. For the large trade houses, the total amount spent on co-op has grown enormously in recent years, and for many publishers, co-op is now one of the largest items in their marketing budget.

Getting books into the high-visibility spaces of bookstores is one thing; persuading consumers to buy the books is quite another. Closing the gap between the stocking of books by retailers and the purchase of books by consumers is known as 'sell-through'. If books don't sell through, then they may be returned by the retailer, thereby reducing the publisher's net sales and increasing the likelihood that they will end up with unsold and unsellable stock that will have to be pulped. So stimulating sell-through is vital for trade publishers—this is the second main arena where the struggle for attention is played out. Traditionally publishers have relied on publicity and advertising in the mainstream media as key ways of bringing their books to the attention of consumers and encouraging them to buy. The publisher's publicists work hard to secure radio and television appearances for the authors of the new books they are publishing and to get prominent reviews in major newspapers like the *New York Times* and *Washington Post*: a big publicity hit in the mainstream media can make a real difference to sales and can trigger a media storm, encouraging others to interview the author or review the book. But these traditional channels are becoming less and less reliable for publicity purposes, both because it is harder to get books into them and because they are less effective than they used to be. As newspapers and other print media like magazines have come under growing financial pressure, in part through the loss of advertising revenue to online media like Google, they have reduced the amount of space devoted to book reviews; many newspapers have closed down their book review sections, and some newspapers and magazines have closed altogether.[7] Books have also become less important for mainstream television, and televised book clubs, like the Oprah Book Club in the USA and the Richard and Judy Book Club in the UK, which once drove sales like nothing else, lost their slots on mainstream TV. With the declining significance of traditional media as channels for marketing and promoting books, publishers have increasingly shifted the focus of their marketing efforts to a variety of more specialized 'micro media', from email, websites, and blogs to social media and online advertising. These new media enable marketers and publicists to be more targeted in their marketing efforts. Instead of placing an expensive ad in a general-circulation newspaper, they can target niche audiences that are more likely to have an interest in the specific content of the book they are seeking to promote. Moreover, by using social media and building on the social media presence of their authors, publishers can help to generate the kind of online chatter and word of mouth that can drive sales.

CHALLENGES AND OPPORTUNITIES
OF THE DIGITAL REVOLUTION

The increasing use of online marketing is just one of the many ways in which trade publishing has been, and is being, transformed by the digital revolution. The impact of the digital revolution has been one of the central concerns of trade publishers since the late 1990s. A large part of this concern has been focused on the question of whether, and to what extent, the traditional format of the book publishing industry—the print-on-paper book—will be replaced by ebooks, and what the implications of this might be in terms of revenue, piracy, and business models. Senior managers in trade houses watched with growing unease as revenues collapsed in the recorded music industry in the early 2000s, undercut both by illicit file sharing and by significantly lower prices for content downloaded through legitimate channels like iTunes, and many wondered whether

---

[7] Wasserman (2007).

trade book sales might suffer a similar fate. While ebook sales were initially very low in the early 2000s, they began to take off in 2008, following the introduction of Amazon's Kindle in November 2007. Ebook sales of trade books increased sharply for several years, and by 2012 ebooks accounted for around 20 per cent of total US trade sales—a dramatic change in just five years. In certain categories of trade books, the percentage was even higher: in romance fiction, ebooks accounted for nearly 60 per cent of sales by 2013 for some of the large US houses, and other categories of genre fiction, like mystery, sci fi and fantasy, were not far behind. However, having grown dramatically in the period from 2008 to 2012, ebook sales then levelled off for most trade publishers; there was continued ebook growth in some categories but decline in others, and the average level of ebook sales remained at around 20 per cent of overall US trade sales. The UK experienced a similar pattern, and ebook sales levelled off in the UK at around 15 per cent of overall sales. For the established trade publishers, the ebook revolution appeared to have plateaued, at least for the time being.

But the digital revolution in the publishing industry was never just about ebooks. From the 1980s on, the digital revolution was already having a profound impact on the nature of the publishing process and the way that books are produced—not only in trade publishing but in every sector of the industry. The entire publishing process, from the point at which an author turns words and sentences into keystrokes which are captured in a digital file to the point at which the final book is printed, has been turned, step by step, into what we could call a 'digital workflow'. Behind the scenes, the book has become a digital file, a database, that is worked on and manipulated in various ways by various people until eventually it is ready to be printed, which today can also be done digitally. This 'hidden revolution' may be invisible to outsiders because the final product, the printed book, may look the same, but this revolution has transformed fundamentally the process by which the book is created.

There are other equally fundamental ways in which the digital revolution is transforming the world of trade publishing. It has transformed the retail sector by making possible the rise of Amazon which, from its origins as a tech start-up in a Seattle garage in 1995, quickly became the largest book retailer in the history of publishing—and one of the world's largest retailers *tout court*.[8] By 2014, Amazon accounted for over 40 per cent of all new book unit sales in the USA, print and digital combined, and it accounted for around 70 of all ebook sales.[9] No other retailer comes anywhere near Amazon's market share of the book business in the USA and the UK, nor has any retailer ever had this kind of market share of the book business in the past. For many publishers, Amazon has now become their single most important account by a considerable margin, both for print books and for ebooks. This puts Amazon in a very powerful position when it comes to negotiating terms of trade with publishers as it is very difficult for publishers to walk away from a retailer that accounts for such a large proportion of its sales.

---

[8] For an excellent account of the rise of Amazon, see Stone (2013).
[9] Research conducted by the Codex Group, reported in Milliot (2014).

The digital revolution has also spurred a tremendous growth in self-publishing. Self-publishing is not new: it began with the so-called vanity presses that emerged in the early and mid-twentieth century. But the digital revolution made possible a completely new model of self-publishing. Many new self-publishing platforms were launched in the early 2000s that enabled authors to self-publish their work very easily and with little or no financial outlay upfront. Self-publishing ceased to be thought of as vanity publishing, as a kind of last resort that authors could take up when all other options were exhausted, and increasingly it was seen by some authors as a positive choice that authors could make for themselves, enabling them to publish their books without having to go through the intermediary of the traditional publishing house. Thanks to the rise of these new digital platforms, vanity publishing gave way to a new kind of 'indie publishing' that was actively embraced by many authors. By using these platforms to publish their own work, authors could take control of the publishing process and earn much higher royalties on the copies sold: on ebooks, for example, authors could earn between 70 and 85 per cent of net receipts, depending on the platform, compared to the typical royalty of 25 per cent of net offered by the traditional trade houses. For those genres where a large proportion of the sales were accounted for by ebooks selling to Kindle users, such as romance, thrillers, sci fi, and fantasy, the idea of self-publishing through Amazon's ebook self-publishing platform, Kindle Direct Publishing (KDP), was becoming an increasingly attractive option for many authors. While many self-published books sell in very small numbers, this is not true of all: there are some authors, like J. A. Konrath and Hugh Howey, who became very successful by self-publishing their work, and there is some evidence to suggest that, by 2016, a substantial proportion of the titles appearing on Amazon's ebook bestseller lists—perhaps as much as a quarter—were self-published books.[10] While accurate figures on the scale of self-publishing are not available, it seems likely that the numbers—both in terms of the numbers of titles being published and the numbers of copies of some titles that are being sold—are large. Self-publishing has become a hidden continent of the publishing world, one that lies largely beyond, and remains largely invisible to, the traditional structures and accounting practices of the publishing industry.

The digital revolution has also opened up the possibility that publishers could develop a more direct relationship with the readers who are the ultimate consumers of the books they publish. Throughout the 500-year history of book publishing, publishers have, for the most part, regarded intermediaries like retailers as their main customers: publishers sold their books to retailers, and they left it to retailers to sell the books to readers. This meant that publishers had very little direct communication with readers: they were primarily B2B rather than B2C businesses, to use the jargon of business studies. It also meant that they knew very little about readers and their purchasing practices. But the digital revolution and the new forms of communication made possible by the Internet have created new opportunities for publishers to learn more about the readers who are

[10] 'February 2016 Author Earnings Report: Amazon's Ebook, Print and Audio Sales', at http://authorearnings.com/report/february-2016-author-earnings-report/

their ultimate customers, to reach out to them with well-targeted marketing campaigns and, indeed, to sell directly to them rather than relying exclusively on sales through intermediaries. These new opportunities opened up by the digital revolution are perhaps the most significant of all, and the extent to which they are taken up by publishers could be among the key factors that shape the changing landscape of trade publishing in the years to come.

REFERENCES

Bourdieu, Pierre (1993a). *The Field of Cultural Production: Essays on Art and Literature*. Cambridge: Polity Press.

Bourdieu, Pierre (1993b). 'Some Properties of Fields', in *Sociology in Question*, by Pierre Bourdieu, trans. Richard Nice, London: Sage.

de Bellaigue, Eric (2004). *British Book Publishing as a Business since the 1960s: Selected Essays*, London: British Library.

Epstein, Jason (2001). *Book Business: Publishing Past Present and Future*, New York: W.W. Norton.

Gillies, Mary Ann (2007). *The Professional Literary Agent in Britain, 1880–1920*, Toronto: University of Toronto Press.

Hepburn, James (1968). *The Author's Empty Purse and the Rise of the Literary Agent*, London: Oxford University Press.

Miller, Laura J. (2006). *Reluctant Capitalists: Bookselling and the Culture of Consumption*, Chicago: University of Chicago Press.

Milliot, Jim (2014). 'BEA 2014: Can Anyone Compete with Amazon?', *Publishers Weekly*, 28 May 28. Available at http://www.publishersweekly.com/pw/by-topic/industry-news/bea/article/62520-bea-2014-can-anyone-compete-with-amazon.html

Schiffrin, André (2000). *The Business of Books: How International Conglomerates Took Over Publishing and Changed the Way We Read*, London: Verso.

Stone, Brad (2013). *The Everything Store: Jeff Bezos and the Age of Amazon*, New York: Little, Brown and Company.

Thompson, John B. (2012). *Merchants of Culture: The Publishing Business in the Twenty-First Century*, 2nd Edition, New York: Penguin.

Wasserman, Steve (2007). 'Goodbye to All That', *Columbia Journalism Review*, Sept.–Oct. Available at https://archives.cjr.org/cover_story/goodbye_to_all_that_1.php

Wischenbart, Rüdiger (2008). *Diversity Report 2008: An Overview and Analysis of Translation Statistics Across Europe* (21 November 2008). Available at http://www.wischenbart.com/diversity/report/Diversity%20Report_prel-final_02.pdf

CHAPTER 16

....

ACADEMIC PUBLISHING

....

SAMANTHA J. RAYNER

ACADEMIC publishers provide a critical set of services to scholars. Without their expertise, co-ordination, and reach, research could not be commissioned, peer reviewed, edited, produced, and disseminated. These processes ensure academic rigour, resulting in trustworthy outputs that form the intellectual capital upon which scholarly reputations, and our collective access to learning and ideas, relies. Academic, or scholarly, publishing is an area that covers a universe of traditional and emerging, constantly changing subjects, formats, and practices, so it is not surprising that attempts to define this are elusive and hard to find. The term 'academic publishing' includes monographs, journals, editions of texts, higher education textbooks, and collections of essays, all of which have undergone some sort of peer review process. Simply put, the field covers the production and dissemination of knowledge and research, but, intricately involved with political issues around education and the value of the knowledge economy, accessibility, and status, it is, and always has been, a complex, innovative, and reflexive industry. As one leading UK academic publisher explains,

> Original, cutting-edge research is the fire that fuels knowledge and education. Without the dissemination of new thought, new ideas, and challenges to current thinking, textbooks don't advance. What we publish today will impact what our children study tomorrow, our social policy, and how businesses are run.
>
> (Burridge 2013)

This emphasizes the potential influence of academic publishing, wherever in the world it takes place. The sheer diversity of different publishing models has meant it has not been possible to show global academic publishing statistics before, or, indeed, comprehensive statistics of any area of publishing as a global industry, but the International Publishers Association is collecting data in 2017 to enable the publication of the first annual world publishing statistics survey in 2018. However, in the UK, the Publishers Association reported that academic and professional publishing was up 10 per cent to

£2.4 billion in 2016, and that while the share of journal subscriptions income fell to 79 per cent the income from Open Access article processing charges increased by 46 per cent to £81m. (Publishers Association 2017) Those statistics show that, in the UK at least, academic publishing is expanding: and that it is changing. The drive to create content that is Open Access, that is, 'peer-reviewed academic research that is free to read online and that anybody can redistribute and reuse, with some restrictions' (Eve 2014: 1) has been one of the transformative factors in academic publishing since the beginning of the twenty-first century. However, the impetus to spread research and knowledge widely has arguably underpinned academic publishing since its beginnings in the late medieval period.

Academic Publishing Origins

When, in the late fifteenth century, printing began to overtake (but not entirely replace) manuscript culture in the West, it 'revolutionised all forms of learning'. (Eisenstein 2005: 3) Before this point learning was communicated via limited, handwritten texts, produced in scriptoria, and situated, in the main, in monasteries or in university towns around Europe. Academic publishing was quite literally circumscribed by the geographical location of manuscripts and the difficulty of travelling to access them, and by the lack of reading skill in the larger population. However, with the coming of the printing press, it was possible to reach more people more quickly, and print smaller, more portable books, pamphlets, and tracts, and this in turn encouraged a wider reading public to emerge. By 1480 there were printing presses in over 110 towns in Western Europe; in 1638 the first printing office in the United States was opened in Massachusetts Bay close to what became Harvard University. The first book in Russia was printed in 1563, the first in Constantinople in 1727, and the first in Greece in 1821. Presses were in use in Abyssinia in 1515, in Goa by 1557, in Macao by 1588, and in Nagasaki by 1590. In China, where printing was already highly developed, the European printing methods were brought in and an initiative, under Father Ruggieri from Naples, collected and translated great works of western science and philosophy into Chinese. (Febvre and Martin 2010: 182–215) The spread of learning was transformed by printing: since the arrival of the World Wide Web and the Internet, in the late twentieth century, another major transformation has occurred, allowing for faster, almost instantaneous access to resources from across the globe. This has brought with it new issues and questions around copyright and IP, a very current and key area of debate as this chapter is being written. In 2004, for example, Google Books announced partnerships with several of the largest research libraries in the world to scan, digitize, and make available texts in their collections, and this initiative has caused ongoing legal battles with publishers who challenge Google's right to reproduce copyrighted work without compensating authors or publishers.

OPEN ACCESS

These large-scale digitization projects underline the ubiquity of the online developments, which, coupled with the explosion of different ways to self-publish (either online via blogs or websites, or via ebooks and ebook providers) have questioned the role of the publisher. This is increasingly and particularly the case in academic publishing, where the value of the publisher's services to the author has become fiercely debated (e.g. Meadows and Wulf 2016). As publishers move away from being content providers to providers of services enhancing and changing the user's access and consumption practices, and as content therefore becomes more open, will the core publisher assets of brand and aggregation continue to hold value?

These debates are most evident in the science subjects, where the main focus is on the costs of journal access; it is no surprise, therefore, that this is the area in which the Open Access (OA) movement has gained the most successful traction. Open Access has its origins in the free culture movement of the late twentieth century, developing alongside the growth of technological innovations. The movement sought to break free from the commercial company boundaries which restricted the use of software to proprietory contexts. It thus confronted copyright practices head on, and was soon being applied to knowledge and the dissemination of that knowledge within the science disciplines. The principles were brought together for the first time in the Budapest (2002), Bethesda (2003) and Berlin Declarations (2003). In the humanities, where imperatives around the need for fast and wide publication are not as pressing, and funding is not as readily available, the Open Access movement has been slower to progress, but it is now one of the key issues within academic publishing, and has strong government support in the UK and in Europe, while in the USA many university presses are exploring OA models (see Crossick 2015; Jisc 2016; Maxwell et al. 2017). Peter Suber, an early advocate of OA, argues that academic authors should embrace it: 'It's enough to know that their employers pay them salaries, freeing them to give away their work, that they write for impact rather than money, and that they score career points when they make the kind of impact they hoped to make' (Suber 2012: 2).

This is one compelling perspective: other voices, particularly in some areas of the creative humanities, argue that their outputs are artistic, and often produced outside of core working hours, and that they should be able to hold onto the right to publish where they choose. It is a zone fraught with anxieties and misapprehensions about what OA means. OA publication still incurs costs, and the questions of who pays, and when, and how, are still obfuscated by a multitude of different business models and approaches (see Jubb 2017: 189-95).

There are two main models, called 'green' and 'gold' OA. The green route is where work is deposited in an institutional repository, and the gold refers to OA from the publisher's website. There are a growing number of additional kinds of OA, such as 'diamond' (free to both authors and readers), but it remains to be seen how the OA landscape will finally establish itself.

The push towards OA is helped by policy: in the UK, the Research Excellence Framework mandates that all journal articles submitted for consideration should be OA, and research funders require that findings and outputs from funded projects are OA, too. Although there are no comparable large-scale reviewing systems in other countries, OA is gaining traction in Europe and the USA via other routes, such as the Digital Public Library of America, funded by the National Endowment for the Humanities, or the OAPEN project, spearheaded by the Netherlands (Eve 2014: 82–3). In Japan and China, OA is continuing to grow in importance, and in India, the National Knowledge Commission recommended an OA policy for academics in 2007 (Eve 2014: 80). In Australia all universities now have an institutional repository, and two of the major research councils require green deposit of articles with a maximum of a twelve-month embargo (Eve 2014: 81).

OA is a global publishing shift, and a helpful starting-point from which to examine other academic publishing issues. Not only does it ask questions about the purpose of research and how it should be disseminated, but it provokes the different groups involved in academic work to reconsider the value of their own role in the publication circuit. All of the various communities of practice that connect via academic publishing help create a structure of complex working relationships. These communities are: scholars, teachers, students, publishers, booksellers, librarians, intermediaries, policy makers, and learned societies and organizations. All these agents collaborate to write, produce, disseminate and preserve academic work; in the twenty-first century these collaborations become more vital, as 'new, genetically modified digital formats force us to rethink what an academic book can be' (Mole 2016: 11).

WHAT IS AN ACADEMIC BOOK?

John Thompson claims that 'there is one key development in the field of academic publishing over the last few decades that stands out above all others: the decline of the scholarly monograph' (Thompson 2005: 93). As academic library budgets shrink, so does the market for book sales. This perceived crisis for the scholarly monograph does not represent the full picture, however. As Geoffrey Crossick reveals via a study conducted for his *Report on Monographs and Open Access*, figures gathered from Cambridge University Press, Oxford University Press, Routledge, and Palgrave all showed 'very significant growth' in the numbers of new monographs being published (Crossick 2015: 21). Sales may be dropping, but there are new types of publication and new kinds of production which means the number of ways books are being consumed and found is increasing rapidly. OA, as discussed above, is just one of these drivers. Michael Jubb says:

> Demand for books is not necessarily expressed in sales: for many academic books, the great majority of readers and readings come via libraries, where demand may be buoyant, and for OA books, demand is expressed almost wholly in views and

downloads. Nevertheless, for books published under traditional models, sales revenues underpin the publishing process. We have referred at several points in this report to declining sales for academic books in the arts and humanities, particularly in the per-title level; increases in prices per title; constraints on library budgets for book purchasing; and reduced exposure to consumers. There is a notable absence, however, of comprehensive and robust data to facilitate a full examination of such trends.   (Jubb 2017: 48)

Jubb's point about the lack of data shows why attempts to precisely map how far the sales of monographs have declined have been so problematical. He also emphasizes that although sales figures currently come from sources like the Publishers Association's annual *Statistics Yearbook*, which collects data from its members, and Nielsen Bookscan, which collects data from the electronic point of sale systems in retail environments, there is no clear definition of what an academic book is for either of these sources, and the Book Industry Communications (BIC) subject codes do not map neatly onto those used by academia. In addition, subjects are often aggregated, and finally, the retail sales data from Bookscan does not cover sales to libraries, bulk institutional sales, or individual titles within custom packs, all 'critically important' parts of the market for academic books (Jubb 2017: 48).

So, the question, 'what is an academic book?' is not an easy one to answer. Not only are the subject codes different, depending on the context in which they were added, but defining them by their origins from an academic publisher throws up dilemmas, too.

University Presses

Academic books are produced by a wide variety of different publishers: the university press is the most traditional, but commercial academic publishers have also grown respectable credentials, and this has created a mixed and dynamic publishing ecosystem for scholars.

In the UK, the university presses based at Oxford (established 1586) and Cambridge (established 1534) have the longest and most prestigious reputations. Known the world over, their heritage in academic publishing is unrivalled, and their brands attract work from top scholars in all subject areas. In the USA, the university press is the dominant part of the academic market, with publishers such as Harvard University Press (established 1913), Chicago University Press (established 1890), and Yale University Press (established 1908) producing lists which include journals and key reference texts. Donald Bean, the business manager of Chicago University Press, was appointed the first president of the American Association of University Presses (AAUP) in 1938. Today the AAUP has 142 members in 14 different countries, including Jamaica, China, New Zealand, South Africa, and Egypt (AAUP, About AAUP). In 2016, a University Press Redux conference was held in the UK, an event stimulated by the Arts and

Humanities Research Council/British Library Academic Book of the Future Project, and delegates represented over forty university presses (Liverpool University Press, Redux). The number of new university presses starting up in the UK is significant: several, like UCL Press and the White Rose University Press are OA only presses, but others, like Goldsmiths Press, are attempting a different business model.

The significance lies in the shift back towards academic institutions, and particularly their libraries, as providers for publication of research, and away from more commercial academic publishers. Although university presses have been around for hundreds of years, the changing needs of researchers, librarians, and policy makers in recent years have provoked a renaissance via university libraries. Research carried out to investigate why this is happening concluded that more growth is on its way (Keene et al. 2016); Lockett and Speicher, two new university press managers, suggest that this is because:

> Libraries are significantly affected by the rise in serial costs, and therefore they can identify significant potential in supporting their own press, both in practice, as a cost saving, and in principle, as a reaction against profiteering. As a department of the library, a significant cost centre already, university presses can be supported in many ways: office space, use of the institutional repository which is usually managed by the library, OA funding often managed by the library, dissemination expertise, and technical infrastructure. Libraries of course also play a crucial role in supporting staff and students at the institution, and as such are embedded in the institution's strategies and make a significant contribution to them—there are mutual benefits to be derived from this relationship, that can help the university press deliver the mission of its institution.   (Lockett and Speicher 2016: 325)

The successful partnerships between academics and academic libraries need nurturing, however: Jubb's Report for the Academic Book of the Future Project concluded that, as libraries' roles are changing significantly, 'there remains the risk of disintermediation in a world in which for many scholars the role of the library is increasingly unseen and/or misunderstood'; this risk means that 'it is critically important that libraries should redouble their efforts to build open lines of communication and active consultation with as wide a range as possible of the academics that they seek to serve' (Jubb 2017: 82).

Alison Mudditt, Director of the University of California Press, summed up the challenges university presses face:

> The current system of scholarly communication is all too often antiquated, inefficient, and slow. Along with increases in quantity of and access to information, we need to develop tools that will help users make more efficient and effective 'expert' use of our accumulating knowledge. We do not just need to publish more; we need to make it easier to find the necessary information from the increasing ocean of information and then to connect it with what we know.   (Mudditt 2016: 333)

There is a recognition then, from all sides, of the tasks that need addressing, and plenty of evidence to show the effort needed to do that is being delivered. Despite the daunting amount of change and adaptation ahead, however, there is a definite optimism about the future: 'university presses can rise phoenix-like through 21st century digital environments and the reworking of scholarly communication frameworks' (Steele 2008: abstract) The sophisticated tools and services that the digital capabilities of the Internet offer mean that academic publishers are the most innovative sector of publishing, utilizing powerful search tools, or tracking and mapping the use and reach of texts, to sell content and support their authors.

COMMERCIAL ACADEMIC PUBLISHERS

For commercial publishers, contexts are both similar and very different. These publishers do not merely have a mission to advance knowledge: their remit includes the need to make the spread of knowledge profitable as well. This means that, in an arena increasingly concerned with OA publication, relationships between these publishers and academics can 'become increasingly strained, as the trajectories of field migration propel publishers in directions that do not coincide with, and in some respects directly conflict with, the aims and priorities of academics' (Thompson 2005: 166).

Size matters: some academic publishers are huge international operations, such as Elsevier, which was founded in 1880 as a small Dutch publishing house focusing on classical scholarship. Now it is a global multimedia publishing business with over 20,000 products for educational and professional science and healthcare communities. Elsevier often comes under attack for its business models, which help create massive profits: in 2010, Elsevier's scientific publishing arm reported profits of £724m on just over £2bn in revenue. This represents a 36 per cent margin—higher than Apple, Google, or Amazon posted that year. (Buranyi 2017) This is a staggering amount; defendants of Elsevier underline that large amounts of that profit are ploughed back into the academic community, via initiatives like the Elsevier Foundation, which funds innovations in health information, research in developing countries, diversity in science and technology for development, but other researchers worry about the ethics of providing content, essentially for free, to a company that takes such a large profit from it. Elsevier's focus is on scientific, technical, and medical (STM) publishing, all very fast-moving areas of research, where speed to publication is often critical. Its success is in large part because it has essential content which users are willing to pay for (e.g. Science Direct), and so, despite predictions to the contrary, it is so far surviving threats to its core business.

Libraries subscribe to journal packages created by companies such as Elsevier, and the costs of these can eat significantly into budgets, often causing tough decisions to be made regarding other content. As Buranyi says, 'it is hard to believe that what is essentially a for-profit oligopoly functioning within an otherwise heavily regulated, government-funded enterprise can avoid extinction in the long run' (Buranyi 2017).

Other commercial publishers, such as Bloomsbury Academic (an independent publisher), or Macmillan (owned by the Holtzbrinck Publishing Group) or Routledge (owned by the Taylor & Francis Group) publish in broader areas covering the STM, professional, humanities, and social sciences disciplines, while smaller publishers, such as Boydell & Brewer, focus on more niche areas like medieval academic publishing, music, and African Studies. To maximize reach, some of these smaller companies, like Boydell, have partnered with initiatives like Cambridge University Press's Cambridge Core, which brings together much of the Press's journal and book content on one platform, along with content from other publishing partners. Commercial academic publishers are responding to the changing needs of researchers, and are now offering services which include author dashboards, where downloads and citations can be viewed, or new ways of publishing, like the short monograph format launched successfully by Palgrave Pivot.

PEER REVIEW

Both commercial and university presses share a commitment to a peer review process, which lies at the heart of the scholarly publishing system. It is, however, 'one of the more paradoxical elements of academic research and dissemination: it is common for academics to complain about unhelpful feedback from their latest review, but the process is simultaneously seen as one of the bedrocks of assuring the quality of research' (Butchard et al. 2017). Peer review comes in many forms: double blind peer review, where neither reviewer nor author knows the name of the person writing, single blind peer review, where the reviewer is given the name of the author, open peer review, where the reviewer's name is revealed, and post-publication peer review, where reviews are invited after the article or book has been published. Peer reviewing activity is rarely counted as a factor in an academic's promotions application, and, as workloads become heavier, the time and effort it takes to conduct peer review, along with questions being raised about the integrity of some peer review processes, mean that this has become an area of keen debate. There is, a recent report stresses, 'an urgent need to address issues with communication, consistency, efficiency and credit outlined by scholars who critique traditional peer review models' (Butchard et al. 2017).

THE CROSS-OVER BOOK

Commercial publishers must factor in economic considerations when choosing which books to publish, but Thompson stresses that this is true even at university presses and contrasts the tension this creates with academics, whose whole field is 'governed largely by a symbolic logic of peer recognition and acclaim (Thompson 2005: 46). This acclaim comes mainly from reviews and citations, but is also the reason why publishing with a trade non-academic publisher can also hold appeal: books published via this route (the cross-over book) can reach much wider audiences, if pitched right, and published with the support of a major publisher's marketing team.

The cross-over book, which is often (but not always) published by a trade publisher, proves that it is possible for an academic book to have a more general readership. The classical scholar Mary Beard, for example, has had considerable sales success with books like *SPQR*, published by Profile Books, which became a *Sunday Times* Top Ten bestseller in 2016. Profile describe themselves as publishers of 'stimulating non-fiction in a wide range of fields, including history, business, economics, science and biography, with a sprinkling of humour' (http://www.profilebooks.com). They are a good example of an independent publisher who has grown a reputation for engaging and high-profile cross-over books; they have expanded with collaborations with other partners like the Wellcome Collection and have developed imprints such as Third Millenium Publishing and Serpent's Tail.

Independent publishers like Profile compete with the larger companies, like Penguin, who also operate in the cross-over academic book market. For Penguin, history and biography and literary criticism lists include international academic authors like Stephen Greenblatt, whose *Swerve: How the Renaissance Began* won the Pulitzer Prize for Non-Fiction in 2012. In the USA, university presses are particularly good at this kind of hybrid book:

> they break out of the narrow circle of specialists and out of a particular discipline, selling to a wider range of academics and students than a typical scholarly monograph would do. On some occasions they may also break out of the academic world and sell to a broader non-academic readership.   (Thompson 2005, 150)

An academic author, then, has a bewildering choice of publisher before them. The drivers towards a trade publisher or an academic one are complex: as Thompson says, in the academic field, 'the importance of a publisher's symbolic capital is accentuated by the existence of various scholarly mechanisms, formal and informal, which endow differential degrees of symbolic reward on academics who publish with certain publishers' (Thompson 2005: 32). Scholars must decide on the best fit for their work, weighing up, for instance, the likely prestige a certain publisher will have with a promotions committee, against the rating another might help attain for, say, the UK's Research Excellence Framework. Often prestige can be conferred on an author just by association with a certain academic editor, who has built a reputation for being the best in an academic discipline. The importance of the role of the editor in academic publishing should not be ignored: often it is only because of the intervention of editors that editions of canonical texts exist in the forms they do, or that monographs or collections of essays ever reach publication. These often untold histories reveal a great deal about the value and impact of academic publishers on the integrity of texts that have been used to take scholarship further, and would provide fruitful research ground of their own (see, e.g., Rayner 2015).

JOURNALS PUBLISHING

Books are just one part of the academic publishing context: journals publishing accounts for £1.8 billion in the UK alone, and worldwide journals account for sales of several billion just in the area of STM publishing (Clark and Phillips 2014: 101–2). Academic journal content is not usually commissioned (except for special issues on particular topics); academics submit articles to the journal, and these are then sent out for peer review, before decisions are made about publication. Journals can be run by academic groups, professional bodies, or learned societies; they can be non-profit or, if published by larger publishing corporations like Elsevier, for significant profits. Journal sales are aimed almost entirely at the academic library market, and the rise of journal platforms and the bundling together of a collection of different journal titles has made the consolidation of these sales easier to manage. Societies may give their members their journal as part of their membership fee package, and the rapid growth of OA models for journal publishing has helped create a more dynamic and accessible route for scholars who need to consult these journals. Enterprises like JISC Collections, which 'works on behalf of the UK higher education sector, to negotiate and license high-quality digital content that meets the requirements of institutions to support academic research, teaching and learning' (Jisc Collections website) have transformed the way scholars work with journals.

There are more STM journals than in any other area, and they are big business for publishers. The fast-moving nature of much of research in these fields means that journals are often the main way to disseminate research, and the exploitation of contact information by publishers so that mailing marketing can target individual researchers to make them aware of new content has helped boost initiatives like the pay-per-view model, or the digitization of back issues. The role of intermediaries in the journal chain should also not be overlooked. For journals, the work that bibliographic data aggregators provides is critical in a context where accurate information can mean the difference between locating an article quickly or very slowly, which has an impact on the level of citations that an article could attract.

Unlike books, journals take time to establish and create an academic brand. As Clark and Phillips emphasize, however, 'once a journal is established, the sales pattern is more predictable than books, the demand for capital lower (as are staff overheads), and the value of sales per employee is higher' (Clark and Phillips 2014: 103).

As digital publishing practices continue to open up new ways of disseminating research, journal publishing is evolving further. The first mega-journal, *PLOS One*, was started in 2006, by the Public Library of Science. The journal covers primary research from any discipline within science and medicine, and has facilitated connections in research which might not otherwise have happened. It has not been without its controversies, but the model, which won the Association of Learned and Professional Society Publishers Publishing Innovation Award in 2009, has spawned other mega-journals, and it looks like this format is here to stay. The mega-journal model engages with the challenge of finding efficiencies in peer review processes, and efforts to keep Article Processing Costs (APCs) down. Cascade journals, where rejected articles from one publication are passed down to another with a focus on the same field, are another result of engaging with these key issues.

Journals publishing is the most innovative area of academic publishing, and as new models arrive, and OA turns others inside out, the questions around peer review processes, about the value that a publisher can offer, new services to authors around metrics and altmetrics, and use and reuse, are stimulating reflection and change within scholarly communication at all levels and within all communities. It is not all positive change, however: alongside the genuine scholarly journals, there has been a growth of online journals which are 'predatory', in that they solicit manuscripts and charge publication fees without providing robust peer review and editorial services. They may promise these services, and entice scholars in with legitimate sounding editorial boards, but they are not legitimate setups. Early career researchers (ECRs), in particular, eager to be published, are the targets for such journals, who employ aggressive email marketing techniques. Research has now been done to expose this practice and to try and educate researchers in how to recognize if they are being scammed, as it is not only ECRs who are falling for these traps:

> Established researchers should beware of predatory journals as well. There are numerous anecdotes about researchers (even deceased researchers) who have been put on a journal's editorial board or named as an editor, who did not wish to be and who were unable to get their names delisted. Aside from this potentially compromising the reputation of an individual that finds him or herself on the board, their affiliation with a potential predatory journal may confer legitimacy to the journal that is not deserved and that has the potential to confuse a naïve reader or author. As our findings indicate, this phenomenon appears to be a clear feature of predatory journals.   (Shamseer et al. 2017: 12)

In an interview with Kelly Cobey and Larissa Shamseer, two of the authors of the research quoted above, they also stressed that:

> The running narrative had been that predatory journals were mainly a problem affecting lower income countries. The fact that this is not the case really demonstrates the universality of the problem—researchers across the globe lack training and knowledge on how to select an appropriate (and legitimate) venue to publish their work in.   (Meadows 2017)

This is a major concern for academic publishing: how can the integrity of publication be protected, so that the intellectual capital it contains is trustworthy and does not contaminate the scholarly communications circuit? In a global environment, where the Internet allows for direct contact of researchers and the fast spread of false information, training to ensure academics are able to recognize genuine operations is going to become more critical than ever before.

TEXTBOOK PUBLISHING

Integrity in the area of higher educational textbook publishing is fiercely protected by the academic publishers who provide for this market, in the main because it generates such large sales. John Thompson's research into the US and UK higher education textbook field gives a very detailed analysis of the differences and similarities between the two countries, and a clear perspective of the stakes this potentially lucrative form of publishing contains (Thompson 2005: 195–306). To begin with, a textbook is 'as slippery and difficult to define as "monograph"' but a good starting point is to say it is 'a book which is written for and used by teachers and students for the purposes of teaching and learning' (Thompson 2005: 196). Thompson admits this is a very broad description, and points out that in higher education, curricula are much more widely diverse than those at school level, where national schemes of education mean children pursue very similar lines of study. The higher education textbook market, in contrast, has to cater for innumerable different courses and syllabi. In the USA, where large numbers of students do take common introductory courses, however, if a publisher can provide a key text of use to all those institutions, and get it adopted, the rewards are high. In this scenario, the book is marketed at the course leader; the academic in charge of setting the reading materials. In this sector of academic publishing, it is therefore the sales rep who has the most vital role: they must connect with the academics, make them aware of new titles, and coax them towards adoption, or, to put it another way, 'the textbook business is somewhat idiosyncratic in that the people who are recommending the books through adoption for their courses are not the ones who have to pay' (Green and Cookson 2012: 118). Thompson contrasts this with the UK market, where he suggests that the modularization of courses has helped to cause a drop in textbook sales at university level, as the students spend much less time dedicated to any one subject or topic: 'the ability to use a book over a long period is one of the most important factors influencing a student's decision to purchase the book' (Thompson 2005: 273).

Textbook sales can be global; if content is customized to different cultural markets, competition to sell into burgeoning academic markets like India and the Arab States can be repaid with strong sales. With the global explosion in higher education (the number of students around the globe enrolled in higher education is forecast to reach 262 million by 2025, with nearly all of this growth in the developing world, more than half in China and India alone), the potential is huge. Against this positive, the counter challenge for publishers is to work to protect copyright, and work out effective systems for monitoring piracy, when there are now so many different geographical areas to cover and so many easy opportunities for copying textbooks illegally. Losing income because of copying is a growing concern, and the quality of the pirated textbooks is harder to detect. The ubiquity of online retail sites like ebay and Amazon mean that students and academics can easily buy books they believe to be legitimate, when in fact they are being provided by pirate book producers.

The issues the textbook market faces are of rapidly changing higher educational contexts, of rising fees for students, making the sale of any books harder, and the need to respond to ever-more flexible materials for study, to help lecturers meet the teaching objectives becoming increasingly monitored and reviewed. There is a hopeful ripple in the UK market, caused by the introduction of the Teaching Excellence Framework, instigated in 2016, which aims to increase the status of teaching within universities. Publishers and booksellers are optimistic that this will herald a renaissance in textbooks and published materials: Scott Hamilton, head of retail at Blackwell and chairman of the Bookseller Association's Academic Booksellers Group said 'we hope the TEF will encourage lecturers to recommend particular titles and place primacy on the most effective books for teaching and learning' (Hamilton 2017). It remains to be seen if this will happen, but the excitement it is causing (and it is significant that academic booksellers are leading the articulation of this) makes it a key area to watch in the future.

CONCLUSIONS

Academic publishing has always engaged, and is still engaging with big questions around the shape of knowledge and its accessibility to readers. Since the first manuscripts began to circulate, debates about authenticity, impact, and dissemination have existed. Arguably these debates are more important than ever in an age where #fakenews is promoted every day, and the rapid increase, and evolving shapes of, academic output defies any clear definition. So many articles, blog posts, and conferences, symposia, and other events are now produced, by all of the different communities involved with academic research, that it is becoming impossible to connect them with meaningful cohesion. This is a major challenge going forwards, but there is plenty of evidence to show how engaged all communities are with the issues academic publishing is facing. As Kathleen Fitzpatrick warned:

> Change is here: we can watch our current publishing system suffocate, leaving the academy not just obsolete but irrelevant, or we can work to create a communication environment that will defy such obsolescence, generating rich scholarly discussions well into the future.   (Fitzpatrick 2011: 196)

REFERENCES

American Association of University Presses (AAUP) (2017). About AAUP. Available at: http://www.aaupnet.org/about-aaup/about-university-presses/snapshot. [Accessed 7 December 2017].

Berlin Declaration on Open Access (2003). https://openaccess.mpg.de/Berlin-Declaration [Accessed 10 November 2017].

Bethesda Statement on Open Access (2003). http://legacy.earlham.edu/~peters/fos/bethesda. htm [Accessed 10 November 2017].

Budapest Open Access Initiative (2002). http://www.budapestopenaccessinitiative.org/. [Accessed 10 November 2017].

Buranyi, Stephen (2017). 'Is the staggeringly profitable business of scientific publishing bad for science?' *The Guardian*, 27 June 2017. https://www.theguardian.com/science/2017/jun/27/profitable-business-scientific-publishing-bad-for-science [Accessed 7 December 2017].

Burridge, Samantha (2013). '5 Minutes with Sam Burridge: "Palgrave Pivot is Liberating Scholarship from the Straitjacket of Traditional Print-Based Formats and Business Models"'. LSE Review of Books, http://blogs.lse.ac.uk/lsereviewofbooks/2013/10/28/palgrave-pivot-100-hours/ [Accessed 8 October 2017].

Butchard, Dorothy, Simon Rowberry, Claire Squires, and Gill Tasker (2017). 'Peer Review in Practice', in *BOOC: Academic Book of the Future*. Edited by Rebecca E. Lyons and Samantha J. Rayner, London: UCL Press.

Clark, Giles and Angus Phillips (2014). *Inside Book Publishing*, 5th Edition, London: Routledge.

Crossick, Geoffrey (2015). *Monographs and Open Access: A Report to HEFCE*. http://www.hefce.ac.uk/media/hefce/content/pubs/indirreports/2015/Monographs,and,open,access/2014_monographs.pdf [Accessed 10 November 2017].

Eisenstein, Elizabeth L. (2005). *The Printing Revolution in Early Modern Europe*, 2nd Edition, Cambridge: Cambridge University Press.

Eve, Martin (2014). *Open Access and the Humanities: Contexts, Controversies and the Future*, Oxford: Oxford University Press.

Febvre, Lucien and Henri-Jean Martin (2010). *The Coming of the Book: The Impact of Printing, 1450–1800*, London: Verso.

Fitzpatrick, Kathleen (2011). *Planned Obsolescence*, New York: New York University Press.

Green, David and Rod Cookson (2012). 'Publishing and communication strategies', in *Academic and Professional Publishing*, Edited by Robert Campbell, Ed Pentz and Ian Borthwick, Oxford: Chandos Publishing, pp. 99–145.

Hamilton, Scott (2017). 'The opportunity of TEF', in *The Bookseller*, 23 January 2017. https://www.thebookseller.com/blogs/opportunity-tef-473871 [Accessed 7 December 2017].

Jisc (2016). *Investigating OA Monograph Services: Final Report*. https://www.oapen.org/content/sites/default/files/u6/Jisc-OAPEN per cent20pilot per cent20Final per cent20report.pdf [Accessed 10 November 2017].

Jisc Collections website: https://www.jisc.ac.uk/jisc-collections [Accessed 8 December 2017].

Jubb, Michael (2017). *Academic Books and Their Futures: A Report to the AHRC and the British Library*. https://academicbookfuture.files.wordpress.com/2017/06/academic-books-and-their-futures_jubb1.pdf [Accessed 10 November 2017].

Keene, C., C. Milloy, V. Weigert, and G. Stone (2016). 'The rise of the new university press: The current landscape and future directions'. Paper presented at the LIBER (Ligue des Bibliothèques Européennes de Recherche—Association of European Research Libraries) Annual Conference, 29 June 2016. Retrieved from http://eprints.hud.ac.uk/28989.

Liverpool University Press (2016). University Press Redux Conference Slides. https://liverpooluniversitypress.co.uk/pages/university-press-redux-slides [Accessed 7 December 2017].

Lockett, Andrew and Lara Speicher (2016). 'New university presses in the UK: Accessing a mission', *Learned Publishing*, 29, pp. 320–9.

Maxwell, John, Alessandra Bordini, and Katie Shamash (2017). 'Reassembling Scholarly Communications: An Evaluation of the Andrew W. Mellon Foundation's Monograph Initiative', *Journal of Electronic Publishing*, 20(1).

Meadows, Alice (2017). 'Illegitimate Journals and How to Stop Them: An Interview with Kelly Cobey and Larissa Shamseer', *Scholarly Kitchen*, 5 December 2017.

Meadows, Alice and Karin Wulf (2016). 'Seven Things Every Researcher Should Know About Scholarly Publishing', *Scholarly Kitchen*, 21 March 2016. https://scholarlykitchen.sspnet. org/2016/03/21/seven-things-every-researcher-should-know-about-scholarly-publishing/ [Accessed 10 November 2017].

Mole, Tom (2016). 'The Academic Book as Socially-Embedded Media Artefact' in *The Academic Book of the Future*. Edited by Rebecca E. Lyons and Samantha J. Rayner, Basingstoke: Palgrave Pivot.

Mudditt, Alison (2016). 'The past, present, and future of American university presses: A view from the left coast', *Learned Publishing*, 29, pp. 330–4.

Profile website, (n.d.). About Us. https://profilebooks.com/about-profile-books. [Accessed 8 December 2017].

Publishers Association (2017). *The Publishers Association Publishing Yearbook 2016*, London: Publishers Association.

Rayner, Samantha J. (2015). 'The Case of the "Curious Document": Malory, William Matthews, and Eugène Vinaver', *Journal of the International Arthurian Society* (JIAS), 3, pp. 120–39.

Shamseer, Larissa, David Moher, Onyi Maduekwe, Lucy Turner, Virginia Barbour, Rebecca Burch, Jocalyn Clark, James Galipeau, Jason Roberts, and Beverley J. Shea (2017). 'Potential predatory and legitimate biomedical journals: can you tell the difference? A cross-sectional comparison', *BMC Medicine*, 15, p. 28 DOI 10.1186/s12916-017-0785-9

Steele, Colin (2008). 'Scholarly Monograph Publishing in the 21st Century: The Future More Than Ever Should Be an Open Book', *The Journal of Electronic Publishing*, 11(2).

Suber, Peter (2012). *Open Access*, Boston, MA: MIT Press.

Thompson, John (2005). *Books in the Digital Age*, Cambridge: Polity.

CHAPTER 17

EDUCATIONAL PUBLISHING

How It Works: Primary and Secondary Education Publishing*

MIHA KOVAČ AND MOJCA K. ŠEBART

INTRODUCTION

ALONGSIDE strident debates on the impact of ebooks on trade publishing and reading practices, another ebook revolution has popped up. For the last two decades, in educational systems all around the world, fierce competition has taken place between, on one side, providers of information technology (IT) equipment and proponents of open educational resources, and on the other, publishers of paid educational content in printed or digital formats. However, only occasionally has this competition taken the form of a clash between printed materials produced by educational publishers and digital learning tools produced by software companies. From the early days of the World Wide Web on, many educational publishers have supplemented their printed textbooks with websites for students and teachers; more recently, they have started to produce digital textbooks and workbooks that can be used with or instead of their printed counterparts. Similarly, teachers, educational enthusiasts, and software companies have been producing websites and apps that supplement or substitute printed learning materials. By using functionalities such as interactivity, augmented reality, and machine learning, some of these substitutes and supplements, produced either by educational publishers or software companies, have significantly surpassed the instructional potential of their printed ancestors. As smartphones have become widespread in developed and developing countries, the digital divide between those who possess IT equipment and those who do not has almost disappeared. All this—at least at first glance—has widely opened classroom doors to digital content.

* This chapter was written as a part of the project The Quality of Slovene Texbooks.

In short, thanks to competition among educational publishers, software providers, and advocates of open access, the educational market is awash with easily accessible digital content. But why, then, has digital content not entirely taken over print in schools, especially considering that the Web opens doors for free access to learning tools in a way that print never did? As we shall see in this chapter, there seem to be three reasons for this. First, the possibilities of digital technologies do not always walk hand-in-hand with the logic of the classroom; second, reading substrates impact cognitive processes; and third, it is not until the last few years that any potentially sustainable business models supporting open access in primary and secondary education have been invented. These factors seem to make the persistence of paper—especially in connection with learning and long-form reading—more than a transitional glitch. However, in recent years they have not stopped the entire field of educational publishing from changing almost beyond recognition. In order to understand these changes, we must first look at the basics of educational publishing.

THE BASICS

In the context of this chapter, we consider educational publishing to refer to any production of print and digital objects that include instructions and recommendations and are used for the transmission of knowledge in primary and secondary education.

Thanks to compulsory school attendance, educational publishers have the broadest audience of all book publishers, since they provide books for entire age cohorts and, for some people at least, textbooks are practically the only books they encounter in their entire life. Yet, regardless of this wide audience, educational publishing remains an almost invisible field within the book industry. Indeed, there are no textbook bestseller charts and textbook authors attract nowhere near the same level of media attention as bestselling fiction and non-fiction writers do. The mainstream media never publish reviews of textbooks, while an announcement concerning the launch of a publication called *New York Review of Textbooks* would likely be interpreted as a rather dull prank for April Fools' Day.

Why is this the case? Quite obviously, there is nothing ground breaking or shocking contained within textbooks that would attract media attention. By definition, their content is determined by national or regional curricula, approval procedures, and examination standards. As such, it represents official knowledge. There are no new 'known unknowns' found within textbooks, since their main goal is to explain widely accepted 'known knowns' in accordance with curricula and/or examination standards and in such a way that is suitable for children at a given development stage. As a result, textbook authors and publishers do not innovate during the process of content production. Their main innovations can instead be seen in the way the content is textualized, visualized, and designed in accordance with pupils' developmental capabilities, curricula, and the development of information technologies. As we shall see, throughout the twentieth century, harsh competition existed between educational publishers and tech providers in relation to inventing new technologies for knowledge transmission and producing new learning tools for in-class education.

In most countries, a set of financial and regulatory mechanisms were introduced in order to lower the financial burden of textbook provision on both parents and schools. Depending on the country, these measures vary from rental schemes to the state purchasing all the learning tools that students need. In the worst-case scenario—for example, if too many rentals occur within a particular rental scheme—such measures have a negative impact on innovation in textbook production due to a lack of resources (see Pingel 2010: 36). Additionally, in many educational systems, teachers use photocopied or digitally copied materials to an extent that arguably surpasses the concept of fair use. In developed countries in particular, governments have sought to compensate authors and publishers for such a breach of copyright by introducing legislation that allows the establishment of collecting societies that negotiate and collect royalty payments from educational institutions and distribute them to copyright owners. The last decade has witnessed the continuous liberalization of free access within the field of education, which has caused a number of educational publishers to experience financial trouble.

Notwithstanding such setbacks, state intervention still has an important impact on the financial turnover, operational modes, and content of educational publishing. While the impact and size of such interventions differ and vary over time, they always exist. As a result, educational publishing has two common features that both stem from state regulation. First, the content of textbooks is to a certain extent pre-determined by educational goals and objectives as contained within national or regional curricula and/or examination standards. Second, the financial turnover of educational publishing depends on state subsidies for the purchasing of learning tools, the regulation of textbook provision, and the regulation of collective rights.

Due to these common features, educational publishing has emerged as a separate publishing field in which different editing and marketing skills are required when compared to those necessary in trade publishing. For example, one of the core skills required in trade publishing is the ability to identify a bestselling author and then promote her or him by organizing as many media appearances as possible, heavily supporting him or her through social media activities, and making the book as visible as possible by means of search engine optimization. However, textbooks are rarely written by only one person. The authorial teams usually comprise a mixture of teachers, specialists, artwork editors, designers, and illustrators. Their success does not depend on mass and social media appearances, but rather on the recognition of their peers (i.e. other teachers). As a result, one of the core editorial competencies in educational publishing is the management of authorial teams in such a way that the end product corresponds with teachers' and pupils' requirements for learning tools that enable the transmission of knowledge as prescribed by curricula and/or examination standards.

Further, textbooks are rarely stand-alone products; workbooks, teachers' guides, audio and video materials, tests, additional exercises for in-class instruction, and similar accompany them. Such learning tools play two different roles. For teachers, they serve to lower their workload, while from the publishers' point of view they are a marketing tool that helps them to lock teachers into their ecosystem. The production of these tools represents a hidden cost that needs to be covered by textbook and workbook sales, which results in their retail prices being higher and the publishers' margins lower than would be the case for stand-alone trade books with similar print-runs.

The origination time for a textbook and a set of accompanying products is usually around five years, and their life span is usually ten years (see Pingel 2010: 35–6). Both time spans exceed the origination and sales times of the majority of trade books. Again, unlike trade publishing, educational publishers rarely generate income through rights sales or exports due to differences in national and regional curricula. Foreign language textbooks represent an important exemption to this rule.

As a result of state interventionism, the people who make the purchasing decisions (in most cases, the teachers, schools, or school districts) do not pay for the textbooks from their own pockets. Consequently, they do not bear the financial burden of their decisions, since the school authorities and/or parents do instead. This renders textbook markets rather imperfect in comparison to the markets for other goods and, additionally, justifies state regulation. Hence, the marketing efforts of educational publishers are not directed towards reading audiences in the same way as the efforts of trade publishing, but rather towards the teachers who choose the books and the civil servants who decide on school budgets. Besides targeting teachers with direct marketing, lobbying among civil servants and regulators has thus became one of the core competencies of educational publishers. The lack of publicly available data concerning textbook provision models indicates that in the majority of countries, most such lobbying takes place backstage rather on stage. Even worse, there are no internationally comparable data on per pupil textbook expenditure and, consequently, surveys such as the Programme for International Student Assessment (PISA) don't look at correlations between textbook usage and the skills and knowledge of students.

More visible and better documented are the approval procedures that are usually introduced by school authorities in order to determine whether textbooks and other learning tools have been properly prepared for use in schools. This is where differences among the educational publishing industries in different countries start to appear.

Approval Procedures

As shown by Repoussi and Tutiaux-Guillon (2010), at the turn of the century in both developed and developing countries, there existed five models of approval procedures:

- In some countries, the state does not interfere in the decisions of teachers regarding which textbooks they will use (model A).
- Conversely, in some countries, the state allows only one textbook per course and the teachers have no choice in what they will use in class (model B).

- Some countries approve more textbooks per class per course, although the teachers are only allowed to choose approved textbooks (model C).
- Some countries approve textbooks, albeit with such approvals being considered to be recommendations and teachers having the freedom to also use non-approved materials (model D).
- In bigger states, there exist regional differences so that some regions use model C and some use model D.

Model B was widely used in communist countries (for more on this, see Kovač and Kovač-Šebart 2003) prior to 1989. As the content of teaching was prescribed by the state and the idea of market competition was alien to communist ideology, there was no need to use more than one textbook per course. Nevertheless, this model did not entirely disappear with the fall of the Berlin Wall, nor did it only exist in communist countries. For example, Greece (which has never been a socialist country) traditionally allows only one textbook per course, with all textbooks being published in a state-owned publishing house. In Hungary, after fifteen years of an open educational market, in the 2010s the government decided to return to a one-textbook-per-course model and hence bought a private textbook publishing house to act as the state educational publisher. Such ideas were also around in many other Central and East European countries. Predominantly due to the rather rapid changeover of governments in the region, their advocates have never had sufficient time to turn them into mainstream ideas and, with the exception of Hungary, the proponents of open educational markets have prevailed.

Accordingly, during the first decade of the new century, model C and model A became common in the majority of developed countries (Wilkens 2011): some countries approved textbooks and some did not, but the huge majority allowed competition among textbooks for the same course.

Countries without a formalized approval system legitimize its absence by arguing that teachers are in the best position 'to decide what is best for their pupils and what is not—including the selection, adoption and use of textbooks' (Wilkens 2011: 67). However, no research projects or international surveys have been conducted to examine teachers' ability to 'decide what is best for pupils' and consequently measure their competence to choose the best textbooks. In addition, there is no evidence concerning the impact of approval procedures on the quality of textbooks, while no internationally assured textbook quality indicators exist that would allow for comparisons among, for example, Greek, Danish, and Slovene textbooks. The reasons for such an absence of evidence are obvious as the search for such indicators rather quickly slips into absurdity. That is, clear-cut evidence concerning textbook quality and the impact of approval procedures could only be produced if parallel realities existed and there were, for example, one Denmark with approval procedures and one without—and comparing the two would reveal correlations and causations among the variables that influence both the quality of textbooks and their role in the instructional process.

As the nearest proxy for textbook quality indicators, Wilkens (2011) compared the 2009 PISA results in countries with and without textbook approval procedures, and she found that during the examined period, the countries without approval procedures achieved better PISA results than the countries with them (Wilkens 2011: 70). Moreover, some authors warn that approval procedures actually slow down innovation in publishing (see, for example, Pingel 2010: 30–40). However, we cannot jump to the conclusion that the absence of approval procedures makes for better PISA results and better textbooks. As stressed by McEwan and Marshall (2004), textbooks and textbook approval procedures are only two components among a much broader mix of variables that determine the quality of education, with the teachers' qualification level and the amount of money spent per student seemingly being the most important variables.

All this leads us to the conclusion that approval procedures were not introduced on the basis of unambiguous proof of their positive impact on education. Just the opposite, we can hypothesize that they are a product of local mores, that is, of the trust and faith that different societies have in educational publishers and in teachers' competence to autonomously conduct their professions. As such, approval procedures seem to appear when legislators distrust teachers' ability to detect and turn down textbooks with didactical and content-related flaws. By introducing such procedures, legislators try to minimize uncertainties in the processes of textbook production and selection.

The geographic distribution of models A and C seems to add emphasis to such a hypothesis. Model C, for example, is most common in Central and Eastern Europe and in Asia (Austria, Slovenia, Slovakia, Croatia, Czech Republic, Latvia, Lithuania, France, Germany, Singapore, Japan, and China), while model A (no state intervention in textbook adoption) is prevalent in countries such as Norway, Sweden, Denmark, Australia, Italy, Finland, Ireland, England, the Netherlands, and Estonia. Models B and D are present in only a few countries (see Wilkens 2011). Therefore, regardless of a few exceptions such as Italy and partially Estonia and the Netherlands, there is a visible geographic pattern in terms of the distribution of these models. The Anglo-Saxon and Nordic countries stick to model A, while continental Europe and Asia predominantly stick to model C.

Similarly as in Chapter 13 looking at Globalization, such a geographic dispersion of approval procedures leads to Hofstede et al.'s (2010) world value research. In their study on cultures and organizations, they developed an uncertainty avoidance index that shows how the members of a given culture feel threatened by ambiguous or unknown situations (Hofstede et al. 2010: 191). Societies with high levels of such anxiety try to reduce any ambiguity that might appear in professional relations and in public life by making rules that would 'make institutions and relations more interpretable and predictable' (Hofstede et al. 2010: 198). Therefore, the higher the uncertainty avoidance index, the higher the drive to produce laws and regulations. In such countries 'there tend to be more—and more precise—laws than in those with weak uncertainty avoidance' (Hofstede et al. 2010: 216).

Unsurprisingly, as shown in Table 17.1, the uncertainty avoidance index (UA index) heavily correlates with the existence of approval procedures. In Western civilization at least, the higher the UA index, the higher the probability that a country will introduce textbook approval procedures. Even more so, the European countries with the highest UA indexes either entirely abolished competition in education markets (Greece and Hungary) or else seriously discussed such an option (Slovenia and Poland).

Table 17.1 Uncertainty avoidance index and approval procedures

Model A	UA index	Model C	UA index	Model B	UA index
Australia	51	Austria	70	Greece	112
England	35	Czech R.	74	Hungary	82
Denmark	23	China	30		
Netherlands	53	Croatia	80		
Estonia	60	France	86		
Finland	59	Germany	67		
Ireland	35	Japan	92		
Italy	76	Latvia	63		
Norway	50	Lithuania	65		
Sweden	29	Poland	93		
		Singapore	8		
		Slovenia	90		
		Slovakia	51		
Average	47.1		57.9 (63.9)*		97
Median	50.5		70		

A visible exception to this rule can be seen in the case of China and Singapore. However, as for many Asian countries, China and Singapore scored highly on the collectivism indexes (for more on this, see Hofstede et al. 2010: 89–133), which means that rules aimed to minimize feelings of uncertainty in Asian societies are often implicit and rooted in tradition, although they are nevertheless there. In short, in Asian cultures, the drive for approving textbooks very likely stems from collectivist rather than anxiety values.

What kind of impact do approval procedures have on publishing processes? Obviously, in countries where such procedures exist, educational publishers need to know how best to design textbook content in order to gain approval as well as how to prepare documentation and properly submit it to the approval committee. All this requires additional work and additional editorial, administrative, and lobbying skills. On the other hand, in countries without approval procedures, teachers are free to choose which instructional tools to use. This opens up additional market opportunities for trade publishers. As a working hypothesis for future research, we can speculate that the absence of approval procedures correlates with more developed trade book publishing. To a significant extent, Figure 13.3. found in Chapter 13 on Globalization adds weight to this hypothesis.

And then, as it is often the case with heavily structured systems, digitization entered through its back doors.

DIGITAL DISRUPTION: IS IT REAL?

No research has yet been conducted on how, when, and why school authorities in a variety of countries decided to introduce digital learning tools into schools. We do not know whether such decisions were taken by school authorities in a top-down fashion or if they happened spontaneously, starting as a bottom-up initiative on the part of teachers and thanks to the marketing efforts of software producers and educational publishers. A brief overview of the available research on these issues also reveals that after the initial euphoria concerning the significant improvement to learning thought to result from digitization, evaluations and research papers started to report controversial results (see, for example, Spitzer 2008; OECD Report, 2015; Selwyn 2016; Wolf 2016).

In order to better understand such developments, we will now make a short history detour towards the introduction of film, radio, and television into educational systems during the twentieth century.

As early as 1913, Thomas Edison proclaimed that 'books in schools will soon be obsolete' as it is 'possible to teach every branch of human knowledge with the motion picture', which he believed would completely change primary and secondary education 'inside of ten years' (Smith 1913). Thirty-two years later, in 1945, William Levenson suggested that 'the time may come when a portable radio receiver will be as common in the classroom as the blackboard' (Cuban 1986: 19). In the 1950s, articles 'in newspapers, magazines and professional journals boosted the merits of classroom television, arguing that its benefits far outweighed any deficits' (Cuban 1986: 28). School authorities in the USA were so thrilled with these developments that they decided to rely totally on television in school districts in American Samoa, where they had to cope with a shortage of teachers. By 1966, four out of every five Samoan pupils were spending from one-third to one-quarter of their classroom time watching television and, in 1968, President Johnson declared the experiment to be a success. Yet, after 1970, more and more voices were raised against the experiment, and both Samoan pupils and teachers complained that television was used too much in classrooms. By 1973, the Samoan authorities had decided to shift authority away from the screen and towards the teacher (see Cuban 1986: 32–3).

This result was similar to the way in which developments during the 1930s and 1940s dried up the arguments of all those who prophesized that textbooks would soon be replaced by movies and radio. In short, regardless of the constant flirting of school authorities with new technologies throughout the twentieth century, during the 1980s print, chalk and blackboards still dominated the classroom as the main instructional tools. Why was this the case?

In his study on the use of technology in the classroom since the 1920s, Larry Cuban (1986) came up with an answer that still has merit. He claimed that engineers and policy makers falsely believed teaching to be a process that could be broken apart, improved, put back together, and mechanically reproduced in the same way as the best teachers perform it in the classroom. However, what technology enthusiasts back then failed to see was the fact that teaching has 'an irrational and emotional component' that cannot be reproduced by machines (Cuban 1986: 88–9). 'Too often forgotten by policy makers intent upon transforming teaching practice is how much classroom learning is anchored in the emotional lives of thirty children and one teacher' stressed Cuban, who also asserted that even 'in the hard core, cognitive skills of analysis emotions fuel the drive for understanding and soften the abrasive edge of calculation' (Cuban 1986: 88–9).

On the other side of the Atlantic at approximately the same time, French linguist and philosopher Jean-Claude Milner (1984) similarly stressed that any serious transfer of knowledge must remain oral regardless of the fact that the development of visual media and new modes of information storage and retrieval had significantly changed instructional processes. In the words of another Frenchman, the development of 'techniques and innovations that affect the means of communication and processes of reproduction, from the monastic copyist to the photocopy' (Rémond 2003 in Moeglin 2005, 17) had a profound impact on education, but only so far as these technologies did not place the educational process as such under a question mark.

Films, radio, and television as learning tools thus failed to conquer educational systems and replace teachers and printed books because they did not meet the realities of classroom dynamics: Engineers and tech enthusiasts might indeed know a lot about technology, but they know less about the nature of the transfer that takes place during educational processes. What they failed to see was that one of most important issues concerning the introduction of technologies into the classroom was not 'what technology will do, but what technology will undo' (Selwyn 2016: 142).

The fact that technologies often clashed with the realities of the classroom indicates that their introduction into schools was more commonly commercially rather than pedagogically driven. This brings us back to the observation at the beginning of this chapter: as the drivers of such changes were not educational publishers but instead film, TV, and radio companies, the history of education during the twentieth century could also be seen as a history of battles among tech providers, media companies, and educational publishers. Until the 1990s, the winners in these battles were the educational publishers.

At least during the early days of their school usage, computers seemed to have a similarly forlorn destiny. After the initial euphoria of the 1980s and 1990s, their usage in schools became marginal, and in 1992, Cuban proclaimed that when 'computer meets classroom, classroom wins', using the same arguments as in the case of radio, film, and television. However, for once he was wrong. At the time of writing this chapter, chalk, blackboard, and print are indeed still around, but due to the rapid and ubiquitous development of digital technologies, the learning tools used in schools have started to irreversibly change. In spring 2017, for example, two articles in the *New York Times* indicated that Google and Facebook were becoming the two main providers of educational tools and platforms in American public schools (see Singer 2017a, 2017b). Not consequently but nevertheless concurrently, the three biggest US educational publishers have either filed for protection under US Chapter 11 legislation (e.g. Cengage and Houghton Mifflin Harcourt) or been taken private (McGraw-Hill) for major restructuring (for more on this, see Wischenbart 2017).

The main reason behind such irreversibility is the all-inclusive media nature of the computer. As stressed by Adriaan van der Weel (2011), a computer is a Universal Machine that 'is more than just a medium for text transmission, the way for example a book is. As a technology that can manipulate symbols the computer can be used for all tasks for which algorithms can be programmed' (2011: 143). As such, tablets, smartphones, and PCs allow for the integration of all media modalities into one ecosystem in which an individual can not only consume, create, store, and redisplay text, audio, and video, but also publish and distribute them as well as search for information. Technological development during the first two decades of the twenty-first century therefore squeezed books, libraries, librarians, television, radio, film screens, printing presses, cameras, microphones, musical instruments, and a variety of distribution channels into one personal device that could be put in a backpack or even in a pocket, and for a price that almost everybody could afford. Similarly, in the field of in-class instructional tools, a hybrid between a personal computer and an LCD projector/smartboard blended chalk, blackboard, radio, television, and motion pictures into one media environment that could be accessed with the devices of both the teacher and pupils.

The difference between the 2010s and the 1980s is therefore the fact that all instructional technologies merged into one media ecosystem, while the devices that allowed access to it became part of the daily attire of teachers and pupils. In this context, the persistence of printed books, blackboards, notebooks, and pencils might be considered as a bizarre confirmation that digitization as such has not yet found the proper *modus vivendi* with regard to the transfer that occurs between teachers and pupils.

Again as stressed at the opening of this chapter, one of the reasons for the persistence of traditional instructional tools might be the fact that media affordances play an important role in their usage. For example, a set of surveys conducted among students (McNeish et al. 2012; Feldstein and Martin 2013) has shown that they stick to printed books when they have to read long and complex texts, while teachers expressed anxiety when e-textbooks were introduced in a top-down fashion by school authorities (Chiu 2017). Similar to students, many researchers print articles and read them on paper when they intend to read them thoroughly (Tenopir et al. 2015). Laboratory research on reading confirmed such results. Mangen et al. (2013) for example, have observed that we remember more when we read from a paper than from a computer or a tablet as the fixity of 'text printed on paper supports a reader's construction of spatial representation of the text by providing unequivocal and fixed spatial cues for text memory and recal' (Mangen et al. 2013). Similarly, Ackerman and Goldsmith (2011) warned that 'common perception of screen presentation as an information source intended for shallow messages may reduce the mobilization of cognitive sources'. As shown by Singer and Alexander (2017), similar findings were reported in thirty-five research articles. On the other hand, a digital instructional environment makes sense when training children in problem solving and team work while virtual reality and gamification make sense in relation to drill exercises, information retrieval, and the visualization of content (see Merchant et al. 2014).

In the 2010s, both surveys and laboratory research therefore indicated that different learning goals required different instructional media. The transfer of classic academic knowledge that requires deep and long form reading and learning by heart remains more paper-oriented, while teamwork and problem solving tends towards digital. This bricolage of learning approaches led to the birth of blended learning that combined traditional classroom methods and instructional technologies with interactive and gamified learning tools and online education.

Similarly as in the case of per pupil textbook expenditure, there are no internationally comparable data available on print and digital learning tools in daily use in school. Consequently, we cannot look for correlations among digitization of education, approval procedures, and uncertainty avoidance indexes.

CONCLUSION

To summarize, during the 2010s we have faced the most pervasive clash between the logic of the classroom and new technologies that has occurred in the modern age. In such a context, the absolute prevalence of digital learning tools would seem to indicate a radical shift in the logic of the classroom in which training in skills should prevail over academic instruction. It is likely that this would make the school of the future unrecognizable for someone who was educated during the twentieth century. As fortune telling is a decidedly unreliable practice, we will avoid predicting the winner in this struggle. What is clear, however, is the fact that technological changes as described in this chapter have affected both educational publishing and the role of the book in contemporary societies on at least three levels.

First, in addition to the supplementary learning materials they produce for teachers, digitization has forced educational publishers to create digital learning resources that either supplement or replace printed materials. According to Clayton Christensen, during the 2010s educational publishing has been in a hybrid stage of development, combining new and old educational technologies in such a way that the innovations were not disruptive to the traditional technologies and approaches (for more on this, see Christensen et al. 2013). The financial problems experienced by the biggest educational publishers in 2016 indicate that they have not developed a sustainable equilibrium between new and old media, nor have they developed a viable business model. Such a negative impact on publishers' margins was amplified by the development of open educational resources as well as the more liberal approach to copyright protection adopted by some developed countries such as Canada (IIPA 2017) and Germany, where two court decisions called into question publishers' rights to receive the revenues generated by collecting societies (see Anderson 2016). Further, as some instructional tools (workbooks, textbooks, stationery, etc.) are sold in many countries in bricks and mortar bookstores, the digitization of education negatively affected the turnover of such enterprises. The demise of bookstores has traditionally been seen as a result of the growth of online book sales and trade ebooks. What remains to be explored is the extent to which the disruption in educational publishing has amplified the disruption in trade publishing.

Second, digital development has changed the skills and competencies necessary in educational publishing. The editors, authors, and marketers of textbooks are ceasing to be solely book people. They are instead becoming masters of all trades, since they need to know how to develop digital learning tools and printed books as well as how to market them to teachers and pupils. Additionally, they need to understand various cognitive processes in order to choose the proper substrate when navigating between paper and screen. All this serves to widen the gap between trade, academic, and educational publishing. If these trends continue, the production of learning tools might become a new field unrelated to traditional publishing. In accordance with such developments in 2017, Pearson as one of the leading educational publishers started to call itself a learning company, without using the word textbook on the opening screens of its website.

Third, as a result of digitization, printed book lost its privileged position in educational systems: it become an *au pair* to the digital learning tools and *vice versa*. This correlates with the broader social and cultural changes that call into question what van der Weel (2011: 90) referred to as the Order of the Book, following Chartier's description of it as an order that 'governs the world of books, and the way in which books and libraries manage to represent—or fail to represent—the world at large'. However, Chartier predominantly discussed the world of books itself, whilst van der Weel (2011: 91) suggested 'also a reverse relationship, with the order that characterises the world of books in fact having come to determine largely the order that obtains in [Western] society'. The fact that schools are ceasing to be bastions of the book could therefore be seen as a result of complex social and cultural processes in which the entire 'readability' of the physical world is transformed. Even more so, as long form reading remains more paper-based and is more common in arts, literature, and history than in the natural sciences, we can assume that the struggle between paper and screen in the classroom might also become an indicator of power relations among different disciplines in primary and secondary education.

If we are correct, educational publishing is becoming a litmus paper of deep changes that are taking place in education. As such, it is becoming one of the main observation areas for those who wish to understand changes in culture and anthropology of contemporary societies.

REFERENCES

Ackerman, R. and Goldsmith, M. (2011). 'Metacognitive regulation of text learning: On screen versus on paper', *Journal of Experimental Psychology: Applied*, 17(1), pp. 18–32.

Anderson, P. (2016). 'No Agreement Yet. Germany's Publishing Copyright Controversy'. Publishing Perspectives, 15 September. Available at http://publishingperspectives.com/2016/09/no-agreement-copyright-controversy-germany-vg-wort/ [Accessed 14 June 2017].

Chiu, T. K. F. (2017). 'Introducing electronic textbooks as daily-use technology in schools: A top-down adoption process', *British Journal of Educational Technology*, 48(2), pp. 524–37.

Christensen, C., M. Horn, and H. Steaker (2013). Is K-12 Blended Learning Disruptive? Clayton Christensen Institute for Disruptive Innovation. Available at www.christenseninstitute.org [Accessed 14 June 2017].

Cuban, L. (1986). *Teachers and Machines. The Classroom Use of Technology since 1920*, New York: Teachers' College, Columbia University.

Cuban, L. (1992). 'Computer Meets Classroom, Classroom Wins', *Education Week*, 13 February. Available at http://www.edweek.org/ew/articles/1992/11/11/10cuban.h12.html [Accessed 14 June 2017].

Feldstein, A. P. and M. M. Maruri (2013). 'Understanding Slow Growth in the Adoption of E-Textbooks', *International Research on Education*, 1(1).

Hofstede, G., G. J. Hofstede, and M. Minkov (2010). *Cultures and Organisations: Software of the Mind*, New York: McGraw Hill

International Intellectual Property Alliance (IIPA). (2017). Special 301 Report on Copyright Protection and Enforcement. Available at http://www.iipawebsite.com/rbc/2017/2017SPEC301CANADA.PDF[Accessed 14 June 2017].

Kovač, M. and M. Kovač-Šebart (2003). *Textbooks at War: A Few Notes on Textbook Publishing in Former Yugoslavia and Other Communist Countries*, Ljubljana: Paradigm, Journal of Textbook Colloquium.

McEwan, P. J., and J. H. Marshall (2004). 'Why does academic achievement vary across countries? Evidence from Cuba and Mexico', *Education Economics*, 12(3), pp. 205–17.

McNeish, J., M. Foster, A. Francescucci, and B. West (2012). 'Why students won't give up paper textbooks', *Journal for Advancement of Marketing Education*, 20(3), pp. 37–48.

Mangen, A., B. R. Walgermo, and B. Kolbjørn (2013). 'Reading linear texts on paper versus computer screen: Effects on reading comprehension', *International Journal on Education Research*, 58, pp. 61–8.

Merchant, Z., E. T. Goetz, L. Cifuentes, W. Keeney-Kennicutt, and T. J. Davis (2014). 'Effectiveness of virtual reality-based instruction on students' learning. Outcomes in K-12 and higher education: A meta-analysis', *Computers & Education*, 70, pp. 29–40.

Milner, J.-C. (1984). *De'l Ecole*, Paris: Le Seuil.

Moeglin, P. (2005). The Textbook and After. Caught in the Web or Lost in the Textbook? Eighth International Conference on Learning and Educational Media. IARTEM. Available at https://iartemblog.wordpress.com/ [Accessed 14 June 2017].

OECD (2015). *Students, Computers and Learning: Making the Connection*, PISA, OECD Publishing. http://dx.doi.org/10.1787/9789264239555-en

Pingel, F. (2010). *UNESCO Guidebook on Textbook Research and Textbook Revision*, 2nd Edition. Paris/Braunschweig: George Eckert Institute for International Textbook Research and UNESCO Education Sector.

Rémond, R. (2003). Préface (Foreword). In *Histoire de l'enseignement et de l'éducation I. Ve siècle av.J.-C.–XVe siècle*. Edited by Michel Rouche (History of Teaching and Education I), Paris: Perrin.

Repoussi, M. and N. Tutiaux-Guillon (2010). 'New trends in history textbook research: Issues and methodologies toward a school historiography', *Journal of Educational Media, Memory and Society*, 2(1), pp. 154–70.

Selwyn, N. (2016). *Is Technology Good for Education?* Cambridge: Polity Press.

Singer, L. M. and P.A. Alexander (2017). 'Reading on paper and Digitally: What the Past Decades of Empirical Research Reveal'. *Review of Educational Research*, DOI: 10.3102/0034654317722961. Available at http://ver.aera.net [Accessed 1 November].

Singer, N. (2017a). 'The Silicon Valley Billionaires Remaking American Schools', *New York Times*, 6 June. Available at https://www.nytimes.com/2017/06/06/technology/tech-billionaires-education-zuckerberg-facebook-hastings.html?_r=0 [Accessed 14 June 2017].

Singer, N. (2017b). 'How Google Took Over the Classroom', *New York Times*, 13 May. Available at https://www.nytimes.com/2017/05/13/technology/google-education-chromebooks-schools.html [Accessed 14 June 2017].

Smith, F. J. (1913). 'The Evolution of the Motion Picture: V—Looking into the Future with Thomas A. Edison', *The New York Dramatic Mirror*, 9 July. Available at http://fultonhistory.com/my%20photo%20albums/All%20Newspapers/New%20York%20NY%20Dramatic%20Mirror/index.html [Accessed 14 June].

Spitzer, M. (2008). *Digitale Demenz*, Munich: Droemer Knaur.

Tenopir, C., D. W. King, L. Christian, and R. Volentine (2015). 'Scholarly article seeking, reading, and use: A continuing evolution from print to electronic in the sciences and social sciences', *Learned Publishing*, 28(2), pp. 93–105.

van der Weel, A. (2011). *Changing Our Textual Minds*, Manchester: Manchester University Press.

Wilkens, H. J. (2011). 'Textbook approval systems and the Program for International Assessment (PISA) results: A preliminary analysis', *IARTEM e-journal*, 4(2), pp. 63–74.

Wischenbart, R. (2017). The Business of Books 2017. It's All About the Consumers. Frankfurt Book Fair white paper. Available at: http://www.buchmesse.de/en/whitepaper/ [Accessed 14 June 2017]

Wolf, M. (2016). *Tales of Literacy for the 21st Century*, Oxford: Oxford University Press.

PART III

PUBLISHING IN PRACTICE

CHAPTER 18

....

ORGANIZATIONAL STRUCTURES IN PUBLISHING

....

FRANIA HALL

INTRODUCTION

....

THIS chapter explores the way publishing has developed into a modern industrial business and how, on facing the digital challenges now impacting the industry, the business needs to evolve away from traditional structures to enable it to redevelop a more flexible and nimble approach to innovation and expansion.

The chapter focuses primarily on the development of traditional publishing houses across different sectors rather than on new, emergent businesses that might be undertaking aspects of publishing as part of their business activity. Companies such as Penguin Random House and Pearson have established management structures that have their roots in the growth of the mass market during the nineteenth century. They have recognizable organizational hierarchies that have evolved out of the management and production thinking which has been mimicked across many sorts of businesses through the twentieth century. Smaller publishing companies also generally adopt this functional approach to the business of publishing. But these structures can make it difficult to manoeuvre a company effectively in response to a rapidly changing environment and so there is an increasing awareness that new approaches to organizational design may be necessary in order for a company to position itself and adapt as needed for a constantly changing digital environment.

HISTORICAL BACKGROUND
AND EMERGING STRUCTURES

As the publishing industry evolved following the invention of the printing press it displayed, from the start, a spirit of entrepreneurship. This opportunity for enterprise developed alongside the objective to promulgate certain theories and theologies: while some early publishers were monasteries and colleges whose aim was to spread their own works and learning, generally publishers were printers, risk takers who looked for opportunities to make money, publishing titles that they selected on the basis that they could sell them. The cost of the print run was entirely borne by the printers so they had to be sure they could sell out an edition. Notwithstanding the ability to print more easily with the press, the costs were still considerable so these early entrepreneurs were taking risks with what they thought customers might want to buy; in the UK these were the printers of St Paul's Churchyard, which became an important and widely recognized market place. To ensure they stood out, these printers needed to build innovative lists or develop reputations for certain types of books. Other printers were focused on disseminating particular religious points of view, paid for by patrons who had certain causes to promote; they might be especially keen to import books of significance from other countries and so developed businesses around this activity.

The ability produce books was one side of the story—for all these early publishers what was critical was a rapidly growing market. Through the two centuries that followed the invention of the press, the socioeconomic climate led to an increase in trade, a growing merchant class, continued technological advances and developments in education and literacy. Improved transport and infrastructure between towns and between countries, an increasingly connected world, an evolving Renaissance movement focused on learning and spreading ideas, complemented by a desire to explore the natural world and travel to new places, all led to new, expanding markets. So the means of production, the ready market, and the ability to reach customers fuelled the growth in the publishing industry (Manguel 1997; Feather 2005).

This market continued to develop. It led to a broadening both of different sorts of participants and of new market opportunities. Printers were still the publishers at this point, most often bookselling too. Various people involved in the trade from papermakers to printers coalesced around guilds and its members reflected the various roles and functions that made up the emerging publishing industry. The printers had to ensure their business was tenable and a protectionist approach to trade developed, as with many other industries, through the grant of rights through the guild. The position of the author, as the embryo industry grew, was not recognized except in a few cases; the material they provided being most often bought outright by the printer as a property which they could then publish and sell on as they wanted. The printer generally undertook most of the roles of the modern day publisher—buying content, producing it, and marketing it.

The following centuries saw this industry continue to develop; individual entrepreneurs stood out as they developed particular skills which reflected a growing sense that a printer was more than a successful marketer but also one that developed their book publishing programme in a particular way—whether selecting on specific lines, editing carefully, designing new layouts and typefaces, innovating with format, working with authors, developing early author brands, creating new distribution routes; such publishers included men like Manutius, Plantin, Rigaud, and Tonson (Manguel 1997; Darnton 2010; Bhaskar 2013).

Continuing socioeconomic change with urbanization, a growing middle class and increasing wealth led both to more educational opportunities as well as more leisure time and so a growing market for books. A burgeoning of the mass market during the nineteenth century led to the continuing development of a publishing industry. At this period the bookseller diverged from the publisher. The growing market put pressure on the existing printer-publisher structures. Impresario booksellers developed their businesses around the growing marketplace, while publishers focused on working with authors, selecting lists, refining the processes of production, and selling products in different formats and editions directed at different sectors of the market. The readership continued to grow through the nineteenth century and entrepreneurial publishers developed their expertise further as they began to specialize in particular areas of the market. Opportunities for expansion to meet the needs of a rapidly growing market led to a proliferation of new entrants in the nineteenth century. Technological developments such as offset litho and monotype allowed publishers to respond to market growth with cheaper production methods. And an evolving finance sector, which allowed companies to raise capital, supported a more systematic approach to business organization. As Feather states, 'the British book trade became a modern industry in every way' (2005: 95).

By the start of the twentieth century the market of readers was continuing to grow as did the search for the next bestsellers that would support publishers in an increasingly competitive market. However, some identified a stagnation in the market around new content as publishers sought to maximize returns on the stock of older successful titles (Feather 2005); as more new content was required the literary agent role developed to become a more formal voice for authors and to help publishers seek out content. At this point, the publisher's role became more focused on the management and production of content; that still led to innovations, however, such as Tauchnitz and Penguin in terms of format and business models. Vertical integration also had an impact as publishers sought to gain the benefits of their own copyrights themselves where possible, rather than sell them on, as had been traditional, so larger publishing companies bought up smaller ones with different expertise so building conglomerates with many imprints representing different sorts of formats for the market.

Through the twentieth century one of the most significant developments, beyond continuing advances in technology that continued to refine the publishing process, was probably the globalization of the industry, particularly in the specialist sector but also in relation to the big consumer houses. From the late 1980s in order to grow effectively and satisfy shareholders with increasing profits, there was a trend towards more mergers and acquisitions in order to develop market 'clout' and gain market share. Businesses needed a broadly generic management structure to merge and develop effectively as international organizations; these structures emerged concurrently through the century as the industry developed and grew increasingly professional.

Organizational Structures and the Emergence of the Value Chain

Structurally, by the late twentieth century a publishing company was broadly recognizable, structured around a traditional management hierarchy: functional areas exist including primarily editorial, production, marketing, sales, operations, and finance, most of which are departments found in any business. They reflected the development of management theory that emerged out of nineteenth-century economics and early twentieth-century theories around production lines and work flows; these evolved from the precepts of organizational thinkers such as Fayol, Taylor, and Weber. Ford's highly influential organization of mass production lines to speed up processes to market, focused the business around the supply chain. Fayol's thinking, developing a theory of management and organization around divisions of work, particularly set up organizations along function forms as can be seen in traditional publishing houses today. Taylor's focus on industrialized efficiency and the nature of organized work also informed the refined structures of management observable across organizations while Weber's theories of a market-driven capitalism focused on developing the bureaucratic model of business to ensure effective management.

Later in the twentieth century Drucker's focus on knowledge workers and productivity influenced the development of an industry that followed functional lines and organizational hierarchies; the industry organized itself broadly around a value chain; this concept, popularized by Porter, was about closely understanding each function's role at each stage of the production process; this analysis then allowed one to understand how value is added to a product as it moves through the chain (Porter 1985). The management structure of a publishing house has therefore evolved along similar lines to many other manufacturing businesses. The concept of the value chain is one that has been examined more explicitly within publishing by Thompson and Clark and Phillips (Clark and Phillips 2008; Thompson 2012); evolved concepts such as the communications circuit (Darnton 2010), and the digital communications circuit (Murray and Squires 2013), loosely adapt this understanding of the flow of publishing through various roles and markets, to reflect more closely upon what each of these roles in publishing essentially does towards the whole. As will be seen, some of these concepts may now need to be revisited.

Current Publishing Structures

So by the end of the twentieth century the traditional mainstream publishing house—whether specialist or consumer, large or small, follows similar lines and it is easy to outline the hierarchy for a typical organization following value-chain based functions.

The product development, as it were the manufacturing industry's research and development department, for the publishing house is situated in the editorial departments; these are the teams surrounding the commissioning or acquisition processes. Unlike some industries, the central product is provided by non-specialist suppliers outside of the organization or the immediate industry; product development is shaped internally but the content itself most often comes from external authors. Unlike specialist suppliers such as typesetters who know the business of publishing and exist and operate within the industry, authors are most generally set outside it. In this way it operates like other creative industry such as music or art, where there is a tradition of talent spotting (both via agents or directly into the house) and this adds a certain gloss to very traditional industrial structures. The content for some sectors may be more in the form of raw material (e.g. legal information) that is refined and structured by the publishing house although the material is available in the public domain. Nevertheless the editorial department provides a crucible for the creative element and brings content skills, market knowledge and production expertise to bear on the author's work to render it publishable (Clark and Phillips 2008; Bhaskar 2013). The filtering and amplification roles of the publisher as identified by Bhaskar reflect the central activity of publishing that is incorporated into every stage of the publishing process.

The editorial department is focused on managing the project and providing an author-facing role. The commissioning editor is more strategically and financially oriented around content acquisition, while editorial work, maybe by a desk editor, continues on the manuscript itself (sometimes called desk editorial by some publishers; at others managed by freelancers via the production departments). The production process overall can encompass many other roles from picture research to design; publishers work with suppliers who (while separate entities, can still be said to exist from within the industry unlike authors) might include typesetters, printers and paper suppliers, digital compilers, warehouse and distribution services, etc. The product is managed by these production departments which work with the editorial teams to ensure smooth processes.

The sales and marketing functions are then similar to those in other industry sectors. The sales teams focus on the actual sale to the customer—whether a wholesale or retail customer, at home or for export, small customers or key accounts (with whom detailed relationships are required). Marketing meanwhile focus on the promotion of that title to potential customers or users to create awareness to drive customers to purchase: this can include traditional paid-for media as well as public relations. Publishers increasingly talk of the paid, earned, owned (and sometimes shared) model of marketing, a model developed across industries evolving with marketing consultants rather than a theoretical model.

There is then the distribution aspect, which is often managed by an operations department overseeing the delivery of print and digital products to the end user via a physical or digital warehouse as well as managing the packaging and shipping to individuals, retailers, and wholesalers, nationally and internationally. The actual warehousing (physical or digital) is often outsourced.

There are certain terms or roles that exist in a publishing structure which are vaguer: the publisher can be at the top of a small publishing house or be a departmental head of a particular subsection of titles in a large company. There are also iterations of the business organizations with, for instance, not-for-profit structures such as university presses.

Further related functions which are more specific to publishing exist. So for instance the teams that might manage rights sales, contracts, permissions can be integral to some publishers. Typically each of these functions will be represented in some way in publishing committee meetings—where the acceptance of new products into the publishing system is managed. And these functions also examine the profit and loss accounts that a company produces, the costs of each function clearly represented at the micro level in the costings of a book right the way up to the company plan and financial accounts. So this follows a traditional economic structure for any typical business focusing on commercial opportunities, monitored though financial management; the job of the business is centred on the success of past products being invested in the development of future products.

STRUCTURAL CHARACTERISTICS OF PUBLISHING IN THE CONTEXT OF THE WIDER CREATIVE INDUSTRIES

With this broad structure in mind what typifies publishing, and indeed many creative industries is their approach to managing risk as they create (or manufacture) cultural products (Hirsch 1972). Product development rests in bringing in new content from talented individuals. This content has to a sell a certain number to cover its costs; after that, to support the organization and bring in profit, it is hoped the title will succeed. It is, however, dependent on a market with changing tastes and consumer behaviours. Spotting where success will come from next therefore proves a challenge as publishers aim to identify a contemporary zeitgeist and publish accordingly, and/or jump on a bandwagon of a particular trend (whether vampire romance, erotica, or adult colouring books). The Pareto rule can often play a part—80 per cent of the income comes from 20 per cent of the books—so for many publishers signing enough books to ensure at least some will become bestsellers is critical. In some specialist markets the opportunities are more predictable but the long-term development of successful titles that will last in a backlist is still a challenging activity. Thompson (2012) identifies some of the myths around the focus on searching for bestsellers. His exploration reveals that the drive to find bestsellers and copy trends does not necessarily lead to a homogenization of the industry as might be expected if taken to the extreme. However, as he notes, the acquisition of bestsellers is still central to the operation of a traditional publishing house (Thompson 2012).

Certain aspects of managing risk are built into this structure. If success depends on a continuous flow of new titles, then identifying and signing swiftly is key and the structure of the business is designed to ensure this. As Hirsch (1972) says, these industries presuppose a surplus of raw material. He examines the way risk is developed and this too has been embedded in the structure across creative industries. Hirsch notes a 'rich assortment of adaptive and "coping" strategies' (1972: 641) have evolved to manage risk, including: the reduction of fixed cost bases where possible (royalties, for instance, allow the costs to be distributed and paid to reflect success or otherwise); talent scouts also allow for expanded networks and they can be rewarded based on success rather than being a costly in-house resource. Literary agents are therefore central to this latter part of the publishing operation and as such form an external arm of the publishing structure. Indeed for Hirsch, 'overproduction is a rational organizational response in an environment of low capital investments and demand uncertainty' (1972: 652). This is something that is very central to the behaviour of publishing organizations and which may well need to change in light of the digital environment.

Publishing industries reflect structures that are similar to many creative industries in terms of creative labour (Hesmondhalgh and Baker 2011; Davies and Sigthorsson 2013; McRobbie 2016). While functions exist as outlined above there is also a considerable element devolved to external agencies, from individual freelancers for editorial to specialist marketing companies for media buying. This follows from Hirsch's summary of ways to manage risk for those producing cultural products. Project-based working is common across the cultural industries; this is not just to manage profitability but also to engender originality, to ensure change and inventiveness (Grabher 2004). A certain fluidity therefore does exist around publishing houses.

This chimes with Handy's concept of the shamrock organization, which presents a picture of the relationship between the organization's core and periphery. A flexible approach to labour is facilitated by a three-way split of the workers: a core group, a contracted specialist staff, and a temporary staff (Handy 2012). This model proves interesting as we shall see later in terms of the trend to projects working but it does not entirely reflect the operations of publishing, compared with, for example, TV production or the music industry. In the TV and music industries the creative personnel brought in are still trained specialists within the creative sector. Each project, needing to be creatively original, draws in freelancers as required. The commissioners, who form the core in Handy's terms, are generally very focused and the companies are small in scale (although strategically powerful). Being somewhat more focused on the mass production of its products, publishing often has a larger central core of employees with a variety of skills (although there are of course very many small companies who have always used freelancers). Creativity is vested in authors outside the organization but, as noted already, they are non-specialists rather than forming part of a specialized body of trained creatives operating as a latent organization (Negus 2002).

ORGANIZATIONS, TECHNOLOGY, AND CHANGE

In the twenty-first century, the technological changes towards a digital world have been significant for publishing. Indeed a report for the EU stated in 2012 'The Media and

Content Industries... are among the industries that have been first and heavily hit by the digital shift' (Simon and Bogdanowicz 2012). For Mintzberg, managing change is an essential part of a company's strategic activity—not something to be done in cycles. A company may well need to put into place mechanisms and structures to cope with continuous change (Mintzberg 1989); the rapidly emerging digital environment is accelerating the need to change and adapt swiftly.

Many aspects of technological change have been integrated into publishing industry structures as they currently exist, whether through production departments automating some typesetting processes or marketing departments developing web expertise. New relationships develop and some new roles emerge (e.g. digital marketers, digital content producers). Some of this change has condensed the value chain within a publisher: technology has taken over some of the traditional roles within the structure (e.g. in-house typesetting) while disintermediation and lower barriers to entry has allowed other entrants to take on some of these roles (e.g. literary agents directly publishing ebooks).

However, integrating digital products into the publishing structure has been more complex. Digital product design has been part of publishing for some time (early digital activities developed in the mid-1990s around CDRom and large specialist databases) but publishing companies have adopted a range of approaches with different degrees of success. Some digital development (e.g. basic ebooks) can sit alongside traditional production work flows successfully; for big specialist publishers large digital departments with new project management approaches have developed reasonably swiftly. But in-between there exists a continuing challenge for publishers—whether to sit the digital activities within a print department or separate it out (often with minimal staff who act as conduits to external software developers). There can be a lack of understanding of the needs of digital product development, anxiety over how best to manage this new category of risk, especially in an increasingly competitive market, and an underlying, unconscious assumption that it should fit within the traditional structure of existing publishing houses.

LEGACY STRUCTURES AND RETHINKING THE VALUE CHAIN

One significant aspect of this has been that publishers struggled with legacy infrastructure. For example, with the increasing digitalization of books for some markets, together with more efficient print-on-demand systems and stock management, warehouses have become less central to publishers' activities. Publishers set up to run a business in a certain way have had to divest themselves of activities they no longer need, such as print works and warehouses. For a global business this can be a considerable undertaking when they are simultaneously having to build new infrastructure to support digital activity (such as digital asset management databases, content management systems, XML first workflows).

Research (Hall 2013) has shown that legacy infrastructure has largely been dealt with by publishers although one particular legacy, the business model, remains a challenge. Reorganization has required time and investment for established publishing houses, while new entrants to the market have emerged with resources allowing a more speedy response to the digital challenge (e.g. Amazon and its self-publishing programme).

Digital change is far reaching. It involves not only the development of new product types and forms, but it has also led to new intermediaries, new types of consumers, a blurring of the boundaries between different sorts of products, new approaches to pricing, and a proliferation of business models and pioneers (Jenkins 2008, Leadbeater 2009, Gauntlett 2011). So for the first time in some time the value chain of the publisher has been significantly disrupted—whether those who control marketplaces are downstream or self-publishers by-passing a publisher altogether.

The product focus of the traditional value chain can entrench companies in a structure centred on the end product and that structure is now breaking apart through disinter-mediation (as a result of digital technology). This disintermediation requires a new approach to the value chain; aspects of the chain that were central to adding value have now been either rendered obsolete or taken over by other organizations up- or down-stream. There is a growing recognition that new value chains need to develop around the customers; it is with customers that the value and meaning resides and so understanding the way customers consume is important (see below in the section 'From product to service'). Commentators observe that the twentieth century has been about refining the product and the supply chain, the twenty-first needs to focus on and understand demand (Nash, 2010). They argue that there is a shift away from content creation to the ways in which the content is filtered, packaged, and consumed (Bilton 2006; Bhaskar 2013).

Therefore rethinking the value chain is becoming more important (Healy 2011; Tian and Martin 2011; Nash 2010; Bhaskar 2013; Hetherington 2014). For some commentators it is even the way of thinking about what publishing does that needs to change—the focus on the container (O'Leary 2011) has led, it could be argued, to the development of a structure that focuses on a limited range of formats, or containers, in favour of content, when really context should determine what a product should look like. The legacy of working within a hardback/paperback format is embedded in the way a publishing house is structured around its work flow and this may have its limitations in terms of future innovation.

TRADITIONAL MANAGEMENT STRUCTURES AND FLEXIBLE ORGANIZATIONS

Similarly other 'traditional' management theorists are coming under scrutiny. Porter's approach provides that a company's differentiation (that which gives the company its competitive edge) must drive the strategy (Porter 2008). That strategy must be embedded across the whole business and reinforced by the structure. This too, for some commentators, limits the ability to change and create. Peters' view, that organizations should continue what they are good at while simultaneously refining their competitive edge, has some truth but maybe does not take into account an increasingly rapid pace of change requiring companies to adapt effectively (Peters and Waterman 1982). These are top-down strategic approaches: for Mintzberg (1989) creativity comes through collective activity and so it is important that organizational structures allow more open and equal-ized actions; a company should not simply follow whatever is imposed by the boardroom (Bilton 2006). Flexible, matrix based organizations that move away from functional approaches are therefore more likely to fit the new creative economies that are emerging; they will cope better with the more fast moving fragmented markets.

Publishers are increasingly aware that the structure they have needs to adapt and change to respond effectively to the changing publishing environment. Research under-taken with twenty-two chief executives, managing directors, and digital operations directors showed that they are all considering changing structures to enable them to respond more effectively to the challenges they face from the digital environment. Examples of the sort of changes they are considering include:

- reviewing company structure;
- looking at a range of people and skills sets;
- developing more skills in-house;
- carrying out more collaborations and partnerships;
- developing new strategies for content development;
- experimenting more with business models (Hall 2016).

This illustrates a recognition within the industry that several elements of the organization of the business need to be adjusted.

DIVERSITY, SKILLS, AND RESTRUCTURING AROUND NEW ROLES

So industry leaders considered that in order to respond effectively to the challenges of twenty-first-century publishing the company structure does need to change. This realization reflects to some extent an understanding of a changing value chain and what is required to restructure around new production processes or to work with new inter-mediaries. But there are some important preoccupations within this list that are critical to publishing organizations beyond the need to restructure. Indeed the need to be posi-tioned so as to benefit from other aspects of change is one driver of organizational change. The ability to collaborate effectively and bring different forms of expertise in-house was recognized as critical, and these skills need to be absorbed and integrated effectively, thus impacting the traditional publishing structure.

While some specific tasks, such as software development, can be outsourced (see below in the section 'In-house to project-based'), this same research shows that publishers have recognized certain areas where they need to bring some further expertise and resources in-house in order to have better control of and flexibililty at the product development stage. Where collaboration becomes central to new product development, so in-house expertise becomes important in order to manage and participate in that collaboration effectively, and equally, with other partners.

There is a growing realization of the need to diversify in terms of the sorts of skills people in the industry have. (This is not ethnic and socio-economic lines diversity; important though that is, it would not have a structural impact.) In this case, the focus is on bringing in different skill-sets from different industries (e.g. software, design, project management, creativity management, innovation strategists, brand managers, and community managers) and to restructure departments to accommodate new ways of working across functions and skill-sets. Generally, new roles have been developing within each of the existing departments. Traditional business structures do have some ability to absorb change; relationship managers and information consultants, for instance, sit within sales and marketing departments in specialist publishers taking on business development roles and working closely with key accounts to customize products. Digital project management expertise, too, is useful for understanding business modelling and planning in order to assess resource allocation and introduce iterative processes of development. Creative management approaches from other creative industries can also be valuable for understanding how structures promote creativity and innovation (Bilton 2006; Kung 2008) and rethinking organizational hierarchies can be informed by these approaches.

FROM PRODUCT TO SERVICE

Developing standardized hierarchies for publishing organizations leads to inflexibility as they are very much focused around the delivery of products in a fixed form. In specialist markets in particular there are new ways of working that mean structures are changing. There is an increasing sense that publishers in certain sectors, with a closer understanding of their customers, can provide not just books but wider services to those customers. Legal publishers, for instance, have spent a lot of time focusing carefully on how their customers work. This has had an impact on the legal products they develop. The same information, say a report of a legal case, may be used by different roles within the legal profession in different ways at different times throughout the day. Structuring content in such a way that it can be delivered in these different ways is something legal publishers have turned their attention to. It goes beyond product: understanding the workflow of customers allows publishers to think about how far they can develop other services, maybe managing legal information, providing resources lawyers can pass on in turn to their customers.

Similarly, in the STM market publishers like Springer Nature, BMJ, and Wiley look at ways to provide other services, such as laboratory information management systems, diagnostic tools, or professional training services and educational technology solutions to their customers. This works in the specialist sector because of their close relationship with their customers and the long-term nature of these relationships. It leads to a changing structure away from one a traditional supply chain to one where departments may be aligned to customer segments and focus on particular types of content. This flexibility then allows the publishers to do more for their customers. Their relationships can go further: publishers can work so closely with their customers in these sectors that they are almost working in partnership to provide highly customized services (e.g. to legal libraries). The emphasis is on working collaboratively and aligning departments; even if there is an internal meta-organization which maintains the old production line for content production, the company is facing outwards according to their customer segments and relationships.

In-house to Project-based

A further result of this is the development of flexible project-based organizations. As new complex services are commissioned, so publishers need to expand in order to develop these projects effectively. Once established, the on-going management is less onerous and, though still important, does not need the same level of specialist staff as required at the development stage of the new service. Such project-based working has led, in some sectors, to an increasing reliance on a highly developed and varied freelance base. Originally freelance lists tended to encompass copy-editors, proofreaders, etc. able to help with the editorial stages of rendering content, together with illustrators and designers who would be specifically commissioned for images and covers (who would not be employed in-house in order to keep the look and visual impacts fresh). This started to expand further as book project managers and packagers were increasingly commissioned by publishers to undertake either complex works or allow publishers to manage workload and crunch points in the year.

This principle has expanded, however, to become, for certain types of projects, particularly in the digital arena, the way that a much wider range of creative and technical expertise can be drawn down to work on the development of a specific project. In some cases organizations have become more simplified and use more freelance labour when required. This model tends to work best for companies that have many large technical projects (again often specialist publishers such as legal publishers which did shift quite dramatically to this model). However, it is interesting to note that this trend may possibly be changing again. The research outlined above based on industry leaders specifically asked if they thought the use of freelance workers was likely to increase and, in general, publishers did not feel this was going to be significantly different. This model, as we have seen, is common throughout the creative industries which depend on freelance labour, a sort of 'gig' economy. It reflects both a recognition of the changing value chain and also a way of managing both risk and cost by not committing too much in the terms of in-house resources.

In a global economy, this trend around project working manifests in different ways. Globally, it is possible to connect creative and production teams so that organizations may have different parts of their activity in different countries. Legal publishers, for instance, may have large managed and hosted databases in the USA, legal expertise in a local market, and rendering and production in India. Similarly academic journal houses will often have editorial and data centres in Asia where information is processed, edited, and formatted ready for holding in a data warehouse. In these cases, all the teams are effectively in-house. Global project teams can come together to develop projects but this requires careful management to ensure it works efficiently in the design and build stage when good access to communication is crucial.

Other organizations take an outsourcing approach, engaging external companies to undertake aspects of their work that may, in the past, have been done in-house. Off-shoring is part of this as companies use external suppliers from overseas. There has been a growth of businesses, in regions like Asia, that can supply services beyond the more traditionally outsourced areas such as printing, warehousing, and data management; they are also employed in activities such as specialized editorial work and managing inspection copy services. This is inspired by a number of factors. As some markets decline or change, for instance, outsourcing is less risky than employing in-house staff. As a company needs to expand and contract around large projects, it cannot afford to keep under-utilized staff during the downtimes. As companies move into newer markets which are unpre-dictable, they may well not want to overcommit to in-house staff. As companies examine how best to cut costs and streamline to boost profits they may look towards cheaper sup-pliers in other countries for certain aspects of their work. For some companies, like Pearson, it has been a critical part of their restructuring to consider off-shoring with cheaper suppliers, and reduce their company head count. It can also help a business to bring in specialists where necessary who can streamline processes and add value as they have focused and detailed knowledge of a specific aspect of publishing; this expertise can be difficult for a large company to develop. This is becoming particularly important as companies look at ways to innovate effectively in new or swiftly changing marketplaces.

For smaller organizations, the flexibility to create on the spot with a group of freelance workers can have its benefits in terms of speed and ease. Conversely however, in certain cases where companies have used outside resources (e.g. for software development) it is actually because of the on-going necessity to continue to develop the service (not just maintain it) that there is a trend towards bringing people back in-house. Firms are finding that this allows for more control over the product as well as the ability to move quickly in an iterative way, and these companies are requiring different skills to come in-house.

INNOVATION AND LEAN ORGANIZATIONS

In the research discussed in the previous sections, industry leaders also noted the need to experiment and develop new content structures. There is an increasing realization of the imperative to change organizational structures in order to innovate effectively. The existing structures, as we have seen, allow for a certain type of product development and risk taking. This innovation exists primarily around content. But developing new digital products involves more innovation of form and different cost structures that cannot be easily fitted into the old methods of funding product development. Publishers find it remarkably difficult to turn the financing structures for book publishing around; digital pricing for instance tends still to reflect, in some way or other, a relationship to print, or at the very least the concept of a book price (as opposed to an app price for instance). Specialist areas have successfully moved to subscription models, but the vestiges of old pricing models still remain in aspects of even the most digital of products. More fundamentally, this reflects the dilemma that publishers face about covering the start-up costs—the fixed costs—for product development. Digital product can require high fixed costs so the break-even point is harder to meet based on the old style of managing risk across lots of books. Publishers have not yet worked out a way to support that cost and this will need a fundamental rethink of the structure of publishing. While print revenues will still be strong in mainstream markets (where indeed ebook sales are plateauing), in order to drive new digital product development (ultimately unavoidable as consumer behaviours change) new business models that allow for upfront investment will be required and new structures are needed to accommodate this.

Experimentation is therefore hindered by traditional business structures for an industry that needs to innovate. New approaches to failure are required that reflect the challenging environment of launching new digital products. Publishers are used to producing products that are finished; everything is done to them to ensure they are polished and can sit waiting to be sold in their final state. But digital development usually requires iterative building, continuous market testing, quality assurance processes, bug fixing, on-going marketing, on-going customer relationships, and support. When innovating around form rather than content more testing needs to take place, whether simply to test that a product works at one end of the scale or in-depth analysis of user journeys at the other. Creative entrepreneurship, so central to the early evolution of publishing, operates well in open flexible structures and methods of innovating in digital businesses often reflect a lean methodology (Ries 2011) that publishers may need to adopt in order to understand effectively how to build innovative digital products going forward. Minimum viable products, continuous market testing, ability to pivot, responsive redirection of resources, understanding how to assess failure and how to learn what has worked effectively, all become key to new product development in a way that traditional structures, designed to produce a book at the end of the value chain are not equipped to do.

Some new start-up publishers have been able to do this by building companies from the ground up around new business models (e.g. publishing specific crowdfunding sites, ebook publishers, app developers, writer services companies, game/book companies). They are able to build structures that can adopt more iterative entrepreneurial approaches which themselves can then evolve. This involves its own challenges but may reflect different sorts of flexible business structures, although funding remains a challenge of these sorts of start ups.

Structures for Collaboration

As noted above, collaboration is one important opportunity for publishers to develop in an increasingly competitive digital marketplace. Publishers recognize that while in print they may operate in direct competition, they may need to work together to build critical mass in digital market places. For some, this is reflected in mergers (e.g. Penguin Random House). For others, it is about being original and fresh, by working with different creative partners. And for some it may be working together to aggregate content. In a market-place where converged media is becoming normal, the customer is not concerned with who the producer of the content is, nor how it is defined (e.g. is it a book or a game) (Jenkins 2008). They look for connectivity and interoperability between their content. Divisions between publishers will not concern them, so if publishers do not work together to solve some of these technical problems, customers will go elsewhere.

For collaboration and partnership theorists Kaats and Opheji (2013), exploratory and entrepreneurial partnerships are important as they reflect an ability to share information where market behaviours are changing as well as to innovate and build new markets. Where companies are challenged by new market entrants, working together can be critical in order to compete effectively; the importance of network behaviour plays to a wider construct of a network society as envisioned by Castells (2000). Understanding working methods around experimentation as well as measuring success and failure differently becomes integral to the way these collaborations work.

In a study of collaboration it is clear that groups of external partners needs to connect and develop ideas together in order to innovate and compete effectively (Kaats and Opheij 2013). But what is particularly interesting is the way these collaborations create blurred boundaries between the different companies involved (in terms of the formation, structure, and operation of the projects). This suggests a new organizational structure is emerging—not quickly perhaps, many traditional approaches still remain dominant in the structure of business. However, it is important to develop a business structure that allows, for certain types of product development, different stakeholders to connect in new ways and allows publishers to experiment and start to innovate more effectively. It may be that some projects will fail more easily following an iterative method of building projects and a new model may move away from an emphasis on a value chain where a fully finished product comes out at the end. Structures need to facilitate connecting with a range of project partners and constructing virtual organizations around them. For new sorts of products this type of fixed structure is not going to be helpful. Building organizational structures that allow greater manoeuvability and flexibility are import-ant. From simply reorganizing so as to face customers (as mentioned above), publishers are now recognizing that they also need to become responsive to partnership building, learning from those partners and managing networks.

Publishing organizations will therefore need to consider structures that allow them to share ideas, inspire creativity, and embed organizational learning. Some companies are developing ways of working that will help promote this. Of the big four trade publishers with a base in London, three have moved into newly designed offices spaces with design remits to encourage collaboration and knowledge sharing to enhance creativity. A number of STM publishers are investing in businesses that move them beyond core publishing activities but which reflect services they can provide to their specialist markets and so are exploring ways to learn from each other and develop converged products.

Networking becomes critical for collaborative activity. One aspect of network theory focuses on which networks allow for increasing creativity and entrepreneurship (Granovetter 1973; Burt 2004) reflecting on which networks structures are the more entrepreneurial. Heebels et al. (2013) explicitly apply network theory around weak and strong ties, reflecting the fact that different publishing roles require different sorts of network ties for an organizational structure to operate effectively. Such network sociality always has been key for publishing organizations (and other creative enterprises): hence the structure of a publishing house has always reflected a form of network behaviour, a para-network, that has often crossed functional lines. For this reason, publishing potentially has the ability to reconstruct itself for new challenges. The links between the personnel within a reasonably flat organization and the strong content thread that runs through the publishing house from author to reader, may well mean that any restructuring required may be easier to manage than it would be in other traditional industries where hierarchies are more entrenched, functional departments more separate, and the organizational order is more vertical.

CONTINUING CHANGE

Publishing companies today are still recognizable according to the twentieth-century structure outlined earlier in the chapter. Editorial and production departments still exist; marketing and sales departments remain important even if their specific activity changes. The freelance base continues to diversify, whether in using animators to supply content or experts in guerrilla marketing to make a splash for a particular title. New departments emerge, most notably digital development where publishers recognize the need to bring more software expertise in-house. There is a proliferation of new roles such as user experience designers and new departments like consumer insight. These will continue to evolve; for instance, consumer insight units currently tend focus on marketing aspects of the business, crunching data, researching markets, and modelling audiences to identify markets for new product ideas, audience engagement, and marketing opportunities. At the present time, they are less concerned with use cases and user journeys, for example, which could be utilized to understand customer behaviour for new digital product development.

But more critically, publishing companies are looking to evolve more flexible ways of working, following different business models of investment in order to innovate and experiment. And as they do so it is likely they will need to become more agile as collaborators and at learning from those collaborations. From the research conducted, it is clear industry leaders recognize that the digital environment is now leading to a continual state of change. Therefore, organizational structures will need to be responsive to this and reflect the ability to adapt. It is likely that some of the structures will change in the coming years even if some functions will remain (although they may be renamed in line with emerging activities). More fundamental change will be necessary, however, to accommodate new styles of innovation; digital product development cannot just be quickly bolted on to existing businesses. Here theories of collaboration and networking are important to understand approaches that may lead to a more creative to outlook on product development. The traditional value chain which focused on similar sorts of products and optimizes the efficient and value-laden production of those products needs to change as the form of the products is changing.

So the organization of the future is one that will have to flex depending on projects balancing the short-term needs of projects with the long-term wider vision. Networks will form a critical part of this and collaborative/cooperative activity will need to be able to maintain that vision at both project and corporate levels.

At one end, small entrepreneurial operations stripped of many functions will operate focusing on segments and customers bringing in services as they are needed. For larger companies, their future organization will have to have a blend of various elements:

1. adopt an approach to networks more akin to those in the wider creative industries, with a broader selection of specialist freelancers to the latent organizations that can surface each time, newly reconfigured for new projects;
2. develop systems that allow for iterative development, reflective of new entrepreneurial organizations;
3. create structures that allow for the quick, efficient assembling of projects—virtual organizations—with other departments that will carry out functions drawn in as needed;
4. build knowledge and learning within the organization with structures that allow for flexibility without dismantling core strengths—a resilient centre with a strong vision is still important.

So it can be seen that creating structures that can be flexible will be important: for instance purpose-built satellite structures that can connect with other companies, reconfigure themselves as needed, and reform for the next collaboration may start to emerge to support innovation. There may be a series of virtual organizations and strong networks that allow for the rapid deployment of talent from a more specialist, wider workforce. Overall they will need to continually evolve and, in order to do that, certain organizational prerequisites need to be in place around flexibility, nimbleness, networking, and learning. Ultimately, the industry is accepting that, unlike their experience of the structures they have had up to now, which have not changed for decades, it is moving into an arena where no structure will remain in place for long.

References

Bhaskar, M. (2013). The *Content Machine: Towards a Theory of Publishing from the Printing Press to the Digital Network*, London: Anthem Press.

Bilton, A. (2006). *Management and Creativity: From Creative Industries to Creative Management*, Malden, MA: John Wiley & Sons.

Burt, R. S. (2004). 'Structural Holes and Good Ideas', *American Journal of Sociology*, 110, pp. 349–99. https://doi.org/10.1086/421787

Castells, M. (2000). *The Rise of the Network Society*. Oxford: Blackwell Publishers.

Clark, G. N. and A. Phillips (2008). *Inside Book Publishing*, 4th edition. London: Routledge.

Darnton, R. (2010). *The Case for Books: Past, Present, and Future: 256*, Reprint edition, New York: PublicAffairs.

Davies, R. and G. Sigthorsson (2013). *Introducing the Creative Industries: From Theory to Practice*, London: SAGE Publications Ltd.

Feather, J. (2005). *A History of British Publishing*, 2nd edition, London; New York: Routledge.

Gauntlett, D. (2011). *Making is Connecting: The Social Meaning of Creativity, from DIY and Knitting to YouTube and Web 2.0*, Cambridge, UK; Malden, MA: Polity Press.

Grabher, G. (2004). 'Learning in Projects, Remembering in Networks? Communality, Sociality, and Connectivity in Project Ecologies', *European Urban and Regional Studies*, 11, pp. 103–23. https://doi.org/10.1177/0969776404041417

Granovetter, M. S. (1973). 'The Strength of Weak Ties', *American Journal of Sociology*, 78, pp. 1360–80.

Hall, F. (2013). *The Business of Digital Publishing: An Introduction to the Digital Book and Journal Industries*, London; New York: Routledge.

Hall, F. (2016). 'Digital Change and Industry Responses: Exploring organizational and strategic issues in the book-publishing industry', *Logos*, 27, pp. 19–31. https://doi.org/10.1163/1878-4712-11112102

Handy, C. (2012). *The Age of Unreason*. London: Random House.

Healy, Michael (2011). 'Seeking permanence in a time of turbulence', *Logos*, 22, pp. 7–15. https://doi.org/10.1163/095796511x580275

Heebels, B., A. Oedzge, and I. van Aalst (2013). 'Social Networks and Cultural Mediators: The Multiplexity of Personal Ties in Publishing', *Industry and Innovation*, 20(8), pp. 701–18. https://doi.org/10.1080/13662716.2013.856621

Hesmondhalgh, D. and S. Baker, (2011). *Creative Labour: Media Work in Three Cultural Industries*, London: Routledge,.

Hetherington, D. (2014). 'Book Publishing: New Environments Call for New Operating Models', *Pub Res Q*, 30, pp. 382–7. https://doi.org/10.1007/s12109-014-9379-y

Hirsch, P. M. (1972). 'Processing Fads and Fashions: An Organization-Set Analysis of Cultural Industry Systems', *American Journal of Sociology*, 77, pp. 639–59.

Jenkins, H. (2008). *Convergence Culture: Where Old and New Media Collide*, 2nd Revised edition, New York: NYU Press.

Kaats, E. and W. Opheij (2013). *Creating Conditions for Promising Collaboration: Alliances, Networks, Chains, Strategic Partnerships*, New York: Springer.

Kung, L. (2008). *Strategic Management in the Media*, London: SAGE Publications Ltd.

Leadbeater, C. (2009). *We-Think: Mass Innovation, Not Mass Production*, 2nd edition, London: Profile Books.

McRobbie, A. (2016). *Be Creative: Making a Living in the New Culture Industries*, Oxford: John Wiley & Sons.

Manguel, A. (1997). *A History of Reading*, London: Flamingo—HarperCollins.

Mintzberg, H. (1989). *Mintzberg on Management: Inside Our Strange World of Organizations*, New York: Simon and Schuster.

Murray, P. R. and C. Squires (2013). 'The digital publishing communications circuit', Book 2.0, 3, pp. 3–23. https://doi.org/10.1386/btwo.3.1.3_1

Nash, R. (2010). 'Publishing 2020', *Publishing Research Quarterly*, 26, pp. 114–18. https://doi.org/10.1007/s12109-010-9155-6

Negus, K. R. (2002). 'The Work of Cultural Intermediaries and the Enduring Distance between Production and Consumption', *Cultural Studies*, 16(4), pp. 501–15. https://doi.org/10.1080/09502380210139089

O'Leary, B. F. (2011). 'Context First: A Unified Field Theory of Publishing', Pub Res Q, 27, 211–219. https://doi.org/10.1007/s12109-011-9221-8

Peters, T. and F. H. Waterman (1982). *In Search of Excellence: Lessons from America's best-run companies*. New York: Harper & Row.

Porter, M. E. (1985). Competitive Advantage, New York: Free Press.

Porter, M. E. (2008). *Competitive Advantage: Creating and Sustaining Superior Performance*, London: Simon and Schuster.

Ries, E. (2011). *The Lean Startup: How Today's Entrepreneurs Use Continuous Innovation to Create Radically Successful Businesses*. London: Crown Business.

Simon, J. P. and M. Bogdanowicz (2012). The Digital Shift in the Media and Content Industries: Policy Brief (Policy Document No. 1/2013), EUR Scientific and Research Series. Luxembourg: European Commission, Joint Research Centre, Institute for Prospective Technological Studies.

Thompson, J. B. (2012). *Merchants of Culture: The Publishing Business in the Twenty-first Century*, 2nd edition, Cambridge: Polity Press.

Tian, X. and B. Martin (2011). 'Impacting Forces on eBook Business Models Development', *Pub Res Q*, 27, pp. 230–46. https://doi.org/10.1007/s12109-011-9229-0

CHAPTER 19

....

BOOK DESIGN

....

PAUL LUNA

Who designs books? This seemingly simple question touches on an important truth: books are 'designed' by their authors and publishers long before any typescript, electronic copy, or cover blurb arrives on the desk of someone whose job title is 'designer'. The author's initial organization of their text, the publisher's conception of the market for the book, and the channels it will be sold through determine much of the physical and visual presentation of the work.

The design function in publishing encompasses the myriad of visual decisions that need to be made today about the presentation of a book to its readers, and which can be grouped into three key areas: branding, cover design, and interior or text design. Some of these design decisions may be taken at a corporate or list level, while others may be in response to the requirements of an individual book; depending on the publisher, designers may work in external agencies, as freelancers, or as part of an in-house team. Looking at the design genres into which printed books fall can help us take a broad view and analyse approaches to design in particular strands of publishing. The role of the designer in publishing is to navigate these genre conventions and expectations and produce efficient and innovative design solutions: book design is an area where fidelity to convention and novelty both have their place.

For more than 500 years the aim of all publishing was to produce a physical product, and therefore design was concerned with the qualities of the book as an object, taking into account its haptic qualities and durability as well as the visual arrangement of text, illustrations, and binding. The development of electronic publishing channels alongside the printed book has radically changed this. Publishers may control every aspect of a physical book's design but, as content providers for electronic distribution, their influence over the appearance of an electronic book and how readers interact with it may be limited by the devices and platforms on which they publish. The design of both the material book and the virtual book therefore need to be considered, because design for publishing involves the creation of both engaging individual artefacts and complex design systems.

BRANDING: DESIGN FROM
THE TOP DOWN

From the earliest days of printing, printers ensured that the reading public recognized their books. Devices identifying the printer appeared on books produced by Aldus Manutius (*c.*1449–1515), the Estiennes (active from 1502), Christopher Plantin (d. 1589) and his successors, and the Elsevirs (active from 1580). The earliest devices appeared next to the colophon, often at the end of the book, moving to the title page as this developed in importance. Bookbinding was a separate activity from printing during the first four centuries of print. This meant that publishers could not effectively brand the outside of their books, as binding designs were separately commissioned by book buyers. Title pages therefore became the publisher's advertising medium, and were designed for display in booksellers' shops. The wording of title pages became filled with selling points, and the printer's or publisher's wood-cut or engraved device identified the book's provenance and confirmed its status and reliability.

Publishers' devices continued to be used on title pages, the wording of which became more and more spare from the start of the twentieth century, as jackets took on the main role in promoting the book at point of sale. But these publishers' devices were neither drawn nor used with absolute consistency, because although publishers believed in the value of designing for recognition, they did not regard conformity to what we would today call a single brand image as necessary beyond the confines of particular series. A different kind of conformity between publications was achieved through the imposition of house style, which in the days of metal type meant the codification of typesetting and layout practices. Exemplified in the United States by the work of Theodore Lowe De Vinne (1828–1914) and in Britain by *Hart's Rules for Compositors and Readers at the University Press, Oxford*, house style was a matter of practicality. Efficiency in typesetting, when a manuscript was divided between compositors, and proofs between proofreaders, required them to work to common standards in spelling, punctuation, and capitalization. The need for house style to be imposed by publishers' copy-editors rather than being left to printers grew as typesetting was transformed by technology from an industrialized craft activity into a semi-automated process where, from the 1980s, typescripts no longer needed to be rekeyed in order to set type. At the same time, designers took on the role of policing layout decisions in text composition that once would have been silently undertaken by printers.

The beginnings of a systematic visual approach that we would recognize today as brand conformity across an entire publishing list can be seen in the Albatross library in the 1930s. The nature of the list—paperback reprints—allowed for much greater conformity to style than a publisher of original works would have accepted. The books were made to a common trimmed size, chosen for its aesthetic proportions as much as its practicality, and different subject areas within the overall list were distinguished only by colour (a device that had been developed earlier by the Tauchnitz reprint library).

The purely typographic design system for both covers and text, designed by Giovanni Mardersteig (1892–1977) in a centred 'new traditionalist' style, set a new benchmark. Covers were set in a new sans serif type, Europa, and highly legible new Monotype seriffed typefaces were used for text (McCleery 2006). These features influenced the subsequent design of Penguin Books from its inception in 1935, and whose covers also eschewed hand-drawn lettering and illustration for plain type.

Penguin subsequently took up the 'total brand' mantle in the post-war years, developing related design systems for its Penguin, Pelican, Puffin, and Peregrine books. The cover design systems refined and developed from 1947 by Jan Tschichold were typographic, and controlled typefaces, sizes, logos, and layout minutely: they were allied to clear rules that controlled the typographic standards required in text composition. But these cover designs adapted badly when the inclusion of illustrations became more and more necessary in a crowded paperback market. A different but still uniform approach was adopted by Germano Facetti (1926–2006) and Romek Marber (b. 1925) in the 1960s. They imposed a modernist grid structure which emphasized the cover image, allowing it to bleed on all sides, and restrained cover typography to minimal, neutral styles. Through all these changes, the Penguin logo remained essentially unaltered since it had been subtly redefined by Tschichold (Baines 2005). A similar attempt at a grid-based cover stand-ardization allied to a highly controlled logo was specified by John McConnell for Faber and Faber in the 1980s; the author's name and title (in a standardized typeface), together with the publisher's imprint floated above any illustration in a rectangular cartouche. These approaches worked because of the relative homogeneity of those publishers' lists at the point that the designs were conceived: as publishers increasingly turned into conglomerates, their corporate design strategies began to separate the identity of the publishers as businesses from the visual presentation of specific lists. Penguin, for example, is now a publisher of books in a wide range of formats, not just pocket paperbacks, and the Penguin logo and the colour orange no longer identify every Penguin book.

Publishers' corporate design systems that were developed from the 1990s recognized this: when Oxford University Press (OUP) embarked on a corporate identity programme in 1996, it was explicitly stated that the system would not intrude on the market-appropriate design of individual lists or books. This was particularly important given the number of markets in which OUP operated. In contrast to the approach of academic publishers such as Springer, whose system standardized the design of books, OUP's programme would only provide standard identification elements that were applicable to all publica-tions across its academic, trade, school, and English language teaching lists. Ultimately these consisted of a wordmark and a concise mission statement, and rules for the colour, sizing, and placement of these elements (Luna 2017b). Recognizing the limits of corporate branding is particularly important in publishing, where author, list, series, or even individual title weighs more heavily in the purchaser's mind than the business from which a book originates, and the opportunity for consumer branding may exist on any one of these levels. Publishers are a conduit through which the consumer receives a product; they are not themselves seen by the public as products, and their use of branding elements reflects this. This is true in large publishing businesses (such as OUP) where a number of publishing lists co-exist. Of course, publishers with a less diffuse range of products still impose standard design elements on their publications: the academic publisher Brill, for example, imposes a standard typeface for text composition (Brill 2011). But for the majority of publishers, and certainly for the larger conglomerates, the pattern is that of OUP's identity guidelines, where the design of individual books is unconstrained except for an identifying logo or wordmark, and only corporate communications are fully constrained by a corporate design system.

BINDINGS, JACKETS, AND COVERS

It was not until the mechanization of bookbinding in the nineteenth century that publishers began to issue works in standard bindings, whether cloth or paper, that could be applied to an entire series. These bindings had to be designed. The arrangement of type on a page was traditionally the domain of the printer, and the separate role of the typographer or book designer working for a publisher, either in-house or as an external consultant, emerged in the nineteenth century. An early example is Joseph Cundall (1818–95), who was both a publisher himself and a designer of books and bindings for other publishers (McLean 1976; Smith 2004).

Nineteenth-century binding designs, whether they were decorative or represented the contents pictorially, were blocked in one or more colours on to cloth or printed on paper sheets that were pasted to the front and back boards. The lettering on bindings, being hand drawn, could escape the rigidity of metal type and, like the lettering on lithographically printed ephemera, adopted a profusion of decorative styles which were integrated with patterns or illustrations. Book jackets were first seen from 1832, but only became a commonplace promotional medium after 1900, as the use of pictorial cloth bindings declined. Jackets had the advantage over blocked bindings in that typeset blurbs, endorsements, and lists of other publications could easily be incorporated. Illustrated jackets initially continued the graphic techniques of flat-colour blocking used in bookbinding, sometimes repeating the designs of the bindings they protected. From about 1920 jackets were typically separately designed from the rest of the book (Roberts 1956; Powers 2001). Typographic jackets used display sizes of metal type, but lettering on jackets was more often hand drawn. This allowed greater flexibility in sizing or condensing lettering so that long titles would fit, especially on spines, and made it easier to integrate lettering with illustrations.

The influence of William Morris (1834–96) and the 'revival of printing' after the 1890s encouraged publishers to look at book design as something that should not simply be left to printers. In the USA, printers such as De Vinne and Daniel Berkeley Updike (1860–1941) and the designer Bruce Rogers (1870–1957) improved the standards of book composition, and essentially set the template for much twentieth-century Anglo-American book design; their work could be plain and functional, but Rogers in particular could also be playful and visually allusive. Rogers also worked briefly in Britain for the university presses at Cambridge and Oxford. The succeeding wave of American book designers, including William Addison Dwiggins (1880–1956), was fully part of the commercial graphic design scene. Dwiggins's work for Knopf and Random House in the 1930s imparted a playful art deco look to jackets, bindings, and text (Kennett 2018). In contrast, the German typographer Jan Tschichold (1902–74) and the Czech designers Ladislav Sutnar (1897–1976) and Karel Teige (1900–51) used the formal elements of modernism (simple geometrical shapes, dynamic composition, photomontage, and bold type) to produce book jackets which succeeded in combining type and photography in new and startling ways (Burke 2007). The post-1945 development of commercial graphic design in the USA, which in many ways married American wit and decoration with European modernism and purity, offered new styles for publishers: the work of Alvin Lustig (1915–55) for New Directions and other publishers is notable for eschewing the 'hard sell' in favour of an allusive graphic approach. Representative illustration was supplanted by the evocative arrangement of discreetly sized type and abstract imagery or photomontage (Heller 2013).

The purely typographic cover had a considerable vogue in mid-twentieth-century Britain, notably in the work of Berthold Wolpe (1905–89) and Michael Harvey (1931–2013). This declined as Letraset and computer-set type overtook hand lettering, but the integration of hand lettering and illustration was revived with the success of designs by Jeff Fisher in the 1990s, notably the influential *Captain Corelli's Mandolin* (Vintage, 1998). Designers turned to increasingly sophisticated desktop applications to combine and customize lettering, type, images, and other elements. This gave rise to new styles of cover artwork that were not limited by the traditional binary choice between an illustrated and a typographic cover. But other significant influences on book cover design came from different kinds of technological change. One was the emergence of online bookselling in the 1990s. The majority of potential buyers now saw book covers, not as full-size physical objects in a bookshop, but in arrays of thumbnails on the websites of online retailers. The ebook caused further disruption. While an online retailer might show an image of the print edition on its website, the file that the reader downloaded might not contain the cover image if the relevant rights had not been negotiated. This dematerialization of the book cover gave rise, paradoxically, to a new interest in the physical aspects of book packaging in the 2010s, as publishers sought to use the distinctive physical qualities of binding materials, blocking, and paper choice as distinctive selling points for print editions, in order to add tactile value to the traditional product and distinguish printed books from the 'flatland' of reading on screen. Some developments were welcome, such as the greater use of matt papers for colour printing, customized rather than generic endpapers and binding materials, and flaps on paperback covers. But features long thought faintly disreputable, such as fake deckle edges, were also seen on mass-market paperbacks. In the 1930s the paperback established its appeal exactly because it was a 'minimum book'; by the 2010s publishers saw the need to maximize the appeal of physical books through physical attributes.

Technology: Constraints and Opportunities

All book design has the aim of generating a visual world for the reader that represents and gives form to the text, and to the reading experience it offers. How it does this is influenced by the technologies available.

For centuries, the main constraint on book design was the separation of text and illustration that was enforced by the limitations of letterpress printing. While woodcuts and later wood engravings could be incorporated into a forme of type, illustrations printed by engraving techniques (and later by lithography) were produced by separate artists and craftsmen, and printed separately, often on different kinds of paper, only to be combined with letterpress text at the bookbinding stage. This separation of text and image was notionally removed by the invention of lithography at the turn of the nineteenth century, but no practical way of composing text for direct use in lithographic printing existed before the invention of commercially practical phototypesetting in the middle of the twentieth century. Up to that point all text had to be composed in metal type, and it was therefore easier to print text by letterpress, separately. In the mid nineteenth century, the engravings that illustrated Dickens's novels were printed on separate pages, while lithography was used for books consisting mainly of illustrations, such as Owen Jones's *Grammar of Ornament* (1856). Later, dictionaries such as the 1882 edition of the *Imperial Dictionary* retained small wood-engraved illustrations within the text, but used lithography for separate, full-page colour illustrations. Initially, photographs could not be reproduced directly by existing printing processes; in the 1880s illustrated magazines such as *The Graphic* had to redraw photographs as wood engravings for reproduction. The invention of the half-tone process towards the end of the nineteenth century allowed continuous-tone photographs to be reproduced mechanically by letterpress. Mid-nineteenth-century book illustrators such as J. E. Millais had their work interpreted as wood engravings by the Dalziel Brothers (Twyman 1998: 85–110). Later artists such as Aubrey Beardsley worked with skilled process engravers to allow fine line work to be printed letterpress in magazines such as *The Yellow Book* (1894–7).

The development of first photogravure and later offset lithography in the first half of the twentieth century offered the prospect of the integrated book, where text and illustrations could be arranged at will on the same printed sheet, so that photographs, line drawings, and text could be freely combined. First exploited in pictorial magazines such as *Life* and *Picture Post*, these techniques coincided with the modernist movement in design, which considered the photograph to be the most urgent and contemporary form of visual communication. The task of integrating photographic images with text became a main concern of modernist book designers such as Jan Tschichold and László Moholy-Nagy, who attempted to offer the reader a simultaneous experience of text and image. The integrated book became established after 1945. An early British example, in the field of popular business and economics, was the series of *Future Books* (1945–7) produced by the pioneering book packagers Adprint, taking their cue from the American business magazine *Fortune* (founded 1930). The four volumes used full-colour gravure and lithographic printing to present charts of pictorial statistics, maps, diagrams, and other kinds of graphic information alongside the text; articles were conceived around their illustrations. The series had a further life as a magazine (Kindel 2017). Titles such as *The Story of Art* (Phaidon, 1950) benefited from what the author Ernst Gombrich described as an 'intense collaboration' between himself and the publisher, with the text being rewritten and new images suggested, so as to enable 'readers as far as possible to have the illustration discussed in the text in front of them, without having to turn the page' (Hollis 2009).

Integration was naturally adopted for art and popular science books, but the integration of text and images in what we can consider as documentary books—which had a close relationship with, and were sometimes linked to, documentary films—was a development of the 1970s. The designer Richard Hollis (b. 1934), working closely with the writer John Berger (1926–2017), created the complex visual relationships of *Ways of Seeing* (BBC/Penguin, 1972) and *A Seventh Man* (Penguin, 1975), where the reader is led through sequences of text and illustration that enhance and reinforce one another. A key feature was the use of a grid that was flexible enough to accommodate varying sizes of illustration, so that the sizing could be used dynamically. Hollis's use of bold type for the text of *Ways of Seeing* was significant: it gave the same visual weight to the text as to the images, avoiding the grey text slabs of a coffee-table book (Hollis 2009).

Hollis worked in a traditional way, marking up a typescript to produce a specification for typesetting, then pasting up the resulting galley proofs on layout sheets with photocopies or sketches of the illustrations. This plan was then used by the typesetter and printer to produce film from which plates were made and the book printed. From the mid-1980s, the combination of computer technologies known as desktop publishing (dtp), and the ease with which authors could present manuscripts electronically which did not need rekeying, changed this, as the files created by a designer on their computer could directly produce film output when handed over to a printer. Overnight, the role of designer changed from specifier to implementer. This had the potential to change the relationship between designers, editors, and authors, and allow these roles to collaborate more closely. The serial process of passing a typescript from editor to designer to typesetter to proofreader could be augmented by a parallel process of designer and editor working together on a text to achieve a design that, through iterative editing and designing, was more closely tailored to the content. This was of most value in publications such as children's non-fiction publishing (the *Oxford Children's Encyclopedia* of 1991 is an interesting early example), and was refined into a characteristic working method by the publisher Dorling Kindersley.

The digital revolution also changed the typographic choices available to the book designer. As well as new display typefaces for use on covers (including a large number that tried to look hand lettered), new text designs emerged. The change of typesetting systems from metal to photocomposition in the 1960s and 1970s had not radically changed the range of typeface choice for book designers. While the cost of creating new designs was lower, typefaces were still proprietary to individual typesetting machine manufacturers, and still required expensive physical equipment. From the launch of the Postscript page description language in 1984, digital type became device-independent—any Postscript digital font could be output on any Postscript-enabled machine, be it a desktop printer, a digital typesetting machine, or a direct-to-plate system. The costs of creating a new typeface were those of design and marketing, not manufacture. The digital publishing environment also encouraged the design of typefaces that were both stronger in weight and sharper in design, intended to be displayed on screen or printed at low and medium resolution. These new typefaces were often highly successful in book design as well, displacing designs based on metal types which had been inadequately redrawn for the phototypesetting process. The typeface Swift (Gerard Unger, 1987), for example, performed well at small sizes in reference books. Traditional typefaces such as Garamond were reworked. Adobe Garamond Premier (Robert Slimbach, 2004) offered designers a range of fonts designed for specific sizes, so that display sizes could be lighter and more elegant, and text and footnote sizes open and clear. Furthermore, there was no longer any significant cost involved in combining several different typefaces in the same publication, and it became feasible for publishers, if they wanted to, to commission their own custom typefaces for corporate and general use.

DESIGN GENRES

At every point in history, a book's format (essentially its page size, but often encompassing the page extent and type of binding) has been related to its expected readership and their likely use of the book (Febvre and Martin 1976: 88–90). For example, scholars and students have read small, pocket editions since they were first produced by the printer Aldus Manutius (c.1449–1515) in the early sixteenth century; illustrated books are necessarily larger and often squarer (both in the shape of their page and in the style of binding) than text-only books; reference works require a sturdy, if plain, library binding; popular novels can be cheaply bound, as long as they have eye-catching covers. These expectations have given rise to distinctive genres of books with recognizable physical characteristics.

Much of a printed book's design is determined by the design genre for which it is intended. When thinking about design, genre can be defined as the interplay between the particular contents and intentions of a text (the 'topic structure'); the constraints of the physical format and the way this affects what can be expressed (the 'artefact structure'); and the opportunities the presentation gives to readers so that they can access information (the 'access structure') (Waller 1987: 139–43). Expectations that individual books comply with design genres are strong among publishers, the book trade, and readers, and, once established, these expectations can be resistant to change. Such change may eventually come about through developments in technology that offer (or require) new ways of designing.

Different genres not only require different overall design approaches, for example in the relationship between cover and interior design, but will also determine the division of labour between art director, designer, illustrator or picture researcher, and typesetter, and the way that the design team interact with editorial staff. Without being an exhaustive list, the following paragraphs identify a number of design genres common in book publishing today, and analyse their design approaches.

Academic books and journals share an emphasis on the typographic design of their text pages, but differ in that a journal article will be submitted for publication in a specified editorial format. Journals issue guidelines that exactly define for the author what hierarchy of heading levels, what style for references, and what kinds of illustration are acceptable; a monograph may be commissioned without such constraints being placed so explicitly on the author. Journals typically present both line and halftone illustrations in the text. Illustrations will be mechanically sized in simple increments to the underlying grid structure (often two-column) and placed on the page in predetermined positions (usually at the top or bottom of pages), with decisions on size and placement being made without concern for subtleties of visual effect or of positioning other than the requirement to fall after any reference in the text. This automation can undermine the use of visual arguments such as comparative or sequential illustrations, which may be split across pages. In monographs and scholarly editions, illustrations (if present) may still be collected together in plate sections, which can improve the quality of reproduction, but breaks the ideally immediate connection between text and image. In all kinds of academic publishing, typographic choices (style of type and mode of justification, positioning of headlines and page numbers) will often be traditional and conservative. Journal design therefore needs the typographer to pay close attention to flexible, modular systems of column grids, illustration and text sizing increments, and rules for make-up and page breaks, so that the design of individual articles can be achieved on an almost automatic basis. Academic monographs may have simpler heading hierarchies than journal articles, but different annotation requirements: for example, on-page footnotes and bibliographies rather than a list of references at the end of the article. Multi-author research works, on the other hand, may adopt the referencing style of journal articles. This relative predictability of content makes many monographs amenable to almost the same level of typographic standardization as journals.

Scholarly editions have long been among the most complex pieces of book typography, because they involve the detailed presentation of textual variants and may include both original and editorial annotation, line and section numbering systems to aid navigation, and parallel texts in different languages. For early modern texts, the representation of archaic typography such as marginal or inset notes also requires care in design and typesetting. For these reasons, unless scholarly editions are part of a prescribed series such as the Oxford Shakespeare, where overarching editorial guidelines determine the appearance of all the component texts, a book-by-book design approach is wisest.

College textbooks, readers, and handbooks share characteristic formats, larger than monographs. Double-column setting may be used in some sections to keep these necessarily long books within a reasonable extent, or to differentiate subsidiary content. The typography of textbooks is less conservative than in monographs or journals, partly because there is pedagogical value in clearly distinguishing the component elements of a chapter to make them explicit to the reader, but also because expenditure on design is more acceptable given the overall investment required in a major textbook. There is more scope in textbooks for careful page layout, but essentially a rule-based page makeup system is still appropriate, as the designer can pre-plan a number of templates for the various pedagogic elements which are used in different combinations as required. Call-outs and panels are a common feature which, along with information graphics (charts and tables), offer readers different points of access into the text. The object is to free the reading process from being simply linear through each chapter; instead, design can support the ease with which readers can look forward, select topics to engage with, and return to review what they have learnt.

Schoolbooks, language teaching, and adult education books typically require page-by-page planning by the designer, and in this respect they resemble magazines rather more than they do books without illustrations. Whereas the key structural component of a textbook is the chapter, and chapters may vary in length according to content, these books are usually planned so that the teaching unit is that of a classroom session, designed to fit a double-page spread or sequence of them, and on which various kinds of text and illustration are integrated. Indeed, given the large print runs involved and the need for production economy, the whole book is likely to have been planned from the outset to be written into a particular number of pages, so that the quantity and kind of illustrations can best be organized. The role of illustration in engaging the reader as well as providing information is considerably greater than in a textbook and this requires an art editor to select and commission illustrators to work with the editorial and design teams. Design is likely to progress through the preparation of sample sections which can be tested in classrooms, so that feedback can inform subsequent iterations of the design. A systematic approach is needed so that the design for students' books is reworked for teachers' books and workbooks. The kind of typographic reticence common in academic publications may be entirely absent in students' books: as long as the hierarchical structure of the text is clearly discernible, there is relative freedom for the designer to make spreads and sections different from one another if that enhances the learning process through engaging and allusive design features; after all, these books can never afford to be dull.

Dictionaries and reference books have always involved the use of economical typography to maximize the amount of information that can be conveyed in a given extent. Printed dictionaries are characterized by an extreme compression of language into a structure of repeating, code-like entries, and the typographic challenge is to present this complexity in a way that is easy to navigate. This can be achieved by carefully mapping the component parts of each entry (headword, pronunciation, labels, senses, variants, compounds) on to clearly differentiated typographic styles, using the full range of typeface variations available, so that the entry structure becomes obvious to the reader. From the 1990s, attempts were made to move away from highly compressed page designs in order to make school and learners' dictionaries more accessible. Entries that were conventionally set as a single paragraph were broken into sub-paragraphs to clarify their structure; this was facilitated by the availability of new digital typefaces. These had more flexible sizing than metal or photoset type, and were issued with many variant weights (Luna 2004). Dictionary illustration has also advanced from the use of small inset illustrations, in the style of wood engravings, to a more innovative use of colour illustration in learners' dictionaries (Luna 2013). But print dictionaries, constrained by space considerations and outdated as soon as they are published, are the genre most challenged by electronic distribution. While this began in the 1980s with the incorporation of publishers' data on dedicated devices, online dictionaries, and dictionaries built into operating systems and applications, are now normal.

Home reference manuals include any kind of infotainment book that can be bought by the general reader who wishes to understand how something works, or to learn a skill or hobby. They share the need for clear organization and explanation with schoolbooks, but they must also entertain. As a result, they place even more emphasis on illustration and high production values, and, unconstrained by syllabus requirements, their formats and extents are often considerably larger. Influences from magazine layout styles can be seen, but the need to encourage longer-term reader engagement usually leads to relatively controlled page designs, because readers perceive regular layouts with fewer visual distractions as indicative of reliability and quality (Moys 2017). Illustrations are used in complex ways to transmit information: single images may identify key subjects or features, sets of images may allow identification through different visual characteristics, while sequences of illustrations explain process and actions (Gillieson 2005). An early example, with only black and white line drawings, was the *Reader's Digest Repair Manual* of 1972. This approach was notably updated in the 1980s by the publishing house Dorling Kindersley. Their strategy was underpinned by developing a bank of high-quality, full-colour images, both photographic and photo-realistic. These were commissioned for use and reuse, and books were planned in units of double-page spreads whose composition depended on striking images—often a central large 'hero' image surrounded by several smaller ones. As significant was the working environment that Dorling Kindersley developed where, within subject areas, designers and editors worked side by side at the same desk, so that designs were developed, and text edited and rewritten to fit as collaboratively as possible. The resulting ease of iterating ideas and the books' focus on their imprint and format rather than on their authors—although authors of the highest quality were commissioned—led at best to highly innovative and highly visual volumes, but sometimes to repetitive and formulaic presentations. Over the decades, Dorling Kindersley has employed greater variation in typographic and graphic styles, and moved away from a regimented house style.

Novels and memoirs are normally the place for typography as plain and conventional as in any academic book. In fact there is a long history of allusive and sympathetic typography in literature. Well-known examples include the visual devices, including a black page, of *Tristram Shandy* (1759–67) and the use of marginal notes and cross-heads to evoke academic writing and newspaper typography respectively in *Ulysses* (1922). Greater flexibility in text composition systems in the 1990s facilitated the inclusion of typographic facsimiles of printed matter in novels such as Jonathan Coe's *What a Carve Up!* (Viking, 1994). Contemporary memoirs such as Edmund de Waal's *The Hare with*

Amber Eyes (Chatto & Windus, 2010) integrate illustrations into the text in a casual, almost inconsequential way, for effect as much as information, but rarely match the genuinely innovative use of completely integrated text and illustrations that characterizes Berger's *Ways of Seeing*.

Art books and books by artists can be thought of as a spectrum of genres where books may be straightforward presentations of images of works of art or architecture, or, when an artist chooses publication as a mode of art practice, can themselves be artworks rather than reproductions of them. For books about art, many galleries and art publishers prefer an ostentatious style, square in format and with heavy, square bindings. Some books act as neutral containers for the art they reproduce, others may allude to the artist under discussion through aspects of their design. A 2003 Phaidon volume on the work of Gordon Matta-Clark, whose site-specific practice involved piercing buildings to reveal their structures, appeared with a large chunk removed from its spine. The book provoked the comment that the designer was 'enter[ing] into competition with the artist', and raises the question of where the boundary lies between the designer's role as conduit of content and that of content creator (Goggin 2009). A different aspect of the designer's responsibility when designing for the serious reproduction of any work of art is the need for fidelity to the artefact and its physical dimensions. This often leads to self-imposed constraints on the cropping or sizing of art images. Ideally, related images should be reproduced at a constant scale, with the whole image reproduced without cropping, so that only details (declared as such) are presented cropped and in close-up (Birdsall 2004). For contemporary media, this fidelity means that reproductions of frames from cinema films or videos should respect the aspect ratio of the original and present the full, uncropped frame.

THE ELECTRONIC BOOK: FORWARDS OR BACKWARDS?

The complexity of all publishing design has been increased by the transition to electronic publishing. Whereas publishers of printed books were responsible for all aspects of the physical appearance of their books, and the way their publications were presented to the reader, the same cannot be said for electronic publications. Here the delivery platform (consisting of hardware and software) imposes its own design constraints, whether physical (the handling quality of the device), system-based (the default aspects of the interface, the screen resolution, and the text composition engine), or resource-based (the availability of fonts to render text). From the early 2000s, dedicated ebook reading devices took most of the design decisions away from publishers, treating the books they presented simply as a stream of words to be rendered in the most basic way possible. Intended for the simple, continuous prose of novels, they imposed defaults on all aspects of text presentation: font, spacing, justification, word-division. The EPUB 3 standard of 2011 (updated to 3.1 in 2017) allows for a reasonable amount of typographic control to be built into dedicated ebook reading devices, so that publishers can define fonts, justification, and spacing, and allows EPUB reader applications to run as software on general-purpose mobile devices (International Digital Publishing Forum 2017). But features defined in the EPUB standard, such as the ability to lock a heading to the text which follows it, are hardly ever implemented in EPUB-reading software. This is a degradation of the typographic standards that have been established in printed books. Such features are not simply typographical niceties, but an integral part of presenting language in a logical way so that the visual presentation reflects the underlying semantic structure of the text. It is an irony that this disregard for the visual rules for structuring text is at its worst when the text that is being rendered is stored in a carefully structured semantic mark-up language, XML.

Electronic editions of books are rightly seen as valuable when the reader is undertaking specific tasks such as search and annotation; they are invaluable when the reader wishes to instantly access the full text of a reference through a hyperlink. However, there are many non-linear reading strategies—turning back, looking forward, and even skipping—which they are less successful at supporting. The integration of illustrations is a particularly weak point, both on desktop and on mobile devices. An XML text stream is a single linear flow, and illustrations embedded in this cannot be laid out with any of the subtlety of a print layout. They are unlikely to be sized with consideration for their content or significance to the text. Layout is the arrangement of text and illustration elements to guide the reader and enhance meaning (Waller 2017). It is effectively lost in many on-screen presentations, unless they are specifically programmed as dedicated websites (for example the New Oxford Shakespeare website, 2016) or are presented as stand-alone apps for mobile devices (such as Faber's innovative *Waste Land* app, 2011).

A distinction can be drawn between fixed and flowed ebooks. When the reader wishes to enlarge the text on a flowed-layout edition, the text is recomposed at the larger size without the danger of text disappearing off the edge of the screen. But this is at the expense of destroying the visual relationships between headings and text or text and image. Fixed-layout ebooks reproduce, as their name implies, page layouts fixed by the designer, which respect text–image and other relationships. However, in order to reproduce what is essentially a printed page on the screen of a mobile device, the page design concept must be simple (as in children's picture books) or suffer from text that is too small to read on all but the largest screens. The EPUB standard supports both approaches, so that fixed-layout ebooks respect the publisher's layout decisions. Both options are equally searchable. This paradox, that the ease of electronic access can be detrimental to the visual enhancement of text that a good design brings, needs to be addressed.

DESIGN SKILLS FOR THE FUTURE

Expertise in design is a fundamental requirement of a publishing business, as design adds value at all levels: at brand level by projecting values and quality; at list and series level by supporting recognition and discoverability; and at individual book level by enhancing the reader experience. Book design practitioners need a wide range of skills, from understanding the context of the books they are working on and the relevant genre conventions, to the ability to understand the variety of electronic text-handling and layout applications and workflows that are current. When considering typeface choice, for example, a designer needs not only to appreciate the basics of typography and legibility, but also to understand the ramifications of cross-platform design. Should the same typeface be used in print, online, and for an ebook? Will they look the same when viewed on paper and on different types of screen, or should different weights or grades be specified depending on the rendering context (Luna 2017a)? Does the designer understand the digital rights aspects of embedding fonts within an app, and have the font manufacturer's end-user licence agreements been observed? Do the fonts contain the correct Unicode ranges to render any non-English language text that may be present? Are any non-Latin typefaces culturally appropriate for the text? Such questions indicate the engagement with technical knowledge that is required by publishing designers, alongside a visual sensibility and an understanding of how design for publishing reflects and presents language through technological means. While far removed from the world of metal typesetting and letterpress printing written about by Hugh Williamson in 1956, design for publishing is still, in his words, 'the practice of an industrial craft' (Williamson 1956).

References

Baines, Phil (2005). *Penguin by Design: A Cover Story 1935–2005*, London: Allen Lane.

Birdsall, Derek (2004). *Notes on Book Design*, New Haven, CT: Yale University Press.

Brill (2011). 'Introducing the "Brill" Typeface to Scholarship'. <http://www.brill.com/sites/default/files/brill_typeface_2011_for_author_use.pdf>.

Burke, Christopher (2007). *Active Literature: Jan Tschichold and the New Typography*, London: Hyphen Press.

Febvre, Lucien and Henri-Jean Martin (1976). *The Coming of the Book*, London: New Left Books.

Gillieson, Katherine (2005). 'Genetics of the "Open" Text', *Eye*, 57, pp. 26–35. <http://www.eyemagazine.com/feature/article/genetics-of-the-open-text>.

Goggin, James (2009). 'The Matta-Clark Complex', in *The Form of the Book Book*. Edited by Sara De Bondt and Fraser Muggeridge, London: Occasional Papers, pp. 23–31.

Heller, Steven (2013). 'Born Modern', *Eye*, 10, pp. 26–37.

Hollis, Richard (2009). 'Ways of Seeing Books', in *The Form of the Book Book*. Edited by Sara De Bondt and Fraser Muggeridge, London: Occasional Papers, pp. 49–60.

International Digital Publishing Forum (2017). 'EPUB'. <http://idpf.org/epub>.

Kennett, Bruce (2018). *W. A. Dwiggins: A Life in Design*, San Francisco, CA: Letterform Archive.

Kindel, Eric (2017). '*Future, Fortune*, and the Graphic Design of Information', in *Information Design: Research and Practice*. Edited by Alison Black, Paul Luna, Ole Lund, and Sue Walker, Abingdon: Routledge, pp. 127–46.

Luna, Paul (2004). 'Not Just a Pretty Face: The Contribution of Typography to Lexicography', in *Proceedings of the Eleventh Euralex International Congress*. Edited by Geoffrey Williams and Sandra Vessier, Lorient: Université de Bretagne Sud, pp. 847–58. <http://centaur.reading.ac.uk/21116/3/Luna_Euralex_final_Text_Pix.pdf>.

Luna, Paul (2013). 'Picture This: How Illustrations Define Dictionaries', in *Typography Papers 9*. Edited by Eric Kindel and Paul Luna, London: Hyphen Press, pp. 153–72.

Luna, Paul (2017a). 'Choosing Type for Information Design', in *Information Design: Research and Practice*. Edited by Alison Black, Paul Luna, Ole Lund, and Sue Walker, Abingdon: Routledge, pp. 479–86.

Luna, Paul (2017b). 'Design', in *A History of Oxford University Press*, Volume IV. Edited by Keith Robbins, Oxford: Oxford University Press, pp. 205–17.

McCleery, Alistair (2006). 'Tauchnitz and Albatross: A "Community of Interests" in English-Language Paperback Publishing, 1934–51', *The Library* 7(3), pp. 297–316. <https://doi.org/10.1093/library/7.3.297>.

McLean, Ruari (1976). *Joseph Cundall: A Victorian Publisher*, Pinner: Private Libraries Association.

Moys, Jeanne-Louise (2017). 'Visual Rhetoric in Information Design: Designing for Credibility and Engagement', in *Information Design: Research and Practice*. Edited by Alison Black, Paul Luna, Ole Lund, and Sue Walker, Abingdon: Routledge, pp. 205–20.

Powers, Alan (2001). *Front Cover: Great Book Jackets and Cover Design*, London: Mitchell Beazley.

Roberts, S. C. (1956). *The Evolution of Cambridge Printing*, Cambridge: Cambridge University Press.

Smith, Margaret M. (2004). 'Joseph Cundall and the Binding Design for the *Illustrated Biographies of the Great Artists*', *The Library* 5(1), pp. 39–63. <https://doi.org/10.1093/library/5.1.39>.

Twyman, Michael (1998). *Printing 1770–1970*, 2nd edition, London: British Library.

Waller, Rob (1987). 'The Typographic Contribution to Language: Towards a Model of Typographic Genres and their Underlying Structures'. PhD thesis, University of Reading. <https://www.academia.edu/5507107/The_typographic_contribution_to_language>.

Waller, Rob (2017). 'Graphic Literacies for a Digital Age: The Survival of Layout', in *Information Design: Research and Practice*. Edited by Alison Black, Paul Luna, Ole Lund, and Sue Walker, Abingdon: Routledge, pp. 177–203.

Williamson, Hugh (1956). *Methods of Book Design: The Practice of an Industrial Craft*, Oxford: Oxford University Press.

CHAPTER 20

PUBLISHING
AND TECHNOLOGY

JOHN W. MAXWELL

PUBLISHING AS HIGH TECHNOLOGY?

FROM the very beginning publishing has fundamentally been about technology—and indeed 'high technology'. But what does that mean? At face value, such an equation is so broad as to be almost meaningless. Let us try it the other way around, then: *publishing is fundamental to our modern understanding of technology*. Despite the fact that many today speak of the printed book as somehow set apart from the world of high tech, the history, present, and future of books and publishing are inextricably tangled with technological innovation and its constitutional relationship with modernity and post-modernity.

When we say 'high technology' we mean technology requiring specialized knowledge or expertise that is beyond the grasp of most people. So, unlike technologies like hammers or soup spoons—which almost anyone can make work—high technology, as in software development, electronics manufacturing, or indeed printing, is possible only with the specialization of knowledge and skills, the accumulation and control of capital and resources, and often very particular configurations of labour. The history of publishing is the history of successive waves of high technology, and the attendant organization of knowledge, labour, and capital. In fact publishing is very much a paradigmatic case—one which provides some of the oldest and most durable examples of such organizational forms. Hence, while publishing relies on technology, it is an activity which has helped define technology in the modern world.

In 1973 the American science fiction writer Arthur C. Clarke famously claimed that, 'Any sufficiently advanced technology is indistinguishable from magic.' The aphorism speaks to our aspirational relationship with technology and innovation: on one level, we see it as rational and governed by predictable rules and models, but on another level, we are

328 JOHN W. MAXWELL

often seduced by the *uncanny* power technology seems to confer. The latest greatest smartphone's features are perhaps the most convenient example of this dual nature, but consider the story of Johannes Fust, who was a creditor and business partner of Johannes Gutenberg in the 1440s and 1450s in Mainz.

As the story goes, Johannes Fust loaned a good deal of money to Gutenberg to develop his innovating printing system and produce his now-famous edition of the Bible (White 2018: 24). But Fust then brought suit against Gutenberg just at this moment his famous Bible edition was being completed. Gutenberg was left with nothing, while Fust and his future son-in-law Peter Schöffer took everything, including the Bibles. Fust went to Paris with a stock of the newly printed Bibles and began selling them. He kept the printing technology strictly secret, and so the Bibles were sold as manuscripts, produced by hand by scribes. But authorities in Paris were soon made aware that the Bibles were uncannily identical. Magic! In fact, *witchcraft* was the charge brought before Johannes Fust, forcing him to reveal the technological secret behind the perfect copies he was attempting to sell. The story is all the more interesting in that Fust—sometimes spelled Faust—is held by some to be the inspiration for the legend of Dr Faustus, who sold his soul to the devil in exchange for 'unlimited knowledge' (see Schafer 1926; Meggs and Purvis 2004: 73).

Fust, along with the hapless Gutenberg, was trading in industrially manufactured items in an era when handcraft was the rule. It is not so surprising that his efforts were interpreted with suspicion by people who had no experience of such things (Eisenstein 2011). Today, we can see Gutenberg's innovations as the beginning of a momentous shift in how the world is organized, the beginnings of industrial capital (that which bankrupted Gutenberg himself), of interchangeable parts, mass production, and economies of scale. Technology theorist Lewis Mumford pointed out that publishing—or printing at least—is the one of the original models of industrial production, and of the industrial revolution (Mumford 2010 [1934]). Of Mumford's framing, Marshall McLuhan wrote, 'Lewis Mumford has suggested that the clock preceded the printing press in order of influence on the mechanization of society. But Mumford takes no account of phonetic alphabet as the technology that had made possible the visual and uniform fragmentation of time' (McLuhan 1965: 147).

Technology is often assessed in terms of its outputs, but it is also important to attend to the transformations it brings about. Industrial manufacturing transformed labour, and the organization of labour; it transformed how people thought about natural resources and the raw materials enlisted in industrial manufacturing. The ability to mass produce texts has one set of effects on the circulation of ideas and the spread of literacy. It has a different set of effects on the manufacture and supply of paper, and ink; on training and the organization of knowledge and skills; on the investment and return in capital and financial resources; on ideas of ownership of equipment, know-how, and ultimately, intellectual property. Technology transforms, or translates, one set of things into another (Callon and Latour 1981). Rags are turned into paper; paper turned into books; men are turned into apprentices, journeymen, guildsmen; populations turned into markets; ideas into property.

Inventions and Innovations

It is common to start the history of publishing with Gutenberg's system of movable type in the 1450s, and this chapter will follow this commonplace milestone. But Gutenberg's innovations relied on several other technologies already in place. An overview introduction to the various technologies of printing is in Keith Houston's overview *The Book* (2016).

Cheap, readily available paper has a very long history beginning with Egyptian papyrus many thousands of years ago, then parchment and vellum, made from specially prepared animal skins (from later centuries BCE), and finally paper itself, credited to a Chinese official of the Han Dynasty in the first century AD (Brokaw and Kornicki 2013). The mass production of paper in Europe didn't happen until the twelfth century, but by the fifteenth century, it was something upon which the first generation of European printers could rely. Ink, probably invented in antiquity in both China and Egypt independently, had been a concoction of charcoal, a stabilizer like gum arabic or animal glue, and water (Houston 2016: 85). Ink was similarly old, 'low tech' by Gutenberg's time.

The book itself—in the sense of the 'codex' form, in which folded gatherings of paper are sewn together at one edge and bound together into a single volume with many pages—is also much older than Gutenberg, probably from the first century CE. By the late Middle Ages, books were common enough in clerical and court contexts, although they were all the products of painstaking handcraft.

The printing press was not itself a significant innovation, but rather an adaptation of technology already in use to press grapes for wine. And even the idea of using a press to print an image was not new to Gutenberg. Woodblock printing, in which an image is carved in relief, inked, and then pressed onto paper, is much, much older. Chinese woodblock printing dates to at least the seventh century CE (Brokaw and Kornicki 2013: xvii), and European examples abound by Gutenberg's time.

Even 'movable type', that which we most closely associate with Gutenberg and the 1450s, pre-dates him significantly, especially in Asia. The idea of creating individual characters that could be assembled to create a text on the printing press can be traced to a number of precursors in East Asia—where printing types were cast in porcelain as early as the eleventh century in by Bi Sheng in China and in metal by the twelfth or thirrteenth century in Korea (Brokaw and Kornicki 2013: xviii–xxx).

The Mass Production of Writing

If the book, printing, and even movable type itself pre-date Gutenberg by centuries, then what is so special about his invention in Mainz in the 1450s? Popular conceptions tend to credit Gutenberg with inventing the mass production of texts (printing) or the interchangeable parts on the press (movable type), but a better way of understanding Gutenberg's invention is the mass production of *type*—the metal letterforms themselves.

In order to set more than a very small amount of type—more than a page at a time—a printer requires a very large number of 'sorts', the individual metal pieces of the alphabet. If the letter 'e' is the most common letter in the English language, think how many little metal 'e's are needed to print something like a book. Johannes Gutenberg came up with a system for creating individual sorts very cheaply, easily, and on demand. A printing operation could thus scale up to the production of an entire book—or even multiple books being produced simultaneously—because Gutenberg's system facilitated the mass production of an almost unlimited number of printing sorts, as needed.

Gutenberg's system involved cutting a master punch for each letter in soft steel which was then hardened. The punch was then used to create a letterform impression in softer metal like copper. Then, a very clever device was clamped together around the impression, making a perfect, regularly sized mould, and a molten lead alloy poured in. The result was a piece of type, with a raised letterform surface ready for ink, and of exactly the right dimensions to fit perfectly alongside the next piece of type, and the next. The mass production of perfectly interchangeable printing sorts made it possible to scale up printing operations so that entire books could be produced.

In the development and perfection of this system, Gutenberg is also credited with innovations in several other critical sub-components: an oil-based ink which would adhere to metal type (ink had traditionally been—and still is, in many cases—water-based); and the specific metal alloy (of lead, tin, and antimony) used to cast individual sorts. If we are to believe the whole story, Gutenberg's contribution is perhaps best cast as a painstaking engineering project rather than an event.

More broadly, though, Gutenberg's innovations do not give us the book, or even the mass-production of pages—these predate Gutenberg by centuries—but rather a more subtle idea: the mass production of letters themselves; indeed, the mass production of writing. This seems to be the innovation which allows books and writing to achieve a social and cultural currency on a scale never before seen.

ALDUS MANUTIUS:
PRINTING TO PUBLISHING

Gutenberg was a printer, but not so much a *publisher* as we might recognize today. His former colleagues Fust and Schoeffer have a much clearer claim to this title, especially with their production of the 1457 Mainz Psalter, the first book to carry a printer's mark crediting its producers. But the modern model of the publisher comes much more clearly from Aldus Manutius, who in the 1490s and early 1500s in Venice developed a substantial publishing operation, blending numerous innovations in typography, editorial vision, and the form of the book itself to pioneer a market-driven, technological powerhouse that continues to serve as inspiration for publishers five centuries later.

Aldus' early career was as a scholar and tutor. The late fifteenth century saw the flourishing of classical and humanist scholarship in Italy—especially in the wake of the fall of

Constantinople in 1453, when collections of classical manuscripts were brought to Venice and other Italian port cities by escaping scholars and nobles. Aldus came of age in this time of relative scholarly riches, teaching Latin and especially Greek to the sons of Italian noblemen. The exact reasons for his turn to the printing profession are not clear, but in the early 1490s Aldus arrived in Venice and began working with printer Andrea Torresani. Between 1494 and his death in 1515, the Aldine press released at least thirty-nine editions in Greek, more than fifty in Latin, plus a number of contemporary Italian works; his lists span classical literature, philosophy, theology, and grammar instruction, and include early editions or indeed *editio princeps* (first printings) of a good deal of what we today would consider the classical canon, including such names as Aristotle, Sophocles, Herodotus. These were editions specially crafted for a scholarly and student audience, carefully edited, typically without marginalia or commentary, designed to be definitive editions for study. Aldus' editions were typically printed in runs of 1000 or more (Lowry 1979).

Aldus' technological innovations are numerous, ranging from the domain of editorial and design (he is credited with the early development of the semicolon) and typography (the Aldine press produced four different Greek typefaces, a number of very influential roman typefaces that are still copied today, and his editions pioneered the use of *italic* type, mimicking the humanist manuscript hand of his contemporaries). Most famously, though, Aldus popularized the *octavo* edition: small format pocket-sized books that could be easily carried with one, bringing the practices of reading and study out of the library and scriptorium and into public and even domestic life. The implications of the wide circulation of pocket-sized books are not unlike the move to mobile Internet-connected devices today, thus ending the 'desktop paradigm'. Taken together, Aldus' many innovations help paint a portrait of a new kind of publisher, tailoring both his operations and his products on numerous levels to meet the needs and desires of an *audience* and *market* he imagined and, critically, brought into being through his publications.

With the Aldine press, we begin to see a model of a publisher who leverages technologies and technological innovations in order to address and serve audiences and publics on a scale hitherto unimagined. Attendant with this scaling up of the written word come the many concerns of the modern, industrial publishing operation: access to capital, inventory management, labour relations, distribution, and marketing.

MECHANIZATION AND ECONOMIES OF SCALE

Gutenberg's system for making movable type—which had spread across Europe in just a few decades—provided a means for the mechanization of writing, of the mass production of letters on the page. But it didn't mechanize much else. The simple printing press of the day allowed for the mass production of pages, and thus the manufacturing of books and pamphlets at scale, but this was still a very labour-intensive process. But, however slow and difficult it may have been, early printing revealed a mode of production qualitatively different from the handcraft production that preceded and indeed still underpinned it. Mass production by printing press allowed printers and publishers to imagine the costs of production at scale, rather than in terms of individual creations.

The industrial revolution came to be based on the idea of 'economies of scale'. In a pure handcraft process like, say, cabinetmaking, it costs the same, in terms of time and labour, to produce the first cabinet as it does the second cabinet, which is the same as the cost to produce the tenth or hundredth cabinet as well. There is no economic advantage or efficiency in *scale*. But in mechanized industrial production, as early printing proved, there is an efficiency in greater scale. The cost of typesetting a page, inking the press, and installing a sheet of paper, will be substantial, in terms of time, labour, and materials. But the cost of taking a *second* impression of the same page will be much, much less. The *incremental* or *marginal cost* of producing just one more unit is drastically reduced. Further, the *unit cost*—that is, the averaged cost of any one single page—effectively declines as the print run increases: the unit cost in a run of 1,000 is much less than in a run of 100, because the *sunk cost* of preparing that first page is amortized over the whole run. If a printer can then sell all 1,000 copies he has made, there will be profit at the end of the day.

Today, we live in a world in which such economies of scale rule almost everything around us. Mobile phones and consumer electronics, for instance, are produced in the *tens of millions* in order to keep the unit costs low—and thus the profit margins high. The cost of producing something like an iPhone in quantities of only a thousand or so would drive the unit costs so high as to make it impossible to bring to market. But the basic logic of this model was worked out by Gutenberg and his immediate successors. Aldus' efforts to create a market for Greek and Latin works involved much more than printing a thousand at a time; it also required the cultivation of a network of both readers (that is, buyers) and middlemen who could distribute and market the books at scale. It didn't hurt that Venice was one of the major trading ports of the day. Aldus' careful consideration of who his audience was, and what they would find appealing, is key to his success. Printing a thousand copies of Sophocles' *Seven Tragedies* would be a quick way to go bankrupt unless one also has a way to distribute and sell most, if not all, of those copies in a timely manner. Mass production also requires a mass audience, and the means to serve it.

The purely technical components of Gutenberg's—or Aldus'—operation are few. They involve a metallurgical operation producing type; a simple system of wooden and metal frames for arranging type in lines and pages; methods for making (or purchasing) both oil-based ink and standard-sized paper, and a press for putting ink on pages. This is, of course, far from the whole story; books needed to be assembled and bound, inventory needed to be organized, distributors and booksellers would have to be organized, inventory distributed (and organized again), and the reading public had to be educated about the availability and desirability of the books. If any of these pieces failed, the publisher would start losing money quickly. The organization and control of the whole system is much harder to see, and yet even more critical to its success.

There are, in effect, at least three technological layers of this early publishing system: there are the overtly 'technical' pieces of industrial manufacturing, mostly found in the press room itself. Second, there are the many instances of handcraft—from editing and typesetting to collating and binding, as well as transportation, warehousing, and selling of finished books. And third there is the organization of the network of labour, money, and social capital that is required to bring books to market at scale.

Technology is therefore only partly about developing clever ways of making physical things like ink, paper, and pages. It is also very much about ways of organizing both material things and people. One important aspect of this organization work is *standardization*. Arguably, Gutenberg's greatest achievement is the moulding device that produced individual type sorts in a form that let them fit neatly together in perfect lines on the press. Gutenberg's type is perhaps the earliest instance of 'interchangeable parts', which would later become one of the hallmarks of industrial production, in which standardized parts come together in a common, regularized production process. But while mechanization demands standardization, industrial production also calls for the standardization of labour and roles. Indeed, as some have argued, the industrial demand for standardized labour—standardized people—makes human beings part of the process of mechanization. The implication for labour and labour relations is immense.

INDUSTRIALIZATION: BETTER, FASTER, CHEAPER

The printing process employed by early printer-publishers like Johann Gutenberg and Aldus Manutius involved a core of mechanization surrounded by large amounts of handcraft and labour. Over the next four centuries, the story of publishing technology is one where, one by one, the labour-intensive parts of the process become mechanized, in the pursuit of faster, cheaper, more consistent production.

The *papermaking* process has gradually shifted from an intensive handcraft operation to enormous mechanized paper mills. In the nineteenth century, fully mechanized, roller-based *Fourdrinier* machines were developed to produce a continuous 'web' of paper, scaling up the speed and efficiency of production immensely—this model of paper production is still used today, as is the handcrafted product, in certain niche contexts.

Improved *printing presses* incorporated more efficient methods of moving paper through the press and better ways of transferring ink to the paper, initially by abandoning the vertical-action wine-press design for iron presses powered by steam, and later by using rollers to move a continuous 'web' of paper in contact with inked surfaces. In the early nineteenth century, the advent of *lithographic* printing replaced the 'relief' technique of inking raised metal type with a system in which ink adheres to the dry part of a special surface—originally stone, hence 'litho', but later via thin aluminum printing plates[1]—which

---

[1] The earliest metal printing plates were made by taking a mould of a printing forme and casting the whole thing in copper. The resulting copper plate could be used again and again, and was especially useful for bits of print used repeatedly from job to job. This technique, called 'stereotyping' gave its name to any thoughtlessly repeated idea. Satisfyingly, the French term for the same thing is *cliché*, a term which derives from the sound made during the casting process!

334 JOHN W. MAXWELL

also allowed the printing of illustrations alongside text. The 'offset' press, developed late in the nineteenth century, transferred ink from a printing plate to a rubber roller and from there to the paper, resulting in significantly greater control and accuracy of inking. Today, the 'offset litho' process is dominant in most commercial printing, scaled up to speeds and production levels unimaginable by the early printers.

Metal type continued to be the foundation of the process, however, until the mid-twentieth century, when typesetting and platemaking finally gave way to a photographic process, with images of type exposed onto film and the resulting film negative used to photo-chemically produce printing plates. *Photographic processing* made much of the printing process vastly more flexible via myriad darkroom techniques. In the 1970s, laser-based (photocopier) technology, in which a laser beam draws an image on a receptive surface, was married with the photographic process; the resulting 'imagesetter' machines could produce incredibly high-quality computer-generated imagery on a photographic negative, from which printing plates could then be made.

The *sewing and binding* of books—for centuries a craft-intensive bespoke process—was itself revolutionized in the nineteenth century. Starched cloth stretched over boards in a specially designed press allowed not just the mechanization of the process, but also made book bindings and covers into a printable surface that could contain text and artwork to identify and advertise the book (Lundblad 2015), making the bindery a core part of the publishing process, and not just an afterthought to printing.

The mechanization of these various processes had significant effects for publishers and printers; they allowed for greater efficiencies, and especially efficiencies of scale (where unit costs decline as print runs increase), and they shifted the industry away from its reliance on skilled craftspeople and instead to industrial labour. This scaling up also made printing cheaper, and with it the numbers and reach of the printed books, magazines, newspapers, and other printed works.

From Mechanizing Type to Digitizing the Word

At the end of the nineteenth century, the last major piece of printing technology that remained wedded to painstaking handcraft was typesetting itself. As in Gutenberg's process in the 1450s, individual sorts needed to be hand-picked from type cases (literally from the UPPER CASE and the lower case) and set, one-by-one, in a composing stick, then transferred to the galley. This is slow, painstaking work that resisted mechanization for hundreds of years.

In the 1890s, two systems emerged almost simultaneously that would finally change this: the *Linotype* machine which cast a whole line of type at a time, and the *Monotype* machine, which cast individual sorts in order. Both machines were driven by a compositor working at a keyboard instead of handling metal type directly. Both machines cast type 'just in time', and so are called examples of 'hot metal' typesetting. Both systems sped up the typesetting process by an order of magnitude, and changed the printing industry enormously (Brewer 1971: ch. 7). The differences between these two systems are worth dwelling on:

The Linotype, developed by the German-American Ottmar Mergenthaler, was an engineering marvel; Thomas Edison famously proclaimed it 'the eighth wonder of the world'. Like a steampunk church organ, it was a great piece of machinery consisting of keyboard, metal-casting system, and a clockwork assembly of key-like brass 'matrices' from which the type would be shaped. A key pressed on the keyboard would cause the appropriate brass matrix to be released from its place in a large magazine. As the compositor typed, the matrices would slide into place until an entire line was ready. Spaces between words could be adjusted by metal wedges in order to achieve perfect justification. Then the entire line was pressed into a mould and hot type metal injected. A few minutes later, a cooling 'slug' emerged from the machine, ready for the printing galley. And the various matrices found their way individually back to the magazine from whence they came. In operation, driven by an electric motor, a Linotype makes a rhythmic, almost musical beat, like the jingling of hundreds of keys. The typesetting floor at a large daily newspaper, with dozens of Linotype machines running simultaneously, would have been orchestral, or at least cacophonous.

The Monotype machine, developed by Tolbert Lanston, had a different design. It was separated into two parts: a compositing system, again driven by a keyboard, and a casting machine which produced type on demand. The two machines were connected via a system based on punched paper tape; the patterns of holes punched in the tape represented the sequence of letters entered on the keyboard, as well as a calculation of the total width of the letters, and therefore the amount of space needed between words on a given line. The paper tape was then fed into the casting machine, and the just-in-time hot metal type produced with the appropriate spacing. As the machine cast individual letters, typos could be fixed by simply replacing a sort; an advantage that gave the Monotype system an edge in some kinds of printing (e.g. books) while the greater speed of Linotype led it to market dominance in other sectors (e.g. newspapers). And the two systems influenced each other over the decades; notably, Linotype machines were soon adapted to paper-tape input, allowing a composition staff—often made up of women—to be managed separately from the printing staff (see Cockburn 1991). The number of compositor stations need not be the same as the number of casting stations, depending on the volume and demands of the operation, not to mention the dynamics of labour relations.

Monotype and Linotype systems were in heavy use in printing up until computer-driven photographic typesetting systems were developed in the 1960s and 1970s. Critically, a few key developments from hot-metal typesetting were enormously influential in the computing paradigm that followed. First was the idea of driving the system via punched paper tape, which is to say, by *code*. The codes inscribed in paper tape, as with telegraph codes for sending early messages over wires, effectively render the alphabet as a series of digits. Those digits, or codes, can then be transferred across time and distance (via wire, or tape, or magnetic media) as well as manipulated or edited in that form—between keyboard and caster. Second, the algorithms and metrics for calculating the width of a particular line, and thus the amount of space needed for proper justification, means that the line is, again, rendered as a set of numbers describing the text. The standardization of both of these systems—first the abstract representation of the letters themselves, and second of information about the sequence of letters—are foundational precursors to modern computing. It is not coincidental that, up until the advent of the smartphone, almost every computer has had a keyboard in front of it. Typesetting machines are very much part of the history of computing.

COMPUTER-BASED TYPESETTING

If the compositor's text can be rendered as an abstract code on paper tape, and then paper tape later used as input for a casting machine, then a computer can be put in the middle of that operation, both as a recipient for the text and as a source for the casting machine. A simple application of this might be for editing and correcting. If the text is entered into a computer, it can be corrected, edited, indexed, stored before it goes to press. More broadly, computers can manage the entire typesetting and composing operation—and they did, especially in the 1970s with the rise of computer-driven photo-typesetting machines. Phototypesetting uses images of letters exposed onto photographic film by way of light, a far quicker and more flexible medium than metal—and much more amenable to being speeded up and processed by computer.

By the 1970s, computer-driven phototypesetting began to overtake metal typesetting in the printing industry, with resulting disruption to both the International Typographical Union, which was at its peak in the 1960s (and was dissolved in the 1980s) and capital (indeed, many dominant manufacturers of typesetting equipment, including the Mergenthaler Linotype Corporation, now sell digital fonts, if they exist at all). By the 1980s, computer-driven laser printing devices occupied both high-end printing shops and office desktops. Typesetting became something handled entirely by software, standardized by Adobe Systems' *PostScript* technology, which effectively made desktop computers and laser printers part of an end-to-end typesetting and page-imaging system. PostScript forms the basis of Adobe's PDF software, which has become the de-facto standard for delivering and viewing page-based files.

THE DIGITAL PARADIGM

In considering the significance of digital technology, it is useful to think about the alphabet itself. As Marshall McLuhan and others have pointed out, the alphabet and alphabetic literacy are fundamental to the development of industrial modernity. In *The Gutenberg Galaxy*, Marshall McLuhan wrote, 'The breaking up of every kind of experience into uniform units in order to produce faster action and change of form (applied knowledge) has been the secret of Western power over man and nature alike' (McLuhan 1962: 93). The phonetic alphabet—developed by the Phoenicians about 3,000 years ago and in evolution ever since—lends itself to such translation by reducing the *material* of representation to just a couple of dozen glyphs (e.g. in English we use just twenty-six letters) that can be assembled and reassembled in a famously infinite number of ways. Digital computing extends this reduction by limiting the material of representation to just *two* states.[2] In our ability to translate wide swaths of media—not just numbers and text but image, audio, video, and beyond—into binary digital code, we have effectively created a master code capable of representing almost any expression.

The standardization of the representation of the alphabet in the early 1960s—in the English-speaking world as the ASCII standard—drew from the very same tradition as early telegraph codes and the perforated tape systems that Monotype and Linotype machines incorporated. The effect of the standard was to establish the digital computer as a text-processing device in addition to its earliest use as a calculating machine—indeed, the computer as a communications medium dates to these earliest years too. By the mid-1960s computer networks were a major area of research, development, and efforts to standardize, and by 1969, an operating ARPAnet, the direct precursor to today's Internet, connected a handful of university sites in the USA. Email inboxes began to fill up immediately.

Standards are only as good as the thinking that goes into them, of course. As global computer networks evolved, the ASCII standard, based on a decidedly anglophone worldview (the ASCII character set includes roughly what is possible to produce on an American-made typewriter) was clearly not up to the multilingual tasks that were asked of it. After decades of 'alternative' and 'extended' character sets, a new standard for representing not just the alphabet but writing systems from around the world was established in the late 1990s: Unicode. Unicode—theoretically at least—represents a possible 128,000 characters (ASCII defines just 127), although individual implementations—such as the character support within a given font—are typically more limited. Unicode is, however, a much more robust standard upon which to build global text processing and publishing systems.

Bottom-up and Top-down Digital

Computers were used in printing and publishing operations as early as the mid-1960s, but effective standards came much later. The ability to enter and store electronic text which could be edited and corrected before further output was an obvious early application. As

---

[2] Etymologically, 'digital computing' almost literally means counting on one's fingers; a computer has only one finger. It can be argued that the turning point in the development of the digital computer, bringing together the formative theorizing of mathematicians Alan Turing and George Boole, was when Claude Shannon in the 1930s realized a *concrete* means of representing binary logic in electronic circuits—thus giving the computer digits to count with.

computer systems became more complex, their own documentation needs began to drive these applications. A notable early example was Unix, a hugely influential multi-user operating system developed at AT&T Bell Laboratories in the early 1970s and effectively 'leaked' out to computer science departments around the world over the next decade.[3] Unix boasted a highly modular design, with components that could be upgraded or added to over time. An early design decision was to embed the system documentation within the system itself, and as a result, the Unix operating system contained a suite of tools (called the 'Documentor's Workbench') that supported the internal system documentation: from text editor, word counter, spell checker to screen-reading tools and—by the mid-1970s—a typesetting application so that the system docs could be output to a phototypesetting machine, and later, to laser printers.

The basic strategy for such computer-driven typesetting was to embed formatting codes within a text document. The codes would be identified or delimited by a special character sequence that distinguished them from the text itself: an early example is a period at the beginning of a line indicating that the rest of that line contained formatting instructions rather than the text itself. In practice, such a system was fairly unwieldy to read and edit; as a result, over time the systems and conventions for these embedded codes became more concise, encapsulating the gory details of machine-specific typesetting codes within a simple shorthand (such as '.BQ' that might indicate that the following text should be formatted as a block quotation). This approach was known as 'generic markup' as the coding convention attempted to be as neutral and device-independent as possible.

Generic markup was taken up as a document-production strategy in earnest by a team at IBM in the 1970s, and this work eventually became enshrined as one of the most significant standards in digital publishing: Standard Generalized Markup Language, or SGML (Goldfarb and Rubinsky 1991). SGML specified a method for embedding information *about* a document within the document, typically using < and > characters as delimiters. The 'metadata' about the text enclosed within those delimiters were known as 'tags' that described the text. A block quotation could delimited by a pair of <block-quotation> tags, serving as an instruction for processing software to format the enclosed text accordingly. Further, SGML specified that pairs of tags must be neatly nested within one another; the result is that a marked-up document, when parsed by processing software, produces a hierarchical graph—a tree-structure—which makes further processing even more flexible.

SGML proved very influential in industrial documentation (esp. military and aerospace firms) but not so much in traditional publishing. But, in the early 1990s, Tim Berners-Lee developed a simple system for making cross-references to documents across the Internet; his system for embedding cross-reference data in a document was based on SGML. Berners-Lee called his system The World-Wide Web, and his embedding language HTML (HyperText Markup Language).

---

[3] Unix or Unix-derived systems form the underpinnings of most operating systems in use today, powering the majority of Internet hosts, iPhones, Androids, mobile devices, and many embedded systems devices.

The conceptual simplicity of generic markup, initially designed to be device-independent with respect to typesetters and printers, made it a robust technology on which to grow a global, massively pluralist network of documents like the World Wide Web. The SGML standard itself was updated with the Internet in mind in 1997 and re-named XML, but HTML itself remains the language of the Web, and is today by far the most dominant publishing technology, with literally trillions of pages of information published in this format.

What You See Is What You Get

At roughly the same time, an entirely different evolution of computer-driven publishing was taking place. At Xerox' Palo Alto Research Centre (PARC) in the 1970s, a group led by Alan C. Kay were interested in developing a 'personal' computer. Kay and his team envisioned a new digital literacy for the twenty-first century, based on widely accessible computing devices. Such a vision would mean a different relationship between individuals and computing technology; it would require portable, wirelessly-networked computers that act as 'personal dynamic media', taking the place of print-based media and indeed print literacy. Xerox PARC developed a host of new technologies over a decade, including desktop computers, peer-to-peer networking, object-oriented programming, and multimedia 'authoring software'. One of the many software applications prototyped at Xerox PARC was a word processor that showed onscreen a direct representation of a finished page—and that could be directly manipulated in real time by a designer via mouse and keyboard.

Xerox famously failed to bring these innovations to market itself (Smith and Alexander 1988), but by the early 1980s, other companies either adopted the technology or spun off from Xerox to develop new applications. Apple Computer's Steve Jobs visited Xerox PARC in 1979 and came away with the idea for the Macintosh. The developers of the word processing application ended up at Microsoft. Adobe Systems, founded on the image-description language PostScript, which allowed onscreen pages to be replicated on high-quality laser printers, was spun off by Xerox engineers John Warnock and Chuck Geschke.

The 'desktop publishing' paradigm took off rapidly after the release of the Apple Macintosh computer in the mid 1980s. A software application, Aldus PageMaker, provided a powerful onscreen design tool for book, magazine, and newspaper production. Apple's *LaserWriter* printer brought laser imaging to the consumer market in 1985, using Adobe's PostScript technology. By the early 1990s, this cluster of software and hardware had matured, and, with the advent of Microsoft Word, became a dominant paradigm for publishing. Printers—and especially typesetting shops—were forced to adapt, or else go out of business. Indeed, the effect on the typesetting profession was cataclysmic. Anyone with a Macintosh could now set type and produce books, magazines, newspapers, posters, and so on. The mass democratization of the tools of the trade were heralded as a boon by many, and decried as the worst thing that ever happened to typography by others. Adobe Systems began to sell typefaces, offering a vast library of digital fonts for sale. Long-established typefoundries (*foundries* indeed!) were lucky if they could compete in such an environment.

However successful the desktop publishing paradigm, its key limitation is clear: the printed page. Desktop publishing software is geared to laying out ink on paper; that is, fixed imagery on a fixed field. With the meteoric rise of the Internet and World Wide Web as a means of publishing and reaching audiences, the traditional page only goes so far. In the online realm, the HTML-dominated world of the web browser has been far more influential. Adobe Systems' PDF software, while enormously successful in its own right, is an odd survival of page-based media in an otherwise screen-based world. Media scholar Lisa Gitelman's book, *Paper Knowledge* (2014) does an excellent job of tracing PDF's survival in the online era.

Adobe's composition software—especially its InDesign and Illustrator tools—have gradually incorporated more and more web-oriented features, but the fundamental premise of the layout of pages in the hands of the designer/compositor has remained somewhat at odds with the dominant trends in online publishing, which have come to have more to do with dynamic, personalized, template-driven content-management systems than with bespoke page design, especially in a pluralistic reading environment populated by desktop computers, laptops, tablets, and mobile phones of all sizes and varieties.

AN ELECTRONIC BOOK?

Regardless of how exactly we produce digital texts and documents, digital publication fundamentally changes the industrial logic of economies of scale. In digital reproduction and distribution, there is no 'incremental cost'. The cost of producing a second copy, or a thousandth copy, or a billionth copy, is effectively zero; the cost isn't exactly zero, because servers, bandwidth, and electricity do cost money. But the cost of making copies is orders of magnitude less than in the industrial manufacturing context. The digital computer and the digital network are copying technologies par excellence; copying is essential to their functioning. This presents difficulties for copyright law, certainly, but it presents even thornier problems for publishing business models with their roots in Gutenberg's revolution.

Yet even so, the ebook has occupied the public imagination since at least the 1990s, existing as a kind of conceptual inevitability: just as we have digital music, digital video, we would of course have to have digital books and magazines. It took until 2007—when Amazon's Kindle launched—for the ebook to become real in the marketplace, but it fulfilled, to some extent, the expectation that readers would in the future turn to electronics instead of paper.

And yet, the ebook is marketed and sold almost exactly as if it were a paper book. It is priced lower, but often not unrecognizably lower; it is sold on a title-by-title basis, and its market performance is still reckoned in units sold, with royalties to authors still paid on more or less the same basis as printed books. With the exception of its weightlessness, there is very little in the ebook of the early twenty-first century to signal that it is in fact a digital product. Rather, the ebook appears to be designed to resemble the printed book in as many ways as possible—particularly in how it travels through sales channels (Rowberry 2015). Despite the seismic disruption we might expect from a technology which completely and utterly changes the economic model of publishing, what we have seen so far in digital books appears to be a sort of 'backeddy' in the larger digital flow, a curious holdover of tropes and modalities from the age of print. At times the ebook ecology—dominated by Amazon's Kindle (reading devices, apps, store, and publishing pathways) but repeated in general shape by a number of much smaller competitors (e.g. Kobo) and edged with partial participation by the likes of Apple (whose iPad and iBooks apps seem to define the upper aesthetic end) and Google, whose vast book-scanning project was stillborn as of 2011 (Somers 2017). Where the open World Wide Web has like a juggernaut plowed through great swathes of western culture, from journalism to match-making, the electronic book seems, by comparison, to have been designed to be as little disruptive to publishers as possible (Bjarnason 2013).

On the other hand, digital technology has brought radical disruption to bookselling. Amazon.com in particular has almost single-handedly revolutionized bookselling: on one hand in capturing a majority of all global book sales—print *and* electronic—and on the other hand in the idea of a bookstore being, in a way, a *front* for a multi-billion dollar Internet-services company. Amazon's dominance of electronic commerce, metadata and inventory management, and especially customer-relations management (CRM) has been near total, an innovative firm who would re-write the rules of business by re-organizing almost every aspect of modern capitalism around ubiquitous, easily scalable digital technology. Amazon's rate of growth and market dominance have outpaced not only its competitors in online retail but also its suppliers—that is, publishers—to the extent that it defies most traditional ways of thinking about the publishing industry. The ebook, to Amazon, seems almost incidental to its larger business operations; the ebook is a way to reduce inventory costs, a way to satisfy impulse buying urges on the part of its customers, but more importantly just one touch-point among many in a long-term customer relations strategy that puts Amazon at the centre of a lifetime of media (and physical goods) consumption for hundreds of millions of people. For Amazon, digital technology wasn't a means to change how books are made, or even read; rather, digital is a means of radically changing how a firm engages with its customers, regardless of the product.

As of 2017, the ebook does not appear to threaten much of the traditional printed book market. Print sales figures, while certainly not growing, seem to be holding their own in the face of ebooks. Prices too—publishers have long worried about downward price pressure brought on by ebooks—have shown signs of resilience, owing to a number of strategic and structural moves by trade publishers. But at the same time, there is also evidence of large new markets emerging in the (Amazon-dominated) ebook space that are outside of traditional trade publishing and book markets.[4] What *appears* to be happening is a large-scale surge of self- (or 'independently') published authors, mostly in genre fiction categories (romance, mystery, science fiction), published and sold almost entirely direct to readers through Amazon. The size and shape of this 'shadow market' are debatable, owing to the lack of concrete data, but it would appear that a viable alternative book market has indeed emerged within the ebook ecosystem. The possibility of a bifurcation of book markets—traditional trade publishers on one side, independent authors on the other—poses fascinating questions for industry observers and theorists!

Whatever may be the case with these self-organizing book markets, it is clear that Amazon's provision of an easy-to-use direct publishing mechanism, wherein an author can upload a text directly to the Kindle store, is a key factor in the rise—and ultimately, in the sustainability—of this market. Amazon's apparent agnosticism about where books come from and to whom they are sold makes the case that Amazon is a platform company first, and a bookseller only secondarily. Amazon seems far more interested in developing automated drones to deliver physical packages (including groceries) than in digital reading systems. Amazon does, however, remain primarily an Internet services company: up until 2017, it was the largest cloud-computing service company in the world, selling web-based infrastructure to a vast array of clients, industries, and indeed governments around the world.

By this view, the ebook represents neither a revolutionary new moment for the book, nor a threat to literacy as we have known it. Rather, as far as companies like Amazon are concerned, books and ebooks are merely parts of a much larger bid to be a general service platform for hundreds of millions of consumers.

Publishing is not reducible to the book trade, of course—no more than publishing technology is reducible to ebooks. The much broader perspective on publishing technology in our time is to look to where digital media makes possible the enlisting and sustenance of communities of interest, which it does at a scale and speed simply unimaginable even a generation ago. Network theorist Yochai Benkler (2002) pointed out that with digital media, many of the 'transaction costs' of social organization fall to near zero. Media theorist Clay Shirky (2008) took this further, noting that the result is the flowering of emergent communities—audiences, publics—online. Digital media therefore facilitates 'economies of scale' in a different way than industrial technology could: allowing things to scale up, but also allowing self-organizing forms at a small scale.

In this sense the World Wide Web is the most interesting publishing context of our time. In facilitating both mass-scale, global activity and small-scale, self-organizing

---

[4] Ebook sales data has been notoriously hard to come by, partly because major players like Amazon simply don't have an incentive to share it as widely as the print book trade has done. It is, therefore, difficult to make confident judgements about ebook trends. The website authorearnings.com, however, is a crowdsourced effort to pool sales data from individual self-published authors. Authorearnings.com provides aggregated statistics that show considerable marketshare, pricing, and sales trends. See http://authorearnings.com

behaviour the Web is, by nearly any measure, the principal publishing technology of our time, even if the vast majority of it has little to do with books, magazines, or industrial publishing formats. The *ubiquity* of web-based technologies today, and their spread into almost all business and social realms, operates even more all-pervasively than print. On some level, all of that activity is in some sense 'publishing'.

Lest we think that the digital media technology is somehow a break from the tradition of books and publishing, it it helpful to remember that publishing has always been a technological endeavour; its 'killer app' has always been the scaling up of audiences—publics—by technological means. What we see on the publishing landscape today is not so much a revolution but a flowering of possibilities: while the printed book trade continues to reach mass audiences as it has done for centuries, and while the periodical press continue to reflect and define the day-to-day and month-to-month issues of concern to millions of people, the Internet and World Wide Web teem with myriad new channels, new forms, and new genres. Some closely resemble the print forms we have known, such as ebooks and online news sources; many do not, and challenge us to think about what we mean when we talk about 'publishing'. If we take a very broad definition of publishing—as nothing less than the infrastructure of modern liberal culture—then publishing and its long relationship to 'high tech' seems very robust indeed.

REFERENCE

Benkler, Yochai (2002). 'Coase's Penguin, or, Linux and "The Nature of the Firm"', *Yale Law Journal*, 112(3). pp. 369–446. http://www.jstor.org/stable/1562247.

Bjarnason, Baldur (2013). 'Which Kind of Innovation?' *Baldur Bjarnason's Notes* (blog). 3 May 2013. https://www.baldurbjarnason.com/notes/the-ebook-innovation/.

Brewer, Roy (1971). *An Approach to Print: A Basic Guide to the Printing Processes*, London: Blandford Press.

Brokaw, Cynthia and Peter Kornicki, eds (2013). *The History of the Book in East Asia*, Farnham: Ashgate.

Callon, Michel and Bruno Latour (1981). 'Unscrewing the Big Leviathan: How Actors Macro-Structure Reality and How Sociologists Help Them to Do So', in *Advances in Social Theory and Methodology: Toward an Integration of Micro- and Macro-Sociologies*. Edited by Karin Knorr-Cetina and Aaron V. Cicourel, Boston: Routledge & Kegan Paul.

Cockburn, Cynthia (1991). *Brothers: Male Dominance and Technological Change*, London: Pluto Press.

Eisenstein, Elizabeth (2011). *Divine Arts, Infernal Machine: The Reception of Printing in the West from First Impressions to the Sense of an Ending*, Philadelphia: University of Pennsylvania Press.

Gitelman, Lisa (2014). *Paper Knowledge: Toward a Media History of Documents*, Durham, NC: Duke University Press.

Goldfarb, Charles and Yuri Rubinsky (1991). *The SGML Handbook*, Oxford: Oxford University Press.

Houston, Keith (2016). *The Book: A Cover-to-Cover Exploration of the Most Powerful Object of Our Time*. New York: WW Norton.

Lowry, Martin (1979). *The World of Aldus Manutius: Business and Scholarship in Renaissance Venice*, Ithaca, NY: Cornell University Press.

Lundblad, Kristina (2015). *Bound to Be Modern: Publisher's Cloth Bindings and the Material Culture of the Book 1840–1914*, New Castle, DE: Oak Knoll Press.

McLuhan, Marshall (1962). *The Gutenberg Galaxy*, Toronto: University of Toronto Press.

McLuhan, Marshall (1965). *Understanding Media: The Extensions of Man*, New York: McGraw-Hill.

Meggs, Philip B. and Alston W. Purvis (2004). *Meggs' History of Graphic Design*, 4th edition, Hoboken, NJ: John Wiley and Sons.

Mumford, Lewis (2010 [1934]). *Technics & Civilization*, Chicago: University of Chicago Press.

Rowberry, Simon Peter (2015). 'Ebookness', *Convergence*, July 2015. https://doi.org/10.1177/1354856515592509.

Schafer, Joseph (1926). 'Treasures in Print and Script', *Wisconsin Magazine of History*, September 1926.

Shirky, Clay (2008). *Here Comes Everybody: The Power of Organizing Without Organizations*, Harmondsworth: Penguin.

Smith, Douglas K. and Robert C. Alexander (1988). *Fumbling the Future: How Xerox Invented, Then Ignored, the First Personal Computer*, New York: Morrow.

Somers, James (2017). 'Torching the Modern-Day Library of Alexandria', *The Atlantic*, 20 April 2017. https://www.theatlantic.com/technology/archive/2017/04/the-tragedy-of-google-books/523320/.

White, Eric Marshall (2018). *Editio Princeps: A History of the Gutenberg Bible*, London/Turnhout: Harvey Miller Publishers.

CHAPTER 21

MARKETING FOR PUBLISHING

ALISON BAVERSTOCK

INTRODUCTION

WITHIN the operation of publishing, marketing and publicity long had a subsidiary role. Editors reigned supreme and shaped the vision for both publishing house and the titles commissioned. No longer. The marketing and public positioning of books has become critical to their success and marketers enjoy increasing clout in both organizational direction and publishing decisions. The scope of marketing has also been extended, from seeking to inform existing customers of new publishing products and services to extending the market for books and reading, including those who do not currently read—whether through habit or low literacy.

The mechanics through which marketing is pursued are however changing. Publishers have always had to balance the delivery of marketing and publicity, informally defined as promotion you do and don't pay for respectively, but new tools such as digital marketing and social media increasingly blur boundaries. The once classic intermediary mechanisms between author and reader—book reviews and serial extracts in the quality press—are changing as new methods of informing markets emerge; their significance increasing as newspaper circulations fall and the impact of book bloggers and 'friends' on social media rises. This chapter will look at how marketing has become, in Claire Squires's words, 'the making of modern literature': seeking to isolate important trends; identify research and principles of practice that both operate internationally and last, and make predictions for the future marketing of the publishing industry's products and services.

The Formalization of Marketing
within Publishing

Plotting publishing activity around industry processes as a measure of sector development, the emergence of marketing was slow. The one consistent point of reference, Unwin's *The Truth about Publishing* (Unwin, 1926 onwards) outlined various aspects of what may today be termed 'marketing' but divided information between chapters; highlighting cross-organizational involvement but no generally established marketing departmental structure. The 'strange irony that there are so few books about book publishing' was the starting point for *Marketing for Small Publishers* (Smith, 1980: 1).

Generic titles were used to support broad understanding (e.g. Kotler 1967 and Baker 1985 on marketing; Mullins 1985 and Buchanan and Huczynski 1985 on organizational behaviour). The concepts of the marketing mix of product, price, promotion, and place; the process of segmenting markets into groups of customers with similar needs; the targeting of those most likely to yield long-term positive outcomes; the creating of positioning statements that are relevant and enticing all helped clarify thinking about what went on within publishing. Kotler's overview of marketing and its sub-fields focused primarily on what managers should do *to* customers to secure their patronage—a push approach. Baker's six years' experience selling steel (1958–64) led to his conviction that success came from doing things *for* customers (a pull approach) which became the basis for 'relationship marketing' in the 1970s. Kotler was concerned with winning the competitive exchange, which implied there are losers, while Baker's interpretation of the marketing concept has always been that marketing 'is concerned with mutually satisfying exchange relationships' (Baker 1976); or a 'win–win' outcome. This was particularly appropriate to the book market where given the low purchase price of most products, marketing aims both to secure immediate purchasers for individual products and turn them into long-term buyers of related products.

While general marketing texts developed an appreciation of marketing within publishing, and helped explore common buyer characteristics, the growth of publishing education within universities was matched by a burgeoning of specific studies of the book business. *Inside Book Publishing* (Clark 1988) and then *How to Market Books* (Baverstock 1990) were written for aspiring/actual entrants to the industry but repurposed once their wider saleability within higher education was realized. The first edition of Lynette Owen's *Selling Rights* (Owen 1991) was followed in 1997 by *Clark's Publishing Agreements: A Book of Precedents* (Clark et al. 2007). Gill Davies' 1994 *Book Commissioning and Acquisition* (Davies 2004) and Carole Blake's *From Pitch to Publication* (Blake 1999) ensued, with Thomas Woll's *Publishing for Profit* (Woll 1999). Claire Squires' *Marketing Literature: The Making of Contemporary Writing in Britain*, (Squires 2007) offered a more considered look at the meaning of marketing within publishing, supported by a series of case studies. Paul Richardson and Graham Taylor's *A Guide to the UK Publishing Industry* (Richardson and Taylor 2008), John B. Thompson's

Books in the Digital Age: The Transformation of Academic and Higher Education Publishing in Britain and the United States (2005) emphasized the role of marketing at the centre of the publishing process. *Merchants of Culture* (Thompson 2010) identified 'Sales and Marketing' as one of six key processes within the industry and for each update of 'Inside Book Publishing' the authors asserted[1] that the chapter that needed most updating was that on marketing (Clark and Phillips 2015). 'The trickle of memoirs' identified by Smith included individual reminiscences of the selling process: touring bookshops with suitcases of books (Hill 1988), and the impact of selling in new locations (Morpurgo 1979; Lewis 2005) but confirmed the industry's generally industry-specific approach to marketing. As the field has grown it has, however, remained porous to ideas from other disciplines, such as Psychology, Sociology and Creative Economy; Daniel Boswell (2017) and Stevie Marsden (2017) have considered the benefits and frustrations of working within this cross-disciplinary area.

How to Define Marketing in Publishing

Early definitions of marketing in publishing (notably Smith, Clark, and Baverstock) relied on evidence from industry practice, the identification of the natural forces advocated by Wendell R. Smith (1956), and wider general literature on marketing. In *Marketing Literature, The Making of Contemporary Writing in Britain* (Squires 2007) the author's definition of marketing is broader and

> goes beyond these activities to encompass the multiplicity of ways in which books are presented and represented in the marketplace: via their reception in the media; their gaining of literary awards; their placement on bestseller lists, to give only a few examples. Marketing is conceived as a form of representation and interpretation, situated in the spaces between the author and the reader—but which authors and readers also take part in—and surrounding the production, dissemination and reception of texts. In *Marketing Literature*, marketing is the summation of multiple agencies operating within the marketplace, by which contemporary writing is actively constructed.
>
> (Squires 2007: 2–3)

This encompassing definition has stood the test of time through the rise of citizen journalism, the growth of self-publishing and rise of the previously unpublished celebrity as author-construct, created by publisher or agent in the expectation of accessing an unserved market with a relevant and timely branded product, the writing resourced elsewhere.

---

[1] Private conversation with author, 2016.

THE PUBLISHING INDUSTRY'S RESISTANCE TO MARKETING

Arthur Bagnall's 1962 legal defence of the UK's Net Book Agreement, had argued that books should be treated differently from other types of retail purchase; that in order to support the stocking of a wide range of titles, booksellers needed to be assured that they would not be undercut by other, principally larger, retail outlets charging less. His argument prevailed and thereafter retail price-maintenance was upheld for just two categories of product: books and pharmaceutical medicines (Dearnley and Feather 2002). This situation lasted until 1995 when the UK Booksellers Association took the decision to no longer defend[2] the Net Book Agreement, although retail price-maintenance survives elsewhere.[3]

Whether or not this long-term separation of publishing from the rest of the business world was helpful, there were conditions that did make the industry different. These differences could be divided into those that arise from nature and nurture; nature including the book as the lasting vehicle for ideas, each one a different product with a separate copyright holder; nurture the specific conditions that have separated the marketers of books from those of other products/services. These include the tendency of most purchasers to buy a title only once; wide-ranging markets for books which make a specific pitch to each segment both impractical and unaffordable; their generally low purchase price, particularly by comparison with other products that compete for consumer spend (computer games, restaurant meals) or contribute to an individual's cultural capital (art, theatre, or concert tickets). The industry also had established sales arrangements with a range of dedicated retail outlets (bookshops) and the arguments for and against government-protection added to a sense of their differentness (Baverstock 1993). In her seminal essay seeking to map the literature in search of a discipline, first presented at the 2006 International Conference of the Book, Simone Murray (2007) divided associated literature into five areas. The most logical for publishing-related marketing, 'Communication, Media, Cultural Studies and Sociology' still offers slim coverage of marketing in publishing, and Murray quotes John Curtain:

> the book sector is the enigma among media industries. Lacking the personalities and politics of television, radio and newspapers, the book is often neglected in any comparative review of contemporary media; yet the book, as a cultural icon, commands a prestige in society which is unique.   (Curtain 1993: 102).

---

[2] This is commonly misunderstood. The legislation enabling resale price-maintenance was not rescinded, rather a decision was taken to no longer defend it.

[3] This includes much of Europe, e.g. Germany, France, Italy, and Spain.

The embedding of marketing structures within publishing took a long time. Long after Unwin, few publishing houses had a marketing department and the publicity role was often part of another function, such as management support or secretarial. Decisions about what to publish tended to be made at editorial meetings at which representative sales/marketing staff might be present, but for information acquisition rather than equal-voting.

The 1980s finally saw the establishment and growth of marketing within the publishing industry, as a practical process and with a steady supply of trained recruits from higher education. The availability of information to support decision making grew significantly. BookData was founded in 1987 (and merged with Whitakers in 2003). Book trade publications supplemented the growing information bank (e.g. bestseller lists, publishers/booksellers' marketing materials and reports from industry analysts such as Nielsen[4] and trade organizations such as Book Marketing Ltd's *Books and the Consumer* Survey[5]).

Bestseller lists, from various sources, gained growing significance; with so many titles competing for attention they offered a rationale both to those stocking and those deciding what to buy. The general media (e.g. print, online, and broadcast) routinely found the industry fascinating if anachronistic; hence a tendency to treat it as an interesting side-show, usually with its own chapter (e.g. Noorda 2018).

> Nielsen enabled publishers to identify trends, analyse comparative sets, track peaks and troughs in the retail calendar and look at the effect of marketing activity on sales, and hence estimate market share and channel performance, benchmark authors and predict likely bestsellers against market competitors. Some thought these processes went too far. Writing of the late 1980s Becky Swift commented:'...people were trying to apply Thatcherite business principles to publishing.... The net effect of this attempt to rationalise book buying, was that the marketer became the publisher, and most editors lost their jobs.... In many ways, what happened at Virago could be seen as a microcosm of the whole industry, which was moving to the idea that sales people could safely predict which books would sell, as opposed to editors.'   (Swift 2012).

Rejecting the notion that publishing success could be predicted by algorithm, Swift established a ground-breaking service offering writers the opportunity to improve their work *before* submission to publishers.

Today a broader strategic view prevails, which includes marketing within the publishing process from the outset, with particular attention paid to branding both lists and authors, in order to promote recognizability and perpetuate longer-term sales. Cover designers seek to offer category-clues to the buyer in a hurry; signalling through cover-layout and supporting quotations that this is the type of book they have enjoyed in the past. Consistent analysis of longer-term trends has enabled the spotting of short-term marketing opportunities, for example the isolation of seasonality as an increasingly important marketing driver, and Valentine's Day, Mothers' Day, and Halloween have

---

[4] *http://www.nielsenbookdata.co.uk   [5] BML became part of Bowker in 2010.

emerged to challenge the publisher's traditional Christmas jamboree, when up to 40 per cent of annual sales might be expected in just one month. In some markets these are highly specific—for example the association between Easter and new crime titles in Scandinavia.

The Widespread Establishment of Marketing in Publishing

As publishing houses developed and institutionally embedded marketing departments within their organizational structures, a number of key issues can be identified, all explored through both sector and academic investigation; often working in collaboration. These include: the emergence of data as a primary driver of activity; the development of new routes to market; the emergence of new online marketing solutions/collaborations, with technical developments supporting marketing's spread; a diversification of the labour pool with wider recognition for marketing skills across the industry; increasing author-participation in marketing—including the option to manage the process themselves through self-publishing.

The Emergence of Data as a Primary Driver of Activity

Long distanced from their consumers as a result of selling through specialist retailers, the demand for customer information became increasingly important to publishers' marketing. Customer and wider market data became vital for market segmentation, decision making about the order for targeting—and a guide to appropriate positioning, with publishers setting up in-house departments to monitor and hopefully predict market trends. With fragmented markets and media, growing unpredictability of consumer leisure patterns given the Internet-fuelled seismic increase in their choices, and reduced consumer attention as they managed several screens at the same time, ensuring 'discoverability' of both consumers and products became increasingly important. How to reach the potential paying customer, and those who buy on their behalf, became the focus of a range of new marketing-related job titles (e.g. market analyst; community liaison/relationship manager; brand manager) all with a strong interest in associated communities, which could be targeted to disseminate a message efficiently—and usually free of charge—on behalf of the publisher.

The Development of New Routes to Market

As traditional marketing routes for published products became increasingly pressurized, new ways of monetizing content dissemination were sought. For example, some chain bookstores introduced charges for what had previously been a standard part of their role, such as prominent (front-of-store) and window display, mounting promotions, and highlighting 'recommended reads'. What had been dubbed 'shared marketing expenditure' became publisher subsidy (through additional discount) or invoiced support. Publishers sought to reduce their costs and increase their negotiating status through consolidation, leading to the emergence of large publishing conglomerations from the eponymous businesses of the nineteenth and twentieth centuries, culminating with the union of Penguin and Random House (2012).

While trade books were largely sold through bookshops, publishers approaching specific markets sought direct contact with customers, for example direct supply through conferences/professional meetings of high-price professional and reference titles which bookshops would be unwilling to stock and marketing of academic textbooks directly to universities through campus-calling.

Direct supply became both possible and more convenient for consumers, particularly given the deregulation of markets and the growth of the freelance economy. Familiarity with direct supply within other consumer purchasing (often with higher profit-margins) increased pressure for swifter publisher-supply; the emergence of a major online retailer (Amazon in 1994) willing to supply items as loss-leaders in order to gain data, raised consumer expectations about required service-levels.

New selling locations fuelled new collaborations. For example, in Australia the discount department store became the principal channel for bulk sales of popular titles.[6] In the US and Europe, the option of selling through out-of-town superstores and garden-centres led to the amalgamated packaging to target the gift market (books with toys, accessories and clothing). Some market-access remains grounded in social rather than economic justification, for example Rosen (2016) reports on US bookshops serving as community hubs, quoting one bookshop owner:

> 'We're constantly growing the store to help the community to see themselves.' For her, that translates into online and in-school book fairs with diverse books, as well as a year-round 'book-angel' program that donates children's books with positive images of African-American children and families to schools and nonprofit centers. The store also has a physical classroom, which she plans to use for events, such as having black medical students talk with middle graders about STEM subjects.
>
> (Rosen 2016)

Similarly the *Financial Times* reported that in US urban neighbourhoods without bookshops, low-cost self-published fiction could reach women with an inclination to read through nailbars and hairdressing salons (Financial Times 2015).

Traditional means of informing the market (e.g. book reviews; third party recommendations; availability in bookshops), which mostly relied on distance between the author/publisher and the consumer), were augmented by new processes (e.g. social media, literary festivals, book groups) which enabled new relationships; for example author/reader, reader/reader, reader/publisher (Hartley 2001; Driscoll 2014). Festival

---

[6] Discussion with Susannah Bowen, Head of Marketing, Cengage Australia.

appearances and book tours similarly by-passed traditional routes to market, with the opportunity for an author signature to add value to a time-specific shared memento that could be sold at full price through a pop-up shop—and potentially resold online at a profit by the marketing-savvy. Gerard Genette (1993) explored the cover's role as 'a threshold or…a vestibule that offers the world at large the possibility of either stepping inside or turning back' and as popular design programmes (e.g. the UK's *Changing Rooms* 1996–2004; franchised in the USA, Australia, and New Zealand) became increasingly popular, product attractiveness, and in particular the cover, became much more important to customers' buying decisions and hence publisher's production and marketing processes (Matthews and Moody 2008). Rachel Noorda has written engagingly about the role of books as cultural reinforcer, helping to shape national identity, and the hence the role of tartanry to reach the 'lived diaspora' receptive to Scottish identity (Noorda 2017).

Libraries sought new ways to preserve their role; emphasizing their part in promoting social mobility by providing locations for information access and entertainment, particularly for hard-to-reach sections of the community. John Sumsion, the UK's first Registrar of PLR,[7] identified differences between consumer borrowing and buying (Sumsion et al. 2002) and research by the National Literacy Trust,[8] the Book Trust,[9] and particularly The Reading Agency[10] (e.g. The Reading Agency and BOP Consulting 2015) confirmed the importance played by wider literacy in societal well-being. As bookshops reduced, publishers built on the customer access offered by libraries, having previously rather taken library sales for granted.

The growing diversification of the media at the end of the twentieth century, and the huge expansion of the Internet from the start of the twenty-first, created new opportunities for the communication of publishers' marketing messages.

Radio had long been a natural medium for the communication of books; publishers seldom able to afford television advertising. The broadcast media, always keen on adversarial structures for programming, became particularly keen to feature those who could articulate an argument and substantiate it with reference to what they had published, and this opened up an additional source of income for some authors. Authors arguably received a disproportionately greater share of media attention compared with other 'creatives/celebrities', perhaps because they were generally more articulate, and often provided cheap copy. New channels also created new opportunities, drawing on latent societal interest in how to write and get published.

Initial coverage on television of book awards (Bragg 1998) and the rise of media book clubs during media prime time such as Oprah Winfrey in the USA and Richard and Judy in the UK proved extremely successful. The latter won HarperCollins the 2006 Award for Expanding the Book Market (*Bookseller*,2006) and an *Observer* poll voted the associated television station's MD the most important figure in British publishing

---

[7] Public Lending Right www.plr.uk.com   [8] www.literacytrust.org.uk
[9] www.booktrust.org.uk   [10] www.readingagency.org.uk*

(McCrum 2006). The trade press repeatedly reported the 'transforming' effect of their selections on subsequent sales (*Bookseller* 2004). David Cooke, Category Manager responsible for the supermarket Tesco's book stocking, recognized the impact of Richard & Judy:

> They have brought different books to new people. Probably 50–60% of all the books they have chosen we wouldn't have listed otherwise. The typical Tesco book buyer only buys one or two books a year, driven by covers and what's very popular.
>
> (Cooke, 2009)

This fuelled further sponsorship collaborations (Jury 2007). These initiatives and other related ways of reaching readers have been explored and analysed (Ramone and Cousins 2011; Fuller and Rehberg 2013).

Marketing processes also began to change, in response to the growing number of stimuli being offered to consumers. In a bid to offer 'category clues' to time-pressured, pre-identified markets, content was increasingly packaged to augment a collective impression. Similarly, marketing budgets were redirected according to 'market forces'. No longer did every title get a guaranteed, if limited, associated marketing spend, and an emerging business model relied on the success of certain high-profile, and often celebrity-based, titles being budgeted to succeed, in the long-term hopefully subsidizing those for which there were lower expectations.

Finally a new area of marketing activity emerged; campaigns intended to reach those with no reading habit at all. Techniques for market segmentation and targeting had long been available to home in on those either without a reading habit, or low literacy levels, but, lacking the means/inclination to purchase, efforts were unlikely to be cost-effective. The turn of the century saw the rise of a range of charitable organizations devoted to marketing involvement in extending literacy, through publicly-funded endeavours, and in this context the efforts of The Chartered Institute of Librarians and Information Providers[11] and Reading Force[12] in the UK and First Book[13] and Literacy for Incarcerated Teens[14] in the USA (and many more) should be highlighted. Led by Gail Rebuck, Random House CEO, the publisher/author collaboration that under-pinned the launch of *Quick Reads* (2006) was particularly significant. The series presented a range of 'short, easy-to-read books by well known-authors'[15] but crucially marketed them as commercially attractive; funded by a variety of charitable/industry support. Similar developments saw books and reading highlighted as life-positives and the rise of bibliotherapy.

---

[11] *http://www.cilip.org.uk/ [http://www.cilip.org.uk/]*

[12] *www.readingforce.org.uk [http://www.readingforce.org.uk/]*

[13] *https://firstbook.org/ [https://firstbook.org/]*

[14] *http://www.literacyforincarceratedteens.org/ [http://www.literacyforincarceratedteens.org/]*

[15] *http://www.bbc.co.uk/skillswise/learners/quick-reads [http://www.bbc.co.uk/skillswise/learners/quick-reads]*

The Emergence of New Online Marketing Solutions/Collaborations

The range of online options for marketing products and services has expanded with dizzying speed (Reed 2013). Encouraging 'word-of-mouth' had long been the aim of publishers, encouraging readers to share information on what they were reading/enjoying as a low-cost and highly targeted marketing support. Online this became a process that could be both intuitive and very rapid, with bloggers and social media taking ideas and spreading them far further than anticipated—hence marketers' search for communicators to both disseminate information—and then write (or have written on their behalf) books for which a wide circulation was built into the commission. The launch of Wren and Rook, as an imprint of Hachette Children's Books in 2016 can be seen as significant in this light. The CEO of Hachette Children's Books commented: 'We weren't producing enough non-fiction for the trade market...there was a commercial need for more trade-facing non-fiction' (Murray Hill 2016). Early titles included books by bloggers and vloggers with a built in marketing reach and, through the boundary-less Internet, strong international sales potential. An early example was the commissioning of a book on sex for young adults by Hannah Witton, a twenty-something vlogger/presenter with 315,000 YouTube subscribers, 75,000 followers on Twitter, and 71,000 followers on Instagram. The endorsements she received were similarly outside those traditionally relied upon within publishing. At the Cosmo Influencer Awards she was named 'Best sex and relationships influencer' and awarded 'Book of the Year' at the 2017 'Summer in the City Awards', launched by an organization aiming 'to create a world of specialised content, including videos, features, quizzes and more, for YouTubers and YouTube fans alike'.[16]

But negative word-of-mouth can spread equally quickly. As networks develop they predict their future fortunes; for example, media that attracts the attention of mid-lifers may in the process rapidly alienate younger customers.

Online platforms secure market-access by developing their usefulness. Publishers, as purveyors of content and ideas, are well placed to benefit. Advertisers use social media platforms like Facebook to target audiences through demographic information, enabling them to match their preferences with products of interest. But against this must be factored high costs per lead; those selling higher-priced products/services may benefit, but publishers of mass-market titles find this unaffordable. And while Internet coverage can add huge value to platforms that dominate web-advertising and online bookselling, this can threaten physical bookshops, the traditional showrooms for book purchase. Given the low profit-margins consistently reported by online retailers, and publishers' inability to make this form of direct selling profitable themselves, the demise of traditional retailers would be a big loss to the industry.

Jamie Criswell and Nick Canty (2014) have explored the processes/outcomes of social media marketing for publishers through detailed analysis of social media posts for two case

---

[16] www.wetheunicorns.com/about-us/

study titles. Comparing sales data from Nielsen BookScan to promote an understanding of the value of social media marketing in publishing, they concluded that 'While social media is less effective at marketing new books written by debut authors with no existing readership, it is none the less an important tool in the marketing plan as it provides a platform to engage with readers around significant events.'

Perhaps the best advice for marketers is to explore the market for their organization/ products and make ongoing investigations into which routes to market deliver the most effective/profitable means of accessing paying/subsidized content purchasers. It is important to ensure communications are matched to the vehicle being used and reflect the brand values of publishing company, author, and associated markets. For example, Twitter engages consumers through conversation rather than hard-sell; YouTube encouraged the rise of book-tubers, communicating with their market. The opportunity to back-up this activity by ensuring product/service availability is open to all: publisher, retailer, author, or syndicate, as appropriate.

The dominance of online has also produced a shift in marketing activity with a focus on search engine optimization (SEO) and discoverability; ensuring accurate title classification in order to benefit from online search algorithms and reach potential customers. This has compromised the marketer's craft of copywriting, requiring more repetition than literary style in the information provided.

Also notable here are the marketing gurus, whose ideas break through into the mainstream vocabulary at regular intervals, for example 'Martini marketing' (Leach 2014; referencing a 1970s drink advertisement; 'any time, any place, anywhere') and other buzz-trends. In a publishing context, these can add energy to marketing planning and delivery, but need careful consideration; give away too much content and there is nothing left to sell.

The Diversification of the Labour Pool—and wider Recognition of Marketing Skills

Traditionally publishing was presented as a series of stages; with marketing both isolatable and separate—and largely at process-end. As marketing's embedding within publishing grew, the associated skills and competencies became increasingly central to the entire business. The value of an ability to predict and orchestrate product sales challenged the previously uniquely editorial route to higher influence. Senior roles were increasingly taken up by those from a marketing background.[17]

This process is typified in the rising profile of rights management. Initially the property of the author(s), ceded through various processes to others, the sale of rights at an early stage in a product's development made the publishing industry's output viable on an international basis; predicted interest in rights sales becoming a key part of whether a

---

[17] In the UK, Bob Osborne of Heinemann Educational was the first managing director from a marketing background (1982); his appointment was quickly followed by others.

potential product merited further consideration. Delivery was expanded and implemented through marketing processes: isolating potential customers; making a series of pitches; securing the deal—and hence the emergence of rights as a marketing-allied activity.

Again based on international communication, resourcing lines for publishing were extended worldwide as process component parts (e.g. marketing services, copy-editing, proofreading, customer services, and production) were internationally sourced, from wherever was able to provide the most cost-effective and reliable service. The effective management of these processes increasingly depended on effective marketing skills and effective communication, with significant consequences for the scale of publishing. It emerged as vital for publishing organizations to be market-focused and have an international outlook.

Broader Recruitment

Recruitment within publishing had traditionally worked against the development of more modern business practices. Both industry size and the ongoing use of low-cost, nepotistic recruitment favoured literary awareness over commercial nous.

Expenditure on publisher training had never been a priority, and many staff learnt on-the-job. The UK Publishers' Association piloted training for publishers in the early 1970s; although the first courses were entirely editorial, once sales and marketing appeared on the programme (1980), these courses attracted growing numbers of editors.[18]

Accompanying this has been a growing awareness that the industry's tradition of recruiting from a largely undiversified demographic—in the process remaining white, middle-class, and seemingly incurious about the reading habits and preferences of others—is both economically and socially disadvantageous. Greater diversity within the industry has promoted a wider understanding of society's content-based needs and hence possibilities for producing broader products/services, generating associated profit.

Today, those organizing marketing conferences in publishing routinely invite speakers from outside the sector and both publishing education and industry professionals are drawing on a broader general body of marketing work, benefiting from a wider understanding of marketing strategies and consumer choices. Dr Paul Delaney has explored how marketing theory can apply in publishing; in particular product differentiation and market segmentation in a product-swamped industry (Delaney 2002). An appreciation that 'books are different' is much less widely accepted.

Increasing Author Participation in Marketing

With notable exceptions (e.g. Charles Dickens' reading tours of North America), authors traditionally relied on publishers to manage communication with their readers and promote sales. Admiring readers would sometimes write to authors care of their

---

[18] Personal conversation with MD Dag Smith.

publishing houses, publishers consolidating and passing on correspondence—or sometimes answering it themselves. Author publicity forms were routinely sent out with contracts, but their function was seldom explained. While publishers appreciated author support with publicity at publication time, they seldom shared theory or ideas, and were particularly ineffective at managing author expectations.

Unwin states in his first edition (1926) that his main rationale is helping 'inexperienced writers to understand some of the technicalities of publishing and thereby to assist them' (1926: 2), but it is clear they should remain distanced until called for. Former publisher Michael Legat's *An Author's Guide to Publishing*, advises authors to 'use every trick you can think of to increase your sales' (1982: 104), but there is little advice on how.

While for some authors there remained an innate distaste for marketing terminology— 'I write books, I do not produce content' (Jauncey 2008) and, not infrequently, an associated 'learned helplessness' (Darwin 2008) this was accompanied by a growing awareness that writers did need to understand the process by which their work reaches their readers, be unembarrassed about trying to promote their work by word-of-mouth and perhaps extend their involvement beyond including flyers in their Christmas cards and following up leads for local talks. As Juliet Gardiner (2000) commented, 'the promotable fiction author who spends, say, a year writing a novel, will now spend considerably more than a year promoting it in a round of press, radio and television interviews, bookshop readings and other events on publication'. Edinburgh University Press's *Handbook of Creative Writing* (Earnshaw 2007) included a section on *The Writer's Life*, confirming the author's role and responsibilities in marketing their work. Exploring the experience of first-time novelists, Nicholas Canty (2012) found that the authors interviewed, almost all of whom were agented, placed significant emphasis on potential publishers' ability to market their work but ended up closely involved themselves:

> One respondent complained: 'I did so much of this [promotional work] myself— I should have been salaried' and another adding 'Although the publisher assigned me a publicist, I did most of the promotion myself'. This may reflect the increasing expectation that authors will be actively involved in the promotion of the book through their blogs and social media platforms, a trend we should expect to continue.
>
> (Canty 2012: 218)

For titles with specific anticipated markets (e.g. academic/educational/professional), the author's involvement in prompting class-adoptions and securing endorsements became vital, particularly as institutional book-purchasing budgets were severely curtailed. For some authors, institutional or individual 'buy-back' became a condition of getting published, hence growing numbers of author experiments with sponsored publishing (e.g. Toksvig 2006).

Authors became increasingly central to publishers' marketing plans. In part this was due to their product knowledge, as original content-creators, but also their growing market-access, which the fragmentation of the media was making ever-harder to predict and reach. Publishers deployed authors in increasing numbers at literary festivals, asking them to recruit endorsers, share contacts, and promote word-of-mouth through social media, ironically further disintermediating themselves. Publishers' regular establishment of 'author-portals', enabling authors/agents to see their sales and media coverage, confirmed they found it necessary to demonstrate the value they added to stakeholders. Jo Royle and colleagues (1999) explored where the brand lay, with publisher or author, and found author names were often more recognizable than those of their publishers and authors' marketing connectedness became part commissioning decisions. A minority of high-profile authors were provided with media training and support, but the vast majority resourced their own associated improved branding—through practice or access to courses run by their professional associations (e.g. The Society of Authors;[19] The Alliance of Independent Authors[20]) and commercial providers, a market some agents and publishers entered (e.g. The Writers' and Artists' Yearbook[21]) through selling individual/group advice on marketing/publishing to potential authors and hosting conferences.

But just as authors were getting more familiar with marketing, many found their standard terms of business were being renegotiated. Intense pressure on margins was encouraging publishers to further reduce costs; through spending less on marketing, cutting author payments (e.g. paying fees rather than royalties; thus cutting authors out of potential profits for successful products), offering either lower levels of editorial intervention and requiring more author involvement. New business models that emerged, such as The Faber Academy,[22] Authonomy,[23] and Macmillan New Writing,[24] all involved increased levels of partnership with the author, and a more proactive authorial role, particularly in generating enthusiasm for their writing. Author Jodi Picoult commented, 'you can't just be a writer, you also have to be your own cheerleader' (Picoult, 2006). When putting forward publishing proposals it became routine practice for academics to be asked if they had any financial 'institutional support' from their university, and they were encouraged to seek the collaboration of their colleagues in promoting their work (Masikunas and Baverstock 2011).

In the longer term, both involvement in their own marketing and the renegotiation of their standard terms were very significant to author–publisher relationships. Publishing had long relied on a mutuality of interests to bind together their stable of authors, accompanied by sketchy and irregular information on sales. Authors delivering events had, however, seen what their audiences looked like and heard the kind of questions they asked. Many set up their own website so they could be contacted directly and as social media developed they 'met' them online daily. It is not a huge leap for them to

[19]   www.societyof authors.org
[20]   *www.allianceofindependentauthors.org [http://www.allianceofindependentauthors.org/]*
[21]   *www.writersandartists.co.uk [http://www.writersandartists.co.uk/]*
[22]   *www.faber.co.uk/academy [http://www.faber.co.uk/academy]*
[23]   *www.authonomy.com [http://www.authonomy.com/]*
[24]   *http://www.panmacmillan.com/imprints/macmillan%20new%20writing [http://www.panmacmillan.com/imprints/macmillan new writing]*

subsequently decide that rather than sharing publishing services with fellow writers they would rather have their own bespoke team.

Enterprising authors took this a stage further, effectively becoming a publishing enterprise in their own right: employing editorial services; contracting them from the house with which they temporarily collaborated; experimenting with team-writing. The latter is particularly interesting. While it is hardly new, being close to the Renaissance model of artist and associated *scuola*, the process offered the marketing advantage of speedier products: quicker production, arguably more directed project control and branding—and hence the better satisfaction of reader-demand. Some of these developments were highly successful: Public Lending Right figures for 2008/9 revealed that James Patterson and Daisy Meadows, two of the most-borrowed authors, were both 'team writing' (BBC News 2009).

Overall, author involvement in the marketing process offered opportunities for self-development, most notably practice in negotiation, with likely significant consequences for publishers, writers, retailers, and all other stakeholders. How author-empowerment will affect publisher–author relationships in future is a significant issue. But battles can certainly be expected over who came up with the ideas, and hence the distribution of associated profits.

The Growth of Self-publishing, Fuelled by Author Understanding of Marketing

Traditionally authors knew little of publishing processes and had sparse involvement with industry personnel beyond their commissioning editor. But increasing involvement in marketing promoted their wider understanding of factors that impinge on their success—and the consequent identification of new opportunities. A notable one is self-publishing.

The first publishers were also booksellers, and it was not uncommon for authors to 'privately publish' a first edition of their own work at their own expense. Publishers would advance the costs of publication; pay themselves back as the titles were sold, charging a commission on every title and then paying the balance to the writer. If a novel did not recover its costs through sales, the author was responsible (Fergus 1997; Raven 2006). All of Jane Austen's novels (apart from *Pride and Prejudice*) were published at the author's financial risk—or 'on commission' as it was termed.

Over time, the two functions of bookselling and publishing separated; publishers, and later agents, began to dominate access to book management; booksellers to selling what was produced. A dependency culture was established: authors on publishers for access to the market; booksellers on publishers for product. And as in any market where the manufacturer controls access to the market, a confidence bordering on arrogance was frequently reported by would-be suppliers (Legat 1982: 145ff). Poorly published and easily identifiable 'vanity publishing' became the only alternative.

In the 1990s, with wider computer availability, publishing organizations began to emerge which empowered authors to publish their work themselves with complete editorial and copyright control, buying in previously publisher-dominated services (editorial, marketing, distribution) according to need. This new availability of services, along with the publisher-induced increased author confidence in the part they could play in marketing their work, made self-publishing an attractive option for a range of publishing goals, from the traditional (e.g. ensuring publication; self-actualization) to the new (e.g. parking a project in a semi-finished format and moving on with something else; creating a project valuable to a specific and identifiable market but unlikely to generate traditional investment). These issues were explored by Poynter (1979) and Baverstock (2011). An awareness that independent editors, on whom the publishing industry had long relied, found their direct employment by self-publishing authors congenial (Baverstock et al. 2015) has significant longer-term implications for the industry.

Looking further ahead, increased author understanding of how publishing and marketing work, and the wider and low-cost availability of publishing services have arguably also fuelled a new type of author–reader relationship: one that is almost entirely unmediated by publishers. Authors can be, if they choose, more informed of relevant marketing techniques and associated processes than their publishers—with whom they may in future be in competition. The irony is that the publishers may end up offering to resume management of their marketing, to give them more time for writing.

Conclusions

Sir Stanley Unwin had no concept of social media marketing; the first editions of Baker and Kotler were in circulation long before bloggers or vloggers. But the underpinning processes behind these new means of market access, communication, and conversion would have fitted their practical and structural instincts: a profound understanding of anticipated customers, the value they access in the products/information being offered and the distillation/communication of key messages likely to prompt purchase/action or involvement.

As each new potential marketing mechanism or trend emerges, usually accompanied by an enthusiastic vocabulary, there is a strong need for stakeholders in publishing's future—existing practitioners, new entrants, researchers, theorists, and students—to evaluate both appropriateness and effectiveness. This needs to take place alongside consideration of the principles discussed in marketing literature, evidence of process-exploration through practice in comparable situations and reflection on likely/actual outcomes—in order to decide how to allocate resources and plan for the future. This is particularly important as momentum for marketing action builds and timeframes reduce; with instant opportunity to be interpreted otherwise than intended.

It is likely that the core marketing principles, processes and opportunities explored in this chapter, both for marketing in general and marketing in publishing, will remain relevant within the publishing industry, the wider creative economy—and the broader range of service companies and individual suppliers involved. But alongside the marketing mix should remain factored the multiplicity of book communication processes and techniques established by publishing marketers, consistently strong on creativity, low on budgets, and consideration of how much—and how helpfully—they impact on each other, given the levels of nudging customers need towards buying decisions will vary significantly, depending on the strength of the associated need and whose money is being spent.

A key consideration within this juggling will be how to ensure that there is something left to pay for. Legat (1982) isolated the importance of 'bandwagon books' and this remains an important issue now rapid market-reach is possible. Marketing and publicity that secure widespread coverage, but leave the customer able to participate in debate without requiring a purchase, yield no associated income (unless provided through third-party funding) with which to support publishers' future developments. While the targeted offering of free material can be a valuable marketing tool, enabling sampling and mass distribution to create a fan-base, the sharing of key ideas as they develop via social media may be particularly damaging to industry coffers.

The growing confidence of the basic content-providers within publishing—the authors—due to their involvement in marketing, and their increased ability to find routes to market other than those offered by traditional publishers, has fuelled a growing debate about sector recruitment; both what gets published and who is doing the publishing. Stick just to markets that are already understood and accessed, and the industry may be targeting a tiny slice of the overall potential for their products and services—and corresponding associated income.

Within this ongoing debate, the discipline of Publishing Studies emerges as increasingly valuable. A blend of academic thinking and practical skills, it leaves those involved well placed to consider practical techniques within the context of wider academic enquiry about rationale, process, and evaluated delivery—and hence to evaluate cross-sector practice for new ideas, and solve future problems we do not as yet even anticipate.

References

Baker, M. J. (1976). *Marketing Theory and Practice*, Basingstoke: Macmillan.

Baker, M. J. (1985). *Marketing Strategy and Management*, Basingstoke: Macmillan.

Baverstock, A. (1990 onwards). *How to Market Books*, London: Kogan Page.

Baverstock, A. (1993). *Are Books Different? Marketing in the Book Trade*, London: Kogan Page.

Baverstock, A. (2011). *The Naked Author*, London: Bloomsbury.

Baverstock, A., R. Blackburn, and M. Iskandarova (2015). 'How is the role of the independent editor changing in relation to traditional and self-publishing models of publication?' *Learned Publishing*, 28(2), pp. 123–31.

BBC News (2009). [online] Available at: http://news.bbc.co.uk/1/hi/entertainment/arts_and_culture/7873127.stm [Accessed 12 November 2010].

Blake, C. (1999). *From Pitch to Publication*, London: Macmillan.

Bookseller (2004). 'The Richard & Judy effect', Issue 5113, 30 January 2004.

Bookseller (2006). 'Retail awards winners', Issue 5249, 22 September 2006.

Boswell, D. (2017). 'What do we write about when we write about publishing?', *Interscript*. Available at: https://www.interscriptjournal.com/online-magazine/what-we-write-about-when-we-write-about-publishing

Bragg, M. (1998). 'Booker on the box', in *Booker 30: A celebration of 30 years of The Booker Prize*, London: Booker, pp. 36–8.

Buchanan, D and A. Huczynski (1985). *Organisational Behaviour*, Harlow: Pearson.

Canty, N. (2012). 'The experience of first time novelists in the UK', *Publishing Research Quarterly* 28, p. 218. https://doi.org/10.1007/s12109-012-9280-5

Clark, C., L. Owen, and R. Palmer (2007). *Clark's Publishing Agreements: A Book of Precedents*, London: Tottell.

Clark, G. (1988, 2000). *Inside Book Publishing: A Career Builder's Guide*, London: Blueprint.

Clark, G. and A. Phillips (2008, 2015). *Inside Book Publishing*, London: Routledge.

Cooke, D. (2009). http://news.bbc.co.uk/1/hi/magazine/8128436.stm [Accessed 5th September 2017].

Criswell, J. and N. Canty (2014). 'Deconstructing Social Media: An Analysis of Twitter and Facebook Use in the Publishing Industry', *Publishing Research Quarterly* 30, p. 352. https://doi.org/10.1007/s12109-014-9376-1

Curtain, J. (1993). *Book Publishing, the Media in Australia: Industries, Texts, Audiences*, ed. Stuart Cunningham and Graeme Turner, Sydney: Allen and Unwin.

Darwin, E. (2008). 'Author empowerment', Response to *Bookseller Blog*. 17 January 2008.

Davies, G. (2004 [1994]). *Book Acquisition and Commissioning*, London: Routledge.

Dearnley, J. and J. Feather (2002). 'The UK bookselling trade without resale price-maintenance—an overview of change 1995–2001', *Publishing Research Quarterly*, 17(4), pp. 16–31.

Delaney, P. (2002). *Literature, Money and the Market: From Trollope to Amis*, Basingstoke: Palgrave Macmillan.

Driscoll, B. (2014). *The New Literary Middlebrow: Tastemakers and Reading in the Twenty-First Century*, London: Palgrave Macmillan.

Earnshaw, S., ed. (2007, 2014). *The Handbook of Creative Writing*, Edinburgh: Edinburgh University Press.

Eyre, C. (2016). HCB launches two new kids' lists. The Bookseller, 22 July 2016 https://www.thebookseller.com/news/hcg-launches-two-new-kids-lists-364036

Fergus, J. (1997). 'The professional woman writer', in E. Copeland and J. McMaster (eds), *The Cambridge Companion to Jane Austen*, Cambridge: Cambridge University Press.

Financial Times (2015). Article on self-publishing; reference to nailbar story dissemination.

Fuller, D. and D. N. Rehberg Sedo (2013). *Reading beyond the Book: The Social Practices of Contemporary Literary Culture*. New York: Routledge.

Gardiner, J. (2000). 'What is an author?' *Publishing Research Quarterly*, 16(1), pp. 255–74.

Genette, G. (1993). *Fiction and Diction*. Trans Catherine Porter, Ithaca, NY: Cornell University Press (originally published in France in 1991).

Hartley, J. (2001). *Reading Groups*, Oxford: Oxford University Press.

Hill, A. (1988). *In Pursuit of Publishing*, London: Heinemann.

Jauncey, J. (2008). Society of Authors in Scotland, Conference. February 2008. Podcast of session. [online] Available at: http://scotlandonsunday.scotsman.com/sos-review/Podcast-Society-of-Authors-in.3808264.jp [Accessed 1 September 2011].

Jury, L. (2007). 'Richard and Judy select Britain's next bestsellers', *The Independent*. http://www.independent.co.uk/arts-entertainment/books/news/richard-and-judy-select-britains-next-best-sellers-430856.html [Accessed 5 September, 2017].

Kotler, P. (1967). *Marketing Management: Analysis, Planning and Control*, Englewood Cliffs, NJ: Prentice-Hall.

Leach, E. (2014). *Welcome to the age of Martini marketing*. The Guardian, Higher Education Network blog https://www.theguardian.com/higher-education-network/blog/2014/mar/21/martini-marketing-higher-education [Accessed 3 September, 2017].

Legat, M. (1982, 1987, 1991). *An Author's Guide to Publishing*, London: Robert Hale.

Lewis, J. (2005). *Biography of Allan Lane*, London: Penguin.

McCrum, R. (2006). 'Our top 50 players in the world of books', *The Observer*. 5 March 2006 Available at: http://www.guardian.co.uk/books/2006/mar/05/features.review [Accessed 1 September 2011].

Marsden, S. (2017). 'Positioning Publishing Studies in the Cultural Economy', *Interscript*. https://www.interscriptjournal.com/online-magazine/positioning-publishing-studies-in-the-cultural-economy

Masikunas, G. and A. Baverstock (2011). 'How well do textbook publishers understand their market?' *International Journal of the Book*, 8(4), pp. 93–102.

Matthews, N. and N. Moody (2008). *Judging a Book by its Cover: Fans, Publishers, Designers, and the Marketing of Fiction*, Farnham: Ashgate.

Morpurgo, J. E. (1979). *Allen Lane, King Penguin*, London: Penguin.

Mullins, L. J. (1985 and subsequent editions). *Management and Organisational Behaviour*, Harlow: Pearson.

Murray, S. E. (2007). 'Publishing Studies: Critically Mapping Research in Search of a Discipline', *Publishing Research Quarterly*, 22(4), pp. 3–25.

Noorda, R. (2017). 'From Waverley to Outlander: Reinforcing Scottish Diasporic Identity through Book Consumption', *National Identities*, 2094), pp. 361–77 http://www.tandfonline.com/eprint/H3H8HJ5JyxZUCtz8uC33/full.

Noorda, R. (forthcoming 2019). 'Entrepreneurship and Marketing in the Publishing Industry', in *Handbook on Marketing and Entrepreneurship*. Edited by I. Fillis, and N. Telford, Cheltenham: Edward Elgar.

Owen, L. (1991). *Selling Rights*, London: Blueprint.

Picoult, J. (2006). Interview in: *The Telegraph Magazine*. 2 September 2006.

Poynter, D. (1979). *The Self-publishing Manual*, California: Para Publishing, 16 editions https://www.amazon.co.uk/Dan-Poynters-Self-Publishing-Manual-Write/dp/1568601425

Ramone, J. and H. Cousins, eds (2011). *The Richard & Judy Book Club Reader: Popular Texts and the Practices of Reading*, Farnham: Ashgate Publishing.

Raven, J. (2006). 'Book production,' in *Jane Austen in Context*. Edited by J. Todd *The Cambridge Edition of the Works of Jane Austen*, Cambridge: Cambridge University Press.

The Reading Agency and BOP Consulting (2015). *The impact of reading for pleasure and empowerment*. https://readingagency.org.uk/news/The%20Impact%20of%20Reading%20for%20Pleasure%20and%20Empowerment.pdf [Accessed 28th December 2017].

Richardson, P. and G. Taylor (2008). *A Guide to the UK Publishing Industry*, London: The Publishers Association.

Reed, J. (2013). *Get up to Speed with Online Marketing*, 2nd edition, London: Pearson.

Rosen, J. (2016). 'A glimmer of hope for black-owned bookstores', *Publishers Weekly*, New York: 263.8 (22 February 2016) https://search.proquest.com/docview/1767981194?rfr_id=info%3Axri%2Fsid%3Aprimo

Royle, J., L. Cooper, and R. Stockdale (1999). 'The use of branding by trade publishers: An investigation into marketing the book as a brand name product', *Publishing Research Quarterly*, 15(4), pp. 3–13.

Smith, K. (1980). *Marketing for Small Publishers*. London: Inter-Action Imprint in association with the Institute for Social Enterprise.

Smith, W. R. (1956). 'Product Differentiation and Market Segmentation as Alternative Marketing Strategies', *Journal of Marketing*, 21(1), pp. 3–8 and reprinted in *Marketing Management*, (1995), 4(3), pp. 63–5.

Squires, C. (2007). *Marketing Literature: The Making of Contemporary Writing in Britain*, London: Palgrave.

Sumsion, J., M. Hawkins, and A. Morris (2002). 'The economic value of book borrowing from public libraries: An optimisation model', *Journal of Documentation*, 58(6): pp. 662–82.

Swift, R. (2012). An interview with Rebecca Swift. https://www.freewordcentre.com/explore/the-future-of-publishing-an-interview-with-rebecca-swift

Thompson, J. B. (2005). *Books in the Digital Age: The Transformation of Academic and Higher Education Publishing in Britain and the United States*, Cambridge: Polity Press.

Thompson, J. B. (2010). *Merchants of Culture: The Publishing Business in the 21st Century*, Cambridge: Polity Press

Toksvig, S. (2006). Foreword. *Courage and Strength: A book of veterans' poetry*. Published in aid of Combat Stress. https://www.cobseo.org.uk/courage-and-strength-a-book-of-veterans-poetry London: Kingston University Press.

Unwin, S. (1926 onwards). *The Truth about Publishing*, London: George, Allan & Unwin.

Woll, T. (1999). *Publishing for Profit*, London: Kogan Page.

CHAPTER 22

....

RIGHTS

....

LYNETTE OWEN

THE concept of copyright is of vital importance to the publishing industry and for many years it was perhaps taken for granted as the intellectual property framework protecting the rights of creators (authors, illustrators, photographers, etc.) and of the businesses who invest in bringing their works to market (publishers). In recent years the relevance of copyright in the digital age has been questioned by a variety of interested parties, not least technology companies such as Google; the educational sector and the public at large, many of whom have grown up with the expectation that content should be instantly and freely available. Despite this, copyright legislation has adjusted continuously to techno-logical developments, and it remains a vital mechanism for recognizing the value of creative content.

Within the publishing industry lies a whole area of exploiting intellectual property through the medium of licensing—an activity which is off at a tangent from the primary publishing process which takes the author's work from manuscript through editing, design, and production to publication, marketing, and dissemination in print and (almost certainly nowadays) also in electronic form. The author as the creator is normally the primary owner of copyright in a work together with all attendant rights; however, most authors will then delegate the handling of such rights to their literary agent or their publisher, depending on the terms of the publishing contract. The role of the agent is to make arrangements with a primary publisher or publishers (i.e. a British agent might make separate arrangements with a UK and a US publisher rather than a single global arrangement); the agent may include a range of subsidiary rights in each such publishing arrangement, or may retain control of some categories of rights (e.g. translation rights and dramatization and documentary rights).

Over the years the sale of rights has become increasingly important to the publishing industry; for some types of publishing, particularly in the area of books highly illustrated in colour, rights sales may make such projects financially viable and may make a crucial contribution to the profitability of the publishing company. Publishers such as Dorling Kindersley were first established on the basis of securing multiple rights deals, printing physical copies for a range of overseas coedition partners.

Why Sell Rights?

The additional opportunities afforded by exploiting various aspects of the intellectual property in a work include a wide range of possible licensing opportunities which—if the work has appropriate potential and the rights are effectively handled—can provide a significant additional source of income for authors, literary agents, and publishers as well as bringing the work to a wider audience in a variety of forms. In some cases, the securing of key licence deals may make a publishing project financially viable—this is more common in the trade sector of publishing, where licence revenue may offset the publisher's investment in a large advance to the author, or co-edition printings of licensed editions by the primary publisher which amortize the high costs of producing books heavily illustrated in colour. In the educational, academic, and professional sectors, it is less likely that potential rights sales will influence the initial publishing decision, but rights revenue is nevertheless welcome and may be crucial in attracting and retaining authors.

In addition to the financial benefits of rights sales (which may vary considerably depending on the project, the type of licence, and the market concerned), licensing provides a means of accessing markets which may be difficult or inappropriate for the original edition to service for reasons of distribution, pricing, or language requirements. Licensing can also build an author's reputation, and in some cases may facilitate the visibility of the publisher's brand in overseas markets, if it appears alongside that of the local licensee.

The History of Rights Business

The trade in rights is not new, but it has expanded and become far more organized and sophisticated over the years, influenced by copyright developments as well as by new opportunities afforded by developments in technology. The USA and the UK did not beome members of a common international copyright convention until the Universal Copyright Convention was established in 1952; before that time, the works of many British authors were published without permission or payment in the USA, a situation often highlighted by Charles Dickens on his reading tours of the USA. Similarly, American authors such as Mark Twain were published without permission or payment in the UK. Details of rights deals can be found in archived publisher's files from early in the twentieth century; arrangements were handled by a range of non-specialist staff, from individual editors to the managing director's secretary. Beatrix Potter[1] and Florence Upton[2] (creator of the golliwog character in a series of books published by Longman) both authorized merchandizing deals for products based on their book characters in the early

---

[1] Lee (2007).   [2] Davis (1992).

years of the twentieth century. Virginia Woolf's correspondence mentions American editions of books published by the Hogarth Press, the publishing house she founded in 1917 with her husband, Leonard Woolf. Her own books were published in the USA by Harcourt Brace.

The range of rights which can be sold has inevitably grown with the advent of new technologies such as radio and television broadcasting, exploitation of books as the basis of cinema films (and now as series available on the Internet through companies such as Netflix and Amazon) and audio recordings (which have progressed from disc to cassette to CD and thence to digital downloads).

Other opportunities for rights trading have opened up when hitherto inaccessible markets have changed—the countries of central and eastern Europe and the former Soviet Union with their state-controlled publishing industries were previously open only for licences of books not considered politically dangerous—primarily scientific and technical titles. Licences had to be negotiated via state copyright agencies and in some cases (e.g. Poland) on the basis of payment in a blocked currency. With major political and economic changes in the region form the early 1990s, these markets opened up to a far wider range of content, to types of books which had not been possible before (e.g. co-editions of lavishly illustrated titles) and on the basis of more normal licensing arrangements.

The People's Republic of China was not a signatory to any international copyright convention until 1992, when it ratified both the Berne and Universal Copyright Conventions. Before that time, many western books were reprinted or translated without permission or payment, although some British educational publishers had succeeded in making licence arrangements for English language teaching courses, again on the basis of blocked currency arrangements. Chinese publishers are now major purchasers of rights, although some content remains politically sensitive. There are similar constraints in Vietnam, which eventually signed the Berne Convention in October 2004.

WHO SHOULD HANDLE RIGHTS SALES?

Nowadays, all licensing arrangements will involve a range of skills to achieve the best deal for author and publisher—imagination and creativity; knowledge of a wide range of markets, some of which may have different copyright regimes and pricing policies; contact with reliable potential licence partners; the ability to negotiate a deal beneficial to both sides and to tie this up in an appropriate licence contract, and administrative skills to keep tabs on a wide range of licence deals at different stages. The question of who is best placed to handle this specialist activity may vary depending on the publishing sector, the status of the author and the resources available within the publishing house. In trade publishing, most established authors in the UK and the USA are represented by literary agents—this is far less the case in Europe, Asia, and Latin America, where authors tend to contract directly with publishers. A well-established literary agency may seek to make separate arrangements with publishers in the major English language markets, granting each an exclusive range of sales territories and designating some territories as open markets where rival editions can compete with each other. Agencies with specialist staff may retain control of foreign language translation rights, which may then be promoted through a network of subagents in individual overseas markets. These are particularly prevalent in central and eastern Europe, Russia, and most markets in Asia. Subagents are generally more active in handling trade titles; they usually have a good knowledge of their own market and hence their services may also be attractive to primary publishers who do not travel to the markets concerned, and who may have concerns about being able to communicate with publishers in these markets. On the negative side, subagents tend to represent many different publishers and by definition have less detailed knowledge of the publications they represent than the primary agent or publisher. As they depend on commission for the deals they negotiate, they sometimes tend to concentrate on the works of authors with already established international reputations.

Some UK and US literary agencies have staff experienced in placing film, television, and merchandising rights; in all these cases, such rights will not form part of the primary publisher's package, although the sale of such rights may well have a positive impact on sales of the original book. Agencies will retain an agreed commission on all deals they handle.

Since the 1960s, the sale of rights has been recognized as a specialized and lucrative activity and today most medium to large trade publishers have specialist rights departments, and publishers keen to exploit rights may seek a broader range of rights than simply the primary right to publish in their agreed sales territory—if a bundle of rights is agreed with the author's agent, this will almost certainly involve their agreeing to higher contractual terms for the work. By contrast, many works published by educational, academic, and professional publishers stem from ideas conceived by the publisher, who will identify the need for a new book on a particular topic and will seek out and commission an appropriate author to undertake the task. Many such authors do not write for a living, but are employed in the education or business sectors; contracts are usually negotiated direct with the publisher and literary agents are rarely involved. The publisher will normally acquire a full range of subsidiary rights from the author in addition to the primary publishing rights, often through a full assignment of copyright to the publisher, and most publishers will have specialist staff to handle rights sales. In most cases the author will receive an advance and royalties on sales of editions of the work produced by the publisher (whether in print or electronic form) and an agreed percentage share of any revenue from each category of rights handled by the publisher.

From the point of view of the publisher, therefore, the optimum position is to acquire as broad a range of rights as possible in order to maximize revenue opportunities which will be shared with the author but which will also offset the publisher's overall investment in bringing the work to market. When acquiring a work, the publisher should have a clear idea of the range of rights required and should be prepared to explain to the author why such rights should be included in the package. If a literary agent is representing the author, much will depend on the bargaining power of each party in the negotiations and whether several publishers are competing for the work, perhaps via a full-scale auction.

Are the interests of the author and the publisher always the same in connection with the licensing of rights? In most cases, their interests should coincide in terms of using licensing as a medium for extending the author's reputation, reaching additional markets, and generating additional revenue for both author and publisher alike. There are, however, some areas where the perceptions and policy of each may diverge—for example, an author may have unrealistic expectations about the scale and value of licences for their book in a particular market (there is often an assumption that languages supported by a large population, e.g. Mandarin and Arabic, may justify enormous print runs). A publisher may wish to avoid or even decline some licence arrangements—one example would be granting translation licences in markets where they expect to sell substantial quantities of the English edition, for example an adoptable student textbook in markets such as Scandinavia or the Benelux countries. Copy for copy, export sales will bring in a higher return than royalties on a licensed edition. In such cases it is vital to explain clearly to the author the market circumstances, and hence the publisher's policy.

INCLUSION OF THIRD PARTY COPYRIGHT MATERIAL

It is worth flagging here an additional issue which is relevant to the licensing potential of a work. If the author wishes to include any third party copyright material in the work—text quoted from other sources, photographs, drawings, maps, graphs, charts., etc—it will be necessary to secure permission to do so from the relevant copyright holders, and in most cases fees will be payable. The task of securing such permission may fall to the author or may be undertaken by the publisher—this will be a matter for agreement between the parties, as will the question of who will cover the cost of such fees. Whoever undertakes the work must have a clear brief on the range of rights to be secured—is the material for publication only in the publisher's own edition or editions of the book, or should permission extend also to any licensed editions, e.g. to a US publisher, a foreign language publisher, or the licensee of some form of digital rights? A project which places the onus on the potential licensee to seek and pay for additional permission to reuse the quoted third party material themselves will be unattractive; broad clearance by the author or the original publisher to include reuse of the material by licensees will increase licensing possibilities but will result in a significantly higher permissions bill.

THE RANGE OF RIGHTS

What types of rights can be licensed? The list constantly changes as some categories rise or fall in importance; some disappear altogether, whilst new opportunities arise, often as a result of new technology.

English Language Rights

For a UK publisher, the ability to license English language rights to publishers in other English language markets such as the USA, Canada, South Africa, and Australasia may be vital if the publisher does not have a network of global subsidiaries or distribution agents; the brand and marketing activities of a local publisher are also likely to produce larger sales than copies of the UK edition sold through a distributor who may be representing the lists of a broad range of other publishers. Territorial licence arrangements are likely to be negotiated either on the basis of local reprint licences based on an advance and royalties, or—for highly illustrated books—may involve the primary publisher printing co-edition copies on behalf of each licensee. Other potential English language licence opportunities might include licences to specialist publishers for large print editions, although this market has been affected by the rise of e-readers and tablets which permit users to increase the font size.

A key area of activity, mainly for English language textbook publishers, is the licensing of low-price reprint editions to publishers in markets such as India and the Philippines, and to some extent in China, where courses in topics such as business are taught at the top universities in English, often by foreign faculty. One drawback of this category of licensing is the tendency of such legitimately licensed editions to 'leak' into other markets such as East Africa or the former republics of the Soviet Union and (more worryingly) into more affluent markets where they can undercut sales of the original publisher's edition, despite the fact that they probably carry clear market restriction notices. This situation has not been helped by the 2013 US Supreme Court decision in the case of *Kirtsaeng v John Wiley & Sons Inc.* In 2008 the US publishers John Wiley brought legal action against a Thai student, Supap Kirtsaeng, who had purchased copies of low-price reprint editions produced by Wiley specifically for sale in a designated Asian market, and had imported them for sale in the USA, undercutting Wiley's full price editions. Wiley won its case in the two lower courts, and when Kirtsaeng appealed, a ban on importation was upheld in the Second Court of Appeal. However, that judgment was overturned by the Supreme Court on the grounds of the doctrine of first sale, that is, that copies legitimately purchased could then be resold without permission from the rightsholder.

Two areas of licensing which were once hugely important have declined substantially in recent years. The first category is that of paperback rights, once licensed by the primary hardback publisher to a specialist paperback publisher. Nowadays most trade publishers can publish in both formats, and are likely to seek to acquire 'vertical' publishing rights, publishing first the hardback edition and then a paperback version or versions a year later. The second category is that of book clubs—once powerful mail order operations which offered books at a discount off the fixed retail price to club members, either purchasing the copies at a very high discount from publishers, or in some cases acquiring reprint licences to print their own editions of titles which were used in large quantities over a long period of time. With the demise of the UK Net Book Agreement in 1997 and the subsequent ability of bookshops, supermarkets, and online retailers such as Amazon to offer substantial discounts, the USP (unique selling point) of book clubs disappeared and they have virtually ceased to exist in the UK.

Some titles, mainly originating in the trade sector, may have potential for the sale of serial rights to newspapers and magazines. The most important category is first serial rights, where a newspaper or magazine may be prepared to pay a substantial sum to publish an extract or series of extracts before the book itself is launched on the market; negotiations may be conducted in great secrecy and involve confidentiality agreements. The most popular categories of book used in this way tend to be biographies or auto-biographies of well-known figures, whether from the world of entertainment, sport, or politics, and at the height of the serial rights market very substantial six-figure sums have been paid by national newspapers, especially for content which might be viewed as sensational or scandalous; at the time of writing, figures are now more modest. Newspapers and magazines hope to increase their readership for issues containing the extracts and to retain at least some of those readers; agents and publishers hope for increased sales of the book in addition to the fees paid for first serial rights, the majority of which go to the author. Against this must be set the fact that it is difficult to secure full approval for exactly what material is used and in what context. Fiction is relatively rarely serialized, but it is possible to license extracts from non-fiction titles in areas such as cookery, gardening, interior design, self-help, and popular business to magazines and to the specialist supplements of national newspapers. Second serial rights, which appear after the book itself is published, are less valuable but nevertheless generate worthwhile publicity.

Translation Rights

Moving away from the English language, a hugely important area is that of translation rights. Literary agents and specialist rights departments in publishing houses devote much of their time to promoting rights to appropriate foreign language publishers and it is a constant challenge to keep up to date with which books 'travel' and appeal across a broad range of countries and cultures—at the time of writing, J. K. Rowling's *Harry Potter* titles[3] have been licensed into seventy-three languages, including Latin and classical Greek. An academic title is likely to have less extensive translation potential, and here rights sellers also have to bear in mind that licensing translation rights for such a book in markets such as the Benelux countries and Scandinavia may have a detrimental effect on English language sales of the book in those markets; it is vital to coordinate policy in this area.

It is currently estimated that approximately 60 per cent of all titles translated world-wide are translated from the English language, which supports the view that English is viewed as the most accessible language, and also the fact that US and UK publishers and literary agents have long been extremely active in promoting rights in their titles.

---

[3] https://en.wikipedia.org/wiki/Harry_Potter_in_translation

Languages such as French, German, Italian, and Spanish generate a far smaller proportion of translated titles worldwide, whilst books in languages regarded as less accessible represent even lower figures. Despite this, the Japanese author Marie Kondo's *The Life-Changing Magic of Tidying*[4] has been translated into some forty languages, whilst the fiction works of Haruki Murakami[5] (a Japanese writer admittedly very influenced by western culture and hence not typical) have been translated into more than fifty languages.

The rationale for buying translation rights may vary according to circumstances—publishers may compete to acquire rights in the work of an international bestselling author, or to meet demands for the latest publishing fad such as mindfulness (or even colouring books, where little or no translation is required). Co-edition publishing can make highly designed and expensive books illustrated in colour accessible to publishers in markets who could not afford to originate such titles themselves. In the academic and professional sectors, there may be a need to acquire up-to-date content written by leading authorities in fields such as business, computing, and medicine. The translation of existing titles can also be a faster way to build a new publishing list than commissioning titles from local authors from scratch. The choice of a translator normally lies with the licensee, unless the original author is well established and has a regular preferred translator or contractual approval of the translator. A major author may also have contractual approval of the final choice of foreign language licensee, particularly if the rights are being auctioned competitively.

By contrast with their outward licensing activities, US and UK publishers are reputed to translate less than 5 per cent of their publishing output annually—the figure of 3 per cent[6] is often quoted. Publishers in markets such as France and Germany publish a far higher proportion of translations—on average between 20 and 30 per cent—whilst publishers in markets such as central and eastern Europe publish even more. Mainland China, a major buyer of rights, acquired around 15,500 titles in 2014, or which 2,655 originated in the UK;[7] the same year, about 8,000 Chinese titles were licensed worldwide, but only 410 of those were licensed to the UK. The reticence of publishers in both the UK and the USA to publish more translations may be for a variety of reasons—an excellent supply of home-grown authors, the acquisition of titles from the other side of the Atlantic or from other English language markets, or a nervousness about translation in terms of the difficulty and cost of finding good translators.

UK publishers—and in particular educational and academic publishers—were pioneers in tackling difficult and transitional markets, visiting central and eastern Europe, the former Soviet Union and China and Vietnam long before many of their overseas competitors; some British publishers still recall conducting licensing activities in countries where currency could not be remitted abroad, and attending book fairs during periods of curfews and martial law. Some of these countries are markets where political and

[4] https.//en.wikipedia.org/wiki/Marie_Kondo
[5] https.//en.wikipedia.org/wiki/Haruki_Murakami
[6] *Translation Statistics from Literature across Frontiers,* May 2015; www.lit-across-frontiers.org/new_translation_statistics_from_laf
[7] GPI Report on China, Publishers Association 2014.

economic changes have made formerly unacceptable content suddenly in high demand. Other markets continued to retain state control over what can be published and censorship remains a real issue which can affect licensing possibilities. Sadly, some markets which had become more liberal after political and economic changes now seem to be reverting to tighter control of the media.

As with English language licences, translation licences can be granted either as arm's length licences, allowing the licensee to print their own editions or—for highly illustrated books—as co-editions, with licensees supplying the original publisher with the translated text imposed to the layout of the original edition, and the primary publisher then undertaking a coordinated co-edition, printing copies for each of their licensees, thus amortizing high origination costs and reducing the manufacturing cost for all the participating publishers.

NON-PRINT LICENCES

Moving away from the realm of print, there are a variety of ways in which a work can be licensed, but much will depend on the nature and suitability of the work in question. A significant area is that of audiobooks which have risen in popularity as the platform moved from cassette to CD to digital download form through companies such as Amazon's Audible. The majority of candidate titles are fiction, popular non-fiction and some business titles. Most of the major UK trade publishers now produce their own audiobooks rather than licensing the rights to specialist audio publishers, but Audible remains the main digital download channel. The move to digital with its virtually unlimited capacity has facilitated a significant move to unabridged rather than abridged audiobooks. The actual reading may be undertaken by the author of the book, particularly if he or she has a distinctive voice (e.g. Alan Bennett) or by actors or personalities with a facility for undertaking this type of work (e.g. Stephen Fry or Martin Jarvis).

Some books may lend themselves to adaptation in dramatic form; a book with dramatization potential could be licensed as the basis for a play (e.g. Michael Morpurgo's *War Horse*) or a musical (e.g. Roald Dahl's *Matilda*)—here payment for a commercial production is usually based on a percentage of the box office receipts. A book might also form the basis of a television programme or serial (e.g. John le Carré's *The Night Manager*) or a series (e.g. the *Inspector Morse* and *Lewis* series based on Colin Dexter's novels, and *The Durrells*, based on Gerald Durrell's *My Family and Other Animals*). Perhaps the most ambitious form of licence is a full-scale cinematographic film. Parties interested in acquiring the film rights in a book could range from a film studio, an independent production company, a producer, a would-be scriptwriter, or an established actor; an initial approach may result in an option being granted on the rights, usually for an initial period of one year while the viability of the project is researched. It is usual for an option to be paid for, but full payment for the rights is made only if the option is actually exercised—this produces the dilemma of having to set an overall price for the rights when there is no guarantee that a film will actually result. The majority of options are not exercised, but despite this a substantial proportion of cinema films are based on books rather than on original screenplays. This is an area where the moral right of integrity of the author may have to be sacrificed, as a waiver is normally required; this can result in characters, locations, and timescales being altered in the film version, as when the recent film version of Paula Hawkins' *The Girl on the Train* was transposed from London to New York; Almodovar's *Julieta* moved the location of Alice Munro's stories from Canada to Spain; while a subplot and tidier ending were grafted on to Julian Barnes' *The Sense of an Ending*. Fiction is the most likely starting-point as the basis of a film, and CGI has greatly facilitated the production of film versions of Tolkien's *The Hobbit* and *Lord of the Rings*, C. S. Lewis's *Chronicles of Narnia* and Patrick Ness's *A Monster Calls*. Non-fiction titles have formed the basis of recent films such as *Trumbo*, *Selma*, and *A United Kingdom*. Sensitive subject matter may mean there is a gap of many years between the appearance of a book and its film version as with *Carol*, the film version of Patricia Highsmith's *The Price of Salt*. In recent years, film and television rights are rarely part of the publisher's package of rights; they are more likely to be retained and handled by the author's literary agent. However, they will almost certainly benefit the publisher's sales of the original book, and many publishers will reissue the book with a TV or film tie-in cover. In the USA, there have been a number of acquisitions by multimedia companies seeking to control content which can be exploited on screen, as when Disney acquired Marvel Entertainment and Warner Brothers acquired DC Comics.

Linked to the sale of film and television rights may be the sale of merchandizing rights, when characters derived from a book may be licensed for a variety of products such as soft toys, clothing, bedlinen, stationery, ceramics, board games, video games, and endorsements for fast food or food products. Interest in merchandizing may come from a wide range of industries with different business models, and is most likely to occur when the book concerned is being turned into a television or film version. These rights may be required as part of the film or television deal—hence the fact that so many merchandizing items based on A. A. Milne's *Winnie the Pooh* books are credited to Walt Disney rather than to the E. H. Shepherd illustrations in the original books. Even if merchandizing rights do lie with the original book publishers, they are sufficiently complex that the publisher may choose to use the services of a merchandizing agent (as for the characters of Beatrix Potter, whose books are still published by the Warne imprint of Penguin Random House). In a recent move, Hachette UK acquired rights to the Enid Blyton estate.

Digital Rights

In recent years there have been increased opportunities for various forms of digital licensing. On the whole, the production of ebooks, enhanced ebooks, and apps has been undertaken by publishers themselves, perhaps with the assistance of digital developers such as Touch Press. Pan Macmillan produced an app based on Douglas Adams's *A Hitchhiker's Guide to the Galaxy* with audiobook extracts read by Stephen Fry and extracts from the original radio series. Egmont UK produced an app based on Michael Morpurgo's *War Horse* with the full text, an audio version read by the author, a filmed stage production, and an interactive timeline of events during the First World War. Faber & Faber produced an app based on T. S. Eliot's *The Waste Land* which includes readings by Ted Hughes. Alec Guinness, Viggo Mortensen, and Eliot himself, as well as images of the original manuscript.

Arrangements with ebook retailers such as Amazon, Apple, and Kobo are distribution deals, while arrangements with ebook library aggregators such as Proquest and Credo are also treated as sales rather than as licences and accounted for accordingly. However, many licences which have previously been confined to the medium of print (e.g. licences to US or foreign language publishers) will nowadays also include a requirement for ebook rights, so publishers granting such licences need to be clear that they control such rights and also to clarify the licensee's proposed distribution and financial models which may vary considerably from country to country.

Other areas of digital licensing include licensing selected content to commercial websites for an agreed period of time (for example, licensing relevant content from a business book to enhance the website of a bank or an investment company, or from a parenting title to a website selling products for children). Reference publishers have long been licensing their lexicographic databases for handheld electronic products such as dictionaries, thesauri, spellcheckers, and crossword solvers produced by companies such as Casio; a good example would be the licensing of the *Oxford English Dictionary* as a reference tool for ebooks on Amazon's Kindle devices.

Licences for the Reading Impaired

An important area of licensing involves granting access to content for the reading impaired, which includes not only the visually impaired but also people with disabilities such as dyslexia or a physical disability which prevents them from holding a book in the normal way. Permission is normally granted free of charge, and ranges from granting the right for an institution such as the RNIB in the UK to produce Braille editions to the supply of accessible files for a student to access a textbook via text-to-speech. The UK Equality Act 2010 protects people with disabilities from discrimination and places an obligation on publishers to make their content accessible to such users. Internationally, the Marrakesh Treaty with similar provisions came into force on 30 September 2016, although it has not yet been ratified by the UK.

PERMISSIONS

There can be additional sources of revenue derived from licensing partial use of a copyright work. The first is the category known in the publishing industry as 'permissions', whereby publishers authorize the use of passages of text, photographs, illustrations, graphs, charts, or maps from one of their own publications in another publication, provided that they themselves have the right to grant such a licence. Rates of payment vary according to the content and the nature and extent of the usage requested; prose is usually charged for at a rate per thousand words, whilst poetry is normally charged for by the line. Charges for illustrations and photographs may vary depending on the context of their reuse: the fee for a photograph reproduced on a book cover will be higher than the fee for the same photograph reproduced to quarter-page size inside the book. Permissions is a reactive function and most publishers will have specialist staff to handle the activity. Some publishers have chosen to semi-automate the permissions function by using services such as RightsLink (provided by the US collective management organization, the Copyright Clearance Center) and in July 2017 a similar service, PLSclear, was launched by the UK Publishers Licensing Services.

Collective Licensing

A second source of income—perhaps favouring educational, academic, and professional rather than trade publishers—comes from collective and so-called 'secondary' licensing. This happens when publishers and authors authorize a central collective management organization—in the case of the UK, the Copyright Licensing Agency (CLA)—to negotiate licences to schools, universities and colleges, government departments, and private businesses, allowing them to make multiple copies of limited amounts of copyright material through photocopying or scanning—for example chapters from textbooks to be included in student coursepacks, copies of journal articles to be used by pharmaceutical companies, copies of legal content to be used by law firms, etc.). The CLA also has bilateral arrangements with similar organizations in a number of other countries to cover the copying of UK copyright material abroad. A share of the revenue from licensing is paid to authors via the Authors Licensing and Collecting Society (ALCS), to visual artists via the Design and Artists Copyright Society (DACS), or the Picture Industry Collecting Society for Effective Licensing (PICSEL) and to publishers via Publishers' Licensing Services (PLS). In the UK, payment to publishers in the 2016–17 period was £32.9 million[8] and such payment goes straight to the bottom line, as authors and visual artists are paid their share of revenue separately.

Most developed countries have collective licensing systems in place, although the models may vary—from the purely voluntary systems in the UK and the USA, the German-Spanish model on the basis of a levy on copying machines, the Dutch model of a statutory licence in the areas of government and education, to the Nordic model which functions on the basis of an extended collective licensing model where the majority of rightsholders agree. The International Federation of Reproduction Rights Organizations

---

[8] PLS Annual Review April 2016–March 2017.

(IFRRO) encourages the establishment of collective management organizations and can advise on how best to design them to suit local circumstances.

CONCLUSION

It can be seen from the above that licensing intellectual property rights is a wide-ranging activity—but of course very few books lend themselves to every aspect of such exploitation. However, the function is crucial to the publishing industry and its importance is often underestimated by comparison with the primary editorial and sales functions—indeed, licence revenue is often wrongly compared with sales turnover, when the publisher share of licensing revenue should rightly be compared with the profit element of such sales. The successful promotion and sale of rights—whether by literary agents or by publishing staff—requires a particular range of skills ranging from creativity, numeracy, negotiating skills, facility with contracts, attention to detail, and people skills. Technology has undoubtedly speeded up communication and has enabled publishers to supply material for assessment by potential licence partners electronically as well as facilitating the promotion of rights to potential buyers via websites. Contact can be made by telephone, Skype, and videoconferencing; however, a great deal of the secret of successful rights selling still depends on building up strong and long-term personal relationships—an experienced rights seller often knows instinctively to which potential publishing partners a new project will appeal, whether it is an illustrated picture book for children or a volume on concrete technology for civil engineers. A substantial amount of rights business is conducted face to face at rights-focused international book fairs such as Frankfurt, London, and Bologna as well as regional fairs such as Beijing, Guadalajara, Abu Dhabi, and Sharjah. Many literary agents and publishing rights staff also undertake sales trips to visit licence partners in their own territories. An additional resource may be the use of online rights trading platforms such as PubMatch and IPR License, where rightsholders can showcase titles available for licence and undertake licence negotiations via the site. Such services are perhaps more useful for smaller publishers who do not have specialist rights staff.

As some indication of the value of rights sales to the UK publishing industry, the annual report[9] commissioned by the Publishers Association (with participation from publishers representing some 70 per cent of the UK trade) showed gross income of £283 million in 2017, an increase of 34 per cent over the previous year. Licensing income generated by literary agents (representing some 70 per cent of UK agents) totalled £136 million.

---

[9] PA Statistics Yearbook 2017, Publishers Association.

REFERENCES

Lee, Linda (2007). *Beatrix Potter: The Extraordinary Life of a Victorian Genius*, London: Allen Lane.

Davis, Norma S. (1992). *A Lark Ascends: Florence Upton, Artist and Illustrator*, Lanham, MD: Scarecrow Press Inc.

Owen, Lynette (2014). *Selling Rights*, 7th Edition, Abingdon: Routledge.

Owen, Lynette, ed. (2017). *Clark's Publishing Agreements: A Book of Precedents*, 10th Edition, London: Bloomsbury Professional.

Jones, Hugh and Christopher Benson, (2016). *Publishing Law*, 5th Edition, Abingdon: Routledge.

CHAPTER 23

....

LIBRARIES

....

ALEX HOLZMAN AND
SARAH KALIKMAN LIPPINCOTT

LIBRARIES occupy a dual role in relation to publishers: that of content consumer or curator and that of content creator. Libraries have long been among the very best customers for publishers' offerings in whatever form. They provide access to millions of volumes of scholarly literature and leisure reading in print and electronic media, as well as serving as community hubs where patrons can consult with experts, learn new skills, and utilize specialized equipment. They also have a long history as publishers of original content, from the production of printed collection catalogues beginning in the seventeenth century to modern efforts to produce portfolios of electronic journals. The digital revolution has transformed the library's role as both collector and creator. The affordances of networked information have led to increased pushes to build unique local collections while providing access to vast quantities of resources through national or regional consortia and have also democratized electronic publishing. Despite these radical changes, the library retains its core mission—providing access to information—and continues to enjoy a symbiotic relationship with the academic and trade publishers who create, assemble, review, and add value to the world's knowledge.

LIBRARIES AS CONTENT CURATORS

....

Selecting, acquiring, and providing access to content remains the cornerstone of library services in both public and academic libraries around the world, although profound changes in technology have transformed many aspects of how libraries fulfil this role. Historically, a library's primary role was to assemble, organize, and interpret vast collections of print materials and media on behalf of a community of users, a function that created efficiencies and economies of scale in a pre-networked environment (Dempsey et al. 2014: 395). Libraries have therefore long been among the very best customers for published content in a range of forms from both commercial and non-profit presses.

Anderson (2014) estimated that, in general, libraries account for around a quarter of total university press sales, and represent the majority of sales in monograph-driven disciplines like history and literary studies. The bulk of science, technology, and maths (STM) subscription revenue comes from sales to libraries while individual subscriptions make up a small, and diminishing, market share (Ware and Mabe 2015: 19). The networked environment has led not only to a prodigious increase in expenditures on electronic resources, but also to interinstitutional collaborations, collection deduplication efforts, and a revaluing of the library's unique materials (Anderson 2013). Libraries sustain large sectors of the academic publishing market, making them not just a customer, but an active partner in shaping the business of publishing. From the Big Deal (large bundles of journal content sold at a considerable discount relative to individual journal sub-scriptions) to Demand Driven Acquisitions (purchases triggered by patron usage), publishers design their business models to appeal to libraries and to align with library workflows. Trends in library collection development practices can exert significant influence on what and how presses publish.

Collection Development Policies and Trends

Collecting practices reflect each library's institutional or community context as well as its resources, its history, and its user base. The academic libraries at large research institutions aspire to provide comprehensive access to scholarly resources across the full breadth of disciplines, a mission that faces growing obstacles as the number and costs of publications increases dramatically each year. Libraries at smaller academic institutions such as regional universities, community colleges, and liberal arts colleges typically collect a narrower range of resources tailored to the teaching and learning mission of their institution and in their institutions' specific areas of strength. They often complement their own relatively small but deep collections through consortial collecting arrangements and inter-library loans. Public libraries tend to focus on general interest trade publications, including fiction and non-fiction books, periodicals, and entertainment media. Their collecting practices often reflect the community in which they are embedded, meaning many build robust collections of foreign language materials. National libraries around the world build their collections based on each country's mandate and traditions, with some aiming to collect a copy of each book published annually in their country.

From Content Scarcity to Information Overload

Modern collection development practices in academic libraries have been shaped by the sheer volume of scholarly resources created each year. Ware and Mabe (2015: 27) identified over 28,000 'active scholarly peer-reviewed English-language journals in late 2014 (plus a further 6,450 non-English-language journals), collectively publishing about 2.5 million articles a year'. The authors further noted that, over the past 200 years, increases in out-put have grown predictably by around 3 per cent for the number of articles published and 3.5 per cent for the number of new journal titles (Ware and Mabe 2015: 28). Meanwhile, data from some of the largest aggregation services providers showed that 54,273 new humanities monographs were published in 2013 (Humanities Indicators, 2015). Even the most well-resourced libraries lack the financial and human resources—and the space—to provide access to all of these materials. Collection development practices therefore do not reflect a desire to collect every possible resource, but to strategically provide access to the materials that the library's stakeholders most need and use. Researchers, particularly in the industrialized world, have access, through the library's print collections, its collection sharing partners, and the open web, to more information than they could ever process. As Hazen (1995: 30) remarked, 'part of the library's job is to make sense of this abundance' through curation activities such as creating discipline-specific resource guides, information maps, and providing aggregated search mechanisms. Librarians must also ensure that electronic and print collections remain up to date and navigable, not only by purchasing selectively, but strategically weeding when necessary.

The evolving nature of the scholarly record has only exacerbated the challenge of vetting, organizing, and stewarding content. While libraries historically focused on monograph and journal collecting, they now must contend with a growing inventory of scholarly outputs, from datasets to born digital and multimedia publications, and dynamic documents meant to evolve over time (Johnson et al. 2015: 13).

Holdings and Expenditures

As of 2012, the 3,793 academic libraries in the USA collectively held over a billion print volumes, of which roughly 9 per cent circulated during the course of that year, according to the National Center for Education Statistics (NCES) (Phan et al. 2014: 8). Libraries expended a total of $2,790,039,494 on 'information resources' in 2014, a figure that includes book and serial backfiles purchases, serials subscriptions, as well as funding for document delivery and inter-library loans, preservation, and other collections-related expenditures (Phan et al. 2014: 10). The Association of Research Libraries (ARL) (2016: 1) reports that its members' average expenditures for materials accounted for roughly 45 per cent of their total expenditures in the 2014–15 fiscal year.

The circulation of print resources has been declining steadily over the past several decades as more readers opt for the convenience and portability of electronic content (Anderson 2011). Library collecting has kept pace with this burgeoning demand. As early as 2007, nearly 90 per cent of academic libraries in the USA reported owning ebooks; patrons would be hard-pressed to find a library that does not offer ebooks at present (Walters 2013). However Walters reported that most libraries remained 'tentative in their acquisition of ebooks' and 'reluctant to divert resources from their print acquisition programs' (2013: 189). Libraries reported holdings of 252.6 million ebooks in 2012, an increase of 52.7 million volumes over the previous year (Phan et al. 2014: 8). Yet, as of 2013, libraries spent on average less than 6 per cent of their acquisitions funds on ebooks (Walters 2013: 189). Journals have reflected this trend tenfold, as many libraries have reduced or eliminated print journal subscriptions, particularly when those journals are available electronically (Association of Research Libraries 2014). A 2012 survey by ARL found that only 2 per cent of bundled journal contracts included print versions (Strieb and Blixrud 2013). A 2016 survey of library directors found that, counterintuitively, respondents 'are increasingly seeing building print collections as more important and as more of a priority, but are devoting fewer resources towards these collections and are increasingly developing policies for de-accessioning these materials when they are also available digitally' (Wolff-Eisenberg 2016).

Online journals and database subscriptions accounted for over 60 per cent of library materials expenditures in 2016, an increase of over 10 per cent from 2010 (Wolff-Eisenberg 2016). As the share of library expenditures on serials has grown, so have tensions around costs and resource allocation. Librarians have questioned the rationale for exorbitant subscription fees and author fees as major commercial publishers report profit margins over 35 per cent (Hu 2016). Commercial publishers have justified rising costs by citing the significant expense of building new digital platforms while maintaining legacy print programmes, as well as the added-value services they provide to both authors and readers.

Although libraries continue to experience budget pressures related to rising costs, they have seen a moderate resurgence in funding in recent years. Public library materials budgets rose an average of 3.7 per cent in 2015 and 2016, a significant increase over the 1.5 per cent reported in 2014 (Peet 2017). Materials budgets in academic libraries are predicted to rise by a global average of 1.2 per cent, although some regions (including North America) anticipate slight declines (Publishers Communication Group 2017).

Purchasing and Licensing Practices

At one time, bibliographers at academic libraries hand-selected each book and serial that would become part of the collection. Many academic libraries still employ bibliographers, selectors, departmental liaisons, or other professional staff with responsibility for collection development, but their roles and the functions they perform have changed dramatically. Rather than sifting through stacks of book slips, librarians typically rely on approval plans and bundled subscriptions to acquire much of the content that meets their needs.

A significant portion of academic library collection development now occurs through bundled purchasing or licensing arrangements. Cox and Cox (2008) found that 95 per cent of large publishers, three-quarters of medium-sized publishers, and 40 per cent of small publishers sell bundled content. Publishers report that individual journal subscriptions have dropped as a proportion of total sales, as bundled sales rise (Ware and Mabe 2015). Large academic libraries, which subscribe to hundreds of journal titles, typically rely on subscription agents to facilitate these transactions. Ware and Mabe (2015) reported that, on average, libraries place about 80 per cent of their business through subscription agents. These agents 'act on behalf of libraries, allowing the library to deal with one or two agents rather than having to manage relationships with large numbers of journal publishers, each with different order processes, terms & conditions, etc.' (Ware and Mabe 2015).

The practice of bundling journal subscriptions has become widely known as the Big Deal, a term that has become increasingly loaded as libraries have expressed discontent at the high prices and restrictive terms it has entailed. Journal subscription costs, especially in the STEM fields, have exacerbated budgetary pressures on academic libraries, leading to large-scale subscription cancellations and a diminishing share of resources allocated to monograph purchasing. According to ARL, serials expenditures rose a remarkable 521 per cent between 1986 and 2015, while overall library materials expenditures rose 352 per cent. Expenditures for one-time resource expenditures (which includes monograph purchasing) rose a meagre 79 per cent, and salaries rose 152 per cent (Association of Research Libraries 2014). A disproportionate amount of these expenditures are directed towards a small group of the largest commercial publishers (Strieb and Blixrud 2013). Notably, several large academic libraries and library consortia—such as Sweden's Bibsam Consortium, France's Le Consortium Couperin, and Florida State University in the USA—have recently cancelled their Big Deal packages or other contracts with major publishers like Elsevier and Springer.

The shift from purchasing to licensing has had significant implications for libraries. Historically, libraries purchased print collections outright, securing the right to possess and lend them in perpetuity. Many publishers have now moved towards licensing their electronic content, meaning that libraries now broker access to much of their collection, rather than owning it outright. Licence agreements also require libraries to adhere to a set of contractual obligations that are typically far more restrictive than copyright law, limiting how these resources can be displayed, downloaded, mined, and used (Thornton 2000). Bundled subscriptions, in particular, have received negative attention from librarians in recent years because libraries retain little power to determine what content is included in the bundle and to cancel individual titles. Libraries have also decried the strict non-disclosure clauses in many of these licences, which prevent them from sharing the terms of the licence or the price they have negotiated with others in the field (Strieb and Blixrud 2013).

The question of cost has become a significant sticking point. Ware and Mabe (2015), citing a 2015 survey conducted by the Association of Research Libraries that found that most licences base pricing on the historic print model, explained that 'the library is offered electronic access to all the titles in the bundle at a price reflecting the library's existing print subscriptions (which are typically retained) plus a top-up fee for electronic-only access to the non-subscribed titles'. However, a range of other pricing models have emerged over the last decade, including usage-based pricing, which has failed to gain much traction, and tiered pricing based on institution size or on institution type (e.g. corporate libraries versus academic). Libraries and publishers have also experimented with innovative purchasing models that attempt to make the most of limited library resources while ensuring patrons can connect to the resources they need. The model that has received the most attention has been Demand-Driven or Patron-Driven Acquisition

(DDA or PDA), in which publishers or vendors provide libraries with a full inventory of their publications, but the titles are only purchased when requested by a patron.

Data-driven Collecting

Flat or declining budgets and increasing costs have led to a growing interest in data-driven decision making for library collection development. Belter and Kaske (2016) argued that 'anecdotal evidence of the value of library journal collections no longer carries the weight it once did, prompting libraries to provide quantitative evidence of value' to justify subscription decisions. In response, libraries have increasingly adopted and developed strategies to analyse the use and impact of their collections to inform their future collecting decisions. These strategies may include analysing electronic usage and circulation statistics, and identifying the works cited in the scholarly work produced by the institution's faculty and students, among others.

Cooperative Collection Development

Libraries have also responded to financial pressures and space constraints by leveraging their long-standing relationships with other libraries, particularly within regional library consortia (Strieb and Blixrud 2013). Cooperative collection development has emerged as a natural outgrowth of libraries' longstanding efforts to facilitate access to materials beyond the library's walls, which have included inter-library loan programmes, the creation of union catalogues (or more modern federated discovery interfaces), and reciprocal borrowing agreements between libraries (Strieb and Blixrud 2013). In a cooperative collection development arrangement, libraries commit to building and maintaining collections in their particular areas of strength. These arrangements allow libraries to build robust collections in the disciplinary specialties of their campus while simultaneously providing their users with access to a broad range of materials in other disciplines. The 'responsibility for collecting marginal, esoteric, or highly specialized research material should be divided up on a coordinated, statewide, or regional basis, although heavily used core materials would still be purchased locally' (Thornton 2000). Cooperative collection development agreements are often formalized through a memorandum of understanding between the participating libraries and/or through the creation of an independent entity to enforce and monitor the agreement. Library consortia have also emerged for the dedicated purpose of pooling resources and leveraging scale to negotiate the best possible subscription rates for electronic resources. Finally, libraries continue to rely heavily on the longstanding practice of inter-library loans (ILL) to connect patrons with the holdings of libraries around the world.

The Digital Revolution

The digital revolution has also become a library revolution. We have already seen how it has affected purchasing patterns and led to licensing models superseding ownership models. But how has the digital revolution changed the way users discover, read, and make use of library materials? And how has it changed what libraries can offer their patrons?

The Library as Place

During the print era, access to a library's materials required a visit to one of its buildings and the resources one could take home were in many cases severely limited. But today both public and academic libraries allow access via their websites to authorized users literally around the world. This is no small thing, although in the blink of an eye it has become a commonplace assumption. And this increased access has led to changes in purchasing schemes. For instance, public libraries now frequently 'purchase' ebooks with a shelf life of twenty-five checkouts. This is meant to replicate in an approximate fashion the shelf life of a physical book and so preserve the revenue stream of book publishers (C Platt 2017, personal communication, 4 October). It is of course a retro way of doing things and likely a bridge to a new model in coming years.

Library buildings themselves have been changed by the digital revolution. Both public and academic libraries now provide numerous public terminals and strong wifi networks for patrons who bring their own digital devices. Patrons use those terminals for everything from job-hunting to posting pictures of the grandchildren on Facebook to conducting research in broad and arcane subjects. Many newspapers and periodicals formerly found in print are now accessed via the library's on-line subscriptions. And as we have seen, ebooks have also found their way into public library markets, although on a relatively small scale because of logistical issues and reader preferences. While public libraries whose readers demand more popular books have tended to the licensing of x number of uses per book, academic libraries often load the metadata for many titles they don't actually hold into their electronic card catalogues (another manifestation of the digital revolution has been the disappearance of the grand wooden catalogue card holders of the print era). Patrons who wish to look at such books can access them seamlessly, but the library does not actually pay for a given title until an 'acquisition' is triggered by a number of uses, however defined in the contract with the publisher. This is the patron-driven acquisitions model.

Academic libraries have been physically transformed in other ways. As the need for space to accommodate both physical devices and areas where people can use devices either singly or collaboratively has increased, books and bound periodicals increasingly have migrated to offsite storage facilities or sometimes been discarded altogether. This has transformed libraries into places that are as much social meeting areas as places for quiet research and contemplation.

The User Experience

The most dramatic impact on usage by library patrons wrought by the digital revolution has been the ability to access library materials 24/7 from remote locations. Whether at their offices or homes or dormitories or conferences in foreign countries, patrons credentialled at a library can tap into its multimedia electronic resources in minutes. This truly is revolutionary, allowing a reallocation of time and work methods beyond the scope of this chapter.

One area we must consider, however, is discovery, where both libraries and publishers have invested tremendous effort. The digital revolution has indeed opened seemingly limitless amounts of information to users of all kinds, but the question of how to locate the best information—whether in terms of currency, accuracy, relevancy, or some other combination of factors, has become vexing. Libraries can create their own searching platforms on their websites, but they are also heavily dependent upon other databases that live on other platforms featuring their own distinctive searching options. Search features from platform to platform have much in common, but each differs in some of its finer details. And scholarly platforms use very different algorithms than commercial platforms such as Google. This can be confusing to researchers. And because each publisher (and author) wants their materials to be discovered, publishers have spent large sums trying to provide libraries with 'robust' metadata. This is a cost that did not exist in a print era.

Another variable in database searches involves what the licence between a library and a platform vendor allows in terms of 'free' display. EBSCO, a major aggregator of thousands of journals and host/manager of various platforms may offer different terms from their competitor, ProQuest, which may differ from Jstor or Project Muse, both non-profit organizations hosting electronic aggregations of books and journals. Some databases include the most recent articles or books; some observe an embargo for a certain length of time. And a researcher who searches a particular database only to find she can view no more than title, author, and abstract can become deeply frustrated.

In short, researchers trained in their fields now require increasing help in maximizing the usefulness of all the discovery mechanisms available to them. And reference librarians constantly have to re-learn what resources are available to them in the fields they service and how best to use them. The questions they now face are different than the ones from twenty years ago. Besides platform and discoverability issues, both researchers and librarians have been working on citation issues that involve citing by URLs, by DOIs (digital object identifiers), by date and place and version, as electronic publications tend to be less stable in both content and location than print ones.

For both libraries and publishers, the digital revolution incurs new costs and savings. Who pays for what and whether the amount of money flowing through the system is sufficient to maintain it remains uncertain.

Open Access

The open access (OA) movement has been the subject of entire books (Suber 2012; Scheufen 2015; Smith and Dickson 2016). It has impacted both libraries and publishers since appearing on the scene in the 1990s and bursting into prominence with the Budapest Open Access Initiative in 2002 and the 2003 Bethesda Statement on Open Access Publishing and the Berlin Declaration on Open Access to Knowledge in the

Sciences (Chan et al. 2002; Berlin Declaration 2003). Some in the open access movement see it as a moral imperative that knowledge be shared; others see OA as a natural response to rapidly increasing costs, especially in journals acquisitions. Either way, its impacts have been many and not always as originally envisioned.

One of the early consequences of the OA movement was the establishment of OA institutional repositories in a wide range of academic libraries throughout the world—4,585 as of December 2017 according to the Registry of Open Access Repositories (Arlitsch and Grant 2018: 267). These immediately became a place where 'non-traditional' or non-peer-reviewed materials could be deposited for any users to see. This included, for instance, such things as on-campus conferences, data sets, and—perhaps both most importantly and in some ways most problematically—pre-finalized versions of scholarly articles. Researchers citing other researchers must now sometimes distinguish which of multiple versions of an article is being quoted at any given time.

Digital repositories have also faced a major problem in the participation rate among local faculty. Despite attempts ranging from cajoling to faculty mandates, even getting 50 per cent of local faculty to deposit their materials has been difficult. As a result, what is and is not in an institutional repository can be difficult to predict and can add to the frustrations of the discovery process among researchers. This is not to say institutional repositories have failed—many house incredibly useful documents, big data, open educational resources, and the like. But as places to collect close to all the original research being published by a faculty, they have so far enjoyed only modest success. Publishers of gated material do not seem to have suffered. However, recent developments, including the acquisition of the popular Digital Commons institutional repository platform by the publishing behemoth Elsevier, point to an increased acknowledgement that service provision may soon eclipse content provision.

Another issue involving institutional repositories is the deposition of PhD theses written at the home university. Many universities now require this and no longer put printed dissertations in their stacks. This would seem a good way to save space and trees, but again as with all new things, unintended consequences ensued. University presses, by far the single largest type of publisher issuing books based on revised dissertations, sometimes declined such books if the 'raw' dissertation were available in an institutional depository. They feared that in an already severely troubled market, some libraries would decline to buy the book if a dissertation involving the same research in a somewhat raw form were already available. This was hardly a universal attitude amongst university press editors, nor was there sufficient proof of the theory's validity, but it was prevalent enough to cause some *angst* and lead to many universities, while still requiring the deposit of all PhD theses, to allow the author to embargo access to it for a period of time, generally a year or two (Truschke 2015).

Finally, institutional repositories and other open access portals will sometimes contain different versions of an article than the journal of record. This comes from publishers allowing pre-final versions (for example, pre-copy-editing) of an article to be posted in repositories. While the research results will not vary, changes in wording can change reader interpretations and lead to confusion in later citations of a work of research. Universal access to one version of a paper and restricted access to another version of the same paper produces a less than ideal transmission of knowledge.

Perhaps of paramount interest to the broader academic community has been the various 'flavours' of open access that have evolved as various interest groups within the community have struggled with the paramount issue open access faces: how to pay the real costs of publication via an open access (i.e. end-user free) format. For the purposes of this article, it is sufficient to say that abandonment of the end user as a source of revenue has left scholars themselves responsible for providing funds sufficient to cover the cost of publishing, a fungible term to be sure. This burden, referred to as author processing costs (APC) is being covered in various ways—by authors themselves, by their institutions, by research grants, and by combinations of all of these.

There have also been initiatives like Knowledge Unlatched that allow publishers to recover first-copy costs by 'pre-selling' books to libraries at lower than customary prices, with a guarantee that upon publication the book will be 'unlatched', that is, available open access.

Sometimes governments, too, have become involved in this issue, mandating open access while either providing some funding, as in the UK, or mandating open access to any research conducted in whole or in part through government funded research. Some countries such as the USA allow an embargo period before research becomes open access, as in the USA. The latter encourages library retention of journals subscriptions in order to ensure that users have access to the most current information, but leaves libraries struggling to stay within their acquisitions budgets.

Of particular concern in some poorer countries is the question of whether the benefits of having access to more research outweighs the new difficulties in procuring funds to publish their own work among scholars in poorer countries.

In short, digital access to information—print, visual, audio—has created enormous opportunities, but library response and indeed the shape of the twenty-first-century library and its relationship to publishing studies remains a work in progress.

Libraries as Content Creators

While libraries have historically occupied the role of content collectors and curators, their expertise in the publishing landscape has created a natural entrée into the role of publisher. Gilman (2015) and others have positioned the growth of library publishing as a strategic response to changes in the role of libraries and an acknowledgement that 'the traditional focal point for libraries—our commercially purchased collections—no longer provide the distinct value that they once did' (2015: 30). As physical barriers to accessing research materials have disappeared, libraries have placed increasing emphasis on their unique collections—such as rare and archival materials, and original content published in their repositories—and less on providing access to the traditionally published materials that are widely available on the web and duplicated in other libraries around the world.

Library publishing capitalizes on the traditional strengths of academic libraries and reflects their long-standing commitment to connecting scholars and the public with information. Libraries tend to adopt unrestrictive Creative Commons licences and platinum Open Access publishing models, where works are free to read and the library fully subsidizes publication, rather than charging author fees. However, some libraries are experimenting with more traditional business models and in some cases even launching their own imprints or full-fledged presses. Unlike traditional scholarly publishers, most libraries focus not on disciplines or subject areas, but on publishing the creative and scholarly output of their local community. In fact, many library-based publishing initiatives require that authors and editors have a connection to the institution.

Although academic libraries have been publishing in some form since the seventeenth century, the past decade has seen a proliferation of library publishing activities (Okerson and Holzman 2015). The Library Publishing Coalition, a professional association founded in 2012, counts dozens of members and includes over 100 library publishers from around the world in its annual inventory. In 2008, Xia (2009 372) identified seventy peer-reviewed journals hosted on Digital Commons, one of the most commonly adopted library publishing platforms. By 2015, Busher and Kamotsky reported that number had skyrocketed to nearly 900 (2015: 65).

Activity in the field remains diverse, however regional hallmarks have emerged. Among North American institutions, the most common model has been hosting Open Access journals and monographs in the institutional repository, without an imprimatur. The level of service provision varies widely across the field, a trend which has given rise to questions about the distinction between hosting and publishing, or what Whyte Appleby et al. (2018: 10) termed the 'publishing-hosting spectrum'. This 'enhanced repository' model generally focuses on publishing campus output, rather than building robust portfolios around disciplines or topic areas. The creation or revival of university press imprints has emerged as another popular model, particularly among library-based publishers in Australia, Europe, and the UK. In this model, the library creates or reclaims a formal press imprint and functions much like any other campus-based press. These presses typically build traditional lists, provide editorial, design, production, and marketing services, and focus on external authors and audiences. Unlike traditional university presses, this new wave of presses generally has an OA focus and may publish both formal, peer reviewed scholarly literature and informal campus outputs, such as data sets and grey literature, often under different imprints. These new presses fulfil an important role in disseminating high quality scholarly content regardless of its market potential. In Australia, for example, the 'need for scholarly publishers that would publish Australian research aimed at specialist audiences was filled by new, library-based university presses, which have been established since 2003 at [Australian National University] ANU, Sydney, Monash, Adelaide and [University of Technology Sydney] UTS' (Mrva-Montoya 2016: 3). In the UK, Lockett and Speicher (2016) reported that five new university presses launched over the course of a single year, and that 'all but one were launched first and foremost as open access presses, based in or supported by their university's library' (2016: 320). Like most library-based publishers, these presses are distinguished by their enthusiastic adoption of new technologies and business models and a commitment to broadening access to scholarship.

Academic libraries in Asia, Africa, and South America have robust histories of campus-based publishing and have also seen a growth in contemporary interpretations of library publishing. Xia (2009) described the longstanding practice among East Asian universities of publishing campus research journals, a practice that Xia advocated as a model for North American institutions. At under-resourced institutions in developing countries, library publishing represents one way of fighting back against the high costs and lack of access to much of the scholarly literature. Although the term 'library publishing' has not been widely adopted in Latin and South America, Santillán-Aldana (2017) characterized libraries as increasingly major contributors to campus-based scholarly publishing efforts in the region. In Africa, where 'researchers have been hamstrung by limited access to relevant and authentic scholarly content to support the growth of their research output'. libraries have an even more acute sense of responsibility to engage in activities that contribute to the open dissemination of knowledge. The library publishing movement is starting to grain traction in nations like South Africa, where four out of the country's twenty-three public academic institutions publish a total of twenty-seven OA scholarly journals (Raju and Pietersen 2016).

Public libraries, which have also historically embraced publishing as a service, are finding this activity aligns well with their modern mission. Examples of public library publishing programmes in the USA date to the late nineteenth century or earlier and many large public libraries have managed robust publishing programmes throughout the twentieth century, often focusing on general reference titles, professional manuals, or out-of-print titles (Conrad 2017). More recently, public libraries have leveraged new self-publishing technologies to bring the power of publishing to their constituents and produce community-oriented content.

Libraries are the very definition of mission-driven publishers. Rather than being defined by a strict set of services or outputs, the field of library publishing is more easily delineated in terms of values and motivations. Traditional mission-driven publishers like university presses rarely stray far from the traditional peer-reviewed monographs and journals, and a small selection of trade or regional interest titles, most often in print or static electronic formats. Library publishers are, at least in theory, content, format, discipline, cost, and platform agnostic, basing their publishing decisions primarily on scholarly merit and on the author or editor's connection to the institution. They measure their success based not on metrics like sales or the volume of publications they produce, but on the more intangible impact their work has in opening access to scholarship.

The genesis of modern library publishing can be traced to the early 2000s, when libraries began to experiment using the institutional repository, a digital portal for archiving campus research, to publish grey literature, electronic theses and dissertations (ETDs), and other original research alongside faculty preprints. Case studies from this era invoke dissatisfaction with the current publishing system to position libraries as key drivers of change and potential partners in the creation of new channels of scholarly communication predicated on openness and long-term stewardship. Wittenberg (2001: 29) recognized 'the possibility of making available scholars' research, writing, and teaching in a form that is timely, widely accessible, and useful to a broad range of users' by leveraging the new publishing technologies available to libraries. Wittenberg described the Electronic Publishing Initiative at Columbia (EPIC)—a collaboration between the Columbia University Press, Libraries, and academic technology group charged with exploring the 'use of technology to develop new organizational and business models for disseminating scholarly content'—and exhorted other libraries to take the lead in the inevitable reinvention of the scholarly publishing system. Crow (2002) evoked publishing original material as one function of a robust institutional repository, and articulated a vision of a global network of digital repositories as the 'foundation for a new disaggregated model of scholarly publishing' (2002: 6). Case and John (2007) and Royster (2008) further established the case for leveraging the institutional repository to publish original scholarly and creative work that does not fit within traditional publishing models, laying the groundwork for library publishing as a distinct subfield with its own identity. A seminal report published by Griffiths et al. (2007), which examined the future of university-based publishing writ large, emphasized the potential value of libraries as publishers, but cautioned them against the peril of institutional repositories that turn into ' "attics" (and often fairly empty ones), with random assortments of content of questionable importance' (2007: 28).

Given this history, most library publishers operate as fully subsidized units of the library, freeing them from the obligation to generate revenue. This model aligns well with libraries' role as OA advocates. As Harboe-Ree (2007: 17) noted, 'librarians are also the group in the scholarly communication value chain most aware of the unsustainability of the current pricing models, and so they are the most motivated to explore initiatives designed to contain or remove costs'. A subset of the library publishing literature explicitly mines this connection, positioning libraries as leaders in promoting access (Vandegrift and Bolick 2014; Chadwell and Sutton 2014). Nearly all library-published journals employ platinum OA (also called diamond or non-APC gold OA) business models; that is, all journals are free to read and charge no author fees (Busher and Kamotsky 2015: 64). Like many OA publishers, library publishers have found themselves defending against the misconception that OA implies low quality or lax standards. Hahn (2008) and Xia (2009), among others, emphasize that library publishers typically hold themselves to the same norms of academic rigour as traditional scholarly publishers and employ the same peer review practices. OA journals represent the bread and butter of many library publishing initiatives (Georgiou and Tsakonas 2010; Perry et al. 2011; De Groote and Case 2014; Sondervan and Stigter 2017). However, libraries have also developed significant book publishing programmes, as attested by a number of recent publications that centre the library's role in exploring and securing the future of the monograph (Adema and Schmidt 2010; Elliott 2015). Open textbook publishing, which aligns well with libraries' teaching and learning missions, has also emerged as a significant area of focus (Billings et al. 2012; Lyons 2014; Sutton and Chadwell 2014).

Library publishing is also tied to discussions about inequities in the scholarly publishing system. Several recent articles explore the social justice implications of library publishing, foregrounding the role of OA publishing in addressing systemic inequities like uneven access to scholarship and underrepresentation of authors of colour and women in the published literature (Inefuku and Roh 2016; Roh 2016).

Library–University Press Collaboration

Academic libraries have cooperated with university presses on occasional projects for many years, sometimes locally, sometimes with presses at other institutions. But the evolving twenty-first-century scholarly communications ecosystem has catalysed an increase in both library–press cooperation and in the number of presses actually reporting directly into their parent institution's library. In 2016 approximately 30 per cent of US university presses reported to their parent institution's library (Watkinson 2016), while that same year in Germany fifteen of twenty-five university presses did the same or were simply a unit in the university library (Muccie et al. 2017).

There are several reasons for this expansion in library–press collaboration. First and perhaps foremost, both presses and libraries have faced increasing financial pressures. Support from central administrations needed to compensate for press budgeted revenue shortfalls has decreased while libraries have for decades been receiving smaller and smaller percentages of the overall university budget. At the same time, press shortfalls have actually increased, in large part because of declines in monograph sales while libraries have had to devote more and more resources to journals licensing and subscribing.

Libraries and presses alike have also come to recognize that their communities of scholars, students, and administrators have changing expectations of them in a digital age. While both institutions are mission-driven, seeking to help scholars and students discover and use all the scholarly content they need, the needs of those constituents have changed. Faculty want to be able to access journals and (to some extent) books, large data sets, and other electronically based source material as well as published books and journal articles. They also want to facilitate broader dissemination of their own work to others. Students—and their parents—want text materials at lower costs than commercial textbook publishers have charged. Administrators want to know that both libraries and presses are attending to local needs and boosting the 'brand' of the university in the most helpful ways, something that has been more of a problem for presses than libraries.

Thus, libraries and presses have begun to collaborate on multiple types of projects. Frequently, they have worked together to digitize materials and make them available on-line on an open access basis. They also team up to apply for outside funding for digitizing and other projects such as the development of open source software to aid dissemination and discovery, platform development, and at times conferences where ideas can be churned.

In the back room, library–press partners have sometimes cooperated on activities like fundraising, human resources, and IT, consolidating overlapping efforts—on platforms, for example—to save time and money. Sometimes they co-sponsor programmes for their communities, and recently some library–press partnerships have undertaken curricular activities with undergraduates, providing both publication outlets and instruction on the researching and publication processes. They have also helped students by developing open access classroom materials. These open educational resources (OERs), by combining the separate kinds of expertise traditionally found in either libraries or presses, provide an example of the possibilities inherent in this still-developing symbiotic relationship.

Finally, libraries and presses have cooperated on managing journals—one example has the press and journal editors preparing articles for publication, then mounting them on open source software managed by the library.

Bringing university presses within the library's orbit requires adjustment on both sides, but as the frequency of the arrangement has increased, so has the cross-institutional effort to share ideas and projects that work with those that don't. Indeed, many library–press partners cite the need for regular meetings between their respective staffs as a top priority before starting any complicated collaborative projects. The first P2L (press to library) summit was held in 2016 and drew twenty-three pairs of press directors and library deans (Muccie et al. 2017), who, in a series of sessions, discussed both the challenges of this evolving relationship and the shared missions of the two units before moving on to the challenges ahead in working together to develop, nurture and disseminate digital scholarship. Future cross-institutional meetings of library–press partners are planned.

While the evolution of the library–press partnership remains mostly a young one with different levels of integration ranging from a simple reporting line to fully integrated status, this blending of units involved in disseminating scholarship offers a prime example of the academic library's shifting roles within the overall scholarly community.

CONCLUSION

We have seen that library functions, library relationships with publishers, and library publishing activities have changed enormously over the past quarter century as the digital revolution has impacted almost every aspect of reader–publisher–library–author relationships. These relationships will continue to evolve as both digital tools are developed and used, and as new business models take place in both libraries and presses. There will be conflicts—subscription prices, open access, the big deal, how to price single copies of items that can now be used by hundreds of readers, when more than one reader can be allowed to access the same material from the same source simultaneously, and so on. But working out these problems will require cooperation as well as some contention.

As libraries take up more of what used to be publishing functions—developing and disseminating their own materials—publishers take up more of what used to be library functions, especially in curation.

But in the end the relationship between libraries and publishers will continue to be symbiotic. Each exists to serve broader communities—in the academic world, the professors and students who use their products and services, and in the public library world a broader audience who require an even wider array of products and services. Publishers, especially academic publishers, rely on libraries as their major consumers; in return, libraries largely rely on publishers for increasingly sophisticated platforms and for most peer review. The two communities work together on standards and on such topics as increasing the ease of discovery for researchers. In some universities, libraries and presses work together directly, with the latter reporting to the former. Although very small numbers in both communities might argue otherwise, libraries and publishers need each other to thrive.

References

Adema, Janneke and Birgit Schmidt (2010). 'From Service Providers to Content Producers: New Opportunities for Libraries in Collaborative Open Access Book Publishing', *New Review of Academic Librarianship* 16(1), pp. 28–43. https://doi.org/10.1080/13614533.2010.509542.

Anderson, Rick (2011). 'Print on the Margins: Circulation Trends in Major Research Libraries', *Library Journal*. http://lj.libraryjournal.com/2011/06/academic-libraries/print-on-the-margins-circulation-trends-in-major-research-libraries/#_.

Anderson, Rick (2013). 'Review of "Can't Buy Us Love: The Declining Importance of Library Books and the Rising Importance of Special Collections"', *Collection Management*, 39(2–3), pp. 227–8. http://www.sr.ithaka.org/sites/default/files/files/SR_BriefingPaper_Anderson.pdf&nid=614

Anderson, Rick (2014). 'How Important Are Library Sales to the University Press? One Case Study', *The Scholarly Kitchen blog*, 23 Jun 2014. https://scholarlykitchen.sspnet.org/2014/06/23/how-important-are-library-sales-to-the-university-press-one-case-study/.

Arlitsch, Kenning and Carl Grant (2018). 'Why So Many Repositories? Examining the Limitations and Possibilities of the Institutional Repositories Landscape', *Journal of Library Administration*, 58(3), pp. 264–281. http://doi.org/10.1080/01930826.2018.1436778.

Association of Research Libraries (2014). 'Expenditure Trends in ARL Libraries, 1986–2015'. Washington, DC: Association of Research Libraries. http://www.arl.org/storage/documents/expenditure-trends.pdf.

Association of Research Libraries (2016). 'ARL University Library Expenditures, 2014–15'. Washington, DC: Association of Research Libraries. http://www.arl.org/storage/documents/university-library-expenditures.pdf.

Belter, C. W. and N. K. Kaske (2016). 'Using bibliometrics to demonstrate the value of library journal collections', *College and Research Libraries*, 77(4), pp. 410–22.

Berlin Declaration on Open Access to Knowledge in the Sciences and Humanities (2003). Berlin: Max Plank Society. Retrieved from http://oa.mpg.de/openaccess-berlin/berlin_declaration.pdf.

Billings, Marilyn S., Sarah C. Hutton, Jay Schafer, Charles M. Schweik, and Matt Sheridan (2012). 'Open Educational Resources as Learning Materials: Prospects and Strategies for University Libraries', *Research Library Issues: A Quarterly Report from ARL, CNI, and SPARC*, 280, pp. 2–10. https://doi.org/10.29242/rli.280.2.

Busher, Casey and Irene Kamotsky (2015). 'Stories and Statistics from Library-Led Publishing', *Learned Publishing*, 28(1), pp. 64–8. http://dx.doi.org/10.1087/20150110.

Case, Mary and Nancy R. John (2007). 'Publishing Journals @UIC', *Research Library Issues: A Quarterly Report from ARL, CNI, and SPARC*, pp. 252–3. http://old.arl.org/bm~doc/arl-br-252-253-uic.pdf.

Chadwell, Faye and Shan C. Sutton (2014). 'The Future of Open Access and Library Publishing', *New Library World*, 115(5/6), pp. 225–36. https://doi.org/10.1108/NLW-05-2014-0049.

Chan, Leslie et al. (2002). Budapest Open Access Initiative. Retrieved from http://www.budapestopenaccessinitiative.org/read.

Conrad, Kathryn M. (2017). 'Public Libraries as Publishers: Critical Opportunity', *Journal of Electronic Publishing*, 20(1). http://dx.doi.org/10.3998/3336451.0020.106.

Cox, J., & Cox, L. (2008). Scholarly publishing practice: Academic journal publishers' policies and practices in online publishing. Third survey. ALPSP. Available at http://www.alpsp.org/ngen_public/article.asp?id=0&did=0&aid=2446&st=scholarly%20publishing%20practice&oaid=0

Crow, Raym (2002). 'The Case for Institutional Repositories: A SPARC Position Paper'. Washington, DC: SPARC. http://sparc.arl.org/sites/default/files/ir_final_release_102.pdf.

De Groote, Sandra L. and Mary M. Case (2014). 'What to Expect When You Are Not Expecting to Be a Publisher', *OCLC Systems & Services: International Digital Library Perspectives*, 30(3), pp. 167–77. https://doi.org/10.1108/OCLC-01-2014-0004.

Dempsey, L., C. Malpas, and B. Lavoie (2014). 'Collection Directions: The Evolution of Library Collections and Collecting', *Portal: Libraries and the Academy*, 14(3), pp. 393–423.

Ehling, Terry (2005). 'DPubs: The Development of an Open Source Publishing System', *Publishing Research Quarterly*, 20(4), pp. 41–3.

Elliott, Michael A. (2015). 'The Future of the Monograph in the Digital Era: A Report to the Andrew W. Mellon Foundation', *Journal of Electronic Publishing*, 18(4). http://dx.doi.org/10.3998/3336451.0018.407.

Gilman, Isaac (2015). 'Adjunct No More: Promoting Scholarly Publishing as a Core Service of Academic Libraries', *Against the Grain*, 26(6), pp. 30–4. http://commons.pacificu.edu/libfac/25.

Georgiou, Panos and Giannis Tsakonas. (2010). 'Digital Scholarly Publishing and Archiving Services by Academic Libraries: Case Study of the University of Patras', LIBER Quarterly 20(2), pp. 242–57. http://doi.org/10.18352/lq.7991

Griffiths, Rebecca J., Matthew Rascoff, Laura Brown, and Kevin M. Guthrie (2007). University Publishing In a Digital Age. New York: Ithaka S+R. https://doi.org/10.18665/sr.22345.

Hahn, Karla L. (2008). 'Research Library Publishing Services: New Options for University Publishing'. Washington, DC: Association of Research Libraries. http://www.arl.org/about/1172-research-library-publishing-services-new-options-for-university-publishing#.WqqaxhPwaAx.

Harboe-Ree, Cathrine (2007). 'Just Advanced Librarianship: The Role of Academic Libraries as Publishers', *Australian Academic & Research Libraries*, 38(1), pp. 15–25.

Hazen, D. (1995). 'Collection Development Policies in the Information Age', *College and Research Libraries*, 56(1), pp. 29–31. https://doi.org/10.5860/crl_56_01_29.

Hu, Jane C. (2016). 'Academics Want You To Read Their Work For Free', *The Atlantic*, 26 January. https://www.theatlantic.com/science/archive/2016/01/elsevier-academic-publishing-petition/427059/.

Humanities Indicators (2015). 'Trends in Academic Books Published in the Humanities and Other Fields'. Washington, DC: American Academy of Arts and Sciences. https://www.humanitiesindicators.org/content/indicatordoc.aspx?i=88.

Inefuku, Harrison and Charlotte Roh (2016). 'Agents of Diversity and Social Justice: Librarians and Scholarly Communication', in *Open Access and the Future of Scholarly Communication: Policy and Infrastructure* Edited by Kevin Smith and Katherine Dickson, Lanham MD: Rowman and Littlefield. http://repository.usfca.edu/librarian/8.

Johnson, L., S. Adams Becker, V. Estrada, and A. Freeman (2015). 'NMC Horizon Report: 2015 Library Edition'. Austin, TX: The New Media Consortium. https://www.nmc.org/publication/nmc-horizon-report-2015-library-edition/.

Lockett, Andrew and Lara Speicher (2016). 'New University Presses in the UK: Accessing a Mission', *Learned Publishing*, 29, pp. 320–9. https://doi.org/10.1002/leap.1049.

Lyons, Charles, ed. (2014). 'Library Roles with Textbook Affordability', Special issue, *Against the Grain*, 26(5). http://www.against-the-grain.com/2016/10/v26-5/.

Muccie, Mary Rose, Joe Lucia, Elliott Shore, Clifford Lynch, and Peter Berkery (2017). *Across the Great Divide: Findings and Possibilities for Action from the 2016 Summit Meeting of Academic Libraries and University Presses with Administrative Relationships (P2L)*, Washington, DC: Association of Research Libraries. http://www.arl.org/storage/documents/across-the-great-divide-2016-p2l-summit.pdf.

Mrva-Montoya, Agata (2016). 'University Presses: An Australian Perspective'. [preprint]. http://hdl.handle.net/2123/15802.

Okerson, A. and A. Holzman (2015). *The Once and Future Publishing Library*, Council on Library and Information Resources: Washington, DC. Retrieved from www.clir.org/pubs/reports/pub166.

Peet, Lisa (2017). 'Keeping Up: Budgets and Funding', *Library Journal*, 1 February. https://lj.libraryjournal.com/2017/02/budgets-funding/keeping-up-budgets-funding/#_.

Perry, Anali Maughan, Carol Ann Borchert, Timothy S. Deliyannides, Andrea Kosavic, and Rebecca R. Kennison (2011). 'Libraries as Journal Publishers', *Serials Review*, 37(3): 196–204. https://doi.org/10.1016/j.serrev.2011.06.006.

Phan, T., L. Hardesty, and J. Hug (2014). 'Academic Libraries: 2012'. U.S. Department of Education, Washington, DC: National Center for Education Statistics. Retrieved from https://nces.ed.gov/pubs2014/2014038.pdf.

Publishers Communication Group (2017). 'Library Budget Predictions for 2017: Results from a Telephone Survey'. http://www.pcgplus.com/wp-content/uploads/2017/05/Library-Budget-Predictions-for-2017-public.pdf.

Raju, R. and J. Pietersen (2016). 'Library as Publisher: From an African Lens'. *Journal of Electronic Publishing*, 20(2). http://dx.doi.org/10.3998/3336451.0020.203.

Roh, Charlotte (2016). 'Library Publishing and Diversity Values: Changing Scholarly Publishing Through Policy and Scholarly Communication Education', *College & Research Libraries News*, 77(2), pp. 82–5. https://doi.org/10.5860/crln.77.2.9446.

Royster, Paul (2008). 'Publishing Original Content in an Institutional Repository', *Serials Review*, 34(1), pp. 27–30. https://doi.org/10.1080/00987913.2008.10765148.

Santillán-Aldana, J. (2017). 'Approaches to Library Publishing Services in Latin America', *Journal of Electronic Publishing*, 20(2). http://dx.doi.org/10.3998/3336451.0020.202.

Scheufen, Marc (2015). *Copyright versus Open Access*, Heidelberg: Springer.

Smith, Kevin L. and Katherine A. Dickson (2016). *Open Access and the Future of Scholarly Communication*, Lanham, MD: Rowman and Littlefield.

Sondervan, Jeroen and Fleur Stigter (2017). 'Sustainable Open Access for Scholarly Journals in 6 Years: The Incubator Model at Utrecht University Library Open Access Journals', *Learned Publishing*. http://dx.doi.org/10.1002/leap.1151.

Strieb, K. L. and J. C. Blixrud (2013). 'The State of Large-Publisher Bundles in 2012', *Research Library Issues: A Report from ARL, CNI, and SPARC*, 282. http://publications.arl.org/rli282.

Suber, Peter (2012). *Open Access*, Boston, MA: MIT Press.

Sutton, Shan and Faye Chadwell (2014). 'Open Textbooks at Oregon State University: A Case Study of New Opportunities for Academic Libraries and University Presses', *Journal of Librarianship and Scholarly Communication*, 2(4). http://doi.org/10.7710/2162-3309.1174.

Thornton, G. A. (2000). 'Impact of Electronic Resources on Collection Development, the Roles of Librarians, and Library Consortia', *Library Trends*, 48(4), pp. 842–56. Retrieved from https://www.ideals.illinois.edu/bitstream/handle/2142/8313/librarytrendsv48i4m_opt.pdf?sequence=1&origin=publication_detail.

Truschke, Andrew (2015). 'To Embargo or Not to Embargo? Strategically Disseminating The Dissertation'. [Blog] *Dissertation Reviews*. Available at: http://dissertationreviews.org/archives/11995.

Vandegrift, Micah and Josh Bolick (2014). '"Free to All": Library Publishing and the Challenge of Open Access', *Journal of Librarianship and Scholarly Communication*, 2(4). http://doi.org/10.7710/2162-3309.1181.

Walters, William H. (2013). 'E-books in Academic Libraries: Challenges for Acquisition and Collection Management', *Portal: Libraries and the Academy*, 13(2), pp. 187–211. http://doi.org/10.1353/pla.2013.0012.

Ware, M. and M. Mabe (2015). 'The STM Report: An overview of scientific and scholarly journal publishing'. International Association of Scientific, Technical and Medical Publishers: The Hague, The Netherlands. Retrieved from http://digitalcommons.unl.edu/scholcom/9.

Watkinson, Charles (2016). 'Why Marriage Matters: A North American Perspective on Press/Library Partnerships', *Learned Publishing*, 29, pp. 342–7. https://doi:10.1002/leap.1044.

Whyte Appleby, Jacqueline, Jeanette Hatherill, Andrea Kosavic, and Karen MeijerKline (2018). 'What's in a Name? Exploring Identity in the Field of Library Journal Publishing', *Journal of Librarianship and Scholarly Communication*, 6(1). http://doi.org/10.7710/2162-3309.2209.

Wittenberg, Kate. (2001). 'The Electronic Publishing Initiative at Columbia (EPIC): A University-Based Collaboration in Digital Scholarly Communication" *Learned Publishing*, 14, pp. 29–32.

Wolff-Eisenberg, Christine (2016). 'US Library Survey 2016'. New York: Ithaka S+R. https://doi.org/10.18665/sr.303066.

Xia, Jingfeng (2009). 'Library Publishing as a New Model of Scholarly Communication', *Journal of Scholarly Publishing*, 40(4), pp. 370–83. http://doi.org/10.1353/scp.0.0052.

CHAPTER 24

BOOKSELLING

NIELS PETER THOMAS

BOOKSELLING is in transition. Both from the point of view of the customer, as well as from the perspective of a publisher, there have been enormous changes in the past few decades to the landscape of how a book is sold, through which sales channels, and by what business models. Many readers remember the rise of chain bookstores, followed by the growth of the ecommerce giant Amazon, today the world's largest and most powerful bookshop. From the perspective of publishers, digitalization has probably been the driver of most changes in the last ten years, also resulting in a completely new landscape of possibilities regarding business models and sales channels (Schrape 2011).

The worldwide market value for books is estimated at around 122 billion euro (143 billion USD) at consumer prices, although there is no consensus about the exact number due to inconsistent data and very different definitions of books and bookselling across countries. To highlight its importance, a market of this size is bigger than that of music, video games, or filmed entertainment (Anderson 2017). The top seven countries for bookselling are the USA, China, Germany, the UK, Japan, France, and India, responsible for roughly 70 per cent of the world market. In all of those markets both print and electronic editions are relevant products, but with highly different market shares: While in China the market share of digital editions is 28 per cent (compare Colombia 24 per cent, Japan 18 per cent), in France the share of electronic editions is only about 2.2 per cent (WIPO 2017).

The market volume in most developed countries is decreasing, and even major emerging countries do not show stable growth in bookselling. Comparing the 2008 and 2016 real market value for books, only China is seeing a significant growth, while Mexico, Brazil, or Russia see a slightly shrinking market (Anderson 2017). An interesting case is Germany: market research shows the number of book buyers in 2016 at the lowest level for more than five years at 30.8 million buyers. From 2012 to 2016, more than 6.1 million book buyers were lost. The trend has continued in 2017, resulting in a shrinking market in real terms, although the remaining book buyers are buying more or more expensive books (Rösler-Graichen 2018). A shrinking number of heavy book buyers and a growing number of non-buyers contribute to weak market development, while at the same time entertainment markets in Germany are growing. Some possible reasons for these trends are discussed by Phillips (2017).

At the same time, the structure of the book market has also changed. The landscape of book buying has changed massively for the two main customer groups: both individual consumers and institutional customers have changed their purchasing habits. Before these changes, bookselling had remained realtively stable for centuries. In the twentieth century, the book trade was divided into retail and wholesale, with few publishers being involved in transactions with end-consumers (Hawker 2016).

Individual customers first saw the rise of large chain bookstores, putting pressure on small independent bookshops. Then Amazon was founded in July 1994, and has since demonstrated remarkable growth, resulting in a major transformation of the book trade. As of today, Amazon has a market share of more than 50 per cent in some territories and some product sectors, developing market power over both consumers and publishers. On one hand, the rise of Amazon has led to the invention and evolution of business intelligence not known to the market before, which is certainly adding value to the market—for example: 'People who bought this book also bought that book...'. On the other hand, the concentration of such huge market power has never favoured consumers in the long run, especially if the remaining independent bookshops come under further commercial pressure and continue to disappear.

Next to their dominance of the print book market, the biggest change that Amazon introduced was the Kindle ebook reader and with it a significant shift towards digital reading. A subsequent innovation for ebooks introduced by Amazon has been Kindle Unlimited, an 'all you can read' subscription similar to recent business models in the music industry (Smith and Telang 2016). While it is not yet clear whether the trend towards ebooks will continue, or whether consumers will eventually go back to print editions, these changes have certainly brought more evolution into the bookselling business than many attempts to disrupt the trade before Amazon.

In this chapter, bookselling does not refer to the legal definition of 'selling', since many ebooks technically are not sold, but rather a temporary or permanent right of use is granted by the bookseller to the book buyer. After providing a systematic overview of book products and business models, the emphasis of this chapter will shift to how the general book trade is organized as an industry. How are books sold, in what form and format, and by whom? The chapter concludes by looking at the pricing process and dynamic effects that the bookselling situation is currently facing, before presenting a few new trends that can already be foreseen for the coming years.

BOOK PRODUCTS AND BUSINESS MODELS

Book content can be consumed and packaged in many different ways: the most obvious of these are in print form and as electronic books. But even within these broad categories, books can be sold in many different forms and products. The following list consists of the most relevant business models, grouped into three categories: first, print books as the main product; second, electronic content as the main product; and third, the main product being a more complex service, where revenue is generated indirectly with book content. Not discussed here are other substitutes for books such as audio books, videos, live events, interactive games, and other media implementations of book content.

Print Book Products and Business Models

Print book sales: the vast majority of revenue in the book market is still generated in a very conventional way by selling print books. While most books are sold individually in different variations (mainly hardcover and softcover, see 'Book pricing' below), both in the history of bookselling and today, there are a few relevant modifications, such as bundling (sets of books) or combinations of print and e-content ('hybrid' books with access to the ebook as a bonus).

Print book rentals: while renting out a print book is not 'bookselling' in the strict sense of the word, it replaces the sale of a book, and therefore is an important business model. Lending books has always been known to libraries, but as a business model it was only recently introduced by online booksellers such as Amazon as an experiment in some markets.

Looseleaf service: A looseleaf publication is similar to a wirebound book where pages are added or replaced on a regular basis. The business model is therefore typically a sub-scription, while the final product resembles a book at any given time. Looseleaf services have been mostly replaced by electronic (periodical) publications.

Book sales clubs: Members of book clubs agree to purchase books that are featured by the club on a subscription basis, and are distributed via mail. Therefore, book clubs can be seen as a hybrid business model to combine a subscription business with independent and individual print books. In advanced markets, book clubs have been in decline faced with competition from online retailers.

Electronic Book Products and Business Models

Individual ebooks: ebooks are sold in various formats—PDF, HTML, EPUB—or on proprietary systems such as the Amazon Kindle (MOBI, AZW, or KF8 format), both with or without DRM protection (Digital Rights Management). Legally selling an ebook is typically not the same transaction as selling a printed book, as the owner often only grants a limited and non-exclusive licence to read the book, which makes it more difficult to resell or inherit used ebooks (Gabrio and Murphy 2014).

Single ebook chapters: Many publishers offer single chapters of ebooks in similar formats to the full book for a reduced price. Obviously, this option is more appropriate for non-fiction than fiction.

Ebook collections: More relevant for academic content is the aggregation of ebooks into collections that are selected by subject area and copyright year. Ebook collections are the prevailing products sold to scientific libraries (Besen and Kirby 2014). The business models are divided into ownership models, where the customer gets permanent access rights to a certain quantity of books, and subscription models, where access to the books is only allowed during the subscription period (Kerby and Trei 2015; Goertzen 2017).

A special form of ebook packages is known as 'variable collections', where the books within the package are selected by the librarian based on actual demand from readers ('patron driven acquisition', PDA). Very often, these packages have a trial period with access to a broad range of books, and a longer regular period with access to those books that proved to be important (Smith and Telang 2016).

Ebook 'flatrate': Similar to large ebook collections, but for individual customers, is a product that allows the customer to read as many books on a subscription basis for a fixed monthly amount. In some cases, the number of books that can be read at the same time is limited, in order to reduce the risk of customers sharing one account (as with Kindle Unlimited). This product is typically offered by a bookseller rather than by a publisher since readers expect books from different imprints to be included in the scheme.

Other ebook products: Especially in B2B bookselling (corporate sales) there are other business models in regular use, for example deposit models where the purchasing company agrees on a certain amount of money, and book content can be accessed as long as this amount is not used up, or combinations of other business models described above.

Book Service Business Models

The following services are not all direct substitutes for selling books, but are very often used in order to be able to offer books cheaplyr or even free of charge. All are alternative possibilities to generate revenues with book content, and are therefore relevant in this context.

Advertisements: Some print or digital books, especially but not limited to non-fiction, may contain advertisements. By generating revenue from advertisements, the price of the book can be reduced, or even offered for free (in the same way as telephone directories).

Printing Subsidies: Printing subsidies are typically requested from first-time or unknown authors in order to make economically feasible a book which would otherwise not be published. In some countries there may be subsidies from the state.

Open access books: A recent trend from (academic) journal publishing is increasingly also being used for books: free online versions of the ebook with typically the author or a funder paying for the publication (BPC, 'book processing charge'). Conceptually, paying a subsidy to publish a book and paying BPC are very similar, which is why book publishers need to ensure they are signalling that OA books are not vanity publishing. The necessity to demonstrate the quality of a book by external reviewers is therefore even more important for OA books than for regular books.

Inter-publisher licensing: Selling content in a B2B business model between publishers is a major revenue source for publishers, and is always specified in terms of publishing a book in a different region, language, or configuration.

THE BOOK TRADE

In most countries, the book trade is a multi-layered wholesale and retail business.[1] Up until the current period, most print books have been sold through this system: a book is published by a publishing company, but sold to the reader by a bookstore. Bookstores can buy the books either directly from the publisher, but in most cases they buy from wholesalers who, as intermediaries, operate large warehouses to enable them to deliver at any time. Sales representatives from publishers introduce their new publications to booksellers, who decide if they want to buy these books to be displayed on the shelves of their shops. Typically, books that are not sold after a certain period of time can be returned to the publisher, and these returns will be taken back at full price, which largely leaves the risk of unsold books with the publisher. Customers can also order other published books which are not stocked in the bookshop, and will then be delivered via wholesalers, in most cases on the next day.

Customers of bookshops are end consumers (readers), or institutional customers such as companies, government or academic institutions (libraries) (Brown 2004). Larger institutional customers often buy directly from publishers or aggregators, who act in a similar way to wholesalers but offer additional products (library software, furniture, etc.) or services to a special group of customers. The traditional refusal of publishers to work directly with their end customers is increasingly seen as a strategic disadvantage. Although many western publishers were originally bookstores that were also active as publishers (and as a result publishers often had an associated book trade), in the twentieth century most of these publishers closed or sold their bookshop activities (Hawker 2016). A recent trend is to invest again in book trade activities to end customers, but typically this is done via online ecommerce web shops.

The inspiration for these web shops is the Internet giant Amazon.com, which in the twenty-first century has undisputedly developed into the largest book retailer in most

---

[1] For the retail situation in China since the 1970s see Liu (2018). China has a retail and wholesale system as well, but obviously ownership and legislation are different when compared to western countries.

countries of the world. Before the emergence of Amazon, large chain bookshops dominated the book market in many western countries and gradually displaced or swallowed up small, independent booksellers. The rapid and ongoing success of Amazon can be explained through the new trade norms they introduced such as free shipping of books, short delivery times, and discounting, as well as an elaborate system of book reviews from end customers, which now guide many readers in their decision making (Hong et al. 2017).

However, chain bookstores and small, independent bookshops will continue to exist because some products and services, such as personal guidance, open shelf browsing, assessing the print quality of the books before purchase are only feasible through a physical presence. While selling ebooks in retail bookshops is possible, and many attempts have been made to increase this business segment, the ebook market is dominated by online web shops, both specialized ebook marketplaces, as well as the large general online booksellers like Amazon (Schröder and Lich 2017). It may be assumed that online book sales are cost effective for most book segments because of reduced operating costs and improved availability of market intelligence about consumer behaviour.

To counteract the pressure from the cost-effective online shops, local bookshops need to be creative to offer a better buying experience in the physical world rather than the virtual world only. This can be done by offering refreshments, events, or adding other kinds of stock (whether seasonal, e.g. before Christmas, or permanent).[2] Items such as stationery and games have become standard in many larger shops.

Additionally, most self-published books are sold exlusively online because they are not stocked by wholesalers, and will be printed on demand only if somebody orders the book (PTO, 'Print-To-Order'). Used books are also almost entirely sold by specialized used bookshops or antiquarian booksellers, and a small fraction of rare books are auctioned.

Book Pricing

In some countries, by law (or business agreement) all books are offered to end customers at a fixed price (under the terms of an FBPL, 'Fixed Book Price Law') so that booksellers have no authority to change the retail price that is decided by the publisher. The key reason for such a law is the assumption that the absence of (ruinous) price wars for books as a cultural asset leads to a greater variety of small and large bookstores and thus to a greater variety of books (van der Ploeg 2004). It is controversial whether such a law has this effect—especially in light of the fact that online booksellers have displaced many smaller retailers despite fixed prices. In most countries with a fixed price system, books with the same content may have different prices if sold under different business models, in different media forms, or with a different binding material (softcover vs. hardcover).

---

[2] For some successful print bookshops, see for example Daunt Books in London or Books Kinokuniya in several Asian countries.

However, with or without a fixed price, publishers or booksellers have to decide a retail price for each book. A few trade norms in pricing are widely accepted: hardcover books typically are sold at a significantly higher price point than softcover books, and ebooks are typically sold at a lower price than the softcover edition. For professional and academic books the higher priced hardcover titles are typically regarded as books for libraries and corporate customers, and the cheaper softcover books are for more price-sensitive individual customers. In fiction, the hardcover titles are most commonly published earlier than the later softcover 'paperback' edition, and therefore results in price differentiation over time. The different types of binding, in both cases, is not so much the reason for the price differentiation, but rather a justification.

Traditionally, many books are priced according to a 'cost-plus' model. A premium is added to the publishing, printing, distribution, and sales costs to determine the retail price. Others are priced in comparison to successful books in the same book segment (competition based), with adjustments according to a few price-driving factors. Price drivers can be based on the product (number of pages, colour images, special type of binding, etc.) but also on other factors (author's fame, reputation of other books in the same imprint, etc.). Demand-based pricing takes into consideration the importance of the content and the current demand of the genre or segment.

The emergence of ebooks and ecommerce retail for print books also allowed the possibility of more specific price differentiation and discrimination. Where legally possible, books are now priced differently according to time, customer, region, and POS (point of sale). The growing number of business models, especially in the ebook market, also adds to the possibilities to differentiate pricing with variations of products sold in different markets. However, most publishers stick to 'nice prices' ending with '.99' or '.95' for the psychological effect of a nice price presentation.

Many publishers change the price of their books over time. While some publishers reduce the price of older books in order to sell remaining stock after a few years, others increase in the price of old books, for example, for academic books where older books have a lower price sensitivity and therefore demand is largely independent of price. Short-term dynamic pricing, which might, for example, be based on printing capacities, is not yet applied widely in the publishing industry (Clerides 2002).

In contract to individual book pricing, the decision making for ebook collection prices has one advantage: since each year the portfolio of published books at a certain publisher will not change much, the price point of previous years can be used as a basis for each year's new prices, with relative changes due to inflation, increased usage, or the growth of content volume within the package.

Current Trends in Bookselling

The above described forces in the retail market for books will probably continue to exist. Economies of scale put cost pressures on smaller, independent bookshops as well as on larger book chains in comparison to bookselling via ecommerce.

While for decades in many countries book revenue grew on a par with the growth of total GDP, book revenue development seems to have been uncoupled from economic growth since the beginning of the twenty-first century (Phillips 2017), and is now plateauing or even shrinking in many countries. Changes in retail, like those described in this chapter, but also competition from other media and other entertainment experiences are possible drivers of this trend. A change in the demographics of many western countries is certainly also accountable for a changing bookselling equilibrium: an ageing society naturally needs other retail structures in contrast to societies with strong population growth. This ageing effect might, in some countries, lead to a modest growth of bookselling revenue because older people read more books on average than adolescents.

What we currently see in the book market is a shift from print to ebooks, although this development is taking place at very different rates in the various book segments. In the consumer market for fiction (and non-fiction) most books are still read in print, but there is growth in the ebook market, and probably most ebooks substitute the sale of a print book. Taking into consideration the tendency of lower prices for ebooks, this development will probably not contribute to a general growth of the book business. For academic books, many publishers already make the majority of their revenue from electronic products, with a clear trend that this shift will continue. However, it does not seem that the cannibalization of print books because of ebook usage will one day be fully completed, as there are many reasons why print books will stay relevant and necessary in academic contexts both for research and learning purposes.

Outlook

We may expect more change and possibly even disruption in the bookselling industry in the near future. Depending on the future development of a few technologies and trends in society, both the consumer book market and institutional (academic) book market are subject to change.

In the fiction and non-fiction consumer market, we will probably see a continuation of the trend towards more products and different business models. In particular, free online content will be a major reason for a change in the book market, shifting revenues from products to services like advertisements. This market trend is also dependent on the invention and market penetration of new generations of reading devices (mobile ebook readers) and the societal trend of a higher 'prioritization of experience over the accumulation of stuff' (Phillips 2017). Ultimately, books compete in the consumer market with any other form of entertainment industry, and in the institutional market with all publication forms, especially journals and specialized databases.

The print books market will in the future probably be affected most by innovation in printing technology, which, in principle, has the power to change the complete wholesale system. If on-demand printing is economically feasible and technically possible at the point of sale (POS) within a short time, wholesaler distribution warehouses will lose out massively in terms of economic relevance and importance. This trend has been expected for some years, but has not materialized so far (Gallagher 2014). It is still unknown whether this will ever happen.

Looking at other media businesses might shed light on a possible big trend in book consumption in the future. The music industry, which has a similar technical and economic structure, has changed completely in the last decade. Today, music is mainly consumed with flatrate offers, and the sale of individual music albums has declined significantly. If this is also a trend for books, then we might see an increased shift to ebook usage and again a reason for further concentration in the book market (Smith and Telang 2016). Taking into account the 'flat rate bias' of consumers this trend might even accelerate (McDonald and Smith Rowsey 2016: 255).

In the long term, new technologies like 'Blockchain' might provide smart solutions for some elements of bookselling, such as a marketplace for used ebooks with guaranteed transfer of access rights from seller to buyer. But it is not yet clear, both economically and technically if blockchain technologies will be the most efficient basis for such transactions.

In the academic book market, there is some potential for further change that builds on current trends. One trend is the convergence of bookselling to the way academic journals are sold. If this 'journalization' of academic books holds, we might see two effects, which are already in place in the market for academic journals: First, a tendency towards 'big deals': instead of individual sales of ebook collections, electronic delivery of all the books from a publisher can be made available through a multi-year subscription contract; second, further momentum for OA books, with OA publishing as the standard in all publication forms. For both individual and institutional ebook markets the future is also dependent on developments regarding illegal piracy of book content. In the consumer book market, being able to reduce the available number of illegal copies will depend on future technical and legal tools. In the institutional book market, piracy will only be overcome if the academic community continues to appreciate the services and resources provided by book publishers.

Overall, bookselling will continue to change, along with societal, economic, and technological changes and innovations (Lake 2016). There are no signals that the book market will disappear in the foreseeable future, but as our understanding of a book as a product evolves, so does the way it is sold.

References

Anderson, P. (2017). 'New BookMap Initiative: Trying To Chart the World Publishing Industry', *Publishing Perspectives*, News, October 23, https://publishingperspectives.com/2017/10/bookmap-launched-to-size-up-world-publishing/ [Accessed 7 July 2018].

Besen, S. and S. Kirby (2014). 'Library Demand for e-Books and e-Book pricing: An Economic Analysis', *Journal of Scholarly Publishing*, 45(2), pp. 128–41.

Brown, S., ed. (2004). *Consuming Books. The Marketing and Consumption of Literature*, Abingdon: Routledge Interpretive Marketing Research.

Clerides, S. (2002). 'Book value: intertemporal pricing and quality discrimination in the US market for books', *International Journal of Industrial Organization*, 20(10), pp. 1385–408.

Gabrio, K. and W. Murphy (2014). E-Book Rights: Advocacy in Action. Proceedings of the Charleston Library Conference. http://dx.doi.org/10.5703/1288284315570

Gallagher, K. (2014). 'Print-on-Demand: New Models and Value Creation', *Publishing Research Quarterly*, 30(2), pp. 244–8.

Goertzen, M. (2017). 'Applying Quantitative Methods to E-book Collections', *Library Technology Reports*, 53(4)

Hawker, J. (2016). 'Selling Words: An Economic History of Bookselling', in R. E. Lyons and S. J. Rayner (eds), *The Academic Book of the Future*, London: Palgrave Macmillan.

Hong, H., D., Xu, D. Xu, G. Wang, and W. Fan (2017). 'An empirical study on the impact of online word-of-mouth sources on retail sales', *Information Discovery and Delivery*, 45(1), pp. 30–5.

Kerby, E. and K. Trei (2015). 'Minding the Gap: ebook package purchasing', *Collection Building*, 34(4), pp. 113–18.

Lake, P. (2016). 'The Future of the Academic Book: The Role of Booksellers', in R. E. Lyons and S. J. Rayner (eds), *The Academic Book of the Future*. London: Palgrave Macmillan.

Liu, Z. (2018). 'Whither the Book Retailing Industry in China: A Historical Reflection', *Publishing Research Quarterly*, 34, pp. 133–46.

McDonald, K. and D. Smith Rowsey, eds (2016). *Netflix Effect*, New York; London: Bloomsbury Academic.

Phillips, A. (2017). 'Have We Passed Peak Book? The Uncoupling of Book Sales from Economic Growth', *Publishing Research Quarterly*, 33, pp. 310–27.

Rösler-Graichen, M. (2018). Der Buchmarkt verliert vor allem jüngere Käufer, Studie des Börsernvereins, 18 Januar 2018, https://www.boersenblatt.net/artikel-studie_des_boersen-vereins.1422566.html, [Accessed 7 July 2018].

Schrape, J. (2011). Der Wandel des Buchhandels durch Digitalisierung und Internet, SOI Discussion Paper 2011–01, Stuttgart.

Schröder, H. and A.-K. Lich (2017). 'Digitale Dienstleistungen im stationären Einzelhandel als Antwort auf die Herausforderungen durch Online-Shops', in *Dienstleistungen 4.0*. Edited by M. Bruhn and K. Hadwich, Wiesbaden: Springer Gabler, pp. 485–510.

Simon, J. (2014). 'E-Book Purchasing Best Practices for Academic Libraries', *Journal of Electronic Resources Librarianship*, 26(1), pp. 68–77.

Smith, M. and R. Telang (2016). *Streaming, Sharing, Stealing: Big Data and the Future of Entertainment*, Boston, MA: MIT Press.

van der Ploeg, F. (2004). 'Beyond the Dogma of the Fixed Book Price Agreement', *Journal of Cultural Economics*, 28(1), pp. 1–20.

World Intellectual Property Organization, ed. (2017). The Global Publishing Industry 2016, A Pilot Survey by IPO and WIPO, http://www.wipo.int/edocs/pubdocs/en/wipo_ipa_pilotsurvey_2016.pdf, [Accessed 7 July 2018].

CODA

CHAPTER 25

THE FUTURE
OF PUBLISHING

Eight Thought Experiments

MICHAEL BHASKAR AND ANGUS PHILLIPS

INTRODUCTION

THROUGHOUT this book the future of publishing has loomed large. Economic, social, technological, and cultural change have, throughout publishing's long history, been constant. Indeed, from intellectual property to industrial workflow, cultural form to retail, publishers were often on the frontlines of change, driving it forward. Yet over the last half-century publishing has, in all likelihood, never seen such fundamental changes to its core business. As has been highlighted by this book, whether it is the consolidation of publishers into major groups or the development of reading technologies that alter the very nature of the codex, such changes impact every aspect of what it means to be a publisher. The open-plan, digital, global workplaces of today's major publishers would be scarcely recognizable to those coming from the mid-twentieth century. This pace of change is unlikely to stop.

Asking what the future holds is not just an academic exercise. Publishing has worldwide revenues of around $121bn, although, factoring in all other forms of publishing, this could plausibly hit $358bn by 2020 (Kozlowski 2016). It employs millions directly, and many more indirectly, from writers and illustrators through to manufacturers of printing machines and forestry managers. Beyond immediate economic concerns, we have seen how publishing underpins and shapes our culture; how it defines many of our great social debates; how it is integral to our education systems and, beyond them, to the constitution of our knowledge and the transmission of information in our societies. Publishing matters, and hence the future of publishing matters. Understanding where it might be heading is significant for all of the above. Using the analysis presented in this book to gain an understanding of this future is crucial. But there is a problem.

BACK TO THE FUTURE OF PUBLISHING

Most activities rely, to some degree, on predicting, or trying to predict, the future. Whether it is governments trying to plan tax income and fiscal expenditure, or businesses trying to forecast the latest consumer trend or breakthrough technology, or even households trying to guess what will happen in their lives next week, huge resources are thrown at the problem of the future. However, not only are we not very good at forecasting in general, but often the more expert one is, the worse one's forecasts are in practice (Tetlock and Gardner 2016). We repeatedly misforecast the future and knowledge is no antidote. Much of the time we fail to hold forecasters to account or rigorously going through what, exactly, was predicted. If we did so we would find, for example, that highly remunerated stock market analysts are frequently much worse at predicting the price of a basket of stocks than pure guesses. In other words you would be better off randomly selecting shares, than having them chosen by many industry leaders.

Publishing and books are also subject to such misforecasts. At a basic level, in trade publishing, almost no publisher is truly capable of spotting a breakout trend until it has either already broken out, or it has reached a kind of hidden social critical mass and suddenly breaks out across the industry. No one predicted the success of Stieg Larsson or E. L. James until they happened; we went from no books on the Danish concept of Hygge to very many in the space of only a few months.

At a macro level, however, the record is similarly poor. Take a few examples. Many predictions have been made about the ebook market, most of which were wrong. For example in 2013 PwC, a respectable source, issued a report arguing that the ebook market would be bigger than print by 2017 (Owen 2013). Yet this did not happen. Interestingly this echoed a PwC forecast from the late 1990s which predicted something similar for the mid-2000s: that ebooks would grow explosively and be worth billions (Gomez 2008). Again, the forecast was not borne out. Predicting what will happen in technology is hard enough; couple the intricate cultural and economic matrix that is publishing and if anything it becomes even harder.

People keep insisting that the market for children's books, and beyond it, the appetite of children for reading, is in grave trouble, threatened by the new digital landscape of social media. Surveys suggest a decline in children's reading (Flood 2015). Research indicates fewer children are reading in their spare time (Harrison 2013). And yet children's books have been the great boom area for trade publishing over the last seven years, hitting record sales figures year after year (Bone 2017). Somehow there is a disconnect here; the predictions are not quite working out. Children's publishing is, at the time of writing, in a far better place than many commentators had thought.

Many of these predictions form part of a familiar genre: the death of publishing and/ or the book. For some, there is a continued willingness to believe in 'the inevitable death of traditional book publishing', as one such piece is titled (Diggs 2016). However, as the Harvard scholar Leah Price has shown, these claims have a storied history (Price 2012).

In the early 1990s the *New York Times Book Review* ran a piece predicting the End of Books. Video and computers were, even then, set to end the era of the book. Like Nietzsche's God, it claimed, books were dead and we have killed them. But Price finds complaints dating from the 1830s that the book is being killed—in that case by the newspaper. Her point is that 'every generation rewrites the book's epitaph; all that changes is the whodunit' (Price 2012). From H. G. Wells writing about a bookless future to Stanislaw Lem's proto-ereader, science fiction writers and futurologists have always predicted that books would disappear. And beyond this it is part of a wider tradition that sees reading, writing, and the book as somehow doomed, a tradition stretching from Socrates to Jonathan Franzen. But despite the idea that books and publishing are doomed, both are still very much here.

The world is innately complex and that complexity makes accurate predictions exceptionally hard, and in some cases virtually impossible. Not many in the publishing industry predicted in 1997 that the fledgling book start-up Amazon would, within twenty years, be responsible for an astonishing 45 per cent of US book sales (Shatzkin 2018). Even a decade later that would have seemed an extraordinary prediction. As would the idea that Amazon would be less about selling books, more a machine for generating patents in areas like machine learning, robotics, and drone technology. And still fewer would have believed that Amazon's market capitalization would dwarf that of the entire publishing industry; that even breaking out subunits of the company, like Cloud Hosting or Advertising would, in the eyes of Morgan Stanley, give those divisions greater market capitalizations than those of the three biggest publishers in the world, Pearson, RELX, and Thomson Reuters, combined. Had those in the publishing industry predicted this, they would, or should, have bought Amazon stock.

Predictions are wrong as often as they are right. Predictions date fast and can lead you down the wrong track. As William Goldman famously said about Hollywood: 'No one knows anything.' The same is true of publishing, both on a day-to-day basis, in that publishers must constantly take risks on the unknown, and in a larger sense, regarding the overall direction of the industry. How then to think of the future?

Thought Experiments

Thought experiments, from Plato's Cave to Rawls' (1971) veil of ignorance, and their attendant methodologies, from historical counterfactuals to retrodiction, have played an important role in the history of thought. Thought experiments exclude the irrelevant: by doing this they focus on the most salient points of a question. They declutter our judgements and views. They force us to reconsider prior assumptions and beliefs; they reveal to us our real opinions about difficult questions. They push circumstances to their limits. Thought experiments are contrived, in contrast to the messiness of the real world, but nonetheless useful. They must take us beyond the immediate, but retain a structural similarity with that they are exploring.

It is not just in philosophy that thought experiments have proved useful: in science for example think of Maxwell's Demon or Schrödinger's Cat. In technology exotic constructs like Von Neumann probes, self-replicating robots that can spread throughout the galaxy, or Dyson spheres, an energy capturing structure built around a star, may seem outlandish, but play an increasing role in how scientists and technologists understand how a space-faring future may play out. This hints at an important role of thought experiments today: in exploring and guiding us through an uncertain future. Thought experiments are not forecasts, but they can pose questions and ideas of what may happen, what could happen, and, in doing so, enable to us to rethink the possible and the likely.

In the field of AI for example, thought experiments that were formerly staples of the philosophy of ethics are gaining traction as a means of understanding a powerful, fast-moving technology whose far-reaching consequences are truly impossible to predict. One of the most famous thought experiments in recent philosophy, John R. Searle's 'Chinese room' was already directed at AI. It was an ingenious thought experiment that sought to describe how, even if a machine appeared to be sentient, this might not be the case (Searle 1980). More recently the Oxford thinker Nick Bostrom has conducted a series of wide-ranging thought experiments about what would happen with the creation of a 'superintelligence' (Bostrom 2017). Indeed, thought experiments are the only practical means of exploring this question. Given that no one can begin to model the consequences of such an event in concrete terms, because it is both unprecedented and potentially far beyond our understanding, we are left only with thought experiments.

In AI these also have an immediate practical force. One of the most discussed thought experiments in ethical philosophy is the so-called 'Trolley Problem' (trolley here being an Americanization of the British 'tram'). First sketched by Philippa Foot in the 1960s it has spawned a literature known as 'Trolleyology' and is even taught as part of the West Point Military Academy course (Edmonds 2015).

In the Trolley Problem five people are tied to a railway track. A trolley is hurtling towards them, certain to kill all five. However, if the trolley deviates onto a spur, thanks to you pulling a lever, it will save their lives; but unfortunately there is one person tied to this track. Do nothing and five people die; actively do something, and one person dies. Many if not most people believe you should, or are obligated, to kill that one person. A 'fat man' version introduces new complexity: the tram is out of control and about to run over five people. You are on a bridge over the track, standing next to a large man. . . . If you push him off the bridge onto the track, his bulk will be sufficient to stop the tram and save the five people, albeit at the expense of his life. Should you do this?

Foot herself believed that we have positive and negative duties. In the case of the first example she believes you have a positive duty to save five lives. However, then think of the 'fat man' scenario in alternative terms: say five people require organ transplants or they will die, does the doctor kill a healthy patient to save them? That is analogous to pushing the fat man off the bridge. The balance of positive and negative duties is, in her view, what decides this basic version of the Trolley Problem. But this view is only the beginning of a vast literature.

All of this may be seen as just a blind alley for philosophers. But this thought experiment now has an all-too real force in the burgeoning field of autonomous vehicles and lethal autonomous weapons, both of which could fundamentally re-order two of the world's most significant industries and, even more importantly, present life and death scenarios on an awesome scale. Autonomous vehicles are already at an advanced stage of development, being trialled in places like California and London. Currently 35,000 people die each year on American roads and, globally, 1.25 million road deaths and 15 million road injuries occur every year (Ross 2017). In a world where autonomous vehicles predominate, having clear answers to the trolley problem, protocols agreed in code and in law, backed by insurers, legislators, manufacturers, and the general public, will be key. Trillions of dollars and above all millions of lives now rest on how we interpret a thought experiment and make it manifest in transportation and weapons algorithms.

If we can't predict the future of publishing, we can still think about it. We can ask various questions of the form 'what if' and then pursue their consequences. We can create miniature narratives based on premises extrapolated from the present and see what happens. We can do this first in a spirit of thinking with a rich intellectual lineage and secondly in terms of the new prevalence of thought experiments at extrapolating into uncertain futures. Thought experiments for publishing can throw the future—and the present—into relief; isolating salient features of publishing and extending them into extremes forces us to reconsider present trajectories. In turn this can help deepen our understanding of publishing and formulate strategies to navigate the future. We do not claim these thought experiments will in any way happen. They likely will not. But, in their various articulations and modalities, they should clarify what is important, what is at stake, and what is within the boundaries of the possible for the future of publishing.

BIG NAME AUTHORS SELF-PUBLISH, ACROSS BOTH ACADEMIC AND TRADE

To date, one brand name author has branched into self-publishing with notable success: J. K. Rowling, the exception that proves the rule that, in general, big name authors have clung to their publishers. Rowling is probably unrivalled in her global recognition and ability to build a platform, Pottermore, for direct sales and world-building. However, it is notable that while she sells her ebooks direct even she has stuck with traditional publishers, Bloomsbury and Little, Brown, for her print books.

Nonetheless it isn't hard to imagine a future in which all authors of significant global sales start to go direct. There are several reasons why this should happen. First, publishers can already be viewed simply as aggregations of services to authors. In the chain of book creation they are responsible for some aspects, say editing, but others are undertaken by separate organizations, say printing or bookselling. Some more vertically integrated publishers, like Sweden's Bonnier or Italy's Feltrinelli, may incorporate the bookselling aspect into the overall business but this isn't core to a publisher. Sometimes a publisher is responsible for representing translation and other rights sales; sometimes this is left to the author or their agent. These aggregations of services have reached an equilibrium, that is, it has appeared that it is optimally efficient to run the book industry in this way and so this particular aggregation of services is the customary form a publisher takes. Now the process of unbundling or disaggregating the services is perhaps gathering steam. We have seen how outsourcing various functions, things like typesetting or copy-editing, to specialist freelancers or new service organizations, including dedicated marketing and publicity agencies, has accelerated over recent years. Publishing is driving its own unbundling.

Eventually this process could become fully realized and the separate functions of a publisher break out into new, independent business units targeted at entrepreneurial big brand authors: there would be an editorial unit, a production and distribution unit, a sales, marketing, and publicity unit; perhaps even a new co-ordinator role to manage all of the pieces. This brings us to the second reason why brand name self-publishing might happen: money. It is likely that successful authors deliver a considerable surplus to publishers; that is, regularly bestselling writers, despite being paid handsomely, are still the cash-cows and engine rooms of publisher profitability. Assuming that the subunits operated as efficiently as within a publisher, and admittedly this could go either way, then there is a substantial financial incentive for authors in the form of the surplus value currently retained by publishers.

Here, therefore, is a possible downward spiral for publishers which would hasten the transition: big name authors leave, damaging the balance sheet, putting pressure on the publisher, hampering its ability to effectively publish and so pushing more authors out. The trends are already in place; the technology and managerial capacity already available; the only question now is the will, the risk appetite, of authors...

Academic publishing too could be part of this dynamic. While many monograph and journals publishers are buttressed by what Martin Eve calls academic symbolic capital—in other words their prestige—new initiatives such as the arXiv platform show how comprehensively new means of communication can gain traction (Eve 2014). As Eve points out, prestige is only a proxy, the ground can shift. Alternate forms of prestige can either grow up organically or be somehow mandated by funding bodies and other power centres within academia. Besides, an academic with Ivy League tenure requires less symbolic capital then a struggling adjunct; for them freedom might be its own reward. If that were to happen, might we see a shift towards an arXiv style model across the board? Academics would upload their work for open review; published material becomes easily accessible online; and then, subsequent to that, specialist agencies could arrange downstream book production and distribution services for a cut of revenue. The slow wheels of academic publishing would turn faster, at the speed of research. While it might feel far fetched, the open access movement has already taken us part of the way there. For whatever reason, a crisis of confidence in major academic names could take us the rest of the way.

Books are Written by AI, According to your Reading Tastes

You have a long flight ahead of you. None of the films on offer seem appealing and you can't sleep. So you decide to read. But read what? Logging in to your new digital device you ask it for a novel, something absolutely gripping featuring helicopters, military commandos, Nazis on the moon, a whirlwind romance and, oh, why not, cats. While even a few years earlier this improbable combination would have been impossible to find, even with sophisticated search and recommendation technology, you are in luck: your device and its inbuilt reading service doesn't scan existing material to find as close as possible a match. Instead it simply writes you the story. Within seconds it has delivered an entirely customized novel of precisely 95,000 words which is absolutely gripping and features helicopters, military commandos, Nazis on the moon, a whirlwind romance and, yes, cats.

It does this not only to your specifications, but with an even deeper understanding of your reading tastes. The system knows every book you have previously purchased, and has analytics on both your reading of these and your reading of its own customized stories. It knows what makes you switch off the device and what keeps you hungrily reading long after bedtime. It surmises which characters you relate to and computes your ideal sentence length and vocabulary for different kinds of material, tasks well beyond the powers of any human writer. Without effort it can deliver you the above novel, but, waiting for your luggage at the airport you realize you want a primer on the economy of the country: it does that too, 10,000 words of pitch-perfect analysis tailored towards your business but with a high level view thrown in.

Publishers, of course, have started to disappear. People still want to read the old classics and publishers' copyrights keep them in business servicing the backlist. But inexorably their market share is shrinking year on year. Some people are 'human only readers' and this sustains some writers albeit on a small scale, analogous to the position of poetry with respect to novels or TV today. For most readers the experience of AI generated work has simply been too good, and the costs too cheap to go back. The ability of the system to deliver uncannily superb material of any kind, idiosyncratic, literary, poetic included, is impossible to resist. The big winners are, of course, the tech companies. Behind the books lies proprietary software centralized on one major platform whose data advantage has made them overwhelmingly the market leader. As you check-in to your hotel this doesn't overly concern you: two great pieces of writing have kept you entertained at marginal cost, pennies. Your reading experience is much the same in form, but the industry behind it is utterly transformed.

Implausible? Certainly beyond the realms of current technology. But advances in AI, driven by deep learning neural networks and reinforcement learning algorithms have been proceeding at pace. The AI lab DeepMind's defeat of the world champion at Go using its AlphaGo software happened far in advance of what was thought possible. With exponentially more combinations than chess it is impossible to 'brute force' winning at Go. But machine learning can try other approaches by estimating optimal strategies. It is not fanciful to say that, based on sufficient training data, they could start to imitate the strings of data that are known as books. Iterating potentially millions or billions of times in a short time span, the improvements could be rapid.

The futurist and scientist Hans Moravec cautions us against believing that some domains, like authoring books, are solely those of human beings. Over time things we believed were the province of the human mind have steadily become that of machines: maths, chess, general knowledge quizzes, Go, investment decisions, medical diagnoses.... Novel writing?

BOOKS DISAPPEAR

What if books disappear from our lives? Publishing has always seen movement in what categories and genres sell better than others, and the industry has been expert in following the latest trend from westerns or horror to erotic fiction. But what happens if we look back and realize that many parts of the market have been steadily eroded, just as the waves wash away at the cliff edge, and another chunk of land falls off into the sea?

We used to buy language dictionaries and they were part of every back to school campaign—now we look up words online rather than walk across to the bookshelf. Our computer helps with grammar and spelling so those guides became redundant. We use translation programmes rather than a print dictionary or phrasebook.

Few can remember general reference titles as those in search of information go online automatically. Online search and Wikipedia replaced the use of encyclopedias and atlases a long time ago. There are apps to identify birds, insects, and flowers, and the stars in the night sky. When pruning the roses or building a patio, we used to consult home reference guides. They helped with DIY projects, changing a fuse, or buying a home. Now we can go on YouTube and watch a video of almost anything, even down to the unboxing of individual products. Also life has changed and few people maintain their own cars or even want to fix a domestic appliance.

The first port of call for students is Google followed by online databases from the library. Journals have moved almost completely online, and specialized books such as academic monographs have followed. Publishers have not seen the diminishing value of textbook sales replaced by equivalent digital sales. In schools the tech companies have arrived, encouraging the use of technology, both hardware and software. The budget for print books has shrunk to near zero, and children are no longer used to seeing books as tools of learning.

There are few water cooler discussions about the latest novel by Ian McEwan or Donna Tartt—instead we discuss *Stranger Things* or *Spiral*. Literary fiction feeds other media but is perceived as rather difficult and time-consuming; authors migrate to writing scripts for shows and films. Sales of literary fiction decline further and genre fiction retreats to an online community of enthusiasts.

With ubiquitous 4G networks, we no longer need print travel guides, and location-based services recommend shops, restaurants, enticing us in with discounts. We go to historic sites, museums, and galleries, and simply point our phones at the relevant view or artefact, summoning up an audio guide.

At home we interact with a smart speaker. Cookery books decline in importance as we search online for the perfect recipe—the Internet of things enables our fridge to recognize ingredients and suggest a dish that can be made in precisely the amount of time we have available.

We don't like our young children to spend too much time on screens so the sales of picture books from celebrities remains buoyant. As children become teenagers, however, the book vanishes from their horizons, seen as static and boring. Instead they become diverted by social media, video and chat, and experiences through virtual reality.

At Your Service

How can we turn the purchase and reading of books into a service? What would happen if a model is taken from the streaming of films or clothing retail and applied to the business of books? The move from product to service has already taken place in academic journals, where users have 24/7 access to huge searchable databases online. How would a service work for trade fiction and non-fiction?

Netflix offers access to films and TV shows for a monthly subscription, with viewing across a range of devices. This model has dealt a body blow to high street rental and the ownership of DVDs and box sets. Many people no longer feel the need to own a TV when they can watch films and TV on their mobile devices; they can also binge watch their favourite shows rather than have to wait for the next episode to be broadcast.

In the area of fashion, the UK retailer ASOS gives its customers the option to try now and pay later, with home delivery of a selection of clothing and the client is only charged for those clothes they want to keep. The other clothes are returned with no need for a refund. The changing-room has been moved from the high street to the bedroom or living-room.

If half the books on our shelves at home are unread, surely this is a waste of the world's resources—how does the reader get round this issue? As owning your media is increasingly regarded as old fashioned and inconvenient, this fits with the desire for our homes to carry a minimalist, uncluttered look. Rather than acquiring stuff, we are more interested in purchasing experiences. Gone is our personal library and the few books we do have on display are turned spine inwards so that the colours do not interfere with the overall look of the room.

To read books we already have Kindle Unlimited, where users can access over one million ebooks and thousands of audiobooks, all for a monthly fee (£7.99 in the UK at the time of writing). Titles include the Harry Potter series and *The Handmaid's Tale* by Margaret Atwood. There are subscription boxes, delivering each month a surprise selection of print titles to our home. What other models are possible? Say we can access, for a monthly subscription, local lending libraries with all the latest print bestsellers plus a carefully curated selection of classic literary fiction. We need never buy a book again. This is a service presently provided by public libraries but the system is under stress due to financial constraints.

Should we wish to purchase a book, perhaps as a special gift, or to furnish our living-room, there is the opportunity to have a copy printed while we have a coffee at a local print shop. Or we can have a number of titles delivered to our door. We can try the first chapters for free, and send back the books that have not piqued our interest. The model of try before you buy is partly financed by authors. Rather than in today's system, where they get paid their royalty regardless of whether the book is completed by the reader—simply from the purchase—authors receive payment once the book is read. Feedback from users not only triggers the royalty but also contributes to the development of the author's next work. Successful authors develop their own service direct to readers—this is facilitated by blockchain technology which enables secure payment services without the need for an intermediary such as Amazon.

TRANSLATION ON DEMAND

The work of the translator has become more prominent in recent years with their skill and name coming more to the fore. In the case of Elena Ferrante, for example, the unwillingness of the author to make public appearances has transformed the translator of the Neapolitan novels, Ann Goldstein, into the face of the author.

With more prominence to translation comes also greater scrutiny, and an example of the criticism applied to a translator's work is Deborah Smith's translation of *The Vegetarian* by Han Kang, winner of the Man Booker International Prize. It came under fire from both Tim Parks, who could not read the original Korean and yet disliked the English version (Parks 2016), and by the Korean academic, Charse Yun, who could read the original and pointed out many differences and omissions from the author's text (Yun 2017). Smith responded by saying: 'Since there is no such thing as a truly literal trans-lation—no two languages' grammars match, their vocabularies diverge, even punctuation has a different weight—there can be no such thing as a translation that is not "creative".'

Can we imagine a future where AI helps to improve and aid the art of translation? The Turing test is whether we can have a text exchange with a computer and to assume that we are in fact talking with a human being. Could an exchange involving a human using a translation programme convince another human correspondent of their language ability?

Earlier versions of Google Translate relied on a huge corpus of books to facilitate its working—so it could supply a perfect translation of the first lines of famous novels simply by consulting the various editions to which it had access. It also relied on the documentation of international organizations, in which human translators have produced texts across different languages. This helped it translate sentences word by word but there was little sense of context and meaning.

More recently Google has moved to an AI approach where the translation programme looks for patterns and comes up with its own translations. This approach had worked with image recognition, where a neural network was given millions of images and learnt how to recognize a cat. Could this now work with language? Gideon Lewis-Kraus writes, 'if you took the entire space of the English language and the entire space of French, you could, at least in theory, train a network to learn how to take a sentence in one space and propose an equivalent in the other. You just had to give it millions and millions of English sentences as inputs on one side and their desired French outputs on the other, and over time it would recognize the relevant patterns in words the way that an image classifier recognized the relevant patterns in pixels' (Lewis-Kraus 2016). This machine learning approach is now paying dividends with a much improved translation programme.

The present route for literary translations can be individual and circuitous. For example, a literal translation may be commissioned first, next to be smoothed out by a native speaker (of the destination language). Or a bridge language may be used—with the translation from one smaller language into another through another version (often the English translation). One barrier to translations appearing is the cost involved, and often publishers have to resort to public subsidy.

As translation programmes improve further, it will become much easier to publish in different languages, and more cost-effective. Programmes will be able to perform the first stage of producing a rough translation, and whilst a high level of intervention may continue for literary fiction, for other texts the need will be greatly reduced. Books will be much more readily available across languages and our access to world literature will be revolutionized. Perhaps one day we will have true translation on demand: a single copy made to order of your desired title.

Ebooks are Free, Print Books Cost Five Times More

'Information wants to be free', cried Silicon Valley. 'No it doesn't', responded the publishing industry. But in digital contexts the price of information is falling and publishers are caught up in this movement, a trend which, if it were to continue indefinitely, would end at digital books becoming free. This is a model we already see emerging with Open Access monograph publishing as practised by UCL Press or Open Book Publishers.

In the trade, there is evidence that not only is the price of ebooks much lower than print, but it is falling over time. Research by digital publisher Canelo, conducted by this author, showed that between two dates in 2016 and 2017 the average price of a print book in the Amazon top 100 increased from £5.66 in February 2016 to £6.15 in October 2017 (Canelo 2017). Meanwhile the price of a top 100 ebook came in at under half that figure: £2.55 in 2016 and £2.43 in 2017. Looking at the average price for just the top 10 books, in 2016 the print was £6.25 and ebooks were £2.85, while 2017 saw £8.19 and £3.19 respectively (the ebook figures for 2017 were skewed by high priced releases from Philip Pullman and Dan Brown). Titles at number one in the chart were priced at £7.49/£0.99 in 2016 and £9.00/£0.98 in 2017. Of the Kindle top 100, 38 were priced at £1 or less in 2016. By 2017 55 were at £1 or less.

While the survey is only a snapshot and cannot be used to draw wholesale conclusions, it only takes a glance at any ebook chart to see that books priced at £0.99/$0.99 are routine. Once the retailers take their cut and, in certain territories VAT is paid, the returns to the publisher and author are negligible on a per unit basis. From here it is only a small albeit still significant step to simply make an ebook free and view it is an audience building exercise; indeed, this is not unheard for publishers (Apple iBooks has a Free Book of the Week, for example).

In the UK, sales of print books and their prices have also been going down. The latter in particular has fallen greatly in real terms since 2000 (Canelo 2017). However, there is now evidence this has, since around 2014/2015, started to go back up. Publishers are putting up the price of their print books with hardbacks leading the charge. If ebooks were a driver of the deflationary cycle, adding price competition to an already competitive market, perhaps now the dynamic has shifted. In an ephemeral digital culture the value of tangibility, beautiful, well-produced books, may go up; in contrast to the weightless world of endless free information, satrapy of the technology giants, print may be finding its place as an antidote. Books are, or could be, once again, artisanal products, not mass produced generic consumer items. Design standards, paper quality, production values: all increase massively in this scenario.

Meanwhile in the digital realm, increasingly its own universe divorced from print, a trend already in evidence as suggested by the almost total discontinuity of titles in those two Amazon top 100s, grinds inexorably to a point of free books, pure audience. Publishing here has finally become two worlds, almost two industries: a high value, low numbers world of print. And a miniscule value, largely self-published world of unlimited free reading.

The Death of Bricks and Mortar Retail: All Books Are Sold via the Internet

It was an average town and the death of the bookstore came slowly. First to go was one of the major chains which one day simply collapsed. Next was the old independent bookshop which had been there forever. Then the supermarkets and other major retail outlets decided that books were no longer worth the trouble; shelf space was better used for simpler and faster moving products. But things carried on.

After all, there was still the last major bookchain, a company that, after some shaky years, had recovered, and was once again at the heart of bookish life. In place of the old independent came a trendy new indie store, which also sold coffee, food, stationery, and crafts, and which stayed open late. In fact for a time it seemed that things were going to be okay; revenues had plateaued but stabilized. But this was only an interregnum before a further shift.

The economics of retail had grown harder. Super-curated shops at the high end and ultra-budget discounters at the low end had found workable niches. Everything in the middle was squeezed. The phenomenon of windowing, whereby customers examined goods in store only to buy them from Internet retailers later, at a discount, had not gone away and was, quietly, intensifying. As shops in the town centre struggled, there were increasing vacancies. The more vacancies, the more the town took on a delipidated air, and the less reason there was for customers to come in and browse.

Footfall, the lifeblood of retail, started leaking away. Demands from landlords and councils did not stop; rental contracts were re-negotiated, but only once the cash position of the book chain was clearly in crisis. Governmental leeway on business rates was non-existent. Corporate white knights occasionally appeared on the horizon, only to conclude that the future wasn't worth the trouble. Debts mounted. Bills went unpaid, and publishers began to withhold key stock. Slowly but surely the position of the chain became steadily worse until one day it went under. Executives from the store tried to revive it, but the market had already moved on.

Meanwhile the indie store had been devoting less and less space to books. No one was buying them. People were, however, buying postcards and coffee in great amounts. The number of book lines on offer diminished, down to thirty, then twenty, then ten, and one day it just didn't seem like a good idea: a few token books left behind the counter were all that was left of its original purpose. Aside from some charity shops there was, eventually, nowhere in the town that sold books, as was the case almost everywhere. Bookshops had ceased to exist. People were still reading of course; but they bought all their books online, both print and digital. It was so much cheaper and more convenient. Publishers, authors, and some readers in the town mourned the loss of bookshops, both for their own sakes and, somehow, they all felt that, with the loss of bookshops, the future of reading, of books, now hung in the balance.

The Resurgence of Analogue

What would happen if current trends continue around the resurgence of analogue, from LPs to film photography? Digital music may be perfect in many ways but it is hard to beat the warm sound produced by an LP played through a decent sound system. There is an authenticity that comes through even the crackles, and the object itself is worthy of preserving and cherishing. A digital download cannot replicate the impact and appeal of the album cover. Physical books offer a tactile experience and a welcome distraction from the screens that pervade our homes and working lives. We enjoy the smell of the paper and the carefully chosen design and typography.

The trend to analogue is accelerated in the light of research providing evidence of worsening health amongst Western populations. Life expectancy declines in many countries and data offers proof of the long-term detriment to our health from the use of mobile devices. Alongside increasing cancer risks, there are grave consequences for mental health through the use of social media. There is a myopia epidemic amongst children using smartphones. Moreover a decline in intelligence is traced to ever-decreasing attention spans.

Silicon Valley executives have for a long time sent their children to schools that prohibit the use of technology for learning, and where pupils are banned from bringing mobile devices into the classroom. Strong reactions arise to the attention economy: a society dominated by the pursuit of likes in social media. VR devices meant that few ever properly engage with the outside world—largely interacting with a souped-up vision of the world around them.

High levels of addiction to the dopamine highs of likes and notifications have led to programmes for weaning adults off social media in order to combat feelings of loneliness, anxiety, and alienation. Dry January is accompanied by a regular digital detox. Fiction is prescribed by doctors to patients in order to rebuild empathy within the individual and society. Freed from their screens, readers rediscover the utility and pleasure of long-form reading.

There are power blackouts around the world as huge resources are required to power digital currencies, server space, and autonomous vehicles. Constant distraction from email and social media has reduced attention spans to a few seconds, and societies see levels of IQ begin to decline. In response to the dumbing down of their societies, governments concerned about the competitiveness of their economies determine to reintroduce books into education at school and university level. Students are required to read whole books and master the arguments for discussion and discursive comment. Investment in public libraries reaps dividends for the wider economy and many rediscover the joys of contemplative reading: during their daily shared commute in a driverless car, in bedrooms free of technological devices, and in those idle moments throughout the day previously filled with constant checking of their mobile phones. The widespread use of automation for many jobs frees up leisure time for reading, and domestic life is revolutionized with robots carrying out household tasks from shopping and cleaning to gardening. Authors are feted and their views are sought on the latest developments in society, as well as on how to encourage children and adults to read more.

Conclusion

No one knows what will happen next in the world of publishing. Aspects of any or all of these scenarios may come to pass, and indeed, there is good reason for thinking they might. But equally all may be wide of the mark. The point is, uncertainty is the condition we operate in and an open mind is hence the only rational response.

One thing is, however, clear. Our age is probably the most turbulent for books and publishing since its modern inception with the printing press, the time of the Renaissance and the Reformation. Information and communications media and technology have, over the past hundred years, and especially the past thirty years, witnessed a transition akin to that of the fifteenth century. In that context it would be foolish not to anticipate further dramatic ruptures and shifts in the landscape of publishing. We cannot predict exactly what they will be; but we can try imagining a future still being written.

References

Bond, David (2017). 'Children's authors pen a tale of record book sales'. *Financial Times* [online]. Available at: https://www.ft.com/content/78d9c896-2a8b-11e7-bc4b-5528796fe35c [Accessed 2 January 2018].

Bostrom, Nick (2017). *Superintelligence: Paths, Strategies, Dangers*, Oxford: Oxford University Press.

Canelo (2017). *Literature in the 21st Century: Understanding Models of Support for Literary Fiction*. London: Arts Council England, [online]. Available at: http://www.artscouncil.org.uk/publication/literature-21st-century-understanding-models-support-literary-fiction [Accessed 8 January 2018].

Diggs, Kallen (2016). 'The Inevitable Death of Traditional Book Publishing'. *Huffington Post* [online]. Available at: https://www.huffingtonpost.com/kallen-diggs/the-inevitable-death-of-t_b_11469768.html [Accessed 20 January 2018].

Edmonds, David (2015). *Would You Kill the Fat Man?: The Trolley Problem and What Your Answer Tells Us about Right and Wrong*. Princeton, NJ: Princeton University Press.

Eve, Martin (2014). *Open Access and the Humanities: Contexts, Controversies and the Future*, Cambridge: Cambridge University Press.

Flood, Alison (2015). 'Sharp decline in children reading for pleasure, survey finds'. *The Guardian* [online]. Available at: https://www.theguardian.com/books/2015/jan/09/decline-children-reading-pleasure-survey [Accessed 8 January 2018].

Ghost, Shona (2017). 'Amazon will become a $1 trillion giant in 2018, says Morgan Stanley'. *Business Insider* [online]. Available at: http://uk.businessinsider.com/morgan-stanley-amazon-facebook-google-trillion-dollar-company-2018-2017-11 [Accessed 2 January 2018].

Gomez, Jeff (2008). *Print is Dead: Books in Our Digital Age*, Basingstoke: Palgrave.

Harrison, Angela (2013). 'Literacy: Fewer children reading in spare time, research suggests'. BBC.co.uk [online]. Available at: http://www.bbc.co.uk/news/education-24387523 [Accessed 8 January 2018].

Kozlowski, Mike (2016). 'Global Publishing Industry will Generate $358 billion by 2020'. *Goodreader* [online]. Available at: https://goodereader.com/blog/e-book-news/global-publishing-industry-will-generate-358-billion-by-2020 [Accessed 26 January 2018].

Lewis-Kraus, Gideon (2016). 'The Great A.I. Awakening', *New York Times Magazine*, 14 December.

Owen, Laura (2013). 'PwC: the U.S. consumer ebook market will be bigger than the print book market by 2017'. *Gigaom* [online]. Available at: https://gigaom.com/2013/06/04/pwc-the-u-s-consumer-ebook-market-will-be-bigger-than-the-print-book-market-by-2017/ [Accessed 2 January 2018].

Parks, Tim (2016). 'Raw and Cooked', *New York Review of Books*, 20 June.

Price, Leah (2012). 'Dead Again: The Death of the Book Through the Ages'. *New York Times* [online]. Available at: http://www.nytimes.com/2012/08/12/books/review/the-death-of-the-book-through-the-ages.html [Accessed 2 January 2018].

Rawls, John (1971). *A Theory of Justice*, Cambridge, MA.: Harvard University Press.

Ross, Alex (2017). *The Industries of the Future*, London: Simon & Schuster.

Searle, J. (1980). 'Minds, brains, and programs', *Behavioral and Brain Sciences*, 3(3), pp. 417–424. doi:10.1017/S0140525X00005756.

Shatzkin, Mike (2018). 'A changing book business: it all seems to be flowing downhill to Amazon'. The Idea Logical Company [online]. Available at: https://www.idealog.com/blog/changing-book-business-seems-flowing-downhill-amazon/ [Accessed 26 January 2018].

Tetlock, Philip and Gardner, Dan (2016). *Superforecasting: The Art and Science of Prediction*, London: Random House Books.

Yun, Charse (2017). 'How the Bestseller *The Vegetarian*, translated from Han Kang's original, caused an uproar in South Korea', *Los Angeles Times*, 22 September.

INDEX

Note: References to Notes will contain the letter 'n' following the page number. Tables and figures are indicated by an italic 't' and 'f' following the page number.